T0210889

Lecture Notes in Computer Science 9033

Commenced Publication in 1973
Founding and Former Series Editors:
Gerhard Goos, Juris Hartmanis, and Jan van Leeuwen

Advanced Research in Computing and Software Science

Subline of Lecture Notes in Computer Science

More information about this series at http://www.springer.com/series/7407

Alexander Egyed · Ina Schaefer (Eds.)

Fundamental Approaches to Software Engineering

18th International Conference, FASE 2015
Held as Part of the European Joint Conferences
on Theory and Practice of Software, ETAPS 2015
London, UK, April 11–18, 2015
Proceedings

 Springer

Editors
Alexander Egyed
Johannes Kepler University
Linz
Austria

Ina Schaefer
Technische Universität Braunschweig
Braunschweig
Germany

ISSN 0302-9743
Lecture Notes in Computer Science
ISBN 978-3-662-46674-2
DOI 10.1007/978-3-662-46675-9

ISSN 1611-3349 (electronic)

ISBN 978-3-662-46675-9 (eBook)

Library of Congress Control Number: 2015934132

LNCS Sublibrary: SL1 – Theoretical Computer Science and General Issues

Springer Heidelberg New York Dordrecht London

Printed on acid-free paper

Springer-Verlag GmbH Berlin Heidelberg is part of Springer Science+Business Media
(www.springer.com)

Foreword

ETAPS 2015 was the 18th instance of the European Joint Conferences on Theory and Practice of Software. ETAPS is an annual federated conference that was established in 1998, and this year consisted of six constituting conferences (CC, ESOP, FASE, FoSSaCS, TACAS, and POST) including five invited speakers and two tutorial speakers. Prior to and after the main conference, numerous satellite workshops took place and attracted many researchers from all over the world.

ETAPS is a confederation of several conferences, each with its own Program Committee and its own Steering Committee (if any). The conferences cover various aspects of software systems, ranging from theoretical foundations to programming language developments, compiler advancements, analysis tools, formal approaches to software engineering, and security. Organizing these conferences into a coherent, highly synchronized conference program enables the participation in an exciting event, having the possibility to meet many researchers working in different directions in the field, and to easily attend talks at different conferences.

The six main conferences together received 544 submissions this year, 152 of which were accepted (including 10 tool demonstration papers), yielding an overall acceptance rate of 27.9%. I thank all authors for their interest in ETAPS, all reviewers for the peer-reviewing process, the PC members for their involvement, and in particular the PC Co-chairs for running this entire intensive process. Last but not least, my congratulations to all authors of the accepted papers!

ETAPS 2015 was greatly enriched by the invited talks by Daniel Licata (Wesleyan University, USA) and Catuscia Palamidessi (Inria Saclay and LIX, France), both unifying speakers, and the conference-specific invited speakers [CC] Keshav Pingali (University of Texas, USA), [FoSSaCS] Frank Pfenning (Carnegie Mellon University, USA), and [TACAS] Wang Yi (Uppsala University, Sweden). Invited tutorials were provided by Daniel Bernstein (Eindhoven University of Technology, the Netherlands and the University of Illinois at Chicago, USA), and Florent Kirchner (CEA, the Alternative Energies and Atomic Energy Commission, France). My sincere thanks to all these speakers for their inspiring talks!

ETAPS 2015 took place in the capital of England, the largest metropolitan area in the UK and the largest urban zone in the European Union by most measures. ETAPS 2015 was organized by the Queen Mary University of London in cooperation with the following associations and societies: ETAPS e.V., EATCS (European Association for Theoretical Computer Science), EAPLS (European Association for Programming Languages and Systems), and EASST (European Association of Software Science and Technology). It was supported by the following sponsors: Semmle, Winton, Facebook, Microsoft Research, and Springer-Verlag.

The organization team comprised:

- General Chairs: Pasquale Malacaria and Nikos Tzevelekos
- Workshops Chair: Paulo Oliva
- Publicity chairs: Michael Tautschnig and Greta Yorsh
- Members: Dino Distefano, Edmund Robinson, and Mehrnoosh Sadrzadeh

The overall planning for ETAPS is the responsibility of the Steering Committee. The ETAPS Steering Committee consists of an Executive Board (EB) and representatives of the individual ETAPS conferences, as well as representatives of EATCS, EAPLS, and EASST. The Executive Board comprises Gilles Barthe (satellite events, Madrid), Holger Hermanns (Saarbrücken), Joost-Pieter Katoen (Chair, Aachen and Twente), Gerald Lüttgen (Treasurer, Bamberg), and Tarmo Uustalu (publicity, Tallinn). Other members of the Steering Committee are: Christel Baier (Dresden), David Basin (Zurich), Giuseppe Castagna (Paris), Marsha Chechik (Toronto), Alexander Egyed (Linz), Riccardo Focardi (Venice), Björn Franke (Edinburgh), Jan Friso Groote (Eindhoven), Reiko Heckel (Leicester), Bart Jacobs (Nijmegen), Paul Klint (Amsterdam), Jens Knoop (Vienna), Christof Löding (Aachen), Ina Schäfer (Braunschweig), Pasquale Malacaria (London), Tiziana Margaria (Limerick), Andrew Myers (Boston), Catuscia Palamidessi (Paris), Frank Piessens (Leuven), Andrew Pitts (Cambridge), Jean-Francois Raskin (Brussels), Don Sannella (Edinburgh), Vladimiro Sassone (Southampton), Perdita Stevens (Edinburgh), Gabriele Taentzer (Marburg), Peter Thiemann (Freiburg), Cesare Tinelli (Iowa City), Luca Vigano (London), Jan Vitek (Boston), Igor Walukiewicz (Bordeaux), Andrzej Wąsowski (Copenhagen), and Lenore Zuck (Chicago).

I sincerely thank all ETAPS SC members for all their hard work to make the 18th edition of ETAPS a success. Moreover, thanks to all speakers, attendants, organizers of the satellite workshops, and to Springer for their support. Finally, many thanks to Pasquale and Nikos and their local organization team for all their efforts enabling ETAPS to take place in London!

January 2015   Joost-Pieter Katoen

Preface

This volume contains the proceedings of FASE 2015, the 18th International Conferences on Fundamental Approaches to Software Engineering, which was held in London, UK, in April 2015 as part of the annual European Joint Conferences on Theory and Practice of Software (ETAPS).

As with previous editions of FASE, this year's papers presented foundational contributions to a broad range of topics in software engineering, including software adaptation, fault localization, model-driven engineering, synthesis, testing, transformation, and verification and validation.

This year we received 80 submissions of which 23 were accepted by the Program Committee for presentation at the conference, constituting an acceptance rate of approximately 28%. Each paper received a minimum of three reviews; acceptance decisions were reached through online discussions among the members of the Program Committee.

Many persons contributed to the success of FASE 2015. The authors of all submitted papers represent the core of such a conference, and we believe that the accepted papers make significant advances in the foundations of software engineering. However, the program could not have been assembled without the great effort of the Program Committee members and their sub-reviewers in critically assessing and discussing the papers: thanks a lot for your active participation! We also express our full gratitude to the Additional Reviewers coming to our aid at the last minute to provide additional insights for papers under dispute, for producing high-quality reviews in a very short time. Finally, we thank Gabriele Taentzer, the FASE Steering Committee Chair, for her timely and accurate responses to our queries about the whole process management, and the ETAPS Steering and Organizing Committees for their coordination work.

We sincerely hope you enjoy these proceedings!

January 2015   Ina Schaefer
                                                                            Alexander Egyed

Organization

Program Committee

David Benavides	University of Seville, Spain
Marsha Chechik	University of Toronto, Canada
Vittorio Cortellessa	University of L'Aquila, Italy
Krzysztof Czarnecki	University of Waterloo, Canada
Alexander Egyed	Johannes Kepler University Linz, Austria
José Luiz Fiadeiro	Royal Holloway, University of London, UK
Bernd Fischer	Stellenbosch University, South Africa
Dimitra Giannakopoulou	NASA Ames Research Center, USA
Stefania Gnesi	Istituto di Scienza e Tecnologie dell'Informazione "A. Faedo", Italy
John Grundy	Swinburne University of Technology, Australia
Mark Harman	University College London, UK
Reiko Heckel	University of Leicester, UK
Valerie Issarny	Inria, France
Einar Broch Johnsen	University of Oslo, Norway
Antónia Lopes	University of Lisbon, Portugal
Henry Muccini	University of L'Aquila, Italy
John Penix	Google Inc., USA
Arend Rensink	University of Twente, The Netherlands
Julia Rubin	IBM Research, Israel
Ina Schaefer	Technische Universität Braunschweig, Germany
Andy Schürr	Technische Universität Darmstadt, Germany
Bran Selic	Malina Software Corp., Canada
Perdita Stevens	University of Edinburgh, UK
Gabriele Taentzer	Philipps-Universität Marburg, Germany
Tetsuo Tamai	University of Tokyo, Japan
Sebastian Uchitel	University of Buenos Aires, Argentina and Imperial College London, UK
Daniel Varro	Budapest University of Technology and Economics, Hungary
Andrzej Wasowski	IT University of Copenhagen, Denmark
Martin Wirsing	Ludwig-Maximilians-Universität München, Germany
Pamela Zave	AT&T Laboratories Research, USA

Additional Reviewers

Abal, Iago
Al-Sibahi, Ahmad Salim
Albarghouthi, Aws
Andriescu, Emil
Anjorin, Anthony
Antkiewicz, Michal
Bae, Kyungmin
Bagheri, Hamid
Belzner, Lenz
Bergmann, Gábor
Boronat, Artur
Bourke, Timothy
Bubel, Richard
Busch, Marianne
Bürdek, Johannes
Corradini, Andrea
Cunha, Alcino
Deckwerth, Frederik
Dimovski, Aleksandar S.
Diskin, Zinovy
Famelis, Michalis
Fantechi, Alessandro
Ferrari, Alessio
Franzago, Mirco
Galindo, José A.
Gotlieb, Arnaud
Guo, Jianmei
Hegedüs, Ábel
Heim, Robert
Heindel, Tobias
Horváth, Ákos
Howar, Falk
Iosif-Lazar, Alexandru Florin
Klarl, Annabelle
Knapp, Alexander
Kroiß, Christian
Kulcsár, Géza
Laarman, Alfons
Leblebici, Erhan
Legay, Axel

Li, Yi
Lochau, Malte
Lucio, Levi
Löwe, Michael
Malavolta, Ivano
Marques, Eduardo R.B.
Martins, Francisco
Mazzanti, Franco
Mehlitz, Peter
Mennicke, Stephan
Mukkamala, Raghava Rao
Olveczky, Peter
Petke, Justyna
Petrocchi, Marinella
Pun, Ka I
Radwan, Marwan
Re, Barbara
Ribeiro, Leila
Ridge, Tom
Ross, Jordan
Rutle, Adrian
Salay, Rick
Saller, Karsten
Santos, André
Schlatte, Rudolf
Semeráth, Oszkár
Senni, Valerio
Stanciulescu, Stefan
Stevens, Perdita
Stolz, Volker
Strüber, Daniel
Störrle, Harald
Tapia Tarifa, Silvia Lizeth
Ter Beek, Maurice H.
Vakili, Amirhossein
Varro, Gergely
Watson, Bruce
Weckesser, Markus
Yu, Ingrid
Zulkoski, Ed

Contents

Models and Synthesis

Testing and Fault Localization

Modeling

Verification

Modeling and Adaptation

Applications

Models and Synthesis

An Institution for Simple UML State Machines

Alexander Knapp[1], Till Mossakowski[2], Markus Roggenbach[3], and Martin Glauer[2]

[1] Universität Augsburg, Germany
[2] Otto-von-Guericke Universität Magdeburg, Germany
[3] Swansea University, UK

Abstract. We present an institution for UML state machines without hierarchical states. The interaction with UML class diagrams is handled via institutions for guards and actions, which provide dynamic components of states (such as valuations of attributes) but abstract away from details of class diagrams. We also study a notion of interleaving product, which captures the interaction of several state machines. The interleaving product construction is the basis for a semantics of composite structure diagrams, which can be used to specify the interaction of state machines. This work is part of a larger effort to build a framework for formal software development with UML, based on a heterogeneous approach using institutions.

Keywords: UML, state machines, interleaving product, institutions.

1 Introduction

The "Unified Modeling Language" (UML [1]) is a heterogeneous language: UML comprises a language family of 14 types of diagrams of structural and behavioural nature. These sub-languages are linked through a common meta-model, i.e., through abstract syntax; their semantics, however, is informally described mainly in isolation. In [2], we have outlined our research programme of "institutionalising UML". Our objective is to give, based on the theory of institutions [3], formal, heterogeneous semantics to UML, that — besides providing formal semantics for the individual sub-languages — ultimately allows to ask questions concerning the consistency between different diagram types and concerning refinement and implementation in a system development. In this paper, we propose a new institution for UML state machines.

Behavioural UML state machines specify the behaviour of model elements, like components, whereas *protocol* UML state machines express usage protocols, like the message exchange over a connector between components. Both variants describe dynamical system behaviour in terms of action effects and messages, where conditions are used to choose between different possibilities of the behaviour. We tackle the well-known resulting problem of integrating specifications of data (i.e., action effects and messages), logic (i.e., conditions), and processes (i.e., state machines) [4,5,6,7] by a two-step semantics: In the first step, we define *institutions of guards and actions* that capture which guards, actions, and messages can be used in order to define a state machine. In general, other UML diagrams like class diagrams or OCL constraints specify these items, i.e., define a suitable environment. In a second step, we then define institutions for behavioural and protocol state machines relative to given institutions of

© Springer-Verlag Berlin Heidelberg 2015
A. Egyed and I. Schaefer (Eds.): FASE 2015, LNCS 9033, pp. 3–18, 2015.
DOI: 10.1007/978-3-662-46675-9_1

guards and actions. However, currently both of our institutions are restricted to "flat", non-hierarchical state machines; in fact, most of the hierarchical features can be reduced to this format [8,9]. A previous UML state machine institution by D. Calegari and N. Szasz [10] encoded all these features on a single (signature) level thus reducing integration flexibility considerably; furthermore, it only comprised behavioural state machines and captured each state machine in isolation. By contrast, we study interacting state machines and the refinement of state machines.

Our institution of behavioural state machines has the peculiarity of being a "programming language-like" institution, in the sense that each sentence essentially has one model, its canonical model. By contrast, our institution of protocol state machines is a "loose semantics" institution where generally a sentence has many models. For system development, we introduce an interleaving product of several state machines in our institution, which allows us to consider refinement for checking the correct implementation of protocols and which ideally could be integrated into the current efforts for providing precise semantics for UML composite structures [11]. Furthermore, we consider the determinism of state machines to foster code generation [12].

The remainder of this paper is structured as follows: In Sect. 2 we provide some background on our goal of heterogeneous institution-based UML semantics and introduce a small example illustrating behavioural and protocol UML state machines. In Sect. 3 we define institutions for these variants of state machines. We study a notion of determinism for state machines, their interleaving, and their refinement based on the institutions in Sect. 4. Finally, in Sect. 5 we conclude with an outlook to future work.

2   Heterogeneous Institution-Based UML Semantics

The work in this paper is part of a larger effort [2] of giving an institution-based heterogeneous semantics to several UML diagrams as shown in Fig. 1. The vision is to provide semantic foundations for model-based specification and design using a heterogeneous framework based on Goguen's and Burstall's theory of institutions [3]. We handle the complexity of giving a coherent semantics to UML by providing several institutions formalising different diagrams of UML, and several institution translations (formalised as so-called institution morphisms and comorphisms) describing their interaction and

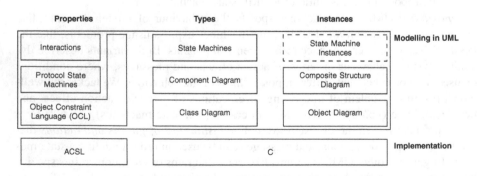

Fig. 1. Languages and diagrams to be considered

information flow. The central advantage of this approach over previous approaches to formal semantics for UML (e.g., [13]) is that each UML diagram type can stay "as-is", without the immediate need of a coding using graph grammars (as in [14]) or some logic (as in [13]). Such coding can be done at verification time — this keeps full flexibility in the choice of verification mechanisms. The formalisation of UML diagrams as institutions has the additional benefit that a notion of refinement comes for free, see [15,16]. Furthermore, the framework is flexible enough to support various development paradigms as well as different resolutions of UML's semantic variation points. This is the crucial advantage of the proposed approach to the semantics of UML, compared to existing approaches in the literature which map UML to a specific global semantic domain in a fixed way.

2.1   Institutions

Institutions are an abstract formalisation of the notion of logical systems. Informally, institutions provide four different logical notions: signatures, sentences, models and satisfaction. Signatures provide the vocabulary that may appear in sentences and that is interpreted in models. The satisfaction relation determines whether a given sentence is satisfied in a given model. The exact nature of signatures, sentences and models is left unspecified, which leads to a great flexibility. This is crucial for the possibility to model UML diagrams (which in the first place are not "logics") as institutions.

More formally [3], an institution $\mathscr{I} = (\mathrm{Sig}^{\mathscr{I}}, Sen^{\mathscr{I}}, \mathrm{Mod}^{\mathscr{I}}, \models^{\mathscr{I}})$ consists of (i) a category of *signatures* $\mathrm{Sig}^{\mathscr{I}}$; (ii) a *sentence functor* $Sen^{\mathscr{I}} : \mathrm{Sig}^{\mathscr{I}} \to \mathrm{Set}$, where Set is the category of sets; (iii) a contra-variant *model functor* $\mathrm{Mod}^{\mathscr{I}} : (\mathrm{Sig}^{\mathscr{I}})^{\mathrm{op}} \to \mathrm{Class}$, where Class is the category of classes; and (iv) a family of *satisfaction relations* $\models^{\mathscr{I}}_{\Sigma} \subseteq \mathrm{Mod}^{\mathscr{I}}(\Sigma) \times Sen^{\mathscr{I}}(\Sigma)$ indexed over $\Sigma \in |\mathrm{Sig}^{\mathscr{I}}|$, such that the following *satisfaction condition* holds for every signature morphism $\sigma : \Sigma \to \Sigma'$ in $\mathrm{Sig}^{\mathscr{I}}$, every sentence $\varphi \in Sen^{\mathscr{I}}(\Sigma)$ and for every Σ'-model $M' \in \mathrm{Mod}^{\mathscr{I}}(\Sigma')$:

$$\mathrm{Mod}^{\mathscr{I}}(\sigma)(M') \models^{\mathscr{I}}_{\Sigma} \varphi \Leftrightarrow M' \models^{\mathscr{I}}_{\Sigma'} Sen^{\mathscr{I}}(\sigma)(\varphi) .$$

$\mathrm{Mod}^{\mathscr{I}}(\sigma)$ is called the *reduct* functor (also written $-|\sigma$), $Sen^{\mathscr{I}}(\sigma)$ the *translation* function (also written $\sigma(-)$).

A *theory* T in an institution consists of a signature Σ, written $sig(T)$, and a set of Σ-sentences; its model class is the set of all Σ-models satisfying the sentences.

An institution $\mathscr{I}$ has the *weak amalgamation property* for a pushout

$$
\begin{array}{ccc}
\Sigma & \longrightarrow & \Sigma_1 \\
\downarrow & & \downarrow \\
\Sigma_2 & \longrightarrow & \Sigma_R
\end{array}
$$

if any pair $(M_1, M_2) \in \mathrm{Mod}^{\mathscr{I}}(\Sigma_1) \times \mathrm{Mod}^{\mathscr{I}}(\Sigma_2)$ that is *compatible* in the sense that M_1 and M_2 reduce to the same Σ-model can be *amalgamated* to a Σ_R-model M_R (i.e., there exists a $M_R \in \mathrm{Mod}^{\mathscr{I}}(\Sigma_R)$ that reduces to M_1 and M_2, respectively). Weak amalgamation allows the computation of normal forms for specifications [17], and implies good behaviour w.r.t. conservative extensions, as well as soundness of proof systems for structured specifications [18].

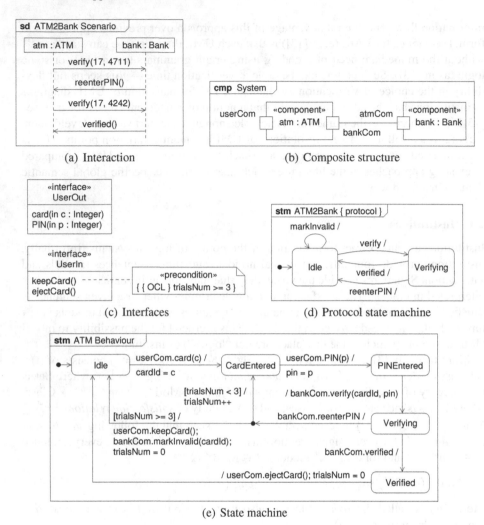

(a) Interaction

(b) Composite structure

(c) Interfaces

(d) Protocol state machine

(e) State machine

Fig. 2. ATM example

2.2 ATM Example

In order to illustrate our approach to a heterogeneous institutions-based UML semantics in general and the institutions for UML state machines in particular, we use as a small example the design of a traditional automatic teller machine (ATM) connected to a bank. For simplicity, we only describe the handling of entering a card and a PIN with the ATM. After entering the card, one has three trials for entering the correct PIN (which is checked by the bank). After three unsuccessful trials the card is kept.

Figure 2(a) shows a possible *interaction* between an atm and a bank, which consists out of four messages: the atm requests the bank to verify if a card and PIN number combination is valid, in the first case the bank requests to reenter the PIN, in the second case the verification is successful.

The composite structure of the ATM-bank system is specified in the *component diagram* in Fig. 2(b). In order to communicate with a bank component, the atm component has a *behaviour port* called bankCom and the bank component has a behaviour port atmCom. Furthermore, atm has a port userCom to a user. Interpreted at the component instance level this *composite structure diagram* also specifies the initial configuration of the system with the component instances atm and bank for the interaction.

Figure 2(c) provides structural information in the form of the interfaces specifying what is provided at the userCom port of the atm instance (UserIn) and what is required (UserOut). An interface is a set of operations that other model elements have to implement. In our case, the interface is described in a *class diagram*. Here, the operation keepCard is enriched with the OCL constraint trialsNum >= 3, which refines its semantics: keepCard can only be invoked if the OCL constraints holds.

The communication protocol on this connector is captured with a *protocol state machine*, see Fig. 2(d). The protocol state machine fixes in which order the messages verify, verified, reenterPIN, and markInvalid between atm and bank may occur.

The dynamic behaviour of the atm component is specified by the *behavioural state machine* shown in Fig. 2(e). The machine consists of five states including Idle, CardEntered, etc. Beginning in the initial Idle state, the user can *trigger* a state change by entering the card. This has the *effect* that the parameter c from the card event is assigned to the cardId in the atm object (parameter names are not shown on triggers). Entering a PIN triggers another transition to PINEntered. Then the ATM requests verification from the bank using its bankCom port. The transition to Verifying uses a *completion event*: No explicit trigger is declared and the machine autonomously creates such an event whenever a state is completed, i.e., all internal activities of the state are finished (in our example there are no such activities). If the interaction with the bank results in reenterPIN, and the *guard* trialsNum < 3 is true, the user can again enter a PIN.

Questions on the model. Given the above diagrams specifying *one* system, the question arises if they actually "fit" together. Especially, one might ask if the diagrams are consistent, and if the different levels of abstraction refine each other. In our ATM example we have:

Example 1 (Consistency). The interface in Fig. 2(c) requires the operation keepCard only to be invoked when the precondition trialsNum >= 3 holds. This property holds for the state machine in Fig. 2(e) thanks to the guard trialsNum < 3.

Example 2 (Refinement). As the only trace of the interaction in Fig. 2(a) is a possible run of the state machine in Fig. 2(e), the interaction refines to the state machine.

Example 3 (Refinement). Similarly, we can consider if the protocol state machine in Fig. 2(d) refines to the product of the state machine of the atm, shown in Fig. 2(e), and of the bank; this essentially means to check for a trace inclusion w.r.t. messages observable on the interfaces, as the protocol state machine has no post conditions.

In order to study, e.g., such a refinement between a protocol state machine and its implementation by state machines, in the following we develop institutions for state machines including a notion of product.

3   Institutions for Simple UML State Machines

We now detail a possible formalisation of a simplified version of UML state machines as institutions. In particular, we omit hierarchical states. Our construction is generic in w.r.t. an institution of *guards*. Then, we give an institutions for the *actions* of a state machine. These fix the conditions which can be used in guards of transitions, the actions for the effects of transitions, and also the messages that can be sent from a state machine. The source of this information typically is a class or a component diagram: The conditions and actions involve the properties available in the classes or components, the messages are derived from the available signals and operations. The sentences of the action institution form a simple dynamic logic (inspired by OCL) which can express that if a guard holds as pre-condition, when executing an action, a certain set of messages is sent out, and another guard holds as post-condition. We then build a family of institutions for *state machines* over the institutions for guards and actions. A state machine adds the events and states that are used. The events comprise the signals and operations that can be accepted by the machine; some of these will, in general, coincide with the messages from the environment. Additionally, the machine may react to completion events, i.e., internal events that are generated when a state of the machine has been entered and which trigger those transitions that do not show an explicit event as their trigger in the diagrammatic representation (we use the states as the names of these events). The initial state as well as the transitions of the machine are represented as sentences in the institution.[1] In a next step, we combine the family of state machine institutions parameterised over actions into a single institution.

3.1   Institution of Guards

We assume that there is an institution of guards. Typically, guards are formulas in some language like OCL. More formally, an *institution of guards* is an institution where signatures are sets, and signature morphisms are functions. We will call the elements of these sets *variables*, but one can think of attributes or properties. Models of a signature V are valuations $\omega : V \to \text{Val}$ into a fixed set of values Val[2]. Model reduct is just composition, that is, given a signature morphism $v : V \to V'$ and a model $\omega' : V' \to \text{Val}$, its v-reduct is $\omega' \circ v$. The nature of sentences $G(V)$ and their translation $G(v) : G(V) \to G(V')$ is left unspecified, as well as the satisfaction relation — we only require the satisfaction condition, which amounts to

$$\omega' \models G(v)(g) \quad \text{iff} \quad \omega' \circ v \models g \, .$$

Example 4. Consider the UML component ATM. A guard signature for ATM would contain the variable trialsNum, leading to sentences such as true, trialsNum $< n$, and trialsNum $== n$ for $n \in \mathbb{N}$.

---

[1] For simplicity, final states are left implicit here. For hierarchical states, they need to be made explicit.

[2] In UML, variables and values would be typed, and variable valuations have to respect the typing. For simplicity, we disregard this here. Moreover, UML queries, could be covered by valuations assigning values in some function space. However, a more elaborate institution would be preferable for OCL.

3.2 Institution of Actions

An object of the category of action *signatures* Sig^{Act} is a triple of sets

$$H = (A_H, M_H, V_H)$$

of actions, messages and variables; and a morphism $H \to H'$ of Sig^{Act} is a triple of functions $\eta : (\eta_A : A_H \to A_{H'}, \eta_M : M_H \to M_{H'}, \eta_V : V_H \to V_{H'})$. The class of action *structures* $\text{Mod}^{\text{Act}}(H)$ for an action signature H consists of transition relations

$$\Omega \subseteq |\Omega| \times (A_H \times \wp(M_H)) \times |\Omega| \,,$$

where $|\Omega| = (V_H \to \text{Val})$ represents the possible configurations of data states, and

$$(\omega, a, \overline{m}, \omega') \in \Omega \quad \text{(also written } \omega \xrightarrow[\Omega]{a,\overline{m}} \omega')$$

expresses that action a leads from state $\omega \in (V_H \to \text{Val})$ to state $\omega' \in (V_H \to \text{Val})$ producing the set of messages $\overline{m} \subseteq M_H$.

The *reduct* $\Omega'|\eta$ of an H'-action structure Ω' along the morphism $\eta : H \to H'$ is given by all transitions

$$\omega_1|\eta_V \xrightarrow[\Omega'|\eta]{a,\eta_M^{-1}(\overline{m})} \omega_2|\eta_V \quad \text{for which} \quad \omega_1 \xrightarrow[\Omega']{\eta_A(a),\overline{m}} \omega_2 \,.$$

An action a is called *deterministic* if $\omega_1 \xrightarrow[\Omega]{a,\overline{m}} \omega_2$ and $\omega_1 \xrightarrow[\Omega]{a,\overline{m}'} \omega_2'$ imply $\overline{m} = \overline{m}'$ and $\omega_2 = \omega_2'$. An action relation Ω is called deterministic if all its actions are deterministic, that is, it is a partial function of type $|\Omega| \times A_H \rightharpoonup \wp(M_H) \times |\Omega|$.

Note that reducts can introduce non-determinism. Given an action signature $(A, M, \{x, y\})$ suppose that a deterministic action a leads to a change of state expressed by the assignment $x := x + y$. Now take the reduct to the signature $(A, M, \{x\})$, i.e., the variable y has been removed. Then a performs a non-deterministic assignment $x := x + y$ where the value for y is non-deterministically guessed.

The set of action *sentences* $\text{Sen}^{\text{Act}}(H)$ for an action signature H comprises the expressions

$$g_{\text{pre}} \to [a]\overline{m} \rhd g_{\text{post}}$$

with $g_{\text{pre}}, g_{\text{post}} \in G(V_H)$ guard sentences over V_H, $a \in A_H$, and $\overline{m} \subseteq M_H$, intuitively meaning (like an OCL constraint) that if the pre-condition g_{pre} currently holds, then, after executing a, the messages $\overline{m}$ are produced and the post-condition g_{post} holds. The *translation* $\eta(g_{\text{pre}} \to [a]\overline{m} \rhd g_{\text{post}})$ of a sentence $g_{\text{pre}} \to [a]\overline{m} \rhd g_{\text{post}}$ along the signature morphism $\eta : H \to H'$ is given by $G(\eta_V)(g_{\text{pre}}) \to [\eta_A(a)]\eta_M(\overline{m}) \rhd G(\eta_V)(g_{\text{post}})$. Finally, the satisfaction relation $\Omega \models_H^{\text{Act}} g_{\text{pre}} \to [a]\overline{m} \rhd g_{\text{post}}$ holds if, and only if, for all $\omega \in (V_H \to \text{Val})$, if $\omega \models g_{\text{pre}}$ and $\omega \xrightarrow[\Omega]{a,\overline{m}'} \omega'$, then $\omega' \models g_{\text{post}}$ and $\overline{m} \subseteq \overline{m}'$. Then the *satisfaction condition* follows.

Example 5. Consider the UML component ATM with its properties cardId, pin, and trialsNum, its ports userCom and bankCom, and its outgoing operations ejectCard() and keepCard() to userCom, and verify() and markInvalid() to bankCom. An action signature for ATM is derived by forming actions and messages over this information, such that it will contain the actions userCom.ejectCard(); trialsNum = 0 and trialsNum++, as well as the messages userCom.ejectCard() and bankCom.markInvalid(cardId). Action sentences over such an action signature could be

true $\to$ [userCom.ejectCard(); trialsNum = 0]{userCom.ejectCard()} $\triangleright$ trialsNum == 0

trialsNum == n $\to$ [trialsNum++]$\emptyset$ $\triangleright$ trialsNum == n+1 .

3.3   Behavioural State Machine Institution

The institution of state machines is now built over the action institution. Let H be an action signature and Ω an action structure over H. An object of the category of state machine *signatures* $\mathrm{Sig}^{\mathrm{SM}(H,\Omega)}$ over H and Ω is given by a triple

$$\Sigma = (E_\Sigma, F_\Sigma, S_\Sigma)$$

of (external) events E_Σ, completion events F_Σ, and states S_Σ with $E_\Sigma \cap F_\Sigma = \emptyset$ and $E_\Sigma \cap S_\Sigma = \emptyset$; and a morphism $\sigma : \Sigma \to \Sigma'$ of $\mathrm{Sig}^{\mathrm{SM}(H,\Omega)}$ is a triple of injective functions $\sigma = (\sigma_E : E_\Sigma \to E_{\Sigma'}, \sigma_F : F_\Sigma \to F_{\Sigma'}, \sigma_S : S_\Sigma \to S_{\Sigma'})$, such that $E_\Sigma \cap M_H = E_{\Sigma'} \cap M_H$ (preservation of internal messages). The class of state machine *structures* $\mathrm{Mod}^{\mathrm{SM}(H,\Omega)}(\Sigma)$ for a state machine signature $\Sigma = (E_\Sigma, F_\Sigma, S_\Sigma)$ over H and Ω consists of the pairs

$$\Theta = (I_\Theta, \Delta_\Theta)$$

where $I_\Theta \in \wp(V_H \to \mathrm{Val}) \times S_\Sigma$ represents the initial configurations, fixing the initial control state; and $\Delta_\Theta \subseteq C_\Sigma \times \wp(M_H) \times C_\Sigma$ with $C_\Sigma = (V_H \to \mathrm{Val}) \times \wp(E_\Sigma \cup F_\Sigma) \times S_\Sigma$ represents a transition relation from a configuration, consisting of an action state, an event pool, and a control state, to a configuration, emitting a set of messages. The event pool may contain both types of events from the signature: external events from signals and operations, and completion events (which are typically represented by states).

Example 6. Consider the state machine of Fig. 2(e) defining the behaviour of ATM. It works over the action signature sketched in the previous example, and its signature is $(E_{\mathrm{ATM}}, F_{\mathrm{ATM}}, S_{\mathrm{ATM}})$ with

$E_{\mathrm{ATM}} = \{\mathrm{card}, \mathrm{PIN}, \mathrm{reenterPIN}, \mathrm{verified}\}$,

$F_{\mathrm{ATM}} = \{\mathrm{PINEntered}, \mathrm{Verified}\}$,

$S_{\mathrm{ATM}} = \{\mathrm{Idle}, \mathrm{CardEntered}, \mathrm{PINEntered}, \mathrm{Verifying}, \mathrm{Verified}\}$.

In particular, the completion events consist of those states from which a completion transition originates.

The *reduct* $\Theta'|\sigma$ of a state machine structure Θ' along the morphism $\sigma : \Sigma \to \Sigma'$ is given by the structure

$$(\{(\omega, s) \mid (\omega, \sigma_S(s)) \in I'\}, \Delta) \quad \text{with}$$

$$\Delta = \{(\omega_1, \sigma_P^{-1}(\overline{p_1}), s_1) \xrightarrow{\overline{m}} (\omega_2, \sigma_P^{-1}(\overline{p_2}), s_2) \mid$$
$$(\omega_1, \overline{p_1}, \sigma_S(s_1)) \xrightarrow[\Delta_{\Theta'}]{\overline{m}} (\omega_2, \overline{p_2}, \sigma_S(s_2))\},$$

where $\sigma_P(p) = \sigma_E(p)$ if $p \in E_\Sigma$ and $\sigma_P(p) = \sigma_F(p)$ if $p \in F_\Sigma$. Here, σ_P^{-1} deletes those events from the event pool that are not present in the pre-image.

The set of state machine *sentences* $Sen^{\mathrm{SM}(H,\,\Omega)}(\Sigma)$ for a state machine signature Σ over H and Ω consists of the pairs

$$\varphi = (s_0 \in S_\Sigma, T \subseteq S_\Sigma \times (E_\Sigma \cup F_\Sigma) \times (G(V_H) \times A_H \times \wp(F_\Sigma)) \times S_\Sigma)$$

where s_0 means an initial state and the transition set T represents the transitions from a state s with a triggering event p (either a declared event or a completion event), a guard g, an action a, and a set of completion events $\overline{f}$ to another state s'. We also write $s \xrightarrow[T]{p[g]/a,\overline{f}} s'$ for such a transition. The translation $\sigma(s_0, T)$ of a sentence (s_0, T) along the signature morphism $\sigma : \Sigma \to \Sigma'$ is given by $(\sigma_S(s_0), \{\sigma_S(s_1) \xrightarrow{\sigma_P(p)[g]/a,\wp\sigma_F(\overline{f})} \sigma_S(s_2) \mid s_1 \xrightarrow[T]{p[g]/a,\overline{f}} s_2\})$. Finally, the *satisfaction relation* $\Theta \models_\Sigma^{\mathrm{SM}(H,\,\Omega)} (s_0, T)$ holds if, and only if $\pi_2(I_\Theta) = s_0$ and Δ_Θ is the least transition relation satisfying[3]

$$(\omega, p :: \overline{p}, s) \xrightarrow[\Delta_\Theta]{\overline{m} \backslash E_\Sigma} (\omega', \overline{p} \lhd ((\overline{m} \cap E_\Sigma) \cup \overline{f}), s') \quad \text{if}$$
$$\exists s \xrightarrow[T]{p[g]/a,\overline{f}} s' . \omega \models g \wedge \omega \xrightarrow{a,\overline{m}}_\Omega \omega'$$

$$(\omega, p :: \overline{p}, s) \xrightarrow[\Delta_\Theta]{\emptyset} (\omega, \overline{p}, s) \quad \text{if}$$
$$\forall s \xrightarrow[T]{p'[g]/a,\overline{f}} s' . p \neq p' \vee \omega \not\models g$$

where $p :: \overline{p}$ expresses that some element p from the pool $\overline{p}$ is extracted, and $\overline{p} \lhd \overline{p}'$ adds the events in $\overline{p}'$ to the pool $\overline{p}$ with respect to some extraction and selection schemes (where completion events are prioritised). The messages on a transition in the structure Θ are only those that are not accepted by the machine itself, i.e., not in E_Σ. The accepted events in E_Σ as well as the completion events are added to the event pool of the target configuration. When no transition is triggered by the current event, the event is discarded (this will happen, in particular, to all superfluously generated completion events). Checking the satisfaction condition

$$\Theta'|\sigma \models_\Sigma^{\mathrm{SM}(H,\,\Omega)} (s_0, T) \Leftrightarrow \Theta \models_{\Sigma'}^{\mathrm{SM}(H,\,\Omega)} \sigma(s_0, T)$$

for a state machine signature morphism $\sigma : \Sigma \to \Sigma'$ is straightforward.

---

[3] Usually, the two cases do not overlap, so the two cases are complete characterisations (iff).

Example 7. Continuing the previous example for the state machine of Fig. 2(e) defining the behaviour of ATM, this state machine can be represented as the following sentence over this signature:

$$(\text{Idle}, \{\text{Idle} \xrightarrow[T]{\text{card[true]}/\text{cardId} = c, \emptyset} \text{CardEntered},$$

$$\text{CardEntered} \xrightarrow[T]{\text{PIN[true]}/\text{pin} = p, \text{PINEntered}} \text{PINEntered},$$

$$\text{PINEntered} \xrightarrow[T]{\text{PINEntered[true]}/\text{bank.verify(cardId, pin)}, \emptyset} \text{Verifying},$$

$$\text{Verifying} \xrightarrow[T]{\text{reenterPIN[trialsNum} < 3]/\text{trialsNum++}, \emptyset} \text{CardEntered}, \ldots\}) \,.$$

In particular, PINEntered occurs both as a state and as a completion event to which the third transition reacts. The junction pseudostate for making the decision whether trialsNum < 3 or trialsNum >= 3 has been resolved by combining the transitions.

3.4   Protocol State Machine Institution

Protocol state machines differ from behavioural state machines by not mandating a specific behaviour but just monitoring behaviour: They do not show guards and effects, but a pre- and a post-condition for the trigger of a transition. Moreover, protocol state machines do not just discard an event that currently does not fire a transition; it is an error when such an event occurs.

For adapting the state machine institution to protocol state machines we thus change the *sentences* to

$$\varphi = (s_0, e \in S_\Sigma, T \subseteq S_\Sigma \times (G(V_H) \times E_\Sigma \times G(V_H) \times \wp(M_H) \times \wp(F_\Sigma)) \times S_\Sigma)$$

where s_0 is the start state and e a dedicated error state, the two occurrences of $G(V_H)$ represent the pre- and the post-conditions, and $\wp(M_H)$ represents the messages that have to be sent out in executing the triggering event (protocol state machines typically do not show completion events). The *satisfaction relation* now requires that when an event e is chosen from the event pool the pre-condition of some transition holds in the source configuration, its post-condition holds in the target configuration, and that all messages have been sent out. Instead of the second clause of Δ_Θ, discarding an event, the error state is targeted when no transition is enabled.

3.5   Flat State Machine Institution

Given an institution of guards, we now flatten the institutions $\text{SM}(H, \Omega)$ for each action signature H and each action structure Ω over H into a single institution SM.[4] The signatures $\langle H, \Sigma \rangle$ consist of an action signature H and a state machine signature Σ, similarly for signature morphisms as well as for structures $\langle \Omega, \Theta \rangle$. As $\langle H, \Sigma \rangle$-sentences we now have both dynamic logic formulas (over H), as well as control transition relations

---

[4] This is an instance of a general construction, namely the Grothendieck institution [19].

(over H and Σ). Also satisfaction is inherited. Only the definition of reducts is new, because they need to reduce state machine structures along more complex signature morphisms: $\langle \Omega', \Theta' \rangle|(\eta, \sigma) = \langle \Omega'|\eta, \Theta'|\sigma|\eta \rangle$ where $\Theta''|\eta = (I_{\Theta''}, \{c_1'', \eta_M^{-1}(\overline{m}''), c_2''\} \mid (c_1'', \overline{m}'', c_2'') \in \Delta_{\Theta''}\})$.

4 Determinism, Interleaving, and Refinement

4.1 Deterministic State Machines

The transition and action relations are not required to be functions. Thus a transition may have multiple choices for the same configuration of states, variables and events. But when moving towards the implementation, deterministic behaviour is desirable.

i-a) A transition set T is called *syntactically deterministic* if it is a partial function of type $S_\Sigma \times (E_\Sigma \cup F_\Sigma) \rightharpoonup G_H \times A_H \times \wp(F_\Sigma) \times S_\Sigma$.

i-b) A transition set T is called *semantically deterministic* if for any two distinct transitions $s \xrightarrow[T]{p[g_1]/a_1, \overline{f}_1} s_1$ and $s \xrightarrow[T]{p[g_2]/a_2, \overline{f}_2} s_2$ sharing the same pre-state s and trigger event p, their guards must be disjoint, that is, there is no $\omega : V_H \rightarrow$ Val satisfying both g_1 and g_2.

ii) A transition relation Δ_Θ is called *deterministic* if and only if it is a partial function of type $C_\Sigma \rightharpoonup \wp(M_H) \times C_\Sigma$.[5]

iii) A state machine structure (Ω, Θ) of SM is called *deterministic* if and only if the corresponding action relation and transition relation are deterministic.

The transition relation Δ_Θ is defined by Ω and T. So it is justified to expect some inheritance of determinism between those.

Theorem 1. *If T is syntactically or semantically deterministic and Ω is deterministic, then Δ_Θ is also deterministic.*

Proof. Consider a configuration $(\omega, p :: \overline{p}, s)$. If there is any transition, then the new state s' and executed action a are determined by $T(s, p) = (g, a, \overline{f}, s')$ (if defined) in the syntactic case. The sent message $\overline{m}$ and the new configuration of the variables ω' result from $\Omega(\omega, a) = (\overline{m}, \omega')$. In the semantic case, at most one guard can be enabled, hence at most one transition in T can fire. □

4.2 Interleaving Product of State Machines

Inside the flat state machine institution SM we can consider the composition of state machines over different action signatures. The composition captures the interplay between different state machines and their communication. The different action signatures represent the local views of the state machines. This composition interleaves the behaviours

---

[5] Note that this function is total if Δ_Θ satisfies some sentence. This originates from the discarding of events that can not be processed in the current state and configuration, which is again a transition.

of the UML state machines. The communication is performed by the exchange of messages which are turned into events, not by synchronisation over shared events.

Given two state machine signatures $\langle H_1, \Sigma_1 \rangle$ and $\langle H_2, \Sigma_2 \rangle$ of SM with $E_{\Sigma_1} \cap E_{\Sigma_2} = \emptyset$ and $S_{\Sigma_1} \cap S_{\Sigma_2} = \emptyset$, we combine these into a single signature $\langle \hat{H}, \hat{\Sigma} \rangle$ of SM by taking the component-wise union for the guard, actions, messages, and variables, the union of events and states for the events, and the product of the state sets for the states. Now consider two state machine structures (Ω_1, Θ_1) over $\langle H_1, \Sigma_1 \rangle$ and (Ω_2, Θ_2) over $\langle H_2, \Sigma_2 \rangle$, respectively. Their *interleaving product* is given by

$$\langle \Omega_1, \Theta_1 \rangle \parallel \langle \Omega_2, \Theta_2 \rangle = (\Omega_1 \parallel \Omega_2, \Theta_1 \parallel \Theta_2) \qquad \text{where}$$

- $\Omega_1 \parallel \Omega_2$ is given by $\omega \xrightarrow[\Omega_1 \parallel \Omega_2]{a, \overline{m}} \omega'$ if for some $i \in \{1, 2\}$: $a \in A_{H_i}$ and $\omega|V_{H_i} \xrightarrow[\Omega_i]{a, \overline{m}}$
  $\omega'|V_{H_i}$ and for $i \neq j \in \{1, 2\}$: $\omega|(V_{H_j} \setminus V_{H_i}) = \omega'|(V_{H_j} \setminus V_{H_i})$
- $\Theta_1 \parallel \Theta_2 = (I_{\Theta_1} \parallel I_{\Theta_2}, \Delta_{\Theta_1} \parallel \Delta_{\Theta_2})$ with, letting $I_{\Theta_i} = (\Gamma_i, s_i)$,

$$I_{\Theta_1} \parallel I_{\Theta_2} = (\{\omega : V_{H_1} \cup V_{H_2} \to \text{Val} \mid \forall j \in \{1, 2\} . \omega|V_{H_j} \in \Gamma_j\}, (s_1, s_2)) \quad \text{and}$$

$$(\omega, p :: (\overline{p}_1 \cup \overline{p}_2), (s_1, s_2)) \xrightarrow[\Delta_{\Theta_1} \parallel \Delta_{\Theta_2}]{\overline{m} \setminus E_{\hat{\Sigma}}} (\omega', (\overline{p}_1 \cup \overline{p}_2) \lhd ((\overline{p}' \cup \overline{m}) \cap E_{\hat{\Sigma}}), (s_1', s_2'))$$

$$\text{iff } \exists i \in \{1, 2\} . (\omega|V_{H_i}, p :: \overline{p}_i, s_i) \xrightarrow[\Delta_{\Theta_i}]{\overline{m}} (\omega'|V_{H_i}, \overline{p}_i \lhd \overline{p}', s_i') \wedge$$
$$\forall j \in \{1, 2\} \setminus \{i\} . (\omega|V_{H_j}, \overline{p}_j, s_j) = (\omega'|V_{H_j}, \overline{p}_j, s_j') .$$

There is also a syntactic version of the interleaving product: given sentences (s_0^1, T_1) and (s_0^2, T_2), their interleaving $(s_0^1, T_1) \parallel (s_0^2, T_2)$ is given by $((s_0^1, s_0^2), T)$ with

$$(s_1, s_2) \xrightarrow[T]{p[g]/a, \overline{f}} (s_1', s_2') \text{ iff } \exists i \in \{1, 2\} . s_i \xrightarrow[T_i]{p[g]/a, \overline{f}} s_i' \wedge \forall j \in \{1, 2\} \setminus \{i\} . s_j = s_j' .$$

The syntactic version is compatible with the semantic interleaving product:

Theorem 2. *If* $\langle \Omega_i, \Theta_i \rangle \models (s_0^i, T_i)$ *for* $i \in \{1, 2\}$, *then* $\langle \Omega_1, \Theta_1 \rangle \parallel \langle \Omega_2, \Theta_2 \rangle \models (s_0^1, T_1) \parallel (s_0^2, T_2)$. $\qquad\square$

Example 8. Consider the composite structure diagram in Fig. 2(b), showing instances atm and bank of the ATM and Bank components, respectively, that are connected through their bankCom and atmCom ports. In execution, atm and bank will exchange messages, as prescribed by their state machines, and this exchange is reflected by the interleaving product which internalises those events that are part of the common signature. On the other hand, messages to the outside, i.e., through the userCom port are still visible.

A system resulting from an interleaving product $\langle \Omega_1, \Theta_1 \rangle \parallel \langle \Omega_2, \Theta_2 \rangle$ represents a state machine in our notation. Thus it can be again part of an interleaving product

$$\langle ((\langle \Omega_1, \Theta_1 \rangle \parallel \langle \Omega_2, \Theta_2 \rangle) \parallel \langle \Omega_3, \Theta_3 \rangle) \rangle .$$

The interleaving product meets the intuitive algebraic properties. Due to the disjoint event sets each event can only trigger at most one machine. Messages are stripped off

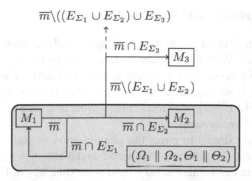

Fig. 3. Messages sent between three machines on transition in machine M_1

the events which can be processed by either of the inner machines, and remaining messages are sent to the third machine, which also extracts its corresponding events as illustrated in Fig. 3. Hence it is impossible that the inner machines consume an event that can also be processed by the third machine. The same behaviour occurs, if the first machine sends a message to a system of the two remaining machines. Thus the distinction in "inner" and "outer" machines becomes obsolete and the interleaving product is associative. Since each machine extracts the events present in its event set, it is not required to consider the order of the machines, and hence the interleaving product is commutative. Finally, we can regard a state machine with no events, no messages, and only one state. In an interleaving product this nearly empty machine would have no effect on the behaviour of the other machine, and thus behaves as a neutral element.

Theorem 3. *The set of state machine structures (over all signatures) with interleaving product $\|$ forms a discrete symmetric monoidal category, which is a "commutative monoid up to isomorphism".* □

It is desirable that the interleaving product of two deterministic machines preserves this determinism. The new action function is determined by the two old ones in such a way, that the new configuration is taken from the configuration of the triggered submachine, which is deterministic, and the missing variable configuration remains untouched. Thus the new action relation is deterministic. The same goes for the transition relation. The sent messages and configuration are determined by the (as argued above) deterministic action relation and the new state and events result from the triggered submachine. However, we need the following prerequisite: Two action relations Ω_1, Ω_2 are called *compatible* if $\Omega_1|(H_1 \cap H_2) = \Omega_2|(H_1 \cap H_2)$.

Theorem 4. *Let (Ω_1, Θ_1) and (Ω_2, Θ_2) be deterministic state machines with both action relations compatible. Then $(\Omega_1 \| \Omega_2, \Theta_1 \| \Theta_2)$ is also deterministic.* □

Using a slightly modified version of the interleaving product construction where messages of shared actions leading to compatible states are united, instead of generating two separate transitions, we can prove:

Theorem 5. *The action institution admits weak amalgamation for pushout squares with injective message mappings.* □

4.3 Institutional Refinement of State Machines

We have defined an institution capturing both behavioural and protocol state machines via different sentences. With the machinery developed so far, we can now apply the institution independent notion of refinement to our institution of state machines. The simplest such notion is just model class inclusion, that is, a theory T_1 refines to T_2, written $T_1 \rightsquigarrow T_2$, if $\mathrm{Mod}^{\mathsf{SM}}(T_2) \subseteq \mathrm{Mod}^{\mathsf{SM}}(T_1)$. (Note that state machines are theories consisting typically of one sentence only.)

However, this is too simple to cover the phenomenon of *state abstraction*, where several states (like Idle, CardEntered, PinEntered and Verified in Fig. 2(e)) in a more concrete state machine can be abstracted to one state (like Idle in Fig. 2(d)) in a more abstract state machine. This situation can be modelled using the institution independent notion of *translation* of a theory T along a signature morphism $\sigma : sig(T) \rightarrow \Sigma$, resulting in a structured theory $\sigma(T)$ which has signature Σ, while the model class is $\{M \in \mathrm{Mod}^{\mathsf{SM}}(\Sigma) \mid M|\sigma \in \mathrm{Mod}^{\mathsf{SM}}(T)\}$, i.e., models are those Σ-models that reduce (via σ) to a T-model. Moreover, sometimes we want to *drop events* (like card in Fig. 2(e)) when moving to a more abstract state machine. This can be modelled by a notion dual to translation, namely *hiding*. Given a theory T and a signature morphism $\theta : \Sigma \rightarrow sig(T)$, the structured theory $\theta^{-1}(T)$ has signature Σ, while the model class is $\{M|\theta \in \mathrm{Mod}^{\mathsf{SM}}(\Sigma) \mid M \in \mathrm{Mod}^{\mathsf{SM}}(T)\}$, i.e., models are all θ-reducts of T-models. Altogether, we arrive at

Definition 1. *An "abstract" (behavioural or protocol) state machine T_1 refines into a "concrete" state machine T_2 via signature morphisms $\theta : sig(T_1) \rightarrow \Sigma$ and $\sigma : sig(T_2) \rightarrow \Sigma$ into some "mediating signature" Σ, if*

$$T_1 \rightsquigarrow \theta^{-1}(\sigma(T_2))$$

in other words, for all Σ-models M

$$M|\sigma \in \mathrm{Mod}^{\mathsf{SM}}(T_2) \Rightarrow M|\theta \in \mathrm{Mod}^{\mathsf{SM}}(T_1)\,.$$

Concerning our original refinement question stated in Ex. 3, we now can argue: As the state machine of the atm, shown in Fig. 2(e) is a refinement of the protocol state machine in Fig. 2(d), using a suitable signature morphism, the interleaving product of the atm and bank state machine, in the syntactic version, will be so as well. As furthermore the protocol state machine has no post conditions, we have established a refinement.

5 Conclusions

We have presented institutions for behavioural and protocol UML state machines and have studied an interleaving product and a notion of determinism. We furthermore presented first steps of how to study refinement in such a context. Our institutions provide the necessary prerequisites for including UML state machines into a heterogeneous institution-based UML semantics and to develop their relationship to other UML sub-languages and diagram types.

An important future extension for the state machine institutions is to add hierarchical states, and to consider refinements from hierarchical to flat state machines. For an integration into the software development process, the study of correct code generation is indispensable. The Heterogeneous Tool Set (Hets [18,20]) provides analysis and proof support for multi-logic specifications, based on a strong semantic (institution-based) backbone. Implementation of proof support for UML state machines (and other kinds of UML diagrams) is under way.

References

1. Object Management Group: Unified Modeling Language. Standard formal/2011-08-06, OMG (2011)
2. Knapp, A., Mossakowski, T., Roggenbach, M.: Towards an Institutional Framework for Heterogeneous Formal Development in UML - A Position Paper. In: De Nicola, R., Hennicker, R. (eds.) Wirsing Festschrift. LNCS, vol. 8950, pp. 215–230. Springer, Heidelberg (2015)
3. Goguen, J.A., Burstall, R.M.: Institutions: Abstract model theory for specification and programming. J. ACM 39, 95–146 (1992)
4. Große-Rhode, M.: Semantic Integration of Heterogeneous Software Specifications. Monographs in Theoretical Computer Science. Springer (2004)
5. Roggenbach, M.: CSP-CASL: A New Integration of Process Algebra and Algebraic Specification. Theo. Comp. Sci. 354, 42–71 (2006)
6. Mossakowski, T., Roggenbach, M.: Structured CSP – A Process Algebra as an Institution. In: Fiadeiro, J.L., Schobbens, P.-Y. (eds.) WADT 2006. LNCS, vol. 4409, pp. 92–110. Springer, Heidelberg (2007)
7. O'Reilly, L., Mossakowski, T., Roggenbach, M.: Compositional Modelling and Reasoning in an Institution for Processes and Data. In: Mossakowski, T., Kreowski, H.-J. (eds.) WADT 2010. LNCS, vol. 7137, pp. 251–269. Springer, Heidelberg (2012)
8. Schattkowsky, T., Müller, W.: Transformation of UML State Machines for Direct Execution. In: VL/HCC 2005, pp. 117–124. IEEE (2005)
9. Fecher, H., Schönborn, J.: UML 2.0 State Machines: Complete Formal Semantics Via core state machine. In: Brim, L., Haverkort, B.R., Leucker, M., van de Pol, J. (eds.) FMICS and PDMC 2006. LNCS, vol. 4346, pp. 244–260. Springer, Heidelberg (2007)
10. Calegari, D., Szasz, N.: Institutionalising UML 2.0 State Machines. Innov. Syst. Softw. Eng. 7, 315–323 (2011)
11. Object Management Group: Precise Semantics of UML Composite Structures. Beta Specification ptc/14-06-15, OMG (2014)
12. Dereziska, A., Szczykulski, M.: Interpretation Problems in Code Generation from UML State Machines — A Comparative Study. In: Kwater, T. (ed.) Computing in Science and Technology 2011: Monographs in Applied Informatics, pp. 36–50. Warsaw University (2012)
13. Lano, K. (ed.): UML 2 — Semantics and Applications. Wiley (2009)
14. Engels, G., Heckel, R., Küster, J.M.: The Consistency Workbench: A Tool for Consistency Management in UML-Based Development. In: Stevens, P., Whittle, J., Booch, G. (eds.) UML 2003. LNCS, vol. 2863, pp. 356–359. Springer, Heidelberg (2003)
15. Mossakowski, T., Sannella, D., Tarlecki, A.: A Simple Refinement Language for CASL. In: Fiadeiro, J.L., Mosses, P.D., Orejas, F. (eds.) WADT 2004. LNCS, vol. 3423, pp. 162–185. Springer, Heidelberg (2005)
16. Codescu, M., Mossakowski, T., Sannella, D., Tarlecki, A.: Specification Refinements: Calculi, Tools, and Applications (2014) (submitted)

17. Borzyszkowski, T.: Logical Systems for Structured Specifications. Theor. Comput. Sci. 286, 197–245 (2002)
18. Mossakowski, T., Autexier, S., Hutter, D.: Development Graphs — Proof Management for Structured Specifications. J. Log. Alg. Program. 67, 114–145 (2006)
19. Diaconescu, R.: Grothendieck Institutions. Applied Cat. Struct. 10, 383–402 (2002)
20. Mossakowski, T., Maeder, C., Lüttich, K.: The Heterogeneous Tool Set, HETS. In: Grumberg, O., Huth, M. (eds.) TACAS 2007. LNCS, vol. 4424, pp. 519–522. Springer, Heidelberg (2007)

Map-Based Transparent Persistence for Very Large Models

Abel Gómez, Massimo Tisi, Gerson Sunyé, and Jordi Cabot

AtlanMod Team, Inria, Mines Nantes, LINA, France
{abel.gomez-llana,massimo.tisi,gerson.sunye,jordi.cabot}@inria.fr

Abstract. The progressive industrial adoption of Model-Driven Engineering (MDE) is fostering the development of large tool ecosystems like the Eclipse Modeling project. These tools are built on top of a set of base technologies that have been primarily designed for small-scale scenarios, where models are manually developed. In particular, efficient runtime manipulation for large-scale models is an under-studied problem and this is hampering the application of MDE to several industrial scenarios.

In this paper we introduce and evaluate a map-based persistence model for MDE tools. We use this model to build a transparent persistence layer for modeling tools, on top of a map-based database engine. The layer can be plugged into the Eclipse Modeling Framework, lowering execution times and memory consumption levels of other existing approaches. Empirical tests are performed based on a typical industrial scenario, model-driven reverse engineering, where very large software models originate from the analysis of massive code bases. The layer is freely distributed and can be immediately used for enhancing the scalability of any existing Eclipse Modeling tool.

Keywords: Model Driven Engineering, Model Persistence, Very Large Models, Key-Value Stores.

1 Introduction

Part of the software industry is embracing the main concepts of Model-Driven Engineering, by putting models and code generation at the center of their software-engineering processes. Recent studies [22], as well as the proliferation of tools related to MDE, testify the increase in popularity of these concepts, which are applied to different contexts and scales. These scales vary from manual modeling activities with hundreds of model elements to very large models, VLMs, with millions of elements. Very large models are especially popular in specific domains such as the automotive industry [10], civil engineering [24], or software product lines [21], or are automatically generated during software modernization of large code bases.

Modeling tools are built around so-called modeling frameworks, that provide basic model-management functionalities and interoperability to the modeling ecosystem. Among the frameworks currently available, the Eclipse Modeling

© Springer-Verlag Berlin Heidelberg 2015
A. Egyed and I. Schaefer (Eds.): FASE 2015, LNCS 9033, pp. 19–34, 2015.
DOI: 10.1007/978-3-662-46675-9_2

Framework [7] (EMF) has become the *de facto* standard for building modeling tools. The *Eclipse marketplace* attests the popularity of EMF, counting more than two hundred EMF-based tools [6] coming from both industry and academia.

However, the technologies at the core of modeling frameworks were designed in the first place to support simple modeling activities and exhibit clear limits when applied to very large models. Problems in managing memory and persisting data while handling models of this size are under-studied and the current standard solution is to use a model/relational persistence layer (e.g., CDO for EMF [3]) that translates runtime model-handling operations into relational database queries. Existing solutions have shown clear performance limits in related work [19,20,23]. In this paper we propose a transparent persistence solution for very large models, that introduces the following innovations:

- The transparent persistence is designed to optimize runtime performance and memory occupancy of the atomic **low-level operations** on models. We argue that this strategy improves execution of model-driven tools on large models in real-world scenarios, without an *ad hoc* support from the tool (differently from similar proposals in related work [19, 20]);
- We propose a **map-based** persistence model for MDE tools, arguing that persisting model graphs directly as maps allows for faster runtime operation with respect to a more obvious graph-database persistence. In this sense this paper presents a novel and different approach completing our previous work [9], in which we built a persistence layer for EMF based on a graph database. We compare the different approaches and discuss the distinct application scenarios for each one.
- Persistence is built around a **database engine**, instead of interfacing with a full-fledged database, and directly manipulates low-level data structures. We argue that this approach (i) gives more flexibility when selecting the data structures that optimize model-specific operations, and (ii) reduces overhead by not requiring translation of model operations into a database query language.

Our persistence layer has been implemented as an open-source prototype[1]. The layer can be plugged into EMF-based tools to immediately provide enhanced support for VLMs. Experimental validation shows that (i) our layer allows handling models that cannot be handled by the standard file-based EMF backend—and even the CDO backend in configurations with little memory—and (ii) that queries perform (up to nine times) faster than the standard relational backend.

The paper is structured as follows: Section 2 motivates the paper by describing a running scenario and the limits of current model-persistence solutions. Section 3 provides an overview of our approach and its main properties. Section 4 describes our publicly-available persistence layer. Section 5 illustrates the experimental evaluation, Section 6 compares our approach with related work and Section 7 concludes the paper.

---

[1] http://www.emn.fr/z-info/atlanmod/index.php/NeoEMF/Map

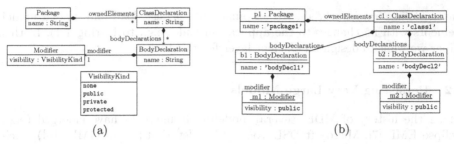

(a)   (b)

Fig. 1. Excerpt of the *Java* metamodel (1a) and sample instance (1b)

2 Motivation

2.1 Running Example

As a running example for this paper we will consider an industrial scenario that uses modeling tools for helping a Java code reverse-engineering and modernization process. The first step in this scenario is parsing the legacy Java codebase (that can be massive) to produce a very detailed Java model. Such model will be then processed by other modeling tools like analyzers or transformers for computer-aided program understanding.

Fig. 1a shows a small excerpt of a possible *Java* metamodel. This metamodel describes *Java* programs in terms of *Packages*, *ClassDeclarations*, *BodyDeclarations*, and *Modifiers*. A *Package* is a named container that groups a set of *ClassDeclarations* through the *ownedElements* composition. A *ClassDeclaration* contains a *name* and a set of *BodyDeclarations*. Finally, a *BodyDeclaration* contains a *name*, and its *visibility* is described by a single *Modifier*.

Fig. 1b shows a sample instance of the *Java* metamodel, i.e., a graph of objects conforming with the metamodel structure. The model contains a single *Package* (`package1`), containing only one *ClassDeclaration* (`class1`). The *Class* contains the `bodyDecl1` and `bodyDecl2` *BodyDeclarations*. Both of them are `public`. Similar instances in large reverse-engineering projects can contain millions of model elements describing the full system code.

Within a modeling ecosystem, all tools that need to access or manipulate models have to pass through a single model management interface. This includes all reverse-engineering, code analysis, and code visualization tools in our running scenario. In some of these ecosystems—as it is the case of EMF—the model management interface is automatically generated from the metamodel of the modeling language. For example, from the metamodel in Fig. 1a EMF produces an API that allows, e.g., to construct the sample instance of Fig. 1b by the code in Listing 1.1.

Without any specific memory-management solution, the model would need to be fully contained in memory for any access or modification. While this approach would be suitable for small models like the one in Fig. 1b, models that exceed the main memory would cause a significant performance drop or the application crash. A possible solution would be a transparent persistence layer in the modeling framework, able to automatically persist, load and unload model elements with no changes to the application code (e.g., to Listing 1.1). In this paper we want to design an efficient layer for this task.

2.2 Persisting Very Large Models

Along the history of MDE, several modeling frameworks have emerged (e.g., Eclipse EMF [7], Microsoft DSL Tools [12], MetaEdit+ [15], GME [16]), each providing a uniform interface to its correspondent ecosystem of modeling tools. Modeling frameworks share a similar, object-oriented conceptual representation of models (e.g., based on OMG's MOF for EMF and GME, on Object-Property-Role-Relationship for MetaEdit+). They differ in the design of the model-management interface and persistence mechanism.

Since the publication of the XMI standard [18], file-based XML serialization has been the preferred format for storing and sharing models and metamodels. The choice was suited to the fact that modeling frameworks have been originally designed to handle human-produced models, whose size does not cause significant performance concerns. However, XML-based serialization results to be inefficient for large models: (i) XML files sacrifice compactness in favor of human-readability and (ii) XML files need to be completely parsed to obtain a navigational model of their contents. The first factor reduces efficiency in I/O accesses, while the second increases the memory required to load and query models and it is an obstacle to on-demand loading. Moreover, XML-based implementations of model persistence require *ad hoc* implementations of advanced features such as concurrent modifications, model versioning, or access control.

The design of additional relational back-ends for model persistence helped solve the problem for medium-size models. For instance, CDO [3] is the standard solution for persisting EMF models where scalability is an issue. It implements a

Listing 1.1. Creation of the sample instance using the generated API (Java-like pseudocode)

```
1  // Creation of objects
2  Package p1 := Factory.createPackage();
3  ClassDeclaration c1 := Factory.createClassDeclaration();
4  BodyDeclaration b1 := Factory.createBodyDeclaration();
5  BodyDeclaration b2 := Factory.createBodyDeclaration();
6  Modifier m1 := Factory.createModifier();
7  Modifier m2 := Factory.createModifier();
8  // Initialization of attributes
9  p1.setName("package1");
10 c1.setName("class1");
11 b1.setName("bodyDecl1");
12 b2.setName("bodyDecl2");
13 m1.setVisibility(VisibilityKind.PUBLIC);
14 m2.setVisibility(VisibilityKind.PUBLIC);
15 // Initialization of references
16 p1.getOwnedElements().add(c1);
17 c1.getBodyDeclarations().add(b1);
18 c1.getBodyDeclarations().add(b2);
19 b1.setModifier(m1);
20 b2.setModifier(m2)
```

client-server architecture with on-demand loading, and transactional, versioning and notification facilities. Although in theory CDO is a generic framework [1, 2, 4, 5], only relational databases are regularly used and maintained[2] and different experiences have shown that CDO does not scale well with VLMs in such a commmon setup [19, 20, 23].

3   Scalable Model-Persistence Layer

In this paper we investigate the problem of persisting very large models and design a solution that improves the state of the art in terms of runtime execution time, memory occupancy, extensibility and compatibility. More precisely, we propose to satisfy a set of requirements, that we consider as necessary for an effective solution for scalable model persistence.

We identify three **interoperability requirements** to guarantee that the solution integrates well with the modeling ecosystem:

1. The persistence layer must be fully compliant with the modeling framework's API. For example, client code should be able to manage models persisted with an alternative persistence manager as if they were persisted using the standard serialization.
2. The underlying persistence backend engine should be easily replaceable to avoid vendor lock-ins.
3. The persistence layer must provide extension points for additional (e.g., domain-specific) caching mechanisms independent from the underlying engine.

Two **performance requirements** represent the improvement we want to achieve over the state of the art:

4. The persistence layer must be memory-friendly, by using on-demand element loading and by removing from memory unused objects.
5. The persistence layer must outperform the execution time of current persistence layers when executing queries on VLMs using the standard API.

In Figure 2, we show the high-level architecture of our proposal particularized for the EMF framework. Our solution consist in a transparent persistence manager behind the model-management interface, so that tools built over the modeling framework would be unaware of it. The persistence manager communicates with a map-database by a driver and supports a pluggable caching strategy. In particular we implement the NeoEMF/Map tool as a persistence manager for EMF on top of MapDB. NeoEMF also supports a graph backend [9].

The architecture answers the interoperability requirements. Requirement 1 is fulfilled by strictly conforming to the base modeling framework. Requirement 2 implies that (i) the APIs must be consistent between the model-management

---

[2] Indeed, only *DB Store* [1], which uses a proprietary Object/Relational mapper, supports all the CDO features and is released in the *Eclipse Simultaneous Release*.

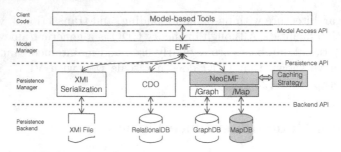

Fig. 2. Overview of the model-persistence framework

framework and the persistence driver (i.e., the module in charge of dealing with the underlying database engine); and (ii) low-level data structures and code accessing the database engine must be completely decoupled from the modeling framework high level code. Maintaining uniform APIs between the different levels allows including additional functionality on top of the persistence driver by using the decorator pattern, such as different cache levels, thus fulfilling Requirement 3.

For fulfilling the performance requirements, we have designed a map-based underlying data model. A map, also called *associative array* or *dictionary*, is an abstract data type composed of a collection of ⟨*key, value*⟩ pairs, such that each possible key appears at most once in the collection. *Hash tables* are typically used to implement maps. A *hash table* is a structure composed by an array of slots in which values are stored. A hash function computes the index of the slot with the correct value. The main advantage of hash tables is that they provide a constant cost on average for searches, insertions and deletions. Maps and hash-maps are one of the most commonly used structures to implement richer data models by their simplicity and performance, specially for data storage. Maps have been used to implement solutions ranging from raw database engines (such as *dbm*, *ndbm*, *MapDB*, etc.) to high level data storage systems (the so called *Key-Value Stores* such as *Oracle NoSQL* or *redis*). The advantage of using a map-based database engine resides in its simplicity, since they are typically provided in the form of software libraries that can be directly embedded in your own solution.

4   NeoEMF/Map

In this section, we describe NeoEMF/Map, our transparent persistence layer for EMF models. The solution is composed of three parts: (i) a memory management strategy, (ii) a map-based data model and (iii) an implementation of atomic model-management operation as low-cost map operations.

4.1   Memory Management

Our memory management strategy combines two mechanisms for lightweight on-demand loading and efficient garbage collection. First we decouple dependencies among objects by assigning a **unique identifier** to all model objects. Then:

- To implement **lightweight on-demand loading**, for each live model object, we create a lightweight delegate object that is in charge of on-demand loading the element data and keeping track of the element's state. Delegates load data from the persistence backend by using the object's unique identifier.
- For **efficient garbage collection** in the *Java Runtime Environment*, we avoid to maintain hard Java references among model objects, so that the garbage collector will be allowed to deallocate any model object that is not directly referenced by the application. Thanks to unique element identification we can obtain this decoupling by replacing references among live objects with collections of identifiers corresponding to the referenced objects.

4.2   Map-Based Data Model

We have designed the underlying data model of NEOEMF/MAP to reduce the computational cost of each method of the EMF model access API. The design takes advantage of the unique identifier defined in the previous section to flatten the graph structure into a set of key-value mappings.

NEOEMF/MAP uses three different maps to store models' information: (i) a *property map*, that keeps all objects' data in a centralized place; (ii) a *type map*, that tracks how objects interact with the meta-level (such as the *instance of* relationships); and (iii) a *containment map*, that defines the models' structure in terms of containment references. Tables 1, 2, and 3 show how the sample model in Fig. 1b is represented using a *key-vale* structure.

As Table 1 shows, keys in the *property map* are a pair, the object *unique identifier*, and the *property* name. The values depend on the *property type* and cardinality (i.e., upper bound). For example, values for single-valued attributes (like the *name* of a Java *Package*) are directly saved as a single literal value as the entry $\langle\langle$'p1', 'name' $\rangle$, 'package'$\rangle$ shows; while values for many-valued attributes are saved as an array of single literal values (Fig. 1b does not contain an example of this). Values for single-valued references, such as the *modifier* containment reference from *BodyDeclaration* to *Modifier*, are stored as a single value (corresponding to the id of the referenced object). Examples of this are the entries $\langle\langle$'b1', 'modifier' $\rangle$, 'm1'$\rangle$ and $\langle\langle$'b2', 'modifier'$\rangle$, 'm2'$\rangle$. Finally, multi-valued references are stored as an array containing the literal identifiers of the referenced objects. An example of this is the *bodyDeclarations* containment reference, from *ClassDeclaration* to *BodyDeclaration*, that for the case of the *c1* object is stored as $\langle\langle$'c1', 'bodyDeclarations' $\rangle$, { 'b1', 'b2' }$\rangle$.

Table 2 shows the structure of the *type map*. The keys are, again, the identifiers of the persisted objects, while the values are named tuples containing the basic information used to identify the corresponding meta-element. For example, the second row of the table specifies the element *p1* is an instance of the *Package* class of the *Java* metamodel (that is identified by the http://java *nsUri*).

Structurally, EMF models are trees. That implies that every non-volatile object (except the root *object*) must be contained within another *object* (i.e., referenced from another *object* via a containment *reference*). The *containment* map is the data structure in charge of maintaining a record of which is the container

Table 1. Property map

KEY	VALUE
⟨'ROOT', 'eContents'⟩	{ 'p1' }
⟨'p1', 'name'⟩	'package1'
⟨'p1', 'ownedElement'⟩	{ 'c1' }
⟨'c1', 'name'⟩	'class1'
⟨'c1', 'bodyDeclarations'⟩	{ 'b1', 'b2' }
⟨'b1', 'name'⟩	'bodyDecl1'
⟨'b1', 'modifier'⟩	'm1'
⟨'b2', 'name'⟩	'bodyDecl2'
⟨'b2', 'modifier'⟩	'm2'
⟨'m1', 'visibility'⟩	'public'
⟨'m2', 'visibility'⟩	'public'

Table 2. Type map

KEY	VALUE
'ROOT'	⟨nsUri='http://java', class='RootEObject'⟩
'p1'	⟨nsUri='http://java', class='Package'⟩
'c1'	⟨nsUri='http://java', class='ClassDeclaration'⟩
'b1'	⟨nsUri='http://java', class='BodyDeclaration'⟩
'b2'	⟨nsUri='http://java', class='BodyDeclaration'⟩
'm1'	⟨nsUri='http://java', class='Modifier'⟩
'm2'	⟨nsUri='http://java', class='Modifier'⟩

Table 3. Containment map

KEY	VALUE
'p1'	⟨container='ROOT', featureName='eContents'⟩
'c1'	⟨container='p1', featureName='ownedElements'⟩
'b1'	⟨container='c1', featureName='bodyDeclarations'⟩
'b2'	⟨container='c1', featureName='bodyDeclarations'⟩
'm1'	⟨container='b1', featureName='modifiers'⟩
'm2'	⟨container='b2', featureName='Mmodifiers'⟩

for every persisted object. Keys in the structure map are the identifier of every persisted object, and the values are named tuples that record both the identifier of the container object and the name of the *property* that relates the container object with the child object (i.e., the object to which the entry corresponds). Table 3 shows in the first row that, for example, the container of the *Package p1* is ROOT through the *eContents* property (i.e., it is a root object and is not contained by any other object). In the second row we find the entry that describes that the *Class c1* is contained in the *Package p1* through the *ownedElements* property.

4.3 Model Operations as Map Operations

As mentioned before, EMF generates a natural *Java* implementation of the concepts described in a metamodel. Operations on model elements are executed by calling the generated methods (mainly *getters* and *setters*). It is worth mentioning that multi-valued *properties* are represented using lists (see Listing 1.1, 16–18), thus, operations on such *properties* are executed using list operators.

Table 4 shows a summary of the minimum and maximum number of operations that are performed on the underlying map-based data structures for each

Table 4. Summary of accesses to the underlying map-based storage system

	LOOKUPS		INSERTS	
METHOD	MIN.	MAX.	MIN.	MAX.
OPERATIONS ON OBJECTS				
getType	1	1	0	0
getContainer	1	1	0	0
getContainingFeature	1	1	0	0
OPERATIONS ON PROPERTIES				
get*	1	1	0	0
set*	0	3	1	3
isSet*	1	1	0	0
unset*	1	1	0	1
OPERATIONS ON MULTI-VALUED PROPERTIES				
add	1	3	1	3
remove	1	2	1	2
clear	0	0	1	1
size	1	1	0	0

model operation. It is noteworthy that all the operations (lookups and inserts) in the underlying maps have always a constant cost. For example getting a *property* always implies a single lookup. Setting a *property* may imply from a single insert to 3 lookups and 3 inserts.

5 Experimental Evaluation

We evaluate the performance of our proposal by comparing different solutions in the running scenario. Based on our joint experience with industrial partners, we have reverse-engineered three models from open-source Java projects whose sizes resemble those one can find in real world scenarios (see Table 5). Moreover, we have defined a set of queries that are executed on those models. The first of these queries is a well-known scenario in academic literature [14]. The others have been selected to mimic typical model access patterns in reverse engineering.

5.1 Selected Backends and Execution Environment

We have selected NEOEMF/MAP, NEOEMF/GRAPH and CDO for a thorough comparison (see Section 6 for a description of NEOEMF/GRAPH and other backends). Only the standard EMF interface methods are used in the

Table 5. Summary of the experimental models

#	MODEL	SIZE IN XMI	ELEMENTS
1	org.eclipse.gmt.modisco.java	19.3MB	80 665
2	org.eclipse.jdt.core	420.6MB	1 557 007
3	org.eclipse.jdt.*	984.7MB	3 609 454

experiments[3] that are hence agnostic of which backend they are running on. Other backends have been discarded because they do not strictly comply with the standard EMF behavior (e.g. *MongoEMF*), they require manual modifications in the source models or metamodels (e.g. *EMF-fragments*), or because we were only able to run a small subset of the experiments on them (e.g. *Morsa*).

All backends use their respective native EMF generated code for the Java MoDisco metamodel and have been tested in their default configurations with the following exceptions: (i) the timeout values for CDO have been increased since the default ones are too low; (ii) for the sake of a fairer comparison, some extended features have been disabled in CDO (e.g. audit views and branches); and (iii) the Neo4j memory buffers have been tweaked in NEOEMF/GRAPH to reduce the memory consumption of the embedded Neo4j engine. CDO maintains its caching and prefetching facilities with their default values. In the case of NEOEMF/MAP and NEOEMF/GRAPH no high-level caching is performed.

5.2   Experiments

Experiment I: Import model from XMI — In this experiment (Table 6) we measure the time taken to load a source experimental model—that has been previously derived from the Java code and saved in XMI—and to save it in the selected persistence backend. The saved models are the ones used in next experiments. This experiment measures the time taken to create models that grow monotonically. Only a single configuration (setting the heap size to 8 GB) is used because the XMI model should be completely loaded into memory before saving it in the backend under study.

Experiment II: Simple model traversal — In this experiment we measure the total time taken to load a model, execute a visitor and unload a model. The visitor traverses the full containment tree starting from the root of the model. At each step of the traversal the visitor loads the element content from the backend. We show the results for the three scalable backends plus the standard XMI-based one. Three different maximum heap sizes have been used in this and the following benchmarks to demonstrate how the different backends perform in different configurations: 8GB for demonstrating the performance in an ideal scenario, and 512MB and 256MB to demonstrate how the loading/unloading mechanisms behave in setups with extremely limited memory. Table 7 shows the results of this experimentation over the test models. NEOEMF/MAP and NEOEMF/GRAPH are abbreviated as N/M and N/G respectively.

Experiment III: Query without full traversal — Results of an example query of this type are shown in Table 8. The query returns all the orphan and non-primitive types by navigating and filtering the *orphanTypes* association.

---

[3] Configuration details: Intel Core i7 3740QM (2.70GHz), 16 GB of DDR3 SDRAM (800MHz), Samsung SM841 SATA3 SSD Hard Disk (6GB/s), Windows 7 Enterprise 64, JRE 1.7.0_40-b43, Eclipse 4.4.0, EMF 2.10.1, NEOEMF/MAP uses MapDB 0.9.10, NEOEMF/GRAPH uses Neo4j 1.9.2, CDO 4.3.1 runs on top of H2 1.3.168.

Table 6. Import model from XMI

Model	NeoEMF/Map	NeoEMF/Graph	CDO
1	9 s	41 s	12 s
2	161 s	1 161 s	120 s
3	412 s	3 767 s	301 s

Table 7. Model traversal (includes loading and unloading time)

	-Xmx8g				-Xmx512m				-Xmx256m			
Model	XMI	N/M	N/G	CDO	XMI	N/M	N/G	CDO	XMI	N/M	N/G	CDO
1	4 s	3 s	16 s	14 s	4 s	3 s	15 s	13 s	4 s	3 s	15 s	13 s
2	35 s	25 s	201 s	133 s	Error[a]	42 s	235 s	550 s	Error[b]	121 s	239 s	650 s
3	79 s	62 s	708 s	309 s	Error[b]	366 s	763 s	348 s	Error[b]	443 s	783 s	403 s

[a]java.lang.OutOfMemoryError: Java heap space
[b]java.lang.OutOfMemoryError: GC overhead limit exceeded

Table 8. Model queries that do not traverse the model

	Orphan Non-Primitive Types									
	-Xmx8g			-Xmx512m			-Xmx256m			
Model	N/M	N/G	CDO	N/M	N/G	CDO	N/M	N/G	CDO	
1	¡1 s[c]	¡1 s[c]	¡1 s[c]	¡1 s[c]	¡1 s[c]	¡1 s[c]	¡1 s[c]	¡1 s[c]	¡1 s[c]	
2	¡1 s[c]	2 s	¡1 s[c]	¡1 s[c]	4 s	¡1 s[c]	¡1 s[c]	5 s	¡1 s[c]	
3	¡1 s[c]	19 s	2 s	¡1 s[c]	19 s	2 s	¡1 s[c]	20 s	2 s	

[c]Execution time is less than the precission used

Table 9. Model queries that traverse the model

	-Xmx8g			-Xmx512m			-Xmx256m		
Model	N/M	N/G	CDO	N/M	N/G	CDO	N/M	N/G	CDO
				Grabats					
1	1 s	11 s	9 s	1 s	10 s	9 s	1 s	11 s	9 s
2	24 s	188 s	121 s	48 s	217 s	558 s	127 s	228 s	665 s
3	61 s	717 s	299 s	367 s	736 s	370 s	480 s	774 s	479 s
				Unused Methods					
1	2 s	17 s	9 s	1 s	15 s	8 s	1 s	16 s	9 s
2	36 s	359 s	131 s	212 s	427 s	1 235 s	336 s	467 s	1 034 s
3	101 s	1 328 s	294 s	884 s	1 469 s	2 915 s	1290 s	1 818 s	Error[d]
				Thrown Exceptions per Package					
1	1 s	10 s	9 s	1 s	10 s	8 s	1 s	10 s	8 s
2	24 s	184 s	120 s	40 s	214 s	544 s	119 s	224 s	666 s
3	62 s	678 s	296 s	360 s	719 s	353 s	450 s	758 s	427 s
				Invisible Methods					
1	1 s	11 s	9 s	1 s	10 s	9 s	1 s	11 s	9 s
2	26 s	263 s	119 s	55 s	399 s	545 s	158 s	733 s	190 s
3	119 s	3 247 s	320 s	412 s	n/a[e]	404 s	496 s	n/a[e]	1 404 s
				Class Declaration Attributes					
1	1 s	10 s	9 s	1 s	10 s	9 s	1 s	10 s	8 s
2	24 s	183 s	120 s	37 s	216 s	540 s	156 s	226 s	670 s
3	61 s	694 s	294 s	261 s	749 s	348 s	457 s	756 s	460 s

[d]java.lang.OutOfMemoryError: GC overhead limit exceeded
[e]Process killed after 2 hours of computation

Table 10. Model modification and saving

	Orphan Non-Primitive Types								
	-Xmx8g			-Xmx512m			-Xmx256m		
Model	N/M	N/G	CDO	N/M	N/G	CDO	N/M	N/G	CDO
1	1 s	11 s	9 s	1 s	11 s	8 s	1 s	11 s	9 s
2	24 s	191 s	118 s	41 s	213 s	536 s	160 s	224 s	723 s
3	62 s	677 s	296 s	356 s	718 s	334 s	472 s	Error[f]	Error[f]

[f]java.lang.OutOfMemoryError: Java heap space

Experiment IV: Queries with full traversal — These queries start their computation by accessing the list of all the instances of a particular element type, and then apply a filtering to this list to select the starting points for navigating the model. In the experience of our industrial partners, this pattern covers the majority of computational-demanding queries in real world scenarios of the reverse-engineering domain. While the first of these queries is well-known in academic literature, the others have been selected to mimic typical model access patterns: (i) *Grabats* [14] returns the set of classes that hold static method declarations having as return type the holding class (i.e., Singleton); (ii) *Unused Methods* returns the set of method declarations that are private and not internally called; (iii) *Thrown Exceptions per package* collects and returns a map of *Packages* with the *Exceptions* that may be thrown by any of the methods declared by its contained classes; (iv) *Invisible Methods* returns the set of method declarations that are private or protected; and (v) *Class Declaration Attributes* returns a map associating each *Class* declaration to the set of its attribute declarations.

Experiment V: Model modification and saving — The last experiment aims to measure the overhead introduced by the transactional support provided by the different back-ends. Table 10 shows the execution times for renaming all method declarations and saving the modified model.

5.3   Discussion

From the analysis of the results, we can observe that NEOEMF/MAP performs, in general, better than any other solution when using the standard API. Only in scenarios with constrained memory the execution times tend equalize due to excessive garbage collection. Nevertheless, other persistence backends tend to be more erratic in those scenarios, running out of memory or presenting big differences in computation times between experiments.

In the XMI import experiment (Table 6) we can observe that NEOEMF/MAP presents import times in the the same order of magnitude than CDO, but it is about a 33% slower for the largest model. The simple data model with low-cost operations implemented by NEOEMF/MAP contrasts with the more complex data model—and operations—implemented by NEOEMF/GRAPH which is consistently slower by a factor between 7 and 9. It can be observed that NEOEMF/MAP is affected by the overhead produced by modifications on big lists that grow monotonically since it does not implement any caching yet.

Table 7 shows that a traversal of a very large model is much faster (up to 9 times) by using the NEOEMF/MAP persistence layer with respect to both a CDO and NEOEMF/GRAPH. However, in scenarios with very constrained memory, some garbage collection overhead can be noticed. Additionally, if load and unload times are considered (which are negligible for NEOEMF/MAP, NEOEMF/GRAPH and CDO), NEOEMF/MAP also outperforms XMI. This is because before executing the traversal, the XMI-based backend needs to parse the whole input model, which is a costly operation. It can also be observed that XMI is unable to load the model into memory for small heap sizes.

Queries that do not require traversing a large part of the model are computed in a negligible time both in NEOEMF/MAP and CDO. NEOEMF/GRAPH shows higher execution times, specially on bigger models (Table 8). In this case, it can be observed that using the rich graph-based data model cannot be exploited when using the standard methods for model traversal.

The fast model-traversal ability of NEOEMF/MAP is exploited by the pattern followed by most of the queries in the modernization domain (Table 9). As a result, NEOEMF/MAP is consistently faster than other backends for all queries, model sizes and heap sizes. Only in few cases NEOEMF/MAP has similar performance to CDO, while in other scenarios NEOEMF/MAP is up to 9 times faster. The low memory consumption of NEOEMF/MAP also is revealed, since there appear cases in which CDO behaves more erratically, running out of memory or experiencing slowness issues caused by the garbage collector.

Typical queries that traverse the model to apply and persist changes perform, in general, significantly better on NEOEMF/MAP (Table 10): 5 times faster on average (on big models) and even up to 9 faster (on small models). In cases with limited memory, however, CDO may present better results than NEOEMF/MAP due to garbage collection overhead. Nevertheless, this is not always the case, and CDO also reveals its tendency to run out of memory in such scenarios.

6 Related Work

As EMF models are designed following an object-oriented paradigm, our model-persistence backend is inspired by object persistence systems for software tools that have been extensively studied in the last three decades [13, 25]. In recent works, different authors have provided some evidence that the use of schema-free databases may improve performance in persisting VLMs. However, most of them have put focus on graph-oriented [8,9] or document-oriented databases [11,19,20]. Although document-oriented databases can be considered a form of *Key-Value Stores*, NEOEMF/MAP is, as far as we know, the only proposal that focus on the optimization of atomic operations by using maps with simple keys and values.

One of the proposals that uses a document-oriented database as its persistence backend is Morsa [19]. It provides on-demand loading capabilities together with incremental updates, and can be used seamlessly to persist models using the standard EMF mechanisms. Performance of the storage backend and their own query language has been reported [19,20]. Our persistence layer resembles Morsa in several aspects (notably in on-demand loading) but we aim at designing an efficient data representation for models, to optimize runtime performance.

Mongo EMF [11] is another alternative to store EMF models in MongoDB databases. Mongo EMF provides the same standard API than previous approaches. However, according to the documentation, the storage mechanism behaves slightly different than the standard persistence backend (for example, for persisting collections of objects or saving bi-directional cross-document containment references). For this reason, Mongo EMF cannot be used without performing any modification to replace another backend in an existing system.

EMF fragments [17] is another NoSQL-based persistence layer for EMF aimed at achieving fast navigation and fast storage of new data. EMF fragments principles are simpler than in other similar approaches. Those principles are based on the EMF proxy mechanism. In EMF fragments, models are automatically partitioned in several chunks (fragments). Unlike our approach, CDO, and Morsa, all data from a single fragment is loaded at a time. Only links to another fragments are loaded on demand. Another characteristic of this approach is that artifacts should be specifically adapted: metamodels have to be modified to indicate where the partitions should be made to get the partitioning capabilities.

NEOEMF/GRAPH—previously known as Neo4EMF [9]—is our graph-based proposal for storing VLMs. In NEOEMF/GRAPH we consider that, since models are a set of highly interconnected elements, graphs are the most natural way to represent them. As we have experienced, however, a significant gain in performance is only obtained when using native queries on the underlying persistence back-end. Although this can be acceptable in some scenarios (as shown in [8,19]), the use of native queries or custom languages implies changes in the client code.

7   Conclusion and Future Work

In this paper we proposed a map-based database persistence layer to handle large models and compared it against previous alternatives based on relational databases and graph databases. Using EMF as the implementation technology, we used queries from some of our industrial partners in the model-driven modernization domain as experiments. The main lesson is that—in terms of performance—typical model-access APIs, with fine-grained methods that only allow for one-step-navigation queries, do not benefit from complex relational or graph-based data structures. Much better results are potentially obtained by optimized low-level data structures, like hash-tables, that guarantee low and constant access times. Additional features that may be of interest in scenarios where performance is not an issue (such as versioning and transactional support provided by CDO) have not been considered.

As further work we want, first, to extend our study on optimized persistence layers for MDE by analyzing caching strategies, especially with reference to element unloading and element prefetching. Caching, and smart prefetching and unloading, aim to (i) alleviate the impact of garbage collection and (ii) reduce the overhead in modifications on lists that grow monotonically. In parallel, we will continue analyzing the benefits of other backends depending on the specific application scenario, such as the graph-based persistence solutions for high-level queries on tools that can drop some of our requirements. In theses cases, for example, bypassing the model access API by translating the queries to high-performance native graph-database queries may provide great benefits.

References

1. CDO DB Store (2014), http://wiki.eclipse.org/CDO/DB_Store
2. CDO Hibernate Store (2014), http://wiki.eclipse.org/CDO/Hibernate_Store
3. CDO Model Repository (2014), http://www.eclipse.org/cdo/
4. CDO MongoDB Store (2014), http://wiki.eclipse.org/CDO/MongoDB_Store
5. CDO Objectivity Store (2014), http://wiki.eclipse.org/CDO/Objectivity_Store
6. Eclipse Marketplace - Modeling Tools (2014),
   http://marketplace.eclipse.org/category/categories/modeling-tools
7. Eclipse Modeling Framework (2014), http://www.eclipse.org/modeling/emf/
8. Barmpis, K., Kolovos, D.S.: Comparative analysis of data persistence technologies
   for large-scale models. In: Proceedings of the 2012 Extreme Modeling Workshop,
   XM 2012, pp. 33–38. ACM, New York (2012)
9. Benelallam, A., Gómez, A., Sunyé, G., Tisi, M., Launay, D.: Neo4EMF, A scalable
   persistence layer for EMF models. In: Cabot, J., Rubin, J. (eds.) ECMFA 2014.
   LNCS, vol. 8569, pp. 230–241. Springer, Heidelberg (2014)
10. Bergmann, G., Horváth, Á., Ráth, I., Varró, D., Balogh, A., Balogh, Z., Ökrös, A.: In-
    cremental evaluation of model queries over EMF models. In: Petriu, D.C., Rouquette,
    N., Haugen, Ø. (eds.) MODELS 2010, Part I. LNCS, vol. 6394, pp. 76–90. Springer,
    Heidelberg (2010)
11. Bryan Hunt: MongoEMF (2014), https://github.com/BryanHunt/mongo-emf/
12. Cook, S., Jones, G., Kent, S., Wills, A.: Domain-Specific Development with Visual
    Studio DSL Tools, 1st edn. Addison-Wesley Professional (2007)
13. Gallo, F., Minot, R., Thomas, I.: The Object Management System of PCTE as a
    Software Engineering Database Management System. SIGPLAN Not. 22(1), 12–15
    (1987)
14. Jouault, F., et al.: An AmmA/ATL Solution for the GraBaTs 2009 Reverse Engi-
    neering Case Study. In: 5th Int. Workshop on Graph-Based Tools (2009)
15. Kelly, S., Lyytinen, K., Rossi, M.: Metaedit+ a fully configurable multi-user and
    multi-tool case and came environment. In: Constantopoulos, P., Vassiliou, Y.,
    Mylopoulos, J. (eds.) CAiSE 1996. LNCS, vol. 1080, pp. 1–21. Springer, Heidelberg
    (1996)
16. Ledeczi, A., Maroti, M., et al.: The generic modeling environment. In: Workshop
    on Intelligent Signal Processing, vol. 17 (2001)
17. Markus Scheidgen: EMF fragments (2014),
    https://github.com/markus1978/emf-fragments/wiki
18. OMG: OMG MOF 2 XMI Mapping Specification version 2.4.1 (August 2011)
19. Espinazo Pagán, J., Sánchez Cuadrado, J., García Molina, J.: Morsa: A Scalable
    Approach for Persisting and Accessing Large Models. In: Whittle, J., Clark, T.,
    Kühne, T. (eds.) MODELS 2011. LNCS, vol. 6981, pp. 77–92. Springer, Heidelberg
    (2011)
20. Pagn, J.E., Molina, J.G.: Querying large models efficiently. Information and Soft-
    ware Technology 56(6), 586–622 (2014)
21. Pohjonen, R., Tolvanen, J.P.: Automated production of family members: Lessons
    learned. In: 2nd International Workshop on Product Line Engineering-The Early
    Steps: Planning, Modeling, and Managing, pp. 49–57 (2002)
22. Ruscio, D.D., Paige, R.F., Pierantonio, A.: Guest editorial to the special issue
    on success stories in model driven engineering. Sci. Comput. Program. 89, 69–70
    (2014)

23. Scheidgen, M., Zubow, A., Fischer, J., Kolbe, T.H.: Automated and Transparent Model Fragmentation for Persisting Large Models. In: France, R.B., Kazmeier, J., Breu, R., Atkinson, C. (eds.) MODELS 2012. LNCS, vol. 7590, pp. 102–118. Springer, Heidelberg (2012)
24. Steel, J., Drogemuller, R., Toth, B.: Model interoperability in building information modelling. Software & Systems Modeling 11(1), 99–109 (2012)
25. Wakeman, L., Jowett, J.: PCTE: The Standard for Open Repositories. Prentice-Hall, Inc., Upper Saddle River (1993)

Composing Message Translators and Inferring Their Data Types Using Tree Automata

Emil Andriescu, Thierry Martinez, and Valérie Issarny

Inria Paris-Rocquencourt,
Domaine de Voluceau, Rocquencourt, Le Chesnay 78153, France

Abstract. Modern distributed systems and Systems of Systems (SoS) are built as a composition of existing components and services. As a result, systems communicate (either internally, locally or over networks) using protocol stacks of ever-increasing complexity whose messages need to be translated (i.e., interpreted, generated, analyzed and transformed) by third-party systems such as services dedicated to security or interoperability. We observe that current approaches in software engineering are unable to provide an efficient solution towards reusing message translators associated with the message formats composed in protocol stacks. Instead, developers must write ad hoc "glue-code" whenever composing two or more message translators. In addition, the data structures of the output must be integrated/harmonized with the target system.

In this paper we propose a solution to the above that enables the composition of message translators according to a high-level user-provided query. While the composition scheme we propose is simple, the inference of the resulting data structures is a problem that has not been solved up to now. This leads us to contribute with a novel data type inference mechanism, which generates a data-schema using tree automata, based on the aforementioned user query.

1 Introduction

Protocols used by modern systems are becoming increasingly complex, while standards bodies are unable to keep pace with the current speed of tech development [16]. At the same time, there is an emerging need to analyze interactions and facilitate interoperability of new as well as legacy systems in the absence of the protocol stack implementations. This need originates from the way systems are designed. Indeed, most modern systems are productive and cost-effective only if they can interoperate with other systems, sharing with them data and functionalities [9]. Additionally, analyzing system interactions at run-time is vital in assuring security in enterprise environments (e.g., protocols in use should be made compatible with corporate firewalls), but can also help in achieving interoperability by automatically discovering/learning functional aspects of the system, such as: application behavior [11], data semantics [10], etc.

Data formats, and in particular message formats, have long represented a barrier to interoperability [3]. This is because software parts often make different assumptions about how data is represented [21]. A crosscutting challenge is further represented by *protocol binding*, i.e., the way protocols are combined to form

© Springer-Verlag Berlin Heidelberg 2015
A. Egyed and I. Schaefer (Eds.): FASE 2015, LNCS 9033, pp. 35–50, 2015.
DOI: 10.1007/978-3-662-46675-9_3

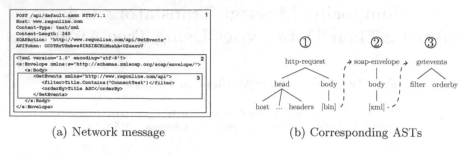

(a) Network message   (b) Corresponding ASTs

Fig. 1. A composed message sample and its corresp. ASTs (leaf nodes omitted)

a protocol stack, which causes systems to exchange messages combining multiple syntaxes (i.e., composite message formats). The resulting message formats can include a mix of text encodings, binary encodings and data serialization formats. As an example, consider the message depicted in Figure 1a. The message combines two distinct data representations: ① a text-based message part that corresponds to the HTTP protocol, and parts ② & ③ that use XML serialization. In the case where individual translators for each independent message format are available (e.g., for parts ①, ② and ③), "glue code" has to be provided in order to compose them. However, to the best of our knowledge, existing methods for the composition of parsers are highly specific to a given parsing method or algorithm (e.g., grammar composition [19], parser-combinators [13], parse-table composition [20]) and cannot be easily generalized. As a result, existing methods do not allow for the systematic composition of message translators out of third-party translators, thereby requiring developers to implement hardcoded adapters in order to process messages.

Additionally, the problem of composing message translators is related to the composition of the associated data structures (or inference of composite data types). The composition of data structures relative to the composition of message translators ensures that composite translators can be seamlessly (or even automatically) integrated with existing systems. For instance, when parsing the message in Figure 1a using a composite translator we would normally obtain three separate data structures, as shown in Figure 1b in the form of Abstract Syntax Trees (AST). Knowledge of the precise constraints on the structure of ASTs is essential if composite translators are to be integrated into other systems. For instance, in Enterprise Service Busses (ESB) [6], service adaptation requires the transformation of messages into a uniform representation (most commonly XML). However, to the best of our knowledge, in all existing ESB implementations, XML data-schemas must be hand-coded by the developers of adaptors. AST composition can be arbitrary, but it should not result in the loss of information. In other words, the AST transformation applied for the composition must be injective, thus invertible. In the context of this paper, we are particularly interested in the *substitution* class of AST transformations, that is, the substitution of a leaf node by a sub-tree. This allows us to represent encapsulated message formats in a hierarchical manner. In Figure 1b, we exemplify such a case of substitution using dotted arrows, as follows: (i) the node labeled [*bin*] in AST ① is substituted by AST ②, and (ii) the node labeled [*xml*] in AST ② is substituted by AST ③. While other compositions are possible (e.g., AST ② could alternatively be appended to the root of AST ①), this particular one closely resembles the way most protocols arrange encapsulated data, therefore being the most intuitive. The tree transformation mentioned above can be easily expressed by adapting already existing mechanisms for XML, such as the XSLT transformation language in combination with the XPath query language. In general, defining the composition of ASTs is rather straightforward. However, inferring the data structure resulting from an AST composition is more complex Indeed, it is already known that for an arbitrary tree transformation, the problem of type inference may not have a solution [12]. While the problem of type inference is quite common in the domains of functional programming languages [2,5] and XML technologies [12,17,18], we are not aware of any solution capable of type inference for the *substitution* class of tree compositions although this kind of transformation is very common in practice (most notably in the XML transformation language XSLT).

Following the above, this paper makes two major contributions to the issue of systematic message translation for modern distributed systems:

1. Starting from the premise that "off-the-shelf" message translators for individual protocols are readily available in at least an executable form, we propose a solution for the automated composition of message translators. The solution simply requires the specification of a composition rule that is expressed using a subset of the navigational core of the W3C XML query language XPath [8].
2. We provide a formal mechanism, using tree automata, which based on the aforementioned composition rule, generates an associated AST *data-schema* for the translator composition. This contribution enables the inference of correct data-schemas, relieving developers from the time-consuming task of defining them. On a more general note, the provided method solves the type inference problem for the *substitution* class of tree compositions in linear time on the size of the output. The provided inference algorithm can thus be adapted to a number of applications beyond the scope of this paper, such as XML Schema inference for XSLT transformations.

There is already a number of systems that can benefit from translator composition such as: Packet Analyzers, Internet Traffic Monitoring, Vulnerability Discovery, Application Integration and Enterprise Service Bus, etc. As a result, our approach can have an immediate impact knowing that current implementations rely on tightly coupled and usually hardcoded message translators, to the detriment of software reuse.

The paper is organized as follows. The next section provides the background of our research focusing on challenges related to message parsing and translator composition, as well as to the problem of AST data-schema inference for a given composition rule. Then, Section 3 details our approach to the systematic composition of message translators, while Section 4 introduces a method to automatically generate AST data-schemas (formalized as Hedge Automata) associated to a given composition of translators. Section 5 assesses our current prototype implementation and its benefits. Finally, Section 6 summarizes our contributions over related work and introduces perspectives for future work.

2 Background

Ideally, message translators may be developed by separate parties, using various technologies, while developers should be able to compose them using an easy to use mechanism. A common challenge in realizing such a mechanism is related to parsing composite message formats. Specifically, one must identify the mechanisms of message encapsulation, that is, the rules upon which one message syntax is combined with another message syntax. However, *"parsers are so monolithic and tightly constructed that, in the general case, it is impossible to extend them without regenerating them from a source grammar"* [20]. Even if the source grammars are made available, composition is still an issue, taking into account that combining two unambiguous grammars may result in an ambiguous grammar, and that the ambiguity detection problem for context-free grammars is undecidable in the general case [1].

2.1 Encapsulated Message Formats

The following investigates in more detail the various cases, from the most complex (also the most general) to the most trivial, of syntax composition to highlight the specific case applying to message composition.

Mutually-recursive Syntax Composition refers to the case where the syntax of two distinct message formats can mutually be included inside one another. A technique commonly used to support this case of composition is *recursive descent parsing* (in particular implemented by parser combinators [22,13]), where a composite parser is defined from a set of mutually recursive procedures. This class of syntax composition has been extensively studied in the domain of extensible programming languages [19,20], where parser composition allows extending the syntax of a "host" programming language, such as Java, with an "extension", such as SQL. Intuitively, the syntax is mutually-recursive because SQL queries can appear within Java expressions, and, at the same time, Java expressions can appear within SQL queries, allowing an unbounded chain of compositions. The same cannot be said about messages exchanged by protocol stacks where mutually-recursive compositions are unlikely given the fixed number of layers.

Syntax Composition represents a restriction of the case above where the inclusion is not mutual. This class includes both *syntax extensions*, which allow expanding the initial language with new message types, as well as *syntax restrictions*, which introduce intentional limitations on the expressiveness of a language, in the same sense explained by Cardelli *et al.* in [4]. The way two syntaxes can be composed to actually reduce the expressiveness of a language is by giving new constraints for existing terminal symbols. For instance, the message in Figure 1a can be successfully parsed by a HTTP parser or by a composed HTTP/SOAP parser. The difference is that the latter will only allow messages that contain SOAP messages in the HTTP *body* section.

Stratified Syntax Inclusion is a special case of syntax composition, which may only restrict the expressiveness of the base language. Commonly, a middleware protocol parser is syntactically "unaware" of encapsulated messages, which are treated as a collection of binary data or arbitrary character strings. Informally, we can say that message parsers should be "forward-compatible" with respect to possible message compositions. Because of this containment property, we can state that whenever two message translators are composed to handle an encapsulated message format, they specialize (or restrict) the set of messages initially accepted. Figure 1a illustrates a concrete example of *stratified syntax inclusion*, where a *SOAP-envelope* message ② is included in the *body* section of an *HTTP request* message ①. The second encapsulation between layers ② and ③ is slightly different because both messages share the same lexical syntax (i.e., XML), but have different data syntax (formulated in terms of XML).

Trivial Inclusion refers to the case where the syntax of composed message formats is delimited by other, more trivial, means. For instance, some protocols compose messages by simply arranging the content in a sequential manner (e.g., one parser analyzes a part of the input, and returns the remaining part in its result). This kind of composition can be easily modeled as a particular case of *stratified syntax inclusion*.

Considering the above cases, we narrow our problem to the case of *stratified syntax inclusion*. While this type of syntax composition is generic enough to capture encapsulation mechanisms implemented by most protocol stacks, it also allows avoiding parsing ambiguity without difficulty. Thanks to the characteristics of stratified syntax inclusion, compositions may be implemented without knowing the internal aspects of translators, as we further present in Section 3.

2.2 Data Type Inference

As far as we know, the problem of inferring the output schema (or the data type) of an arbitrary tree transformation has not yet been solved, while it is known that, in general, a transformation might not be recognizable by a schema [12].

In [12], Milo *et al.* propose an approach capable of type inference for queries over semistructured data, and in particular XML. However, the query mechanism for node selection that is proposed is only capable of vertical navigation, meaning that the language does not allow conditions on the ordering of nodes (horizontal navigation), which is particularly required for selecting ordered nodes of an AST. In [17], Papakonstantinou *et al.* propose an improved approach that can infer Data Type Definitions (DTDs) for views of XML documents. In their work, *views* are in fact subtrees that are selected using a query language capable of both vertical and horizontal selection conditions. The solution can be easily generalized to select *views* from multiple trees/sources. However, it is not capable of merging the results from different XML languages, as it is required in the case of translator composition.

CDuce [2] is a language for expressing well-typed XML transformations. Specifically, CDuce can automatically infer non-recursive data types corresponding to a provided XML transformation. CDuce does not propose a high-level tree composition mechanism, but rather provides a language where XML queries and transformations can be implemented using a low-level form of navigational patterns that are non-compliant with the XPath standard. In [5], an extension was provided, which essentially allows implementing XPath-like navigation expressions by pattern matching and to precisely type them. While this improves the query mechanism, it does not solve the limitations of the transformation mechanism which, in our understanding, is limited to disjoint trees concatenated in the result. We mention that the problem of type inference is related, but different to the problem of static type checking for XSLT transformations [23,18], which intends to verify that a program always converts valid source documents into also valid output documents for the case were both input and output schemas are known.

Considering the above, none of the approaches solve the AST type inference problem for the *substitution* class of transformations, which applies whenever two or more message translators are combined. In the next section, we introduce our approach for translator composition and detail the *substitution* transformation that is applied.

3   Message Translator Composition

Translator composition includes two mutually-dependent problems, the composition of parsers and the composition of un-parsers (also referred to as message composers). Because of space restrictions, we only discuss the first one in detail, while the latter can be easily deduced from our presentation.

Definition 1 (Message Translator). *A message translator comprises a parsing function* $P : M \rightarrow T(\Sigma)$ *that takes as input a bit-string and outputs a tree, and the inverse* $C = P^{-1}$ *where:*

— $M \subseteq \{0,1\}^*$
— $T(\Sigma)$ *is a set of finite ordered, unranked, directed, and rooted trees* [1] *labelled over the finite alphabet* $\Sigma = \Sigma_0 \cup \{\beta, 0, 1\}$, *where* Σ_0 *is a set of labels, not including the set of* binary labels $\{0, 1\}$, *neither the* binary-subtree label β [2].

In Figure 2, we detail our method of composing message translators in the form of two block diagrams, corresponding to the composition of, respectively, parser functions and the inverse composer functions.

Parser composition requires three inputs, (i) a parser P_1, (ii) a query $\mathcal{Q}$ that identifies parts of the output of P_1 which contains the encapsulated data, encoded in an auxiliary message format, and a parser P_2 that corresponds to the auxiliary message format. Informally, the method works as follows. First, the stratified

---

[1] A finite ordered tree t over a set of labels Σ is a mapping from a finite prefix-closed set of positions $\mathcal{P}os(t) \subseteq N^*$ into Σ as explained in [7].

[2] Note that since elements of T represent ASTs, arbitrary data can be included only as leaf nodes, in the form of an ordered sequence of binary labels, by convention, under a β-labeled node. Such a structure (e.g., $\beta \rightarrow 1011...$) is equivalent to a bit-string $b \in \{0,1\}^*$. We use this convention to avoid having an infinite label alphabet, such as $\Sigma_0 \cup \{0,1\}^*$, that would be outside the scope of regular tree automata theory.

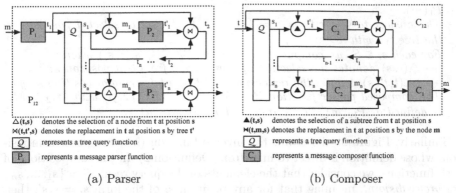

△(t,s) denotes the selection of a node from t at position s
⋈(t,t',s) denotes the replacement in t at position s by tree t'
$\boxed{Q}$ represents a tree query function
$\boxed{P_1}$ represents a message parser function

▲(t,s) denotes the selection of a subtree from t at position s
⋈(t,m,s) denotes the replacement in t at position s by the node m
$\boxed{Q}$ represents a tree query function
$\boxed{C}$ represents a message composer function

(a) Parser   (b) Composer

Fig. 2. Message translator composition mechanism

input message is parsed using the parser P_1, which corresponds to the first
stratum of the message. The query Q is then used to select positions in the
resulting AST which correspond to encapsulated messages (of a second format).
Then, the AST of the composite message is obtained by substituting in the initial
tree every position that belongs to an answer to Q by trees resulting from the
parsing of the encapsulated messages using P_2.

To better exemplify this mechanism, we consider the stratified message presented in Figure 1 (the leaf nodes containing message data values are omitted).
The first stratum (or layer) ① of the message consists of a HTTP request message. By passing this message through a HTTP translator, we obtain an AST
representation similar to Tree ①. Knowing that the sub-tree [bin] attached to
the *body* node contains (encapsulates) SOAP message syntax we may pass this
data to a SOAP translator to be interpreted. To support this kind of composition
for all trees of the form of Tree ①, which may be an infinite set, we must generalize the composition mechanism. To do so, we can define the node-selection
requirements as a *unary* (or *node-selecting*) *tree query* [18].

In the context of this paper, we consider a tree-query to be a subset of
the navigational core of the W3C XML query language XPath [8], which we
represent formally in Section 4 as *tree query automata*. Using the XPath syntax, we can write $T_{HTTP}[/request/body/] \rightarrow T_{SOAP}$, meaning that the translator T_{HTTP} is composed with translator T_{SOAP} such that, for a given composite message, all nodes selected by the query */request/body/* are substituted with an AST corresponding to T_{SOAP}. While this example is trivial,
more complex queries are supported. For instance, defining the composition
between a HTTP translator and a MIME-type translator can be specified as
$T_{HTTP}[/request/head/header[key =' Content - Type']/value] \rightarrow T_{MIME}$,
making use of an XPath predicate that enables the selection of a node that
contains a specific value.

Formally, we introduce the following definition for parser composition:

Definition 2 (Parser Composition). *Given two message parsers $P_1 : M_1 \rightarrow$
$T_1(\Sigma_1)$, $P_2 : M_2 \rightarrow T_2(\Sigma_2)$ and a user-defined tree query Q for $t_1 \in T_1(\Sigma_1)$, we
define the composed parser $P_{12} : M_{12} \rightarrow T_{12}(\Sigma_1 \cup \Sigma_2)$ as follows (see Figure 2a):*

— *For a stratified message $m \in M_1$, we apply the query $\mathcal{Q}$ on t_1, where $t_1 = P_1(m)$.*
— *The answer to $\mathcal{Q}$ for t_1 is $S = \{s_1, ..., s_n\}$, the set of selected positions in the tree t_1, with $n \geq 0$.*
— *For each $s_i \in S$, we compute $t_{i+1} = \bowtie(t_i, P_2(\triangle(t_i, s_i)), s_i)$ where:*
    — *$\triangle(t, s)$ denotes the selection of a bit-string from t at position s;*
    — *$\bowtie(t, t', s)$ denotes the replacement in t of a bit-string at position s by t'.*
— *The composed parser function $P_{12} : M_{12} \to T_{12}(\Sigma_1 \cup \Sigma_2)$, with $M_{12} \subseteq M_1$, is defined as $P_{12}(m) = t_{n+1}$ ($t_{n+1} = t$ in Figure 2a).*

Similarly, Figure 2b illustrates the inverse function (i.e., composer composition, whose definition is direct to infer from Definition 2). In the compositions of both functions, we consider that the elements of the query result $S = \{s_1, ..., s_n\}$ are *prefix-disjoint*, meaning that for any position s_i of the form $s_i = s_j s'$, then $i = j$. This property ensures that the *selection* $\triangle(t, s)$ and *replacement* $\bowtie(t, t', s)$ operations for a query result S on a *tree* t can be performed in an arbitrary order.

We observe that the aforementioned composition method is part of a wider class of *result-conversion* mechanisms. Most notably, the Scala (`http://www.scala-lang.org/`) programming language implements a result-conversion *parser combinator*. A result-conversion combinator, denoted $P\,\hat{}\,\hat{}\,f$, is defined as a higher-order function, which takes as input a parser function P and a user-defined function f that is applied on the result of P. The modified parser succeeds exactly when P succeeds. This method is particularly relevant to our case because it is purely defined on the output data type, and thus it does not require any knowledge about the input message syntax. However, in our case, the function f is not arbitrary, since it is represented by a user query.

By applying the composition mechanism defined above, we are able to compose message translators as black-box functions, which, in turn, allows the translation of composite messages (for the case of *stratified syntax inclusion*) to and from a uniform tree representation. However, the constraints on the structure of this tree representation (i.e., the data-schema) are unknown. In the next section, we provide a formal mechanism by which we are able to automatically generate a *data-schema* for the resulting ASTs.

4   Data-Schema Composition

Data-schema languages share unranked tree automata as theoretical foundation [15]. In what follows, we use top-down non-deterministic finite hedge automata [14] (or, equivalently, hedge grammars) to model AST languages. Below, we first recall the basic definitions associated with tree automata.

4.1   Definitions

Definition 3 (NFHA). *A top-down non-deterministic finite hedge automaton (NFHA) is a tuple $\mathcal{A} = (Q, \Sigma, Q_0, \Delta)$ where Q is a finite set of states, Σ is an alphabet of symbols, $Q_0 \subseteq Q$ is a subset of accepting states, and Δ is a finite set of transition rules of the type $q \to a(R)$ where $q \in Q$, $a \in \Sigma$, and $R \subseteq Q^*$ is a regular language over Q.*

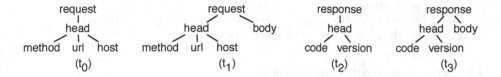

Fig. 3. Sample ASTs (leaf and β nodes omitted)

Additionally, we introduce the definition of $\mathcal{A}$-derivations, which we use as a helper mechanism to describe the process of tree evaluation by a hedge automaton.

Definition 4 ($\mathcal{A}$-derivations). *Given an automaton $\mathcal{A}$, $\mathcal{A}$-derivations are defined inductively as follows. A tree $r \in T(Q)$ with $r = q(r_1 \ldots r_n)$ is a derivation from a state $q \in Q$ for a tree $t \in T(\Sigma)$ with $t = a(t_1 \ldots t_n)$ if:*

— *There exists a transition rule $q \to a(R) \in \Delta$ such that $q_1 \ldots q_n \in R$,*
— *For all $1 \le i \le n$, r_i is an $\mathcal{A}$-derivation from $q_i \in Q$ for t_i.*

A tree $t \in T(\Sigma)$ is accepted by an automaton $\mathcal{A}$ if there exists a derivation from a state $q_0 \in Q_0$ for t.

Example 1 (NFHA). Consider the automaton $\mathcal{A}^b = (Q^b, \Sigma^b, Q_0^b, \Delta^b)$ that recognizes the language $L(\mathcal{A}^b) = \{t_0, t_1, t_2, t_3\}$ containing the trees shown in Figure 3. The automaton is defined as follows:

— $Q^b = \{q_0, q_1, ..., q_{10}\}$, $Q_0^b = \{q_0, q_1\}$,
— $\Sigma^b = \{request, response, head, body, ...\} \cup \{\beta, 0, 1\}$,
— $\Delta^b = \{q_0 \to request(q_3\, q_2?), q_1 \to response(q_4\, q_2?), q_2 \to body(q_{10}),$
  $q_3 \to head(q_5\, q_6\, q_7), q_4 \to head(q_8\, q_9), q_5 \to method(q_{10}), q_6 \to url(q_{10}),$
  $q_7 \to host(q_{10}), q_8 \to code(q_{10}), q_9 \to version(q_{10}), q_{10} \to \beta(q_\beta)\}$,
  q_β is a state that accepts any sequence of $\{0, 1\}$ leaves.

The $\mathcal{A}_b$-derivation for the tree $t_0 = request\langle head\langle method\, url\, host\rangle\rangle$ (shown in Figure 3) is the tree $r = q_0\langle q_3\langle q_5\langle q_{10}\langle q_\beta\rangle\rangle\, q_6\langle q_{10}\langle q_\beta\rangle\rangle\, q_7\langle q_{10}\langle q_\beta\rangle\rangle\rangle\rangle$, where $r \in T(Q^b)$, thus, we can say that t_0 is accepted by $\mathcal{A}^b$.

While data-schemas are formalized as NFHA, we introduce a second type of tree automata, which we use to formalize tree queries. Informally, a query automaton is a tree automaton with the attachment of a set of "marked" states that are used to model node-selection.

Definition 5 (Query NFHA). *A query NFHA is a pair $\mathcal{Q} = (\mathcal{A}, Q_m)$ where $\mathcal{A}$ is a top-down NFHA over a set of states Q, and $Q_m \subseteq Q$ is a subset of marked states. Given a query $\mathcal{Q} = (\mathcal{A}, Q_m)$ and a tree t, a set S of positions in t is an answer to $\mathcal{Q}$ for t if there exists an $\mathcal{A}$-derivation r for t such that S is the set of positions of all nodes in r that are in Q_m.*

Example 2 (Query NFHA). Consider the tree query $\mathcal{Q}^p = (\mathcal{A}^p, Q_m^p)$, which applied on trees from $L(\mathcal{A}^b)$, selects the node labeled *body* that is a child node of the tree root. Intuitively, this query should return an empty set of positions S for the trees t_0 and t_2, and a single position when applied on t_1 and t_3. This query is defined as follows:

— $Q^p = \{q_0, q_1, q_2, q_T\}$, $Q^p_0 = \{q_0, q_1\}$, $\Sigma^p = \Sigma^b$, $Q^p_m = \{q_3\}$,
— $\Delta^p = \{q_0 \rightarrow request(q_T, q_2), q_1 \rightarrow response(q_T, q_2), q_2 \rightarrow body(q_3),$
  $q_3 \rightarrow \beta(q_\beta)\}$, q_T is a state which accepts all trees.

4.2   Tree Automata Composition

We now present a method for composing two hedge automata $\mathcal{A}^b$ and $\mathcal{A}^e$ based on the composition rules defined using a query NFHA $\mathcal{Q}$. The resulting automaton $\mathcal{A}$ recognizes a tree language corresponding to the substitution defined by $\mathcal{Q}$.

Let $\mathcal{Q} = (\mathcal{A}^q, Q_m)$ be a query NFHA, where $\mathcal{A}^q = (Q^q, \Sigma^b, Q^q_0, \Delta^q)$.

Given two trees t^b (base tree) and t^e (extension tree), we note $t^b[\mathcal{Q} \leftarrow t^e]$ the tree obtained by substituting t^e in t^b at every position that belongs to an answer to $\mathcal{Q}$ for t^b.

Given two sets of trees T^b and T^e, we note $T^b[\mathcal{Q} \leftarrow T^e]$ the set of trees of the form $t^b[\mathcal{Q} \leftarrow t^e]$ where $t^b \in T^b$ and $t^e \in T^e$.

Since the composition performs the intersection between the base automaton and the query, we can suppose without loss of generality that the base automaton and the query share the same alphabet. Furthermore, it is worth noticing that the query can restrict the language recognized by the base automaton. However, in practice, we consider mostly queries that are expressed using XPath: such a query accepts all trees, even if the XPath query does not select any node in some of these trees.

We consider the following core XPath language:

```
path ::= '/' relative-path
relative-path ::= step[pred] | step[pred] '/' relative-path
                | step[pred] '//' relative-path
step ::= label | '*'
pred ::= path | not(path) | pred and pred | pred or pred | true
```

We restrict `pred` to predicates that can be recognized by Boolean combinations of paths (with the usual set-to-Boolean interpretation: a path is true if and only if it matches at least one node). This ensures that these predicates can be recognized by hedge automata. Indeed, the transformation from an XPath to a query automaton is straightforward, and it is done inductively over the structure of the path. The most relevant construction is `step[pred]` `'/'` `relative-path`: given the query automata A_P (with initial state Q_P) for `pred` and A_R for `relative-path`, a new accepting state q_0 is introduced with the transition $q_0 \rightarrow step(q_T * q_P q_T *)$ and the resulting automaton is intersected with A_R. Resulting automata are completed such that they accept all trees, even in the case that no node is selected.

For an arbitrary tree transformation, type inference may not have a solution [12]. It is thus important to prove that for the *substitution* class of tree transformations, which we defined in Section 3, all resulting AST languages are recognizable:

Proposition 1. *Given a query $\mathcal{Q}$ and two finite hedge automata:*
$\mathcal{A}^b = (Q^b, \Sigma^b, Q^b_0, \Delta^b)$ and $\mathcal{A}^e = (Q^e, \Sigma^e, Q^e_0, \Delta^e)$,
the language $L(\mathcal{A}^b)[\mathcal{Q} \leftarrow L(\mathcal{A}^e)]$ is recognizable by a finite hedge automaton $\mathcal{A}$.

Algorithm 1. Tree automata composition

```
 1: procedure COMPOSE(A^b, A^e, Q)
 2:     A = (Q, Σ, Q_0, Δ);
 3:     Q ← Q^e; Σ ← Σ^b ∪ Σ^e; Q_0 ← Q_0^q; Δ ← Δ^e; S ← Q_0^b × Q_0^q
 4:     while S ≠ ∅ do
 5:         (b, q) ∈ S; S ← S \ {(b, q)}
 6:         if q ∉ Q_m^q then
 7:             for all b → a(R^b) ∈ Δ^b do
 8:                 for all q → a(R^q) ∈ Δ^q do
 9:                     R ← {(q_1, q_1'), (q_2, q_2'), ..., (q_n, q_n') | ∃n, q_1...q_n ∈ R^b, q_1'...q_n' ∈ R^q}
10:                     Δ ← Δ ∪ {(b, q) → a(R)}
11:                     S' ← {(b', q')|(b', q') occurs in R}
12:                     S ← S ∪ (S' \ Q)
13:                     Q ← Q ∪ S'
14:                 end for
15:                 if q = q_⊤ then
16:                     Δ ← Δ ∪ {(b, q) → a(R^b)}
17:                     S' ← {(b', q_⊤)|b' occurs in R}
18:                     S ← S ∪ (S' \ Q)
19:                     Q ← Q ∪ S'
20:                 end if
21:             end for
22:         else
23:             for all b → a(q_f) ∈ Δ^b, q_f ∈ Q^b do
24:                 for all q_0 ∈ Q_0^e do
25:                     Δ ← Δ ∪ {(b, q) → a(q_0)}
26:                 end for
27:             end for
28:         end if
29:     end while
30:     return A
31: end procedure
```

Proof. It suffices to consider $A = ((Q^b × Q^q) ∪ Q^e, Σ^b ∪ Σ^e, Q_0^q, Δ^e ∪ Δ)$, where $Δ$ contains all the transitions rules of the form $(b, q) → a(R)$ when:

— either $b → a(R^b) ∈ Δ^b$ and $q → a(R^q) ∈ Δ^q$ and R is the set $(q_1, q_1^q)...(q_n, q_n^q)$ when $q_1...q_n ∈ R^b$ and $q_1^q...q_n^q ∈ R^q$.
— or $q ∈ Q_m$ and $b → a'(q_f) ∈ Δ^b$ and there exists $q_0 ∈ Q_0^e$ such that $q_0 → a(R) ∈ Δ^e$.

R is regular since R is recognized by the product of the automata that recognize respectively R^b and R^q. Based on this result, in Algorithm 1 we provide the procedure to generate A. Next, we provide a proof that the algorithm is guaranteed to terminate with an answer for any valid input.

Proposition 2. *The Algorithm 1 terminates for all valid inputs.*

Proof. Let $α ∈ ℕ ∪ \{ω\}$ be the number of loop iterations within the while loop between Lines 5 and 31 (possibly $ω$ in case of non-termination). For every $i < α$, let U_i be the value of $S ∪ (Q^b × Q^q) \ Q$ at Line 5 at the ith loop iteration. The loop satisfies $U_{i+1} ⊊ U_i$ for every i such that $i + 1 < α$. Therefore $(U_i)_{i<α}$ is a sequence of strictly decreasing finite sets, thus, necessarily, $α ≠ ω$.

Complexity. The size of the resulting automaton is $O(|Q^e| + |Q^b| × |Q^q|)$ and the running time is linear in the size of the output. The worst case is reached for a family of pairs of automata $(\mathcal{A}_i^b, \mathcal{Q}_i)_i$ where, for every pair of automata $(\mathcal{A}_i^b, \mathcal{Q}_i)$, every pair of states is reachable during synchronous exploration of $\mathcal{A}_i^b$ and $\mathcal{Q}_i$.

5 Assessment

We have implemented a prototype of the proposed approach to the systematic composition of message translators, in the form of a Java library, which is available as open-source [3]. The library implements both the translator composition mechanism presented in Section 3, as well as the type inference algorithm introduced in Section 4. The purpose of this implementation is to be integrated in systems requiring high adaptability to new protocol stacks. Such systems include Enterprise Service Buses, Firewalls, Network Analyzers, etc.

While the underlying source code closely follows the formal mechanisms (such as tree automata) and algorithms presented in the paper, we further concerned ourselves with making this library usable for non-expert developers by adhering to well-established standards. Specifically, the following abstractions are concretized, as follows: (i) AST types which are internally modeled as top-down NFHAs, are transformed both on the input and output to RelaxNG (http://relaxng.org/) or XSD (www.w3.org/TR/xmlschema-1/) schema documents, and (ii) AST query inputs, which we model as query NFHAs, are to be provided using a subset of the XPath query language (www.w3.org/TR/xpath/).

Translator Support. A prerequisite of any composition is the existence of individual translators for each protocol. In our current implementation, we integrated translators for common middleware protocols like HTTP and SOAP, as well as generic translators for extensible formats such as XML and JSON. It is important to mention that while SOAP message formats are XML-based, they are more restrictive with respect to the messages accepted, and SOAP translators also produce more compact ASTs for the same messages. It is thus interesting to have protocol-specific translators, even when the protocol itself uses an extensible data format. Other translators may be easily integrated, although the creation of associated ASTs and AST data-schemas is currently hardcoded. To overcome this limitation, we are working on a solution that will automatically inspect third-party translators using reflection and generate the two according to the data-model used by the translators.

Translator Composition in Wireshark. To better asses the utility of our approach, we discuss our contributions in relation to the well-known open-source packet analyzer software Wireshark (http://www.wireshark.org/docs/dfref/). The role of Wireshark is to capture network packets, to parse their content and to present the information to the user in a structured format for analysis. Figure 4a depicts the representation of a HTTP/SOAP message in

---

[3] The project's Git repository can be checked out through anonymous access using a GIT client: `git clone https://gforge.inria.fr/git/iconnect/iconnect.git` (sourcecode located under the subproject mtc). Additionally, the repository can be browsed via the Git Repository Browser using the same URL. The mtc project is located under `projects/iconnect/iconnect.git/tree/mtc/` .

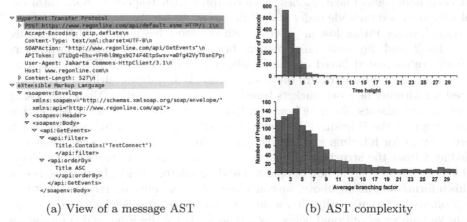

(a) View of a message AST   (b) AST complexity

Fig. 4. Use of translators (aka packet dissectors) in Wireshark

the Wireshark graphical user interface. Wireshark provides two mechanisms for composing translators (which they call dissectors). The first involves writing "glue-code" as an extension of an already existing dissector implemented in the C language. A more advanced solution (postdissectors and chained dissectors), which is similar to our composition approach uses the scripting language Lua (http://wiki.wireshark.org/Lua/Dissectors) to define compositions. However, postdissectors have to be implemented in Lua, thus eliminating the possibility of using already compiled, third-party, translators. Unlike the substitution-based composition that we introduce for ASTs, Wireshark uses a much simpler approach where disjoint trees are concatenated in the result. This can be observed in Figure 4a for the trees *Hypertext Transfer Protocol* and *eXtensible Markup Language*. In Wireshark, message ASTs do not have an associated data-schema, meaning that neither individual ASTs, nor ASTs resulting from a dissector chaining can be validated or inspected before runtime. Thus, the benefit of using our composition approach in a Packet Analysis software like Wireshark, enables: (i) composition/integration of third-party translators with already existing translators, and (ii) run-time validation and static-analysis/inspection of AST data types. The second is particularly beneficial when resulting data have to be further processed (e.g., data mining and machine learning) and stored (e.g., in a relational data base) rather than simply presented to the user.

Development Effort. Our entire approach is based on the assumption that developers are able to define XPath queries on message ASTs, in order to identify positions where data corresponding to composed protocols is located. In this case, it is important to estimate if this operation is effortless for developers in the general case. To this end, we conducted an analysis of AST type complexity on the 1317 protocols supported by Wireshark, focusing on two aspects that may influence the effort required to specify queries: tree height and branching factor. Intuitively, the tree height is proportional to the length of a query, when using only child axis (denoted '/'), and can prove complex to write in case of deep trees. Further, high branching factors (i.e., the average number of children at each node) also make queries more complex with respect to horizontal exploration, based on node order and sibling axis. As we show in Figure 4b, both parameters are rather low in general, with the most frequent tree height being of value 2, and the most most frequent branching factor of 4. The parameters above are estimated based on the Display Filter Reference of Wireshark. Display Filters in Wireshark are quite similar to AST queries, although they are used for filtering network packets based on a predicate, rather than composing message translators. We note however, that this is only an empirical estimation knowing that the Wireshark Display Filter Reference only includes fields which are relevant for filtering, and that the hierarchical nature of message fields was deduced from the structure of field names. Furthermore, in the Display Filter Reference there is no notion of optional and mandatory fields. In the absence of this information, in the above, we considered that all fields are required. For this reason, we had to manually filter a small number of protocols which define an extensive number of optional fields (e.g., 1634 fields for the Financial Information eXchange Protocol –FIX–).

As a conclusion, we argue that the approach introduced in this paper enables developers to design composite translators seamlessly as opposed to implementing hand-coded adapters. This statement is supported by the empirical evaluation above showing that, in the general case, the XPath queries that must be provided by the developers have a low complexity.

6   Conclusions

In this paper, we presented a method for composing message translators for complex protocols stacks by reusing already exiting translator components. For systems like Packet Analyzers, Firewalls, Enterprise Service Buses, etc., the reuse of third-party translators is critical since they must constantly evolve to support an increasing number of protocol stacks. The composition approach that we introduced in this paper functions as a purely "black-box" mechanism, thus allowing the use of third-party parsers and message serializers independently of the parsing algorithm they use internally, or the method by which they were implemented/generated. Our solution goes beyond the problem of translator composition by inferring AST data-schemas relative to translator compositions. This feature allows newly generated translators to be seamlessly (or even automatically) integrated with existing systems. On a more general note, the provided inference method solves the type inference problem for the substitution class of tree compositions. This contribution has a wider domain of applications beyond the specific scope of this paper, such as the inference of XML schemas for XSLT transformations.

We implemented a prototype of the approach, which is released as open-source, to showcase its benefit in reducing development time by enabling seamless integration of message translators as reusable software components. As a part of our future work, we intend to integrate the aforementioned prototype with an Enterprise Service Bus. This will in particular allow us to further assess the benefits of the proposed message translator composition in real-life applications.

Acknowledgements. This work has been partly supported by an ANRT CIFRE grant. The authors gratefully acknowledge the suggestions and advice from Dr. Roberto Speicys Cardoso, Dr. Ajay Kattepur and Eng. Georgios Mathioudakis.

References

1. Basten, H.: Ambiguity detection methods for context-free grammars. Master's thesis, Universiteit van Amsterdam (2007)
2. Benzaken, V., Castagna, G., Frisch, A.: Cduce: An xml-centric general-purpose language. In: Proc. of ACM SIGPLAN ICFP 2003 (2003)
3. Blair, G.S., Bennaceur, A., Georgantas, N., Grace, P., Issarny, V., Nundloll, V., Paolucci, M.: The role of ontologies in emergent middleware: Supporting interoperability in complex distributed systems. In: Kon, F., Kermarrec, A.-M. (eds.) Middleware 2011. LNCS, vol. 7049, pp. 410–430. Springer, Heidelberg (2011)
4. Cardelli, L., Matthes, F., Abadi, M.: Extensible grammars for language specialization. In: DBPL (1994)
5. Castagna, G., Im, H., Nguyen, K., Benzaken, V.: A core calculus for XQuery 3.0 (2013), http://www.pps.univ-paris-diderot.fr/~gc/papers/xqueryduce.pdf
6. Chappell, D.: Enterprise service bus. O'reilly Media (2004)
7. Comon, H., Dauchet, M., Gilleron, R., Löding, C., Jacquemard, F., Lugiez, D., Tison, S., Tommasi, M.: Tree Automata Techniques and Applications (2007), http://tata.gforge.inria.fr/ (release October 12, 2007)
8. DeRose, S., Clark, J.: XML Path Language (XPath) Version 1.0. W3C recommendation, W3C (1999)
9. Gallaher, M., O'Connor, A., Dettbarn, J., Gilday, L.: Cost Analysis of Inadequate Interoperability in the U.S. Capital Facilities Industry. U.S. Department of Commerce, Technology Administration, NIST (2004)
10. Joachims, T.: Text categorization with suport vector machines: Learning with many relevant features. In: Nédellec, C., Rouveirol, C. (eds.) ECML 1998. LNCS, vol. 1398, pp. 137–142. Springer, Heidelberg (1998)
11. Merten, M., Steffen, B., Howar, F., Margaria, T.: Next Generation LearnLib. In: Abdulla, P.A., Leino, K.R.M. (eds.) TACAS 2011. LNCS, vol. 6605, pp. 220–223. Springer, Heidelberg (2011)
12. Milo, T., Suciu, D.: Type inference for queries on semistructured data. In: PODS (1999)
13. Moors, A., Piessens, F., Odersky, M.: Parser combinators in Scala. KU Leuven, CW Reports vol:CW491 (2008)
14. Murata, M.: Hedge automata: a formal model for XML schemata (1999), http://www.xml.gr.jp/relax/hedge_nice.html
15. Murata, M., Lee, D., Mani, M., Kawaguchi, K.: Taxonomy of XML schema languages using formal language theory. In: ACM TOIT (2005)
16. Narayanan, V.: Why I quit writing internet standards (2014), http://gigaom.com/2014/04/12/why-i-quit-writing-internet-standards/
17. Papakonstantinou, Y., Vianu, V.: DTD Inference for Views of XML Data. In: PODS (2000)
18. Schwentick, T.: Automata for XML—A Survey. JCSS (2007)
19. Schwerdfeger, A.C., Van Wyk, E.R.: Verifiable Composition of Deterministic Grammars. In: PLDI (2009)
20. Schwerdfeger, A.C., Van Wyk, E.R.: Verifiable Parse Table Composition for Deterministic Parsing. In: SLE (2010)

21. Shaw, M.: Architectural issues in software reuse: It's not just the functionality, it's the packaging. ACM SIGSOFT Software Engineering Notes (1995)
22. Swierstra, S.D.: Combinator parsers - from toys to tools. ENTCS 41 (2000)
23. Tozawa, A.: Towards Static Type Checking for XSLT. In: ACM DocEng (2001)

On-the-Fly Synthesis of Scarcely Synchronizing Distributed Controllers from Scenario-Based Specifications

Christian Brenner[1], Joel Greenyer[2], and Wilhelm Schäfer[1]

[1] Software Engineering Group,
Heinz Nixdorf Institute
University of Paderborn, Germany
{cbr,wilhelm}@uni-paderborn.de
[2] Software Engineering Group
Leibniz Universität Hannover, Germany
greenyer@inf.uni-hannover.de

Abstract. Distributed systems consist of subsystems that usually need to coordinate with each other. Each subsystem must decide its actions locally, based on its limited knowledge. However, these decisions can be interdependent due to global requirements, i.e., one subsystem may need to know how another one decided. Complex communication can be required to exchange this knowledge. With rising complexity, a correct manual implementation of all subsystems becomes unlikely. Therefore, our goal is to automate the implementation process as far as possible. This paper presents a novel approach for the automatic synthesis of a distributed implementation from a global specification. In our approach, MSDs—a scenario-based specification language—can be used to intuitively, but formally define the requirements. The resulting implementation comprises one automaton for each subsystem, controlling its behavior. Contrary to similar approaches, we automatically add communication behavior to the system only when local knowledge is insufficient.

1 Introduction

Advanced driver-assistant systems with inter-vehicle communication or decentralized production systems are examples of software-intensive, distributed systems where multiple components interact with each other and the environment to fulfill complex, sometimes critical requirements. These requirements often span multiple components, which must synchronize so that each component has sufficient information about the overall system state in order to act accordingly. Architectural constraints may prohibit the direct communication between certain components or may require economical use of channels; also the time needed for exchanging additional synchronization messages can be an issue. Therefore, the naive approach of full synchronization among all components is usually not feasible. With rising complexity, implementing a global specification correctly and with feasible synchronization becomes an extremely difficult task.

© Springer-Verlag Berlin Heidelberg 2015
A. Egyed and I. Schaefer (Eds.): FASE 2015, LNCS 9033, pp. 51–65, 2015.
DOI: 10.1007/978-3-662-46675-9_4

In this paper, we propose a novel algorithm for synthesizing distributed controllers from a Modal Sequence Diagram (MSD) specification. MSDs [9] are a variant of Live Sequence Charts (LSCs) [4], which allow engineers to describe what the system components of a system may, must, or must not do.

Approaches for synthesizing distributed controllers from MSD/LSC specifications have been described previously. One part of these approaches considers the question whether a distributed implementation exists where the subsystems exchange messages exactly as defined in the specification, without adding extra messages for synchronization among the distributed subsystems. The engineers have to manually ensure that this property is fulfilled by explicitly specifying all necessary communication. This becomes harder with rising complexity, increasing the chance of errors. The other part of these approaches asks whether a distributed implementation of a specification exists where extra synchronization messages can be added. The existing approaches of this kind automatically add synchronization messages such that all subsystems have perfect information about the global state of the system—even when this information is not required to act correctly according to the specification. This causes a large overhead due to the unnecessary communication and removes all parallelism from the system. In real-time systems, this unnecessary communication can even lead to a violation of timing requirements. But even when timing is not an issue, the given architecture might not allow all subsystems to communicate.

Contrary to existing approaches, our automatic algorithm introduces synchronization messages *scarcely*, only when the subsystems could not otherwise avoid violating the specification. Moreover, these synchronization messages are only added where allowed by the given architecture. Our algorithm explores candidate implementations of an MSD specification *on-the-fly* and can often find a solution without constructing all alternatives. This is an advantage over related approaches that start with constructing a maximal global controller and then attempt to distribute it. A further advantage over most related approaches is that we consider specifications where also *assumptions* can be described on how the system's environment may, will, or will not behave.

This paper is structured as follows. Section 2 introduces the foundations and a running example. Section 3 introduces our distributed synthesis approach. We illustrate its application for the running example in Sect. 4. We present related work in Sect. 5 and conclude with Sect. 6.

2   Foundations

As an example, we consider a simple production system with one robot arm and a press (see sketch in Fig. 1). Blanks arrive on a feed belt where, at its end, a sensor detects the arrival of a blank and whether it is intact or broken. The arm must remove broken blanks and move intact ones to the press, where the blanks are pressed into plates. After pressing, the arm must transport the pressed plates to a deposit belt. We assume that until the arm has delivered the plate or removed a broken blank, no new blanks will arrive.

The system has two software controller components. One receives signals from the sensor and controls the robot arm, the other controller controls the press. Figure 1 shows the requirements (R1-R5) and assumptions (A1, A2).

2.1 MSD Specifications

MSDs are a variant of LSCs [4,10], proposed by Harel and Maoz as a formal interpretation of UML sequence diagrams [9]. MSDs specify the interaction behavior of components or *objects*. We consider open systems with controllable *system objects* and uncontrollable *environment objects*. Together, these objects form the *object system*. An MSD specification consists of an object system and a set of MSDs, which can be *requirement MSDs* and *assumption MSDs*.

Lifelines, Messages, MSD Semantics. An MSD contains lifelines that each represents one object. Objects can exchange messages. A message has a name and one sending and one receiving object. We only consider *synchronous* messages, where the sending and receiving of a message together form a single *event*, also called *message event*. A *run* of a system is an infinite sequence of events.

We model the object system by a UML composite structure diagram (CSD, see Fig. 1). System objects have a rectangular shape; environment objects have a cloud-like shape. Connectors define which objects can exchange messages.

An MSD contains *(diagram) messages* that have a name and a sending and receiving lifeline. They also have a *temperature* and an *execution kind*, which indicate safety and liveness requirements, as we will explain shortly. The temperature can be either *hot* or *cold*. The execution kind can be either *executed* or *monitored*. In Fig. 1, the temperature and execution kind is annotated by labels (c,m), (c,e), (h,m), (h,e) next to the messages. In addition, the hot message arrows are colored red; cold message arrows are colored blue. Monitored messages have a dashed arrow; the arrows of executed messages have a solid line.

A message in an MSD can be *unified* with a message event if the sending and receiving object of the message event are represented by the sending and receiving lifeline of the diagram message. If a message event occurs that can be unified with the first message of an MSD (we assume that there is always exactly one first message), then an *active copy* of the MSD, also called *active MSD*, is created. The active MSD progresses as further events occur that can be unified with subsequent messages. This progress is indicated by the *cut*, which marks messages that have been unified. The MSD labeled R1 in Fig. 1 shows the cut as a dashed horizontal line spanning all lifelines (the cut is not part of the specification, but only part of its interpretation). The cut here indicates that the events `intactBlank` and `blankToPress` occurred. There can be several active MSDs at the same time. The occurrence of `blankToPress` for example also activated the MSDs labeled R2 and R4. If the cut reaches the end of the MSD, the active copy of the MSD is terminated and discarded.

A message in an active MSD is called *enabled* if the cut is immediately in front of the message on the sending and receiving lifeline. If a hot message is

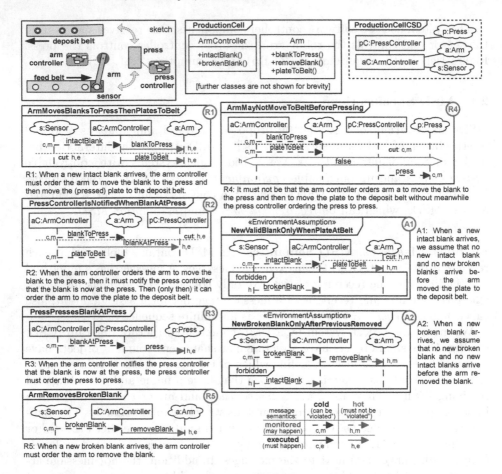

Fig. 1. The production cell MSD specification

enabled, the cut is also hot; otherwise the cut is cold. If an executed message is enabled, the cut is also executed; otherwise the cut is monitored. Labels also indicate the cut temperature and execution kind in Fig. 1.

If a message event occurs that can be unified with a message in the same MSD that is not currently enabled, this is called a *violation*. If the cut is hot, a violation must not happen. If it does, this is called a *safety violation*. If the cut is cold, a violation is allowed to happen and results in a premature termination of the active MSD (*cold violation*). If the cut is executed, this means that the cut must eventually progress, otherwise this is called a *liveness violation*.

An MSD can also contain *conditions*. In this paper, we only have, and thus only explain, the hot `false` condition in MSD R4, depicted by a red hexagon. In this case, the cut must not reach the condition, otherwise this is a safety violation. This MSD is an example of an *anti-scenario*, which describes a sequence of events that must not happen; in this case `blankToPress` followed by `plateToBelt`.

The only way this sequence is allowed to happen is if press occurs in between, which leads to a cold violation in the cut illustrated in Fig. 1.

Assumption MSDs, Satisfying an MSD Specification. A run of a system is *accepted* by an MSD iff it does not lead to a safety or liveness violation of this MSD. The set of all runs accepted by an MSD D is also called the *language* of this MSD, $L(D)$. Given a set of MSDs $M = \{D_1, \ldots, D_n\}$, the *language* of this set of MSDs, $L(M)$, is the set of runs accepted by all the MSDs in the set, $L(M) = \bigcap_{i=1}^{n} L(D_i)$.

We consider MSD specifications MS that comprise two sets of MSDs, *requirement MSDs* G (for "guarantees") and *assumption MSDs* A. The set of runs *satisfying* an MSD specification, $L(MS)$, is defined as $L(MS) = \overline{L(A)} \cup L(G)$, where $\overline{L(A)}$ is the set of all runs not in $L(A)$. Intuitively, a run satisfies an MSD specification iff it satisfies the requirements or does not satisfy the assumptions.

We consider open systems consisting of *environment objects* and *system objects*. Usually, we use assumption MSDs to constrain the possible behavior of the environment, hence we also call these MSDs *environment assumptions*. Assumption MSDs have the additional label «EnvironmentAssumption»; the MSDs A1 and A2 in Fig. 1 are examples for such assumption MSDs. Moreover, we assume, as also Harel et al. [10], that the system objects can send any finite number of messages between two messages sent by environment objects.

The Specification State Graph. An MSD specification induces a transition system that we call the *specification state graph (SSG)*. This graph is the basis for our algorithm. The SSG consists of states and transitions; the transitions are labeled with message events and a state represents a set of active MSDs with a particular configuration of cuts. The start state is a state with no active MSDs. The cut configuration of the other states is the configuration that results after any sequence of message events that corresponds to a path in the SSG from the start state to that state. Transitions labeled with system events are *controllable*; those with environment events are *uncontrollable*. The SSG can be considered a *game graph*, representing a game played by the system against the environment.

The synthesis must create a strategy for choosing controllable transitions such that always eventually a *goal* state can be reached (Büchi condition). The primary form of goal state is a state without any enabled executed message in any active requirement MSD. In these states, intuitively, the system currently has no obligations to do anything and waits for the next environment event to happen. While calculating this strategy, the algorithm must assume that the environment can do anything to keep the system from reaching such a state. The strategy must avoid safety violations of requirement MSDs, unless they coincide with safety violations of assumption MSDs; this represents behavior that we assume is not possible to occur in the environment. Moreover, safety violations in requirement MSDs are allowed while executed messages are enabled in assumption MSDs; this represents environment behavior that we assume is not complete—maybe here the environment only achieves a violation of the requirements at the expense of finally violating the assumptions, too. These latter states are also goal states.

More formally, a *strategy* is a subset of transitions of an SSG. A strategy is *winning* under the following two conditions. *W1*: The SSG, by taking only these strategy transitions, contains no deadlocks and no cycles without goal states. *W2*: If a strategy includes an outgoing uncontrollable transition of a state, it must include all outgoing uncontrollable transitions of that state. Intuitively, *W2* means that if the environment makes a move, the strategy must consider all its possible moves; *W1* means that the Büchi condition is satisfied.

2.2   The Controller System

Our synthesis approach generates a *controller system* consisting of *controllers* that together implement a given MSD specification. We consider controllers to be deterministic finite-state automata that define which messages are sent at what point in time for one object each. A set of controllers CS is called a *controller system* if each system object is controlled by a controller.

We call an event *controllable by an object* if the object sends the event. We call it *observable by an object* if the object sends or receives the event. Events are controllable/observable for a controller if they are controllable/observable for the object it controls. We call transitions controllable/observable for an object or controller if their event is controllable/observable.

By parallel composition, a controller system can be mapped to an equivalent *global (controller) automaton*. Given an MSD specification for the same object system, the states of the global automaton correspond to states of the specification's SSG. We call an SSG state *reachable* for a controller system iff there exists a sequence of events for which there is a corresponding path in the global automaton as well as in the SSG (starting from their resp. start states). The transitions between the SSG states that are reachable for a controller system define a *strategy corresponding to the controller system*.

3   Algorithm for Distributed Synthesis

Our algorithm creates a controller system that implements a given MSD specification—provided that an implementation is possible. A controller system implements a specification iff it corresponds to a winning strategy (see Sect. 2.1) in the SSG. Such a controller system is a *solution* for the distributed synthesis.

Our algorithm systematically generates *candidate controller systems* (in short *candidates*), i.e., controller systems which might be extensible towards a solution. These candidates are extended in such a way that an increasing number of SSG states fulfill the winning conditions. The algorithm backtracks if it finds that a candidate cannot be extended into a solution. To allow for this systematic search, the candidates are maintained as nodes in a graph structure called the *candidate graph (CG)*. The algorithm performs a depth-first search (DFS) in the CG to approach a solution (cf. Fig. 2):

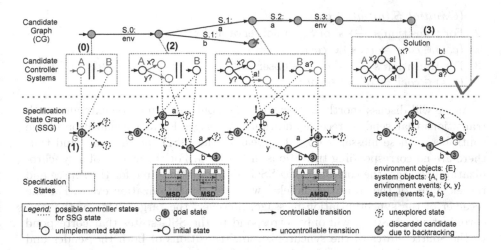

Fig. 2. Overview of the algorithm

The initial CG consists of a candidate with only the start state for each controller of a system object (0). We assume that environment objects can send any sequence of environment events and, hence, we do not need to construct controllers for them. In each step, the algorithm considers a *current candidate*. The algorithm finds all states in the SSG that are reachable for this current candidate. Then the algorithm checks whether any of these currently reachable SSG states violate the winning conditions (cf. Sect. 2.1) (1). We call these SSG states *unimplemented states*. If no such state exists, the candidate is a solution and the DFS terminates (3). Otherwise, the DFS extends the CG by constructing a successor candidate (2). The successor candidate is created by extending a copy of the current candidate and adding transitions and states to ensure that one of the previously unimplemented SSG states fulfills the winning conditions and becomes *implemented*. If this is possible, the algorithm performs the next step with the successor candidate. If an unimplemented state cannot be implemented, i.e., a candidate is not extensible towards a solution, the DFS backtracks.

We explain the two procedures of *computing unimplemented states* and *creating successor candidates* in more detail in Sect. 3.1 and 3.2.

3.1 Computation of Reachable Unimplemented SSG States

Identifying reachable unimplemented SSG states works as follows:

Identify Reachable SSG States. We call a specification state s and a controller state c *corresponding* if there is a sequence of events after which the specification is in state s and the controller is in state c. We call a controller transition t_c and a specification transition t_s *corresponding* if the source states are corresponding and both transitions are labeled with the same event. The algorithm computes these correspondences according to the following definition of the relation *corr* of corresponding states of an SSG S for a controller C:

1. $(C.initial, S.initial) \in corr$.
2. For transition $s \xrightarrow{e} s'$ of S, e unobservable for C:
   $(c, s) \in corr \Rightarrow (c, s') \in corr$.
3. For transition $s \xrightarrow{e} s'$ of S, e observable for C (it exists $c \xrightarrow{e} c'$ in C):
   $(c, s) \in corr \Rightarrow (c', s') \in corr$.

As we will discuss shortly in Sect. 3.2, the controllers may be extended with transitions that send or receive additional messages for synchronization of the controllers. These messages do not appear in the MSD specification, and thus there are no corresponding transitions in the SSG. For the sender of a synchronization message, the corresponding SSG states are the same for the source and target states of the transition labeled with the synchronization event. For the receiver of the synchronization message, however, the target state of the synchronization transition will only correspond to the SSG states that correspond to the source states of the synchronization transitions of both the sender and receiver. Intuitively, the sender of a synchronization message conveys its information about the possible global system states to the receiver. Conversely, the receiver does not convey its information about the global state to the sender, because we assume that the receiver cannot block the sending of messages.

The definition of the relation $corr$ is extended as follows.

4. For synchronization sending transition $c \xrightarrow{synch!} c'$ in C:
   $(c, s) \in corr \Rightarrow (c', s) \in corr$.
5. For transition $c \xrightarrow{synch?} c'$ in C that receives a synchronization message sent by transition $c2 \xrightarrow{synch!} c2'$ in another controller $C2$:
   $(c, s) \in corr \wedge (c2, s) \in corr \Rightarrow (c', s) \in corr$

Determine Whether Reachable SSG States are Implemented. We call an event e *implemented in a reachable SSG state* s if the sending and receiving objects either are environment objects or their controllers define a sending/receiving transition for e in *all* their controller states that are corresponding to s. Additionally, the outgoing transition for e in the SSG state s may close a loop of SSG transitions for other implemented events only if that loop includes a goal state. The latter is required to fulfill winning condition *W1* (see Sect. 2.1). We call an SSG transition *implemented* if its event is implemented.

We call a *goal* state implemented if all outgoing transitions labeled with environment events are implemented (cf. condition *W2* in Sect. 2.1). (In goal states, there is no obligation for the system to send messages.)

We call a *non-goal* state *implemented* if it has at least one outgoing transition labeled with a system event that is implemented. Intuitively, there must be at least one message that the system can send. In some cases, it may be that the system can send no message, but there is at least one assumption MSD in an executed cut, i.e., the environment must yet complete a particular sequence of events. In this case, the system can wait for environment events. Hence, a non-goal state is also implemented if there is an assumption MSD in an executed cut and all outgoing transitions labeled with environment events are implemented.

Since we require all reachable states to be implemented, the corresponding strategy does not contain any deadlock state (cf. condition *W1* in Sect. 2.1).

3.2   Creation of Successor Candidate

When the algorithm finds any unimplemented SSG states for the current candidate (called CC in the following), it picks any state s of these and creates a successor candidate CC' by copying CC. The algorithm attempts to add transitions and states to CC' such that s becomes implemented. These additions depend on whether or not s is a goal state.

If s is a goal state, the algorithm checks the following conditions:

1. No other successor candidate CC'' of CC already exists in which all *uncontrollable* events are implemented in s.
2. No controller in CC is sending in s.

Condition 1 ensures that the algorithm will not attempt to construct the same successor candidate twice. Condition 2 ensures that environment events are considered only in states in which the system does not send anything, because we assume that the system is always faster than the environment.

If both conditions are met, the algorithm adds receiving transitions to the controllers of CC' such that all uncontrollable events in s are implemented. Otherwise, the algorithm handles s in the same way as a non-goal state.

If s is not a goal state, the algorithm picks any unimplemented *controllable* event e that fulfills the following conditions:

1. No other successor candidate CC'' of CC already exists in which e is implemented in s.
2. The sender controller C of e does not send another event in s.
3. Implementing e in s does not close a loop of implemented SSG transitions without a goal state.

Condition 1 ensures that no candidate for the same combination of e and s is constructed again which was previously found to inevitably lead to a losing strategy. Condition 2 ensures that controllers remain deterministic, i.e., they send only one event in each state. Condition 3 is necessary to fulfill winning condition *W1* (cf. Sect. 2.1). The algorithm checks condition 3 by performing a DFS from the successor state of the SSG transition for e in s via transitions that are implemented for CC and stopping at goal states. Thus the DFS only reaches s if this transition closes a loop without goal state in the strategy.

If such an event e exists, the algorithm adds sending transitions to all states of C in CC' that correspond to s (and adds receiving transitions to the receiving controller, if applicable), such that e is implemented. If no such event e exists, the algorithm searches an unimplemented controllable event e that fulfills conditions 2 and 3, *but not 1*. Then, a successor candidate for implementing e was already created, but the DFS backtracked. If C in a state corresponding to s also corresponds to other SSG states s', this backtracking may have been necessary because sending the event e was problematic in s': It can be that, while e must be sent in s, sending e in s' violates the specification. Since C cannot distinguish these states, it must send the same message in both of them. The algorithm then checks whether there is another controller C' that can distinguish at least one such state s' from s. If a C' exists, the algorithm adds transitions to the controllers in CC' such that one or several controllers C' send synchronization messages to C. These allow C to distinguish s from other states s'. If a synchronization was added, CC' is extended as above to make s implemented for CC', without affecting s'. Note that we only add synchronization messages when a path via connectors in the CSD (cf. Sect. 2.1) exists such that C' can send messages to C. We search such a path via a DFS on the CSD.

If still no such event e could be found, but an assumption MSD is in an executed cut in s, the system may wait for the environment in s. Then, the algorithm attempts to implement all environment events as discussed above for goal states. In all other cases, the algorithm discards CC and backtracks to its predecessor CC_p. In the attempt to create a new successor for CC_p, the same SSG state s that was picked when constructing CC as successor of CC_p is picked again. This ensures that the algorithm will not attempt to implement other SSG states when s is unimplementable. In this case, no solution can be reached by extending CC_p and the algorithm needs to backtrack again.

3.3　Removal of Duplicates

After each modification of the CG, the algorithm checks all new candidates and all new controller states for duplicates. It merges the duplicates into one, combining their incoming transitions/edges. We consider candidates as duplicates whenever all their controllers are *identical*. We consider controllers as identical when their sets of states and transitions are identical. Controller transitions are identical if their source and target state and their event are identical. Controller states are identical if they correspond to the same SSG states and if the set of (other) controllers to which synchronization messages have been sent is identical. The latter is necessary because sending a synchronization message must lead to a new controller state—despite identical corresponding states—so that the message will not be sent repeatedly.

3.4　Correctness

In the following, we informally argue for the correctness of our algorithm.

Termination. Our algorithm generally is a DFS on the CG that terminates if the graph is finite. The CG is finite if the number of candidates for the given specification is finite. This, in turn, depends on the maximum number of controller states and transitions. Without considering synchronization transitions, the maximum number of controller states is bounded by the size of the power set of SSG states, as new controller states are created only for new sets of corresponding SSG states. Each synchronization transition adds an additional controller state for the sender controller as it must distinguish the state before sending the message from the state after sending. However, synchronization transitions are only added in cases where a controller needs information from other controllers to send. Thus, in the worst case, for each SSG state an additional state will be added to all controllers except the one receiving the synchronizations. The number of controller transitions is bounded by the number of controller states and the number of events in the specification, which we assume to be finite. Thus, the total number of candidates depends on the number of system objects and the size of the SSG, which we both also assume to be finite. In conclusion, the CG is finite as well. Computation of the corresponding states requires further DFS runs, but these are performed on the (finite) SSG. Thus, *the algorithm is guaranteed to terminate.*

Correctness of the Resulting Solution. If the DFS terminates with a solution, that solution is a candidate with no reachable unimplemented SSG states. The conditions for an SSG state to be implemented directly correspond to the conditions *W1* and *W2* for a winning strategy (cf. Sect. 2.1 and 3.1), except for the requirement to include goal states in circles of implemented transitions in the SSG. However, the algorithm checks for loops without goal states and does not close them by adding transitions to a candidate. Thus, only loops with goal states remain and the strategy defined by all implemented transitions between the reachable states is a winning strategy. Consequently, *the candidate returned by the algorithm is a valid implementation for the given specification.*

4   Example Execution of the Distributed Synthesis

We illustrate our algorithm by showing its execution on the example MSD specification presented in Fig. 1 (cf. Sect. 2). Figure 3 shows for several steps of the algorithm snapshots of the candidate controller system CS that has been constructed up to that point, the SSG S, and the CG.

a.1 The snapshot shows the algorithm's models after initialization. The specification defines two system objects: the PressController pC and the ArmController aC. Thus, the algorithm creates initial states for the two controllers, which both correspond to the initial state $S.0$ of the SSG. The initial state is a goal state and the algorithm needs to consider all possible environment events in this state. These are intactBlank and brokenBlank, both leading to new SSG states.

a.2 The algorithm creates a new candidate which has receiving transitions in aC for brokenBlank and intactBlank, making the SSG states $S.1$ and $S.2$ reachable, but also making $S.0$ implemented. The controller aC can observe both messages and "knows" in which SSG state the system is, either $S.1$ or $S.2$. Thus, the new transitions lead to two new controller states corresponding to one SSG state each. The controller pC, however, cannot observe this message and cannot distinguish $S.1$ and $S.2$ from $S.0$. All three correspond to $pC.0$ (state 0 of pC). The algorithm checks for the reachable states $S.0$, $S.1$, and $S.2$, whether they are unimplemented, which is the case for $S.1$ and $S.2$.

a.3 The algorithm selects $S.1$. Since $S.1$ is not a goal state, the algorithm must pick an enabled system event, which here can only be removeBlank. It adds

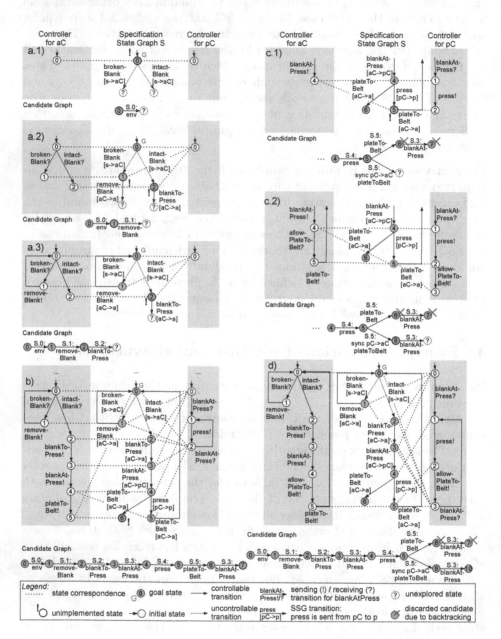

Fig. 3. Algorithm steps performed for the example (excerpts)

a transition to aC that sends this event. The algorithm determines that this transition leads back to $S.0$. As all outgoing transitions in $S.0$ are observable for aC, the transition's target state only corresponds to $S.0$. For this set of corresponding states, the controller state $aC.0$ already exists in aC. Thus, the transition leads to $aC.0$. Now, $S.0$ and $S.1$ are implemented, while $S.2$ is not.

b The figure then skips several steps until, in the step before snapshot b, the addition of a controller transition closes the second loop to the goal state $S.0$ in the SSG. Like in step a.3, the algorithm has extended aC to send events as a reaction to an environment event. It sends the second event, blankAtPress, to pC. Hence, the algorithm adds a receiving transition for blankAtPress to pC. The target state $pC.1$ in pC can then distinguish $S.4$ from the other states and sends press. In $S.5$, plateToBelt is sent, which closes the loop to $S.0$, but also makes $S.6$ reachable from $S.4$, because $aC.4$ corresponds to both, $S.4$ and $S.5$. The closing of the loop to $S.0$ and the subsequent events until blankAtPress are not observable by pC. To compute the corresponding states for $pC.2$, the algorithm performs a DFS starting in $S.0$ via unobservable transitions for pC. Since $S.2$ is among the states found by the DFS, the event blankAtPress was implemented by adding a receiving transition in $pC.2$. However, $S.6$ remains unimplemented.

c.1 Because $S.6$ turns out to be a deadlock state (due to a safety violation in a requirement MSD) which cannot be implemented, the DFS backtracks until candidate 5 to prevent reachability of $S.6$.

c.2 The algorithm again attempts to implement $S.5$. The CG shows that immediately sending plateToBelt in $S.5$ was already attempted unsuccessfully. However, it was not yet attempted with prior synchronization to help aC distinguish $S.4$ from $S.5$. The algorithm finds a controller that can distinguish these states, namely pC, since $pC.2$ only corresponds to $S.5$. Therefore, the algorithm adds a synchronization message allowPlateToBelt from pC to aC, telling aC that $S.5$ has been reached and sending plateToBelt is safe now. Consequently, a controller transition sending plateToBelt is added to aC. Note that allowPlateToBelt was not defined in the specification.

d After the synchronization, the algorithm will never need to consider plateToBelt in $S.4$ and, thus, never need to consider the deadlock state $S.6$. It just has to implement blankAtPress in $S.3$ as discussed for snapshot b. Then, all reachable SSG states are implemented and the algorithm terminates successfully. Snapshot d shows the final result. We omitted the correspondences of some controller states for reasons of visualization.

5   Related Work

Harel et al. [7] describe an approach for controller synthesis from LSCs based on the creation of a product automaton; a distributed implementation is then formed by fully-synchronized copies of a centralized controller. Contrary to our approach, this procedure introduces additional synchronization messages even when the local information of the controllers is sufficient to fulfill the specification. The approach may thus introduce a vast amount of superfluous messages in the generated implementation that degrades its runtime performance.

In later works, Harel et al. [8], and similarly Bontemps et. al. [1], synthesize distributed implementations from LSCs, but they do not add any additional messages not defined in the specification. Therefore, unlike our approach, they cannot handle cases where the local controllers need to share their knowledge about the global state to fulfill the specification.

Sun and Dong [13] present a synthesis approach for LSCs that constructs a distributed implementation in the form of a CSP (Communicating Sequential Processes) system. However, the implementation they create is only valid if the LSC specification already guarantees that, regardless of the behavior of the system, no situation can be reached where liveness requirements cannot be fulfilled without violating safety requirements. Our approach does not have this restriction, because it backtracks in such situations.

While the following approaches do *not* consider LSC/MSD-specifications, they are related as they also model the local knowledge of subsystems.

Halle and Bultan [6] construct local views of subsystems to decide whether a given automata-based protocol can be implemented by a distributed system without additional communication. They mention as possible future work to add additional messages that are required to implement the protocol. However, they do not actually present any such algorithm in the paper.

Finkbeiner and Schewe [5] consider the distributed synthesis problem for specifications using ω-regular tree languages. They take into account the limited knowledge of the synthesized subsystems but, contrary to our approach, they do not consider additional communication to extend this knowledge. Thus, their approach does not work in cases requiring additional communication.

Like our approach, Katz et al. [11] and Peled and Schewe [12] model the local knowledge of subsystems and use synchronizations when this local knowledge is insufficient. However, their approach requires as an input an existing implementation model of a distributed system given as a Petri net. New safety requirements are provided in a textual form. Their algorithm modifies the given system such that these new requirements are fulfilled.

6   Conclusion

In this paper, we presented a new approach for synthesizing implementation models for distributed systems based on scenario-based MSD specifications. We presented an algorithm that synthesizes a controller automaton for each subsystem such that they in combination fulfill the specification. The core novelty is that our algorithm keeps track of the local knowledge of the subsystems about the global state. It adds additional synchronizations whenever a subsystem needs to react based on messages that it cannot observe. We demonstrated the application of our approach on an example specification.

We implemented our distributed synthesis algorithm as an Eclipse plug-in based on our SCENARIOTOOLS tool suite [3]. We evaluated our approach by executing it on the production cell example presented in the previous sections. Furthermore, we applied it on several variants with a higher number of arms and presses. We then manually validated that the controllers created by the algorithm are a correct implementation of these MSD specifications.

In future works, we will extend our synthesis algorithm to take into account real-time behavior and asynchronous communication. Our new timed play-out for SCENARIOTOOLS [2] paves the way for these extensions. Furthermore, we plan to evaluate the algorithm's performance for larger systems and aim to reduce its runtime by preventing unnecessary re-computation of intermediate results.

References

1. Bontemps, Y., Heymans, P., Schobbens, P.-Y.: Lightweight formal methods for scenario-based software engineering. In: Leue, S., Systä, T.J. (eds.) Scenarios: Models, Transformations and Tools. LNCS, vol. 3466, pp. 174–192. Springer, Heidelberg (2005)
2. Brenner, C., Greenyer, J., Holtmann, J., Liebel, G., Stieglbauer, G., Tichy, M.: Scenariotools real-time play-out for test sequence validation in an automotive case study. In: Proc. of 13th Int. Workshop on Graph Transformation and Visual Modeling Techniques, GT-VMT 2014 (2014)
3. Brenner, C., Greenyer, J., Panzica La Manna, V.: The ScenarioTools play-out of modal sequence diagram specifications with environment assumptions. In: Proc. of 12th Int. Workshop on Graph Transformation and Visual Modeling Techniques, GT-VMT 2013 (2013)
4. Damm, W., Harel, D.: LSCs: Breathing life into message sequence charts. In: Formal Methods in System Design, vol. 19, pp. 45–80. Kluwer (2001)
5. Finkbeiner, B., Schewe, S.: Uniform distributed synthesis. In: Proc. of 20th IEEE Symp. on Logic in Computer Science, pp. 321–330 (2005)
6. Halle, S., Bultan, T.: Realizability Analysis for Message-based Interactions Using Shared-State Projections. In: Proc. of 18th ACM SIGSOFT Int. Symp. on Foundations of Software Engineering, FSE 2010, Santa Fe, New Mexico (2010)
7. Harel, D., Kugler, H.: Synthesizing state-based object systems from LSC specifications. Foundations of Computer Science 13(1), 5–51 (2002)
8. Harel, D., Kugler, H.-J., Pnueli, A.: Synthesis revisited: Generating statechart models from scenario-based requirements. In: Kreowski, H.-J., Montanari, U., Orejas, F., Rozenberg, G., Taentzer, G. (eds.) Formal Methods in Software and Systems Modeling. LNCS, vol. 3393, pp. 309–324. Springer, Heidelberg (2005)
9. Harel, D., Maoz, S.: Assert and negate revisited: Modal semantics for UML sequence diagrams. Software and Systems Modeling (SoSyM) 7(2), 237–252 (2008)
10. Harel, D., Marelly, R.: Come, Let's Play: Scenario-Based Programming Using LSCs and the Play-Engine. Springer (2003)
11. Katz, G., Peled, D., Schewe, S.: Synthesis of distributed control through knowledge accumulation. In: Gopalakrishnan, G., Qadeer, S. (eds.) CAV 2011. LNCS, vol. 6806, pp. 510–525. Springer, Heidelberg (2011)
12. Peled, D., Schewe, S.: Practical distributed control synthesis. In: Yu, F., Wang, C. (eds.) Proc. Int. Workshop on Verification and Infinite State Systems (INFINITY 2011). EPTCS, vol. 73, pp. 2–17 (2011)
13. Sun, J., Dong, J.S.: Synthesis of distributed processes from scenario-based specifications. In: Fitzgerald, J.S., Hayes, I.J., Tarlecki, A. (eds.) FM 2005. LNCS, vol. 3582, pp. 415–431. Springer, Heidelberg (2005)

Testing and Fault Localization

BPEL Integration Testing

Seema Jehan, Ingo Pill, and Franz Wotawa

Institute for Software Technology
Graz University of Technology, Austria
{sjehan,ipill,wotawa}@ist.tugraz.at

Abstract. Service-oriented architectures, and evolvements such as
clouds, provide a promising infrastructure for future computing. They encapsulate an IP core's functionality for easy access via well-defined business
and web interfaces, and in turn allow us to flexibly realize complex software
drawing on available expertise. In this paper, we take a look at some challenges we have to face during the task of testing such systems for verification purposes. In particular, we delve into the task of test suite generation,
and compare the performance of two corresponding algorithms. In addition, we report on experiments for a collection of BPEL processes taken
from the literature, in order to identify performance trends with respect
to fault coverage metrics. Our results suggest that a structural reasoning
might outperform a completely random approach.

1 Introduction

Today, service oriented architectures (SOAs) are an important instrument for
software design [28], and they might become ubiquitous in future computing -
be it mobile apps, cloud applications, or the realization of public and private
business processes. As their backend, web services encapsulate an intellectual
property (IP) core's individual functionality and provide a web interface for easy
and flexible access of our own or a third party's expertise and developments. In
this context, BPEL originated almost a decade ago as OASIS[1] standard for
modeling and executing such business processes that implement a desired functionality drawing on web services. Non-functional requirements can be defined,
for instance, in Service Level Agreements (SLAs).

Aside exacerbated issues regarding controllability and observability, the fact
that we have only partial knowledge about some system parts (i.e. third party
web services) - as Friedrich et al. discussed in [24] - makes diagnosis and repair
of these systems a cumbersome and very complex task. In [31], we envisioned an
integrated testing and diagnosis approach that considers such a system's BPEL
processes. Extracting a control-flow graph from a BPEL model, and annotating
it with (most likely partial) knowledge about invoked web services in the form
of pre- and postconditions, we proposed to use constraint representations as
reasoning model for such an approach [19].

---

[1] Organization for the Advancement of Structured Information Standards, see
https://www.oasis-open.org.

© Springer-Verlag Berlin Heidelberg 2015
A. Egyed and I. Schaefer (Eds.): FASE 2015, LNCS 9033, pp. 69–83, 2015.
DOI: 10.1007/978-3-662-46675-9_5

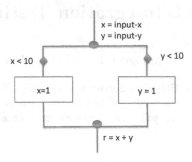

Fig. 1. Flow Example

In our current work, we take a closer look at the task of creating an efficient test suite for functional verification purposes. Complementing earlier work (see Section 4), we focus on path extraction and symbolic execution. Extending [17], we experiment in Section 3 with two path-oriented variants of systematically generating test suites for synchronous, executable BPEL processes (see Section 2). In particular, we compare the performance of test suites generated (a) in an entirely random fashion with (b) a structural approach of exploring the paths in a process' control structure. In this context, we define a test suite's efficiency in terms of its capability to detect an original BPEL process' mutations (specifically in relation to consumed resources). Extending our earlier work and definitions, we support also the flow activity (limited to branches that do not share variables) that allows designers to model also concurrent computations.

Since considering all of a system's feasible runs in the control structure is likely to be infeasible for practical purposes, i.e., in terms of test case generation and execution, specific questions of ours were whether a random approach achieves the desired performance, and how (and to which extent) the variation of certain parameters affects a verdict. Using several example BPEL processes from the literature, we aimed at discovering common trends by bringing several designs to the picture, elaborating on our first ideas proposed in [17].

The general idea of the algorithms compared in Section 3 is to traverse a BPEL process' flow graph in order to extract the necessary inputs and expected outputs for real executions and in turn generate test cases. Our work can be understood best via illustrations for a simple concurrent BPEL process like the one depicted in Figure 1. For our example, an execution starts with assigning the input values to the respective variables, and the subsequent flow activity defines two branches that are triggered if their respective guards ($x < 10$ and $y < 10$) are activated. In both branches, individual activities then offer new value assignments, where after the branches join again, the variables x and y are summed up. An execution then follows a *run* in the graph, where, in contrast to a path as we have been using in our earlier work for sequential programs [17,31], more than one branch may be active simultaneously. Deriving a flow graph from the BPEL process, and annotating it with our partial knowledge about called web services (and other available knowledge) in the form of pre- and postconditions (to be added as conditions and assignments), our test case generation algorithms still select paths, but to a corresponding run's model we add also all the parallel branches that might be traversed as well (depending on the actual assignment and the corresponding evaluation of the guards). Deriving a satisfying variable assignment for a constraint representation of this model, we can derive a corresponding test-case, and in turn, following different strategies for choosing paths, test suites.

Since we have only partial knowledge about invoked external services, we consider our work to fall in the category of active grey-box testing approaches [19]. In our title, we use the term integration testing, as from a certain and important point of view, we test the integration of all a system's components when orchestrated by the BPEL process.

Presently, most research in the field of SOA testing focuses on passive, rather than active testing. Factors here are related costs (i.e. for invoking external web services), execution times (see our experiments in Section 3), and the impact of an environment's dynamic effects (e.g. of the network). We, however, believe that active testing issues in the SOA domain should not be neglected either. In fact, they have become more critical in emerging concepts such as clouds and similar distributed architectures, where faults affect performance for a multitude of users and trust in correctness is an issue of utmost importance.

2   Basic Definitions and Test Case Generation

For our reasoning, we use a specific control-flow graph and annotate it with our knowledge about web services using the concept of pre- and postconditions. In order to support BPEL's flow constructs, we extend our BPEL Flow Graph introduced in [19] as follows. Such flow constructs allow for possibly concurrent branches that are activated by individual and optional guards. If such guards are not specified, we assume them to be *True* for simplifying our description.

Definition 1. *An* Extended BPEL Flow Graph *G is a tuple $(V, B, E, v_0, F, \gamma_C (v \in V), \gamma_A(v \in V), \gamma_P(v \in V), \gamma_G(v \in B), \gamma_B(v \in V \setminus B))$, where V is a finite set of vertices representing BPEL process activities, $B \subset V$ is the finite set of fork activity vertices (where a run might branch), $E \subseteq V \times V$ is a finite set of directed edges representing the connections between BPEL activities (edge $e = (v_1, v_2) \in E$ connects v_1 to v_2), $v_0 \in V$ is the start vertex, $F \subseteq V$ is the set of leaf vertices (with no outgoing edges), and the functions $\gamma_C(v)$ and $\gamma_A(v)$ map vertices $v \in V$ to activity conditions and assignments respectively. If v is in B, $\gamma_P(v \in V)$ returns the complementing join activity vertice (and vice versa), and $\perp$ otherwise. Function $\gamma_G(v \in B)$ returns a list of tuples (e_i, TG_{e_i}) for all of a fork vertice v's outgoing edges e_i and their transition guards TG_{e_i} (if there is no guard specified, we assume True so that this branch is always enabled). For any vertice v in $V \setminus B$, the function $\gamma_B(v \in V \setminus B)$ returns the closest predecessor in B if there is such a node, and $\perp$ otherwise.*

An extended BPEL flow graph thus covers a process' structural concept, and via a vertex' labels defined by $\gamma_C(v \in V)$ and $\gamma_A(v \in V)$, we are able to annotate vertices by specifying additional (likely partial) knowledge about activities.

If there are no concurrent computations, an actual execution follows a path in the flow graph, a fact that we exploited in earlier work [17,19] in order to derive corresponding test cases by searching for a satisfying variable assignment to the conditions and assignments encountered along a path.

Definition 2. *A finite path π of length n in an Extended BPEL flow graph G as of Def. 1 is a finite sequence $\pi = \pi_1\pi_2...\pi_n$ such that (1) for any $0 < i \leq n$: $\pi_i \in V$, (2) $\pi_1 = v_0$, (3) for any $0 < i < n$, the edge $e = (\pi_i, \pi_{i+1})$ is in E, and (4) $\pi_n \in F$. $|\pi|$ denotes the length of a path π. We use $f(\pi)$ to refer to the last vertex in π.*

Definition 3. *A finite path segment π in an Extended BPEL flow graph G is defined like a path, but does not have to start in G's initial state v_0, and neither is $f(\pi)$ required to be in F of G.*

For parallel computations, an execution does not follow a single path but features parallel branches, so that we introduce the following definition of a run.

Definition 4. *A finite run r of length n in an Extended BPEL Flow Graph G as of Def. 1 is a finite sequence $r = r_1r_2...r_n$ such that (1) for any $0 < i \leq n$: $r_i \in V$, (2) $r_1 = v_0$, (3) $r_n \in F$, and (4) for any $0 < i < n$, either the edge $e = (r_i, r_{i+1})$ is in E, or if $\gamma_B(p_i) \neq \perp$ then there has to be some $i < j \leq n$ such that (a) there is no $i < k < j$ with $r_k = \gamma_P(\gamma_B(r_i))$ and (b) edge $e = (r_i, r_j)$ is in E. $|r|$ denotes the length of run r. With $f(r)$ we refer to the last vertex in r.*

Obviously, the activities in parallel branches may interleave, as usually there is no defined total order of all the events in the parallel branches, but only a partial one within each individual branch. Part (4) of Def. 4 ensures this partial order. As we will see by the following two definitions, while an actual execution defines a run, in general this is not the case in the other direction.

For one, due to some conflict in the conditions and assignments along a run r, r might actually be infeasible. Accordingly, we have to check a run's collected assignments and conditions for a satisfying assignment in order to determine if such a run is even possible.

Definition 5. *A feasible run r is a run as of Def. 4 s.t. the conditions and assignments encountered along the run are feasible. It is complete, iff for all satisfied transition guards TG_{e_i} at all $v \in B$ visited by r, the corresponding branch started by edge e_i is present in r.*

A corresponding satisfying assignment for a complete run r defines a valid test case. In earlier work neglecting concurrent constructs, we computed test cases by choosing paths in the flow graph and deriving test cases directly from a satisfying assignment for a path's collected conditions and assignments. Now, via the triggered guards, an individual assignment defines which branches are actually executed, so that pre-selecting which branches are to be taken (specifically if there are many, broad, and/or nested flow activities) and then asking for a satisfying assignment might lead to a lot of infeasible instances and thus bad test suite generation performance. Therefore, we still choose paths π in G, but for identifying an actual *execution*, we derive the following run-constraints model for path π (in analogy to our path constraints in earlier work). Complementing π's constraints, all branches of encountered flow constructs are to be modeled, where only the ones being part of π are specifically required to be active.

Definition 6. *For a path $\pi = \pi_1\pi_2...\pi_n$ in some Extended BPEL flow graph G as of Def. 1, we create the* run-constraints $C(\pi)$ *as follows. For each $l \in \gamma_G(\pi_i)$ of a $\pi_i \in B$, we define a branching variable b_l. Let scope be an initially empty list of these branching variables, where we can append a variable b_l via append(scope, b_l), and ask for the last variable with $b_l = $ last(scope) (which will be $\perp$ if the list is empty) as well as remove the last variable via drop(scope). Furthermore, let stop be an initially empty list of vertices in G which we can access with the same functions as scope. Then let $C(\pi)$ be the union of the constraints as derived by traversing π from π_1 to $f(\pi)$ (possibly recursively) as of Def. 7, where in recursive calls the original path can be referred to as π^o, and where variables are replaced by indexed variables in order to implement a static single assignment form (see [10]).*

Definition 7. *For a given path segment π in G, its branching variables and lists scope and stop, we do the following: Let Π be an initially empty list of tuples (v, b_m, π') such that v is a vertex, b_m is a branching variable, and π' is a path segment in G. Then, traversing π from π_1 to $f(\pi)$ do as follows.*

1. *if $\pi_i = $ last(stop), then for each (π_i, b_m, π') in Π do: First, remove (π_i, b_m, π') from Π, and then add constraints for π' as of this Definition for a local scope having b_m as it sole element, computing the local branching variables for π', and assuming a local empty stop list. When there is no more (π_i, b_m, π') in Π, call drop(scope) and drop(stop).*
2. *if $\pi_i \notin B$ then (a) add constraints $\gamma_C(\pi_i) \cup \gamma_A(\pi_i)$ if last(scope) $= \perp$ and proceed with Step 1 for π_{i+1}, or (b) add constraints $(b_l \rightarrow \gamma_C(\pi_i)) \cup (b_l \rightarrow \gamma_A(\pi_i)) \cup (\neg b_l \rightarrow \gamma'_A(\pi_i))$ for $b_l = $ last(scope) $\neq \perp$ and $\gamma'_A(\pi_i)$ replacing every assignment of a variable in $\gamma_A(\pi_i)$ with an assignment of the variable's old value (so that we are always synchronized in respect of the SSA indices when arriving at the join activity, regardless of which branch was active).*
3. *if $\pi_i \in B$ then do as follows. For $l = ((\pi_i, \pi_{i+1}), TG_l) \in \gamma_G(\pi_i)$, add the constraints $b_l \rightarrow TG_l$ and $TG_l \rightarrow b_l$, and append b_l to scope, append $\gamma_P(\pi_i)$ to stop, but add the constraint b_l only if $\pi = \pi^o$. Then find for each $m = ((\pi_i, v), TG_m) \in \gamma_G(\pi_i)$ s.t. $m \neq l$ a path segment π' leading from v to $\gamma_P(\pi_i)$, and add the tuple $(\gamma_P(\pi_i), b_m, \pi'')$ s.t. π'' equals π' but with the last vertex $(\gamma_P(\pi_i))$ removed to Π, as well as add constraints $b_m \rightarrow TG_m$ and $TG_m \rightarrow b_m$.*

In detail, the static single assignment form means that we use indexed variables (i.e. "temporal" variable instances clocked by assignments), such that, whenever a variable is assigned a value, the index is incremented for further referrals along the run. This process, described in principle in earlier work [19], ensures that every variable along a run is defined only once, but might be referred to many times. Note that our approach is similar to symbolic execution, which is a very well-known technique in testing [20]. Similar to symbolic execution, we compute conditions that belong to a particular execution run. In our case, we convert each run condition into a constraint satisfaction problem.

The basic step in Def. 7 is the second one, since there we collect a visited node's conditions and assignments in order to model the run's constraints. The scope variable (as assigned in Step 3) tells us if a node is visited in a branch of a fork activity, so that the corresponding conditions and assignments are of interest only if the branch is active. Note that (only) for branches being part of the original path π^o, the corresponding branch variables are required to be true (active). Since we model relevant path segments that might not be part of the run determined by the actual assignment, we have to make sure that in the SSA form all the branches (that is, the variable indices) get synchronized. To this end, for an inactive branch (s.t. the branching variable is false), each assignment is "replaced" with a propagation of the last (in a temporal sense) valid value known, so that regardless of the actually active branches, the correct value is assigned to the variables referenced afterwards. Step 3 is responsible for establishing a node visit's scope, and choosing which concurrent branches will have to be modeled (stored in Π). Whenever we reach the end of a branch, we ensure in Step 1 that the necessary complementing branches in Π are contained in the model.

Via run constraints for a path π, we can derive an assignment for a feasible, complete run to be stored as testcase. The only thing that has do be done is to filter the propagation assignments synchronizing the branches, which can be done easily since the assignment contains the branching variables.

Definition 8 (Test Case and Test Suite). *A test case for a BPEL Flow Graph G is a variable assignment that makes a complete run r in G feasible. A test suite TS is a set of test cases.*

For assessing a test suite's quality, we consider its effectiveness in identifying mutated versions of the original BPEL flow graph. Therefore, we introduce the concept of mutants, which are variants of the original BPEL program.

Definition 9. *A Mutant is an altered version G' of an original program G. The mutant G' is equivalent to G, if and only if they do not differ in their behavior.*

We use a Mutation tool [4] to generate faulty versions of BPEL processes. Those versions we use to check whether a test suite is able to "kill" the mutants.

Definition 10. *A mutant G' is killed by a test suite TS, if there is some test case t ∈ TS such that the output triggered for G' differs from that for G.*

Note that a mutant not killed might either be equivalent [16] to the original process (which would have to be checked manually), or the test suite is simply

```
1: procedure STRUCTRUNS(G, MaxLen)
2:     initialize test suite S ← ∅
3:     compute the set P of all paths π s.t. |π| ≤ MaxLen, where for vertices v ∈ B,
   we create for each (eᵢ, TG_{eᵢ}) in γ_G(v), a path s.t. TG_{eᵢ} is enabled.
4:     for each path π ∈ P do
5:         check the satisfiability of run-constraints C(π) as of Def. 6
6:         if C(π) is satisfiable then
7:             add a corresponding test case to S
8:         end if
9:     end for
10:    return test suite S.
11: end procedure
```

Fig. 2. Our structural TCG algorithm STRUCTRUNS

not able to trigger the mutant in the right way in order to make it unveil itself as a mutant. The higher the mutation score (the percentage of killed mutants), the better we consider a test suite's effectiveness at fault detection to be.

In earlier work [19], we introduced the ALLPATHS test suite generation algorithm that considers all possible paths through a BPEL flow graph (with no parallel computations) up to a certain path length. The algorithm takes two inputs, i.e., the flow graph G and the maximum length $MaxLen$, and traverses the flow graph using a depth-first search strategy, returning a test suite covering all the corresponding feasible paths. Assuming there is no interaction between the parallel branches, we can derive the variant given in Figure 2, supporting also parallel computations. The STRUCTRUNS algorithm is thus also search based, and the only difference is that we derive *run-constraints* as of Def. 6 instead of collecting only the assignments and conditions along the path itself (path-constraints) as in [19]. If such a run-constraints model is satisfiable, the relevant corresponding variable assignments are saved as test case.

Considering limited resources, agile testing requirements, and the fact that computing all paths might be too time consuming for larger BPEL processes (as could be executing the tests), we previously proposed also a random algorithm [17]. This algorithm extracts a desired number of random testcases, limited in length by a given parameter. Like for the ALLPATH algorithm, we can easily derive a variant RANDOMRUNS (see Fig. 3) supporting flow constructs via considering a path's run-constraints as of Def. 6 instead of its path constraints [17].

3   Empirical Evaluation

Our empirical evaluation's goal was to analyze the performance of the STRUCTRUNS and the RANDOMRUNS algorithms. In particular, we have been interested in the coverage and mutation scores obtained when using said algorithms for test suite generation. In the latter context, our main objective was to compare the algorithms. The initial underlying surmise was that STRUCTRUNS should perform better than RANDOMRUNS with respect to coverage and mutation scores.

```
1: procedure RANDOMRUNS(G, Len, numTC)
2:     initialize test suite S ← ∅
3:     while |S| < numTC do
4:         initialize path π ← v₀
5:         while |π| < maxLen do
6:             pick random v ∈ V s.t. ∃e = (f(π), v) ∈ E
7:             add v to π: π ← πv
8:             if f(π) ∈ F then
9:                 if run-constraints C(π) (see Def. 6) are satisfiable then
10:                        add a corresponding test case to S
11:                    end if
12:                else
13:                    increment infeasible paths
14:                end if
15:            end while
16:        end while
17:    return test suite S
18: end procedure
```

Fig. 3. TCG algorithm RANDOMRUNS based on random paths

For our empirical evaluation, we considered ten examples of synchronous BPEL processes. These examples include activities like Receive, Reply, Assign, If, Else if, While, Invoke, Sequence and Flow. The three SOA processes *Loan*, *LoanCov* and *SquaresS* are available from the mutation tool repository [4], where we used the *Loan* example also in the evaluation presented in [18]. *LoanCov* is a slight variant of the *Loan* example, and *SquaresS* computes the obvious arithmetic function. The SOA example *ATM* is a simplified version of the process discussed in [3]. With *Triangle*, we implemented also a typical example from software engineering studies (see [21]). This *Triangle* process decides for a given triangle whether it is equilateral, isosceles, or scalene. Similarly, *Bmi* is another famous example taken from software testing papers. *Calc* is our last example with Sequence activity that implements basic calculator functionalities, i.e., addition, subtraction, multiplication, and division for given input values. The examples *Flow* and *Flow3* are simple hand-crafted examples using Flow construct, whereas *Order* is a variant of an Ordering Service from the BPEL specification document.

We implemented both algorithms, STRUCTRUNS and RANDOMRUNS, in Java. All the experiments ran on a 13" MacBook Pro (Late 2011) with a 2.4 GHz Intel Core i5, 4 GB 1333 MHz DDR3, running under OS X 10.7.2.

Tables 1 and 2 offer the experiments' details when using the STRUCTRUNS and RANDOMRUNS algorithms respectively. The number of a BPEL process' activities is given by n, the desired maximum path length by mL, the number of derived paths is labeled p, the minimum and maximum lengths of derived paths are given in columns labeled miP and maP respectively, and the minimum and maximum numbers of constraints derived for any path are reported as miC and maC respectively. *GenT* defines the total time in milliseconds it took us to derive a corresponding test suite S. The most interesting values, however, are

Table 1. Experimental results for the STRUCTRUNS TCG algorithm

Prog	n	mL	p	miP	maP	miC	maC	GenT	Cov	Mut	ExecT
Loan	16	10	2	8	9	9	11	176	76.9	68.50	629,271
		15	3	8	12	9	13	227	100.0	87.64	966,228
		20	3	8	12	9	13	247	100.0	87.64	962,418
Atm	27	10	1	9	9	12	12	68	35.2	21.77	468,613
		15	5	9	15	12	20	569	100.0	80.64	2,411,368
		20	5	9	15	12	20	985	100.0	80.64	2,442,709
SquareS	7	10	3	7	10	12	17	200	100.0	88.51	726,955
		15	5	7	15	12	32	566	100.0	89.65	1,279,305
		20	8	7	19	12	42	830	100.0	89.65	2,421,234
LoanCov	27	10	3	8	10	11	11	293	64.0	52.54	1,346,072
		15	5	8	13	11	15	433	100.0	71.03	1,971,916
		20	5	8	13	11	15	467	100.0	71.03	1,971,476
Triangle	22	10	1	7	7	9	9	354	38.0	12.34	870,823
		15	4	7	15	9	25	477	92.0	66.04	2,289,147
		20	5	7	16	9	26	718	100.0	71.03	2,651,180
Bmi	15	10	5	7	9	9	9	485	100.0	90.00	1,081,270
Calc	30	10	4	5	10	6	20	248	40.0	38.63	1,633,480
		15	9	5	15	6	32	591	100.0	98.37	3,496,140
Flow	11	15	1	11	11	14	14	156	83.3	54.00	450,463
Flow3	11	15	2	11	11	11	11	243	100.0	83.30	326,788
OrderFlow	24	25	2	24	24	41	41	378	100.0	61.00	366,954

Table 2. Experimental results for the RANDOMRUNS TCG algorithm with len = 40

Prog	n	rP	miP	maP	miC	maC	GenT	miCov	maCov	avgCov	miMut	maMut	avgMut	stdev	ExecT
Loan	16	1	8	12	9	13	451.0	46.1	69.2	51.49	24.71	52.80	39.21	15.28	526,905
		2	8	12	9	13	445.0	46.1	76.9	66.89	24.71	68.53	55.16	17.51	696,221
		3	8	12	9	13	641.0	46.1	100.0	86.14	24.71	87.64	67.41	17.13	884,560
Atm	27	1	9	14	11	20	479.0	41.1	52.9	50.54	21.77	45.96	33.70	12.58	447,316
		3	9	15	11	20	644.4	35.2	76.4	54.66	21.77	66.12	48.22	15.03	1,111,243
		5	9	15	11	20	897.5	47.0	100.0	65.85	48.38	80.64	59.59	9.74	1,821,139
SquareS	7	3	7	13	12	27	405.3	100.0	100.0	100.00	83.90	89.65	88.50	1.71	808,907
		5	7	25	12	57	728.2	100.0	100.0	100.00	83.90	89.65	88.85	1.80	1,232,068
		8	7	21	12	47	872.9	100.0	100.0	100.00	88.50	89.65	89.54	0.36	1,930,244
LoanCov	16	3	8	13	11	15	926.3	47.3	89.4	64.15	33.33	55.73	43.98	11.77	1,325,958
		5	8	13	11	15	811.3	47.3	94.7	75.74	34.97	61.74	52.89	7.82	1,884,014
Triangle	22	1	7	12	9	15	475.0	33.3	66.6	50.00	12.96	45.37	26.47	15.04	1,002,234
		4	7	15	9	26	654.0	33.3	83.3	74.20	12.96	58.95	44.41	14.39	1,818,729
		5	7	15	9	26	646.0	75.0	91.6	85.00	37.96	69.75	59.35	9.86	2,722,881
		7	7	15	9	26	915.4	75.0	91.6	84.10	37.34	65.74	57.75	7.78	2,800,813
Bmi	15	1	7	9	9	9	158.7	60.0	60.0	60.00	29.09	52.72	42.09	9.99	406,481
		3	7	9	9	9	737.7	60.0	80.0	74.00	45.45	72.72	64.27	10.61	733,752
		5	7	9	9	9	700.0	70.0	90.0	83.00	60.90	81.81	73.18	7.68	1,049,588
		7	7	9	9	9	797.4	80.0	100.0	87.00	62.72	90.00	77.72	7.59	1,436,189
		10	7	9	9	9	816.8	90.0	100.0	92.00	80.90	90.00	83.00	3.71	2,240,604
		12	7	9	9	9	678.5	90.0	100.0	97.00	80.90	90.00	87.27	4.39	2,645,961
		15	7	9	9	9	852.7	90.0	100.0	98.00	80.90	90.00	88.18	3.83	2,737,402
		17	7	9	9	9	877.1	90.0	100.0	97.00	80.90	90.00	87.27	4.39	3,726,332
Calc	30	4	5	25	6	38	703.6	35.0	70.0	46.00	29.73	57.18	39.90	10.28	1,529,496
		9	5	24	6	56	822.7	40.0	100.0	68.00	38.23	84.64	59.31	15.72	2,930,746
Flow	11	1	11	11	13	23	768.4	83.3	83.3	83.30	54.54	54.54	54.54	1.17	374,245
Flow3	11	1	11	11	11	17	545.5	50.0	83.3	66.65	42.66	52.00	43.60	6.56	283,808
		2	11	11	13	19	884.7	83.3	100.0	91.65	52.00	70.66	67.73	5.65	333,727
Order	24	1	23	23	42	42	826.6	47.0	94.1	65.84	40.84	52.11	45.35	5.81	264,348
		2	23	23	42	42	1059	47.0	100.0	82.33	42.25	60.56	52.53	7.99	348,207

those for *Cov* and *Mut* that give us the percentage of covered activities and killed mutants, respectively. The overall test execution time the mutation tool took to compute mutation coverage (in milliseconds) is given in the columns labeled *ExecT*. That is, for the RANDOMRUNS algorithm, we computed 10 samples per row and report the minimum, maximum, and average values for coverage and mutation scores respectively, with also *GenT* referring to the average value over these 10 samples. For the mutation score, we also report on the standard deviation *stdev*. In Table 2, *rP* defines the desired amount of test cases.

Taking a look at Tables 1 and 2, we obtained the following general observations. First, for both algorithms, the test suite generation time was always a fraction of the time needed for executing the mutation tool. That is, whereas the test suite generation time never exceeded 1 second for any example, test execution took up to slightly over an hour. Hence, in the SOA domain, test execution seems to be very time consuming, even for smaller examples. Second, when considering the time required to come up with a test suite of the same size, overall generation time is almost equivalent for both algorithms. Finally, when taking average values into account (but even for the best cases of RANDOMRUNS), the STRUCTRUNS algorithm performs better in terms of coverage and mutation scores for most of the examples.

We recorded also the number of infeasible paths encountered, where we report on corresponding results for the *Calc* example in Table 3. Please note that up to a path length of 20, we saw no infeasible paths for the STRUCTRUNS algorithm. For the random approach, however, we see how the number of infeasible paths increases if we raise the desired number of test cases (for a given, fixed maximum path length). The longer test cases allowed for this variant, very early ran into issues in this respect. That is, for $|S| = 4$ we already had to dismiss 3 infeasible paths at most (over 10 samples), increasing to 8 paths for a test suite of size 9. As also for 9 test cases, we could reach only a mutation score of 80%, this raises the question of how many random paths we would need in order to achieve the same mutation score as with the STRUCTRUNS algorithm.

To the end of answering this question, we considered the *BMI* BPEL process, and test suite sizes *rP* of 1, 3, 5 7, 10, 12 ,15, and 17 (see Table 2). The coverage attained for 12 to 17 paths was roughly the same, with the execution time increasing from approximately 45 minutes to 62 minutes on average. In Figure 4 we summarize our findings using a box plot diagram, where the grey box indicates the bounds given by the average value and the standard deviation. We see that the results are converging to the same mutation score as obtained when using STRUCTRUNS. That is, for 7 test cases or more, the random algorithm provided the same 100% activity coverage and maximum mutation score of around 90% as the STRUCTRUNS algorithm did. For 12 test cases and above, also the average mutation score got in the same range. However, the time needed for generating a test suite with similar average performance almost doubled for RANDOMRUNS. Moreover, also due to the higher number of test cases, the execution time was higher for the random approach. That is, for test suite sizes of 10 and above, and using the STRUCTRUNS algorithm, it was less than half of that as when using

Table 3. Infeasible paths for the RANDOMRUNS TCG algorithm

Prog	rP	min InP	max InP	avg InP
Calc	4	0	3	0.4
Calc	9	0	8	1.4

the RANDOMRUNS algorithm. The random approach took 700 milliseconds on average for computing five paths, achieving an average mutation score of 73.18% (ranging between 60.9 and 81.81 percent), while the STRUCTRUNS took (smaller) 485 milliseconds to compute 5 paths for a given maximum length of 10, offering a (higher) mutation score of 90% percent.

It is also worth mentioning that there were many surviving mutants for each of the examples used in our empirical evaluation. The highest achieved mutation score was 90%. In order to investigate the non killed mutants, we inspected the surviving mutants manually for the *BMI* example. We found out that by adding five additional test cases, we were able to reach a mutation score of 95%. The remaining mutants were equivalent ones. Hence, we conclude that there is still room for improving the test case generation process, in order to deliver an algorithm with an improved performance.

4   Related Research

Exploiting constraints for software testing is an attractive concept. Gotlieb et al. [15] extracted test cases from programs via a constraint representation of its source code. Whereas our work is quite close to this in principle, the application domain and constraint extraction process are different. In our case we exploit also a component's pre- and postconditions, because, as a matter of fact, a SOA's services' actual implementations are hardly available. In this respect we differ also from [7], where, in contrast to our BPEL flow graph, Bentakouk et al. translate a BPEL model into a symbolic transition system (STS) used to extract test cases from. They issue specific warnings for situations where their approach is incomplete due to time-out violations in the construction of the STS. Similar work was presented in [29].

In the context of web service testing, literature reports on mainly three model based testing techniques, i.e., *symbolic execution*, *petri nets*, and *model checking* [9]. Yuan et al. [34] presented a graph search based test case generation of BPEL processes that exploits matrix transformations of control flow graphs, path coverage, and a node classification depending on incoming and outgoing edges. While their approach is close, we differ in the use of pre- and postconditions added to the test paths, aiming to solve the test oracle problem. A slight difference is also in the use of the MINION constraint solver [14] rather than Lp.

The underlying idea behind [32], which relies on an extended Control Flow Graph (XCFG), is to extract all sequential paths from the XCFG, and to combine them into concurrent test paths. Constraints are then collected from these

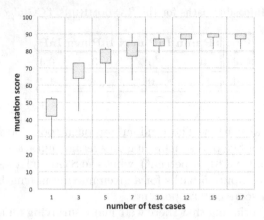

Fig. 4. RANDOMRUNS: Mutation score as function of the number of test cases for *BMI*

concurrent test paths via backward substitution. In contrast, we transform each sequential path directly into a set of constraints, each set independently checked for satisfiability. For unsatisfiable constraints, the corresponding path is discarded, satisfiable ones produce the corresponding variables used to execute the path. These values define a test case to be included in the test suite.

Also model checking [9] can be exploited in the context of web service testing. For this, BPEL specifications are converted into a formal modeling language like PROMELA [13]. Defining test criteria as formal properties, in a language such as LTL [30], a model checker can be used to search for violations of the properties by the BPEL model. The actual test cases then are derived from the counter examples provided by the model checker for such violations. Zhen et al. [36] applied the same idea to web services and BPEL processes, addressing the state space explosion problem inherent with model checking. Moreover, they also developed a tool for the generation of JUnit test cases for automated test execution. Model based testing techniques using Petri Nets have also been explored extensively. Petri Nets are attractive for modeling concurrent processes and their synchronization, and can be categorized into Plain Petri Nets [27], Colored Petri Nets [33] and High-level Petri Nets. Dong [11] developed a tool for test case generation of BPEL processes using High-level Petri Nets. The basic approach is to build a reachability graph from which test cases can be extracted. The approach has a very high space complexity.

For test case execution, we use [23], where we convert the abstract test cases manually to executable ones accepted by the BPELUnit tool [22]. This tool supports simulated as well as real-life testing, accommodating many BPEL engines like Active VOS [1], Oracle BPEL Process Manager [5], and Apache ODE [2]. For simulated testing, a BPEL process is not deployed, rather the intended engine is called through a debug API. In real-life testing mode, a business process is actually deployed and the partner web services are tested using mocks.

The survey of Zakaria et al. [35] gives a very good comparison of different unit testing approaches applied to BPEL processes. One key issue pointed out there is the lack of an empirical evaluation. Surprisingly, only 1 out of 27 considered studies provides results on real-life BPEL processes.

Random testing has been successfully used in practice. For example, Faigon [12] reports on experience gained in random testing of a compiler. He mentions that a simple Random IR (Intermediate Representation) Generator was able to find more than half of all the bugs reported by customers in just one night. Other applications include testing graphical user interfaces (GUIs). In GUI testing, dump and smart monkeys [26,6] are used, where the latter makes use of a simplified model of the application in order to guide testing to some extent. Arnold [6] reports that monkeys are able to find more than 25 % of the bugs when used early in the development cycle. Hence, random testing can be effectively used in practice. In contrast to these papers, we apply random testing on a model obtained from the source code directly.

5 Conclusions

Summarizing, we report on experiments with two test suite generation algorithms that implement orthogonal strategies for creating functional tests for synchronous executable BPEL processes. That is, the STRUCTRUNS variant derives test cases covering all feasible paths up to a given length, and the RANDOMRUNS variant derives a desired number of test cases covering a random selection of feasible paths (and successor states in a path), also limited by a predetermined length. Our initial surmise that by construction, the STRUCTRUNS variant should offer better performance in terms of achievable mutation scores and activity coverage, but might be infeasible in practical terms (s.t. a random approach might be favorable) was confirmed by our experiments. However, the experiments showed also that the random approach was inferior in terms of generation time (and execution time). That is, for the BMI example, even computing 3 random paths took us 50 % longer to construct, than all the five paths for a maximum length of 10. While we saw that for the SOA domain, construction time is negligible in comparison to test execution time, our random setup was quite inferior also in the achieved mutation scores for the BMI example and a comparable execution time. We draw several conclusions from this. First, our observations regarding execution times show that one definitely has to employ some strategic reasoning for designing test suites in the context of BPEL process testing. Our tests also showed that, at least our examples might not favor the use of longer paths as allowed for the random approach, in comparison to the shorter paths derived for the STRUCTRUNS variant. For a completely random approach, longer path lengths must be allowed however, due to the random choice of the successor states (i.e. in the context of loops). Thus an approach mixing a random component with some structural reasoning should be the subject of future research. Such research will also aim at accommodating those five manual tests that allowed us to improve the mutation score for the BMI example, and will be subject to stimuli from realistic [8] and search-based test-case generation [25].

Acknowledgement. The research leading to these results has received funding from the Austrian Science Fund (FWF) under project references P23313-N23 and P22959-N23.

References

1. Active VOS engine, http://www.activevos.com
2. Apache ODE, http://ode.apache.org/
3. JBoss example,
   http://docs.jboss.com/jbpm/bpel/v1.1/userguide/tutorial.atm.html
4. MuBPEL- a mutation testing tool for WS-BPEL,
   https://neptuno.uca.es/redmine/projects/sources-fm/wiki/MuBPEL
5. Oracle BPEL Process Manager,
   http://www.oracle.com/technetwork/middleware/bpel
6. Arnold, T.R.: Visual Test 6 Bible. IDG Books Worldwide, Inc., Foster City (1998)
7. Bentakouk, L., Poizat, P., Zaïdi, F.: A formal framework for service orchestration testing based on symbolic transition systems. In: Proc. of the 21st IFIP WG 6.1 Int. Conf. on Testing of Software and Communication Systems and 9th Int. FATES Workshop, pp. 16–32 (2009)
8. Bozkurt, M., Harman, M.: Automatically generating realistic test input from web services. In: International Symposium on Service-Oriented System Engineering (SOSE), pp. 13–24 (December 2011)
9. Bozkurt, M., Harman, M., Hassoun, Y.: Testing Web Services: A Survey. Tech. Rep. TR-10-01, Dep. of Computer Science, King's College London (January 2010)
10. Brandis, M.M., Mössenböck, H.: Single-pass generation of static assignment form for structured languages. ACM TOPLAS 16(6), 1684–1698 (1994)
11. Dong, W.: Test case generation method for BPEL-Based Testing. In: Int. Conf. on Computational Intelligence and Natural Computing, vol. 2, pp. 467–470 (June 2009)
12. Faigon, A.: Testing for zero bugs, http://www.yendor.com/testing/
13. Garcia-fanjul, J., Tuya, J., Riva, C.D.L.: Generating Test Cases Specifications for BPEL Compositions of Web Services Using SPIN (2006),
   http://citeseerx.ist.psu.edu/viewdoc/summary?doi=10.1.1.60.9287
14. Gent, I.P., Jefferson, C., Miguel, I.: Minion: A fast scalable constraint solver. In: Proceedings of ECAI 2006, Riva del Garda, pp. 98–102. IOS Press (2006)
15. Gotlieb, A., Botella, B., Rueher, M.: Automatic test data generation using constraint solving techniques. In: ACM SIGSOFT International Symposium on Software Testing and Analysis, pp. 53–62 (1998)
16. Grün, B.J.M., Schuler, D., Zeller, A.: The impact of equivalent mutants. In: Proceedings of the IEEE Int. Conf. on Software Testing, Verification, and Validation Workshops, ICSTW 2009, pp. 192–199 (2009)
17. Jehan, S., Pill, I., Wotawa, F.: SOA testing via random paths in BPEL models. In: 10th Workshop on Advances in Model Based Testing; 2014 IEEE Seventh Int. Conf. on Software Testing, Verification and Validation Workshops (ICSTW), pp. 260–263 (2014)
18. Jehan, S., Pill, I., Wotawa, F.: Functional SOA testing based on constraints. In: 8th Int. Workshop on Automation of Software Test (AST), pp. 33–39 (2013)

19. Jehan, S., Pill, I., Wotawa, F.: SOA grey box testing - a constraint-based approach. In: 5th Int. Workshop on Constraints in Software Testing, Verification and Analysis; 2013 IEEE Sixth Int. Conf. on Software Testing, Verification and Validation Workshops (ICSTW), pp. 232–237 (2013)
20. King, J.C.: Symbolic execution and program testing. Commun. ACM 19(7), 385–394 (1976), http://doi.acm.org/10.1145/360248.360252
21. Langdon, W.B., Harman, M., Jia, Y.: Efficient Multi-objective Higher Order Mutation Testing with Genetic Programming. J. Syst. Softw. 83(12), 2416–2430 (2010)
22. Lübke, D.: Bpel Unit (2006), http://bpelunit.github.com
23. Mayer, P., Lübke, D.: Towards a BPEL unit testing framework. In: Workshop on Testing, Analysis, and Verification of Web Services and Applications, pp. 33–42 (2006)
24. Mayer, W., Friedrich, G., Stumptner, M.: On computing correct processes and repairs using partial behavioral models. In: European Conf. on Artificial Intelligence (ECAI), pp. 582–587 (2012)
25. McMinn, P., Shahbaz, M., Stevenson, M.: Search-based test input generation for string data types using the results of web queries. In: 5th Int. Conf. on Software Testing, Verification and Validation (ICST), pp. 141–150 (April 2012)
26. Nyman, N.: Using monkey test tools. Software Testing & Quality Enineering Magazine (January/February 2000)
27. Ouyang, C., Verbeek, E., van der Aalst, W.M.P., Breutel, S., Dumas, M., ter Hofstede, A.H.M.: Formal semantics and analysis of control flow in WS-BPEL. Sci. Comput. Program. 67(2-3), 162–198 (2007)
28. Papazoglou, M.P., Traverso, P., Dustdar, S., Leymann, F.: Service-oriented computing: a research roadmap. Int. J. of Cooperative Information Systems 17(2), 223–255 (2008)
29. Paradkar, A., Sinha, A.: Specify once test everywhere: Analyzing invariants to augment service descriptions for automated test generation. In: Bouguettaya, A., Krueger, I., Margaria, T. (eds.) ICSOC 2008. LNCS, vol. 5364, pp. 551–557. Springer, Heidelberg (2008)
30. Pnueli, A.: The temporal logic of programs. In: 18th Annual Symposium on Foundations of Computer Science (FOCS), pp. 46–57 (1977)
31. Wotawa, F., Schulz, M., Pill, I., Jehan, S., Leitner, P., Hummer, W., Schulte, S., Hoenisch, P., Dustdar, S.: Fifty shades of grey in SOA testing. In: 9th Workshop on Advances in Model Based Testing; 2013 IEEE Sixth Int. Conf. on Software Testing, Verification and Validation Workshops (ICSTW), pp. 154–157 (2013)
32. J., Li, Z., Yuan, Y., Sun, W., Yan, J.Z.: BPEL4WS Unit Testing: Test case generation using a concurrent path analysis approach. In: 17th Int. Symp. on Software Reliability Engineering (ISSRE), pp. 75–84. IEEE Computer Society (2006)
33. Yang, Y., Tan, Q., Xiao, Y.: Verifying web services composition based on hierarchical colored petri nets. In: 1st Int. Workshop on Interoperability of Heterogeneous Information Systems, IHIS 2005, pp. 47–54. ACM (2005)
34. Li, Z., Yuan, W.S.Y.: A graph-search based approach to BPEL4WS test generation. In: Int. Conf. on Software Engineering Advances, p. 14 (October 2006)
35. Zakaria, Z., Atan, R., Ghani, A.A.A., Sani, N.F.M.: Unit testing approaches for BPEL: A systematic review. In: 16th Asia-Pacific Software Engineering Conference, pp. 316–322. IEEE Computer Society (2009)
36. Zheng, Y., Zhou, J., Krause, P.: A model checking based test case generation framework for web services pp. 715–722 (April 2007)

Facilitating Reuse in Multi-goal Test-Suite Generation for Software Product Lines

Johannes Bürdek[1], Malte Lochau[1], Stefan Bauregger[1], Andreas Holzer[2],
Alexander von Rhein[3], Sven Apel[3], and Dirk Beyer[3]

[1] TU Darmstadt, Germany
[2] TU Wien, Austria
[3] University of Passau, Germany

Abstract. Software testing is still the most established and scalable quality-assurance technique in practice. However, generating effective test suites remains computationally expensive, consisting of repetitive reachability analyses for multiple test goals according to a coverage criterion. This situation is even worse when testing entire software product lines, i.e., families of similar program variants, requiring a sufficient coverage of all derivable program variants. Instead of considering every product variant one-by-one, family-based approaches are variability-aware analysis techniques in that they systematically explore similarities among the different variants. Based on this principle, we present a novel approach for automated product-line test-suite generation incorporating extensive reuse of reachability information among test cases derived for different test goals and/or program variants. We present a tool implementation on top of CPA/TIGER which is based on CPACHECKER, and provide evaluation results obtained from various experiments, revealing a considerable increase in efficiency compared to existing techniques.

Keywords: Software Product Lines, Automated Test Generation, Symbolic Model Checking, CPACHECKER, CPA/TIGER.

1   Introduction

Software-product-line engineering [15] has become a key technology to cope with the variability of highly-configurable (software) systems, prevalent in various application domains today. In recent years, software product lines (SPL) have found their way into numerous industrial application domains, e.g., automotive, information and mobile systems [29]. SPL engineering aims at developing a family of similar, yet well-distinguished software products based on a common core platform, where commonality and variability among the family members (product variants) are explicitly specified in terms of *features*. Each feature corresponds to (1) user-visible product characteristics in the problem domain, relevant for product configuration, as well as to (2) composable implementation artifacts for (automated) assembling of implementation variants. This philosophy of extensive *reuse* of common feature artifacts among product variants facilitates a remarkable gain in efficiency compared to one-by-one variant development [15].

© Springer-Verlag Berlin Heidelberg 2015
A. Egyed and I. Schaefer (Eds.): FASE 2015, LNCS 9033, pp. 84–99, 2015.
DOI: 10.1007/978-3-662-46675-9_6

For SPLs to obtain full acceptance in practice, established quality-assurance techniques have to be lifted to become *variability-aware* as well, to also benefit from reuse principles [24, 26, 27]. Various promising attempts have been proposed, enhancing respective model-checking and software-testing techniques to efficiently verify entire families of software products instead of every single variant [4, 12, 14, 16]. In practice, systematic software testing remains the most established and elaborated quality-assurance technique, as it is directly applicable to real-world applications at any level of abstraction [28]. Furthermore, testing allows for a realistic and controllable trade-off between effectiveness and efficiency. In particular, white-box test generation aims at (automatically) deriving sample inputs for a given program under test to meet certain *test goals*. Thereupon, the derivation of an entire *test suite* is usually guided by test-selection measures by means of coverage criteria, e.g., *basic-block coverage* and *condition coverage* [8]. Coverage criteria impose multiple, arbitrarily complex test goals, thus requiring *sets* of test-input vectors to achieve a complete coverage [8]. Depending on the concrete application domain and the respective level of mission-/safety-criticality, it is imperative, or even enforced by industrial standards, to guarantee a certain degree of code coverage for every delivered product [11]. The computational problem underlying automated test generation consists of expensive reachability analyses of the program state space. Symbolic model checking has emerged in the past as a promising approach for fully automated white-box test generation using counterexamples as test inputs [7]. However, in case of large sets of complex test goals, scalability issues still hinder efficient test-case generation when being performed for every test goal anew. This is even worse when generating test inputs for covering entire product-line implementations. To avoid product-by-product (re-)generation of test cases with many redundant generation runs, a family-based test-generation approach must enhance test-suite-derivation techniques to be likewise applicable to product-line implementations [12, 24].

In this paper, we present a novel approach for efficient white-box test-suite generation that guarantees multi-goal test coverage of product-line implementations. The approach systematically exploits reuse potential among reachability-analysis results by means of similarity among test cases

- derived for different test goals [8], and/or
- derived for different product variants [12].

The interleaving of both techniques leads to an incremental, coverage-driven exploration of the state space of the product line under test implemented in C enriched with feature parameters [19]. We implemented an SPL test-suite generator for arbitrary coverage criteria on top of CPA/TIGER which is based on CPACHECKER [9], a symbolic model checker using the CEGAR approach [13]. In our evaluation, we consider sample product-line implementations of varying sizes to investigate the general applicability of the novel test-suite-derivation approach, as well as the gain in efficiency obtained from the reuse of reachability analyis results. The results reveal a considerable improvement in efficiency compared to test-suite-generation approaches without systematic reuse.

```
1  int func(int x, int y, int z) {
2     int a;
3     if (x < y)
4        a = x;
5     else
6        a = y;
7     z = z - a;
8     return z;
9  }
```

(a) Sample C-Code   (b) CFA

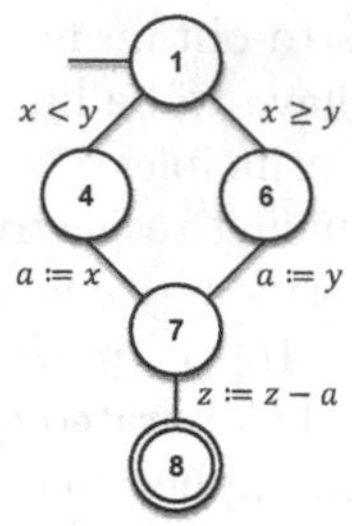

Fig. 1. C Code and CFA Representation of a Program Under Test

2 Background

In this section, we give a brief overview on the general principles and notions of white-box test-case derivation and its application to software product lines.

2.1 White-Box Test-Suite Derivation

Consider the C code snippet in Fig. 1(a) implementing a simple function func that takes three integer parameters, x, y and z, subtracts the smaller value of x and y from z, and returns the result. The program operates on a set $V = \{x, y, z, a\}$ of typed program variables, where the subset $\{x, y, z\} \subseteq V$ constitutes *input variables* of the program. The purpose of test-case derivation is to systematically derive sample vectors of concrete *input values*, one for each input variable, to stimulate and therefore investigate a particular behavior of the program under test. For example, executing the given sample program with the *input vector* $[x = 1, y = 2, z = 3]$ enforces a test run that traverses the if branch in Lines 3 – 4. In addition to the input vector, a test case often further consists of a *test oracle*, i.e., a specification of the intended outcome of running the test, e.g., by means of the expected return value of a function in case of unit testing. Hence, a *test case* consists of a pair of an input vector and a test oracle, e.g., $([x = 1, y = 2, z = 3], [z = 2])$. To properly test a program, typically a whole *set* of test cases is required. However, due to the large and even (theoretically) unbounded size of input-value domains (integer in this example), exhaustive testing is, in general, infeasible, or even impossible. To guide the selection of appropriate subsets of input vectors into a *test suite*, various adequacy criteria have been proposed [28]. Concerning white-box testing, in particular, *code-coverage measures* refer to syntactic program elements as multiple *test goals* to be covered by a test suite. For this purpose, an abstract representation of the program under test is considered, e.g., a control-flow automaton (CFA) [8], as shown in Fig. 1(b). Nodes of the CFA refer to program locations (program-counter valuations), and edges denote control transfers between locations according to the syntactic structure of the program. Edges referring to (blocks of) operations are labeled with respective value assignments on program variables, whereas edges referring control-flow branches are labeled with corresponding predicates (assumptions) over program-variable values. Covering a test goal on a CFA means to find an input vector that traverses a CFA path that matches this goal. For instance, applying *statement coverage* to the CFA of Fig. 1(b), the statements in Lines 4, 6, and 7 each constitute a test goal, where the aforementioned test case ($[x = 1, y = 2, z = 3], [z = 2]$) covers the goals 4 and 7. To obtain complete statement coverage, a further test case, e.g., ($[x = 2, y = 1, z = 3], [z = 2]$), is required to cover the else branch (Lines 5 – 6). Hence, both test-input vectors in combination constitute a *complete* test suite for statement coverage.

Statement coverage is one of the weakest code-coverage criteria, solely ensuring a small subset of the reachable program state space to be actually explored. In the context of safety-critical systems, coverage criteria such as MC/DC [11] comprise more complex test-goal specifications including sets of pairs (ℓ, φ) of program locations ℓ together with predicates φ over program variables in V. Coverage criteria not only define quality measures for existing test suites, but also serve as test-end criteria during test-suite generation. Therefore, a test-suite generator iterates over the set of test goals and derives a satisfying test case for each test goal. For example, statement coverage selects the program locations 4, 6, 7 as test goals and starts with location 7, which is trivially reached by any input vector, e.g., $[x = 1, y = 2, z = 3]$. In addition, location 4 is also already covered by this test case. Thus, results of test-case generation may be *reused* among test goals to reduce test-generation/execution efforts.

2.2   Test-Suite Derivation for Product-Line Implementations

The program in Fig. 1 implements a fixed functionality without any behavioral variability, as apparent, e.g., in software product lines [15]. In a product line, features are related to dedicated artifacts within the solution space. These artifacts are composable into product variants derivable for a given configuration, thus facilitating systematic reuse of artifacts among product-family members at any level of abstraction [1]. At source-code level, features may occur as implementation parameters annotating dedicated pieces of code as feature-specific implementation variability, e.g., using C preprocessor [19].

Consider the product-line implementation func-spl in Fig. 2(a) (line breaks are added for better readability), which extends the example from Fig. 1(a) by variability. Therein, #ifdef conditions over (Boolean) feature parameters annotate those code pieces being conditionally compiled into a variant implementation depending on the feature selection. In the example of Fig. 2, feature parameters control that, from x and y, either the smaller (LE) or the greater value (GR) is either added (PLUS) or subtracted (MINUS) from z. In the case of subtraction, feature NOTNEG ensures the result not to be negative for positve input values.

The set of features, together with constraints limiting their possible combinations, are usually captured in a *variability model*. Here, we limit our attention to a representation in terms of propositional formulae over Boolean feature

```
 1  int func-spl(int x, int y,
                  int z) {
 2      int a;
 3      #ifdef LE
 4      if (x < y)
 5          a = x;
 6      else
 7          a = y;
 8      #elsif GR
 9      if (x > y)
10          a = x;
11      else
12          a = y;
13      #endif
14      #ifdef PLUS
15      z = z + a;
16      #elsif MINUS
17      #ifdef NOTNEG {
18      if ((z - a) < 0)
19          a = a * (-1);
20      }
21      #endif
22      z = z - a;
23      #endif
24      return z;
25  }
```

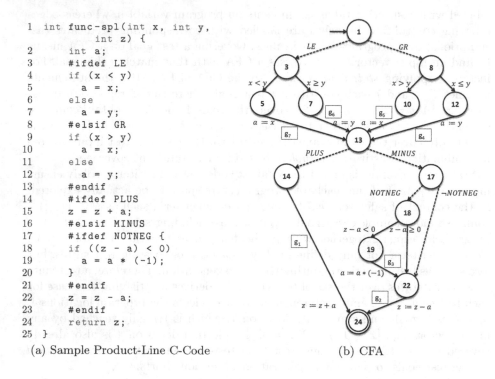

(a) Sample Product-Line C-Code   (b) CFA

Fig. 2. Parameterized C-Code and CFA Representation of a Product-Line Under Test

variables [5]. For our example in Fig. 2(a), the variability model states that

$$(\mathsf{LE} \veebar \mathsf{GR}) \wedge (\mathsf{PLUS} \veebar \mathsf{MINUS}) \wedge (\mathsf{NOTNEG} \rightarrow \mathsf{MINUS})$$

holds, where $\veebar$ denotes exclusive or. The features LE and GR, as well as PLUS and MINUS denote alternative choices, whereas NOTNEG is an optional feature, only selectable in combination with MINUS. Thus, there are 6 valid configurations.

The inherent variability of product-line implementations has to be taken into account also during test-case derivation [12]. The enhanced CFA representation for the example of Fig. 2 is depicted in Fig. 2(b), where each *variation point* is represented as an additional (dashed) branch edge labeled over respective feature constraints. Hence, actual test runs, i.e., the code parts traversed and the final results computed for a test case applied to a product-line implementation, depend on the configuration of the product variant under test. For instance, the input vector $[x = 1, y = 2, z = 3]$ traverses the if branch (Lines 4 – 5) only if feature LE is selected, and the else branch (Lines 11 – 12) if feature GR is selected. Next, either Line 15 is executed for feature PLUS, or Line 22 for feature MINUS. In the latter case, the execution of Line 19 for feature NOTNEG further depends on whether LE or GR is selected, whereas the if branch (Lines 18 – 19) is not covered and Line 19 is skipped in both cases. Finally, the expected value returned in Line 24, again, depends on the selected feature combination, i.e., $[z = 4]$ for LE and PLUS, $[z = 2]$ for LE and MINUS, $[z = 5]$ for GR and PLUS, and $[z = 1]$ for GR and MINUS, whereas feature NOTNEG does not affect the outcome of the test run.

To cope with behavioral variability, the derivation of test cases must be *variability-aware*. Therefore, a test-case specification is extended to a triple, e.g., $([x = 1, y = 2, z = 3], [z = 2], \phi)$, where ϕ denotes the *presence condition*, i.e., a propositional formula over feature parameters constraining the set of configurations for which this test case is *valid*. In the example, $\phi = $ LE $\wedge$ MINUS holds, i.e., this test case is (re-)usable for configurations with and without feature NOTNEG. In the same way, the notion of code coverage must be adapted to product-line implementations. For instance, concerning location 19, the input vector $[x = 1, y = 3, z = 2]$ covers this location on configurations with GR, MINUS, and NOTNEG being selected, whereas in program variants with feature LE instead of GR, location 19 remains uncovered. In contrast, input vector $[x = 3, y = 2, z = 1]$ covers location 19 on both program variants, and, together with input vector $[x = 2, y = 3, z = 1]$, the resulting test suite achieves complete statement coverage for the entire product line.

To summarize, a systematic approach for variability-aware, yet efficient test-suite derivation for complete product-line coverage has to take both dimensions of reuse into account: among test goals as well as among variants.

3   Test-Suite Generation for Product Lines

In this section, we introduce an approach for white-box test-suite generation for covering entire product-line implementations based on symbolic model checking. The approach incorporates systematic reuse of reachability-analysis results among different test goals as well as different product variants.

3.1   Test-Case Generation Based on Symbolic Model Checking

The derivation of test inputs for covering a particular test goal requires a *reachability analysis* of the state space of the program under test. Model checking has been extensively investigated as a viable technique for automating the evaluation of respective *reachability queries*. The basic idea of those approaches is to pass the (negated) test goal to the model checker to derive a counterexample serving as test input for covering that goal [7].

Considering white-box testing in particular, symbolic model checking has recently shown promising performance improvements when applied to derive test inputs for a given program under test [8]. Symbolic test-input derivation for a test goal consisting of a pair (ℓ, φ) is performed in two interleaved steps.

1. Find a path through the CFA of the program under test to location ℓ.
2. Derive input values satisfying the *path condition* for ℓ and state predicate φ.

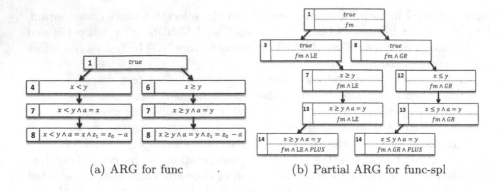

(a) ARG for func   (b) Partial ARG for func-spl

Fig. 3. ARG for C Program and Product-Line Implementation

For Step 2, the model checker uses an abstract reachability graph (ARG) as central data structure to symbolically represent the reachable program state space [7]. Based on the approach of lazy abstraction [6], the ARG is iteratively constructed and refined for any possible CFA path reaching ℓ, until either a satisfying variable assignment has been found, or the path conditions of all possible paths leading to (ℓ, φ) turn out to be unsatisfiable.

The fully-explored ARG for the program in Fig. 1(a) is depicted in Fig. 3(a). Each ARG path refers to some path of the CFA in Fig. 1(b), where the accumulated state predicates over program variables denote the path condition to be satisfied by input values to reach that location in a concrete execution. Fresh temporal variables, e.g., z_0, z_1, are introduced using SSA encoding. For instance, for the ARG path $1, 4, 7, 8$, derived for test goal $(\ell = 8, \varphi = \langle x < y \rangle)$, there is an initial variable assignment satisfying the respective path condition as well as φ, whereas, for path $1, 6, 7, 8$, no such assignment exists.

Formally, the set V of program variables is typed over a compound domain $\mathcal{D}$, where we limit our considerations to $\mathcal{D} = \mathbb{B} \cup \mathbb{Z}$, i.e,. Boolean and Integer variables. Thereupon, the labeling alphabet of a CFA is given as $\mathcal{L}(V) = \mathcal{L}_{assume}(V) \cup \mathcal{L}_{assign}(V)$, where $\mathcal{L}_{assume}(V) = (V \to \mathcal{D}) \to \mathbb{B}$ comprises the sub-alphabet of *predicates* over V, and $\mathcal{L}_{assign}(V) = (V \to \mathcal{D}) \to (V \to \mathcal{D})$ denotes the sub-alphabet of (blocks) of *value assignments* on V. We refer to elements of the labeling alphabet as $a \in \mathcal{L}(V)$.

Definition 1 (Control-Flow Automaton). *A CFA is a triple (L, ℓ_0, E), where L is a finite set of control locations, $\ell_0 \in L$ is the initial control location, and $E \subseteq (L \times \mathcal{L}(V) \times L)$ is a labeled transition relation.*

For a CFA to be well-structured, we require each node except termination nodes to have either exactly one outgoing edge labeled over $\mathcal{L}_{assign}(V)$, or all outgoing edges labeled with mutually excluding predicates from $\mathcal{L}_{assume}(V)$. A *concrete execution* of a program traverses some path of the corresponding CFA, denoted

$$\ell_0 \xrightarrow{a_0} \ell_1 \xrightarrow{a_1} \cdots \xrightarrow{a_{k-1}} \ell_k,$$

where $(\ell_i, a_i, \ell_{i+1}) \in E$, $0 \le i < k$, holds. Semantically, a concrete execution corresponds to a sequence

$$\pi = (\ell_0, c_0) \xrightarrow{a_0} (\ell_1, c_1) \xrightarrow{a_1} \cdots \xrightarrow{a_{k-1}} (\ell_k, c_k)$$

of *program states*, i.e., pairs (ℓ_i, c_i), $0 \le i < k$, of locations $\ell_i \in L$ and current values of program variables given by a mapping $c_i : V \to \mathcal{D}$, such that either

- $c_{i+1} = a_i(c_i)$ if $a_i \in \mathcal{L}_{assign}(V)$, or
- $c_{i+1} = c_i$ and $c_i \models a_i$, if $a_i \in \mathcal{L}_{assume}(V)$

holds. Based on this notion of program-execution semantics, input-variable assignments of an initial program state c_0 constitute a (concrete) test-case-satisfying test goal (ℓ, φ) iff there is a concrete program execution reaching some state (ℓ, c_k) with $c_k \models \varphi$. Stepping from concrete excutions to symbolic-execution semantics is done by predicate representation of (sets of) concrete data values in program states: a set of possible program-variable assignments, called a *region*, in a program location is symbolically characterized by a *state predicate* $r \in \mathcal{L}_{assume}(V)$, where $R(V)$ denotes the set of all regions over V. For constructing symbolic executions, the *strongest postcondition* operator $sp_V : (R(V) \times \mathcal{L}(V)) \to R(V)$ is defined such that, for $r' = sp_V(r, a_i)$ and for each $c_i \models r$, either

- $c_{i+1} = a_i(c_i)$ and $c_{i+1} \models r'$, if $a_i \in \mathcal{L}_{assign}(V)$, or
- $c_i \wedge a_i \models r'$, if $a_i \in \mathcal{L}_{assume}(V)$

holds. The symbolic representation of regions as predicates supports *abstraction*, i.e., omitting information about the state space that is not necessary for the analysis: the *abstract states* might *over-approximate* sets of concrete states. Based on these notions, an ARG is defined as follows.

Definition 2 (Abstract Reachability Graph). *An ARG of a CFA (L, ℓ_0, E) is a triple (S, s_0, T), where $S \subseteq (L \times R(V))$ is a set of abstract program states, $s_0 = (l_0, true) \in S$ is the initial abstract program state, and $T \subseteq (S \times E \times S)$ is a labeled transition relation, where $(\ell, r) \xrightarrow{e} (\ell', r') \in T$ if $e = (\ell, a, \ell') \in E$ and $r' \models sp_V(r, a)$.*

An ARG is *complete*, if it contains, for every concrete execution π of a program, a corresponding abstract path

$$(\ell_0, r_0) \xrightarrow{e_0} (\ell_1, r_1) \xrightarrow{e_1} \cdots \xrightarrow{e_{k-1}} (\ell_k, r_k),$$

with $c_i \models r_i$, $0 \le i \le k$. For deriving a test case that covers goal (ℓ, φ), it is often sufficient to only partially explore the ARG until an abstract state (ℓ, r) with $r \models \varphi$ is found, for which an initial program state c_0 with $c_0 \models r_0$ exists. Although being much more efficient than explicit state-space exploration in many cases, this process has to be repeated until every reachable test goal is covered by, at least, one input vector.

Symbolic test-case generation is applicable to derive test cases from product-line implementations as shown in Fig. 2. Formally, a product line enhances a single program implementation by adding a set of distinguished Boolean (read-only) input variables $V_F \to \mathbb{B}$ to the set of program variables V_P, thus leading to $V = V_P \cup V_F$. Based on the concept of *variability encoding* [25], preprocessor-based, compile-time variability can be transformed into run-time variability using plain `if-then-else` statements over feature variables in a fully-automated way [19]. Similarly, the feature model can be represented as propositional formula $FM \in \mathcal{L}_{assume}(V_F)$ over V_F [5]. Correspondingly, (partial and complete) product configurations are denoted as $\gamma \in \mathcal{L}_{assume}(V_F)$, where $\gamma \models FM$. Based on this encoding, the derivation of a test case satisfying a test goal (ℓ, φ) can be performed as described before. Starting with feature model FM as initial path condition, ARG regions $r = (pc \wedge \phi) \in R(V_P \cup V_F)$ now is a conjunction of two separated parts: (1) a *path condition* $pc \in \mathcal{L}_{assume}(V_P)$ over program variables V_P restricting the inputs and (2) a *presence condition* $\phi \in \mathcal{L}_{assume}(V_F)$ over feature variables V_F restricting the feature selections for which the test case is valid.

The partially explored ARG for test goal $(\ell = 14, true)$ in the CFA of Fig. 2(b) is shown in Fig. 3(b). The path condition and the presence condition are separated by a dashed line, for better readability. Path $1, 3, 7, 13, 14$ suffices to cover the goal on complete configurations with feature LE, whereas for configurations with feature GR, the additional path $1, 8, 12, 13, 14$ is required. As location 14 is only reachable in variants with feature PLUS, this ARG is sufficient to derive inputs for covering the test goal on every variant in which that goal is reachable.

Definition 3 (Complete Product-Line Test Suite). *Let G be a set of test goals on a product-line implementation. A set C_{TS} of initial program states is a complete product-line test suite, if for each $g = (\ell, \varphi) \in G$ and for each $\gamma \in \mathcal{L}_{assume}(V_F)$ with $\gamma \models FM$ it holds that, if $(\ell_0, \gamma) \xrightarrow{e_0} \cdots \xrightarrow{e_{k-1}} (\ell, r_k)$ with $r_k \models \varphi$ exists, then there exists $c_0 \in C_{TS}$ with $c_0 \models \gamma$ and c_0 covering g.*

To achieve complete coverage of product-line implementations, test-case derivation has to be repeated for each test goal (ℓ, φ) until it is covered by, at least, one valid test case on each program variant in which the test goal is reachable.

3.2   Reuse of Reachability-Analysis Results

We now describe an efficient approach for deriving a test suite for multi-goal coverage of product lines. The approach incorporates systematic reuse of reachability information that is already obtained from a (partially explored) ARG during test-case derivation for other test goals and program variants. The overall approach consists of two phases: (1) incremental ARG exploration until sufficient reachability information is obtained to cover each test goal on every program variant in which it is reachable; (2) derivation of concrete test-input data from ARG path conditions for reachability counterexamples. In the first phase, ARG exploration is guided by repetitively traversing paths of the CFA until every test

---

Algorithm 1. Abstract Product-Line Test-Suite Derivation

Input: CFA (L, ℓ_0, E), Feature Model FM, Test Goals $G = \{g_1, g_2, \ldots, g_n\}$
Output: Abstract Test Suite TS
1: $TS := \{\}$; **for all** $g \in G : CS[g] := FM$
2: **for all** $g = (\ell, \varphi) \in G$ **do**
3:      $r_0 := CS[g]$
4:      **if** $(\ell_0, r_0) \xrightarrow{e_0} \cdots \xrightarrow{e_{k-1}} (\ell_k, r_k)$ with $\ell = \ell_k, r_k = (pc_k, \phi_k)$, and $pc_k \models \varphi$ **then**
5:          **for all** $g' = (\ell_i, \varphi') \in G$ with $0 \leq i \leq k$, $r_i = (pc_i, \phi_i)$, and $pc_i \models \varphi'$ **do**
6:              **if** $\nexists \phi_j \in \mathcal{L}_{assume}(V_F) : TS[g', \phi_j] \neq undef \wedge \phi_i \models \phi_j$ **then**
7:                  $TS[g', \phi_i] := pc_i; CS[g'] := CS[g'] \wedge \neg \phi_i$
8:              **end if**
9:          **end for**
10:     **else**
11:         $G := G \setminus \{g\}$
12:     **end if**
13: **end for**

---

goal $g' = (\ell_i, \varphi') \in G$ from a set G of test goals is covered. The corresponding region r_i of the ARG state (ℓ_i, r_i) that is reached via the CFA path then contains the path condition pc_i, as well as the presence condition ϕ_i for concrete test input data.

The general procedure for the first phase is outlined in Alg. 1. The algorithm incorporates two reuse strategies for reachability-analysis results during ARG exploration: (1) reuse of reachability information for multiple product variants and (2) reuse of reachability information for multiple test goals. The algorithm operates on the CFA of the product-line implementation, the corresponding feature model FM, and a finite set G of test goals of the form $g = (\ell, \varphi)$. The data structure TS (test suite), holding the result of the algorithm, maps test goals g together with presence conditions ϕ onto path conditions pc, such that each concrete input vector satisfying pc covers g on every program variant whose configuration satisfies ϕ. In addition, the map CS (cover set) assigns to every test goal g a predicate over feature variables, denoting the subset of product configurations on which g is *not yet* covered. The cover set of every test goal $g \in G$ is initialized with FM (Line 1), thus requiring a reachability analysis of g for every valid product configuration. The algorithm iterates over the set of not yet completely processed test goals from G (Lines 2 – 13), and incrementally refines the ARG, correspondingly. To consider test goal $g \in G$, reachability analysis is initialized with region $r_0 = CS[g]$ (Line 3), thus restricting the search to the subset of product configurations on which g is not yet covered by a previous ARG refinement. If a further ARG refinement succeeds to obtain a feasible ARG path reaching g on configurations from the remaining product subset (Line 4), then TS is updated (Line 5 – 9) and otherwise, g is removed from the working set G (Line 11). In the first case, the ARG path potentially not only covers g, but may be also (re-)used to (partially) cover further test goals in G. In particular, every test goal $g' \in G$ (including g) whose location ℓ_i lies on the ARG path reaching g

TG	TC	CFA Path	Presence Condition
g_1	tc_1	1,3,5,13,14,24	LE ∧ PLUS
g_7	tc'_1	1,3,5,13	LE
g_1	tc_2	1,8,10,13,14,24	GR ∧ PLUS
g_5	tc'_2	1,8,10,13	GR
g_2	tc_3	1,8,12,13,17,18,19,22,24	GR ∧ MINUS ∧ NOTNEG
g_3	tc'_3	1,8,12,13,17,18,19,22	GR ∧ MINUS ∧ NOTNEG
g_4	tc''_3	1,8,12,13	GR
g_2	tc_4	1,3,7,13,17,18,19,22,24	LE ∧ MINUS ∧ NOTNEG
g_3	tc'_4	1,3,7,13,17,18,19,22	LE ∧ MINUS ∧ NOTNEG
g_6	tc''_4	1,3,7,13	LE
g_2	tc_5	1,3,7,13,17,22,24	LE ∧ MINUS
g_2	tc_6	1,8,10,13,17,22,24	GR ∧ MINUS

	g_1	g_2	g_3	g_4	g_5	g_6	g_7
P_1	tc_1	–	–	–	–	tc''_4	tc'_1
P_2	–	tc_5	–	–	–	tc''_4	tc'_1
P_3	tc_2	–	–	tc''_3	tc'_2	–	–
P_4	–	tc_6	–	tc''_3	tc'_2	–	–
P_5	–	tc_4	tc''_4	–	–	tc''_4	tc'_1
P_6	–	tc_3	tc'_3	tc''_3	tc'_2	–	–

P_1 : LE, PLUS
P_2 : LE, MINUS
P_3 : GR, PLUS
P_4 : GR, MINUS
P_5 : LE, MINUS, NOTNEG
P_6 : GR, MINUS, NOTNEG

(a) Test-Case Derivation for func-spl   (b) Test-Goal Coverage for func-spl

Fig. 4. Sample SPL Test-Suite Derivation

and whose predicate φ' is satisfied by the path condition pc_i of the respective ARG state may be added to TS (Line 5). If g' is already covered by a previously obtained ARG path with presence condition ϕ_j, it is added to TS only if ϕ_i is not subsumed by any those existing ϕ_j in TS, i.e., $\phi_i \not\models \phi_j$ (Line 6). Thus, the corresponding path condition pc_i is added for g' and ϕ_i to TS and the cover set of g' is further restricted, accordingly (Line 7).

After termination, TS contains an *abstract, symbolic* product-line test suite in the sense that it provides enough reachability information to derive in the second phase a *concrete* test suite that completely covers the entire product-line implementation. In particular, for each pair (g, ϕ) with $TS[g, \phi] = pc$, a concrete test suite C_{TS} contains an initial program state c_0 with $c_0 \models pc$ as test input being applicable to all program variants whose configuration complies ϕ. The following result essentially relies on the soundness of ARG refinement (Line 4).

Theorem 1. *A concrete test suite C_{TS} obtained from the abstract test suite TS generated by Algorithm 1 is a complete product-line test suite (cf. Def. 3).*

A sample application of Alg. 1 to the example from Fig. 2 is illustrated in Fig. 4, considering statement coverage. The resulting set of test goals $G = \{g_1, \ldots, g_7\}$ are attached (in boxes) to the CFA edges in Fig. 2(b). Fig. 4(a) lists the iterations over G, where each horizontal line marks the next iteration of the outer loop. Starting with test goal g_1, the corresponding ARG path obtained for test case tc_1 traverses the CFA such that the resulting path condition requires the features LE and PLUS. In addition, test case tc_1 is reusable as test case tc'_1 covering g_7. The presence condition of tc'_1 is, therefore, weakened to LE, as the predicate requiring PLUS does not occur in the respective sub-path. A further ARG exploration is required to finally cover g_1 also on those configurations with GR instead of LE selected. After termination, six abstract test cases have been generated explicitly to cover all products $P_1 - P_6$, as summarized in the table in Fig. 4(b). In contrast, considering every single test goal on every program variant anew without any information reuse would have required at least 20 reachability-analysis steps.

4   Evaluation

To investigate the effects of the two proposed reuse strategies, we compare both of them to a product-by-product (PbP) product-line test-suite generation approach. For quantifying the effects of reuse among product variants, we apply a family-based (FB), i.e., variability-aware, generation approach, whereas for the reuse among test goals (TG), we apply a PbP approach. Finally, we combine both reuse strategies (FBTG) to measure potential synergies. The two product-by-product approaches are regarded for comparison purposes. These considerations led us to the following research questions.

- **RQ1:** Do the presented reuse strategies improve the *efficiency* of product-line test-suite generation in terms of CPU time and model-checker calls?
- **RQ2:** Does a family-based approach decrease testing *effectiveness* by leaving more test goals uncovered than a product-by-product approach due to the presumably more complex control-flow of product-line implementations after variability encoding?

To answer the research questions, we implemented a product-line test-suite generator based on CPA/TIGER[1], a test-case generator on top of CPACHECKER[2], which is a software model checker for C programs. Internally, CPACHECKER uses CFA and ARG representations and applies the CEGAR approach, as described in Sect. 3. Furthermore, we use FQL[3] (FShell Query Language), which is part of CPA/TIGER, to specify complex coverage criteria. For a variability-aware generation of product-line test suites, we integrated a BDD-based feature-parameter analysis into CPA/TIGER and added further code to determine which test goals of which variants are covered by a given test case. For our experiments, we selected two subject systems that are well-known from several benchmarks, e.g., in context of product-line verification and feature interaction detection [3].

- *Mine-Pump (MP)* implements a water pump system based on the CONIC project [20]. The product-line implementation has 279 LoC, 7 features, e.g., a methane sensor, and 64 configurations.
- *E-Mail (EM)* is based on a model of an e-mail system developed by Hall [18]. The product-line implementation we used has 233 LoC, 4 features, e.g., encryption and automatic forwarding, and 8 configurations.

As coverage criterion, we applied *Basic-Block Coverage*, i.e., each basic statement block constitutes a test goal. Our measurements, e.g., the CPU time and the number of model-checker calls, were obtained by hooking into the test-case generator. We performed our evaluation on a E5-2650 (2 GHz) machine with 30 GB of RAM. CPA/TIGER ran with value-based analysis, an overall timeout of 24 h, and a timeout per test goal of 900 s, i.e., if a test goal had not been reached after 900 s, the next test goal was processed. Table 1 summarizes the

---

[1] http://forsyte.at/software/cpatiger/
[2] http://cpachecker.sosy-lab.org/
[3] http://forsyte.at/software/fshell/fql/

Table 1. Overview of Evaluation Results (#TG: Test Goals, #TC: Test Cases, #CPA: Model-checker Calls, t: CPU Time)

		#TG	processed	feasible	infeasible	timeout	#TC	#CPA	t (in h)
MP	PbP	3792	3792	3298	490	4	3298	3720	13.9
	TG	3792	3792	3300	490	2	427	847	3.7
	FB	93	93	42	1	50	52	145	24
	FBTG	93	81	42	1	38	46	127	24
EM	PbP	1084	1084	804	280	0	800	1874	32.9
	TG	1084	1084	804	280	0	169	533	10.4
	FB	198	131	78	16	37	154	285	24
	FBTG	198	160	91	30	39	103	224	24

results of our experiments. Compared to PbP, we observe the following effects: (1) the number of model-checker calls and generated test cases have been reduced by both reuse strategies, (2) TG led to high time savings, and (3) FB led to more timeouts. For test goals not reached by FB within 24 h, we extrapolated the results.

Considering **RQ1**, both reuse strategies are able to drastically reduce the number of test cases to be generated, as well as the generation time in terms of model-checker calls. However, a decrease of CPU time was only observable for TG, whereas FB led to increased CPU time compared to PbP due to the additional control-flow for variability encoding. The number of model-checker calls and generated test cases has been further reduced when using both reuse strategies in combination (FBTG), compared to applying them independently. Furthermore, we obtained no valuable CPU time results for the FB and the FBTG approaches due to timeouts after 24 h. Finally, concerning **RQ2**, we observed that more test goals stayed uncovered using FB/FBTG than using PbP/TG since more CPU time is required, which leads to more timeouts. This might be avoided by increasing the overall timeout, as well as the test-goal timeout.

5   Related Work

In previous work, the problem of generating test suites for product-line coverage has been investigated in the context of model-based (black-box) testing [12]. There, the explicit-state model checker SPIN has been used for reachability analysis, with a posteriori reasoning about test-case reuse among product variants, but without any reuse of reachability results among test goals. Applying CPACHECKER for product-line verification has been proposed [3], incorporating BDD analysis for reuse of verification results [2]. Reuse of reachability analysis results for different test goals [7, 8] has been presented and implemented as CPA/TIGER on top of CPACHECKER and corresponding reuse concepts have been applied to intermediate verification results [10]. Both approaches are limited to single systems without variability. Recent approaches for variability-aware product-line analysis can be roughly categorized into four strategies: sample-based, family-based, feature-based, and incremental techniques [27]. Most of these approaches consider the adoption of formal methods for product-line verification [26]. Similar to the problem of test generation, these approaches are, in general, also concerned with exploring the state space of entire product lines incorporating inherent variability. Family-based SPL analysis approaches focus on lifting static analysis and model-checking techniques to entire product lines. Some of those approaches also use symbolic model-checking techniques, handling features as special inputs, as in our approach [14,16]. However, those approaches consider a family-based evaluation of one particular model-checking query without systematic reuse of analysis results. Feature-based [21], as well as incremental SPL model-checking techniques [22], perform a step-wise state-space exploration similar to the CEGAR approach, but, again, considering a single query instead of multiple analysis/test goals. Finally, incremental approaches focus on step-wise test-suite refinement and retest selection inspired by regression testing, where the test-case generation approach is out of scope [17,23].

6 Conclusion

We presented a test-suite-generation approach for efficiently achieving complete multi-goal test-coverage of product-line implementations. Our approach exploits similarity information to facilitate systematic reuse of reachabiltity information among product-line variants. To this end, we extended the test-suite generator CPA/TIGER and presented evaluation results showing a considerable gain in efficiency compared to approaches without reuse. In addition, we plan to further improve reuse strategies, e.g, by fully adopting the concepts from previous work [8] and considering optimization criteria for the ordering of test goals.

Acknowledgments. This work has been supported by the German Research Foundation (DFG) in the Priority Programme SPP 1593: Design For Future – Managed Software Evolution (SCHU 1309/6-1, AP 206/5), by the DFG grants AP 206/4 and AP 206/6, as well as by the Austrian National Research Network S11403 and S11405 (RiSE) of the Austrian Science Fund (FWF), and by the Vienna Science and Technology Fund (WWTF) through grant PROSEED.

References

1. Apel, S., Batory, D., Kästner, C., Saake, G.: Feature-Oriented Software Product Lines. Springer (2013)
2. Apel, S., Beyer, D., Friedberger, K., Raimondi, F., von Rhein, A.: Domain Types: Abstract-Domain Selection Based on Variable Usage. In: Bertacco, V., Legay, A. (eds.) HVC 2013. LNCS, vol. 8244, pp. 262–278. Springer, Heidelberg (2013)
3. Apel, S., Rhein, A.: v., Wendler, P., Grösslinger, A., Beyer, D.: Strategies for Product-Line Verification: Case Studies and Experiments. In: ICSE, pp. 482–491. IEEE Press (2013)
4. Asirelli, P., ter Beek, M.H., Fantechi, A., Gnesi, S.: A Model-Checking Tool for Families of Services. In: Bruni, R., Dingel, J. (eds.) FORTE and FMOODS 2011. LNCS, vol. 6722, pp. 44–58. Springer, Heidelberg (2011)
5. Batory, D.: Feature Models, Grammars, and Propositional Formulas. In: Obbink, H., Pohl, K. (eds.) SPLC 2005. LNCS, vol. 3714, pp. 7–20. Springer, Heidelberg (2005)

6. Beyer, D., Henzinger, T.A., Jhala, R., Majumdar, R.: The software model checker BLAST. Int. J. Softw. Tools Technol. Transfer 9(5-6), 505–525 (2007)
7. Beyer, D., Chlipala, A.J., Henzinger, T.A., Jhala, R., Majumdar, R.: Generating Tests from Counterexamples. In: ICSE, pp. 326–335. IEEE Press (2004)
8. Beyer, D., Holzer, A., Tautschnig, M., Veith, H.: Information Reuse for Multi-goal Reachability Analyses. In: Felleisen, M., Gardner, P. (eds.) ESOP 2013. LNCS, vol. 7792, pp. 472–491. Springer, Heidelberg (2013)
9. Beyer, D., Keremoglu, M.E.: CPACHECKER: A Tool for Configurable Software Verification. In: Gopalakrishnan, G., Qadeer, S. (eds.) CAV 2011. LNCS, vol. 6806, pp. 184–190. Springer, Heidelberg (2011)
10. Beyer, D., Löwe, S., Novikov, E., Stahlbauer, A., Wendler, P.: Precision Reuse for Efficient Regression Verification. In: ESEC/FSE 2013, pp. 389–399. ACM (2013)
11. Chilenski, J.J., Miller, S.P.: Applicability of Modified Condition/Decision Coverage to Software Testing. Software Engineering Journal 9(7), 193–200 (1994)
12. Cichos, H., Oster, S., Lochau, M., Schürr, A.: Model-Based Coverage-Driven Test Suite Generation for Software Product Lines. In: Whittle, J., Clark, T., Kühne, T. (eds.) MODELS 2011. LNCS, vol. 6981, pp. 425–439. Springer, Heidelberg (2011)
13. Clarke, E., Grumberg, O., Jha, S., Lu, Y., Veith, H.: Counterexample-Guided Abstraction Refinement. In: Emerson, E.A., Sistla, A.P. (eds.) CAV 2000. LNCS, vol. 1855, pp. 154–169. Springer, Heidelberg (2000)
14. Classen, A., Heymans, P., Schobbens, P.-Y., Legay, A.: Symbolic Model Checking of Software Product Lines. In: ICSE, pp. 321–330. ACM (2011)
15. Clements, P., Northrop, L.: Software Product Lines: Practices and Patterns. Addison-Wesley (2001)
16. Cordy, M., Classen, A., Schobbens, P.Y., Heymans, P., Legay, A.: Simulation-Based Abstractions for Software Product-Line Model Checking. In: ICSE, pp. 672–682. IEEE (2012)
17. Engström, E.: Exploring Regression Testing and Software Product Line Testing - Research and State of Practice. Lic dissertation, Lund University (May 2010)
18. Hall, R.J.: Fundamental Nonmodularity in Electronic Mail. ASE 12, 41–79 (2005)
19. Kästner, C., Giarrusso, P., Rendel, T., Erdweg, S., Ostermann, K., Berger, T.: Variability-Aware Parsing in the Presence of Lexical Macros and Conditional Compilation. In: OOPSLA, pp. 805–824. ACM (2011)
20. Kramer, J., Magee, J., Sloman, M., Lister, A.: CONIC: An Integrated Approach to Distributed Computer Control Systems. Computers and Digital Techniques 130, 1–20 (1983)
21. Li, H.C., Krishnamurthi, S., Fisler, K.: Interfaces for Modular Feature Verification. In: ASE 2002, pp. 195–204. IEEE (2002)
22. Lochau, M., Mennicke, S., Baller, H., Ribbeck, L.: DeltaCCS: A Core Calculus for Behavioral Change. In: Margaria, T., Steffen, B. (eds.) ISoLA 2014, Part I. LNCS, vol. 8802, pp. 320–335. Springer, Heidelberg (2014)
23. Lochau, M., Schaefer, I., Kamischke, J., Lity, S.: Incremental Model-Based Testing of Delta-Oriented Software Product Lines. In: Brucker, A.D., Julliand, J. (eds.) TAP 2012. LNCS, vol. 7305, pp. 67–82. Springer, Heidelberg (2012)
24. McGregor, J.D.: Testing a Software Product Line. Tech. Rep. CMU/SEI-2001-TR-022, Software Engineering Inst (2001)
25. Post, H., Sinz, C.: Configuration Lifting: Verification Meets Software Configuration. In: ASE, pp. 347–350. IEEE (2008)
26. Schaefer, I., Hähnle, R.: Formal Methods in Software Product Line Engineering. Computer 44(2), 82–85 (2011)

27. Thüm, T., Apel, S., Kästner, C., Schaefer, I., Saake, G.: A Classification and Survey of Analysis Strategies for Software Product Lines. ACM Comput. Surv. 47(1), 6:1–6:45 (2014)
28. Utting, M., Legeard, B.: Practical Model-Based Testing: A Tools Approach. Morgan Kaufmann (2007)
29. Weiss, D.M.: The Product Line Hall of Fame. In: SPLC, p. 395. IEEE (2008)

Just Test What You Cannot Verify!*

Mike Czech, Marie-Christine Jakobs, and Heike Wehrheim

University of Paderborn, Germany
mczech@mail.upb.de, {marie.christine.jakobs,wehrheim}@upb.de

Abstract. Today, software verification is an established analysis method which can provide high guarantees for software safety. However, the resources (time and/or memory) for an exhaustive verification are not always available, and analysis then has to resort to other techniques, like testing. Most often, the already achieved *partial* verification results are discarded in this case, and testing has to start from scratch.

In this paper, we propose a method for combining verification and testing in which testing only needs to check the residual fraction of an uncompleted verification. To this end, the partial results of a verification run are used to construct a *residual program* (and residual assertions to be checked on it). The residual program can afterwards be fed into standard testing tools. The proposed technique is sound modulo the soundness of the testing procedure. Experimental results show that this combined usage of verification and testing can significantly reduce the effort for the subsequent testing.

1 Introduction

Today, software verification has reached industrial size programs, with a large number of tools providing an automatic analysis (see e.g. the annual software verification competition [5]). Still, verification tools might fail in analyzing the program at hand. This might have two reasons: (1) the resources necessary for a complete verification are not available, e.g. because an "on-the-fly" analysis is needed, or (2) the property to be verified is beyond reach of the verification technology, e.g. when complex structural properties are involved. In this case, software engineers need to resort to other analysis techniques, for instance the most widely used method of *testing* [4]. In this case, the work done in a prior, but incomplete verification run is usually discarded, and testing is started from scratch, again considering the complete program and set of properties to be analyzed. This seems to be an unnecessary waste of time and effort.

In this paper, we present a method for combining verification and testing in such a way that a testing run following an unfinished verification run *need just test those parts of the program which have not been verified.* Prior combinations of verification and testing most often follow other principles: either one of the techniques is used to generate likely properties which the other technique then

---

* This work was partially supported by the German Research Foundation (DFG) within the Collaborative Research Centre "On-The-Fly Computing" (SFB 901).

A. Egyed and I. Schaefer (Eds.): FASE 2015, LNCS 9033, pp. 100–114, 2015.
DOI: 10.1007/978-3-662-46675-9_7

has to check (e.g. for likely invariants [29] or potential error locations [6]), or information computed by one technique is used to enhance the other technique (e.g. test data used for abstraction refinement [27]). Computation of *residual programs* (or properties) is employed in none of these approaches. The only other work aiming at a reduction of one parts of the analysis is [12]. They use a value analysis to compute potential errors (so called alarms), and use program slicing [32] on the statements occurring in alarms to reduce the effort of successive testing. The first static analysis is therein executed on the whole program and only the dynamic analysis has a reduced effort. Here, we introduce a true divide-and-conquer type of combining static and dynamic analysis: verification is doing one part (basically as much as it can under restricted resources) and testing is then simply doing the rest.

Our technique is based on conditional model checking [7], which allows to save the information computed in a verification run (complete or incomplete) in the form of a so-called *condition*. In [7], this condition is given to a second, different verifier to complete verification. Here, we will use the condition to compute a residual program for a subsequently running testing tool. Two guiding principles lead the construction of residual programs: on the one hand, we do not want to test program parts which already have been verified w.r.t. the properties under interest, and on the other hand, we need to generate syntactically correct programs again such that these can be fed into standard testing tools. Here, we will propose two techniques for this, both fulfilling these guidelines, which have however different consequences for the testing step. Technique 1 uses the condition itself to generate a residual program, building the synchronous product of condition and original program thereby removing the already verified parts. This usually leads to a residual program which is structurally different from the original program. The second technique uses the condition to extract a *slice* of the original program (thus obtaining a syntactic subprogram) which is then used as residual program.

Our technique can be proven to be sound modulo soundness of the testing tool, i.e., if the testing tool could faithfully show absence of errors our combined technique would be able to definitely state safety of programs. We have implemented our technique using the software analysis tool CPACHECKER [9] as verification tool and the concolic testing tool KLEE [10] for dynamic analysis. Using the results of our experiments we will also discuss which of the two residual program construction techniques is more suitable for which type of program.

2   Background

For the description of our approach, we assume programs to be written in a simple imperative language using assignments, assume and assert statements on integer variables only.[1] Following [8] describing configurable program analysis (the verification framework we employ later), we model programs as *control-flow automata* (CFA) $P = (L, G, l_0)$, where L is the set of control locations,

---

[1] In our experiments we use programs written in C intermediate language (CIL) [28].

```
10 : if ( flag )
11 :     if (x>=0)
13 :         r:=1;
         else
14 :         r:=0;
         else
12 :     r:=x%2*x%2;
15 : assert  r>=0;
16 :
```

```
10 : s:=0;
11 : if (x<=0)
12 :     assert s>=0;
         else
13 :     i:=1;
14 :     while (i<=x)
15 :         s:=s+i ;
16 :         i:=i+1;
17 :     assert s>0;
18 :
```

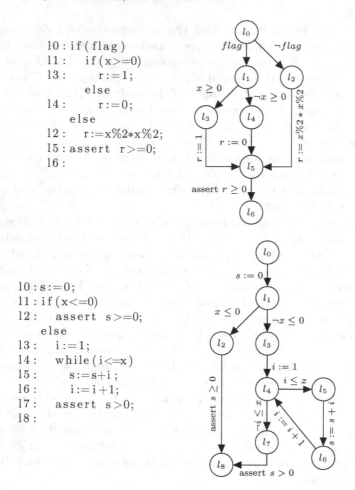

Fig. 1. Example programs EVEN/SIGN and SUM and their CFAs

$G \subseteq L \times Ops \times L$ the control flow edges and l_0 the program entry location. The set Ops contains all assignments, assume and assert statements. Figure 1 shows our example programs EVEN/SIGN and SUM and their CFAs. Program EVEN/SIGN computes – depending on the value of variable $flag$ – either the sign of variable x or whether x is even or odd. Program SUM sums up all integer values in interval $[0; x]$. The assert statement states the property to be checked. Indicator r describing if x is even/odd is expected to be non-negative. Sum s is non-negative and positive if $x > 0$. Note, the property (sum positive if $x > 0$) stated in line 7 of SUM is only true when neglecting overflows. Both CFAs contain two assume edges per condition of an if- or while-statement (one per valuation), and one assignment and assertion edge for each assignment and assertion, respectively.

The semantics of a program $P = (L, G, l_0)$ is given by a labeled transition system $T(P) = (C, G, \rightarrow)$ consisting of a set of concrete states C, the labels G

(the control-flow edges of the program) and a transition relation $\rightarrow \subseteq C \times G \times C$. We write $c \xrightarrow{g} c'$ for $(c, g, c') \in \rightarrow$. Let V denote the set of all integer variables of program P. A *concrete state* c either assigns to any variable $v \in V$ a value $c(v)$ and to the program counter a control location $c(pc) \in L$ or it is the error state, $c = c_{err}$, denoting that an assertion is violated. A transition $c \xrightarrow{(l,op,l')} c'$ is contained in $T(P)$ if $c \neq c_{err}$ and $c(pc) = l$ and either op is an assume statement, $c \models op$, $c'(pc) = l'$ and $\forall v \in V : c(v) = c'(v)$, or $op \equiv v := expr$ is an assignment and $c'(pc) = l'$, $c' = c[v \mapsto expr]$ or $op \equiv \texttt{assert } cond$ and either $c \models cond$ and $c'(pc) = l'$ and $\forall v \in V : c(v) = c'(v)$ or $c \not\models cond$ and $c' = c_{err}$. We call $c_0 \xrightarrow{g_0} c_1 \xrightarrow{g_1} \cdots \xrightarrow{g_{n-1}} c_n$ a *path* of program P if $c_0 \neq c_{err}$, $c_0(pc) = l_0$ and $\forall 0 \leq i < n : c_i \xrightarrow{g_i} c_{i+1}$. Intuitively, a path of a program describes a (partial) execution of P. We denote the set of all paths of P by $paths(P)$.

Finally, we are interested in program safety. In our case this means that none of program P's executions violates an assertion. All (partial) executions of P, that are all paths in $paths(P)$, are safe. Formally, a path $c_0 \xrightarrow{g_0} c_1 \xrightarrow{g_1} \cdots \xrightarrow{g_{n-1}} c_n \in paths(P)$ is *safe* if $c_n \neq c_{err}$. Let $paths_{safe}(P) \subseteq paths(P)$ denote the set of safe program paths. Then, a program P is *safe* if $paths_{safe}(P) = paths(P)$.

Unfortunately, a verification tool may fail to prove a program safe, e.g. due to resource limits it only proves that a subset of the program paths are safe. We use conditional model checking (CMC) [7] to describe which paths are proven safe by the verification tool and which paths still need to be verified. CMC can be used with any verification tool that keeps track of its (abstract) state space exploration in form of a reachability graph. Subtrees of the reachability graph which are completely verified are aggregated into a single safe state. For all other parts there is a one to one correspondence between the reachability graph and the *condition* generated by CMC. Coming back to our example programs EVEN/SIGN and SUM (Fig. 1), we assume that the verification tool only verified the left branch of the (outer) if statements. Figure 2 shows the conditions for these partial verifications. The rectangle node is the safe state. Since the left branch of each program has already been verified, it directly ends in the safe state. For the unproven right part of program EVEN/SIGN there is one automaton state per CFA location and if two of these CFA locations are connected by an edge g, then there is an edge between the corresponding automaton states and the label is the CFA edge g. For the unproven right part of program SUM we see that the verifier already revealed that the while loop is executed at least once and that it unrolled the while loop once (see path q_3, q_4, q_5, q_6).

Formally, a conditition can be defined as follows. For the details of the condition construction and the CMC approach we refer the reader to [7].[2]

Definition 1. *A* condition *for a program* $P = (L, G, l_0)$ *is a four-tuple* $C_P = (Q, \delta, q_0, q_s)$, *where* Q *is a set of states,* $\delta \subseteq Q \times G \times Q$ *a transition function,* q_0 *the initial state and* q_s *the safe state. The transition function ensures that the safe state is never left, i.e.,* $\forall g \in G : (q_s, g, q_s) \in \delta$. *A run of* C_P *is a sequence of states* $q_0 q_1 \ldots q_n$ *such that* $\forall 0 \leq i < n \; \exists (q_i, \cdot, q_{i+1}) \in \delta$.

---

[2] Note that, the condition is called assumption automaton in [7].

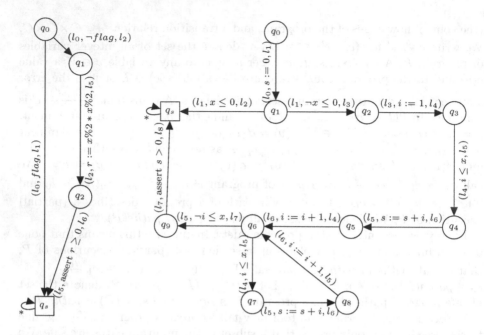

Fig. 2. Conditions showing partial verification result for programs EVEN/SIGN and SUM

We further assume that the verification tools produce conditions C_P for programs P fulfilling the following well-formedness properties. These properties ensure that the condition correctly summarizes the work done by the verification tool. Note, our verification tool CPACHECKER always generates well-formed conditions.

Path Coverage. Every program path is described by a run of the condition. Formally, for all paths $c_0 \xrightarrow{g_0} c_1 \xrightarrow{g_1} \cdots \xrightarrow{g_{n-1}} c_n \in paths(P)$ there exists a run $q_0 q_1 \ldots q_n$ s.t. $\forall 0 \leq i < n : (q_i, g_i, q_{i+1}) \in \delta$.

Safety. If the tail of a program path is subsumed by the safe state of the condition, then the program path is safe. Formally, all paths $c_0 \xrightarrow{g_0} c_1 \xrightarrow{g_1} \cdots \xrightarrow{g_{n-1}} c_n \in paths(P)$ are safe for which a run $q_0 q_1 \ldots q_n$ exists s.t. $\forall 0 \leq i < n : (q_i, g_i, q_{i+1}) \in \delta$ and $\exists k < n \forall k \leq j \leq n : q_j = q_s$.

If a program has been completely verified and is safe, then the condition consists of two states only, namely q_0 and q_s. Given a condition describing which program paths are verified and which not, our idea is to provide to a test tool only the non-proven program paths in form of a residual program. Next, we describe two techniques to compute such a residual program, one based on subprogram extraction and the other on slicing.

3 Extraction of Residual Program from Condition

Our first technique extracts a subprogram from program P which contains only the unproven program paths. The idea is that the subprogram P' results from

Just Test What You Cannot Verify!   105

(a) Residual program of EVEN/SIGN   (b) Residual program of SUM

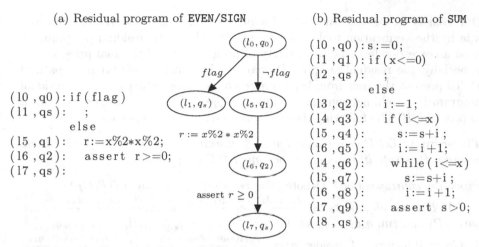

```
(10 , q0 ): if ( flag )
(11 , qs ):   ;
       else
(15 , q1 ):   r:=x%2*x%2;
(16 , q2 ):   assert r>=0;
(17 , qs ):
```

```
(10 , q0 ): s :=0;
(11 , q1 ): if ( x<=0)
(12 , qs ):    ;
       else
(13 , q2 ):    i :=1;
(14 , q3 ):    if ( i<=x)
(15 , q4 ):      s:=s+i ;
(16 , q5 ):      i:=i+1;
(14 , q6 ):    while ( i<=x)
(15 , q7 ):      s:=s+i ;
(16 , q8 ):      i:=i+1;
(17 , q9 ):    assert s>0;
(18 , qs ):
```

Fig. 3. Source code of residual program constructed by synchronization of example programs and respective condition, also CFA for residual program of EVEN/SIGN

the syntactic, synchronous composition of program P and condition C_P. Subprogram P' starts in the initial locations of P and C_P and may only execute an operation if both P and C_P agree that the execution step is possible in the current situation. Furthermore, executions of P' stop if C_P determines that all possible extensions of the execution are already proven safe (C_P reaches safe state q_s). The subprogram extracted this way is the residual program used for further validation. Note, the residual program is not necessarily a syntactic subprogram. Its branching structure may be different. Nevertheless, all verified program executions are excluded from the residual program.

Figure 3 shows the source code for the residual programs extracted in the described way for our example programs (Fig. 1) and the respective conditions from Fig. 2. For program EVEN/SIGN also its CFA is given. The locations of the residual programs are a product of original program location and condition state. Moreover, the residual program contains an edge from location (l, q) to location (l', q') if an edge $g = (l, op, l')$ in the original program and a transition (q, g, q') in the condition exist. Furthermore, it stops in locations $(\cdot, q_s)$. Both residual programs remove the proven program part but since in the condition for program SUM the while loop is unrolled already once, the residual program of program SUM has more locations than program SUM. The following definition now formally describes the explained construction of the residual program.

Definition 2. *Let $P = (L, G, l_0)$ be a program and $C_P = (Q, \delta, q_0, q_s)$ a well-formed condition for P. The residual program extracted from P and C_P, denoted by residual_program_of(P, C_P), is a program $P' = (L', G', l'_0)$ inductively defined as follows:*

1. $(l_0, q_0) \in L'$,
2. *if $(l, q) \in L'$, $q \neq q_s$, $g = (l, op, l') \in G$ and $(q, g, q') \in \delta$, then $(l', q') \in L'$ and $((l, q), op, (l', q')) \in G'$.*

Our goal is to validate the part of a program that has not yet been proven safe by the verification tool. Since we plan to check the residual program, we need a correspondence between safety of program P and residual program P'. Especially, the residual program P' may not lack any unsafe program path of P. To prevent the user from being bothered by non-existing bugs, the residual program P' should not contain new unsafe program paths that are not contained in program P. The following theorem guarantees these properties.

Theorem 1. *Let P be a program and C_P a well-formed condition for P. Then, program P is safe iff $residual\_program\_of(P, C_P)$ is safe.*

Proof (by contraposition). Denote $P' = residual\_program\_of(P, C_P)$

"$\Rightarrow$" If P is unsafe, exists $c_0 \xrightarrow{(l_0, op_0, l_1)} c_1 \xrightarrow{(l_1, op_1, l_2)} \dots \xrightarrow{(l_{n-1}, op_{n-1}, l_n)} c_{err} \in$ $paths(P)$ and run $q_0 q_1 \dots q_n$ s.t. $\forall 0 \leq i < n : q_i \neq q_s \land (q_i, (l_i, op_i, l_{i+1}), q_{i+1}) \in$ δ (C_P well-formed). Consider $p = c'_0 \xrightarrow{((l_0, q_0), op_0, (l_1, q_1))} c'_1 \xrightarrow{((l_1, q_1), op_1, (l_2, q_2))}$ $\dots \xrightarrow{((l_{n-1}, q_{n-1}), op_{n-1}, (l_n, q_n))} c_{err}$ s.t. $\forall 0 \leq i < n : c'_i(pc) = (l_i, q_i) \land \forall v \in V :$ $c_i(v) = c'_i(v)$. By construction of P' and definition $p \in paths(P')$. P' is unsafe.

"$\Leftarrow$" If P' is unsafe, exists a path $c_0 \xrightarrow{((l_0, q_0), op_0, (l_1, q_1))} c_1 \xrightarrow{((l_1, q_1), op_1, (l_2, q_2))}$ $\dots \xrightarrow{((l_{n-1}, q_{n-1}), op_{n-1}, (l_n, q_n))} c_{err} \in paths(P')$. Now, consider $p = c'_0 \xrightarrow{(l_0, op_0, l_1)}$ $c'_1 \xrightarrow{(l_1, op_1, l_2)} \dots \xrightarrow{(l_{n-1}, op_{n-1}, l_n)} c_{err}$ s.t. $\forall 0 \leq i < n : c'_i(pc) = l_i \land \forall v \in V :$ $c_i(v) = c'_i(v)$. By construction of P' and definition $p \in paths(P)$. P is unsafe.

4   Residual Program via Slicing

Our second technique uses program slicing [32] to compute the residual program that describes the unproven part of the program. Program slicing is a technique for extracting those parts of a program which may affect a so-called *slicing criterion*. Slicing usually computes executable subprograms which is important since we want to give the residual program to a testing tool. We use slicing in the following way: First, we use the condition to identify those assertions of program P that have not been fully proven by the verification tool. Then, we take these assertions as slicing criteria to get those program parts of P which influence the unproven assertions. The obtained program slice is the residual program.

Next, we are coming to the details. First, we need to identify the set of unproven assertions. Given a well-formed condition C_P, we only know that assertions which at most occur in transitions of the form $(q_s, \cdot, q_s) \in \delta$ are not violated. Hence, any assertion `assert cond` that occurs in a transition $(q, (\cdot, \text{assert } cond, \cdot), q') \in \delta, q \neq q_s$ must be in the set of unproven assertions.[3] Looking at our example conditions (Fig. 2), we see that one unproven assertion in each condition, `assert r ≥ 0` and `assert s > 0`, respectively, exists.

---

[3] Our implementation represents `assert cond` by `if(¬cond) __assert_fail(...)`. We only add assertions if a transition with `__assert_fail(...)` exists. Thus, we do not add proven assertions which are on a program path that is not completely proven.

To distinguish between same assertions (same operation) used on different CFA edges, we use the CFA edge to describe an assertion. Hence, for our examples the sets of unproven assertions are $S_{C_{\text{EVEN/SIGN}}} = \{(l_6, \texttt{assert } r \geq 0, l_7)\}$ and $S_{C_{\text{SUM}}} = \{(l_7, \texttt{assert } s > 0, l_8)\}$. Generally, the set of unproven assertions is defined as follows.

Definition 3. *Let P be a program and $C_P = (Q, \delta, q_0, q_s)$ a well-formed condition for P. The set S_{C_P} of unproven assertions is defined as*

$$S_{C_P} = \{g \mid \exists (q, g, q') \in \delta \wedge q \neq q_s \wedge g \equiv (\cdot, \texttt{assert } \cdot, \cdot)\} \ .$$

To ensure that we do not miss any bug, we must assure that the computed set of unproven assertions S_{C_P} is complete. This means that if an unsafe path in the original program exists that violates assertion a, then a is contained in the set of unproven assertions. The following lemma gives us this property.

Lemma 1. *Let P be a program and C_P a well-formed condition for P. If P is unsafe, then an assertion $g \in S_{C_P}$ from the set of unproven assertion is violated.*

Proof (by contradiction). Let P be unsafe. By definition an unsafe program path exists. Let $p = c_0 \xrightarrow{g_0} c_1 \xrightarrow{g_1} \cdots \xrightarrow{g_{n-1}} c_{err} \in paths(P)$ be an arbitrary unsafe path. Since p unsafe, $g_{n-1} \equiv (\cdot, \texttt{assert } \cdot, \cdot)$. Assume $g_{n-1} \notin S_{C_P}$. Since C_P well-formed, exists run $q_0 q_1 \ldots q_n$ s.t. $\forall 0 \leq i < n : (q_i, g_i, q_{i+1}) \in \delta$. Since $g_{n-1} \notin S_{C_P}$, it follows that $q_{n-1} = q_n = q_s$. Contradiction to well-formedness (safety) of C_P.

After computation of the set S_{C_P} of unproven assertions from condition C_P, we now generate the residual program via slicing. The general idea of slicing is to delete those statements from the program that do not influence the semantic property defined by the slicing criteria. Typical slicing criteria are the variable values at certain program location. We are interested in the evaluation of the computed, unproven assertions at the location they are defined. Slicing should delete those statements which do not influence evaluation of any assertion in S_{C_P}. Looking at our example programs (Fig. 1) and the sets of unproven assertions $S_{C_{\text{EVEN/SIGN}}} = \{(l_6, \texttt{assert } r \geq 0, l_7)\}$ and $S_{C_{\text{SUM}}} = \{(l_7, \texttt{assert } s > 0, l_8)\}$, we see that we cannot delete any statement in program EVEN/SIGN. Every statement influences the evaluation of the assertion. In program SUM only the right branch of the if statement influences the assertion in $S_{C_{\text{SUM}}}$. Hence, slicing deletes the statements of the left branch. The resulting program slice, the residual program, for SUM and $S_{C_{\text{SUM}}} = \{(l_7, \texttt{assert } s > 0, l_8)\}$, is the residual program shown in Fig. 4. Here, we refrain from defining the computation of program slices but just define constraints on the constructed slice, which standard slicing technique will however give us. Slicing only removes program statements (CFA edges). Technically, a statement is removed by deleting the respective CFA edge (l, op, l'). To keep the initial location l_0, we do not relink l's predecessors. Instead, we relink successors of l' to l. Furthermore, locations without predecessors and successors are removed. The following definition describes the structural appearance of a program slice obtained from a program by deletion of some the program's statements.

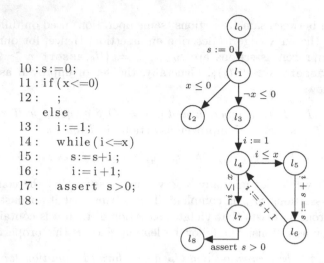

```
10 : s:=0;
11 : if (x<=0)
12 :    ;
      else
13 :    i:=1;
14 :    while (i<=x)
15 :       s:=s+i;
16 :       i:=i+1;
17 :    assert s>0;
18 :
```

Fig. 4. C code and CFA of residual program constructed by slicing of program SUM using slicing criterion $SC_{SUM} = \{(l_7, \mathtt{assert}\ s > 0, l_8)\}$

Definition 4. *Let $P = (L, G, l_0)$ be a program. A slice of P is a program $P' = (L', G', l_0')$ with $L' \subseteq L$, $l_0' = l_0$ and if $(l, op, l') \in G'$, then a sequence of locations $l_1 \ldots l_n$, $n \geq 2$, exists with $l_1 = l$, $l_n = l'$, $(l_{n-1}, op, l') \in G$, $\forall 1 \leq i < n - 1 : (l_i, \cdot, l_{i+1}) \in G \wedge l_i \notin L'$.*

So far, we defined the structural appearance of a program slice. In addition we require that the behavior of program slice and original program is identical w.r.t. the slicing criterion. In general, a slicing criterion is a set of program statements of interest. Since program statements are defined by CFA edges and we are only interested in unproven assertions, the slicing criterion is a set of assertion edges, namely the set of unproven assertions. In this case, original program and a program slice behave identically w.r.t. the slicing criterion – we call the program slice sound w.r.t. the slicing criterion – if the following holds. If an arbitrary execution of the original program violates an assertion g_a in the slicing criterion, then an execution of the program slice exists, that violates the corresponding assertion g_a' in the program slice. Formally, this is stated as follows.

Definition 5. *Let $P = (L, G, l_0)$ be a program and SC a slicing criterion, $SC \subseteq G_{assert} = \{g \mid g \in G \wedge g \equiv (\cdot, \mathtt{assert}\ \cdot, \cdot)\}$. Then, a program slice $P' = (L', G', l_0)$ of program P is sound w.r.t. the slicing criterion SC if for any concrete state $c_0 \in C$ the following holds: if there is a path $c_0 \xrightarrow{g_0} c_1 \cdots \xrightarrow{g_{n-1}} c_{err} \in paths(P) \wedge g_{n-1} = (l, \mathtt{assert}\ expr, l') \in SC$ in program P, then there is also a path $c_0 \xrightarrow{g_0'} c_1' \cdots \xrightarrow{g_{m-1}'} c_{err} \in paths(P') \wedge g_{m-1}' = (\cdot, \mathtt{assert}\ expr, l')$ in program slice P'.*

We use dependence based slicing [23] to compute a program slice w.r.t a slicing criterion SC. The work in [2] ensures that the computed slice obtained from dependence based slicing is sound w.r.t. SC. That is why, in the latter we assume that the residual program, the program slice computed from program P and slicing criterion S_{C_P} is sound w.r.t. S_{C_P}.

Remember, our goal is the validation of the non-proven part of the original program. Validating the residual program obtained from slicing the original program using the set of unproven assertions as slicing criterion is planned as one option. That is why, we need some correspondence between the original program and this residual program. Especially, the residual program must only be safe if the original program is safe. The following theorem ensures this property

Theorem 2. *Let P be a program, C_P a well-formed condition for P and P' a slice of program P which is sound w.r.t. the set of unproven assertions S_{C_P} (the slicing criterion). P is safe if P' is safe.*

Proof (by contraposition). If P is unsafe, exists a path $c_0 \xrightarrow{(l_0, op_0, l_1)} c_1 \xrightarrow{(l_1, op_1, l_2)}$ $\dots \xrightarrow{(l_{n-1}, op_{n-1}, l_n)} c_{err} \in paths(P)$ and $op_{n-1} \equiv \mathtt{assert}\ cond$. Due to lemma 1 $(l_{n-1}, op_{n-1}, l_n) \in S_{C_P}$. Since slice P' is sound, P' is unsafe.

Note that the two presented residual program construction techniques can be combined as follows. Given a program P and a condition C_P for P, first, use the technique extraction of residual program from condition and compute program $P' = (L', G', l'_0) = residual\_program\_of(P, C_P)$. Take all assertions in P' as unproven assertions, $S_{C'_P} = \{g \mid g \in G' \land g \equiv (\cdot, \mathtt{assert}\ \cdot, \cdot)\}$, and apply the technique residual program via slicing to get program slice P'' sound w.r.t. $S_{C'_P}$. Program P'' is the input for testing in the combined approach.

5   Experimental Results

In our experiments, we studied the actual benefits of our techniques for combined verification and testing. For that, we examined whether a partial verification run with subsequent testing is faster than a complete verification. Furthermore, we determined whether a residual program reduces the test effort. Finally, we compared all three techniques, the two techniques for construction of residual programs as well as their combination, with the naive approach always testing the complete program.

For (partial) verification we used the configurable software analysis tool CPACHECKER (svn r13520). We configured CPACHECKER to use predicate analysis[4] and to produce a condition after partial verification. Also, the residual program from condition is generated by CPACHECKER. We sliced the original program and the residual program from condition with the help of the source code analysis platform Frama-C (v.Neon-20140301) [17]. Finally, we utilized the concolic test tool KLEE (v.git-20140327) [10] to generate the test-case suites. We evaluated our techniques on our examples, on two programs called **search**

---

[4] Our technique allows the usage of arbitrary analyses, e.g. value analysis or even sequential combinations of analyses as illustrated in [7].

Table 1. Experimental Results

Program	Verification		Verification+Testing				Program Size				#Tests			
	V	p.V	P	C	S	C+S	P	C	S	C+S	P	C	S	C+S
EVEN/SIGN	2.71	2.71	**2.8**	3.15	3.45	3.59	51	43	51	**34**	3	**2**	3	**2**
SUM	3.66	3.48	**4.54**	4.68	5.52	5.64	49	51	**48**	49	2	3	**1**	3
search	7.55	4.17	5.51	5.73	5.73	**5.29**	217	243	201	**167**	14	17	14	**8**
sort	16.28	11.23	**11.88**	12.94	12.32	13.61	760	780	**569**	574	19	19	15	**14**
get_tag	9.71	4.11	4.71	**4.64**	5.1	5.35	415	248	**159**	199	16	8	**6**	8
mim7to8	21.58	14.34	20.8	23.18	**17.07**	20.16	939	1142	**538**	966	48	79	**28**	48
esc_uri	72.07	49.91	**50.56**	52.5	51.35	53.61	808	1052	**638**	757	29	51	**26**	38

and sort, which allow the user to select one from popular array search and array sort algorithms, as well as 3 programs constructed from the Verisec benchmark [26]. Each of the three programs looks at one test case in the benchmark and allows to select between the different variants of that test case available in the benchmark. Except for our examples, all assert statements checked the absence of buffer-overflows. Furthermore, every program was preprocessed with CIL [28]. All programs are error free excluding overflows which the verification tool assumes not to happen. Moreover, the test tool found the errors regarding overflows if they are part of the test tool's input program. Our experiments were performed on a 2.4 Ghz Intel Core 2 Duo Arch Linux system with 4GB memory and statement coverage, measured with gcov from the GNU Compiler Collection (v.4.8.2) [1], was always about 90-100% for all generated test-case suites.

Table 5 shows our results. All times are given in seconds. Columns V and p.V show the times for complete and partial verification. The times for EVEN/SIGN are the same because due to the modulo operator used in EVEN/SIGN CPACHECKER was not able to prove the full program using predicate analysis. The next four columns show the total times for partial verification and subsequent testing for all four approaches: testing complete program (P), residual program from condition (C), residual program constructed via slicing (S) and the combination of the latter two (C+S). Total time includes the time for partial verification, construction of residual program (if any, e.g. slicing time) and test generation time. The last 8 columns reflect the test effort. First, the sizes of the programs put into the test tool are given in number of control locations. Thereafter, the number of generated test cases per test suite is depicted. The smallest total time, program size and number of tests for each evaluated benchmark program is presented in bold.

Our experiments show that in most cases, partial verification with subsequent testing is faster than a complete verification and thus, enables "on-the-fly" analysis. Surprisingly, the naive approach testing always the complete program performs best in half of the cases. We believe that this is not a general weakness of our approaches. In fact, KLEE performs well even for large programs (much larger than ours) and currently constructing the residual program takes a significant amount of time. The following comparison of program size and number of tests will support our position. In contrast to total execution times, program size and number of tests are usually lower for the two residual program approaches based on slicing (S,C+S) than for the complete program but this is rarely true for the residual program from condition (C). In case of the slicing approaches, testing following a partial verification benefits from residual program construction. Moreover, none of the two slicing approaches (S, C+S) always outperforms the other. As already seen for our example programs EVEN/SIGN and SUM which approach performs better depends on the partial verification, e.g. do assertions exist which are only partially verified or do loops exist which are only partially verified. Hence, strategies choosing the correct technique need to be developed considering e.g. the program structure and the condition.

6 Related Work

There are a number of different approaches combining verification and testing which we shortly discuss here. VART [29] uses testing to identify likely invariants and exclude intentionally invalidated invariants after update. Bounded model checking determines the invariants from the likely invariants and checks the non-invalidated invariants on the updated program. In unit checking [20] a LTL formula specifies program paths being suspicious. A model checker explores these paths. A satisfying assignment to the respective path condition is used for test generation. Approaches like [31,30] check if a model satisfies a property and then verify that the implementation is consistent with the model.

Like us, many approaches use collaboration of verification and testing to either verify a program or find bugs. The approaches in [25,33,19,3,13,21,27] describe (interleaved) collaboration of verification and testing in which testing assists to find a proof. [33] generalizes test observations to a likely abstraction. A theorem prover checks the abstraction. If this check fails, the counterexample is used to compute the next input for testing and generalization starts again. [27] uses testing to choose a good abstraction configuration for the analysis. [21] uses test data to simplify invariant constraints. [25,19,3,13] including Synergy [19] and Dash [3] search for errors and proofs at the same time. Test information (e.g. unavailability of concrete counterexample) is used for refinement of abstraction in case of spurious abstract counterexamples. Abstract counterexamples are used to derive a test for a concrete counterexample. In our approaches collaboration is purely sequential, first verification, then testing, and testing does not assist verification.

A different class of collaborating approaches [6,15,16,18,12] uses static analysis to detect potential bugs and then test if the bugs really exist in the program. DyTa [18] first detects potential defects with a static analyzer, then identifies branching conditions which must be valid to trigger a defect, and adds an assume statement for this condition to guide test input generation via symbolic execution. BLAST [6] reports error locations considered reachable and computes a test input for every error path, a satisfying assignment for the symbolic error path. Check'n'Crash [15] and DSD-Crasher [16] use ESC/Java to identify potential errors and compute a satisfying assignment to the error condition for every potential error. These assignments are given to JCrasher to generate JUnit tests. SANTE [12] uses a static abstract interpretation based value analysis to compute alarms. Then, it instruments the program with special error branches to enable alarm guided test generation and computes one or more program slices, depending on the configuration. These program slices are subject to test generation. Our second approach can be understood as testing potential defects. Any unproven assertion is a potential defect. In contrast to all the other approaches, we do not verify the whole program and we believe that an error found by our verification tool is a real bug. Nevertheless, similar to SANTE [12] in configuration ALL (computing a single slice) we also apply slicing using the non-verified assertions instead of the alarms as slicing criteria.

Further approaches [24,7,14] divide the program like we do. One part of the program is verified, the other is tested. Program partitioning [24] takes the opposite direction. It first tests. Then, it removes the sufficiently tested paths and verifies the residual program. In contrast to our approaches the residual program in [24] is always a subgraph of the original one. Conditional model checking [7] produces an assumption automaton to sum up the verification work and thus partitions the program. In [7] the technique is used to verify the non-verified partition by a second verifier. It is only mentioned that the technique can be used to guide test generation. We describe two approaches for actual guidance. Christakis et al. [14] instrument the program with assumptions and assertions describing the verification effort already done. The subsequent testing tool is guided to test the assumptions or the validated property but in contrast to our approaches, the tested program is not simplified by slicing or deletion of program paths.

Conditioned program slicing [11] and its extension [22] provide a general model for the extraction of those program parts which keep the behavior of a program statement w.r.t. a set of program executions. Hence, their idea is similar to our extraction of a residual program from condition and our combined approach. An important difference between our approaches and [11,22] is that we use a structural description of the program executions (the condition) and [11,22] require a logic formula on a subset of the input variables. We think that it is non-trivial to transform our condition into a logic formula needed for conditioned program slicing.

7   Conclusion

In this paper we presented a new way of combining verification and testing. The approach divides the labor of safety checking onto verification and testing, testing only having to analyze those parts of the program which have not been verified. To this end, we presented two ways of constructing residual programs for testing. We implemented both techniques and experimentally evaluated them on a number of example programs. The experiments showed that in almost all cases the subsequent testing following an incomplete verification could benefit from residual program construction.

As future work we in particular would like to work on strategies for dividing the available amount of time into the part for verification and that for testing. Furthermore, the experiments so far indicate that the program's syntactical structure might influence what residual program construction technique works better, so that the choice for the technique could be based on the program at hand. Another line of improvement could be a parallelization of the two techniques since they are completely independent.

References

1. Gnu compiler collection, https://gcc.gnu.org (accessed: October 13, 2014)
2. Barraclough, R.W., Binkley, D., Danicic, S., Harman, M., Hierons, R.M., Kiss, Á., Laurence, M., Ouarbya, L.: A trajectory-based strict semantics for program slicing. Theoretical Computer Science 411(11-13), 1372–1386 (2010)
3. Beckman, N.E., Nori, A.V., Rajamani, S.K., Simmons, R.J.: Proofs from tests. In: ISSTA 2008, pp. 3–14. ACM (2008)
4. Bertolino, A.: Software testing research: Achievements, challenges, dreams. In: Briand, L.C., Wolf, A.L. (eds.) International Conference on Software Engineering, ISCE 2007, Workshop on the Future of Software Engineering, FOSE 2007, Minneapolis, MN, USA, May 23-25, pp. 85–103 (2007)
5. Beyer, D.: Status report on software verification. In: Ábrahám, E., Havelund, K. (eds.) TACAS 2014 (ETAPS). LNCS, vol. 8413, pp. 373–388. Springer, Heidelberg (2014)
6. Beyer, D., Chlipala, A.J., Henzinger, T.A., Jhala, R., Majumdar, R.: Generating tests from counterexamples. In: ICSE 2004, pp. 326–335. IEEE Computer Society (2004)
7. Beyer, D., Henzinger, T.A., Keremoglu, M.E., Wendler, P.: Conditional model checking: A technique to pass information between verifiers. In: FSE 2012, pp. 1–11. ACM (2012)
8. Beyer, D., Henzinger, T.A., Théoduloz, G.: Configurable software verification: Concretizing the convergence of model checking and program analysis. In: Damm, W., Hermanns, H. (eds.) CAV 2007. LNCS, vol. 4590, pp. 504–518. Springer, Heidelberg (2007)
9. Beyer, D., Keremoglu, M.E.: CPACHECKER: A Tool for Configurable Software Verification. In: Gopalakrishnan, G., Qadeer, S. (eds.) CAV 2011. LNCS, vol. 6806, pp. 184–190. Springer, Heidelberg (2011)
10. Cadar, C., Dunbar, D., Engler, D.: KLEE: unassisted and automatic generation of high-coverage tests for complex systems programs. In: OSDI 2008, pp. 209–224. USENIX Association (2008)
11. Canfora, G., Cimitile, A., De Lucia, A.: Conditioned program slicing. Information and Software Technology 40(11-12), 595–607 (1998)
12. Chebaro, O., Kosmatov, N., Giorgetti, A., Julliand, J.: Program slicing enhances a verification technique combining static and dynamic analysis. In: SAC 2012, pp. 1284–1291. ACM (2012)
13. Chen, J., MacDonald, S.: Towards a better collaboration of static and dynamic analyses for testing concurrent programs. In: PADTAD 2008, pp. 8:1–8:9. ACM (2008)

14. Christakis, M., Müller, P., Wüstholz, V.: Collaborative verification and testing with explicit assumptions. In: Giannakopoulou, D., Méry, D. (eds.) FM 2012. LNCS, vol. 7436, pp. 132–146. Springer, Heidelberg (2012)
15. Csallner, C., Smaragdakis, Y.: Check 'N' Crash: Combining static checking and testing. In: ICSE 2005, pp. 422–431. ACM (2005)
16. Csallner, C., Smaragdakis, Y.: DSD-Crasher: A hybrid analysis tool for bug finding. In: ISSTA 2006, pp. 245–254. ACM (2006)
17. Cuoq, P., Kirchner, F., Kosmatov, N., Prevosto, V., Signoles, J., Yakobowski, B.: Frama-c. In: Eleftherakis, G., Hinchey, M., Holcombe, M. (eds.) SEFM 2012. LNCS, vol. 7504, pp. 233–247. Springer, Heidelberg (2012)
18. Ge, X., Taneja, K., Xie, T., Tillmann, N.: DyTa: Dynamic symbolic execution guided with static verification results. In: ICSE 2011, pp. 992–994. ACM (2011)
19. Gulavani, B.S., Henzinger, T.A., Kannan, Y., Nori, A.V., Rajamani, S.K.: SYNERGY: a new algorithm for property checking. In: SIGSOFT FSE 2006, pp. 117–127. ACM Press (2006)
20. Gunter, E., Peled, D.: Model checking, testing and verification working together. Formal Aspects of Computing 17(2), 201–221 (2005)
21. Gupta, A., Majumdar, R., Rybalchenko, A.: From tests to proofs. In: Kowalewski, S., Philippou, A. (eds.) TACAS 2009. LNCS, vol. 5505, pp. 262–276. Springer, Heidelberg (2009)
22. Harman, M., Hierons, R., Fox, C., Danicic, S., Howroyd, J.: Pre/post conditioned slicing. In: ICSM 2001, pp. 138–147 (2001)
23. Horwitz, S., Reps, T., Binkley, D.: Interprocedural slicing using dependence graphs. In: PLDI 1988, pp. 35–46. ACM (1988)
24. Jalote, P., Vangala, V., Singh, T., Jain, P.: Program partitioning: A framework for combining static and dynamic analysis. In: WODA 2006, pp. 11–16. ACM (2006)
25. Kroening, D., Groce, A., Clarke, E.: Counterexample guided abstraction refinement via program execution. In: Davies, J., Schulte, W., Barnett, M. (eds.) ICFEM 2004. LNCS, vol. 3308, pp. 224–238. Springer, Heidelberg (2004)
26. Ku, K., Hart, T.E., Chechik, M., Lie, D.: A buffer overflow benchmark for software model checkers. In: ASE 2007, pp. 389–392. ACM (2007)
27. Naik, M., Yang, H., Castelnuovo, G., Sagiv, M.: Abstractions from tests. In: POPL 2012, pp. 373–386. ACM (2012)
28. Necula, G.C., McPeak, S., Rahul, S.P., Weimer, W.: CIL: Intermediate language and tools for analysis and transformation of C programs. In: Nigel Horspool, R. (ed.) CC 2002. LNCS, vol. 2304, pp. 213–228. Springer, Heidelberg (2002)
29. Pastore, F., Mariani, L., Hyvärinen, A.E.J., Fedyukovich, G., Sharygina, N., Sehestedt, S., Muhammad, A.: Verification-aided regression testing. In: ISSTA 2014, pp. 37–48. ACM (2014)
30. Rusu, V., Marchand, H., Tschaen, V., Jéron, T., Jeannet, B.: From safety verification to safety testing. In: Groz, R., Hierons, R.M. (eds.) TestCom 2004. LNCS, vol. 2978, pp. 160–176. Springer, Heidelberg (2004)
31. Sharygina, N., Peled, D.: A combined testing and verification approach for software reliability. In: Oliveira, J.N., Zave, P. (eds.) FME 2001. LNCS, vol. 2021, pp. 611–628. Springer, Heidelberg (2001)
32. Tip, F.: A survey of program slicing techniques. Journal of Programming Languages 3(3) (1995)
33. Yorsh, G., Ball, T., Sagiv, M.: Testing, abstraction, theorem proving: Better together? In: ISSTA 2006, pp. 145–156. ACM (2006)

Evaluation of Measures for Statistical Fault Localisation and an Optimising Scheme*

David Landsberg[2], Hana Chockler[1], Daniel Kroening[2], and Matt Lewis[2]

[1] King's College London
[2] University of Oxford

Abstract. *Statistical Fault Localisation* (SFL) is a widely used method for localizing faults in software. SFL gathers coverage details of passed and failed executions over a faulty program and then uses a measure to assign a degree of *suspiciousness* to each of a chosen set of program entities (statements, predicates, etc.) in that program. The program entities are then inspected by the engineer in descending order of suspiciousness until the bug is found. The effectiveness of this process relies on the quality of the suspiciousness measure. In this paper, we compare 157 measures, 95 of which are new to SFL and borrowed from other branches of science and philosophy. We also present a new measure optimiser Lex_g, which optimises a given measure g according to a criterion of single bug optimality. An experimental comparison on benchmarks from the Software-artifact Infrastructure Repository (SIR) indicates that many of the new measures perform competitively with the established ones. Furthermore, the large-scale comparison reveals that the new measures Lex_{Ochiai} and Pattern-Similarity perform best overall.

1 Introduction

Software engineers use fault localization methods in order to focus their debugging efforts on a subset of program entities (such as statements or predicates) that are most likely to be causes of the error. Since the attempts to reduce the number of faults in software are estimated to consume $50 - 60\%$ of the development and maintenance effort [6], accurate and efficient fault localization techniques have the potential to greatly reduce the overall effort of software development.

In statistical fault localisation (SFL), statistical information on passing and failing executions of a faulty program is gathered and analysed [1, 3, 14–16, 33]. Based on the resulting data, SFL assigns a degree of suspiciousness to each member of a chosen set of program entities of the program under test. Essentially, the degree of suspiciousness depends on the number of appearances of this entity in the passing and failing executions. There are many approaches to computing this degree, and naturally, entities that cause the error are hoped to have the highest degree of suspiciousness. The program entities are inspected by the user in descending order of suspiciousness until the bug is found. SFL has been considered a highly effective and efficient way for localising faults in software [31].

---

* Supported by UK EPSRC EP/J012564/1 and ERC project 280053.

A. Egyed and I. Schaefer (Eds.): FASE 2015, LNCS 9033, pp. 115–129, 2015.
DOI: 10.1007/978-3-662-46675-9_8

Our Contributions. The contributions of this paper are as follows:

1. We introduce and motivate 95 new measures (borrowed from other areas of science and philosophy) to SFL. These measures are divided into five categories: similarity, prediction, causation, confirmation and custom.
2. We formally prove that over 50 measures are equivalent to others for the purpose of ranking suspicious entities.
3. We experimentally compare the measures on the Siemens test suite along with five larger programs: space, grep, gzip, sed and flex[1]. We show that many of the new measures perform competitively, with an optimised version of PatternSimilarity outperforming all pre-existing SFL measures on the benchmarks.
4. We introduce a new measure-optimising scheme Lex_g and show Lex_{Ochiai} outperforms all other measures on the benchmarks.

Along with providing two new best performing measures, to the best of our knowledge, this research provides one of the largest scale SFL studies to date in three ways. Firstly, it contains the largest experimental study over C programs in SFL, consisting of the largest number (and largest sized) C programs. Secondly, it introduces and compares the largest number of measures. Thirdly, it contains results for the largest number of ranking equivalence proofs (see [21]).

Related Work. Research in SFL is largely driven by the construction or introduction of new suspiciousness measures. Experimental results assess the quality of measures by applying them to known benchmarks [1, 2, 17, 19, 21, 25, 26, 30]. Theoretical results have included formal properties and equivalence proofs of different measures [20, 21, 31].

A similar paper to ours is the paper by Lucia et al. [19], which compares association measures on C and Java Programs. However, Lucia et al. conclude that there is no measure which is clearly the best, whereas we show our new measure Lex_{Ochiai} is a robust overall top performer. Another similar paper is the paper by Naish [21], who set the standards for proving equivalences between suspiciousness measures, discuss optimal measures and compare a (smaller) set of measures against a (smaller) set of benchmarks.

A recent paper by Yoo et al. [32] analyses fault localisation in conjunction with prioritisation. The problem studied in [32] is deciding the best course of action when a fault is found. Their approach is complementary to ours (and applied to a similar set of benchmarks) and can also be applied in conjunction with the measure we construct in this paper.

Xie et al. develop a theoretical approach to proving that some measures are better than others [31]. However, their proof relies on several critical simplifying assumptions (in particular, the bug must be contained in a single line of code or block). Bugs that are more realistic often break this assumption, invalidating the proof on realistic examples. We impose no such theoretical restrictions.

---

[1] From the Software Artifact Infrastructure Repository at http://sir.unl.edu

On a more general level, Parnin et al. [22] raise the question of whether fault localisation techniques are useful at all. The paper compared the efficiency of fault localisation with and without the automated tool Tarantula [14]. They reported that experts are faster at locating bugs using the tool for simple programs, but not for harder ones. However, their study is limited in its ability to generalize, as their experiments included only two small, single-bug programs (Tetris and NanoXML, 2K/4K LOC respectively) and is limited to the Tarantula tool.

Paper Structure. The rest of the paper is organised as follows. In Section 2, we present the informal ideas and formal definitions of SFL and discuss the 62 previously used suspiciousness measures. In Section 3, we discuss 95 measures that have not yet been applied to SFL and demonstrate that these new measures are well suited to SFL. We briefly outline proofs of equivalence of many of these measures when applied to SFL. Section 4 presents the experimental results of applying the non-equivalent measures to the benchmarks. We summarize our results in Section 5. Due to lack of space, the complete ranking equivalence proofs, results tables and tables containing definitions of measures are only in the extended version of this paper. The extended paper, the data set and the code used to perform the experiments are available from `http://www.cprover.org/sfl/`.

2   Definitions and Notations

In this section, we introduce the basic definitions and notations of SFL, and survey the established measures. We also present a small motivating example.

2.1   Definitions

Let a program under test (PUT) **P** be an ordered set of *program entities*, such that $\mathbf{P} = \langle C_1, \ldots, C_n \rangle$, where $n \in \mathbb{N}$. Program entities can be statements, branches, paths, or blocks of code (see, for example, [15, 17, 29]). Let a test suite **T** be an ordered set of test cases $\mathbf{T} = \langle t_1, \ldots, t_m \rangle$, where m is the size of the test suite. Each test case t_i is a Boolean vector of length n (where n is the number of program entities) such that $t_i = \langle b_1^i, \ldots, b_n^i \rangle$, where $b_j^i \in \{0, 1\}$, where we have $b_j^i = 1$ iff C_j is covered by t_i. We represent each program entity C_i by the set of test cases where C_i is 1. The last program entity C_n is the error statement E, which is 1 if the test case *fails* and 0 if it *passes*. A convenient way to store this information is using *coverage matrices*, in which the i-th row of the j-th column represents whether test case t_i covers program entity C_j, an example of which is given in Table 1.

For each program **P**, test suite **T** and program entity C_i we can construct this program entity's *contingency table* [24]. This table can be symbolically represented as a vector of four elements denoted as $\langle a_{ef}^i, a_{ep}^i, a_{nf}^i, a_{np}^i \rangle$, where a_{ef}^i is the number of failing test cases in **T** that cover C_i, a_{ep}^i is the number of passing test cases in $\mathbf{T}$ that cover C_i, a_{nf}^i is the number of failing test cases in $\mathbf{T}$ that do not cover C_i and a_{np}^i is the number of passing test cases in $\mathbf{T}$ that do not cover C_i. For each program entity, we can calculate its contingency table for a test suite. See Table 2 for an example. We let $F_i = a_{ef}^i + a_{nf}^i$, $P_i = a_{ep}^i + a_{np}^i$ and $T_i = F_i + P_i$. For each test suite and C_i and C_j, $F_i = F_j$ and $P_i = P_j$. When the context is clear we drop numerical indices, writing, for instance, C and a_{ef} instead of C_i and a_{ef}^i.

A *suspiciousness measure* m maps a contingency table $\langle a_{ef}^i, a_{ep}^i, a_{nf}^i, a_{np}^i \rangle$ to a real number [21]. Roughly speaking, for a test suite and faulty program, the higher the output of the measure the more suspicious the program entity C_i is assumed to be with respect to containing a bug. The output of each suspiciousness measure is the *suspiciousness score* that is assigned to each program entity (we also say that a program entity is *ranked* according to its suspiciousness score). The program entities are then ordered according to their degree of suspiciousness and are investigated in descending order by the user until the bug is found.

A probability space for each test suite is defined as follows. Given a program $\mathbf{P}$ and test suite $\mathbf{T}$, we identify a probability space (Ω, S, Pr), where the sample space $\Omega = \{t_1, \ldots, t_n\}$ is the set of test cases, the set of events S is the power-set of the set of program entities, where $Pr \colon S \to [0, 1]$ is a probability function with the usual signature. Assuming the axioms and language of classical probabilistic calculus and given the definitions of a_{ef}^i, a_{nf}^i, a_{ep}^i, a_{np}^i above, we can identify $Pr(C_i \cap E)$, $Pr(\neg C_i \cap E)$, $Pr(C_i \cap \neg E)$ and $Pr(\neg C_i \cap \neg E)$ with $\frac{a_{ef}^i}{T_i}$, $\frac{a_{ep}^i}{T_i}$, $\frac{a_{np}^i}{T_i}$ and $\frac{a_{nf}^i}{T_i}$ respectively. Using probabilistic calculus, this is sufficient to generate the other probabilistic expressions we need. Probabilistic expressions may also be translated into algebraic form in the obvious way. For example, $P(E|C_i)$ is equal to $\frac{a_{ef}^i}{a_{ep}^i + a_{ef}^i}$.

Naish's notion of *single-bug optimality* [20] is based on the observation that if a program contains only a single bug, then all failing traces cover that bug. Formally, a measure m is *single-bug optimal* if (1) when $a_{ef} < F$, the value returned is less than any value returned when $a_{ef} = F$ and (2) when $a_{ef} = F$ and $a_{np} = k$, the value returned is greater any value returned when $a_{np} < k$ [20].

We use Naish's notion of *ranking equivalence* between suspiciousness measures, defined as follows. Two suspiciousness measures m_1 and m_2 are said to be *monotonically equivalent* if $(m_1(\boldsymbol{x}) < m_1(\boldsymbol{y})) \Leftrightarrow (m_2(\boldsymbol{x}) < m_2(\boldsymbol{y}))$ for all vectors $\boldsymbol{x}$ and $\boldsymbol{y}$. Many suspiciousness measures turn out to be monotonically equivalent on domains in which the measures share the same program and test suite [21]. In other words, they are monotonically equivalent on domains in which the number of failing test cases F and the number of passing test cases P is the same for the vectors $\boldsymbol{x}$ and $\boldsymbol{y}$. This property is called *ranking equivalence* [21].

2.2 Motivating Example

In this section, we present a simple motivating example to illustrate a typical instance of SFL. Consider the faulty program *minmax.c* in Figure 1 (taken from [12]). The program has six program entities $\langle C_1, C_2, C_3, C_4, C_5, E \rangle$, where E is the specification. The program fails to satisfy the specification *least $\leq$ most*.

```
int main () { // C1
  int inp1, inp2, inp3;
  int least = inp1;
  int most = inp1;

  if (most < inp2)
    most = inp2;   // C2
  if (most < inp3)
    most = inp3;   // C3
  if (least > inp2)
    most = inp2;   // C4 (Bug!)
  if (least > inp3)
    least = inp3;  // C5
  assert(least <= most);
  // E (Specification)
}
```

Fig. 1. minmax.c

The reason for the failure is the bug at C_4, which should be an assignment to *least* instead of an assignment to *most*. To locate the fault, we collected coverage data from ten test cases t_1 to t_{10}. Three of them fail and seven pass. The coverage matrix for these test cases is given in Table 1. We compute contingency tables for each program entity using the coverage matrix and give the table for C_4 as an example (Table 2). We then apply a suspiciousness measure to assign a degree of suspiciousness to each of the program entities. We use the Wong-II measure [30] $a_{ef} - a_{ep}$ as a simple example.

Table 1. Coverage matrix for minmax.c

	C_1	C_2	C_3	C_4	C_5	E
t_1	1	0	1	1	0	1
t_2	1	0	0	1	1	1
t_3	1	0	0	1	0	1
t_4	1	1	0	0	0	0
t_5	1	0	1	0	0	0
t_6	1	0	0	0	1	0
t_7	1	0	0	1	1	0
t_8	1	0	0	0	0	0
t_9	1	1	0	0	1	0
t_{10}	1	1	1	0	0	0

Table 2. Contingency table for C_4

	E	$\neg E$
C_4	3	1
$\neg C_4$	0	6

The user then investigates the program entities in descending order of suspiciousness until the fault is found (ignoring E). In this example, Wong-II ranks C_4 the highest with a score of 2 and thereby successfully identifies the bug within the most suspicious program entity.

2.3   Established Measures

We include 62 measures selected by Naish [21] and Lo [19] in our comparison. To motivate many of these measures to SFL, Naish et al. discuss desirable formal properties [20]. One important property that has been discussed is *monotonicity*: for a fixed number of passed and failed tests, a measure should strictly increase as a_{ef} increases and strictly decrease as a_{ep} decreases [14,20,31]. Examples of some prominent measures from [21] are Wong-I $= a_{ef}$, Wong-II $= a_{ef} - a_{ep}$, Naish $= a_{ef} - \frac{a_{ep}}{a_{ep}+a_{np}+1}$, Zoltar $= \frac{a_{ef}}{a_{ef}+a_{nf}+a_{ep}+\frac{10000 a_{nf} a_{ep}}{a_{ef}}}$, Jaccard $= \frac{a_{ef}}{a_{ef}+a_{nf}+a_{ep}}$, Ochiai $= \frac{a_{ef}}{\sqrt{(a_{ef}+a_{nf})(a_{ef}+a_{ep})}}$ [1], Tarantula $= \frac{\frac{a_{ef}}{a_{ef}+a_{nf}}}{\frac{a_{ef}}{a_{ef}+a_{nf}}+\frac{a_{ep}}{a_{ep}+a_{np}}}$ [14][2], Kulczynski-II $= \frac{1}{2}(\frac{a_{ef}}{a_{ef}+a_{nf}}+\frac{a_{ef}}{a_{ef}+a_{ep}})$, and M2 $= \frac{a_{ef}}{a_{ef}+a_{np}+2(a_{nf}+a_{ep})}$.

3   New SFL Measures

In this section we introduce 95 new suspiciousness measures that have not yet been applied in SFL. We organise them into five different groups: *similarity, predictive, causal, confirmation* and *custom* measures. Their application to SFL is motivated in terms of different proposed criteria about what a suspiciousness measure should exactly capture. We discuss such criteria at the beginning of each paragraph and the reader is referred to the full paper for the definitions of the new measures. We identify over 50 measures which are ranking equivalent and summarise interesting monotonic simplifications of some measures. The introduction of many measures has the benefit of consolidating the results concerning top performing measures. Furthermore, we introduce a new measure optimiser, which we later show can be used to construct the best performing measure on our benchmark suite.

3.1   New SFL Measures from the Literature

Similarity Measures. The first proposed criterion is that a suspiciousness measure should measure how similar a program entity C is to the error E. This motivates the use of similarity measures in SFL and has been discussed in the literature [20, 21]. Indeed, many of the measures of the previous section are similarity measures (such as Jaccard) that were originally used in different domains. The new similarity measures we include in our experiments are available in the survey of [5] and are as follows: 3w-Jaccard, Baroni-Urbani-Buser-I and II, Braun-Blanquet, Bray-Curtis, Cosine, Cole, Chord, Dennis, Dispersion, Driver&Kroebner, F&M, Faith, Forbes-I, Forbes-II, Fossum, Gower, Gower-Legendre, Hellinger, Johnson, Lance-Williams, MCconnaughey, Michael, Mountford, Nei-Li, Otsuka, PatternSimilarity, ShapeSimilarity, SizeSimilarity, Vari, Simpson, Sorgenfrei, and Sokal&Sneath-I, II, III, IV, V and Tarwid.[3]

---

[2] Strictly, this is an algebraic simplification of the original Tarantula measure.

[3] In some cases, a distance measure m has been converted to a similarity measure for our purposes, using the convention of $-$distance $\equiv$ similarity.

The measure PatternSimilarity $= -\frac{4(a_{ep}a_{nf})}{(a_{ef}+a_{ep}+a_{nf}+a_{np})^2}$, which is used in clustering [5], is of particular interest and we discuss it later in more detail.

Prediction Measures. The second proposed criterion is that a suspiciousness measure should measure the degree by which the execution of a program entity C *predicts* the error E. This motivates the use of what we loosely call *prediction* measures. Many of these measures are commonly used in epidemiology and diagnosis to estimate how well a test result predicts a disease or successful treatment [9,11]. The prediction measures we include in our experiments are as follows: Positive predictive value (PPV) $= P(E|C)$, Negative predictive value (NPV) $= P(\neg E|\neg C)$, Sensitivity $= P(C|E)$, Specificity $= P(\neg C|\neg E)$, Youden's J, Positive Likelyhood, Tetrachoric, Relative risk, Z-ratio, Peirce, Pearson-I, II and III [24], Pearson-Heron I and II, Anderberg-II, Tanimoto, Mutual Info, Simpson, Gilbert&Wells and Goodman&Kruskal (see the surveys [5,9,11,27]).

Causal Measures. The third proposed criterion is that a suspiciousness measure should measure the degree by which the execution of a program entity C has the power to cause the error E. This motivates the use of measures of causal power/strength to SFL. Such measures are principally found in the domain of philosophy of science [10] and artificial intelligence [23] and many of their formal properties have been shown [10]. Examples of causal measures are Suppes $= P(E|C)-P(E|\neg C)$, Eels $= P(E|C)- P(E)$, Lewis $= \log\frac{P(E|C)}{P(E|\neg C)}$, Fitelson $= \log\frac{P(E|C)}{P(E)}$ [10]. The other causal measures considered are: Pearl-I, II, III and IV Fitelson II and III Korb I, II and III, Cheng and Good.

Confirmation Measures. The fourth proposed criterion is that a suspiciousness measure should measure the degree by which the execution of a program entity H is a hypothesis which explains the error E. This motivates the use of measures of explanation (sometimes called evidential/inductive/confirmation measures) to the domain of SFL. Such measures have been developed in the domain of philosophy of science [13] and many of their formal properties have been proven [8]. Some example confirmation measures are Earman $= P(H|E) - P(H)$, Joyce $= P(H|E) - P(H|\neg E)$, Milne $= \log\frac{P(H|E)}{P(H)}$, and Good-II $= \log\frac{P(H|E)}{P(H|\neg E)}$ [13]. The other measures considered are Carnap-I and II, Crupi, Rescher, Kemeny, Popper-I, II, and III, Levi, Finch-I, Gaifman and Rips.

3.2 Ranking Equivalent Measures

Naish proved that many different suspiciousness measures are in fact equivalent for the purposes of ranking suspiciousness entities [21]. We extend Naish's work by providing many of the remaining equivalence proofs (over 50) for the measures in this paper (see the full paper for the proofs). Proving ranking equivalences is essential in determining a maximal set of inequivalent measures to investigate and allows us to ignore the remainder in experimentation. Furthermore, using equivalence proofs we can find some elegant monotonic simplifications which identify the underlying "essence" of some of the new suspiciousness measures, which may be used to guide future development. For instance, of our new measures (established measures are bracketed), we have found that Sensitivity is ranking equivalent to a_{ef} (as is Wong-I), Specificity to a_{np}, PPV to $\frac{a_{ef}}{a_{ep}}$ (as is Tarantula), NPV to $\frac{a_{np}}{a_{nf}}$, YulesQ to $\frac{a_{ef}a_{np}}{a_{ep}a_{nf}}$, F1 to $\frac{a_{ef}}{a_{ep}+a_{nf}}$ (as is Jaccard), SizeSimilarity to a_{ef}-a_{ep} (as is Wong-II) and PatternSimilarity to $-a_{nf}a_{ep}$.

3.3 A New Custom Measure

We propose the fifth criterion for suspiciousness measures: that a measure should be tailored to particular features concerning software errors (similar ideas had been proposed in [21] and Wong-III [30]).

We motivate our measure as follows. Firstly, following work by Naish [21], we state that our measure should be *single bug optimal* as defined in Section 2.1, because of deeper reasoning pertaining to Occam's razor. That is, we think the simplest hypothesis for explaining the error should be investigated first, and as the simplest hypothesis is that the program contains a single bug, the measure should be single bug optimal.

Secondly, although we state that the measure should be single bug optimal, we diverge from Naish [21] insofar as we do not make the *single fault assumption* – that the program contains only a single bug. This is because there exist programs with multiple bugs and our goal is to construct a measure that provides a complete solution to the problem of SFL. Consequently, it still remains to work out how to rank the suspiciousness of entities when no bug is covered by all bad traces. In this case, the suspiciousness of each program entity is determined by an existing measure g which is chosen on its ability to deal with multiple bugs and by success in experimentation. We account for this in the second condition of our measure below. For a measure g, we define our *measure optimising scheme* Lex_g as follows. Let x be the vector $\langle a_{ef}, a_{ep}, a_{nf}, a_{np} \rangle$. Then,

$$Lex_g(x) = \begin{cases} a_{np} + 2 & \text{if } a_{ef} = F \\ g(x) & \text{otherwise.} \end{cases} \qquad (1)$$

In Equation 1, g stands for an internal measure, and can represent any measure appropriately scaled from 0 to 1. The intuition behind our optimising scheme is that g should rank each program entity in terms of suspiciousness as it usually does, except in the case where that entity is covered by every failing trace, in which case it should be investigated by the user as a matter of top priority. Based on its performance in our experiments, we choose Ochiai as the internal measure g, hence called Lex_{Ochiai}.

The following theorem states the optimality of our scheme (see the full paper for the proof).

Theorem 1. *Lex_g is single bug optimal.*

Lex_g can be considered as an optimising scheme which "converts" an appropriately scaled measure g into a single-bug optimal measure. The name of our scheme is derived from its underlying idea — to lexically order two different classes of entities in terms of suspiciousness.

4 Experiments

In this section we describe the results of empirical evaluation of the measures. First we describe the experimental setup; then, we discuss our two means of assessment – an average scoring method and a Wilcoxon rank sum significance test. We conclude the section with the presentation and the analysis of the results.

Table 3. Table of benchmarks

Program	Vs	LOC	TC	FTC	PE	FPV	Program	Vs	LOC	TC	FTC	PE	FPV
tcas	41	173	1608	38	53	1.61	replace	32	563	5542	96	218	1.79
schedule	9	410	2650	80	146	1.45	gzip	3	7996	214	126	1223	3.33
schedule2	10	307	2710	27	126	1.10	space	38	9126	13585	1439	976	5.21
tot_info	23	406	1052	83	116	1.04	sed	2	11990	360	210	2378	5.50
print_tks	7	563	4130	69	179	1.14	grep	3	13229	750	304	1785	17.33
print_tk2	10	508	4115	206	196	1.00	flex	2	14230	567	71	3092	29.50

4.1 Experimental Setup

The benchmarks are listed in Table 3. For each program, the table specifies the number of faulty versions (Vs), the number of lines of code in the original version of the program (LOC), the number of test cases (TC), the average number of failing test cases per version (FTC), the number of program entities of the original version of the program (PE), and the average number of faulty lines of code per version (FPV)[4].

The benchmarks are obtained from the Software Information Repository [7]. The versions of sed, grep, flex, and gzip used are the same as ones used in Lo [18], the versions of the Siemens and space test suites are the same as the ones used in Naish [21]. The Siemens test suite consists of tcas, schedule, schedule2, totinfo, print tokens, print tokens2 and replace. Overall, the experimental setup consists of 180 program versions, with over a million lines of code in total, and an average of 2.88 buggy lines per version.

The Siemens test suite is a widely used set of benchmarks in the domain of SFL [1, 2, 17, 25, 26, 30]. Space was additionally included by Naish [21]. The second set of benchmarks, consisting of versions of *gzip*, *grep*, *flex* and *sed*, has been used to assess SFL in [18]. In this paper, we demonstrate experimental

---

[4] Note that some program versions contain no faults. This happens when the fault appears in a non-executable line of code, such as a macro definition. These versions are removed from the experiment following [21].

results on the union of the sets of benchmarks used in these papers, making our evaluation, to the best of our knowledge, the largest set of C programs used to evaluate measures for SFL. Moreover, the set of measures in our evaluation is, to the best of our knowledge, the largest set of measures ever compared over any set of benchmarks in SFL.

Each test case was executed for each of the faulty programs and the result (pass or fail) recorded together with the set of the lines of code that were executed during this test (this data was extracted using GCOV). The pass or fail result was decided based on the output of the program and its comparison with the original program on the same input. Crashes were recorded as failures. The collected coverage data was used as an input to the measures, which assigned a suspiciousness score to each program entity (statements) in the (mutant) program and sorted the lines of code in the descending order of suspiciousness. To assign a score, we added a small *prior constant* (0.5) to each cell of each program entity's contingency table in order to avoid divisions by zero, as is convention [21].

We experimented over a range of different prior constants (PC) in between 0 to 1, and did not discover any significant or noteworthy differences in results. The exception was for the PatternSimilarity measure (for which we used the ranking equivalent measure $-a_{nf}a_{ep}$ in our implementation). We discovered that this measure was optimised if we set the PC to $a_{nf} = 0.1$ and $a_{ep} = 0.5$. The optimised version of PatternSimilarity is henceforth called PattSim2, and the unoptimised PattSim1.

4.2   Methods of Assessment

We use two means of assessment: an average scoring method and a Wilcoxon rank-sum significance test. We discuss the details here.

To score how well a measure performs on a benchmark, we introduce the *best, worst* and *average* scoring methods [1, 21, 30]. Formally, where m is a measure, n is the number of program entities in the program, b is a bug with the highest degree of suspiciousness of any bug and *bugs* is the number of faulty lines in the program, we define $best(m) = (|\{x|m(x) > m(b)\}|/n) \times 100$ and $worst(m) = (|\{x|m(x) > m(b)\}|/n) \times 100$ and $avg(m) = best(m) + ((worst(m) - best(m))/(bugs + 1))$. For our evaluation we use the *avg* scoring method [21], which gives us the percentage of non-buggy program entities which we'd expect an engineer to examine before locating a bug, given the number of faulty lines in the program. To get the *avg* score for a benchmark, we take the mean *avg* of the scores of all the versions in that benchmark. To get the overall *avg* score, we take the mean of the 12 benchmark scores.

We performed a second means of assessment using Wilcoxon rank-sum tests. The Wilcoxon rank-sum test is a non-parametric statistical test which tests whether one population of values is significantly larger than another population [28]. Using this test, we were able to establish which measures were significantly better than others, by comparing each measure's 12 average scores for each benchmark.[5] To establish a baseline for localisation efficiency, we included a measure (Rand) which assigns each program entity a random suspiciousness score.

4.3 Results

We now present our experimental data and quantify their significance. We first discuss Table 4. The average scores for those suspiciousness measures with a higher score than the random measure are listed in Table 4. Equivalent measures are represented by one measure per equivalence class (with preference given to measures already established in SFL), and the new measures are in bold. Note that (thirteen) additional potential sets of equivalences are suggested by the equal scores in the table.

Table 4. Overall *avg* scores for measures

Name	Score	Name	Score	Name	Score	Name	Score
Lex$_{Ochiai}$	13.74	Ample2	16.48	**Keynes**	18.22	InfoGain	19.93
PattSim2	13.88	**Dennis**	16.66	**Good2**	18.22	JMeasure	19.95
Zoltar	13.92	**Popper1**	16.87	**Finch1**	18.22	Ochiai2	20.40
Naish	14.01	**Korb3**	16.93	**Forbes1**	18.22	**SokSneath5**	20.40
PattSim1	14.21	2WaySupport	16.93	Tarantula	18.22	MI	20.53
WongIII	14.23	YulesQ	17.11	Interest	18.22	**Peirce**	22.37
Kulc2	14.41	**NPV**	17.15	AddedValue	18.22	Leverage	23.20
M2	14.52	**Rescher**	17.15	SebagSch	18.22	BinaryNaish	23.34
Ochiai	15.25	**Lewis**	17.16	OddMultiplier	18.22	WongI	23.43
Conviction	15.65	AMean	17.17	Example	18.22	Confidence	23.43
Certainty	15.65	Stiles	17.27	Zhang	18.22	Fleiss	23.61
Crupi	15.88	GMean	17.27	**Korb2**	18.24	Scott	23.86
Michael	16.00	Phi	17.27	1WaySupport	18.24	Faith	24.49
Klosgen	16.31	Jaccard	17.40	Laplace	18.42	LeastCont.	25.83
Mountford	16.41	CBISqrt	17.68	**Suppes**	18.62	WongII	25.85
YoudensJ	16.48	**Popper2**	17.74	**Pearson1**	18.62	Gower	26.41
Earman	16.48	Cohen	17.98	SokSneath4	18.65	GoodKrus	26.64
Carnap1	16.48	Kappa	17.98	HMean	18.65	**Specificity**	27.20
Carnap2	16.48	CBIlog	18.11	**Good**	19.26	Anderberg2	27.25
Levi	16.48	**Likelyhood**	18.22	**PearlII**	19.26	**FagerMc**	29.10
Dispersion	16.48	GilbertW	18.22	**Cheng**	19.26	Rand	31.74

We first make some general observations about the table. Some prominent established measures appear quite low on the list, such as Jaccard and Tarantula. It is interesting that Tarantula (which is equal to $P(E|C)$), performs worse than NPV (which is equal to $P(\neg E|\neg C)$). Also, some established measures appear quite high on the list, such as Zoltar and Naish. Thus, our larger-scale

---

[5] Following a convention on small sample sizes, we applied continuity correction by adjusting the Wilcoxon rank statistic by 0.5 towards the mean value when computing the z-statistic.

comparison accentuates the successes and failures of established measures. The top-performing measures from each of our newly introduced categories of similarity, confirmation, predictive, causal and custom measures are PattSim2, Crupi, NPV, Lewis and Lex_{Ochiai}, respectively. As we can see, many new measures are competitive with established ones. Finally, Rand's average score was consistently between 30–38% on reruns, which is what one might expect given an average of 2.88 bugs per program version.

We now discuss PattSim2. We saw that PattSim2 has an elegant monotonic reduction to $-a_{nf}a_{ep}$, and performs particularly well despite its relative simplicity, coming in the second place. Note that the difference between the results for PattSim2 and PattSim1 was a consequence of changing the prior constant (PC) (the details of which are discussed in the experimental setup section) in order to try and optimise the PatternSimilarity measure. We experimented in this way with this measure, because we noticed (as a theoretical observation) that by lowering the prior constant for a_{nf} it became a measure that converged to being single bug optimal. PattSim2 is a statistically significant improvement over PattSim1 using $p = 0.02$. We emphasise that we did not observe that changing the PC for our other top measures resulted in improvements in terms of their relative position in Table 4. We believe this is because the simplified ranking equivalent version of PatternSimilarity $= -a_{nf}a_{ep}$ used in our experiments is an extremely simple measure, and is consequently altered significantly by small adjustments (such as PC), where other measures are not.

We now discuss Lex_{Ochiai}. This is our new optimising scheme Lex_g with Ochiai as the internal measure g, and it is the top performer. Most of the measures can be used as a submeasure g for Lex_g and achieve a better score than all other measures below Lex_{Ochiai} in the table. To this end, Lex_{Stiles}, Lex_{M2}, and $Lex_{Wong-III}$ are the runners up. Thus, Lex_g can be viewed as a good measure optimiser on our benchmarks. Lex_{Ochiai} achieved the best score for three of the twelve benchmarks (Tcas, Totinfo, Schedule2, Replace, Gzip, Flex, Grep), the second best score for two (PrintTokens, PrintTokens2) and performed less well (towards the bottom end) in the remaining three, but never went below a score of 18.77 for such benchmarks (meaning it still has a good score in cases where other measures are ranked higher). Lex_{Ochiai} still maintains the top overall average score if the test is run on the small programs alone (i.e. the Siemens test suite, with a score of 17.83) and comes a close third with a score of 8.02 on the larger programs alone (after PattSim2 and Zoltar which score 7.53 and 7.76, respectively). If the worst score is used instead of the average, Lex_{Ochiai} still has the top overall score (22.32). Overall, these results support the claim that Lex_{Ochiai} is a robust and top-performing suspiciousness measure.

We now discuss our significance tests. Firstly, Rand was significantly better than Loevinger, TwoWaySupportVariation, CollectiveStrength, and GiniIndex, using $p = 0.05$. We believe this is sufficient to conclude that these measures are ineffective in SFL. Lex_{Ochiai} was significantly better than all measures using $p = 0.29$. Using $p = 0.05$, it was significantly better than everything that scored below and including Peirce in the fourth column of Table 4, and was additionally significantly better than Good, PearlII, Cheng and Infogain. Thirdly, PattSim2 was significantly better than everything below and including Leverage in the fourth column (apart from Fleiss and Scott), and was additionally better than MI, Jmeasure, Infogain, Cheng, PearlII, Good, Hmean, SokSneath4, Pearson1, Suppes, Mountford and PattSim1. In general, PattSim2 was significantly better than all the measures below it on Table 4 using $p = 0.21$ (apart from Zoltar $p = 0.92$).

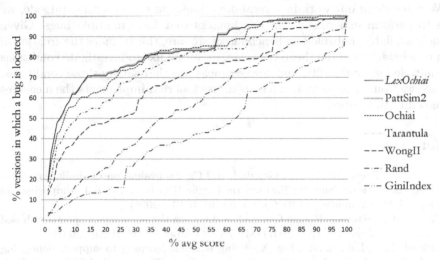

Fig. 2. Graphical comparison of prominent measures

Finally, we discuss Fig. 2, which compares the performance of some prominent measures graphically. For each measure, a line is plotted as a function of the avg scores for each of the 180 program versions. If $y\%$ of those versions have an average score $\leq x\%$, a point is plotted on the graph at (x, y). For example, for the Rand measure, 50% of the versions have an average score lower than 58%. Lex_{Ochiai} and PattSim2 have an almost aligned performance.

5   Conclusions and Future Work

We presented what is, to the best of our knowledge, the largest comparative analysis of suspiciousness measures on C programs for SFL to date, comparing 157 different measures on 12 C programs, constituting over a million lines of examined code. Out of these measures 95 are new to the domain of SFL. We taxonomised these measures into five different classes: similarity, association, causation, confirmation and custom measures. We demonstrated that each class is applicable to SFL, and that many measures are in fact equivalent in terms of ranking, thus reducing the space of measures for experimental consideration.

We defined a new custom measure optimiser Lex_g, which can admit any other measure g as its inner measure. Our experimental results demonstrate that our new measures Lex_{Ochiai} and PattSim2 achieve the best average scores over other measures and are significantly better than many of them with $p = 0.05$.

We conjecture that the top performance of Lex_{Ochiai} is owed to a strong a priori component (single bug optimality), together with an experimentally vindicated a posteriori component (using the Ochiai measure as a submeasure). Our second best performer, PattSim2, is ranking equivalent to $-a_{nf}a_{ep}$, demonstrating the success of an extremely simple measure.

We will extend our work in several directions. On the experimental side, we plan to perform experiments on benchmarks that have multiple bugs. Given publicly available multiple-bug benchmarks are rare, this includes the creation of such benchmarks. On the theoretical side, we would like to investigate conditions for multiple-bug optimality, and develop measures that satisfy those conditions. Finally, we would like to create an easy-to-use tool that implements the measures discussed in this paper.

References

1. Abreu, R., Zoeteweij, P., van Gemund, A.J.C.: An evaluation of similarity coefficients for software fault localization. In: Pacific Rim International Symposium on Dependable Computing (PRDC), pp. 39–46. IEEE (2006)
2. Abreu, R., Zoeteweij, P., van Gemund, A.J.C.: On the accuracy of spectrum-based fault localization. In: TAICPART-MUTATION, pp. 89–98. IEEE (2007)
3. Briand, L.C., Labiche, Y., Liu, X.: Using machine learning to support debugging with Tarantula. In: International Symposium on Software Reliability (ISSRE), pp. 137–146. IEEE (2007)
4. Carnap, R.: Logical Foundations of Probability. University of Chicago Press (1962)
5. Choi, S.S., Cha, S.H., Tappert, C.: A Survey of Binary Similarity and Distance Measures. Journal on Systemics, Cybernetics and Informatics 8, 43–48 (2010)
6. Collofello, Woodfield: Evaluating the effectiveness of reliability-assurance techniques. Journal of Systems and Software, 745–770 (1989)
7. Do, H., Elbaum, S., Rothermel, G.: Supporting controlled experimentation with testing techniques: An infrastructure and its potential impact. Empirical Softw. Eng, 405–435 (2005)
8. Eells, E., Fitelson, B.: Symmetries and asymmetries in evidential support. Philosophical Studies 107, 129–142 (2002)
9. Everitt, B.: The Cambridge Dictionary of Statistics. CUP (2002)
10. Fitelson, B., Hitchcock, C.: Probabilistic measures of causal strength. In: Illari, P.M., Russo, F., Williamson, J. (eds.) Causality in the Sciences. Oxford University Press, Oxford (2011)
11. Fletcher, R., Suzanne, W.: Clinical epidemiology: the essentials. Lippincott Williams and Wilkins (2005)
12. Groce, A.: Error explanation with distance metrics. In: Jensen, K., Podelski, A. (eds.) TACAS 2004. LNCS, vol. 2988, pp. 108–122. Springer, Heidelberg (2004)
13. Huber, F.: Confirmation and induction, http://www.iep.utm.edu/conf-ind/
14. Jones, J.A., Harrold, M.J.: Empirical evaluation of the Tarantula automatic fault-localization technique. In: ASE, pp. 273–282. ACM (2005)

15. Liblit, B., Naik, M., Zheng, A.X., Aiken, A., Jordan, M.I.: Scalable statistical bug isolation. In: SIGPLAN Not., pp. 15–26 (2005)
16. Liu, C., Fei, L., Yan, X., Han, J., Midkiff, S.P.: Statistical debugging: A hypothesis testing-based approach. IEEE Trans. Softw. Eng. 32(10), 831–848 (2006)
17. Liu, C., Yan, X., Fei, L., Han, J., Midkiff, S.P.: SOBER: Statistical model-based bug localization. SIGSOFT Softw. Eng. Notes, 286–295 (2005)
18. Lucia, Lo, D., Jiang, L., Budi, A.: Comprehensive evaluation of association measures for fault localization. In: International Conference on Software Maintenance (ICSM), pp. 1–10. IEEE (2010)
19. Lucia, Lo, D., Jiang, L., Thung, F., Budi, A.: Extended comprehensive study of association measures for fault localization. Journal of Software: Evolution and Process 26(2), 172–219 (2014)
20. Naish, L., Lee, H.J.: Duals in spectral fault localization. In: Australian Conference on Software Engineering (ASWEC), pp. 51–59. IEEE (2013)
21. Naish, L., Lee, H.J., Ramamohanarao, K.: A model for spectra-based software diagnosis. ACM Trans. Softw. Eng. Methodol, 1–11 (2011)
22. Parnin, C., Orso, A.: Are automated debugging techniques actually helping programmers? In: International Symposium on Software Testing and Analysis (ISTA), pp. 199–209. ACM (2011)
23. Pearl, J.: Probabilities of causation: three counterfactual interpretations and their identification. Synthese 1-2(121), 93–149 (1999)
24. Pearson, K.: On the theory of contingency and its relation to association and normal correlation (1904)
25. Pytlik, B., Renieris, M., Krishnamurthi, S., Reiss, S.: Automated fault localization using potential invariants. Arxiv preprint cs.SE/0310040 (2003)
26. Renieris, M., Reiss, S.P.: Fault localization with nearest neighbor queries. In: ASE, pp. 30–39 (2003)
27. Tan, P.-N., Kumar, V., Srivastava, J.: Selecting the right interestingness measure for association patterns. In: Knowledge Discovery and Data Mining (KDD), pp. 32–41. ACM (2002)
28. Wilcoxon, F.: Individual comparisons by ranking methods. Biometrics Bulletin 1(6), 80–83 (1945)
29. Wong, W.E., Qi, Y.: Effective program debugging based on execution slices and inter-block data dependency. Journal of Systems and Software 79(7), 891–903 (2006)
30. Wong, W.E., Qi, Y., Zhao, L., Cai, K.-Y.: Effective fault localization using code coverage. In: Computer Software and Applications Conference (COMPSAC), pp. 449–456. IEEE (2007)
31. Xie, X., Chen, T.Y., Kuo, F.-C., Xu, B.: A theoretical analysis of the risk evaluation formulas for spectrum-based fault localization. ACM Trans. Softw. Eng. Methodol., 31:1–31:40 (2013)
32. Yoo, S., Harman, M., Clark, D.: Fault localization prioritization: Comparing information-theoretic and coverage-based approaches. ACM Trans. Softw. Eng. Methodol. 22(3), 19 (2013)
33. Zhang, Z., Chan, W.K., Tse, T.H., Jiang, B., Wang, X.: Capturing propagation of infected program states. In: ESEC/FSE, pp. 43–52. ACM (2009)

Modeling

A Generalized Formal Framework
for Partial Modeling

Rick Salay and Marsha Chechik

University of Toronto, Canada
{rsalay,chechik}@cs.toronto.edu

Abstract. Uncertainty is pervasive within software engineering, nega-
tively affecting software quality as well as development time. In previous
work, we have developed a language-independent partial modeling technique called *MAVO* that allows a software modeler to explicitly express
and reason about model uncertainty. The cost of such a broadly applicable technique was to focus exclusively on the syntactic aspects of models.
In addition, we have found that while *MAVO* expresses uncertainty at
the model level, it is often more natural to do so for the entire submodels.

In this paper, we introduce a new language-independent formal framework for partial modeling called *GMAVO* that generalizes *MAVO* by
providing the means for addressing model semantics and allowing uncertainty to be specified at the granularity of a submodel. We then show
that *GMAVO* is sufficiently general to express Modal Transition Systems
(MTSs) – an established "semantics-aware" partial behavioral modeling
formalism.

1 Introduction

Uncertainty is pervasive in software modeling. It can be introduced in various
ways including inconsistencies [2], competing design alternatives [21], problem-
domain uncertainties [22], conflicting stakeholder opinions [16], etc.

Partial behavioral modeling [9,6] has been extensively investigated. For example, Modal Transition Systems [9] extend Labelled Transition Systems (LTSs)
by allowing the designer to annotate some transitions to indicate that they are
possible but not required to be present in the resulting system. In our previous work [18], we presented a partial modeling technique called *MAVO* that
generalizes this approach in two ways. First, it expands the types of partiality
annotations to express richer kinds of uncertainty, and second, it allows these
annotations to be used with an *arbitrary* modeling language whose syntax is
defined using metamodels.

For example, the top model P1 in Fig. 1 is a UML class diagram that uses
MAVO annotations. The "maybe" annotation M is used with Hovercraft to
express that the modeler is uncertain whether or not to include it and which class
should be its superclass. The uncertainty about which class attribute numOfDoors
belongs in is expressed by putting it in a "variable" class C1 marked with the
annotation V. The "set" annotation S is used to represent uncertainty about how
many securityRelated attributes there will be. Annotations S and V are used

© Springer-Verlag Berlin Heidelberg 2015
A. Egyed and I. Schaefer (Eds.): FASE 2015, LNCS 9033, pp. 133–148, 2015.
DOI: 10.1007/978-3-662-46675-9_9

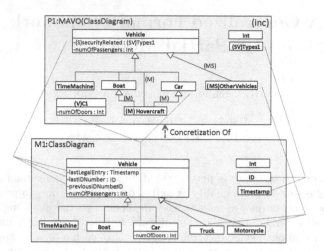

Fig. 1. An example *MAVO* model, a concretization of it and the refinement relation connecting them. To avoid visual clutter, only non-identity mappings are shown.

with `Types1` to represent a set of classes that can include new or existing classes. Annotations M and S are used with `OtherVehicles` and `super(OtherVehicles, Vehicle)` to indicate that the modeler thinks that there may be other, not yet known, vehicle classes. Finally, the "incomplete" annotation INC is used for all of `P1` (top right)to indicate uncertainty about whether more elements may still need to be added to the model.

We have investigated many aspects of *MAVO* including refinement [17], reasoning [18], change propagation [19] and pragmatic issues with its usage [5]. While *MAVO* is broadly applicable, it has some limitations that have led us to seek a more general treatment of partial modeling. First of all, to achieve language-independence, we had to focus purely on language syntax and ignore semantics. Thus, formalisms like MTSs which do take semantics into account (MTSs encode sets of possible and required traces that the system can take and allow reasoning over such traces) cannot be expressed by *MAVO*. The second, more pragmatic, limitation is that *MAVO* allows expression of uncertainty on the level of individual model elements, whereas our experience indicates that it is often expressed more naturally on the submodel level. For example, if we are uncertain about a design alternative, then this typically includes many model elements. Finally, often more precise expressions of uncertainty than *MAVO* can express are required, and it has not been clear how to incorporate such richer constraints. For example, in `P1` of Fig. 1, we may want to say that `Hovercraft` must be a subclass of exactly one of the three classes indicated but *MAVO* does not allow this type of detail – the M annotations allow it to be a subclass of multiple classes.

The investigation of these limitations motivated a search for a more general partial modeling framework; however, rather than attempting to generalize *MAVO* directly, we have developed an entirely new framework from "first principles", using Category Theory, calling it Generalized *MAVO*, or *GMAVO*.

∀x:Property ∃c:Class·ownedAttribute(c,x)
∀x:Property·(∃c:Class·type(x,c))⇔¬(∃d:Datatype·type(x,d))
∀x:Property ∃c1, c2:Class·type(x,c1)∧type(x,c2)⇒c1=c2
∀x:Property ∃d1, d2:Datatype·type(x,d1)∧type(x,d2)⇒d1=d2
∀x:Property, c1,c2:Class·ownedAttribute(c1,x)∧ownedAttribute(c2,x)⇒c1=c2

Fig. 2. An adapted and simplified metamodel of the UML class diagram language shown as a type graph and a set of well-formedness constraints in first order logic

Category theory has been shown to be useful for expressing general formal patterns, particularly having to do with modeling, e.g., graph grammars and transformation systems [3], model merging [15] and model synchronization [1]. Our objective in this paper is to provide similar foundations for partial modeling.

In this paper, we describe *GMAVO* and show that it is a generalization of *MAVO* and is sufficiently general to encode semantics-aware partial behavioral modeling formalisms such as MTSs. Specifically, the paper makes the following contributions: (a) We define the general *GMAVO* framework for partial modeling that addresses both syntactic and semantic partiality and that can be used with any modeling language satisfying certain properties; (b) We show that the MTS formalism can be derived within *GMAVO* and can be soundly generalized to express richer kinds of partiality for LTSs; (c) We show that *MAVO* and a related partial modeling language called *May* models, can be derived within *GMAVO* and that these can be extended to address the expressive limitations discussed above. Note that this paper focuses on the theoretical aspects of *GMAVO* and we leave pragmatic issues such as usability for future work.

The rest of this paper is organized as follows: In Sec. 2, we give the required background about *MAVO*. In Sec. 3, we introduce *GMAVO* without Category Theory for the simple case when a model consists of a set of untyped elements. In Sec. 4 we give the more general case of *GMAVO* using Category Theory. In Sec. 5, we apply *GMAVO* to derive and generalize the *MAVO*, *May* model and MTS formalisms. In Sec. 6, we discuss related work and finally, in Sec. 7, we give conclusions and suggest future work.

2   Background

In this section, we briefly review the concepts of *MAVO* and its current formalization introduced in [18].

Models and Metamodels. In this paper, a model is a typed graph [3] – a graph with a graph homomorphism to a type graph that defines the types of the nodes and edges. The term *atom* denotes either a node or edge of a graph. A type graph with a set of well-formedness constraints is called a *metamodel*. The metamodel of the class diagrams in Fig. 1 is given in Fig. 2. (Note that the class diagrams in Fig. 1 are expressed using their concrete syntax rather than their abstract syntax as a typed graph.)

Partial Models. A model with partiality information is called a *partial* model. Partiality information often takes the form of model annotations. Semantically, a partial model represents the set of different possible *concrete* (i.e., non-partial) models that would resolve the uncertainty represented by the partiality:

Definition 1 (Partial Model). *A partial model P over a metamodel T consists of a* base model, *denoted bs(P), and a set of annotations.* [P] *denotes the set of models conforming to T, called the* concretizations *of P. A partial model is refined by reducing its set of concretizations.*

The base model is the underlying model in which the annotations are stripped away. As uncertainty is incrementally resolved, the partial model is refined, reducing the set of concretizations until only one concretization remains. Note that we can treat a concretization as the equivalent *ground* partial model – i.e., one that has exactly one concretization, itself. Model M1 in Fig. 1 is a concretization of *MAVO* partial model P1 and the lines connecting them define the relation showing how M1 refines P1.

MAVO **Partial Models.** The *MAVO* partial modeling language uses four types of partiality annotations, each adding support for a different type of uncertainty in a model, summarized in Table 1(a):

May partiality allows a modeler to express uncertainty about the presence of a particular atom in a model by annotating it with either M, to indicate that it "may exist" or E, to indicate that it "exists". A *May* annotation is refined by changing an M to E or removing the atom altogether. For example, in Fig. 1, M-annotated class Hovercraft is refined by removing it. The ground annotation E is the default if an annotation is omitted.

Abs partiality allows a modeler to express uncertainty about the number of atoms in the model by letting her annotate atoms as P, representing a "particular", or S, representing a "set". A refinement of an *Abs* annotation elaborates the content of S atoms by replacing them with a set of S and P atoms. For example, in Fig. 1, the S-annotated class OtherVehicles is refined by splitting it into classes Truck and Motorcycle. The ground annotation P is the default if an annotation is omitted.

Var partiality allows a modeler to express uncertainty about distinctness of individual atoms in the model by annotating an atom to indicate whether it is a "constant" (C) or a "variable" (V). A refinement of a *Var* annotation involves reducing the set of variables by merging them with constants or other variables. For example, in Fig. 1, the V-annotated class C1 is refined by merging it with class Car. The ground annotation C is the default if an annotation is omitted.

OW partiality allows a modeler to explicitly state whether her model is incomplete (i.e., can be extended) (INC) or complete (COMP). In contrast to the other types of partiality, here the annotation is at the level of the entire model. An INC-annotated model is refined by adding zero or more atoms and to optionally change the annotation to COMP. For example, in Fig. 1, model INC-annotated model P1 is refined by making it complete. The ground annotation COMP is the default if an annotation is omitted.

MAVO **Semantics.** For a given *MAVO* model, the semantics defines the set of concretizations it represents. In [18], we defined it formally by translating a *MAVO* model to an equivalent first-order theory whose set of models, in the model-theoretic sense, defines the set of concretizations of the *MAVO* model.

Table 1. (a) Summary of *MAVO* annotations. *May*, *Abs* and *Var* annotations apply to each atom while *OW* annotations apply to the entire model. (b) Summary of constraints used to define *MAVO* semantics.

	Partiality Type	Target	Non-ground annotation	Ground annotation (default)
(a)	*May*	atom	M (may exist)	E (exists)
	Abs	atom	S (set)	P (particular)
	Var	atom	V (variable)	C (constant)
	OW	model	INC (incomplete)	COMP (complete)

	Partiality Type	*MAVO* constraint
(b)	*May*	$(\text{E})a \Rightarrow \exists x \in M \cdot \langle a, x \rangle \in R$
	Abs	$(\text{P})a \Rightarrow \forall x, x' \in M \cdot \langle a, x \rangle \in R \land \langle a, x' \rangle \in R \Rightarrow x = x'$
	Var	$(\text{C})a \Rightarrow \forall x \in M \cdot \langle a, x \rangle \in R \Rightarrow \neg \exists a' \in P \cdot a' \neq a \land (\text{C})a' \land \langle a', x \rangle \in R$
	OW	$(Comp)P \Rightarrow \forall x \in M, \exists a \in P \cdot \langle a, x \rangle \in R$

We summarize the essence of this formalization in Table 1(b) in terms of a relation R mapping a *MAVO* model P to one of its concretizations M such as is illustrated in Fig. 1. Each atom that has an E, P or C annotation adds a constraint on the concretization. If an atom has multiple annotations, it adds all the corresponding constraints. In addition, if the COMP annotation for P is present, then this also adds a constraint. The E annotation on an atom a in P adds the constraint that there must exist *at least one* atom in M mapping to a. The P annotation adds the constraint that there must be *at most one* atom in M mapping to a. The C annotation on an atom a adds the constraint that any atom of M mapping to a must not also map to another atom of P annotated with C. Finally, the COMP annotation on P adds the constraint that every atom of M must map to some atom of P.

The concretizations of P are all models M that simultaneously satisfy all of the constraints added by the annotations. For example, model M1 in Fig. 1 satisfies the constraints added by the *MAVO* class diagram P1 and thus is a concretization of P1.

3   A Formal Partial Modeling Framework for Sets

Our objective with partial modeling can be expressed as follows: given a model type T, use a T-model plus additional information (e.g., annotations), to represent a set of T-models (i.e., its set of concretizations). In this section, we consider the simplest model type – a set of untyped elements, and develop a rich partial modeling language over it. In Sec. 4, we use Category Theory to generalize this language to arbitrary model types.

To consider a set M as a partial model, we require a way to interpret M as a "set of sets". A general way to do this is to take M to represent the set of sets that are on the other end of every possible relation with M. Fig. 3 shows an example of a relation R between M and a concretization K. The figure also

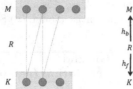

Fig. 3. A concretization K of M related by R and the equivalent expression as a span of two functions

shows an alternate way to represent R as a *span* of two functions (h_b and h_f), which is the representation used in this paper.

By itself, this kind of partial model is not very interesting – each M can only be used to represent one set of sets. We thus give a more general form:

Definition 2. *Given a set M, let $sp(M)$ denote the set of spans with M on one end. A partial model P is a pair $\langle M, \Phi \rangle$, where the set M is its base model and Φ is a constraint that is satisfied by a subset of $sp(M)$.*

The possible sets of concretizations of P representable by this definition depends on the expressiveness of the language over which Φ is defined.

First note that the span in Fig. 3 consists of the two functions h_b and h_f. Injectivity and surjectivity are two fundamental properties a function can have, and we can define a language for Φ in terms of these constraints on h_b and h_f; however, such a language admits only 16 possible constraints.

To get a more fine-grained control over expressing uncertainty, we use another generic idea, that of a "subset". Fig. 4 shows how a subset can be used with injectivity and surjectivity to define more constraints for Φ. S is a subset of set M where α is the injective function giving the embedding of S into M (shown by the red rectangle). The subset S *induces* a corresponding span $\langle g_b, g_f \rangle$:

- Set R_S is the subset of R that is mapped by h_b to the (the embedding of) S. Injective function α_S gives the embedding of R_S into R (shown by the red rectangle).
- Function g_b is h_b restricted to R_S.
- Function g_f is defined as $h_f \circ \alpha_S$, where $\circ$ is function composition.

We can use this setup to express more fine-grained partiality on spans $\langle h_b, h_f \rangle$ by applying injectivity/surjectivity constraints to g_b and g_f instead of directly to h_b and h_f. This is the core strategy of *GMAVO*.

Connection to *MAVO*. A remarkable thing is that the four possible applications of injectivity/surjectivity constraints to g_b and g_f *behave the same way as the four types of partiality in MAVO* discussed in Sec. 2. Specifically, (1) constraining g_b *to be surjective* forces the span $\langle h_b, h_f \rangle$ to map every element of S in M to at least one element in K. Thus, it is equivalent to the *May* partiality where each element of S within M is annotated with E, and it is annotated with M everywhere else in M. (2) Constraining g_b *to be injective* forces the span $\langle h_b, h_f \rangle$ to map every element of S in M to at most one element in K. Thus, it is

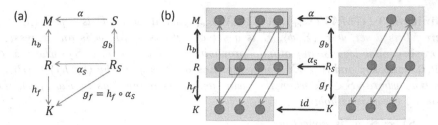

Fig. 4. Using injectivity and surjectivity constraints with subsets: (a) a commutative diagram describing the general case; (b) an illustration

equivalent to the *Abs* partiality where each element of S within M is annotated with P, and it is annotated with S everywhere else in M. (3) Constraining g_f to be *injective* forces the span $\langle h_b, h_f \rangle$ to map every element of K to at most one element in S. Thus, it is equivalent to the *Var* partiality where each element of S within M is annotated with C, and it is annotated with V everywhere else in M. (4) Constraining g_f to be *surjective* forces the span $\langle h_b, h_f \rangle$ to map every element of K to at least one element in S. Thus, it is equivalent to the *OW* partiality when $S = M$, and M is annotated with COMP.

This final case seems to suggest why *OW* partiality is not applied at the element level like the other *MAVO* annotations but it also shows how to generalize it to apply at the element level. This constraint implies that all elements in a concretization must map to some element of S - i.e., that S is complete. While this captures the idea of complete/incomplete scope when applied to the entire set M (i.e., when $S = M$), the meaning is less clear when applied to some $S \subset M$. Thus we conclude, at least temporarily, that *OW* partiality only "makes sense" at whole model level. We revisit this conclusion and discuss related future work in Sec. 7.

Additional Generalizations. The discussion above justifies our description of *GMAVO* as "generalized *MAVO*". However, two additional generalizations are also possible. First, we note that Fig. 4(a) suggests two more general constraints: $R_S = \emptyset$ forces the span $\langle h_b, h_f \rangle$ to map *no elements of S in M* to an element of K, while $R_S = R$ forces the span $\langle h_b, h_f \rangle$ to map *no elements outside of S in M* to an element of K. Thus, these are both ways of forcing some elements of M to always be absent in a concretization. Clearly, asserting $R_S = R$ for subset S is equivalent to asserting that $R_S = \emptyset$ for subset $M \setminus S$; thus, we only need one of these two constraints. (As we will see in Sec. 5, these are not necessarily equivalent when we generalize beyond sets and the constraint $R_S = R$ is the more expressive one to use.)

Another evident generalization over *MAVO* is to consider multiple different constrained subsets of M simultaneously. That is, we can identify subsets $S_1, \ldots, S_n$, compute the span $\langle g_b, g_f \rangle$ for each, and constrain it using a combination of the five constraints discussed above. As a final generalization, we allow boolean expressions of these constraints to be specified.

The resulting Generalized *MAVO* partial modeling language over sets, which we call $GMAVO_{Set}$, incorporates all of these features.

Definition 3 (*GMAVO$_{Set}$*). *A* GMAVO$_{Set}$ *partial model P is a pair $\langle M, \Phi \rangle$, where M is a set, $\Phi = \langle \Sigma, \phi \rangle$, Σ is a set of subsets of M, ϕ is an expression in propositional logic using atomic propositions of the form $x(S)$, where $x \in \{\texttt{E}, \texttt{P}, \texttt{C}, \texttt{Comp}, \texttt{A}\}$, and $S \in \Sigma$. The semantics of P is given by $\langle h_b, h_f \rangle \in [P]$ iff ϕ is true where $\forall S \in \Sigma$, when the span $\langle g_b, g_f \rangle$ is induced as in Fig. 4(a), the following conditions hold:*

$\texttt{E}(S) \iff g_b$ *is surjective;*
$\texttt{P}(S) \iff g_b$ *is injective;*
$\texttt{C}(S) \iff g_f$ *is injective;*
$\texttt{Comp}(S) \iff g_f$ *is surjective;*
$\texttt{A}(S) \iff R_S = R.$

As an illustration, the example span in Fig. 4(b) satisfies the constraints $\texttt{E(S)}$, $\texttt{C(S)}$ and $\texttt{Comp(S)}$ because g_b is surjective and g_f is both injective and surjective. Thus, it would be a concretization of $\langle \texttt{M}, \langle \{\texttt{S}\}, \texttt{C(S)} \vee \texttt{P(S)} \rangle \rangle$ but not a concretization of $\langle \texttt{M}, \langle \{\texttt{S}\}, \texttt{E(S)} \wedge \texttt{P(S)} \rangle \rangle$.

4   The Generalized Framework

In this section, we generalize *GMAVO$_{Set}$* to arbitrary model types using Category Theory.

The property of a function being injective/surjective is generalized to arbitrary categories as the property of a morphism being a monomorphism/epimorphism. Instead of subsets, we use subobjects S. Furthermore, the commutative diagram in Fig. 4(a) can be interpreted in any category that has pullbacks along monomorphisms: the span $\langle g_b, g_f \rangle$ is induced by taking the pullback along the monomorphism α and morphism h_b into M to produce the span $\langle \alpha_S, g_b \rangle$ and then computing g_f as $h_f \circ \alpha_S$. We summarize this in the following definition.

Definition 4 (*GMAVO$_C$*). *Given a category C that has all pullbacks of monomorphisms, a GMAVO$_C$ partial model P is a pair $\langle M, \Phi \rangle$, where M is a C object, $\Phi = \langle \Sigma, \phi \rangle$, Σ is a set of subobjects of M, ϕ is an expression in propositional logic using atomic propositions of the form $x(S)$, where $x \in \{\texttt{E}, \texttt{P}, \texttt{C}, \texttt{Comp}, \texttt{A}\}$ and $S \in \Sigma$. The semantics of P is given by $\langle h_b, h_f \rangle \in [P]$ iff ϕ is true, where $\forall S \in \Sigma$, when the span $\langle g_b, g_f \rangle$ is induced as in Fig. 4(a), the following conditions hold:*

$\texttt{E}(S) \iff g_b$ *is an epimorphism;*
$\texttt{P}(S) \iff g_b$ *is a monomorphism;*
$\texttt{C}(S) \iff g_f$ *is a monomorphism;*
$\texttt{Comp}(S) \iff g_f$ *is an epimorphism;*
$\texttt{A}(S) \iff R_S = R.$

Thus, GMAVO can be applied to any modeling language whose corresponding category has the property of having all pullbacks of monomorphisms. Furthermore, the choice of category C is central to determining the nature of the partiality that *GMAVO$_C$* exhibits. For example, when we work in the category **Set**, the five constraints are independent - i.e., for a given set S it is possible for any subset of the five constraints to hold. This is not true for all categories. The ability for *GMAVO* to move beyond the syntactic limits of *MAVO* is also due to the choice of category used. For example, if **C** is chosen to be a category where the morphisms between models are purely structural, the partiality will be syntactic. However, by choosing a category in which the morphism corresponds to a semantic notion of refinement for the language (e.g., simulation for LTS's), we get partiality over language semantics. This is illustrated in the next section.

5   Application

In this section, we show how *MAVO*, MTSs and a third partial modeling language called *May* models can be expressed as special cases of *GMAVO*. For each partial modeling language, we define a translation to $GMAVO_C$ for an appropriate choice of **C** and then show that this translation produces semantically equivalent partial models.

5.1   Deriving *MAVO* from *GMAVO*

Given a metamodel T for a modeling language, we can define the natural "syntactic category" T for the modeling language where the objects are typed graphs and the morphisms are typed graph homomorphisms. Further, let T^{wf} be the subcategory of T containing only well-formed typed graphs according the well-formedness constraints of T. A typed graph homomorphism is a graph homomorphism that preserves atom types. For example, the syntactic category **CD** for Class Diagrams has class diagrams as objects (i.e., typed graphs based on metamodel in Fig. 2) and class diagram morphisms as morphisms. Thus, a class diagram morphism maps **Class** nodes to **Class** nodes, **super** edges to **super** edges, etc.

The category **CD** is suitable for *GMAVO* because it has all pullbacks – in fact, every syntactic category T defined as above has all pullbacks since the category of typed graphs has pullbacks [3]. However, we have a difficulty: we need to restrict K in the *GMAVO* diagram of Fig. 4(a) to be an object of $\mathbf{CD}^{wf}$ since *MAVO* only allows concretizations that are well-formed class diagrams. Furthermore, it is too restrictive to just use the category $\mathbf{CD}^{wf}$ for the entire diagram because *MAVO* allows base models (i.e., model M in the diagram) to be not well-formed. For example, if we want to express that a class attribute is maybe an **Int** or maybe a **String**, the resulting *MAVO* base model is not well formed because the attribute has two types. For the current paper, we just use **CD** and leave addressing the two-category situation within *GMAVO* for future work.

We now define a translation Υ_{MAVO} from *MAVO* models to *GMAVO* models:

Definition 5 (Υ_{MAVO}). *Given a metamodel T, let P be a MAVO model over T and let $M = bs(P)$, i.e., M is the base model of P. Let S_E, S_P and S_C be the smallest submodels of M containing all* E, P, *and* C-*annotated elements of*

M, respectively. We define the model $\Upsilon_{MAVO}(P)$ to be GMAVO$_T$ model $\langle M, \Phi \rangle$, where $\Phi = \langle \Sigma, \phi \rangle$, $\Sigma = \{S_E, S_P, S_C\}$ and ϕ is an expression of form $\text{E}(S_E) \wedge \text{P}(S_P) \wedge \text{C}(S_C) \wedge x$ where $x = true$, if P has the INC annotation and $x = \text{Comp}(M)$, otherwise.

Proposition 1. *Given a metamodel T, and MAVO T model P, the GMAVO model $\Upsilon_{MAVO}(P)$, defined as in Def. 5, has the same set of concretizations as P.*

For the *MAVO* model P1 in Fig. 1, all atoms are found in at least one of S_E, S_P or S_C and some, such as class Vehicle, are in all three. We can interpret the concretization relation depicted in Fig. 1 as a span $\langle h_b, h_f \rangle$ of class diagram homomorphisms – note that if an atom mapping is not shown, it is the identity mapping. It is possible then to verify that when we restrict $\langle h_b, h_f \rangle$ to each of S_E, S_P and S_C to get span $\langle g_b, g_f \rangle$, g_b is surjective for S_E, injective for S_P and g_f is injective for S_C. Note that since P1 is INC-annotated, there is no requirement for Comp(P1) to hold, and so h_f does not need to be surjective (although, for the concretization M1, it happens to be surjective).

Discussion. The encoding of *MAVO* within *GMAVO* directly shows why *MAVO* is limited. First, it is only defined for the syntactic category of a modeling language and so it can't deal with semantic information. Second, it is limited to constraints on three submodels rather than allowing constraints on arbitrary submodels. Finally, the form of the propositional formula restricts its expressiveness. Thus *GMAVO* represents a natural evolution and generalization of *MAVO*.

It is important to note, however, that the restrictions on *MAVO* also make it easier to use with model editing tools. For example, in order to constrain arbitrary submodels with *GMAVO*, a way of identifying these submodels is required and this may lead to visually cluttered model. We discuss this further in Sec. 7.

5.2 Deriving May Models from *GMAVO*

A *May* model [4] is equivalent to a *MAVO* model restricted to only using M annotations and with the addition of a propositional formula, called the *May formula*, expressed over the M-annotated atoms. The May formula gives *May* models an additional expressive power because it can exclude undesirable concretizations. For example, the class diagram in Fig. 1 has M annotations on the class Hovercraft and the three possible superclass relations it could have. With *MAVO* semantics, the concretizations include the cases where Hovercraft could have multiple superclasses; however, what if the system implementation language chosen does not support multiple inheritance? If the example was expressed using a *May* model instead of *MAVO*, the restriction to single inheritance could be expressed with the May formula $\phi_{May}^{hover} = (\text{super}(H, B) \wedge \neg \text{super}(H, V) \wedge \neg \text{super}(H, C)) \vee (\neg \text{super}(H, B) \wedge \text{super}(H, V) \wedge \neg \text{super}(H, C)) \vee (\neg \text{super}(H, B) \wedge \neg \text{super}(H, V) \wedge \text{super}(H, C))$ where we used the abbreviations H, B, V, and C to denote Hovercraft, Boat, Vehicle and Car, respectively.

We give the translation of *May* models to *GMAVO* as follows:

Definition 6 (Υ_{May}). *Let P be a May model over T, with ϕ_P being the May formula of P and model M being the base model of P. Let S^0 be the largest submodel of M containing no M-annotated elements in P. For each M-annotated atom a, let S_a be the smallest submodel of M containing a. We define the model $\Upsilon_{May}(P)$ to be GMAVO_T model $\langle M, \Phi \rangle$, where $\Phi = \langle \Sigma, \phi \rangle$ and*

- *$\Sigma = \{S^0\} \cup \{S_a | a$ is an M-annotated atom of $M\}$ and,*
- *$\phi = \text{P}(M) \wedge \text{C}(M) \wedge \text{Comp}(M) \wedge \text{E}(S^0) \wedge \phi_m$, where ϕ_m is obtained by replacing each propositional variable a in ϕ_P with the formula $(\text{E}(S_a) \veebar \text{A}(M \setminus S_a))$.*

Here, $M \setminus S_a$ is the complement of subgraph S_a in M.

As an illustration of the construction, consider the *May* model P1' we get from P1 in Fig. 1, if we ignore all annotations except M annotations and use ϕ_{May}^{hover} (defined above) as the May formula. Let N1' be the base model of P1'. Thus for P1' (and using the abbreviations from above), we have that S^0 contains all atoms except classes H and OtherVehicles and their super class relations. S_{H} contains only class H, $S_{\text{super(H,V)}}$ contains relation super(H, V) and classes H and V, etc. We then substitute $(\text{E}(S_{\text{super(H,V)}}) \veebar \text{A}(\text{N1'} \setminus S_{\text{super(H,V)}}))$ for each occurrence of super(H, V) in ϕ_{May}^{hover}, etc.

The following proposition shows the correctness of Υ_{May}.

Proposition 2. *Given a May model P over metamodel T, the GMAVO model $\Upsilon_{May}(P)$ obtained via Def. 6, has the same set of concretizations as P.*

5.3 Deriving the MTS Formalism from *GMAVO*

In this section, we show that the MTS partial modeling formalism [9] that has been proposed for expressing uncertainty within LTSs is an instance of *GMAVO*. In contrast to the cases of *MAVO* and *May* models, the category we use is not syntactic. We begin with basic definitions.

Definition 7 (Labelled Transition System). *[8] An LTS over action alphabet A is a tuple $\langle S, \Delta, s_0 \rangle$, where S is the set of states, $\Delta \subseteq S \times A \times S$ is the transition relation and $s_0 \in S$ is the initial state. We write $s \rightarrow_a s'$ when $\langle s, a, s' \rangle \in \Delta$.*

An LTS is represented by a directed graph with edges labelled with actions representing transitions. The standard approach to defining an MTS is to identify a subset of the transition relation that represents *required* transitions.

Definition 8 (Modal Transition System). *[9] An MTS M is a tuple $\langle S, \Gamma, \Delta, s_0 \rangle$, where $\langle S, \Delta, s_0 \rangle$ is an LTS and $\Gamma \subseteq \Delta$. We refer to Δ as the set of possible transitions and Γ as the set of required transitions. We refer to the LTSs $\langle S, \Delta, s_0 \rangle$ and $\langle S, \Gamma, s_0 \rangle$ as the underlying possible and required LTSs of M, respectively. We write $s \rightarrow_a s'$ when $\langle s, a, s' \rangle \in \Gamma$, and $s \dashrightarrow_a s'$ when $\langle s, a, s' \rangle \in \Delta$.*

Like an LTS, an MTS represents behaviours but it allows some transitions to be uncertain. Specifically, if a transition is possible but not required, then it is

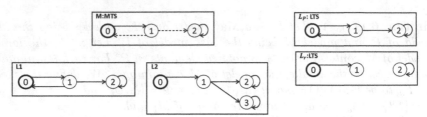

Fig. 5. An example MTS and two of its implementations

considered to be "maybe". Thus, the behaviours of the underlying possible and required LTSs are the *possible* and the *required behaviors*, respectively.

We can also view an MTS as the set of LTSs that "implement" it, i.e., as a partial LTS. Intuitively, an implementation of an MTS is an LTS that includes all required behaviours and excludes behaviours that are not possible. This can be expressed formally in terms of the simulation relation [11].

Definition 9 (Implementation). *[9] Given an MTS $M = \langle S, \Gamma, \Delta, s_0 \rangle$ where L_p and L_r are the underlying possible and required LTSs of M, respectively, an LTS $L = \langle S', \Delta', s_0' \rangle$, a relation $R \subseteq S \times S'$ and its opposite $R^{op} \subseteq S' \times S$ defined as $R^{op} = \{\langle s', s \rangle | \langle s, s' \rangle \in R\}$, we say that L is an implementation of M iff the following conditions hold: (1) L_p simulates L via R and (2) L simulates L_r via R^{op}.*

Fig. 5 shows an example MTS and two LTSs, L1 and L2, that are its implementations. The underlying possible (L_p) and required (L_r) LTSs are also shown.

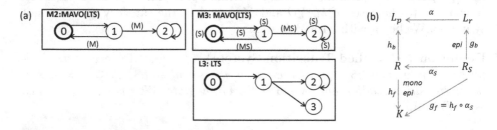

Fig. 6. (a) Two attempts at expressing an MTS as a *MAVO* model; (b) GMAVO encoding of an MTS expressed as a diagram in category **LTS**(A)

We now express MTSs as a *GMAVO* model. First note that the application of *MAVO* (i.e., over the syntactic category of LTSs), does not work for expressing MTSs. Fig. 6(a) illustrates the problem. The *MAVO* LTS model M2 on the left of the figure has implementation L1 from Fig. 5 as one of its concretizations but not implementation L2. Thus, M2 under-approximates M. On the other hand, the *MAVO* model M3 in Fig. 6(a) has both implementations as its concretizations but it also has L3 which is not an implementation of M. Thus, M3 over-approximates M. Clearly, no combination of *MAVO* annotations will eliminate L3 while preserving L2. Thus, there is no *MAVO* LTS that can exactly capture the set of implementations of M as concretizations.

The reason for the failure of *MAVO* is that the concept of MTS implementation is a *semantic* notion relying on the simulation relation whereas *MAVO* uses the syntactic category of LTSs with homomorphism as the morphism. Since *GMAVO* is applicable to any category, we address this problem by switching to a category of LTSs in which the morphism is based on the simulation relation. We define simulation morphisms as follows:

Definition 10 (Simulation Morphism). *Given LTSs* $L = \langle S, \Delta, s_0 \rangle$ *and* $L' = \langle S', \Delta', s_0' \rangle$, *a simulation morphism* $f : L' \to L$ *is a pair of relations* $\langle R \subseteq S' \times S, R_\Delta \subseteq \Delta' \times \Delta \rangle$, *where* L *simulates* L' *via* R^{op} *and* R_Δ^{op} *contains all pairs of transitions* $\langle s \to_a t, s' \to_a t' \rangle$ *that witness the simulation.*

Thus, a simulation morphism is a simulation relation between states augmented with the corresponding relation between the transitions that define the simulation. Based on this morphism, we define the required category.

Definition 11 (LTS(A)). *Let* **LTS**(A) *be the category with LTSs over action set A as objects and simulation morphisms as the morphisms.*

Note that **LTS**(A) has pullbacks along monomorphisms. Various categories have been used in other work on LTSs [20]. We define a translation Υ_{MTS} from MTS models to *GMAVO* models:

Definition 12 (Υ_{MTS}). *Given MTS* $M = \langle S, \Gamma, \Delta, s_0 \rangle$ *where* L_p *and* L_r *are the underlying possible and required LTSs of M, respectively. We define the model* $\Upsilon_{MTS}(M)$ *to be the* GMAVO$_{LTS(A)}$ *model* $\langle L_p, \Phi \rangle$, *where* $\Phi = \langle \Sigma, \phi \rangle$, $\Sigma = \{L_p, L_r\}$ *and* $\phi = \{\mathbb{E}(L_r) \wedge \mathbb{C}(L_p) \wedge \mathtt{Comp}(L_p)\}$.

The constraints defined in the above definition are shown diagrammatically in Fig 6(b). The next proposition shows the correctness of Υ_{MTS}.

Proposition 3. *Given MTS M, the set of implementations of M is the same as the set of concretizations of* GMAVO *model* $\Upsilon_{MTS}(M)$.

Discussion. Standard extensions of the MTS formalism are also possible to express using *GMAVO*. For example, a Disjunctive MTS (DMTS) [10] extends the MTS formalism by generalizing a required transition into a set of alternative transitions from a common state, exactly one of which must be used in an implementation. We can express this kind of constraint by using a separate submodel for each alternative transition and expressing the corresponding propositional formula over the existence of these transitions. This kind of fine-grained control was illustrated with the *GMAVO* encoding for *May* models.

Additionally, the *GMAVO* encoding creates the possibility of giving sound semantics to other kinds of extensions to the MTS formalism. For example, MTSs only allow transitions to be annotated as "maybe" but *GMAVO* can allow this uncertainty for states too. This is accomplished by removing these states from L_r. Another possibility is to allow for "variable" states and transitions by replacing the constraint $C(L_p)$ with $C(L_c)$ for some submodel L_c of L_p. Whether these kinds of extensions are of practical use for MTS applications is outside the scope of this paper and is left for future work.

6   Related Work

In this section, we discuss work related to partial modeling.

Modeling with Uncertainty. Uncertainty in software systems has been studied from the perspective of the inherent uncertainty in the environment. For example, research in self-adaptive systems (e.g., [14]) regards uncertainty in the context of changing environmental parameters. In contrast, we are examining the epistemic uncertainty of the modeler herself regarding the information in the model. This kind of uncertainty is reducible rather than being fixed, and possibilistic (i.e., producing sets of alternatives) rather than being probabilistic. Techniques for managing epistemic and reducible uncertainty have been studied in the past (e.g., [7]); however, the aim of these approaches is typically to understand and mitigate its consequences or to manage its associated risks. On the other hand, we aim to support the expression of uncertainty and reasoning about it.

Modeling Sets of Models. Partial models are a formalism for encoding a set of models into a single modeling artifact. Other formalisms that use the same abstraction pattern to capture sets of related and/or similar models include metamodels (e.g., [12]) and software product lines [13]. Although such formalisms implement the same abstraction pattern and may have similar expressive powers, they have a different intent. Metamodels are used to characterize a modeling language while product lines define a set of desired product variants. Unlike metamodels, the focus of partial models is to express what is still unknown. Unlike product lines, only one of the possibilities a partial model expresses is desirable while the others are eliminated as uncertainty is resolved. Partial models are inherently transient in the development process – the objective is to make them "go away" by resolving the uncertainty. On the other hand, metamodels and product lines are both long-lived artifacts that are carefully engineered and used many times.

7   Conclusion

Partial modeling provides a means for addressing uncertainty in software engineering. Although several partial modeling languages have been proposed and studied, there has been no unifying treatment of these languages. In this paper, we have addressed this gap by proposing a general formal framework for partial modeling languages using Category Theory, called *GMAVO*. We showed how existing partial modeling languages can be instantiated within *GMAVO* and how this can suggest sound ways to increase their expressiveness.

As part of future work, we intend to examine several issues. First, our analysis of OW partiality suggested that it is pragmatically useful only when applied to the entire model. Another intuitively meaningful interpretation of a complete submodel is "this submodel should be the same in all concretizations". We are exploring refinements of $GMAVO$ that capture this interpretation. Second, the fact that syntactic partiality on $MAVO$ and May models requires us to work with two categories needs further study on how best to incorporate this situation within $GMAVO$. Third, although $GMAVO$ provides greater expressive power than $MAVO$, the usability implications must be considered. Some early work has already been done in the context of alternative notations for $MAVO$ [5]. Finally, since $GMAVO$ can be defined over an arbitrary category, we are exploring the meaning of partiality for other semantic categories of models or even entities other than models.

References

1. Diskin, Z.: Algebraic Models for Bidirectional Model Synchronization. In: Czarnecki, K., Ober, I., Bruel, J.-M., Uhl, A., Völter, M. (eds.) MODELS 2008. LNCS, vol. 5301, pp. 21–36. Springer, Heidelberg (2008)
2. Egyed, A., Letier, E., Finkelstein, A.: Generating and Evaluating Choices for Fixing Inconsistencies in UML Design Models. In: Proc. of ASE 2008, pp. 99–108 (2008)
3. Ehrig, H., Ehrig, K., Prange, U., Taentzer, G.: Fundamentals of Algebraic Graph Transformation, vol. 373. Springer (2006)
4. Famelis, M., Chechik, M., Salay, R.: Partial Models: Towards Modeling and Reasoning with Uncertainty. In: Proc. of ICSE 2012, pp. 573–583 (2012)
5. Famelis, M., Santosa, S.: MAV-Vis: A Notation for Model Uncertainty. In: Proc. of MiSE 2013, pp. 7–12 (2013)
6. Fischbein, D., D'Ippolito, N., Brunet, G., Chechik, M., Uchitel, S.: Weak Alphabet Merging of Partial Behavior Models. ACM Trans. Softw. Eng. Methodol. 21(2) (2012)
7. Islam, S., Houmb, S.H.: Integrating Risk Management Activities into Requirements Engineering. In: Proc. of RCIS 2010, pp. 299–310 (2010)
8. Keller, R.: Formal Verification of Parallel Programs. Communications of the ACM 19(7), 371–384 (1976)
9. Larsen, K.G., Thomsen, B.: A Modal Process Logic. In: Proc. of LICS 1988 (1988)
10. Larsen, P.: The Expressive Power of Implicit Specifications. In: Leach Albert, J., Monien, B., Rodríguez-Artalejo, M. (eds.) ICALP 1991. LNCS, vol. 510, pp. 204–216. Springer, Heidelberg (1991)
11. Milner, R.: Communication and Concurrency. Prentice-Hall, New York (1989)
12. OMG. Meta Object Facility (MOF) (2006)
13. Pohl, K., Böckle, G., Linden, F.V.D.: Software Product Line Engineering: Foundations, Principles, and Techniques. Springer-Verlag New York Inc. (2005)
14. Ramirez, A.J., Cheng, B.H.C., Bencomo, N., Sawyer, P.: Relaxing Claims: Coping with Uncertainty While Evaluating Assumptions at Run Time. In: France, R.B., Kazmeier, J., Breu, R., Atkinson, C. (eds.) MODELS 2012. LNCS, vol. 7590, pp. 53–69. Springer, Heidelberg (2012)
15. Sabetzadeh, M., Easterbrook, S.: View Merging in the Presence of Incompleteness and Inconsistency. J. Requirements Engineering 11(3), 174–193 (2006)

16. Sabetzadeh, M., Nejati, S., Chechik, M., Easterbrook, S.: Reasoning about Consistency in Model Merging. In: Proc. of LWI 2010 (2010)
17. Salay, R., Chechik, M., Gorzny, J.: Towards a Methodology for Verifying Partial Model Refinements. In: Proc. of VOLT 2012 (April 2012)
18. Salay, R., Famelis, M., Chechik, M.: Language Independent Refinement Using Partial Modeling. In: de Lara, J., Zisman, A. (eds.) Fundamental Approaches to Software Engineering. LNCS, vol. 7212, pp. 224–239. Springer, Heidelberg (2012)
19. Salay, R., Gorzny, J., Chechik, M.: Change Propagation due to Uncertainty Change. In: Cortellessa, V., Varró, D. (eds.) FASE 2013. LNCS, vol. 7793, pp. 21–36. Springer, Heidelberg (2013)
20. Sobociński, P.: Relational Presheaves as Labelled Transition Systems. In: Pattinson, D., Schröder, L. (eds.) CMCS 2012. LNCS, vol. 7399, pp. 40–50. Springer, Heidelberg (2012)
21. van Lamsweerde, A.: Requirements Engineering - From System Goals to UML Models to Software Specifications. Wiley (2009)
22. Ziv, H., Richardson, D., Klösch, R.: The Uncertainty Principle in Software Engineering (1996)

Performance-Based Software Model Refactoring in Fuzzy Contexts*

Davide Arcelli[1], Vittorio Cortellessa[1], and Catia Trubiani[2]

[1] Università degli Studi dell'Aquila, L'Aquila, Italy
[2] Gran Sasso Science Institute, L'Aquila, Italy
{davide.arcelli,vittorio.cortellessa}@univaq.it
catia.trubiani@gssi.infn.it

Abstract. The detection of causes of performance problems in software systems and the identification of refactoring actions that can remove the problems are complex activities (even in small/medium scale systems). It has been demonstrated that software models can nicely support these activities, especially because they enable the introduction of automation in the detection and refactoring steps. In our recent work we have focused on performance antipattern-based detection and refactoring of software models. However performance antipatterns suffer from the numerous thresholds that occur in their representations and whose binding has to be performed before the detection starts (as for many pattern/antipattern categories).

In this paper we introduce an approach that aims at overcoming this limitation. We work in a fuzzy context where threshold values cannot be determined, but only their lower and upper bounds do. On this basis, the detection task produces a list of performance antipatterns along with their probabilities to occur in the model. Several refactoring alternatives can be available to remove each performance antipattern. Our approach associates an estimate of how effective each alternative can be in terms of performance benefits. We demonstrate that the joint analysis of antipattern probability and refactoring benefits drives the designers to identify the alternatives that heavily improve the software performance.

Keywords: Software Performance, Model Refactoring, Performance Antipatterns.

1 Introduction

In the software development domain, there is a high interest in the early validation of performance requirements because it avoids late and expensive fixes to consolidated software artifacts. Model-based approaches, pioneered under the name of Software Performance Engineering (SPE) by Smith [1], aim at producing performance models early in the development cycle and using quantitative

---

* This work has been partially supported by the European Office of Aerospace Research and Development (EOARD), Grant/Cooperative Agreement (Award no. FA8655-11-1-3055).

A. Egyed and I. Schaefer (Eds.): FASE 2015, LNCS 9033, pp. 149–164, 2015.
DOI: 10.1007/978-3-662-46675-9_10

results from model solutions to refactor the design with the purpose of meeting performance requirements [2].

Nevertheless, the problem of interpreting the performance analysis results is still quite critical. A large gap in fact exists between the representation of performance analysis results and the feedback expected by software designers. The former usually contains numbers (e.g., mean response time, throughput variance, etc.), whereas the latter should embed design alternatives useful to overcome performance problems (e.g., split a software component in two components and re-deploy one of them). The results interpretation is today exclusively based on the analysts' experience and therefore it suffers from lack of automation.

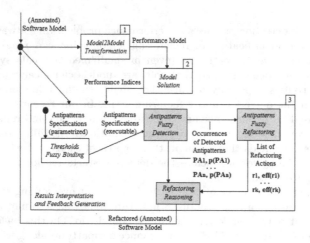

Fig. 1. Model-based software performance refactoring process

Figure 1 illustrates a model-based software performance refactoring process. It includes three main operational steps: (1) the *Model2Model Transformation* step takes as input an annotated[1] software model and generates a performance model [3]; (2) the *Model Solution* step takes as input a performance model and produces a set of performance indices [4]; (3) the *Results Interpretation and Feedback Generation* macro step takes as input both the software model and the performance indices to detect possible performance problems, and it provides a refactored (annotated) software model where problems have been removed. In particular, the refactored model is obtained with a semantics-preserving transformation that aims at improving the quality of the original software model. In other words, the functional aspects of this latter model have to remain unaltered after the transformation. For example, the interaction between two components might be refactored to improve performance by sending fewer messages with larger data per message.

---

[1] Software model annotations support the performance analysis by specifying parameters like workload, resource demands, etc.

A number of approaches have been recently introduced for this macro step [5, 6] (see more details in Section 2), while we were working on the detection and refactoring of *technology-independent* performance antipatterns [7–10]. *Performance antipatterns* [11] are well-known bad design practices that lead to software products suffering from poor performance. A specific characteristic of performance antipatterns is that they contain numerical parameters that represent thresholds referring to either performance indices (e.g., *high*, *low* device utilization) or design features (e.g., *many* interface operations, *excessive* message traffic).

Both the detection and solution of performance antipatterns are heavily affected by multiplicity and estimation accuracy of thresholds that an antipattern requires. For this reason, in our previous work we have experimented the influence of thresholds with respect to these two activities. We have conducted a sensitivity analysis on a case study by varying the numerical values of several thresholds for different antipatterns. Then, we have quantified threshold variations with the support of recall and precision metrics, and derived useful findings for dealing with performance antipatterns on software models [12].

The motivation of this paper stems from two main reasons:
(i) due to the stochastic nature of the process of Figure 1, it would not be realistic to assume that threshold values can be exactly determined;
(ii) it is difficult to identify refactoring actions that quicken the convergence of the whole process of Figure 1.
In this paper we introduce an approach that aims at overcoming these limitations, by providing a *thresholds fuzzy binding* that does not assign exact values to antipattern thresholds, but it works on their lower and upper bounds to make fuzzy the context of antipatterns detection and refactoring.

In such context we envisage (see Figure 1): (i) a detection task that produces a list of performance antipattern occurrences $PA_1, \ldots, PA_n$, along with their probabilities to occur, i.e. $p(PA_1), \ldots, p(PA_n)$, and (ii) a refactoring task that produces a list of available refactorings $r_1, \ldots, r_k$ with their effectiveness, i.e. $eff(r_1), \ldots, eff(r_k)$, in terms of expected performance benefits.

The contribution of this paper is to introduce:
1. A method for associating to each detected performance antipattern PA_i the probability of occurring, i.e. $p(PA_i)$.
2. A technique that estimates the *effectiveness* of each available refactoring action r_j, i.e. $eff(r_j)$, in terms of expected performance benefits.
3. A *Refactoring Reasoning* step that jointly analyzes the antipattern probability and refactoring benefits to drive the designers towards the identification of refactoring actions that quicken the process convergence. The output is a design alternative, i.e. a new (refactored) software model that undergoes the same process[2].

---

[2] Note that we intend to provide here an instrument to help the process convergence, hence a performance analyzer can decide to limitedly use this instrument, for example by stopping the detection and the refactoring steps before all antipatterns and refactoring actions have been devised (for sake of processing time), and then reasoning on a reduced set of alternatives.

The remainder of the paper is organized as follows. Section 2 presents related work. Section 3 describes our approach to deal with the fuzzy antipattern detection and refactoring. Section 4 illustrates the application of our approach to a case study, i.e. an e-commerce system. Finally, Section 5 concludes the paper by outlining the most challenging research topics in this area.

2 Related Work

In literature there are some approaches that deal with the problem of improving the performance of software systems based on analysis results.

Xu et al. [5] present a semi-automated approach to find configuration and design improvement on the model level. Based on a Layered Queueing Network (LQN) model, two types of performance problems are identified, i.e, bottleneck resources and long paths. Then, rules containing performance knowledge are applied to solve the detected problems. However, the approach is notation-specific, in fact it is based on LQN rules, and it does not incorporate heuristics to rank the solutions, as suggested in this paper.

Parsons et al. [13] present a framework for detecting performance antipatterns in Java EE architectures. The method requires an implementation of a component-based system, which can be monitored for performance properties. However, the limitation of this approach is that it cannot be used in early development stages, running EJB systems are required for the detection of performance problems.

Diaz Pace et al. [14] present the ArchE framework that assists the software architect during the design to create architectures that meet quality requirements. However, defined rules are limited to improve modifiability only. A simple performance model is used to predict performance metrics for the new system with improved modifiability.

In previous work [15] we proposed an approach for automated feedback generation from software performance analysis results, based on model-driven techniques. Support to rank and solve antipatterns has been provided in [16] however thresholds have been estimated with heuristics. As future work we plan to compare our guilt-based approach with the one presented in this paper to further investigate pros and cons of the two approaches.

3 Probability-Effectiveness Approach

In this section we describe our approach by providing details on the shaded boxes of Figure 1 that represent the focus of this paper.

3.1 Antipatterns Fuzzy Detection

Performance antipatterns have been originally defined in natural language [11]. Hence, we first tackled the problem of providing a more formal representation by introducing first-order logic rules that express a set of system properties under which an antipattern occurs [17].

As stated in Section 1, performance antipatterns are very complex (as compared to other software patterns) because they are founded on design characteristics (e.g., *many* usage dependencies, *excessive* message traffic) and performance results (e.g., *high*, *low* utilization), hence thresholds must be introduced. For example, a Blob occurs when a component requires a *lot* of information from other ones, it generates *excessive* message traffic that lead to *over utilize* the device on which it is deployed or the network involved in the communication. The logic-based formula of the Blob antipattern has been defined in [17] and reported in Equation (1), where $sw\mathbb{E}$ and $\mathbb{S}$ represent the set of all software components and services, respectively.

$$\exists swE_x, swE_y \in swE, S \in \mathbb{S} \mid$$
$$(F_{numClientConnects}(swE_x) \geq Th_{maxConnects}$$
$$\vee F_{numSupplierConnects}(swE_x) \geq Th_{maxConnects})$$
$$\wedge F_{numMsgs}(swE_x, swE_y, S) \geq Th_{maxMsgs} \tag{1}$$
$$\wedge (F_{maxHwUtil}(P_{xy}, all) \geq Th_{maxHwUtil}$$
$$\vee F_{maxNetUtil}(P_{swE_x}, P_{swE_y}) \geq Th_{maxNetUtil})$$

In our previous work [17] we defined some heuristics to estimate thresholds numerical values. For example, the $Th_{maxConnects}$ threshold (that represents the maximum bound for the number of usage relationships a software component is involved in) has been estimated as the average number of usage relationships, with reference to the entire set of software components in the software system, plus the corresponding variance. In [12] we considered ranges of values around these average values, but the main issue was to set a suitable width to capture the actual bad practices.

To overcome such problem, in this paper we move a step ahead by determining thresholds' lower and upper bounds, thus to make fuzzy the detection step. In fact, the logic-based representation of antipatterns allows us to move the detection process in a fuzzy context by defining the probabilities associated to the logical predicates involved in antipatterns specifications. Thresholds' lower and upper bounds can be defined by examining the whole system and calculating the minimum and maximum values of the observed properties. For example, Table 1 reports the description of thresholds included in the Blob specification along with strategies to derive lower and upper bounds.

In order to calculate the probability of occurrence for each antipattern, we firstly consider the probabilities associated to logical basic predicates separately, and then we properly combine them following their logical operators, i.e. *AND* ($\wedge$), *OR* ($\vee$).

Each logical basic predicate is associated to a probability value of occurrence based on its *distance* from lower and upper bounds, respectively. In particular, we consider how far a specific design characteristic or a performance index is from the thresholds' upper bound (in case of maximum boundaries) or thresholds' lower bound (in case of minimum boundaries). This quantity is normalized

Table 1. Thresholds specification for the Blob antipattern

	Threshold	Description	Lower Bound	Upper Bound
Design	$Th_{maxConnects}$	Maximum bound for the number of connections in which a component is involved	$LBTh_{maxConnects}$ is the minimum number of connections among all the components	$UBTh_{maxConnects}$ is the maximum number of connections among all the components
	$Th_{maxMsgs}$	Maximum bound for the number of messages sent by a component in a service	$LBTh_{maxMsgs}$ is the minimum number of messages sent among all the components	$UBTh_{maxMsgs}$ is the maximum number of messages sent among all the components
Performance	$Th_{maxHwUtil}$	Maximum bound for the hardware device utilization	$LBTh_{maxHwUtil}$ is the minimum hardware utilization among all the devices	$UBTh_{maxHwUtil}$ is the maximum hardware utilization among all the devices
	$Th_{maxNetUtil}$	Maximum bound for the network link utilization	$LBTh_{maxNetUtil}$ is the minimum utilization among all the network links	$UBTh_{maxNetUtil}$ is the maximum utilization among all the network links

over the difference between thresholds' upper and lower bounds. For example, for the Blob antipattern the number of connections of a certain swE_x software component ($F_{numClientConnects}(swE_x)$) is compared to the corresponding threshold upper bound ($UBTh_{maxConnects}$) and lower bound ($LBTh_{maxConnects}$). The probability formula for this basic predicate is reported in Equation (2):

$$1 - ((UBTh_{maxConnects} - F_{numClientConnects}(swE_x))/$$
$$(UBTh_{maxConnects} - LBTh_{maxConnects})) \quad (2)$$

We combine these probabilities to obtain the probability of an antipattern occurrence, following the classic probability theory formulas for independent events, that are as follows for the union of two events, (i.e., the probability of $(A \vee B)$ in the logical formula):

$$P(A \cup B) = P(A) + P(B) \quad (3)$$

and as follows for the intersection of two events (i.e., the probability of $(A \wedge B)$ in the logical formula):

$$P(A \cap B) = P(A) * P(B) \quad (4)$$

The experimentation shows that the hypothesis of independency does not compromise the validity of the approach.

3.2   Antipatterns Fuzzy Refactoring

In this section we provide an answer to a significant research question that arises when choosing a refactoring to apply on the model: "How to quantify the *effectiveness* of a refactoring action?".

To answer this question, we first observe that in case of systems representable as separable Queueing Networks (this is our case), it is well-known that the more the load of the system is balanced among nodes, the better the response time and throughput are [4, Ch. 5]. This means that, among all the available refactorings, we should prefer to apply the one(s) resulting in a more balanced system. Hence, we need a way to quantify the *equilibrium point* of a system configuration in terms of node utilization, because utilization is the index that more directly relate to the load distribution in the system. Given the utilizations of the system's nodes in a configuration, we consider the mean utilization value as the equilibrium point.

It is evident that, the closer the utilizations of all nodes are to the mean value, the closer that configuration is to the equilibrium point. Hence, given the utilization of each node for a configuration (namely *config*), we can estimate the distance from the equilibrium point by considering the *variance* among the nodes utilizations, denoted with $var(config)$.

In order to compute $var(config)$ we need a technique to estimate the node utilizations $\bar{U}' = \{u'(n_1), u'(n_2), ..., u'(n_k)\}$ after the application of a refactoring r. In this paper we consider the following refactorings because they represent foundational actions, and it is possible to build many complex refactorings from their combination:

- *redeploy(Component c, Node n)*: this action moves a software component c to the node n. Such refactoring action is aimed at improving the utilization of the node where the component c was deployed. In a performance model, this results in moving the resource demand of c to n.
- *split(Component c, Node n)*: this action split a software component c in two new components c_1' and c_2', by properly distributing the connections of c between them, while taking into account the functional responsibilities of c. c_1' remains on the node where c was deployed, whereas c_2' is deployed on n. Such refactoring action is aimed at reducing the number of connections of c in an efficient way. In a performance model, this results in moving part of the resource demand of c to n.

To estimate $\bar{U}'$, we define the *unitary cost of a resource demand on a node n*, namely $uc(n)$, as follows:

$$uc(n) = \frac{u(n)}{\displaystyle\sum_{c \in D(n)} rd(c)} \qquad (5)$$

where $rd(c)$ is the resource demand of a component c and $D(n)$ is the set of all components c that are currently deployed on n.

Hence, given two distinct nodes n_i and n_j, with $uc(n_i)$ and $uc(n_j)$ respectively, if we are moving $rd(c)$ from n_i to n_j, then

$$\bar{U}' = \{u'(n_i), u'(n_j)\} \bigcup \bar{U}_k \qquad (6)$$

where

- $u'(n_i) = u(n_i) - rd(c) * uc(n_i)$
- $u'(n_j) = u(n_j) + rd(c) * uc(n_j)$
- $\bar{U}_k = \displaystyle\bigcup_{k \neq \{i,j\}} \{u(n_k)\}$

It is worth to notice that an algebraic approximation of future utilizations due to refactoring actions cannot be easily extended to nodes not directly involved in the split/redeploy refactorings, although they could be affected by the propagation of refactoring effects. Hence, we here introduce the assumption that utilizations of these nodes (other than $u'(n_i)$ and $u'(n_j)$) do not change after refactoring.

The above definitions based on resource demands can be straightforwardly applied to the case of mass storage resources and, in general, to any resource that in a queueing network model can be represented as a service center with queue. However, for sake of simplification, we only refer to CPU resources in our case study. For other types of resources, such as RAMs, the concepts of utilization and resource demands are not applicable as they are, so these definitions do not hold. Hence, for all cases where resources like RAM could be critical, a different quantification of performance improvements due to refactoring has to be introduced.

After estimating utilizations of each possible refactored configuration $config'$, we can estimate $var(config')$.

At this point, with respect to the research question that we have arisen above, we intend to distinguish if a refactoring r_i is *better* than a refactoring r_j. For this goal, denoting by $config'_i$ and $config'_j$ the configurations resulting from r_i and r_j respectively, if $var(config'_i) < var(config'_j)$ then we assess r_i as better than r_j. This is because r_i results in a more balanced refactored configuration (i.e. one that is closer to the equilibrium point) than r_j.

Now, starting from the performance shown by an initial model, we make a distinction between *beneficial* and *non-beneficial* refactorings. In particular, a refactoring r is *beneficial* if it results in a refactored configuration $config'$ that shows better performance than the ones shown by the initial configuration $config_{Initial}$. Conversely, r is *non-beneficial* if performance do not improve by applying it.

With this distinction in mind, we define the *effectiveness* of a refactoring r as $eff(r) = var(config_{Initial}) - var(config')$. Basing on $eff(r)$, we can now classify the set of available refactorings. In particular, we consider r as a *beneficial* refactoring if $eff(r) > 0$, otherwise as *non-beneficial*. In practice, the $eff(r)$ value suggests the degree of influence that r can provide to the performance of the resulting configuration, i.e. $config'$.

3.3   Refactoring Reasoning

As shown in Figure 1, the refactoring reasoning operational step takes as input: (i) the list of detected antipatterns associated with their probability of occurrence; (ii) the list of refactoring actions associated with their effectiveness. Several strategies can be devised to make use of this knowledge, for example:

- *High probability*: while looking at the list of detected antipatterns it is possible to identify the ones that most likely represent a bad practice, and then to apply (one of) the most effective refactorings to (one of) them;

- *High effectiveness*: while looking at the list of refactoring actions it is possible to identify the ones that most likely provide a performance improvement, and then to apply (one of) the most effective refactorings to (one of) the most likely occurring antipatterns;
- *High combination of probability and effectiveness*: while looking at the list of detected antipatterns and refactoring actions it is possible to combine the $(probability, effectiveness)$ values to identify the ones that most likely provide a performance improvement while removing bad practices.

The goal of providing probability and effectiveness values for antipatterns is to introduce an ordering in the list of detected antipatterns, where highly ranked antipatterns are the most promising causes for performance problems as well as the most promising candidates to solve such problems. The key factor of our approach is to consider the thresholds' lower and upper bounds thus to evaluate the whole system. We first assign a probability to each antipattern, and then we estimate the effectiveness of its refactoring actions on the basis of the achieved equilibrium point.

4   Case Study: E-Commerce System (ECS)

E-Commerce System (ECS) is a web-based system that manages business data related to books and movies. A *Guest* may invoke the *BrowseCatalog* service, whereas a *Customer* may invoke two services, i.e., *Login* and *MakePurchase*. Several software components and hardware platforms have been defined in ECS. For the sake of simplicity we name components $C1, \ldots, C6$ and platforms $n1, \ldots, n3$, in particular $C1$ and $C2$ are deployed on $n1$, $C3$ and $C4$ are deployed on $n2$, and $C5$ and $C6$ are deployed on $n3$.

Among all system services, we focus here on the *MakePurchase*, which is triggered whenever a customer wants to purchase a book or a movie, after authentication. We assume that a performance requirement have been defined on the *MakePurchase* service, i.e. its average response time must not exceed 90 seconds. Such requirement must be fulfilled under a workload of 100 customers. The performance analysis has been conducted by transforming the software model into a Queueing Network (QN) model [18] and by solving the latter with the Java Modeling Tools (JMT) [19].

The considered requirement is violated because, under a workload of 100 users purchasing a product, the mean time elapsed in the server-side for each request (i.e., the average response time at the server-side) is 93.79 seconds that is larger than the stated requirement.

4.1   ECS: Antipatterns Fuzzy Detection

As stated in Section 3.1, antipatterns fuzzy detection is performed by assigning a probability value for the logic basic predicates. In the following we illustrate our approach applied to the Blob occurrences of the ECS case study, however other antipatterns (i.e., the Concurrent Processing System and the Pipe and Filter [11]) have been detected and analyzed.

Table 2 reports the observed values of the ECS case study. In particular the first column reports all the software components listed as candidates for the Blob occurrence. The remaining columns reports the values coming from the application of functions defined in the Blob logic-based specification (see Equation 1). For example, in the first row of Table 2 we can notice that the $C1$ component has 3 connections, it sends 11 messages, and it is deployed on an hardware platform with an utilization of 57%. In the lower part of Table 2 we report thresholds' upper and lower bounds that have been calculated across all the system features.

Table 2. EHS: Thresholds upper and lower bounds for the Blob antipattern

Component	$F_{numClientConnects}(swE_x)$	$F_{numMsgs}(swE_x, swE_y, S)$	$F_{maxHwUtil}(P_{xy}, all)$
C1	3	11	0.57
C2	5	16	0.57
C3	7	25	0.87
C4	6	22	0.87
C5	1	4	0.41
C6	3	13	0.41
Upper Bound	7	25	0.87
Lower Bound	1	4	0.41

Table 3. EHS: Fuzzy detection for the Blob antipattern

Component	p(A)	p(B)	p(C)	p(Blob)
C1	0.33	0.33	0.34	0.04
C2	0.67	0.57	0.34	0.13
C3	1	1	1	1
C4	0.83	0.86	1	0.71
C5	0	0	0	0
C6	0.33	0.43	0	0

Table 3 reports the values calculated according to Equations (4) (3), and it is structured as follows. The first column report the set of all the software components. The subsequent three columns report the probabilities of the sub equations (namely A, B, C) included in the Blob specification. For Blob occurrence the event A is associated to the sub equation related to the number of connections, and it is calculated using the formula reported in Equation (2). For example, Table 3 shows that the $C1$ component is associated with p(A) calculated as: 1- (7-3/7-1) = 1 - 4/6 = 0.33. The last column reports the p(Blob) that represents the probability of occurrence for the corresponding components. For example, Table 3 shows that the $C1$ component is associated to a probability equal to 0.04 (= 0.33 * 0.33 * 0.34) that basically represents the confidence associated in the detection of the $C1$ component as a Blob occurrence.

Similarly to Table 3 fuzzy detection of antipatterns have been performed to estimate the Concurrent Processing Systems (CPS) and Pipe & Filter occurrences. Numerical values are reported in Section 4.3.

4.2 ECS: Antipatterns Fuzzy Refactoring

Figure 2 shows the classification of the refactored configurations vs the initial one: on the x-axis the refactoring efficiencies ($eff(r)$) are reported, whereas the y-axis represents the response time (RT, calculated by simulating the underlying performance model) of the corresponding refactored configuration.

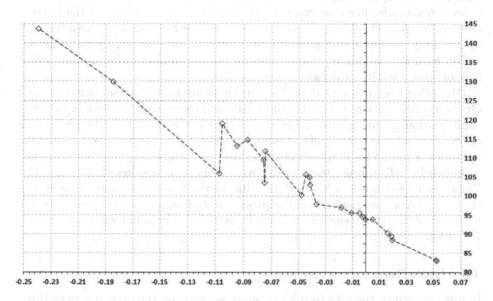

Fig. 2. Refactoring effectiveness vs. system response time

Our approach bases on the conjecture that we mentioned in Section 3.2, i.e. "we consider r as a *beneficial* refactoring if $eff(r) > 0$, otherwise as *non-beneficial*.". Hence, basing on our approach, there are 6 beneficial actions, whereas all the remaining ones are non-beneficial. To validate this, we simulated each refactored configuration, obtaining its response time and comparing it to the one of the initial configuration (i.e. the point with $x = 0$ in Figure 2). Given this knowledge, we computed *recall* and *precision* of our approach on the ECS case study[3]. In particular, the recall is 100%, because all the 5 actual beneficial refactored configurations (i.e. the 5 right-most points) have been retrieved; instead, the precision is 83.33%, because among the 6 refactored configurations that we computed (i.e. the 6 points with $x > 0$), 5 were actually beneficial.

The conjecture above is true for all the points of Figure 2, except for the point $(0.005, 93.79)$, i.e. the first point in the positive side of x-axis. This is due to the fact that the corresponding refactoring $Split(C1, n3)$ is a *border-line case*; in fact, by simulating the resulting refactored configuration several times,

---

[3] Precision and recall are well-known metrics aimed at quantifying the effectiveness of a technique for pattern recognition or information retrieval [20]. High recall means that the technique has returned most of the relevant results, while high precision means that it has returned substantially more relevant results than irrelevant ones.

some times the response time deteriorates, other times it improves. Note that, in this experimentation, we simulated each refactored configuration just once. As a future work, it would be interesting to take into account this "pathological uncertainty", by simulating N times each refactored configuration, and counting how many times it actually results in a better configuration with respect to the initial one. Thus, the existence of borderline cases influences precision. In fact, if at least one border-line case exists, then the precision is strictly less than 100%. Our conjecture still holds up to borderline cases. However, since we are interested in directing the user to obtain the best benefit (if one exists), by choosing the action with the maximum effectiveness we can be confident that if that action is beneficial, then it is the most beneficial one.

Observing Figure 2, we can notice that there are some "classification errors". Given a configuration, it is not well-classified if there exists at least a different configuration having greater effectiveness (thus, it is considered better by our approach) and lower RT (thus, actually it is not better) at the same time. Our approach made 6 classification errors on the case study: one error with respect to beneficial refactorings and 5 errors with respect to non-beneficial ones. The former can be discarded, because it is due to the border-line case. Concerning the latter errors, we notice that the probability of making a classification error increases while effectiveness decreases; in fact, for very small values of $eff(r)$, RT is very high.

4.3   ECS: Refactoring Reasoning

In our case study, the refactoring reasoning is based on the occurrences of three different performance antipatterns, i.e., *Blob*, *CPS* and *P&F*. Figure 3 shows the summary of our experimentation coming from the antipatterns fuzzy detection and refactoring steps of the model-based software refactoring process (see Figure 1): each (x, y) point is related to a considered antipattern and a refactoring action, where x is the antipattern occurrence probability, and y is the refactoring effectiveness. We are obviously interested to upper right-most points.

Figure 3 shows that if we use the *High probability* strategy (see Section 3.3) for the Blob antipattern, occurrences associated with a high probability are actually the ones that most likely provide a performance benefit.

For example, concerning the Blob antipattern: (i) points $(1, y)$ refer to component $C3$ that has a probability of occurrence equal to one, and two of its refactoring actions bring a system performance improvement, e.g. one is $Split(C3, n3)$ as labeled in the figure; (ii) points $(0.71, y)$ refer to component $C4$ that has a probability of occurrence equal to 0.71, and three of its refactoring actions have been experimented to be beneficial for the system, e.g. one is $Split(C4, n3)$ as labeled in the figure; (iii) all the remaining points correspond to low or zero probabilities of occurrence and refer to components $(C1, C2, C5, C6)$ for which refactoring effectiveness is very low.

Interestingly, in Figure 3 we can notice that CPS antipattern occurrences associated with a high probability may not imply a performance improvement. In our ECS case study we found that in case of the $(n2, n3)$ CPS occurrence,

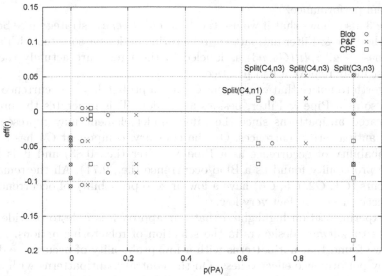

Fig. 3. Probability of antipattern occurrence vs. refactoring effectiveness

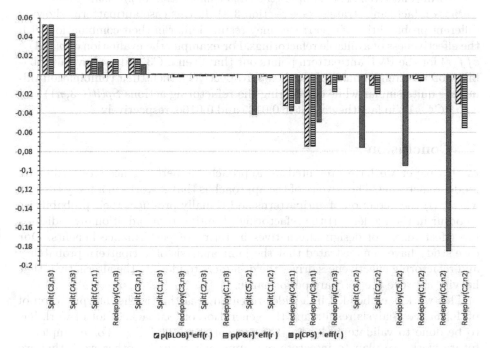

Fig. 4. Refactoring vs. probability of antipattern occurrence multiplied by refactoring effectiveness

which has a probability of one, no refactoring actions are actually beneficial for the system performance.

Figure 3 also shows that if we use the *High effectiveness* strategy (see Section 3.3) for the Pipe & Filter antipattern, refactoring actions associated with a high effectiveness, e.g. $Split(C4, n3)$ as labeled in the figure, are actually the ones that most likely remove a bad practice.

It is worth to notice that component $C3$ has a probability of occurrence equal to one also as a Pipe & Filter, besides as a Blob. This generates the problem of duplicated antipatterns since the same model element may represent two different antipattern occurrences. On the contrary, component $C4$ has a quite high probability of occurrence as a Pipe & Filter (i.e., 0.83) and it is larger than the probability found as a Blob occurrence (i.e., 0.71). All the remaining components ($C1$, $C2$, $C5$, $C6$) have a low or zero probability of occurrence and their effectiveness is in fact very low.

The experimentation highlighted that our approach is able to provide some guidelines to software designers in the selection of refactoring actions. In particular, we found that antipatterns with a low probability of occurrence do not entail any performance effectiveness. On the contrary, antipatterns with a high probability of occurrence may include beneficial refactoring actions but their effectiveness is not guaranteed in advance.

Figure 4 shows the product between probability of antipattern occurrence and refactoring effectiveness, to support the *High combination of probability and effectiveness* refactoring strategy (see Section 3.3). In this case antipatterns showing different probabilities of occurrence may result similar in their combination with the effectiveness of available refactorings. For example, the evaluation of $p(PA) * eff(r)$ for the P&F antipattern points out that even if $C3$ and $C4$ have a probability of occurrence equal to 1 and 0.83, respectively, then their combination values are quite similar while considering the refactoring actions $Split(C3, n1)$ and $Split(C4, n1)$, in fact they result in 0.0165 and 0.0166, respectively.

5   Conclusion

In this paper we have presented an approach for performance-based software model refactoring. The novelty of the approach is that it works in a fuzzy context where: (i) the detection of antipatterns additionally produces their probabilities to occur in the model; (ii) the refactoring of antipatterns additionally indicates the effectiveness of design alternatives in terms of performance benefits. Our case study have demonstrated that the joint analysis of antipattern probability and refactoring effectiveness drives the designers to identify the alternatives that heavily improve the software performance.

This work is embedded in a wider research area that is the interpretation of performance analysis results and the generation of feedback. A lot of work has to be done to validate and refine the presented methodology. For example, as future work, we plan to integrate our approach with the other work that we have conducted up today in this area, particularly with respect to [16]. Moreover, we are facing the problem of using the effectiveness of refactoring actions to decide the most promising model changes that can rapidly lead to remove performance problems. In this direction several interesting issues have to be faced, such as: (i) the consideration of multiple resources at the same time (e.g. a split can relieve the CPU load while aggravating the network occupancy due to increased interactions), (ii) the simultaneous application of multiple refactoring actions.

References

1. Smith, C.U.: Introduction to software performance engineering: Origins and outstanding problems. In: Bernardo, M., Hillston, J. (eds.) SFM 2007. LNCS, vol. 4486, pp. 395–428. Springer, Heidelberg (2007)
2. Woodside, C.M., Franks, G., Petriu, D.C.: The Future of Software Performance Engineering. In: Briand, L.C., Wolf, A.L. (eds.) FOSE, pp. 171–187 (2007)
3. Cortellessa, V., Marco, A.D., Inverardi, P.: Model-Based Software Performance Analysis, pp. 1–190. Springer (2011)
4. Lazowska, E., Kahorjan, J., Graham, G.S., Sevcik, K.: Quantitative System Performance: Computer System Analysis Using Queueing Network Models. Prentice-Hall, Inc. (1984)
5. Xu, J.: Rule-based automatic software performance diagnosis and improvement. Perform. Eval. 69, 525–550 (2012)
6. Martens, A., Koziolek, H., Becker, S., Reussner, R.: Automatically improve software architecture models for performance, reliability, and cost using evolutionary algorithms. In: ICPE, pp. 105–116 (2010)
7. Cortellessa, V., Di Marco, A., Eramo, R., Pierantonio, A., Trubiani, C.: Digging into UML models to remove performance antipatterns. In: ICSE Workshop Quovadis, pp. 9–16 (2010)
8. Trubiani, C., Koziolek, A.: Detection and solution of software performance antipatterns in palladio architectural models. In: International Conference on Performance Engineering (ICPE), pp. 19–30 (2011)
9. Arcelli, D., Cortellessa, V., Trubiani, C.: Antipattern-based model refactoring for software performance improvement. In: ACM SIGSOFT International Conference on Quality of Software Architectures (QoSA), pp. 33–42 (2012)
10. Cortellessa, V., De Sanctis, M., Di Marco, A., Trubiani, C.: Enabling Performance Antipatterns to arise from an ADL-based Software Architecture. In: Joint Conference on Software Architecture and European Conference on Software Architecture, WICSA/ECSA (2012)
11. Smith, C.U., Williams, L.G.: More New Software Antipatterns: Even More Ways to Shoot Yourself in the Foot. In: International Computer Measurement Group Conference, pp. 717–725 (2003)
12. Arcelli, D., Cortellessa, V., Trubiani, C.: Experimenting the influence of numerical thresholds on model-based detection and refactoring of performance antipatterns. ECEASST 59 (2013)
13. Parsons, T., Murphy, J.: Detecting Performance Antipatterns in Component Based Enterprise Systems. Journal of Object Technology 7, 55–91 (2008)
14. Diaz-Pace, A., Kim, H., Bass, L., Bianco, P., Bachmann, F.: Integrating quality-attribute reasoning frameworks in the arche design assistant. In: Becker, S., Plasil, F., Reussner, R. (eds.) QoSA 2008. LNCS, vol. 5281, pp. 171–188. Springer, Heidelberg (2008)

15. Cortellessa, V., Di Marco, A., Eramo, R., Pierantonio, A., Trubiani, C.: Approaching the Model-Driven Generation of Feedback to Remove Software Performance Flaws. In: EUROMICRO-SEAA, pp. 162–169. IEEE Computer Society (2009)
16. Trubiani, C., Koziolek, A., Cortellessa, V., Reussner, R.: Guilt-based handling of software performance antipatterns in palladio architectural models. Journal of Systems and Software 95, 141–165 (2014)
17. Cortellessa, V., Di Marco, A., Trubiani, C.: An approach for modeling and detecting software performance antipatterns based on first-order logics. Software and System Modeling 13, 391–432 (2014)
18. Cortellessa, V., Mirandola, R.: PRIMA-UML: a performance validation incremental methodology on early UML diagrams. Sci. Comput. Program. 44, 101–129 (2002)
19. Casale, G., Serazzi, G.: Quantitative system evaluation with Java modeling tools. In: International Conference Performance Engineering, pp. 449–454. ACM (2011)
20. Frakes, W.B., Baeza-Yates, R.: Information retrieval: data structures and algorithms. Prentice-Hall, Inc., Upper Saddle River (1992)

Analyzing Conflicts and Dependencies of Rule-Based Transformations in Henshin*

Kristopher Born, Thorsten Arendt, Florian Heß, and Gabriele Taentzer

Philipps-Universität Marburg, Germany
{born,arendt,hessflorian,taentzer}@informatik.uni-marburg.de

Abstract. Rule-based model transformation approaches show two kinds of non-determinism: (1) Several rules may be applicable to the same model and (2) a rule may be applicable at several different matches. If two rule applications to the same model exist, they may be in conflict, i.e., one application may disable the other one. Furthermore, rule applications may enable others leading to dependencies. The critical pair analysis (CPA) can report all potential conflicts and dependencies of rule applications that may occur during model transformation processes. This paper presents the CPA integrated in Henshin, a model transformation environment based on the Eclipse Modeling Framework (EMF).

1 Introduction

Rule-based model transformation systems can control the application of rules not only by explicit control mechanisms but also by causal dependencies of rule applications. Hence, these causal dependencies influence their execution order. If, e.g., a rule creates a model element, it can be used in subsequent rule applications. It can also happen that two rule applications overlap in a model element and one rule is to delete it while the other one requires its existence. For a better understanding of this implicit control flow, it is interesting to analyze all potential causal dependencies of rule applications for a given rule set.

The *critical pair analysis* (CPA) for graph rewriting [6] can be adapted to rule-based model transformation, e.g., to find conflicting functional requirements for software systems [7], or to analyze potential causal dependencies between model refactorings [9] which helps to make informed decisions on the most suitable refactoring to apply next. The CPA reports two different forms of potential causal dependencies, called conflicts and dependencies.

The application of a rule r_1 is in *conflict* with the application of a rule r_2 if

- r_1 deletes a model element used by the application of r_2 (**delete/use**), or
- r_1 produces a model element that r_2 forbids (**produce/forbid**), or
- r_1 changes an attribute value used by r_2 (**change/use**).[1]

---

* This work was partially funded by the German Research Foundation, Priority Program SPP 1593 "Design for Future – Managed Software Evolution".

[1] Dependencies between rule applications can be characterized analogously.

© Springer-Verlag Berlin Heidelberg 2015
A. Egyed and I. Schaefer (Eds.): FASE 2015, LNCS 9033, pp. 165–168, 2015.
DOI: 10.1007/978-3-662-46675-9_11

In our work, we extended Henshin [2], a rule-based model transformation language adapting graph transformation concepts and being based on the Eclipse Modeling Framework (EMF) [5]. Our extension computes all potential conflicts and dependencies of a set of rules and reports them in form of critical pairs. Each critical pair consists of the respective pair of rules, the kind of potential conflict or dependency found, and a minimal instance model illustrating the conflict or dependency. The analysis can be fine-tuned by a number of additional options to be set. The adoption of graph transformation theory to EMF model transformation requires to check the transformation rules for preserving model consistency and the resulting minimal model for being a valid EMF model [4].

The next section introduces a running example and discusses expected results; afterwards the new analysis tool is presented.

2   Model Transformation with Henshin

EMF is a common and widely-used open source technology in model-based software development. It extends Eclipse by modeling facilities and allows for defining (meta-)models and modeling languages by means of structured data models.

Henshin is an EMF model transformation engine based on graph transformation concepts. Since refactoring is a specific kind of model transformation, refactorings of EMF-based models can be specified in Henshin and then integrated into a refactoring framework such as EMF Refactor [3]. To demonstrate the main idea, we limit ourselves to one rule of a refactoring example for class modeling [8]. Rule Move_Attribute (Figure 1(a)) specifies the shift of an attribute from its owning class to an associated one along a reference. It is shown in abstract syntax. Objects and references tagged by ⟨⟨preserve⟩⟩ represent unchanged model elements, elements tagged by ⟨⟨create⟩⟩ represent new ones whereas those tagged by ⟨⟨delete⟩⟩ are removed by the transformation.

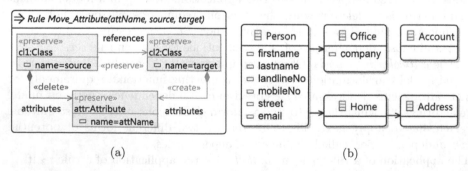

(a)   (b)

Fig. 1. Henshin refactoring rule (a) and class model Address Book(b)

Modifying the class model in Figure 1(b) by the refactoring specified in Figure 1(a), we observe two potential problems: (1) The attribute landlineNo of class Person can be shifted to either class Home or class Office (by refactoring Move_Attribute). However, if it is shifted to class Home the other refactoring becomes inapplicable (and vice versa). This means, refactoring Move_Attribute is in conflict with itself. (2) The attribute `street` of class `Person` can be shifted to class `Address` via class `Home` (by two applications of `Move_Attribute` along existing references). The second shift is currently not possible since class `Home` does not have an attribute so far, i.e., refactoring `Move_Attribute` may depend on itself. Graph transformation theory allows us to analyze such conflicts and dependencies at specification time by relying on the idea of the CPA.

3 Tooling

The provided CPA extension of Henshin can be used in two different ways: Its application programming interface (API) can be used to integrate the CPA into other tools and a user interface (UI) is provided supporting domain experts in developing rules by using the CPA interactively.

After invoking the analysis, the rule set and the kind of critical pairs to be analyzed have to be specified. Furthermore, options can be customized to stop the calculation after finding a first critical pair, to ignore critical pairs of the same rules, etc. The resulting list of critical pairs is shown and ordered along rule pairs. Figure 2 depicts an example for the analysis of rule `Move_Attribute`, in which the delete/use-conflict (1) corresponds to the example discussed above.

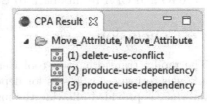

Fig. 2. The result view

The subsequent dependency results differ in their target of the second attribute movement. The first produce/use-dependency (2) represents the case of moving the attribute back to the original class, which leads to a smaller minimal model with only two classes referencing each other, as depicted in Figure 3. The highlighting by enclosing hash marks is the most important information, since the enclosing element is the cause of the dependency.

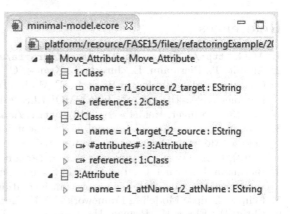

Fig. 3. Minimal model of a dependency

The link between 2:`Class` and 3:`Attribute` is created by the first rule application and is required by the second application. Since all elements and values in the minimal model may be matched by the first and the second rule application, there is a generic approach to represent attribute values. Value `r1_source_r2_target`, e.g., means that it must conform to value `source` in rule `r1` and value `target` in rule `r2`, respectively (compare Fig. 1(a)). The second dependency reported in Figure 2 is the handling of two consecutive attribute shifts, also described in Section 2.

The current version of the tool can analyze rules with negative application conditions and attributes of primitive data types. Positive application conditions shall be supported in the future. In order to avoid improper results, the rules are checked regarding these prerequisites. Further checks ensure that the rules are consistent to the properties defined in [4]. The LHS, RHS and intersection graphs of each rule are checked to comply to Definition 3 in [4], e.g., each node must have at most one container, there is no containment cycle. Furthermore, rules have to ensure consistent results, i.e., have to comply to Def. 6 in [4], ensuring e.g. that containment edge deletion and creation is restricted to edge redirection. The rule shown in Figure 1(a) is consistent to this definition. Internally, the CPA extension of Henshin is based on the graph transformation tool AGG [1]. Dedicated exporter and importer translate EMF meta-models and Henshin rules to AGG and CPA results back to EMF models.

4   Conclusion

The model transformation tool Henshin has been extended by a critical pair analysis to inspect rule sets for dependencies and conflicts. An interactive user interface is provided allowing the inspection of each critical pair in detail.

For the future, we intend to support also a confluence check of critical pairs, for which the CPA is a first step. The tool download as well as additional information on the CPA in Henshin, especially with respect to the translation between Henshin and AGG, can be found at [8].

References

1. AGG, http://user.cs.tu-berlin.de/~gragra/agg/
2. Arendt, T., Biermann, E., Jurack, S., Krause, C., Taentzer, G.: Henshin: Advanced Concepts and Tools for In-Place EMF Model Transformations. In: Petriu, D.C., Rouquette, N., Haugen, Ø. (eds.) MODELS 2010, Part I. LNCS, vol. 6394, pp. 121–135. Springer, Heidelberg (2010), http://www.eclipse.org/henshin/
3. Arendt, T., Taentzer, G.: A tool environment for quality assurance based on the Eclipse Modeling Framework. Automated Software Engineering 20(2), 141–184 (2013), http://www.eclipse.org/emf-refactor
4. Biermann, E., Ermel, C., Taentzer, G.: Formal foundation of consistent EMF model transformations by algebraic graph transformation. SoSyM 11(2), 227–250 (2012)
5. Eclipse: Eclipse Modeling Framework (EMF), http://www.eclipse.org/emf
6. Ehrig, H., Ehrig, K., Prange, U., Taentzer, G.: Fundamentals of Algebraic Graph Transformation. Monographs in Theoretical Computer Science. Springer (2006)
7. Hausmann, J.H., Heckel, R., Taentzer, G.: Detection of Conflicting Functional Requirements in a Use Case-Driven Approach: A Static Analysis Technique Based on Graph Transformation. In: ICSE, pp. 105–115. ACM (2002)
8. Tool download and installation, http://www.uni-marburg.de/fb12/swt/cpa
9. Mens, T., Taentzer, G., Runge, O.: Analysing refactoring dependencies using graph transformation. Software and System Modeling 6(3), 269–285 (2007)

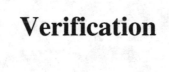

Verification

Translation Validation for Clock Transformations in a Synchronous Compiler

Van Chan Ngo, Jean-Pierre Talpin, Thierry Gautier, and Paul Le Guernic

INRIA Rennes - Bretagne Atlantique, 35042 Rennes Cedex, France
{firstname,lastname}@inria.fr

Abstract. Translation validation was introduced as a technique to formally verify the correctness of code generators that attempts to ensure that program transformations preserve the semantics of input program. In this work, we adopt this approach to construct a validator that formally verifies the preservation of clock semantics during the SIGNAL compiler transformations. The clock semantics is represented as a first-order logic formula called *clock model*. We then introduce a *refinement* which expresses the preservation of clock semantics, as a relation on clock models. Our validator does not require any instrumentation or modification of the compiler, nor any rewriting of the source program.

Keywords: Formal Verification, Translation Validation, Certified Compiler, SMT Solver, Synchronous Data-Flow Languages.

1 Introduction

Motivation. Synchronous programming languages such as SIGNAL, LUSTRE and ESTEREL propose a formal semantic framework to give a high-level specification of safety-critical software in automotive and avionics systems [10,13,2]. As other programming languages, synchronous languages are associated with a compiler. The compiler takes a source program, analyses and transforms it, performs optimizations, and finally generates executable code for a particular hardware platform or in some general-purpose programming languages. However, a compiler is a large and very complex program which often consists of hundreds of thousands, if not millions, lines of code, divided into multiple sub-systems and modules. The compilation process involves many analyzes, program transformations and optimizations. Some transformations and optimizations may introduce additional information, or constrain the compiled program. They may refine its meaning and specialize its behavior to meet a specific safety or optimization goal. Consequently, it is not uncommon that compilers silently issue an incorrect result in some unexpected context or inappropriate optimization goal. To circumvent compiler bugs, one can entirely rewrite the compiler with a theorem proving tool such as COQ [8], or check that it is compliant to the DO-178C documents [22]. Nonetheless, these solutions yield a situation where any change of the compiler (e.g., further optimization and update) means redoing the proof.

© Springer-Verlag Berlin Heidelberg 2015
A. Egyed and I. Schaefer (Eds.): FASE 2015, LNCS 9033, pp. 171–185, 2015.
DOI: 10.1007/978-3-662-46675-9_12

Another approach, which provides ideal separation between the tool under verification and its checker, is trying to verify that the output and the input have the same semantics. In this aim, *translation validation* was introduced in the 90's by Pnueli et al. [20,21], as a technique to formally verify correctness of code generators. Translation validators can be used to ensure that program transformations do not introduce semantic discrepancies, or to help debugging the compiler implementation.

Contribution. We consider the SIGNAL compiler, in the first two phases, The *clock information* and *Boolean abstraction* are computed. The next phase is *static scheduling* and the final phase is the *executable code generation*. Obviously, one can prove that the input program and its transformed program at the final phase have the same semantics. However, we believe that a better approach consists in separating the concerns and proving for each phase the preservation of different kinds of semantic properties. In the case of a synchronous compiler such as SIGNAL, the preservation of the semantics can be decomposed into the preservation of *clock semantics*, *data dependencies*, and *value-equivalence* of variables [18].

This paper focuses on constructing a validator that proves the preservation of clock semantics in the first two phases of the SIGNAL compiler. The clock semantics of the source program and its transformed counterpart are formally represented as *clock models*. A clock model is a first-order logic formula with *uninterpreted functions*. This formula deterministically characterizes the presence/absence status of all discrete data-flows (input, output and local variables of a program) manipulated by the specification at a given logic instant. Given two clock models, a *correct transformation* relation between them is checked by the existence of their *refinement* relation, which expresses the semantic preservation of clock semantics. In the implementation, we apply our translation validation to the first two transformation steps of the compiler.

The remainder of this paper is organized as follows. Section 2 introduces the SIGNAL language. Section 3 presents the abstraction that represents the clock semantics in terms of first-order logic formula. In Section 4, we consider the definition of correct transformation on clock models which formally proves the conformance between the original specification and its transformed counterpart. The application of the verification process to the SIGNAL compiler, and its integration in the Polychrony toolset [19] is addressed in Section 5. Section 6 presents related works and concludes our work.

2   The SIGNAL Language

SIGNAL [5,11] is a polychronous data-flow language that allows the specification of multi-clocked systems, called *polychrony models*. SIGNAL handles unbounded sequences of typed values $x(t)_{t \in \mathbb{N}}$, called *signals*, denoted as x. Each signal is implicitly indexed by a logical *clock* indicating the set of instants at which the signal is present, noted C_x. At a given instant, a signal may be present where it holds a value, or absent where it holds no value, denoted by $\bot$. Given two signals, they are *synchronous* iff they have the same clock. A process, written P or Q, consists of the synchronous composition of equations over signals x, y, z, written $x := y$ op z or $x := \text{op}(y, z)$, where op is an operator. In particular, a process can be used as a basic pattern, by means of an interface that describes its parameters and its input and output signals. Moreover, a process can use other subprocesses, or even other processes as external parameters. A program is a process and the language is modular.

Data Domains. Data types consist of usual scalar types (Boolean, integer, float, complex, and character), enumerated types, array types, tuple types, and the special type **event**. It is a subtype of the Boolean which has only one value, **true**.

Operators. The core language consists of two kinds of "statement" defined by the following primitive operators: four operators on signals and two operators on processes. The operators on signals define basic processes with implicit clock relations while the operators on processes are used to construct complex processes with the parallel composition operator. In the *delay* operator, inf and sup denote the greatest lower bound and the least upper bound.

- *Stepwise Functions:* $y := f(x_1, ..., x_n)$, where f is a *n-ary* function on values, defines a basic process whose output y is synchronous with $x_1, ..., x_n$ ($C_y = C_{x_1} = ... = C_{x_n}$) and $\forall t \in C_y, y(t) = f(x_1(t), ..., x_n(t))$.
- *Delay:* $y := x\$1$ **init** a defines a basic process such that y and x are synchronous ($C_y = C_x$), $y(t_0) = a$, and $\forall t \in C_y \wedge t > t_0, y(t) = x(t^-)$ with $t_0 = \inf\{t' | x(t') \neq \bot\}, t^- = \sup\{t' | t' < t \wedge x(t') \neq \bot\}$.
- *Merge:* $y := x$ **default** z defines a basic process which specifies that y is present iff x or z is present ($C_y = C_x \cup C_z$), and that $y(t) = x(t)$ if $t \in C_x$ and $y(t) = z(t)$ if $t \in C_z \setminus C_x$.
- *Sampling:* $y := x$ **when** b where b is a Boolean signal, defines a basic process such that $\forall t \in C_x \cap C_b \wedge b(t) = true, y(t) = x(t)$, and otherwise, y is absent ($C_y = C_x \cap [b]$, where $[b] = \{t \in C_b | b(t) = \text{true}\}$).
- *Composition:* If P_1 and P_2 are processes, then $P_1 | P_2$, also denoted as $(|P_1 | P_2|)$, is the process resulting of their parallel composition. This process consists of the composition of the systems of equations. The composition operator is commutative, associative, and idempotent.
- *Restriction:* P **where** x, where P is a process and x is a signal, specifies a process by considering x as local variable to P (i.e., x is not accessible from outside P).

Clock Relations. Clock relations can be defined explicitly: $y := \hat{}x$ specifies that y with **event** type is the clock of x, C_x. The synchronization $x \hat{=} y$ means that x and y have the same clock. The clock extraction from a Boolean signal is denoted by a unary *when*: **when** b. The clock union $x \hat{+} y$ defines a clock as the union $C_x \cup C_y$. In the same way, the clock intersection $x \hat{*} y$ and the clock difference $x \hat{-} y$ define clocks $C_x \cap C_y$ and $C_x \setminus C_y$.

Example. The following SIGNAL program emits a sequence of values FB, FB $- 1,...$, 2, 1, from each value of a positive integer signal FB coming from its environment. We can see that the clock of the output signal is more frequent than that of the input. The following diagram illustrates one possible execution of the program DEC.

```
process DEC=
(? integer FB; ! integer N) //FB is input signal and N is
   output signal
 (| FB ^= when (ZN<=1) //FB is present when ZN holds a value
     smaller than 1
  | N := FB default (ZN-1)
  | ZN := N$1 init 1 //ZN takes the previous value of N
  |)
where integer ZN end; //ZN is defined as a local signal
```

t	.	.	.	.	.	.	.	.	.
FB	6	⊥	⊥	⊥	⊥	3	⊥	⊥	2
ZN	1	6	5	4	3	2	1	3	2	1
N	6	5	4	3	2	1	3	2	1	2
C_{FB}	t_0						t_6			t_9
C_{ZN}	t_0	t_1	t_2	t_3	t_4	t_5	t_6	t_7	t_8	t_9
C_N	t_0	t_1	t_2	t_3	t_4	t_5	t_6	t_7	t_8	t_9

3 Clock Model

In SIGNAL, clocks play a much more important role than in other synchronous languages, they are used to express the underlying control (i.e., the synchronization between signals) for any conditional definition. This differs from LUSTRE, where all clocks are built by sampling the fastest clock. We consider the following equation with the primitive operator *sampling*, where x and y are numerical signals, and b is a Boolean signal: $y := x$ when b. To express the control, we need to represent the status of the signals x, y and b. We use a Boolean variable $\hat{x}$ to capture the status of x: ($\hat{x} = $ true) means x is present, and ($\hat{x} = $ false) means x is absent. In the same way, the Boolean variable $\hat{y}$ captures the status of y. For b, two Boolean variables $\hat{b}$ and $\tilde{b}$ are used to represent its status: ($\hat{b} = $ true $\wedge \tilde{b} = $ true) means b is present and holds a value true; ($\hat{b} = $ true $\wedge \tilde{b} = $ false) means b is present and holds a value false; and ($\hat{b} = $ false) means b is absent. Hence, at a given instant, the clock relations of the equation above can be encoded by the formula: $\hat{y} \Leftrightarrow (\hat{x} \wedge \hat{b} \wedge \tilde{b})$

3.1 Abstraction

Let $X = \{x_1, ..., x_n\}$ be the set of all signals in program P consisting of input, output, register (corresponding to *delay* operator), and local signals, denoted by I, O, R and L, respectively. With each signal x_i, based on the encoding scheme proposed in [12], we attach a Boolean variable $\widehat{x_i}$ to encode its clock and a variable $\widetilde{x_i}$ of same type as x_i to encode its value. The composition of processes corresponds to logical conjunctions. Thus the clock model of P will be a conjunction $\Phi(\mathrm{P}) = \bigwedge_{i=1}^{n} \phi(eq_i)$, whose atoms are $\widehat{x}_i, \widetilde{x}_i$, where $\phi(eq_i)$ is the abstraction of statement eq_i, and n is the number of statements in the program. In the following, we present the abstraction corresponding to each SIGNAL operator.

Stepwise Functions. The functions which apply on signal values in the stepwise functions are usual logic operators (**not, and, or**), numerical comparison functions ($<, >, =, <=, >=, /=$), and numerical operators ($+, -, *, /$). In our experience working with the SIGNAL compiler, it performs very few arithmetical optimizations and leaves most of the arithmetical expressions intact. Every definition of a signal is determined explicitly by the input and register signals, otherwise program can not be compiled. This suggests that most of the implications will hold independently of the features of the numerical comparison functions and numerical operators and we can replace these operations by *uninterpreted functions.* By following the encoding procedure of [1], for every numerical comparison function and numerical operator (denoted by $\square$) occurring in an equation, we perform the following rewriting: i) Replace each $x \square y$ by a new variable $v_{\square}^i$ of the same type as the return value by $\square$. Two stepwise functions $x \sqcup y$ and $x' \square y'$ are replaced by the same variable $v_{\square}^i$ iff x, y are identical to x' and y', respectively; ii) For every pair of newly added variables $v_{\square}^i$ and $v_{\square}^j$, $i \neq j$, corresponding to the non-identical occurrences $x \square y$ and $x' \square y'$, add the implication $(\widetilde{x} = \widetilde{x'} \wedge \widetilde{y} = \widetilde{y'}) \Rightarrow \widetilde{v_{\square}^i} = v_{\square}^j$ into the abstraction $\Phi(\mathrm{P})$. The abstraction $\phi(y := f(x_1, ..., x_n))$ of stepwise functions is defined by induction as follows: $\phi(\mathbf{true}) = \mathbf{true}$ and $\phi(\mathbf{false}) = \mathbf{false}$; $\phi(y := x) = (\widehat{y} \Leftrightarrow \widehat{x}) \wedge (\widehat{y} \Rightarrow (\widetilde{y} = \widetilde{x}))$; $\phi(y := x) = (\widehat{y} \Leftrightarrow \widehat{x}) \wedge (\widehat{y} \Rightarrow (\widetilde{y} = \widetilde{x})) \wedge (\widehat{x} \Rightarrow \widetilde{x})$ if x is an **event** signal; $\phi(y := \mathbf{not}\ x) = (\widehat{y} \Leftrightarrow \widehat{x}) \wedge (\widehat{y} \Rightarrow (\widetilde{y} \Leftrightarrow \neg\widetilde{x}))$; $\phi(y := x_1\ \mathbf{and}\ x_2) = (\widehat{y} \Leftrightarrow \widehat{x_1} \Leftrightarrow \widehat{x_2}) \wedge (\widehat{y} \Rightarrow (\widetilde{y} \Leftrightarrow \widetilde{x_1} \wedge \widetilde{x_2}))$; $\phi(y := x_1\ \mathbf{or}\ x_2) = (\widehat{y} \Leftrightarrow \widehat{x_1} \Leftrightarrow \widehat{x_2}) \wedge (\widehat{y} \Rightarrow (\widetilde{y} \Leftrightarrow \widetilde{x_1} \vee \widetilde{x_2}))$; $\phi(y := x_1 \square x_2) = (\widehat{y} \Leftrightarrow \widetilde{v_{\square}^i} \Leftrightarrow \widehat{x_1} \Leftrightarrow \widehat{x_2}) \wedge (\widehat{y} \Rightarrow (\widetilde{y} = \widetilde{v_{\square}^i}))$.

Delay. Considering the *delay* operator, $y := x\$1\ \mathbf{init}\ a$, its encoding $\phi(y := x\$1\ \mathbf{init}\ a)$ contributes to $\Phi(\mathrm{P})$ with the following conjunct: $(\widehat{y} \Leftrightarrow \widehat{x}) \wedge (\widehat{y} \Rightarrow ((\widetilde{y} = m.x) \wedge (m.x' = \widetilde{x}))) \wedge (m.x_0 = a)$. This encoding requires that at any instant, signals x and y have the same status (present or absent). To encode the value of the output signal as well, we introduce a memorization variable $m.x$ that stores the last value of x. The next value of $m.x$ is $m.x'$ and it is initialized to a in $m.x_0$.

Merge. The encoding of the *merge* operator, $y := x\ \mathbf{default}\ z$, contributes to $\Phi(\mathrm{P})$ with the following conjunct: $(\widehat{y} \Leftrightarrow (\widehat{x} \vee \widehat{z})) \wedge \widehat{y} \Rightarrow ((\widehat{x} \wedge (\widetilde{y} = \widetilde{x})) \vee (\neg\widehat{x} \wedge (\widetilde{y} = \widetilde{z})))$

Sampling. The encoding of the *sampling* operator, $y := x\ \mathbf{when}\ b$, contributes to $\Phi(\mathrm{P})$ with the following conjunct: $(\widehat{y} \Leftrightarrow (\widehat{x} \wedge \widehat{b} \wedge \overline{b})) \wedge (\widehat{y} \Rightarrow (\widetilde{y} = \widetilde{x}))$

Composition. Consider the composition of two processes P_1 and P_2. Its abstraction $\phi(\mathrm{P}_1|\mathrm{P}_2)$ is defined as follows: $\phi(\mathrm{P}_1) \wedge \phi(\mathrm{P}_2)$

Clock Relations. Given the above rules, we can obtain the following abstraction for derived operators on clocks. Here, z is a signal of type **event**: $\phi(z := \hat{\ }x) = (\widehat{z} \Leftrightarrow \widehat{x}) \wedge (\widehat{z} \Rightarrow \widetilde{z})$; $\phi(x\hat{\ } = y) = \widehat{x} \Leftrightarrow \widehat{y}$; $\phi(z := x\hat{\ }+ y) = (\widehat{z} \Leftrightarrow (\widehat{x} \vee \widehat{y})) \wedge (\widehat{z} \Rightarrow \widetilde{z})$;

$\phi(z := x \,\hat{*}\, y) = (\hat{z} \Leftrightarrow (\hat{x} \wedge \hat{y})) \wedge (\hat{z} \Rightarrow \bar{z}); \; \phi(z := x \,\hat{-}\, y) = (\hat{z} \Leftrightarrow (\hat{x} \wedge \neg \hat{y})) \wedge (\hat{z} \Rightarrow \bar{z});$
$\phi(z := \text{when } b) = (\hat{z} \Leftrightarrow (\hat{b} \wedge \bar{b})) \wedge (\hat{z} \Rightarrow \bar{z}).$

Example. Applying the abstraction rules above, the clock semantics of the program DEC is represented by the following formula $\Phi(\text{DEC})$, where ZN $<= 1$ and ZN -1 are replaced by two fresh variables ZN1 and ZN2, and encoded by two uninterpreted function symbols $\text{v}^1_{<=}$ and v^1_-, respectively.

$$(\widehat{FB} \Leftrightarrow \widehat{ZN1} \wedge \widetilde{ZN1}) \wedge (\widehat{ZN1} \Leftrightarrow \widetilde{v^1_{<=}} \Leftrightarrow \widehat{ZN}) \wedge (\widehat{ZN1} \Rightarrow (\widetilde{ZN1} = \widetilde{v^1_{<=}}))$$
$$\wedge (\widehat{ZN} \Leftrightarrow \widehat{N}) \wedge (\widehat{ZN} \Rightarrow (\widetilde{ZN} = m.N \wedge m.N' = \widetilde{N})) \wedge (m.N_0 = 1)$$
$$\wedge (\widehat{N} \Leftrightarrow \widehat{FB} \vee \widehat{ZN2}) \wedge (\widehat{N} \Rightarrow ((\widehat{FB} \wedge \widetilde{N} = \widehat{FB}) \vee (\neg \widehat{FB} \wedge \widetilde{N} = \widetilde{ZN2})))$$
$$\wedge (\widehat{ZN2} \Leftrightarrow \widetilde{v^1_-} \Leftrightarrow \widehat{ZN}) \wedge (\widehat{ZN2} \Rightarrow (\widetilde{ZN2} = \widetilde{v^1_-}))$$

In the following sections, we denote input, output, register, memorization and local variables used in a clock model by $I_{clk}, O_{clk}, R_{clk}, M_{clk}$ and L_{clk}, respectively. Note that the memorization variables are introduced only by the translation into clock models, they are not original in the SIGNAL programs.

Definition 1 (Clock Configuration). *Consider a clock model $\Phi(\text{P})$ over the set of variabels $\hat{X}$. A clock configuration $\hat{I}$ is an interpretation over $\hat{X}$ such that it is a model of the first-order logic formula $\Phi(\text{P})$.*

For instance, $(\widehat{FB} \mapsto \text{true}, \widehat{N} \mapsto \text{true}, \widehat{ZN} \mapsto \text{true}, \widetilde{FB} \mapsto 6, \widetilde{N} \mapsto 6, \widetilde{ZN} \mapsto 1)$ is a clock configuration of $\Phi(\text{DEC})$.

3.2   Concrete Clock Semantics

We rely on the basic elements of *trace semantics* [14] to define the clock semantics of a synchronous program. For each $x_i \in X$, we use $\mathbb{D}_{x_i}$ to denote its domain of values, and $\mathbb{D}^{\perp}_{x_i} = \mathbb{D}_{x_i} \cup \{\perp\}$ to denote its domain of values with absent value, where $\perp \notin \mathbb{D}_{x_i}$ denotes the absent value. Then, the domain of values of X with absent value is defined as $\mathbb{D}^{\perp}_X = \bigcup_{i=1}^{n} \mathbb{D}_{x_i} \cup \{\perp\}$

Definition 2 (Clock Events, Clock Traces). *Given a non-empty set X, the set of clock events on X, denoted by $\mathcal{E}c_X$, is the set of all possible interpretations I over X. The set of clock traces on X, denoted by $\mathcal{T}c_X$, is defined by the set of functions T_c defined from the set $\mathbb{N}$ of natural numbers to $\mathcal{E}c_X$, denoted by $T_c : \mathbb{N} \longrightarrow \mathcal{E}c_X$.*

An interpretation I is an assignment of values from X to $\mathbb{D}^{\perp}_X$. The assignment $I(x) = \perp$ means x holds no value while $I(x) = v$ means that x holds the value v. The natural numbers represent the instants, $t = 0, 1, 2, ...$, a trace T_c is a chain of clock events. We denote the interpreted value of a variable x_i at instant t by $T_c(t)(x_i)$.

Definition 3 (Restriction Clock Trace). *Given a non-empty set X, a subset $X_1 \subseteq X$, and a clock trace T_c being defined on X, the restriction of T_c onto X_1 is denoted by $X_1.T_c$. It is defined as $X_1.T_c : \mathbb{N} \longrightarrow \mathcal{E}c_{X_1}$ such that $\forall t \in \mathbb{N}, \forall x \in X_1, X_1.T_c(t)(x) = T_c(t)(x)$.*

Let X be the set of all signals in program P. We write $[[\text{P}]]_c$ to denote the clock semantics of P which is defined as the set of all possible clock traces on X. For any subset $X_1 \subseteq X$, the set of all restriction clock traces on X_1 defines the clock semantics of P on X_1, denoted by $([[\text{P}]]_c)_{\setminus X_1}$.

Let $\Phi(\text{P})$ be the clock model of the program P. We now define the *concrete clock semantics* of a clock model based on the notion of clock configurations. Given a clock configuration $\hat{I}$, the set of clock events according to $\hat{I}$ is the set of interpretations I such that for every signal x_i, if x_i holds a value then $\widehat{x}_i$ has the value $\texttt{true}$ (x_i is present), and $\widehat{x}_i$ holds the same value as x_i. Otherwise, $\widehat{x}_i$ has the value $\texttt{false}$ (meaning x_i is absent). The set of clock events according to $\hat{I}$ and the set of all clock events of $\Phi(\text{P})$ are computed as follows:

$$
\begin{aligned}
S_{\mathcal{E}c_X}(\hat{I}) \quad &= \{I \in \mathcal{E}c_X \mid \forall x_i \in X, (I(x_i) = \hat{I}(\widehat{x}_i) \wedge \hat{I}(\widehat{x}_i) = \texttt{true}) \\
&\quad \vee (I(x_i) = \perp \wedge \hat{I}(\widehat{x}_i) = \texttt{false})\} \\
S_{\mathcal{E}c_X}(\Phi(\text{P})) &= \bigcup\nolimits_{\hat{I} \models \Phi(\text{P})} S_{\mathcal{E}c_X}(\hat{I})
\end{aligned}
$$

With a set of clock events $S_{\mathcal{E}c_X}(\Phi(\text{P}))$, the concrete clock semantics of $\Phi(\text{P})$ is defined by the following set of clock traces $\Gamma(\Phi(\text{P})) = \{T_c \in \mathcal{T}c_X \mid \forall t, T_c(t) \in S_{\mathcal{E}c_X}(\Phi(\text{P}))\}$. For any subset $X_1 \subseteq X$, the concrete clock semantics of $\Phi(\text{P})$ on X_1 is defined as $\Gamma(\Phi(\text{P}))_{\setminus X_1} = \{X_1.T_c \mid T_c \in \mathcal{T}c_X \text{ and } \forall t, T_c(t) \in S_{\mathcal{E}c_X}(\Phi(\text{P}))\}$. Due to the lack of space, we do not present the proof of soundness of our abstraction.

4   Clock Model Translation Validation

We adopt the translation validation approach [20,21] to formally verify that the clock semantics is preserved for every transformation of the compiler. In order to apply the translation validation to the transformations, we capture the clock semantics of the original program and its transformed counterpart by means of clock models. Then we introduce a *refinement* relation which expresses the preservation of clock semantics, as relation on clock models.

4.1   Clock Refinement

Let $\Phi(\text{A})$ and $\Phi(\text{C})$ be two clock models of programs A and C, to which we refer respectively as a source program and its transformed counterpart produced by the compiler. We denote the sets of all signals in A, C by X_A and X_C, respectively. The corresponding sets of variables which are used to construct the clock models are denoted by $\widehat{X_A}$ and $\widehat{X_C}$. Consider the finite set of common signals $X = X_A \cap X_C$ and the set of common variables which are used to construct the clock models is $\widehat{X} = \widehat{X_A} \cap \widehat{X_C}$, we say that A and C have the same clock semantics on X if $\Phi(\text{A})$ and $\Phi(\text{C})$ have the same set of concrete restriction clock traces on X:

$$
\forall X.T_c.(X.T_c \in \Gamma(\Phi(\text{C}))_{\setminus X} \Leftrightarrow X.T_c \in \Gamma(\Phi(\text{A}))_{\setminus X})
$$

In fact, the compilation makes the transformed program more concrete. For instance, when the SIGNAL compiler performs the "endochronization" which is used to generate the sequential executable code, the signal with the fastest clock is always present in the generated code. Moreover, compilers perform transformations and optimizations for removing or eliminating some redundant behaviors of the source program (e.g., eliminating subexpressions, trivial clock relations). Consequently, the above requirement is too strong to be practical. Hence, we have to relax it as follows:

$$\forall X.T_c.(X.T_c \in \Gamma(\Phi(\mathtt{C}))_{\backslash X} \Rightarrow X.T_c \in \Gamma(\Phi(\mathtt{A}))_{\backslash X})$$

It expresses that every restriction clock trace of $\Phi(\mathtt{C})$ is also a clock trace of $\Phi(\mathtt{A})$ on X, or $\Gamma(\Phi(\mathtt{C}))_{\backslash X} \subseteq \Gamma(\Phi(\mathtt{A}))_{\backslash X}$. We say that $\Phi(\mathtt{C})$ is a *correct clock transformation* of $\Phi(\mathtt{A})$, or $\Phi(\mathtt{C})$ is a clock refinement of $\Phi(\mathtt{A})$ on X, denoted by $\Phi(\mathtt{C}) \sqsubseteq_{clk} \Phi(\mathtt{A})$.

Proposition 1. *The clock refinement is reflexive and transitive*

Proof. Proposition 1 is proved based on the clock refinement definition. $\Phi(\mathtt{P}) \sqsubseteq_{clk} \Phi(\mathtt{P})$ since $\Gamma(\Phi(\mathtt{P}))_{\backslash X} \subseteq \Gamma(\Phi(\mathtt{P}))_{\backslash X}$. For every clock trace $X.T_c \in \Gamma(\Phi(\mathtt{P_1}))_{\backslash X}$, $\Phi(\mathtt{P_1}) \sqsubseteq_{clk} \Phi(\mathtt{P_2})$ on X implies $X.T_c \in \Gamma(\Phi(\mathtt{P_2}))_{\backslash X}$. Since $\Phi(\mathtt{P_2}) \sqsubseteq_{clk} \Phi(\mathtt{P_3})$ on X, we have $X.T_c \in \Gamma(\Phi(\mathtt{P_3}))_{\backslash X}$, or $\Phi(\mathtt{P_1}) \sqsubseteq_{clk} \Phi(\mathtt{P_3})$ on X.

4.2   Adaptation to SIGNAL Compiler

We will adapt the definition of the above general clock refinement to the case of the SIGNAL compiler. We need to consider the following factors [4]. A first consideration is that the programs take the inputs from their environment and the register values. Then, they calculate the outputs to react with the environment. In general, the programs can use some local variables to make the output calculations. However, from the outside, the natural observation of the programs is the snapshot of the values of the input and output signals. In our context, it is the snapshot of the presence of the input and output signals. For example, for the program DEC, the observation is the tuple of the presence of the signals (FB, N) at a considered instant.

A second consideration is that in the compilation process of the SIGNAL compiler, the local signals in the source program do not necessarily have counterparts in the transformed program. However, all input and output signals are preserved in the transformations and are represented by identical names in the transformed program. Moreover, all signals in the R set are also preserved in the transformations. Therefore, it is natural to choose the snapshot of the presence of the input and output signals to be the observation for the transformed program.

These considerations let us adapt the above definition of clock refinement as follows. Let X_A and X_C be the sets of all signals in the source program A and its counterpart transformed program C. We write X_{IO} to denote the set of common input and output signals. We say that C is correct transformation of A if at any instant, the tuples of values representing the presence of the signals in X_{IO} are the same in both programs. In other words, $\Phi(\mathtt{C}) \sqsubseteq_{clk} \Phi(\mathtt{A})$ on X_{IO}.

4.3   Proving Clock Refinement by SMT

Our aim is proving that $\Phi(\text{C})$ refines $\Phi(\text{A})$ on X_{IO}. Let $\widehat{X_A}$, $\widehat{X_C}$ and $\widehat{X_{IO}}$ be the set of variables which are used to construct $\Phi(\text{A})$, $\Phi(\text{C})$ and the set of common variables between the two clock models. For every variable in the clock model $\Phi(\text{C})$ except the common variables in $\widehat{X_{IO}}$, we added "c" as superscript to distinguish them from the variables in the clock model of the input program. The standard way of proving the existence of the clock refinement is based on the following elements:

- The identification of a *variable mapping* that maps the non input/output variables from the clock model $\Phi(\text{A})$ to the non input/output variables in the clock model $\Phi(\text{C})$. We denote the mapping by: $\widehat{X_A} \setminus \widehat{X_{IO}} = \alpha(\widehat{X_C} \setminus \widehat{X_{IO}})$
- The premises of a rule such that if the premises hold, then the conclusion, $\Phi(\text{C})$ refines $\Phi(\text{A})$, is **true**. The premise is presented in Fig. 1.

For a variable mapping $\widehat{X_A} \setminus \widehat{X_{IO}} = \alpha(\widehat{X_C} \setminus \widehat{X_{IO}})$,

Premise $\forall \hat{I}$ over $\widehat{X_A} \cup \widehat{X_C}.(\hat{I} \models \Phi(\text{C}) \Rightarrow \hat{I} \models \Phi(\text{A}))$

Conclusion $\Phi(\text{C}) \sqsubseteq_{clk} \Phi(A)$ on X_{IO}

Fig. 1. Rule CLKREF

The rule CLKREF indicates that for any interpretation $\hat{I}$ over $\widehat{X_A} \cup \widehat{X_C}$ such that the variable mapping is evaluated to **true**, $\hat{I}$ is a clock configuration of $\Phi(\text{C})$ then it is also a clock model of $\Phi(\text{A})$. Then there exists a clock refinement for $(\Phi(\text{C}), \Phi(\text{A}))$. The rule CLKREF is sound based on the following theorem.

Theorem 1. *For a variable mapping* $\widehat{X_A} \setminus \widehat{X_{IO}} = \alpha(\widehat{X_C} \setminus \widehat{X_{IO}})$, *if the formula* $\Phi(\text{C}) \Rightarrow \Phi(\text{A})$ *is valid, then* $\Phi(\text{C}) \sqsubseteq_{clk} \Phi(\text{A})$ *on* X_{IO}.

Proof. To prove it, we have to show that for every interpretation $\hat{I}$ over $\hat{X} = \widehat{X_A} \cup \widehat{X_C}$ such that it is evaluated to **true**. If $\hat{I} \models (\Phi(\text{C}) \Rightarrow \Phi(\text{A}))$, then $\Gamma(\Phi(\text{C}))_{\setminus X_{IO}} \subseteq \Gamma(\Phi(\text{A}))_{\setminus X_{IO}}$. Given $X_{IO}.T_c \in \Gamma(\Phi(\text{C}))_{\setminus X_{IO}}$, it means that $\forall t, T_c(t) \in S_{\mathcal{E}c_X}(\Phi(\text{C}))$. Since for every interpretation $\hat{I}$, $\hat{I} \models \Phi(\text{C})$ implies that $\hat{I} \models \Phi(\text{A})$, thus $S_{\mathcal{E}c_X}(\Phi(\text{C})) \subseteq S_{\mathcal{E}c_X}(\Phi(\text{A}))$ under the variable mapping. We get $T_c(t) \in S_{\mathcal{E}c_X}(\Phi(\text{A}))$ for every t. Therefore, we have $T_c \in \Gamma(\Phi(\text{A}))$.

Consider a variable $x \in \widehat{X_A} \setminus \widehat{X_{IO}}$, the mapping α_x of the variable mapping defines the value of x in the clock model $\Phi(\text{A})$ α-related to the value represented by the clock model $\Phi(\text{C})$. We therefore need to describe the mappings α_x for $x^c \in \widehat{X_C} \setminus \widehat{X_{IO}} = M_{clk} \cup R_{clk} \cup L_{clk}$. Recall that every register signal s, we introduce memorization variables $m.s$, $m.s'$ in the clock model $\Phi(\text{A})$, and the corresponding memorization variables $m.s^c$, $m.s'^c$ in the clock model $\Phi(\text{C})$. Therefore, we define the following instance of the α mapping for each register signal s: $\tilde{s} = \tilde{s}^c \Rightarrow m.s = m.s^c \wedge m.s' = m.s'^c$.

For example, the mapping for the variables $m.N$, $m.N'$, $m.N^c$, and $m.N'^c$ will be given by the formula: $\tilde{N} = \tilde{N}^c \Rightarrow m.N = m.N^c \wedge m.N' = m.N'^c$.

It remains to define the instance of the mapping α for variables $\hat{l}, \tilde{l} \in R_{clk} \cup L_{clk}$ in the clock model $\Phi(\mathtt{A})$ which correspond to the local or register signal named l in the program. In a SIGNAL program, one signal is defined by an equation $l = eq$, if we follow the definitions of all output and local signals in this equation and apply successively substitutions, then we get that the equation is constructed only by the input and register signals. This property is yielded since the SIGNAL program is determinate, meaning that all definitions of signals are defined determinately by the input and register signals, and the compilers rejects all non-determinate program. Equivalently, in the corresponding clock model $\Phi(\mathtt{A})$, the output, register and local variables are determinately defined by the input I and memorization M variables. The definition is written in the clock model in the form $\hat{l} \Leftrightarrow \hat{f} \wedge (\hat{l} \Rightarrow \tilde{l} = \tilde{f})$ or $\hat{l} \Leftrightarrow \hat{f} \wedge (\hat{l} \Rightarrow \tilde{l} = \tilde{f}) \wedge \tilde{f}_0$, where $\hat{f}$, $\tilde{f}$ and $\tilde{f}_0$ are the formulas which define the clock relation, the value, and the initial value of the signal l in the clock model $\Phi(\mathtt{A})$. Therefore, we define the following instance of the α mapping in the clock model corresponding to each register or local signal l: $\hat{l} \Leftrightarrow \hat{f} \wedge (\hat{l} \Rightarrow \tilde{l} = \tilde{f})$ or $\hat{l} \Leftrightarrow \hat{f} \wedge (\hat{l} \Rightarrow \tilde{l} = \tilde{f}) \wedge \tilde{f}_0$.

For example, the mapping for the variables $\widehat{ZN}$ and $\widetilde{ZN}$ in the clock model $\Phi(\mathtt{DEC})$ corresponding to the local variable ZN in the program DEC will be given by the formula: $(\widehat{ZN} \Leftrightarrow \hat{N}) \wedge (\widehat{ZN} \Rightarrow (\widetilde{ZN} = m.N \wedge m.N' = \tilde{N})) \wedge (m.N_0 = 1)$.

Therefore, the variable mapping $\widehat{X_A} \setminus \widehat{X_{IO}} = \alpha(\widehat{X_C} \setminus \widehat{X_{IO}})$ is expressed as the following formula:

$$\bigwedge_{m.s \in M}(\tilde{s} = \tilde{s}^c \Rightarrow m.s = m.s^c) \wedge \bigwedge_{\hat{l}, \tilde{l} \in S \cup L}(\hat{l} \Leftrightarrow \hat{f} \wedge (\hat{l} \Rightarrow \tilde{l} = \tilde{f})) \text{ or}$$
$$\bigwedge_{m.s \in M}(\tilde{s} = \tilde{s}^c \Rightarrow m.s = m.s^c) \wedge \bigwedge_{\hat{l}, \tilde{l} \in S \cup L}(\hat{l} \Leftrightarrow \hat{f} \wedge (\hat{l} \Rightarrow \tilde{l} = \tilde{f}) \wedge \tilde{f}_0)$$

To solve the validity of the formula $(\Phi(\mathtt{C}) \Rightarrow \Phi(\mathtt{A}))$ in Theorem 1 under the variable mapping, a SMT solver is needed since this formula involves non-Boolean variables and *uninterpreted functions* (using a SAT solver would not be sufficient). A SMT solver decides the satisfiability of arbitrary logic formulas of linear real and integer arithmetic, scalar types, other user-defined data structures, and uninterpreted functions. If the formula belongs to the decidable theory, the solver gives two types of answers: sat when the formula has a model (there exists an interpretation that satisfies it); or unsat, otherwise. In our case, we will ask the solver to check whether the formula $\neg(\Phi(\mathtt{C}) \wedge \widehat{X_A} \setminus \widehat{X_{IO}} = \alpha(\widehat{X_C} \setminus \widehat{X_{IO}}) \Rightarrow \Phi(\mathtt{A}))$ is unsatisfiable, since this formula is unsatisfiable iff $\models (\Phi(\mathtt{C}) \wedge \widehat{X_A} \setminus \widehat{X_{IO}} = \alpha(\widehat{X_C} \setminus \widehat{X_{IO}}) \Rightarrow \Phi(\mathtt{A}))$. In our translation validation, the clock models which are constructed from Boolean or numerical variables and uninterpreted functions belong to a part of first-order logic which has a *small model* property according to [3]. The numerical variables are involved only in some implications with *uninterpreted functions* such as $(\tilde{x} = \tilde{x}' \wedge \tilde{y} = \tilde{y}') \Rightarrow \widetilde{v_\square^i} = \widetilde{v_\square^j}$.

In addition, the formula is quantifier-free. This means that the check of satisfiability can be established by examining a certain finite cardinality of models. Therefore, the formula can be solved efficiently and significantly improves the scalability of the solver.

5   Implementation

This section describes the implementation of our validator and some adaptation when the translation validation is applied to the real SIGNAL compiler. We also show the previously unknown bugs have been detected so far by our validator.

5.1   Towards Certified Compiler

Given a program P, with an unverified compiler, the compilation process can be represented in the following pseudo-code, where $Cp(P)$ is the compilation step from the source program P to either compiled code $IR(P)$ or compilation errors:

```
if (Cp(P) is Error) then
    output Error;
else output IR(P);
```

Now, the compilation is followed by our refinement verification which checks that the transformed program $IR(P)$ refines P w.r.t. the clock semantics:

```
if (Cp(P) is Error) then
    output Error;
else if (Φ(IR(P)) ⊑_clk Φ(P)) then
    output IR(P);
else output Error;
```

This will provide a formal guarantee as strong as that provided by a certified compiler in case the correctness of the validator is proved. We describe the main components of the implementation which is integrated in the existing POLY-CHRONY toolset [19] to prove the preservation of clock semantics of the SIGNAL compiler. We are interested here in the first phase: *clock calculation* and *Boolean abstraction* where the intermediate forms of the source program of are expressed in the SIGNAL language itself.

At a high level, our validator, which is depicted in Figure 2, works as follows. First, it takes the input program P and its transformed counterpart P_BASIC_TRA, and constructs the corresponding clock models. These clock models are combined as the formula $(\Phi(\text{P\_BASIC\_TRA}) \Rightarrow \Phi(\text{P}))$. In the solving phase, it checks the validity of the formula $\Phi(\text{P\_BASIC\_TRA}) \Rightarrow \Phi(\text{P})$. The result of this check can be exploited for the preservation of clock semantics of the transformations. If the formula is not valid then it emits a compiler bug. Otherwise, the compiler continues its work. The same procedure is applied for the other steps of the compiler. Finally, our verification process asserts that $\Phi(\text{P\_BOOL\_TRA}) \sqsubseteq_{clk} \Phi(\text{P\_BASIC\_TRA}) \sqsubseteq_{clk} \Phi(\text{P})$ along the transformations of the compiler. We delegate the checking of the clock refinement to a SMT solver. For our experiments, we consider the YICES [9] solver, which is one of the best solvers at the SMT-COMP competition [23].

5.2   Detected Bugs

So far, our validator has revealed three previously unknown bugs in the compilation of the SIGNAL compiler. The first problem was introduced when multiple

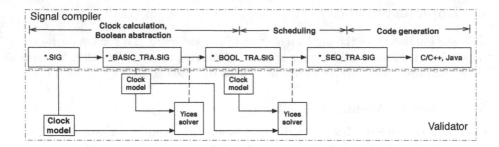

Fig. 2. The Integration within POLYCHRONY Toolset

constraints condition a clock such as in the following segment of SIGNAL program and its clock calculation part in transformed programs:

```
// P_BASIC_TRA.SIG                    // P_BOOL_TRA.SIG
| CLK_x := when (y <= 9)             | when Tick ^= C_z ^= C_CLK
| CLK := when (y >= 1)               | when C_z ^= x ^= z
| CLK_x ^= CLK                       | C_z := y <= 9
| CLK ^= XZX_24                      | C_CLK := y >= 1
// P.SIG
| x ^= when (y <= 9)
| x ^= when (y >= 1)
```

In the transformed counterpart P_BASIC_TRA, the introduction of signal XZX_24 and the synchronization between CLK and XZX_24 cause the incorrect specification of clocks, the signal x might be absent when XZX_24 is absent, which is not the case in P, nor in P_BOOL_TRA). This bug was caught by our validator when it found that $\Phi(\text{P\_BOOL\_TRA}) \not\sqsubseteq_{clk} \Phi(\text{P\_BASIC\_TRA})$.

The second problem is the wrong implementation of xor operator as shown in the followng program. The validator detects this bug with the fact that $\Phi(\text{P\_BASIC\_TRA}) \not\sqsubseteq_{clk} \Phi(\text{P})$.

```
// P.SIG                             // P_BASIC_TRA.SIG
| b3 := (true xor true) and b1      | CLK_b1 := ^b1
                                     | CLK_b1 ^= b1 ^= b3 | b3 := b1
```

The last problem detected was not found by the translation validation but was indirectly discovered when trying to apply it. It occurred in a program in which a *merge* operator with a constant signal was used, such as $y := 1$ default x. In this case, the code generation phase of the compiler dealt wrongly with the *clock context* of a constant signal by introducing a syntax error in the generated C code. The bug and its fix are given by:

```
// Version with bug          // Version without bug
if (C_y) {                   if (C_y) {
    y = 1; else y = x;           if (C_y) y = 1; else y = x;
    w_ClockError_y(y);           w_ClockError_y(y);
}                            }
```

6   Related Work and Conclusion

The notion of translation validation was introduced in [20,21] by A. Pnueli et al. to verify the code generator of SIGNAL. In that work, the authors define a language of symbolic models to represent both the source and target programs, called *Synchronous Transition Systems* (STS). A STS is a set of logic formulas which describes the functional and temporal constraints of the whole program and its generated C code. Then they use BDD [6] representations to implement the symbolic STS models, and their proof method uses a solver to reason on constraints over signals. The drawback of this approach is that it does not capture explicitly the clock semantics. Additionally, for a large program, the formula is very large, including numerical expressions that cause some inefficiency. Moreover, the whole calculation of a synchronous program or the corresponding generated code is considered as one atomic transition in STS, thus it does not capture the data dependencies between signals and does not explicitly prove the preservation of abstract clocks in the compiler transformations.

Another related work is the static analysis of SIGNAL programs for efficient code generation [12]. In a similar way as we do, the authors formalize the abstract clocks and clock relations as first-order logic formulas with the help of interval abstraction technique. The objective is to make the generated code more efficient by detecting and removing the dead-code segments (e.g., segment of code to compute a data-flow which is always absent). They determine the existence of empty clocks, mutual exclusion of two or more clocks, or clock inclusions, by reasoning on the formal model using a SMT solver.

Some other works have adopted the translation validation approach in verification of transformations, and optimizations. In [16], the translation validation is used to verify several common optimizations such as common subexpression elimination, register allocation, and loop inversion. The validator is simulation-based, that means it checks the existence of a simulation relation between two programs. Leroy et al. [15,7] used this technique to develop the COMPCERT high-assurance C compiler. The programs before and after the transformations and optimizations of the compiler are represented in a common intermediate form, then the preservation of semantics is checked by using symbolic execution and the proof assistant COQ. It also has shown that translation validation can be used to validate advanced loop optimizations such as software pipelining as in [25]. Tristan et al. [24] recently proposed a framework for translation validation of LLVM optimizer. For a function and its optimized counterpart, they compute a shared value-graph. The graph is *normalized* (roundly speaking, the graph is reduced). After the normalizing, if the outputs of two functions are represented by the same sub-graph, they can safely conclude that two functions are equivalent.

With the same purpose, in the work of [17], we encode the source SIGNAL programs and their transformations with *Polynomial Dynamical Systems* (PDS), and we prove that the transformations preserve the abstract clocks and clock relations of the source programs. This approach uses simulation relation in model checking techniques, and it suffers from the increasing of the state-space when it deals with large programs. On the contrary, in our present work, the abstract clocks and clock relations are described as a logic formula over Boolean variables. Thanks to the efficiency of SMT solver implementation in processing formulas over Boolean variables and uninterpreted functions, our approach can deal with large programs whose number of variables is large. This situation generally makes the state-space explosion problem in model checking techniques.

The present paper provides a proof of correctness of a the synchronous dataflow compiler. We have presented a technique based on SMT solving to prove the preservation of clock semantics during the compilation. Namely, we have shown that implicit clock relations, describing the discrete timing model of a dataflow specification, are preserved in their implementation. The desired behavior of a given source program and the transformed one are represented as clock models. A refinement relation between source and transformed programs is used to express the preservation, which is checked by using a SMT solver. We have constructed and integrated our validator within the POLYCHRONY toolset to prove the correctness of the SIGNAL compiler.

We believe that our validator must have the following features to be effective and realistic. First, we do not modify or instrument the compiler, and we treat the compiler as a "black box". Hence the validator is not affected by some future update or modification of the compiler. We only need some additional information about the mapping between original names and potential new names of local variables. Our approach consists in applying formal methods to the compiler transformations themselves in order to automatically generate formal evidence that the clock semantics of the source program is preserved during program transformations, as per applicable qualification standard. Second, it is important that the validator can be scaled to large programs. For this purpose, we represent the desired program semantics using a scalable abstraction and we use efficient SMT libraries [9] to achieve the expected goals: traceability and formal evidence. Moreover, this approach provides an attractive alternative to develop a certified compiler for a synchronous language since in general the validator is much smaller and easier to verify than the compiler it validates.

References

1. Ackerman, W.: Solvable Cases of the Decision Problem. Study in Logic and the Foundations of Mathematics. North-Holland, Amsterdam (1954)
2. Berry, G.: The Foundations of Esterel. In: Proof, Language and Interaction: Essay in Honor of Robin Milner, MIT Press (2000)
3. Borger, E., Gradel, E., Gurevich, Y.: The Classical Decision Problem. Spinger-Verlag (1996)
4. Besnard, L., Gautier, T., Le Guernic, P., Talpin, J.-P.: Compilation of Polychronous Data Flow Equations. In: Synthesis of Embedded Software. Springer (2010)
5. Benveniste, A., LeGuernic, P.: Hybrid Dynamical Systems Theory and the Signal Language. IEEE Transactions on Automatic Control 35(5), 535–546 (1990)
6. Bryant, R.: Graph-based Algorithms for Boolean Function Manipulation. IEEE Transactions on Computers, C 35(8), 677–691 (1986)
7. Inria, The CompCert Project, http://compcert.inria.fr

8. Inria, The Coq Proof Assitant, http://coq.inria.fr

9. Dutertre, B., de Moura, L.: Yices Sat-solver (2009), http://yices.csl.ri.com

10. Gamatié, A.: Designing Embedded Systems with the Signal Programming Language: Synchronous, Reactive Specification, pp. 971–978. Springer, New York (2009) ISBN 978-1-4419-0940-4

11. Kahn, G. (ed.): FPCA 1987. LNCS, vol. 274. Springer, Heidelberg (1987)

12. Gamatié, A., Gonnord, L.: Static Analysis of Synchronous Programs in Signal for Efficient Design of Multi-Clocked Embedded Systems. In: ACM SIG-PLAN/SIGBED Conference on Languages, Compilers, Tools and Theory for Embedded Systems - LCTES 2011, Chicago, IL, USA (April 2011)

13. Halbwachs, N.: A Synchronous Language at Work: the Story of Lustre. In: 3th ACM-IEEE International Conference on Formal Methods and Models for Codesign, MEMOCODE 2005 (July 2005)

14. Le Guernic, P., Gautier, T.: Advanced Topics in Data-flow Computing, Chapter Data-flow to von Neumann: the Signal Approach, pp. 413–438. Prentice-Hall (1991)

15. Leroy, X.: Formal Certification of a Compiler Back-end, or Programming a Compiler with a Proof Assistant. In: 33rd Symposium Principles of Programming Languages, pp. 42–54. ACM Press (2006)

16. Necula, G.C.: Translation Validation for an Optimizing Compiler. In: Proceeding PLDI 2000 Proceedings of the ACM SIGPLAN 2000 Conference on Programming Language Design and Implementation, pp. 83–94 (May 2000)

17. Ngo, V.C., Talpin, J.-P., Gautier, T., Le Guernic, P., Besnard, L.: Formal Verification of Compiler Transformations on Polychronous Equations. In: Derrick, J., Gnesi, S., Latella, D., Treharne, H. (eds.) IFM 2012. LNCS, vol. 7321, pp. 113–127. Springer, Heidelberg (2012)

18. Ngo, V.C.: Formal Verification of a Synchronous Data-flow Compiler: from Signal to C. In: PhD thesis (2014)

19. Inria/Espresso, Polychrony Toolset,
http://www.irisa.fr/espresso/Polychrony

20. Pnueli, A., Siegel, M., Singerman, E.: Translation Validation. In: Steffen, B. (ed.) TACAS 1998. LNCS, vol. 1384, pp. 151–166. Springer, Heidelberg (1998)

21. Pnueli, A., Shtrichman, O., Siegel, M.: Translation Validation: From Signal to C. In: Olderog, E.-R., Steffen, B. (eds.) Correct System Design. LNCS, vol. 1710, pp. 231–255. Springer, Heidelberg (1999)

22. RTCA, DO-178C, http://rtca.org

23. Stump, A., Deters, M.: SMT-Comp (2009), http://www.smtcomp.org/2009

24. Tristan, J.-B., Govereau, P., Morrisett, G.: Evaluating Value-graph Translation Validation for LLVM. In: ACM SIGPLAN Conference on Programming and Language Design Implementation, California (June 2011)

25. Tristan, J.-B., Leroy, X.: A Simple, Verified Validator for Software Pipelining. In: 37th Principles of Programming Languages, pp. 83–92. ACM Press (2010)

Symbolic Detection of Assertion Dependencies for Bounded Model Checking

Grigory Fedyukovich[1], Andrea Callia D'Iddio[2], Antti E.J. Hyvärinen[1], and Natasha Sharygina[1]

[1] Formal Verification Lab of the Faculty of Informatics,
Università della Svizzera italiana, Lugano, Switzerland
[2] University of Rome Tor Vergata, Rome, Italy

Abstract. Automatically generating assertions through static or runtime analysis is becoming an increasingly important initial phase in many software testing and verification tool chains. The analyses may generate thousands of redundant assertions often causing problems later in the chain, including scalability issues for automatic tools or a prohibitively large amount of information for final processing. We present an algorithm which uses a SAT solver on a bounded symbolic encoding of the program to reveal the implication relationships among spatially close assertions for use in a variety of bounded model checking applications. Our experimentation with different applications demonstrates that this technique can be used to reduce the number of assertions that need to be checked thus improving overall performance.

1 Introduction

An important part of many of the approaches for increasing software quality through formal methods is to infer potential correctness properties from a program. Such properties can be obtained in the form of assertions from the source code, or behavior observed during run time [19,6,17,13,24]. The assertions can then be verified against the source code using static-analysis methods such as model checking [5,22]. In the paper, we study how Bounded Model Checking [1] (BMC) can be used in verifying assertions generated by automated software analysis.

We propose a generic framework for identifying implication relations between assertions, and study how obtaining information about the implication relation between assertions can be used in finding redundant assertions. This knowledge becomes useful when the number of assertions generated automatically grows large. For instance, in our experiments, independently on the settings of the assertion synthesiser, the number is typically in the order of hundreds and sometimes much higher.

The machine-generated assertions are often redundant in the sense that a BMC algorithm only needs to verify a subset of these assertions and can safely skip the rest if the verification was successful. This observation opens new opportunities for speeding up the computationally expensive BMC algorithms.

A. Egyed and I. Schaefer (Eds.): FASE 2015, LNCS 9033, pp. 186–201, 2015.
DOI: 10.1007/978-3-662-46675-9_13

For example, the DAIKON program invariant generator [10] might produce the following set of assertions for a return value of a function:

$A_1 : \mathtt{assert}(\mathtt{ret} = 0); A_2 : \mathtt{assert}(\mathtt{ret} \leq 0); A_3 : \mathtt{assert}(\mathtt{ret} \geq 0);$

Clearly if the assertion A_1 holds then also the assertions A_2 and A_3 hold. In this paper we formalize the intuition that an assertion may imply other assertions and provide an algorithm and an implementation for discovering such implications for programs written in the C language. In our experiments detecting assertions that are implied to avoid redundant checking consistently decreases the time required to compute the set of true assertions in programs where such redundancy exists. We observe a similar positive result in a model checking approach based on *function summarization* [24] where the summary sizes typically decrease by 30% as a result of our algorithm.

Our approach is ultimately based on determining whether an assertion in the software implies another assertion using a SAT query on a propositional encoding of the program. The number of queries in a straightforward approach would be quadratic in the number of assertions which for realistic programs is infeasible. To achieve a level of performance required for a practical approach we use an analysis that is sensitive to the control flow of the program, to the SAT query, and to the distance between assertions to filter out checks which either cannot result or would very unlikely result in detected implications. These optimizations result in the approach having a relatively low overhead and they do not compromise the soundness of the verification approach.

BMC has proven particularly successful in safety analysis of software and has been implemented in several tools, including CBMC [4], LLBMC [18], VeriSoft [14], and FunFrog [24]. While BMC assumes a loop-free approximation of the program, there are several recent techniques for transforming programs into loop-free programs which, if successful, do not sacrifice soundness or completeness of the verification results. Examples of such techniques include unwinding assertions [4], automatic detection of recursion depth [12], k-induction [9], and loop summarization [15]. While we believe that these techniques are compatible with our method for computing assertion implications, we leave this study for future work.

Related Work. To the best of our knowledge both the approach for detecting implications between assertions using bounded model checking and the use of the detected implications to remove redundant assertions for enhancing bounded model checking are new. The implementation of DAIKON [10] includes an approach for pruning dependent assertions. Our approach extends this by considering also assertions that do not appear in the same program location, and by using propositional logic in deducing the relations between assertions. While [8] presents several approaches for generating assertions in implicative form as potential invariants for recursive algorithms, our goal is at removing redundant implied assertions. Furthermore, [8] detects potential implications through procedure return analysis, a straightforward static analysis, clustering, random selection, and context-sensitive analysis, but applies to assertions at the same program location. Yang et al. [26] further extended the idea of assertion implications to the case of software evolution (to reflect the change impact between program versions). In contrast to these approaches, our method uses BMC encoding and is able to identify redundant assertions at different program locations. A related approach complementary to ours is presented in [16] where the idea is to lift assertions located in the nested function calls towards the main function to achieve verification performance speedup.

We identify two main approaches for synthesizing assertions for a program. The *dynamic invariant detection* exploits software executions obtained, for instance, from regression test suites, to generate likely invariants (see, e.g., [10,19,6]); while the *static invariant detection* uses static analysis of the source code and symbolic execution to construct potentially helpful invariants (see, e.g., the HOUDINI tool [13]). For our experimentation we selected one representative assertion synthesizer from both approaches: the dynamic invariant synthesizer BCT [17], and a tool based on the CPROVER [4,24] framework for static invariant generation.

Finally, decreasing the sizes of function summaries computed through Craig interpolation [7] can be done through proof compression [3] and the careful selection of interpolation algorithms [23]. This work provides an orthogonal approach where the interpolant is optimized on a higher level by dropping unnecessary verification conditions using domain-specific information.

This paper is organized as follows. Section 2 formalizes the bounded model checking framework we use in the paper. Section 3 explains in detail the basic ideas to detect implications between assertions and the techniques to implement them. Section 4 shows the applications of the approach and the experimental results. Section 5 summarizes the results of our work and discusses open problems and starting points for future work.

2   Preliminaries

Our discussion is based on the *unwound static single assignment* (USSA) approximation of the program, where loops and recursive function calls are unwound up to a fixed limit, and each variable is only assigned once. We have implemented the computing of assertion implications for the C language, but follow the usual approach of presenting the theory in a simpler abstract language to render the discussion more approachable. The USSA approximation serves as an intermediary step in transforming a program to a propositional formula for software bounded model checking. It also serves as a framework for unambiguously defining the assertion implications in Sec. 3 and gives a natural interpretation for a distance between assertions in Sec. 3.4.

The USSA approximation is heavily influenced by techniques used in software bounded model checking (see, e.g. [4]) and consists of an ordered sequence of assignments called instructions, guarded by Boolean valued enabling conditions:

Definition 1. *An* Unwound Static Single Assignment *(USSA) approximation is a finite sequence* $U = (S_1, S_2, \ldots, S_n)$ *of guarded instructions* S_i *having the form* $C \to I$ *where* C *is a condition, called* guard, *and* I *is an instruction.*

```
void main(){
  int x, y, z;
  x = some_value();
  y = some_value();
  if (x >= y){
    if (y >= 0){
      assert(x >= 0);
      z = x + y;
      assert(z >= 0);
    }
  }
  x = some_value();
  y = some_value();
  z = f(x, y);
  assert(z >= 0);
  assert(z >= x + y);
  assert(x <= z - y);
}

int f(int a, int b){
  int i = 0;
  while (i < a + b){
    if (i < a){
      i = i + a;
    } else {
      i = i + b;
    }
  }
  assert(i >= a + b);
  return i;
}
```

$$true \rightarrow x_1 := some\_value_1; \qquad (1)$$
$$true \rightarrow y_1 := some\_value_2; \qquad (2)$$
$$x_1 \geq y_1 \wedge y_1 \geq 0 \rightarrow assert(x_1 \geq 0); \qquad (3)$$
$$x_1 \geq y_1 \wedge y_1 \geq 0 \rightarrow z_1 := x_1 + y_1; \qquad (4)$$
$$x_1 \geq y_1 \wedge y_1 \geq 0 \rightarrow assert(z_1 \geq 0); \qquad (5)$$
$$true \rightarrow x_2 := some\_value_3; \qquad (6)$$
$$true \rightarrow y_2 := some\_value_4; \qquad (7)$$
$$true \rightarrow \mathbf{f}_{a_1} := x_2; \qquad (8)$$
$$true \rightarrow \mathbf{f}_{b_1} := y_2; \qquad (9)$$
$$true \rightarrow \mathbf{f}_{i_1} := 0; \qquad (10)$$
$$(\mathbf{f}_{i_1} < \mathbf{f}_{a_1} + \mathbf{f}_{b_1}) \wedge (\mathbf{f}_{i_1} < \mathbf{f}_{a_1}) \rightarrow \mathbf{f}_{i_2} := \mathbf{f}_{i_1} + \mathbf{f}_{a_1}; \qquad (11)$$
$$(\mathbf{f}_{i_1} < \mathbf{f}_{a_1} + \mathbf{f}_{b_1}) \wedge (\mathbf{f}_{i_1} \geq \mathbf{f}_{a_1}) \rightarrow \mathbf{f}_{i_3} := \mathbf{f}_{i_1} + \mathbf{f}_{b_1}; \qquad (12)$$
$$(\mathbf{f}_{i_1} < \mathbf{f}_{a_1} + \mathbf{f}_{b_1}) \rightarrow \mathbf{f}_{i_4} := \mathbf{phi}(\mathbf{f}_{i_2}, \mathbf{f}_{i_3}, (\mathbf{f}_{i_1} < \mathbf{f}_{a_1})); \qquad (13)$$
$$(\mathbf{f}_{i_1} \geq \mathbf{f}_{a_1} + \mathbf{f}_{b_1}) \rightarrow \mathbf{f}_{i_5} := \mathbf{f}_{i_1}; \qquad (14)$$
$$true \rightarrow \mathbf{f}_{i_6} := \mathbf{phi}(\mathbf{f}_{i_4}, \mathbf{f}_{i_5}, (\mathbf{f}_{i_1} \leq \mathbf{f}_{a_1} + \mathbf{f}_{b_1})); \qquad (15)$$
$$(\mathbf{f}_{i_6} < \mathbf{f}_{a_1} + \mathbf{f}_{b_1}) \wedge (\mathbf{f}_{i_6} < \mathbf{f}_{a_1}) \rightarrow \mathbf{f}_{i_7} := \mathbf{f}_{i_6} + \mathbf{f}_{a_1}; \qquad (16)$$
$$(\mathbf{f}_{i_6} < \mathbf{f}_{a_1} + \mathbf{f}_{b_1}) \wedge (\mathbf{f}_{i_6} \geq \mathbf{f}_{a_1}) \rightarrow \mathbf{f}_{i_8} := \mathbf{f}_{i_6} + \mathbf{f}_{b_1}; \qquad (17)$$
$$(\mathbf{f}_{i_6} < \mathbf{f}_{a_1} + \mathbf{f}_{b_1}) \rightarrow \mathbf{f}_{i_9} := \mathbf{phi}(\mathbf{f}_{i_7}, \mathbf{f}_{i_8}, (\mathbf{f}_{i_6} < \mathbf{f}_{a_1})); \qquad (18)$$
$$(\mathbf{f}_{i_6} \geq \mathbf{f}_{a_1} + \mathbf{f}_{b_1}) \rightarrow \mathbf{f}_{i_{10}} := \mathbf{f}_{i_6}; \qquad (19)$$
$$true \rightarrow \mathbf{f}_{i_{11}} := \mathbf{phi}(\mathbf{f}_{i_9}, \mathbf{f}_{i_{10}}, (\mathbf{f}_{i_6} \leq \mathbf{f}_{a_1} + \mathbf{f}_{b_1})); \qquad (20)$$
$$true \rightarrow assert(\mathbf{f}_{i_{11}} \geq \mathbf{f}_{a_1} + \mathbf{f}_{b_1}); \qquad (21)$$
$$true \rightarrow \mathbf{f}_{ret_1} := \mathbf{f}_{i_{11}}; \qquad (22)$$
$$true \rightarrow z_2 := \mathbf{f}_{ret_1}; \qquad (23)$$
$$true \rightarrow assert(z_2 \geq 0); \qquad (24)$$
$$true \rightarrow assert(z_2 \geq x_2 + y_2); \qquad (25)$$
$$true \rightarrow assert(x_2 \leq z_2 - y_2); \qquad (26)$$

(a) C code   (b) USSA approximation (bound = 2)

Fig. 1. Converting a C program into USSA

In the process of constructing the USSA approximation the program loop conditions and branches are encoded into guards, while the rest of the encoding consists of constructing assignments. Given an unwinding limit k, a while loop is transformed into a chain of k nested if constructs in order to represent at most k iterations of the loop. Similarly, recursive functions are inlined k times. To encode values which depend on if branches and while loops we use the phi-function, which returns its first or second argument depending on the truth value of its third argument as follows:

$$\mathbf{phi}(e_1, e_2, e_3) = \begin{cases} e_1 & \text{if } e_3 \text{ is true;} \\ e_2 & \text{otherwise.} \end{cases}$$

Finally, guarded assignment S can be annotated with guarded assertions of the form $A = C \to assert(C')$ evaluated right after S.

Instead of giving an exact definition for the process of constructing the USSA approximation we give an artificial but illustrative example in Fig. 1 showing how a program written in the C language, on the left, is transformed into the USSA approximation on the right. The program consists of two functions main and f in addition to a nondeterministically treated function some_value.[1] The call from main to f is inlined on lines 10 - 22. Function input and output parameters are assigned on lines 8, 9, and 23; and the loop inside f is unwound 2 times on lines 11 - 15 and again on lines 16 - 20. The six assertions in C code appear on the USSA approximation on lines 3, 5, 24, 25, 26, and 21.

Propositional Encoding. Given a USSA approximation U, the propositional formula $\pi(U)$ consists of the propositional encoding of all guarded assignments of U. We extend the definition of the propositional encoding operator π to guards C and *arguments* C' of assertions A. Once the USSA approximation is converted into a propositional formula, determining the validity of the assertions with respect to the program reduces to conjoining the negations of the assertions and then deciding the unsatisfiability of the resulting formula.

3   The Assertion Implication Relation

The aim of the techniques presented in this paper is to enable efficient analysis of a program with respect to a large number of assertions. We are interested in determining whether, in a given USSA approximation, there are assertions A, A' such that A' holds whenever A holds in all executions of the USSA approximation. For performance reasons we do not compute the above, but instead the *assertion implication relation* (AIR), which consists of a subset of such pairs where the implication follows from the statements between the assertions A and A'. In cases where the program contains this type of redundancy in assertions and AIR is not empty, the information can often be used to significantly improve the efficiency of model checking.

Definition 2. *Given a USSA approximation* $(S_1, \ldots, S_n)$ *containing two assertions* $A_i = C_i \to assert(C'_i)$ *and* $A_j = C_j \to assert(C'_j)$, *we say that the assertion* A_i *locally implies the assertion* A_j *iff* $1 \le i < j \le n$ *and the following formula is valid:*

$$(\pi(C_i) \to \pi(C'_i)) \land \pi(S_{i+1}, \ldots, S_{j-1}) \to (\pi(C_j) \to \pi(C'_j))$$

An alternative way of viewing the definition is to say that A_i locally implies A_j iff the *Hoare triple*

$$\{C_i \to C'_i\}(S_{i+1}, \ldots, S_{j-1})\{C_j \to C'_j\}$$

---

[1] To simplify the discussion we ignore arithmetic overflows and underflows. However, the implementation does not have the limitation.

is valid. Given the valid local implication relation between assertions A_i and A_j, we will refer to A_i as a *stronger* assertion, and to A_j as a *weaker* assertion. Notably, this relation is transitive, but not symmetric.

We present a high-level overview of the algorithm for detecting assertion implications (DAI) in Algorithm 1. The algorithm computes the AIR from a USSA approximation provided as an input. We compute the implication relation in two phases: (i) by detecting classes of *dependent* assertions AD using a syntactic analysis on the USSA approximation first directly on the variables in the USSA form (line 1) and then extending the variable dependency to assertions (line 2); and (ii) by detecting implications among the elements of AD using the propositional encoding of the USSA approximation (line 3) with queries to SAT solvers. In the following subsections we describe in details the three subroutines of the algorithm.

Algorithm 1. DAI(P)

Input: A USSA approximation $P = (S_1, \ldots, S_n)$
Output: AIR — the assertion implication relation
Data:
VD — disjoint sets of variables corresponding to the variable dependency classes;
AD — The assertion dependency relation
1: $VD \leftarrow$ dependent variables in P (see Def. 3)
2: $AD \leftarrow$ dependent assertions in P based on VD (see Def. 4)
3: $AIR \leftarrow \{(i,j) \in AD \mid \text{IMPLIES}(i,j) = true\}$

3.1 Detecting Dependent Variables

We say that two variables x and y are *dependent* when the value of x potentially affects the value of y. The idea of variable dependencies dates back to *program slicing* [25]. We adapt this notion to the USSA approximation of a program, and create dependencies from the assignments and the guards. For example, after the execution of a guarded assignment $G \rightarrow x := E$, the updated value of x may depend on the values of variables in E and G. However, due to the final propositional encoding the assignment creates potential dependency also from x to all the variables in E and G. To obtain an over-approximation of the dependency relation, it is enough to assume that all the variables in a guarded instruction depend on each other. The dependency relation is reflexive, transitive and symmetric and therefore an equivalence relation which groups all variables into *dependency classes*. This leads to the following definition of the dependency relation:

Definition 3. *Two variables x, y are said to be* directly dependent *if there exists a guarded instruction $S = C \rightarrow I$ such that $\{x, y\} \subseteq Vars(S)$. The general dependency relation is the transitive closure of direct dependency.*

Computing the dependency relation from the USSA form can be done efficiently with a union-find algorithm. Furthermore, since the local implication only considers guarded instructions between two assertions, it is sufficient to compute the dependency between two assertions that are currently being checked.

3.2 Finding Assertion Dependencies

To speed up the assertion checking by reducing the number of implication checks, the dependency relation should be extended from variables to assertions. Two assertions A and A' are said to be dependent if there exists a variable x in A and a variable x' in A' such that x and x' are dependent. Unlike a variable, if an assertion A depends on an assertion A', and the assertion A' depends on an assertion A'', this does not imply that A depends on A'', since the dependencies might result from variables not shared by A and A''.

The assertion dependency relation of a USSA approximation is constructed using a variable dependency relation (line 2 of DAI). This is an iterative procedure over the set of assertion pairs. For each pair, it explores the dependency classes of the variables involved in the assertions. If two assertions contain variables of the same dependency class, the assertions are dependent and are going to be included into the relation AD. The dependency of assertions is defined as follows:

Definition 4. *Two assertions* $A_1 = C_1 \rightarrow assert(C_1')$ *and* $A_2 = C_2 \rightarrow assert(C_2')$ *are* dependent *if there is a variable* $x_1 \in Vars(A_1)$ *and a variable* $x_2 \in Vars(A_2)$ *such that* x_1 *and* x_2 *are dependent.*

Example 1. Based on the definitions 3 and 4, the dependent assertions in Fig. 1(b) include $assert(x_1 \geq 0)$ and $assert(z_1 \geq 0)$ on lines 3 and 5; $assert(z_2 \geq x_2 + y_2)$ and $assert(x_2 \leq z_2 - y_2)$ on lines 25 and 26; and $assert(f_{i_{11}} \geq f_{a_1} + f_{b_1})$ and $assert(z_2 \geq x_2 + y_2)$ on lines 21 and 25. The assertions $assert(z_1 \geq 0)$ and $assert(z_2 \geq 0)$ on lines 5 and 24 are not dependent since the set of common symbols is empty (program variables x, y, and z were reassigned independently on the previous values).

3.3 Finding Assertion Implications

In the last phase of constructing AIR, the assertion dependency relation is refined to contain only the pairs of assertions (A, A') such that A locally implies A'. This is done by constructing the formula corresponding to Def. 2 and invoking the SAT solver through the IMPLIES call on line 3 in Algorithm 1.

Example 2. The assertion implication relation computed from the USSA approximation given in Fig. 1(b) consists of $(assert(x_1 \geq 0), assert(z_1 \geq 0))$ on lines 3 and 5, and $(assert(z_2 \geq x_2 + y_2), assert(x_2 \leq z_2 - y_2))$ on lines 25 and 26.

Finally, the AIR defines an *assertion implication graph* representing all revealed implication relationships between the guarded assertions. More formally,

Definition 5. *Given a USSA approximation* $U = (S_1, \ldots, S_n)$, *the* assertion implication graph *of* U *is a graph* $G_U = (V, E)$ *where*

$$V = \{A_i \in U \mid A_i \text{ is an assertion}\}$$

and

$$E = \{(A_i, A_j) \mid A_i \text{ locally implies } A_j \text{ in } U\}.$$

The algorithms proposed in this section are able to detect implications of assertions only in forward direction (i.e., the assertion on the left-hand side of an implication should be located before the assertion on the right-hand-side according to the USSA approximation). However the algorithms might be adapted to deal also with reverse direction. The next subsection will consider other optimizations making the approach applicable in practice.

3.4 Further Optimizations

Given a USSA approximation with k assertions, if Algorithm 1 identifies all assertions as dependent, the total number of assertion implication checks is $k(k-1)/2$. For USSA approximations containing thousands of assertions this number can be prohibitively large. On the other hand, if an assertion implication check needs to be performed between two assertions, one of which is close to the beginning of the USSA approximation and the other which is close to the end of the USSA approximation, the resulting formula might be very large. This often results in the check being computationally expensive. In the experiments we use a threshold to skip checking dependencies of assertions if there are more than n instructions between them in the USSA approximation. For example, none of the pairs of assertions (line 3 and 24; line 3 and 25; line 5 and 26) will be checked for a threshold 5. In our applications this does not break the soundness of the approach, since checking a subset of pairs of assertions will just under-approximate the assertion implication graph. In case when an assertion implication remains undetected, the approach will need to perform more work compared to the case when the assertion implication would have been discovered.

4   Applications

Algorithm 1 returns the assertion implication relation AIR, which then can be used for various BMC applications that deal with large sets of assertions. In this section we present two of those applications, namely *Optimizing Assertion Checking Order* and *Assertion Implication Checking in Function Summarization*.

We will study two research questions related to two different applications of assertion implication checking in this section.

R1 In the first application a BMC tool checks the validity of a set of assertions. We determine whether the number of verification runs can be reduced by skipping assertions whose validity is implied by already performed checks and AIR.

R2 In the second application a BMC tool constructs *function summaries* based on a set of assertions. We study whether excluding weak assertions using AIR reduces the size of function summaries.

Implementation. We implemented the approach for detecting assertion implications (DAI) as a preprocessor for the FUNFROG [24] tool. FUNFROG is built on top of CBMC [4], features interpolation-based function summarization (see the description in Section 4.2) for C programs, and uses the OPENSMT solver [2] for solving propositional formulas and interpolation.

The tool uses the CPROVER[2] framework. In particular, it accepts a precompiled GOTO-BINARY, a representation of the C program in an intermediate GOTO-CC language which is further unwound to create the USSA approximation. The analysis is then conducted on this USSA approximation. For each pair of assertions being checked, the analysis identifies the USSA steps corresponding to the assertions and the instructions between them. The USSA form is then bit-blasted and sent to OPENSMT for solving. FUNFROG was run with the default configuration which employs for instance an implementation of slicing [24].

We evaluated the performance of FUNFROG+DAI in summarization-based BMC on a range of academic and industrial benchmarks widely used in model checking experiments. The assertions for the benchmarks were obtained from the user, the BCT dynamic assertion generator [17] that internally uses DAIKON [10], and static invariant synthesizers implemented in FUNFROG [24]. In the rest of the section, we describe the details of both applications and provide experimental evidence of the positive effect from using DAI.

4.1   Optimizing Assertion Checking Order

Dynamic analysis tools such as DAIKON are often used for producing assertions. Such tools observe program behavior to form a set of the expressions over values of the program variables, which is then turned into a set of assertions V. Since the assertions are obtained by monitoring the execution of the program over a limited set of input parameters, there is no guarantee that such assertions hold for every execution of the program. BMC is used in [20] to check which of those assertions hold. While precise, a model checking run might consume a significant amount of time and require high amounts of memory. Therefore any optimization in the process immediately renders the technique more applicable to a wider set of benchmarks.

Given the USSA approximation U of a program that contains a set of assertions $V \subseteq U$, let $G_U = (V, E)$ be its assertion implication graph. We propose to traverse G_U during the BMC run to minimize the search for holding assertions and avoid checking all assertions one by one. Our solution is based on the two following ideas: 1) If an assertion A_i is proven to hold, all weaker assertions A_j (i.e., $\{A_j \in V \mid (A_i, A_j) \in E\}$) are implicitly proven to hold. 2) If an assertion A_k is proven to fail, all stronger assertions A_j (i.e., $\{A_k \in V \mid (A_j, A_k) \in E\}$) are implicitly proven to fail.

We further expand these ideas into the two complementing strategies for the efficient detection of assertions which hold in the program. We denote the nodes of G_U that do not have incoming edges as $\{A_s\}$. These correspond to the *strongest* assertions in the program. Similarly, we denote the edges with no

---

[2] http://www.cprover.org/

Table 1. Verification of a set of assertions by FUNFROG and FUNFROG+DAI. The timing values are given in seconds.

Bench	#USSA Steps	#Asserts	#Checks	Strategy	#DAI Impl	DAI Time	FUNFROG+DAI	FUNFROG
token_ring	11769	108	34	F	90	36.5	312.4	498.0
mem_slave	2843	146	116	F	61	24.6	70.9	108.9
ddv	537	152	103	F	93	14.9	162.1	240.2
diskperf	1730	192	34	B	172	75.8	65.5	332.5
s3	1733	131	47	B	265	4.4	20.6	55.5
cafe	2686	146	101	B	97	42.2	216.3	301.8

outgoing edges as $\{A_w\}$, and these correspond to the *weakest* assertions in the program.

In the first (*forward*) strategy, a BMC tool traverses G_U starting from $\{A_s\}$ in the depth-first order. For each assertion node A_i, if there exists a holding predecessor A_j, the BMC tool concludes that A_i also holds. Otherwise, it verifies the program with respect to A_i. This strategy is efficient in cases when there are many holding assertions in the program.

Example 3. Given the USSA approximation in Fig. 1(b) and its assertion implication graph, in the forward strategy, a BMC tool starts with checking the assertion $assert(x_1 \geq 0)$ on line 3 and proves that it holds. Then, the tool skips checking assertion $assert(z_1 \geq 0)$ on line 5. Next, the tool proves $assert(z_2 \geq x_2 + y_2)$ on line 25 and skips checking $assert(x_2 \leq z_2 - y_2)$ on line 26. To terminate model checking, the tool iteratively checks assertions $assert(f_{i_{11}} \geq f_{a_1} + f_{b_1})$ on line 21 and $assert(z_1 \geq 0)$ on line 24. The forward strategy results in checking 4 of 6 assertions. We expect the overall performance speed up to be approximately 30%.

In the second (*backward*) strategy, a BMC tool traverses G_U in reverse, starting from $\{A_w\}$. For each assertion node A_k, if there exists a failing successor A_j, the BMC tool concludes that A_k also fails. Otherwise, it verifies the program with respect to A_k. This strategy is efficient in cases when there are many assertions which fail in the program.

Example 4. Given the USSA approximation in Fig. 1(b) and its assertion implication graph, in the backward strategy, a BMC tool explicitly checks all 6 assertions. Since all assertions hold in the given example, this strategy does not produce any performance speed up.

Experiments. We report the effect of DAI on the assertion checking in Table 1. In the experiment we are given a benchmark (represented as a USSA form with the corresponding **#USSA Steps**) and a set of assertions (**#Asserts**). First, FUNFROG+DAI constructs the *AIR* (that reveals **DAI Impl** implications and takes **DAI Time** (*excluded from* **FunFrog+DAI**)). Then, FUNFROG+DAI proceeds to assertion verification following one of the two strategies (**Strategy** = **F** (forward) or **B** (backward)), in which **#Checks** was actually performed. Finally, we compare the time spent on verification by **FunFrog+DAI** with the time needed to verify each assertion by the vanilla **FunFrog**. The assertions for these benchmarks come from the BCT tool.

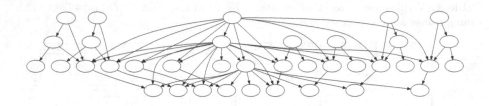

Fig. 2. The assertion implication relation for benchmark instance mem_slave. Note that the figure only contains assertions that imply another assertion.

In all our benchmarks FUNFROG+DAI is able to reduce the total number of checks needed to perform the verification. In the best case scenario we observe run times that are more than two times faster than the vanilla FUNFROG (see, diskperf). Note that for benchmarks containing many redundant assertions it is possible to detected more implications than the number of existing assertions in the code. For example, the benchmark instance s3 has 131 assertions but over 200 implications. We illustrate the redundancy of assertions in Fig. 2 showing the assertion implication relation computed for the benchmark instance mem_slave.

4.2   Assertion Implication Checking in Function Summarization

FUNFROG is an incremental model checker that maintains a set of *function summaries* in order to speed up consequent verification runs and checking correctness of software upgrades [11]. FUNFROG relies on partitioning the assertion set V into smaller disjoint subsets $\{\mathcal{A}\}_0^k$. Each set $\mathcal{A}_i \subseteq V$ is then checked with a separate run of the model checker. FUNFROG encodes the program into the USSA approximation (see Sec. 2 and Fig. 1). FUNFROG conjoins the USSA approximation with disjunction of the negations of the assertions $a \in \mathcal{A}_i$ to be checked. The resulting *BMC formula* ϕ_i is then bit-blasted and sent to the SAT solver. If it is proven that ϕ_i is unsatisfiable then the program is correct with respect to $\mathcal{A}_i$ and the proof of unsatisfiability can be used to over-approximate function behaviors by means of Craig interpolation.

In propositional logic, for every unsatisfiable pair of formulas (A, B) there exists an interpolant I that can be constructed from the proof of unsatisfiability [21] and has the properties that $A \rightarrow I$ and $I \wedge B$ is unsatisfiable [7]. For each function call f and the set of assertions $\mathcal{A}_i$, we define the BMC formula ϕ_i as $\phi_i \equiv A_f \wedge B_{\mathcal{A}_i}$, where A_f encodes the function call f and $B_{\mathcal{A}_i}$ encodes the rest of the program and the assertions from the set $\mathcal{A}_i$. Given a proof of unsatisfiability, we use an interpolating solver to generate the *function summary* for the function call f as an interpolant I_f, such that $A_f \rightarrow I_f$.

While verifying the program with respect to another set of assertions $\mathcal{A}_j \neq \mathcal{A}_i$, the BMC formula ϕ_j is constructed in such a way that the precise encoding of function calls is replaced by a function summary. By construction, a summary is accurate enough to prove the set of assertions $\mathcal{A}_i$. However, for $\mathcal{A}_j$, it may contain infeasible error paths due to the over-approximating nature of Craig interpolants. In this case, ϕ_j is satisfiable, and FUNFROG identifies the summaries responsible for the satisfiability. To continue the verification, FUNFROG needs to replace responsible summaries by the precise function representations. It is worthwile to try to avoid this scenario through better organization of the checking since the procedure is computationally expensive and requires another FUNFROG iteration. On the other hand, if ϕ_j is unsatisfiable then the substitution of summaries was sufficient to prove $\mathcal{A}_j$. In such cases verification with summaries is often faster than with the exact encoding. Independently of the result of the SAT solver, the size and the logical strength of Craig interpolants in ϕ_j affect the verification behavior of FUNFROG [23].

The assertion implication graph $G_U = (V, E)$ can be used to reduce the size of function summaries. We propose to construct each subset $\{\mathcal{A}\}_0^k$ of V while traversing G_U. The method is based on the following observation. If each assertion $A \in \mathcal{A}_i$ is implied by some assertion $A' \in \mathcal{A}_j$ then the summaries constructed from BMC formula ϕ_j will be sufficient to prove both $\mathcal{A}_j$ and $\mathcal{A}_i$. On the other hand, if no implication is found between assertions $A \in \mathcal{A}_j$ and $A' \in \mathcal{A}_i$ then there is no guarantee that the summaries constructed from ϕ_j will be sufficient to prove $\mathcal{A}_i$. We propose to use the AIR to identify the set of strongest assertions and perform the verification only on this set. As a result we expect to obtain a strong summary that due to the simplicity of the resulting formula will be more compact (as our following experimental results confirm).

Example 5. Consider the example in Fig. 1. There are six assertions, which can be verified one by one[3], having been partitioned into singleton sets. Two of them (A_1 and A_2 at lines 3 and 5 respectively) are located before the function f is called, and do not rely on the function behavior. After one of them is verified, the summary of function f is going to be created. A likely summary of function f with respect to the assertions A_1 and A_2 is simply the formula $I_{f,A_1} \equiv I_{f,A_2} \equiv true$.

There are three assertions after call to f. Once they are verified, the summary reflects the behavior of f (lines 24, 25, 26): (A_3): $true \rightarrow assert(z_2 \geq 0)$, ($A_4$): $true \rightarrow assert(z_2 \geq x_2 + y_2)$, ($A_5$): $true \rightarrow assert(x_2 \leq z_2 - y_2)$. For example, after verifying assertion A_3, the summary of function call f should reflect that the return value of the function f is never negative, i.e., $I_{f,A_3} \equiv f_{ret} >= 0$. In the next run, while verifying assertion A_4, the function call f is replaced by the previously computed summary I_{f,A_3} which relates the returned variable and a constant 0. Since A_4 relies on a more sophisticated relation over the return value and the values of input/output parameters, this substitution is likely to lead to a spurious counterexample and, consequently, to an expensive further refinement, i.e., repeating verification from scratch.

Similarly, after successful verification of A_4, a new summary I_{f,A_4} is generated. The summary relates the return value and the values of input/output parameters (i.e., $I_{f,A_4} \equiv f_{ret} \geq f_a + f_b$). After two iterations, the resulting summary of f is a conjunction $I_{f,A_3,A_4} \equiv I_{f,A_3} \wedge I_{f,A_4}$. In the next run, while

---

[3] We intentionally chose only holding assertions to demonstrate how summary construction and its usage works.

Table 2. Creation of function summaries by FunFrog and FunFrog+DAI. The timing values are given in seconds.

Benchmark	#USSA Steps	#Asserts	#DAI Impl	DAI Time	#V	#Cl	#V'	#Cl'
floppy	15076	721	134	26.38	228357	11973	228659	12879
diskperf	6000	47	7	0.083	150413	49362	162902	83625
gd_simp	673	21	5	0.138	6091	15420	12119	33504
two_expands	183	4	1	0.033	735	1221	1087	2277
p2p_joints	759	146	24	1.71	158034	452427	307897	902016
goldbach	7502	1344	65	25.82	6159	13455	13237	34689

verifying assertion A_5, the function call f is replaced by I_{f,A_3,A_4}. Since A_5 is essentially the same as A_4, this substitution should be sufficient, so no refinement is needed to complete verification.

In this example, assertion implication checking can be used to simplify the model checking process in two ways. First, the AIR reveals that $A_4 \rightarrow A_5$, i.e., it is enough to show that A_4 holds to show that A_5 also holds. Second, no dependency is detected between A_3 and A_4, suggesting that no matter in which order the two are checked, it is likely that a refinement is needed afterwards. In order to avoid the expensive refinement procedure, it makes sense to combine the two assertions into a single verification run.

Experiments. Table 2 reports statistics on constructing function summaries with FunFrog when DAI was used as a preprocessor. Similarly to the experiment from Sec. 4.1, we are given a benchmark (with the size of **#USSA Steps**) and a set of assertions (**#Asserts**). First, FunFrog+DAI constructs the AIR (with **DAI Impl** relations). Then FunFrog+DAI obtains the set of strongest assertions to be encoded to the BMC formula, solved and used to create function summaries. Finally, we calculate the total number of variables and clauses in the resulting summary formula (**#V** and **#Cl** respectively). We compare these values with the ones collected after the vanilla FunFrog run (**FunFrog** time, **#V'** and **#Cl'** respectively). For these benchmarks we obtained the assertions using the CPROVER library underlying FunFrog.

The experimentation demonstrates that on our benchmark set the proposed approach improves the performance and the effect of BMC in the context of interpolation-based function summarization. Using particular optimization techniques (i.e., threshold for assertion locations and timeout for implication checks), in many cases it was possible to reduce the overhead of performing the implication checks. Note that at least in these benchmarks the construction of AIR requires a considerably smaller amount of time than needed for the actual assertions checking in the classic BMC approach.

5   Summary and Future Work

We presented a simple but effective approach to reveal the implication relationships between spatially close assertions. This technique addresses the problems arising from large number of redundant assertions in bounded model checking and, as our experimentation on benchmarks containing redundant assertions demonstrates, in many cases reduces the total verification time. We observe a similar positive result in a model checking approach based on function summarization, where the summary sizes typically decrease by 30%.

As a potential future optimization we consider improving the condition in Def. 2. A propositional encoding π considers the instructions between a pair of assertions but does not take into account the variables assigned with equal values before the first assertion. For instance, in Fig. 1(b), $assert(\mathbf{f}_{i_{11}} \geq \mathbf{f}_{a_1} + \mathbf{f}_{b_1})$ and $assert(z_2 \geq x_2 + y_2)$ on lines 21 and 25 imply each other, but the implication between them can be proved only if two additional assignment instructions (on lines 8 and 9) are added to the SAT-query. While including all the USSA program to every implication query would likely be overly expensive, including parts of this information to the checking process would potentially increase the number of detected implications and pay off as a result of decreased assertion checks.

The assertion implication checking could be further improved heuristically by using more intelligent ways of ordering assertion implication checking. One approach for ordering the checking is to identify *likely implications*, as discussed in [8]. Another interesting source of assertions that is not discussed in this work is to consider also semantical properties of pointers and stack contents. However for this to work in practice it is likely that an alias analysis should be performed as a preprocessing step to reduce the number of assertion candidates.

Acknowledgements. We thank the reviewers for their valuable feedback. The work was supported by the SNF project number 138078. This work has been done during an internship of the second author at the Formal Verification Lab of the Faculty of Informatics, Università della Svizzera italiana, Lugano, Switzerland. The second author would like to thank the Verification Lab for this important collaboration, and at the same time he thanks Prof. Maurizio Talamo from the Tor Vergata University of Rome, for strongly encouraging this collaboration.

References

1. Biere, A., Cimatti, A., Clarke, E., Zhu, Y.: Symbolic model checking without bDDs. In: Cleaveland, W.R. (ed.) TACAS 1999. LNCS, vol. 1579, pp. 193–207. Springer, Heidelberg (1999)
2. Bruttomesso, R., Pek, E., Sharygina, N., Tsitovich, A.: The openSMT solver. In: Esparza, J., Majumdar, R. (eds.) TACAS 2010. LNCS, vol. 6015, pp. 150–153. Springer, Heidelberg (2010)
3. Cabodi, G., Lolacono, C., Vendraminetto, D.: Optimization techniques for Craig interpolant compaction in unbounded model checking. In: DATE 2013, pp. 1417–1422. ACM DL, EDA Consortium San Jose (2013)
4. Clarke, E., Kroning, D., Lerda, F.: A tool for checking ANSI-C programs. In: Jensen, K., Podelski, A. (eds.) TACAS 2004. LNCS, vol. 2988, pp. 168–176. Springer, Heidelberg (2004)
5. Clarke, E.M., Emerson, A.: Synthesis of Synchronization Skeletons for Branching Time Temporal Logic. In: Kozen, D. (ed.) Logic of Programs 1981. LNCS, vol. 131, Springer, Heidelberg (1982)

6. Cobb, J., Jones, J.A., Kapfhammer, G.M., Harrold, M.J.: Dynamic invariant detection for relational databases. In: Proc. International Workshop on Dynamic Analysis 2011, pp. 12–17. ACM (2011)

7. Craig, W.: Three uses of the Herbrand-Genzen theorem in relating model theory and proof theory. JSL 22(3), 269–285 (1957)

8. Dodoo, N., Donovan, A., Lin, L., Ernst, M.D.: Selecting predicates for implications in program analysis (2002),
http://homes.cs.washington.edu/~mernst/pubs/invariants-implications.ps

9. Donaldson, A.F., Kroening, D., Rümmer, P.: Automatic analysis of scratch-pad memory code for heterogeneous multicore processors. In: Esparza, J., Majumdar, R. (eds.) TACAS 2010. LNCS, vol. 6015, pp. 280–295. Springer, Heidelberg (2010)

10. Ernst, M.D., Cockrell, J., Griswold, W.G., Notkin, D.: Dynamically discovering likely program invariants to support program evolution. IEEE Transactions on Software Engineering 27(2), 99–123 (2001)

11. Fedyukovich, G., Sery, O., Sharygina, N.: eVolCheck: Incremental Upgrade Checker for C. In: Piterman, N., Smolka, S.A. (eds.) TACAS 2013 (ETAPS 2013). LNCS, vol. 7795, pp. 292–307. Springer, Heidelberg (2013)

12. Fedyukovich, G., Sharygina, N.: Towards Completeness in Bounded Model Checking Through Automatic Recursion Depth Detection. In: Braga, C., Martí-Oliet, N. (eds.) SBMF 2014. LNCS, vol. 8941, pp. 96–112. Springer, Heidelberg (2015)

13. Flanagan, C., Rustan, K., Leino, M.: Houdini, an annotation assistant for eSC/Java. In: Oliveira, J.N., Zave, P. (eds.) FME 2001. LNCS, vol. 2021, pp. 500–517. Springer, Heidelberg (2001)

14. Ivancic, F., Yang, Z., Ganai, M.K., Gupta, A., Ashar, P.: Efficient SAT-based bounded model checking for software verification. TCS 404(3), 256–274 (2008)

15. Kroening, D., Sharygina, N., Tonetta, S., Tsitovich, A., Wintersteiger, C.M.: Loop summarization using state and transition invariants. Formal Methods in System Design 42(3), 221–261 (2013)

16. Lal, A., Qadeer, S.: A program transformation for faster goal-directed search. In: Proc. FMCAD 2014, pp. 147–154. IEEE (2014)

17. Mariani, L., Pastore, F., Pezzè, M.: Dynamic analysis for diagnosing integration faults. IEEE Transactions on Software Engineering 37(4), 486–508 (2011)

18. Merz, F., Falke, S., Sinz, C.: LLBMC: Bounded Model Checking of C and C++ Programs Using a Compiler IR. In: Joshi, R., Müller, P., Podelski, A. (eds.) VSTTE 2012. LNCS, vol. 7152, pp. 146–161. Springer, Heidelberg (2012)

19. Nguyen, T., Kapur, D., Weimer, W., Forrest, S.: Using dynamic analysis to discover polynomial and array invariants. In: Proc. ICSE 2012, pp. 683–693. IEEE (2012)

20. Pastore, F., Mariani, L., Hyvärinen, A.E.J., Fedyukovich, G., Sharygina, N., Sehestedt, S., Muhammad, A.: Verification-aided regression testing. In: Proc. ISSTA 2014, pp. 37–48. ACM (2014)

21. Pudlák, P.: Lower bounds for resolution and cutting plane proofs and monotone computations. Journal of Symbolic Logic 62(3), 981–998 (1997)

22. Queille, J.-P., Sifakis, J.: Specification and verification of concurrent systems in CESAR. In: Dezani-Ciancaglini, M., Montanari, U. (eds.) Programming 1982. LNCS, vol. 137, pp. 337–351. Springer, Heidelberg (1982)

23. Rollini, S.F., Alt, L., Fedyukovich, G., Hyvärinen, A.E.J., Sharygina, N.: PeRIPLO: A framework for producing effective interpolants in SAT-based software verification. In: McMillan, K., Middeldorp, A., Voronkov, A. (eds.) LPAR-19 2013. LNCS, vol. 8312, pp. 683–693. Springer, Heidelberg (2013)

24. Sery, O., Fedyukovich, G., Sharygina, N.: FunFrog: Bounded model checking with interpolation-based function summarization. In: Chakraborty, S., Mukund, M. (eds.) ATVA 2012. LNCS, vol. 7561, pp. 203–207. Springer, Heidelberg (2012)
25. Weiser, M.: Program slicing. In: Proc. ICSE 1981, pp. 439–449. IEEE (1981)
26. Yang, G., Khurshid, S., Person, S., Rungta, N.: Property differencing for incremental checking. In: Proc. ICSE 2014, pp. 1059–1070. ACM (2014)

Verification of Loop Parallelisations

Stefan Blom, Saeed Darabi, and Marieke Huisman

University of Twente, The Netherlands

Abstract. Writing correct parallel programs becomes more and more difficult as the complexity and heterogeneity of processors increase. This issue is addressed by parallelising compilers. Various compiler directives can be used to tell these compilers where to parallelise. This paper addresses the correctness of such compiler directives for loop parallelisation. Specifically, we propose a technique based on separation logic to verify whether a loop can be parallelised. Our approach requires each loop iteration to be specified with the locations that are read and written in this iteration. If the specifications are correct, they can be used to draw conclusions about loop (in)dependences. Moreover, they also reveal where synchronisation is needed in the parallelised program. The loop iteration specifications can be verified using permission-based separation logic and seamlessly integrate with functional behaviour specifications. We formally prove the correctness of our approach and we discuss automated tool support for our technique. Additionally, we also discuss how the loop iteration contracts can be compiled into specifications for the code coming out of the parallelising compiler.

1 Introduction

Parallelising compilers aim to detect loops that can be executed in parallel. However, this detection is not perfect. Therefore developers can typically also add compiler directives to declare that a loop is parallel. Any loop annotated with such a compiler directive is assumed to be parallel by the compiler.

This paper discusses how to verify that loops that are declared parallel by a developer can indeed safely be parallelised. This is achieved by adding specifications to the program that when verified guarantee that the program can be parallelised without changing its behaviour. Our specifications stem from permission-based separation logic [5,6], an extension of Hoare logic. This has the advantage that we can easily combine the specifications related to non-functional properties such as data race freedom with functional correctness properties.

Concretely, for each loop body we add an *iteration contract*, which specifies the iteration's resources, i.e., the variables read and written by one iteration of the loop. We prove that if the iteration contract can be proven correct without any further annotations, the iterations are independent and the loop is parallelisable. If a loop has dependences, we can add additional annotations that capture these dependences. These annotations specify how resources are transferred to another iteration of the loop. We then identify a class of annotation patterns

© Springer-Verlag Berlin Heidelberg 2015
A. Egyed and I. Schaefer (Eds.): FASE 2015, LNCS 9033, pp. 202–217, 2015.
DOI: 10.1007/978-3-662-46675-9_14

for which we can prove that the loop can be vectorised because they capture forward dependences. Finally, we also discuss how the verified iteration contract (including possibly functional property specifications) can be translated into a verifiable contract for the parallelised or vector program, written as a kernel.

Our approach is motivated by our work on the CARP project[1]. As part of this project the PENCIL language has been developed [1]. It is a high-level programming language designed to ease the programming of many-core processors such as GPUs. Its core is a subset of sequential C, imposing strong limitations on pointer-arithmetic. However, it should be noted that our approach also is applicable to other programming languages or libraries that have a similar parallel loop construct, such as OpenMP [7], parallel_for in C++ TBB [21] and Parallel.For in .NET TPL [13].

The main contributions of our paper are the following:

- a specification technique, using iteration contracts and dedicated transfer annotations that can capture loop dependences;
- a soundness proof that loops respecting specific patterns of iteration contracts can be either parallelised or vectorised; and
- compilation of iteration contracts to kernel contracts for the parallelised or vectorised program.

An earlier paper sketching the idea of iteration contracts to capture dependences appeared in PLACES 2014 [3]. However, the current paper additionally proves soundness of the approach, and defines specification compilation.

The remainder of this paper is organised as follows. After some background information, Section 3 explains how iteration contracts precisely capture dependences. Soundness of the approach is proven in Section 4. Then Section 5 discusses tool support for iteration contracts, and Section 6 discusses compilation of specifications. Finally, we conclude with related and future work.

2   Background

We first provide some background on data dependence and separation logic.

Loop Dependences. Given a loop, there exists a *loop-carried dependence* from statement S_{src} to statement S_{sink} in the loop body if there exist two iterations i and j of that loop, such that: (1) $i < j$, and (2) instance i of S_{src} and instance j of S_{sink} access the same memory location, and (3) at least one of these accesses is a write. The *distance* of a dependence is defined as the difference between j and i. We distinguish between *forward* and *backward* loop-carried dependences. When S_{src} syntactically appears before S_{sink} (or if they are the same statement) there is a *forward loop-carried dependence*. When S_{sink} syntactically appears before S_{src} there is a *backward loop-carried dependence*.

Example 1 (Loop-Carried Dependence). The examples below show two different types of loop-carried dependence. In (a) the loop has a *forward loop-carried dependence*, where L_1 is the source and L_2 is the sink, as illustrated by considering

---

[1] See http://www.carpproject.eu/

iteration 1 and 2 of the loop. In general, the ith element of the array a is shared between iteration i and $i - 1$. In (b) the loop has a *backward loop-carried dependence*, because the sink of the dependence (L_1) appears before the source (L_2).

```
     for(int i=0;i<N;i++){          iteration = 1          iteration = 2
(a)  L₁: a[i] = b[i] + 1;           L₁: a[1] = b[1] + 1;   L₁: a[2] = b[2] + 1;
     L₂: if(i>0) c[i]=a[i−1]+2;}    L₂: c[1] = a[0] + 2;   L₂: c[2] = a[1] + 2;

     for(int i=0;i<N;i++){          iteration = 1          iteration = 2
(b)  L₁: a[i] = b[i] + 1;           L₁: a[1] = b[1] + 1;   L₁: a[2] = b[2] + 1;
     L₂: if(i<N−1) c[i]=a[i+1]+2;}  L₂: c[1] = a[2] + 2;   L₂: c[2] = a[3] + 2;
```

The distinction between forward and backward dependences is important. Independent parallel execution of a loop with dependences is in general unsafe, because it may change the result. However, for loops with forward dependences only, parallelisation is possible if appropriate synchronisation is inserted. This is called *vectorised execution*.

Separation Logic. Our approach to reason about loop (in)dependences uses permission-based separation logic to specify which variables are read and written by a loop iteration. Separation logic [17] is an extension of Hoare logic [11], originally proposed to reason about pointer programs. Separation logic is also suited to reason modularly about concurrent programs [15]: two threads working on disjoint parts of the heap do not interfere and thus can be verified in isolation.

The basis of our work is a separation logic for C [22], extended with fractional permissions [6,5] to denote the right to either read from or write to a location. Any fraction in the interval $(0, 1)$ denotes a *read permission*, while 1 denotes a *write permission*. Permissions can be split and combined, but soundness of the logic prevents the sum of the permissions for a location over all threads to exceed 1. This guarantees that if permission specifications can be verified, the program is free of data races. In earlier work, we have shown that this logic is suitable to reason about kernel programs [4].

We write $\mathbf{Perm}(e, \pi)$ to denote that a thread holds an access right π to the location denoted by expression e. Permissions are combined using *separating conjunction* ($**$), which is the resource-sensitive extension of *conjunction*. For example $\mathbf{Perm}(x, 1/2) ** \mathbf{Perm}(y, 1/2)$ indicates that a thread holds read permissions to access locations x and y, and these permissions are disjoint. If a thread holds $\mathbf{Perm}(x, 1/2) ** \mathbf{Perm}(x, 1/2)$, this can be merged into a write permission $\mathbf{Perm}(x, 1)$.

3   Dependence Specifications

The classical way to specify the behaviour of a loop is by means of an invariant that has to be preserved by every iteration of the loop. However, loop invariants offer no insight into possible parallel executions of the loop. Instead we consider every iteration of the loop in isolation. First, we introduce our way of specifying them. Then, we propose a way of verifying our annotations.

```
for(int i=0; i < N; i++) /*@
    requires Perm(a[i],1) ** Perm(b[i],1/2);
    ensures  Perm(a[i],1) ** Perm(b[i],1/2);
@*/ { a[i]= 2 * b[i];      }
```

Listing 1. Iteration contract for an independent loop

3.1   Iteration Contracts

Each iteration is specified by its *iteration contract*, such that the precondition of the iteration contract specifies the resources that a particular iteration needs, and the postcondition specifies the resources that become available after the execution of the iteration. In other words, we treat each iteration as a specified block [10]. For convenience, we present our technique on non-nested for-loops with K statements that are executed during N iterations.[2] Each statement S_k labelled by L_k consists of an atomic instruction I_k, which is executed if a guard g_k is true, i.e., we consider loops of the following form:

  for(int j=0; j < N; j++){ *body(j)* }

where $body(j) \equiv L_1$: **if**(g_1) I_1; ... L_K: **if**(g_K) I_K;

There are two extra restrictions. First, the iteration variable j cannot be assigned anywhere in the loop body. Second, the guards must be expressions that are constant with respect to the execution of the loop body, i.e., they may not contain any variable that is assigned within the iteration.

Listing 1 shows an example of an *independent loop* with its iteration contract. This contract requires that at the start of iteration i, permission to write a[i] is available, as well as permissions to read b[i]. Further, the contract ensures that these permissions are returned at the end of iteration i. The iteration contract implicitly requires that the *separating conjunction of all iteration preconditions* holds before the first iteration of the loop, and that the *separating conjunction of all iteration postconditions* holds after the last iteration of the loop. For example, the contract in Listing 1 implicitly specifies that upon entering the loop, permission to write the first N elements of a must be available, as well as permission to read the first N elements of b.

To specify *dependent loops*, we need to specify what happens when the computations have to *synchronise* due to a dependence. During such a synchronisation, permissions should be transferred from the iteration containing the source of a dependence to the iteration containing the sink of that dependence. To specify such a transfer we introduce two annotations: **send** and **recv**:

  //@ L_S: **send** ϕ **to** L_R, d;
  //@ L_R: **recv** ψ **from** L_S, d;

A **send** specifies that at label L_S the permissions and properties denoted by formula ϕ are transferred to the statement labelled L_R in iteration $i + d$, where i is the current iteration and d is the distance of dependence. A **recv** specifies that permissions and properties as specified by formula ψ are received.

---

[2] Our technique can be generalized to nested loops as well.

(a)   for(int i=0; i < N; i++) /*@
          requires **Perm**(a[i],1) ∗∗ **Perm**(b[i],1/2) ∗∗ **Perm**(c[i],1);
          ensures **Perm**(b[i],1/2) ∗∗ **Perm**(a[i],1/2) ∗∗ **Perm**(c[i],1);
          ensures i>0 ==> **Perm**(a[i−1],1/2);
          ensures i==N−1 ==> **Perm**(a[i],1/2); @*/
       {   a[i]=b[i]+1;
          //@ L1:if (i< N−1) send **Perm**(a[i],1/2) to L2,1;
          //@ L2:if (i>0) recv **Perm**(a[i−1],1/2) from L1,1;
          if (i>0) c[i]=a[i−1]+2; }

(b)   for(int i=0; i < N; i++) /*@
          requires **Perm**(a[i],1/2) ∗∗ **Perm**(b[i],1/2) ∗∗ **Perm**(c[i],1);
          requires i==0 ==> **Perm**(a[i],1/2);
          requires i < N−1 ==> **Perm**(a[i+1],1/2);
          ensures **Perm**(a[i],1) ∗∗ **Perm**(b[i],1/2) ∗∗ **Perm**(c[i],1);   @*/
       {   //@ L1:if (i>0) recv **Perm**(a[i],1/2) from L2,1;
          a[i]=b[i]+1;
          if (i < N−1) c[i]=a[i+1]+2;
          //@ L2:if (i < N−1) send **Perm**(a[i+1],1/2) to L1,1; }

Listing 2. Iteration contracts for loops with loop-carried dependences

The **send** and **recv** annotations can be used to specify loops with both forward and backward loop-carried dependences. Listing 2, shows specified instances of the code in Example 1.

We discuss the annotations for part (a) in some detail. Each iteration i starts with a write permission on a[i] and c[i], and a read permission ($\frac{1}{2}$) on b[i]. The first statement is a write to a[i], which needs write permission. The value written is computed from b[i], for which a read permission is needed. The second statement reads a[i−1], which is not allowed unless read permission is available. This statement is not executed in the first iteration, because of the condition $i > 0$. For all subsequent iterations, permission must be transferred. Hence a **send** annotation is specified before the second assignment that transfers a read permission on a[i] to the next iteration (and in addition, keeps a read permission itself). The postcondition of the iteration contract reflects this: it ensures that the original permission on c[i] is released, as well as the read permission on a[i], which was not sent, and also the read permission on a[i−1], which was received. Finally, since the last iteration cannot transfer a read permission on a[i], the iteration contract's postcondition also specifies that the last iteration returns this non-transferred read permission on a[i].

The **send** annotations indicate an order in which the iterations have to be executed, and thus how the loop can be parallelised. Any execution that respects this order yields the same behaviour as the sequential execution of the loop. For the forward dependence example, this means that it can be vectorised, i.e. we add appropriate synchronisation to the parallel program to ensure permissions can be transferred as specified. However, for the backward dependence example, only sequential execution respects the ordering.

3.2   Verification of Iteration Contracts

To prove the correctness of an iteration contract, we propose appropriate program logic rules. As mentioned above, an iteration contract implicitly gives rise to a contract for the loop. The following rule says that if the iteration contract is correct for any execution of the loop body then this contract is true:

$$\frac{\{P(j)\}\ body(j)\ \{Q(j)\}\quad \forall j.j \in [0 \cdots N)}{\{\bigstar_{j=0}^{N-1} P(j)\}\ \mathbf{for}(\mathbf{int}\ j{=}0;j{<}N;j{+}{+})\{\ body(j)\ \}\ \{\bigstar_{j=0}^{N-1} Q(j)\}}$$

Note that this rule for a loop with an iteration contract is a special case of the rule for parallel execution, which allows arbitrary blocks of code to be executed in parallel (see e.g. [15]).

The rules for the **send** and **recv** are similar in spirit to the rules that are typically used for permission transfer upon lock releasing and acquiring, see e.g. [9]. In particular, **send** is used to give up resources that the **recv** acquires. This is captured by the following two proof rules:

$$\overline{\{P\}\ \mathbf{send}\ P\ \mathbf{to}\ L, d\ \{\mathrm{true}\}} \qquad \overline{\{\mathrm{true}\}\ \mathbf{recv}\ P\ \mathbf{from}\ L, d\ \{P\}} \qquad (1)$$

Receiving permissions and properties that were not sent is unsound. Therefore, **send** and **recv** statements have to be properly matched, meaning that:

(i) if S_r is the statement $\mathbf{if}(g_r(j))\ \mathbf{recv}\ \psi(j)\ \mathbf{from}\ L_s, d$; then S_s is the statement $\mathbf{if}(g_s(j))\ \mathbf{send}\ \phi(j)\ \mathbf{to}\ L_r, d$;

(ii) if the **recv** is enabled in iteration j, then d iterations earlier, the **send** should be enabled, i.e.,

$$\forall j \in [0, \cdots, N).g_r(j) \implies j \geq d \wedge g_s(j - d) \qquad (2)$$

(iii) the information and resources received should be implied by those sent:

$$\forall j \in [d, \cdots, N).\phi(j - d) \implies \psi(j) \qquad (3)$$

In other words, the rules in Eq.1 cannot be used unless the syntactic criterion (i) and the proof obligations (ii) and (iii) hold.

4   Soundness of the Approach

Next, we show that a correct iteration contract capturing a loop independence or a forward loop-carried dependence indeed implies that a loop can be parallelised or vectorised, while preserving the behaviour of the sequential loop.

To construct the proof, we first define the semantics of the three loop execution paradigms: sequential, vectorised, and parallel. We also define the instrumented semantics for a loop specified with an iteration contract. Next, to prove the soundness of our approach we show that the instrumented semantics of an independent loop is equivalent to the parallel execution of the loop, while the instrumented semantics of a loop with a forward dependence is an extension of the vectorised execution of the loop. Functional equivalence of two semantics is shown by transforming the computations in one semantics into the computations in the other semantics by swapping adjacent independent execution steps.

4.1   Semantics of Loop Executions

To keep our formalisation tractable, we split the loop semantics into two layers. The upper layer determines which sequences of atomic statements, called *computations*, a loop can have. The lower layer defines the effect of each atomic statement, and we do not discuss this further here, as this is standard.

As above, we develop our formalisation for non-nested loops with K guarded statements. We instantiate the loop body for each iteration of the loop, so we have $(L_i^j : \mathbf{if}(g_i^j)\ I_i^j;)$ as the instantiation of the ith statement in the jth iteration of the loop. We refer to this instance of statements as S_i^j. The semantics of a statement instance $[\![S_i^j]\!]$ is defined as the atomic execution of the instruction I_i^j labelled by L_i^j provided its guard condition g_i^j holds, otherwise it behaves as a skip. If we execute iterations one by one in sequential order and we preserve the program order of the loop body, we will have a sequence of statement instances starting from S_0^0 and ending at S_K^{N-1}. Intuitively this is the semantics of the sequential execution of the loop.

Definition 1. *A computation c is a finite sequence $t_1, t_2, ..., t_m$ of statement instances such that t_1 is executed first, then t_2 is executed and so on until the last statement t_m.*

To define the set of computations describing the parallel and vectorised semantics of a loop, we define auxiliary operators *concatenation* and *interleaving*. We define two versions of concatenation, plain concatenation $(++)$ and *synchronised concatenation* $(\#)$, which prevents data races between statements by inserting a barrier b that acts as a memory fence:

$$C_1 ++ C_2 = \{c_1 \cdot c_2 \mid c_1 \in C_1, c_2 \in C_2\}$$
$$C_1 \# C_2 = \{c_1 \cdot b \cdot c_2 \mid c_1 \in C_1, c_2 \in C_2\}$$

We lift concatenation to multiple sets as follows:

$$\mathsf{Concat}_{i=1}^N C_i = C_1 ++ \cdots ++ C_N$$
$$\mathsf{SyncConcat}_{i=1}^N C_i = C_1 \# \cdots \# C_N$$

Next, interleaving defines how to weave several computations into a single computation. This is parametrised by a *happens-before* order $<$, in order not to violate restrictions imposed by the program semantics. To define the interleaving operator ($\mathsf{Interleave}_<$), we use an auxiliary operator that denotes interleaving with a fixed first step: ($\mathsf{Interleave}_<^i$):

$$\mathsf{Interleave}_<^{i=1..N} c_i = \mathsf{Interleave}_<(c_1, \cdots, c_n) = \bigcup_{i=1}^n \mathsf{Interleave}_<^i(c_1, \cdots, c_n)$$
$$\mathsf{Interleave}_<^i(\epsilon, \cdots, \epsilon) = \{\epsilon\}$$
$$\mathsf{Interleave}_<^i(c_1, \cdots \epsilon \cdots, c_n) = \emptyset$$
$$\mathsf{Interleave}_<^i(c_1, \cdots s_i c_i \cdots, c_n) = \emptyset \text{ , if } \exists j \neq i, s \in c_j.s < s_i$$
$$\mathsf{Interleave}_<^i(c_1, \cdots s_i c_i \cdots, c_n) = \{s_i \cdot s \mid s \in \mathsf{Interleave}_<(c_1, \cdots c_i \cdots, c_n)\} \text{ , otherwise}$$

where ϵ is the empty computation. We use two happens-before orders: *program order* (PO), which maintains the order of statements executed by the same thread and *specification order* (SO), which extends program order by also enforcing that for every matching pair of **send** and **recv**, the **send** statement happens-before the **recv** statement. Both orders maintain the order between a barrier and the statements preceding and following it.

Now we are ready to define the semantics of the different loop executions. *Sequential execution* simply executes all steps sequentially, *parallel execution* allows any interleaving that preserves program order within the loop body and *vectorised execution* executes multiple iterations in lock-step.

Definition 2. *Suppose we have a loop LP in standard form.*

- *Its* sequential execution semantics *is* $[\![LP]\!]^{Seq} = \mathsf{Concat}_{j=0}^{N-1}\mathsf{Concat}_{i=1}^{K}[\![S_i^j]\!]$
- *Its* parallel execution semantics *is* $[\![LP]\!]^{Par} = \mathsf{Interleave}_{\mathsf{PO}}^{j=0..N-1}\mathsf{Concat}_{i=1}^{K}[\![S_i^j]\!]$
- *Its* vectorised execution semantics *for vector length V is*

$$[\![LP]\!]^{Vec(V)} = \mathsf{Concat}_{v=0}^{(N/V)-1}\mathsf{SyncConcat}_{i=1}^{K}\left(\mathsf{Interleave}_{\emptyset}^{j=vV..vV+V-1}[\![S_i^j]\!]\right)$$

We define the *instrumented semantics* to capture the behaviour of *LP* in the presence of its specifications. This semantics contains all possible computations respecting the specification order (SO). It is formalised by parametrising the interleaving operator with SO.

Definition 3. *The instrumented semantics of* LP *is*

$$[\![LP]\!]^{Spec} = \mathsf{Interleave}_{\mathsf{SO}}^{j=0..N-1}\mathsf{Concat}_{i=1}^{K}[\![S_i^j]\!]$$

4.2   Correctness of Parallel Loops

In the previous section, we defined the semantics of parallelised and vectorised executions in terms of possible traces of atomic steps. This section proves, under certain conditions, that each of those traces is safe and yields the same result as sequential execution, where safe means that the execution of the trace is data race free. Equivalence is established by considering traces modulo reordering independent steps and while ignoring steps that make no modifications. First, we formally define these notions. Then we present our correctness theorems.

To determine if two steps are independent and/or can cause a data race, we need to know for every atomic step (t) which locations in memory it writes ($\mathsf{write}(t)$), which locations in memory it reads ($\mathsf{read}(t)$) and by which thread it is executed. We define the set of accessed locations as $\mathsf{access}(t) = \mathsf{write}(t) \cup \mathsf{read}(t)$. Now we define a *data race* in a trace as a pair of statements that both access a location, where at least one access is a write, and are not ordered by the happens-before relation:

Definition 4. *A computation contains a* data race *with respect to a happens-before order* $<$, *if it contains two steps* s *and* t, *such that* $\mathsf{write}(s) \cap \mathsf{access}(t) \neq \emptyset \wedge \neg(s < t \vee t > s)$.

To reason about different execution orders, equivalence of executions is defined in terms of swapping the order of steps which are not in the happens-before relation. The following proposition states that this does not change the end result of a data race free computation.

Proposition 1. *In a data race free computation, swapping two adjacent statements which are unordered in the happens-before relation does not change the behaviour of that computation.*

Proof. Because the statements are unordered and the computation is data race free, the set of locations written by one of the actions cannot affect the set of locations accessed by the other. Hence neither step can see the effect of the other.   □

The traces in the different semantics do not just differ by their order, but also by steps that are used to enforce synchronisation. To compare the functional result of two threads, we only look at the steps in those traces that actually modify locations that are relevant to the program semantics.

Definition 5. *Given two computations c_1 and c_2. The computations c_1 and c_2 are functionally equivalent if* $\mathsf{mods}(c_1) = \mathsf{mods}(c_2)$, *where*

$$\mathsf{mods}(c) = \begin{cases} \epsilon & \text{, if } c = \epsilon \\ \mathsf{mods}(c') & \text{, if } c = t \cdot c' \wedge \mathsf{write}(t) = \emptyset \\ t \cdot \mathsf{mods}(c'), & \text{, if } c = t \cdot c' \wedge \mathsf{write}(t) \neq \emptyset \end{cases}$$

The correctness of the various loop semantics depends on the correctness of the instrumented semantics:

Theorem 1. *Given a loop with a valid specification.*

1. *All computations in $[\![LP]\!]^{Spec}$ are data race free.*
2. *All computations in $[\![LP]\!]^{Spec}$ and $[\![LP]\!]^{Seq}$ are functionally equivalent.*

Proof. 1. Because there is a valid specification, all invariants of separation logic hold. In particular, for every location the sum over all threads of the permissions held for that location cannot exceed 1.

   Suppose that a statement s occurs before t where one writes a location l and the other accesses it and they are not ordered by happens-before ($s \not< t$). If s needs a fraction p permission on l then we can trace which threads hold the permission when t is executed. It cannot be the thread that executes t, because that implies $s < t$. The fraction q held for t and p are thus held at the same time. Because $p = 1$ or $q = 1$, we have $p + q > 1$. This contradicts the invariant.

2. We prove that every computation in $[\![LP]\!]^{Spec}$ is functionally equivalent to the single computation $[\![LP]\!]^{Seq}$, by showing that any computation can be reordered until it is the sequential computation using Prop. 1.

   Assume that the first n steps of the given computation are in the same order as the sequential computation. Then step t_{n+1} in the sequential execution has to be somewhere in the given sequence. Because each sequence contains the same steps and the sequential computation is in happens-before order, all of the steps that have to happen before t_{n+1} are already included in the prefix. Hence, step t_{n+1} is independent of all of the steps after the prefix and before itself in the given sequence and can be swapped with them one-by-one until it is the next step. We then repeat until the whole sequence matches.   □

The correctness of parallelisation of independent loops is an immediate corollary of this theorem.

Corollary 1. *Given a loop with a valid specification, that does not make use of* **send** *or* **recv**.

1. *All computations in* $[\![LP]\!]^{Par}$ *are data race free.*
2. *All computations in* $[\![LP]\!]^{Par}$ *and* $[\![LP]\!]^{Seq}$ *are functionally equivalent.*

Proof. If the specification does not make use of **send** or **recv** then program order coincides with specification order and the result follows from Theorem 1.   □

This proof is straightforward because in this case, the program order and synchronisation order coincide, thus the set of parallel executions is equivalent to the set of instrumented executions. However, if the specifications use **send** and **recv** then some parallel execution order may contain data races. But if the **send** occurs before the matching **recv** in the loop then vectorisation is possible.

Theorem 2. *Given a loop with a valid specification, such that every* **send** *occurs before the matching* **recv** *in the body, and V that divides N.*

1. *All computations in* $[\![LP]\!]^{Vec(V)}$ *are data race free.*
2. *All computations in* $[\![LP]\!]^{Vec(V)}$ *and* $[\![LP]\!]^{Seq}$ *are functionally equivalent.*

Proof. Because every **send** occurs before the matching **recv**, every computation that may occur in $[\![LP]\!]^{Vec(V)}$ can also occur in $[\![LP]\!]^{Spec}$. That is, we can construct a specification order sequence in which the computational steps occur in the same order and in which the happens-before relation on the vectorised sequence are more restrictive than those in the specification order sequence. Hence all vectorised sequences are data race free because all specification order sequences are data race free (Theorem 1). Moreover, every vectorised computation is functionally equivalent to a specification order sequence and thus functionally equivalent to $[\![LP]\!]^{Seq}$ (Theorem 1).   □

5   Tool Support

After discussing the soundness of our approach, we now turn to tool support as provided by the VerCors tool set. The VerCors tool set was originally developed to reason about multi-threaded Java programs, but it has been extended to support verification of OpenCL kernels [4] and parallel loops. The tool set leverages

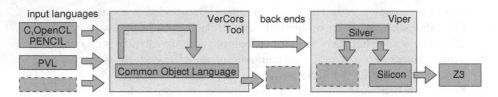

Fig. 1. VerCors tool set overall architecture

existing verification technology: it encodes programs via several program transformation steps into Silver programs [12]. Silver is an intermediate language for
separation logic-like specifications, used by the Viper project [12,23]. Verification
of the encoded program uses the Silver verification framework. Figure 1 sketches
the overall architecture of the tool set, where dashed boxes are other front-ends
and back-ends that are not relevant for this paper.

Encoding into Silver. For the verification of parallel loops, we only use the
encoding into Silver, using the Silicon verifier. We describe this encoding below.

To verify our iteration contracts using the Silicon verifier, we encode the
behaviour of parallel loops and the **send/recv** annotations as method contracts.
The idea is that every loop annotated with an iteration contract is encoded by
a call to the method loop_main, whose contract encodes the application of the
Hoare Logic rule for parallel loops, instantiated for the specific iteration contract.

/*@ **requires** (\forall* int j;0<=j && j<N; pre(j));
     ensures (\forall* int j;0<=j && j<N; post(j)); @*/
loop_main(**int** N,free(S)));

We also need to verify that every iteration respects the iteration contract. This
is encoded by a method, parametrised by the loop variable, containing the loop
body, and specified by the iteration contract.

/*@ **requires** (0<=j && j<N) ** pre(j);
     ensures post(j); @*/
loop_body(**int** j,**int** N,free(S))){ *body*; }

Within the body there may be **send** and **recv** statements.

//@ L_s: **if** ($g_s(j)$) { **send** $\phi(j)$ **to** L_r, d;}
//@ L_r: **if** ($g_r(j)$) { **recv** $\psi(j)$ **from** L_s, d;}

The guards are untouched, but the statements are replaced by method calls

//@ L_s: **if** ($g_s(j)$) { send_s_to_r(j,N,free($\phi(j)$));}
//@ L_r: **if** ($g_r(j)$) { recv_s_to_r(j,N,free($\psi(j)$));}

where   **requires** $\phi(j)$;   **ensures** $\psi(j)$;
           send_s_to_r(**int** j,**int** N,free(S)));   recv_s_to_r(**int** j,**int** N,free(S)));

Finally, we need to check that the proof obligations in Eq. 2 and 3 hold.

Verification Examples. In Section 3, we illustrated our approach by specifying
loops with different data dependencies in Listings 1, and 2. These examples are

$$\begin{array}{ll}
\textbf{for}(\text{int } j{=}0; j < N; j{+}{+}) & \textbf{requires } \phi(\textbf{tid}); \\
\quad \textbf{requires } \phi(j); & \textbf{ensures } \psi(\textbf{tid}); \\
\quad \textbf{ensures } \psi(j); & \text{loop}() \\
\quad \{ L_1 \colon \textbf{if } (g_1(j)) \{ I_1(j); \} \quad \Rightarrow & \quad \{ C_1(\textbf{tid}); \\
\qquad \vdots & \qquad \vdots \\
\quad L_K \colon \textbf{if } (g_K(j)) \{ I_K(j); \} \} & \quad C_K(\textbf{tid}); \}
\end{array}$$

Fig. 2. Vectorisation of a loop with a forward loop-carried dependence

verified automatically by the tool. Moreover, the tool is also able to verify the functional correctness of loops. For example, to verify the functional correctness of the program in Listing 2(a), we could add the following specifications:

requires b[i]==i;
ensures   a[i]==i+1 ** b[i]==i ** (i>0 ==> c[i]==i+2);

to its iteration contract. To make this verify, the property a[i]==i+1 has to be added to the **send** resource formula and a[i−1]==i has to be added to the **recv** resource formula. To see the fully annotated examples, we refer to http://www.utwente.nl/vercors.

6 Compiling Iteration Contracts to Kernel Specifications

Above, we discussed verification of loop parallelisability in high-level sequential programs. Typically, we want to be sure that when we parallelise the program, the resulting low-level parallel code is still correct. To support this, we define how a specification of the original program can be translated into a specification of the low-level code. In particular, this section shows how iteration contracts are translated into OpenCL kernel specifications [4], such that if the code is compiled using a basic parallelising compiler, without further optimisations, the compiled code is correct w.r.t. the compiled specification.

Independent loops. Given an independent loop, the basic compilation to kernel code is simple: create a kernel with as many threads as there are loop iterations and each kernel thread executes one iteration. Moreover, the iteration contract can be used as the thread contract for each parallel thread in the kernel directly. The size of the work-group can be chosen at will, because no barriers are used.

Forward loop-carried dependences. If the loop has forward dependences then the kernel must mimic the vectorised execution of the loop. Consider the specified loop on the left of Figure 2, for simplicity, we assume that both the number of threads and the size of the working group are N. Basic vectorisation results in the kernel on the right of Figure 2, where:

– if $I_k(j)$ is a **send** statement then it is ignored: $C_k(j) \equiv \{\}$

```
kernel Ref {
  global int[tcount] a,b,c;

  requires Perm(a[tid],1) ** Perm(b[tid],1/2) ** Perm(c[tid],1) ** b[tid]==tid;
  ensures  Perm(a[tid],1/2) ** Perm(b[tid],1/2) ** Perm(c[tid],1);
  ensures  tid>0 ==> Perm(a[tid−1],1/2);
  ensures  tid==tcount−1==>Perm(a[tid],1/2);
  ensures  a[tid]==tid+1 ** b[tid]==tid ** (tid>0==>c[tid]==tid+2);

  void main(){
    a[tid]=b[tid]+1;
    barrier(global){
      requires tid<tcount−1 ==> Perm(a[tid],1/2) ** a[tid]==tid+1;
      ensures  (tid>0==>Perm(a[tid−1],1/2)) ** (tid>0==>a[tid−1]==tid);}
    if (tid>0)  c[tid]=a[tid−1]+2;
  }
}
```

Listing 3. Kernel implementing the loop with forward dependence

- if $I_k(j)$ is a **recv** statement with a matching **send** statement at L_i, then it is replaced by a barrier $C_k(j) \equiv$

    barrier(){**requires** $g_i(j) ==> \phi_S(j)$; **ensures** $g_k(j) ==> \phi_R(j)$;}

    where the barrier contract specifies how the permissions are exchanged at the barrier (cf. [4]).
- if $I_k(j)$ is any other statement then it is copied: $C_k(j) \equiv$ **if** $(g_k(j))\{ I_k(j); \}$

Listing 3 shows the kernel that is derived in this way from the forward dependence example in Listing 2(a).

7   Related Work

Verification of High-Level Parallel Constructs. Recently, almost all major programming languages have been augmented by high-level parallelisation constructs. Verification of these high-level constructs has been investigated in different works. Salamanca et al. [19] present an integration of a runtime loop-carried dependence checker in OpenMP. Compared to their approach, we propose a static approach to detect loop-carried dependences, that is valid for all possible executions.

Radoi et al. [16] employ the restricted thread structure of parallel loops to specialise a set of static data race detection techniques and make them practical for the verification of Java 8 loop-parallelism mechanism [20]. In comparison, their method cannot distinguish between vectorised and parallel loop executions, while our approach propose different specification patterns for each of these executions. Also, they use a specialised data race techniques for Java 8 collections, while we investigate the problem in a more general sense.

Barthe et al. [2] propose a new program synthesis technique which produces SIMD code for a given innermost loop. They exploit the *relational verification* approach to prove functional equivalence of the generated SIMD code and the original sequential code, while we employ permission-based separation logic to prove such an equivalence for both vectorised and parallel loop executions.

Automated Loop Verification. Gedell et al. [8] employ automated first-order reasoning in order to deal with parallelisable loops instead of interactive proof techniques, such as induction. They transform a loop into a universally quantified update of state changes by the loop body. The extraction of quantified state update for a particular loop iteration is intuitively similar to the idea of iteration contracts in our method. Their technique only works for parallelisable loops where there is no loop-carried dependence, while our iteration contracts idea addresses both dependent and independent loops.

Parallelising Compilers. From parallelising compilers perspective, our approach can complement the current static dependence analysis techniques. Specifically, in case of *input-dependent semantics* where static analysis cannot decide whether a loop is independent or not [14,18].

8   Conclusion and Future Work

This paper proposes how to verify compiler directives about loop parallelisation. Each loop is specified by its iteration contract and in the presence of loop-carried dependence, additional **send/recv** annotations are added to the iteration specifications to indicate how the iterations synchronise with each other. We prove that loops without **send/recv** annotations are parallelisable, and for a specific pattern of **send/recv** annotations the loop is vectorisable. As an additional result, we propose how the high-level iteration contracts can be compiled into low-level kernel contracts.

In addition to the verification of compiler directives, our approach can be employed to detect possible loop parallelisations even where (in)dependence cannot be determined from static analysis of program text.

The method described is modular in the sense that it allows us to treat any parallel loop as a statement, thus nested loops can be dealt with simply by giving them their own iteration contract. Alternatively one iteration contract can be used for several nested loops.

As future work we plan to investigate how the verifier and the parallelising compiler can support each other. We believe this support can work in both ways. First of all, the parallelising compiler can use verified annotations to know about dependences without analysing the code itself. Conversely, if the compiler performs an analysis then it could emit its findings as a specification template for the code, from which a complete specification can be constructed. This might extend to a set of techniques for automatic generation of iteration contracts.

Acknowledgement. This work is supported by the ERC 258405 VerCors project and by the EU FP7 STREP 287767 project CARP.

References

1. Baghdadi, R., Cohen, A., Guelton, S., Verdoolaege, S., Inoue, J., Grosser, T., Kouveli, G., Kravets, A., Lokhmotov, A., Nugteren, C., Waters, F., Donaldson, A.F.: PENCIL: Towards a Platform-Neutral Compute Intermediate Language for DSLs. CoRR, abs/1302.5586 (2013)
2. Barthe, G., Crespo, J.M., Gulwani, S., Kunz, C., Marron, M.: From relational verification to SIMD loop synthesis. In: PPoPP, pp. 123–134 (2013)
3. Blom, S., Darabi, S., Huisman, M.: Verifying parallel loops with separation logic. In: PLACES, pp. 47–53 (2014)
4. Blom, S., Huisman, M., Mihelčić, M.: Specification and verification of GPGPU programs. In: Science of Computer Programming (2014)
5. Bornat, R., Calcagno, C., O'Hearn, P., Parkinson, M.: Permission accounting in separation logic. In: Palsberg, J., Abadi, M. (eds.) POPL, pp. 259–270. ACM (2005)
6. Boyland, J.: Checking interference with fractional permissions. In: Cousot, R. (ed.) SAS 2003. LNCS, vol. 2694, pp. 55–72. Springer, Heidelberg (2003)
7. Dagum, L., Menon, R.: OpenMP: an industry standard API for shared-memory programming. IEEE Computational Science & Engineering 5(1), 46–55 (1998)
8. Gedell, T., Hähnle, R.: Automating verification of loops by parallelization. In: LPAR, pp. 332–346 (2006)
9. Haack, C., Huisman, M., Hurlin, C.: Reasoning about java's reentrant locks. In: Ramalingam, G. (ed.) APLAS 2008. LNCS, vol. 5356, pp. 171–187. Springer, Heidelberg (2008)
10. Hehner, E.: Specified blocks. In: Meyer, B., Woodcock, J. (eds.) VSTTE 2005. LNCS, vol. 4171, pp. 384–391. Springer, Heidelberg (2008)
11. Hoare, C.: An axiomatic basis for computer programming. Communications of the ACM 12(10), 576–580 (1969)
12. Juhasz, U., Kassios, I.T., Müller, P., Novacek, M., Schwerhoff, M., Summers, A.J.: Viper: A verification infrastructure for permission-based reasoning. Technical report, ETH Zurich (2014)
13. Microsoft TPL, http://msdn.microsoft.com/enus/library/dd460717.aspx
14. Oancea, C.E., Rauchwerger, L.: Logical inference techniques for loop parallelization. SIGPLAN Not 47(6), 509–520 (2012)
15. O'Hearn, P.W.: Resources, concurrency and local reasoning. Theoretical Computer Science 375(1–3), 271–307 (2007)
16. Radoi, C., Dig, D.: Practical static race detection for java parallel loops. In: ISSTA, pp. 178–190 (2013)
17. Reynolds, J.: Separation logic: A logic for shared mutable data structures. In: Logic in Computer Science, pp. 55–74. IEEE Computer Society (2002)
18. Rus, S., Pennings, M., Rauchwerger, L.: Sensitivity analysis for automatic parallelization on multi-cores. In: Proceedings of the 21st Annual International Conference on Supercomputing, ICS, pp. 263–273. ACM (2007)
19. Salamanca, J., Mattos, L., Araujo, G.: Loop-carried dependence verification in openMP. In: DeRose, L., de Supinski, B.R., Olivier, S.L., Chapman, B.M., Müller, M.S. (eds.) IWOMP 2014. LNCS, vol. 8766, pp. 87–102. Springer, Heidelberg (2014)

20. State of the Lambda: Libraries Edition, http://cr.openjdk.java.net/
    ~briangoetz/lambda/lambda-libraries-final.html
21. Threading Building Blocks, http://threadingbuildingblocks.org
22. Tuch, H., Klein, G., Norrish, M.: Types, bytes, and separation logic. In: Hofmann, M.,
    Felleisen, M. (eds.) POPL, pp. 97–108. ACM (2007)
23. Viper project website, http://www.pm.inf.ethz.ch/research/viper

Model-Based Formal Reasoning about Data-Management Applications*

Carolina Dania and Manuel Clavel

IMDEA Software Institute, Madrid, Spain
{carolina.dania,manuel.clavel}@imdea.org

Abstract. Data-management applications are focused around so-called CRUD actions that create, read, update, and delete data from persistent storage. These operations are the building blocks for numerous applications, for example dynamic websites where users create accounts, store and update information, and receive customized views based on their stored data. Typically, the application's data is required to satisfy some properties, which we may call the application's data invariants. In this paper, we introduce a tool-supported, model-based methodology for proving that all the actions possibly triggered by a data-management application will indeed preserve the application's data invariants. Moreover, we report on our experience applying this methodology on a non-trivial case study: namely, an application for managing medical records, for which over eighty data invariants need to be proved to be preserved.

1 Introduction

Model-Driven Architecture (MDA) [13] supports the development of complex software systems by generating software from models. Of course, the quality of the generated software depends on the quality of the source models. If the models do not properly specify the system's intended behavior, one should not expect the generated system to do so either. Experience shows that even when using powerful, high-level modelling languages, it is easy to make logical errors and omissions. It is critical not only that the modelling language has a well-defined semantics, so one can know what one is doing, but also that there is tool support for analyzing the modelled systems' properties.

ActionGUI [2] is a methodology for the model-driven development of secure data-management applications. It consists of languages for modelling multi-tier systems, and a toolkit for generating these systems. Within this methodology, a secure data-management application is modelled using three interrelated models:

1. A *data model* defines the application's data domain in terms of its classes, attributes, and associations. It also defines the application's *data invariants*, i.e., the properties about the application's data that are required to be satisfied in every state.

---

* This work is partially supported by the Spanish Ministry of Economy and Competitiveness Project "StrongSoft" (TIN2012-39391-C04-01 and TIN2012-39391-C04-04).

© Springer-Verlag Berlin Heidelberg 2015
A. Egyed and I. Schaefer (Eds.): FASE 2015, LNCS 9033, pp. 218–232, 2015.
DOI: 10.1007/978-3-662-46675-9_15

2. A *security model* defines the application's security policy in terms of autho-rized access to the actions on the resources provided by the data model.
3. A *graphical user interface (GUI) model* defines the application's graphical interface and application logic.

From these models, ActionGUI generates complete, ready-to-deploy, security-aware web applications, along with all support for access control.

In this paper, we enhance ActionGUI with a tool-supported, model-based methodology for proving the *invariant preservation* property, i.e., that all the action possibly triggered by an application will indeed preserve the application's data invariants. In a nutshell, our approach, which was first informally sketched in [6], consists of the following three steps. Suppose that we are interested in checking whether a sequence $\mathcal{A} = \langle act_1, \ldots, act_{n-1} \rangle$ of data actions preserves an invariant ϕ of an application's data model $\mathcal{D}$. We proceed as follows: (Step 1) From the data model $\mathcal{D}$, we automatically generate a new data model $\mathrm{Film}(\mathcal{D}, n)$ for representing all sequences of n states of $\mathcal{D}$. Notice that some of these sequences will correspond to executions of $\mathcal{A}$, but many others will not. (Step 2) We constrain the model $\mathrm{Film}(\mathcal{D}, n)$ in such a way that it will represent exactly the sequences of states corresponding to executions of $\mathcal{A}$. We do so by adding to $\mathrm{Film}(\mathcal{D}, n)$ a set of constraints $\mathrm{Execute}(\mathcal{D}, act_i, i)$ capturing the execution of the action act_i upon the i-th state of a sequence of states, for $i = 1, \ldots, n-1$. (Step 3) We prove that, for every sequence of states represented by the model $\mathrm{Film}(\mathcal{D}, n)$ constrained by $\bigcup_{i=1}^{n-1} \mathrm{Execute}(\mathcal{D}, act_i, i)$, if the invariant ϕ is satisfied in the first state of the sequence then it is also satisfied in the last state of the sequence.

Organization. After describing in more detail the three steps of our methodology, we report on our experience applying it to a non-trivial case study. We conclude with a brief discussion on related and future work.

2   Modelling Sequences of States (Step 1)

A data model provides a data-oriented view of a system, the idea being that each state of a system can be represented by an *instance* of the system's data model. In this section, however, we introduce a special data model: one whose instances do not represent states of a system but instead *sequences of states* of a system. We begin recalling the notions of ActionGUI data models and object models. Notice that, for the sake of readability, we have moved the technical definitions to Appendix A.

2.1   Data Models

ActionGUI employs ComponentUML [1] for data modelling. ComponentUML provides a subset of UML class models where *entities* (classes) can be related by *associations* and may have *attributes*. A formal definition of ComponentUML data models is given in the Appendix A (Definition 2).

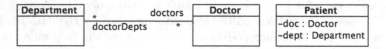

Fig. 1. EHR: A sample data model

Example 1. Consider the ComponentUML model EHR shown in Fig. 1. It consists of three entities: Patient, Department, and Doctor.

Patient. It represents patients. The doctor treating a patient is set in the attribute doc and the department where a patient is treated is set in the attribute dept.

Department. It represents departments. The doctors working in a department are linked to the department through the association-end doctors.

Doctor. It represents doctor's information. Departments where a doctor works are linked to the doctor's information through the association-end doctorDepts.

2.2 Object Models

Object models represent *instances* of data models, consisting of *objects* (instances of entities), with concrete attribute *values*, and *links* (instances of associations). A formal definition of ComponentUML object models is given in the Appendix A (Definition 3).

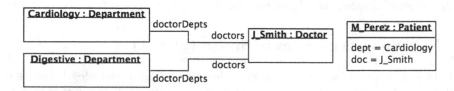

Fig. 2. Inst_EHR: A sample object model

Example 2. Consider the ComponentUML object model Inst_EHR shown in Fig. 2. It represents an instance of the ComponentUML model EHR shown in Fig. 1. In particular, Inst_EHR represents a state of the system in which there are only two departments, namely, Cardiology and Digestive; one doctor, namely, J_Smith, working for both departments; and one patient, M_Perez, treated by doctor J_Smith in the department of Cardiology.

Let $\mathcal{D}$ be a data model. In what follows, we denote by $\llbracket \mathcal{D} \rrbracket$ the set of all instances of $\mathcal{D}$.

2.3 Data Invariants

Data invariants are properties that are required to be satisfied in every state of a system.

In ActionGUI we use Object Constraint Language (OCL) [15] to formalize a system's data invariants. OCL is a strongly typed textual language. Expressions either have a primitive type, a class type, a tuple type or a collection type. OCL provides: standard operators on primitive data, tuples, and collections; a dot-operator to access the values of the objects' attributes and association-ends in the given object model; and operators to iterate over collections. OCL includes two constants, null and invalid, to represent undefinedness. Intuitively, null represents unknown or undefined values, whereas invalid represents error and exceptions. To check if a value is null or invalid, OCL provides the boolean operator oclIsUndefined().

OCL expressions are written in the context of a data model and can be evaluated on any object model of this data model. The evaluation of an OCL expression returns a value but does not alter the given object model, since OCL evaluation is side-effect free. Let $\mathcal{D}$ be a data model, let $\mathcal{I} \in [\![\mathcal{D}]\!]$ be an object model, and let $expr$ be an OCL expression. In what follows, we denote by $[\![expr]\!]^{\mathcal{I}}$ the result of evaluating $expr$ in $\mathcal{I}$. Also, let Φ be a set of data invariants over $\mathcal{D}$. Then, we denote by $[\![\mathcal{D}, \Phi]\!] \subseteq [\![\mathcal{D}]\!]$ the set of all the *valid* instances of $\mathcal{D}$ with respect to Φ. More formally,

$$[\![\mathcal{D}, \Phi]\!] = \{\mathcal{I} \in [\![\mathcal{D}]\!] \mid [\![\phi]\!]^{\mathcal{I}} = \text{true, for every } \phi \in \Phi\}.$$

Example 3. Suppose that the following data invariants are specified for the data model EHR in Fig. 1:

1. *Each patient is treated by a doctor.*

   Patient.allInstances()→forAll(p|not(p.doc.oclIsUndefined()))

2. *Each patient is treated in a department.*

   Patient.allInstances()→forAll(p|not(p.dept.oclIsUndefined()))

3. *Each patient is treated by a doctor who works in the department where the patient is treated.*

   Patient.allInstances()→forAll(p|p.doc.doctorDepts→includes(p.dept))

Clearly, the object model Inst_EHR in Fig. 2 is a valid instance of EHR with respect to the data invariants (1)–(3), since they evaluate to true in Inst_EHR.

2.4 Filmstrip Models

Next, we introduce the notion of *filmstrips* to model sequences of states of a system. Given a data model $\mathcal{D}$, a $\mathcal{D}$-*filmstrip model* of length n, denoted by $\text{Film}(\mathcal{D}, n)$, is a new data model which contains the same classes as $\mathcal{D}$, but now:

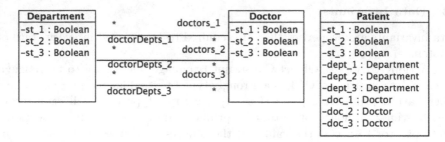

Fig. 3. Film(EHR,3): a filmstrip model of length 3 of EHR

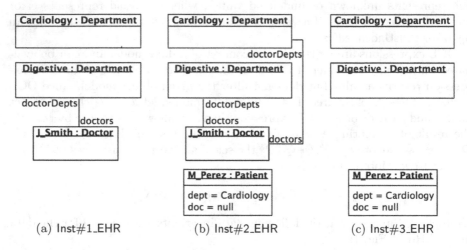

Fig. 4. Three instances of EHR

- To represent that an object may have different attribute values and/or links in each state, each class c contains n different "copies" of each of the attributes and association-ends that c has in $\mathcal{D}$. The idea is that, in each instance of a filmstrip model, the value of the attribute at (respectively, association-end as) for an object o in the i-th state of the sequence of states modelled by this instance is precisely the value of the i-th "copy" of at (respectively, as).
- To represent that an object may exist in some states, but not in others, each class c contains n "copies" of a new boolean attribute st. The idea is that, in each instance of a filmstrip model, an object o exists in the i-th state of the sequence of states modelled by this instance if and only if the value of the i-th "copy" of st is true.

A formal definition of ComponentUML filmstrip models is given in Appendix A (Definition 4).

Example 4. In Fig. 3 we show the filmstrip model Film(EHR, 3). Consider now the three instances of EHR shown in Fig. 4. The first instance (Inst#1_EHR)

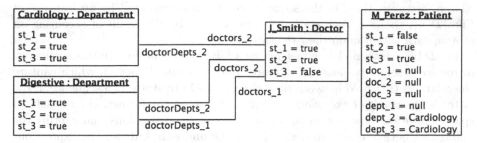

Fig. 5. An instance of Film(EHR, 3)

corresponds to a state where there are two departments, Cardiology and Digestive, and one doctor, J_Smith, working in Digestive. The second instance (Inst#2_EHR) is like the first one, except that now J_Smith also works in Cardiology and, moreover, there is a patient, M_Perez, who is treated in Cardiology, but has no doctor assigned yet. Finally, the third instance (Inst#3_EHR) is like the second one, except that it does not contain any doctor. In Fig. 5 we show how the sequence ⟨Inst#1_EHR, Inst#2_EHR, Inst#3_EHR⟩ can be represented as an instance of Film(EHR, 3).

To conclude this section, we introduce a function Project(), which we will use when reasoning about filmstrip models. Let $\mathcal{D}$ be a data model and let ϕ be an expression. Project($\mathcal{D}, \phi, i$) "projects" the expression ϕ so as to refer to the i-th state in the sequences represented by the instances of Film($\mathcal{D}, n$), for $n \geq i$. A formal definition of Project() is given in Appendix A (Definition 5).

Example 5. Consider the data invariants (1) and (3) presented in the Example 3. Then,

Project(EHR, (1), 1) =

  Patient.allInstances()→select(p|p.st_1)→forAll(p|not(p.doc_1.oclIsUndefined()))

Project(EHR, (3), 1) =

  Patient.allInstances()→select(p|p.st_1)→forAll(p|p.doc_1.doctorDepts_1
    →includes(p.dept_1))

Recall that Patient.allInstances()→select(p|p.st_1) refers to the instances of the entity Patient which exist in the first state of the sequences of states modelled by Film(EHR, 3), while .doc_1 and .doctorDepts_1 refer, respectively, to the value of the attribute doc and the links through the association-end doctorDepts of the instances of the entity Patient also in the first state of the aforementioned sequences of states.

3   Modelling Sequences of Data Actions (Step 2)

As explained before, given a data model $\mathcal{D}$ and a positive number n, the instances of the filmstrip model Film($\mathcal{D}, n$) represent sequences of n states of the system.

Notice, however, that, in the sequence of states represented by an instance of Film$(\mathcal{D}, n)$, the $(i + 1)$-th state does not need to be the result of executing an atomic data action upon the i-th state.

Let $\mathcal{D}$ be a data model and let act be a CRUD data action. In this section we introduce a set of boolean OCL expressions, Execute$(\mathcal{D}, act, i)$, which capture the relations that hold between the i-th and $(i+1)$-th states of a sequence, if the latter is the result of executing the action act upon the former. For the sake of space limitation, however, we only provide here the expressions that capture the differences between the two states, $(i + 1)$-th and i-th, but not the expressions that capture their commonalities.

As expected, we define Execute$(\mathcal{D}, act, i)$ by cases. In ActionGUI, we consider the following *atomic data actions*: *create* or *delete* an object of an entity; *read* the value of an attribute of an object; and *add* or *remove* a link between two objects. [1]

Action create. For act the action of creating an instance new of an entity c, the difference between the states $(i+1)$-th and i-th can be captured by the following expressions in Execute$(\mathcal{D}, act, i)$:

- $new.\text{st\_}i = \mathsf{false}$.
- $new.\text{st\_}(i + 1) = \mathsf{true}$.
- $new.at\_(i + 1) = \mathsf{null}$, for every attribute at of the entity c.
- $new.as\_(i + 1) \rightarrow \mathsf{isEmpty}()$, for every association-end as of the entity c.

Action delete. For act the action of deleting an instance o of an entity c, the difference between the states $(i+1)$-th and i-th can be captured by the following expressions in Execute$(\mathcal{D}, act, i)$:

- $o.\text{st\_}i = \mathsf{true}$.
- $o.\text{st\_}(i + 1) = \mathsf{false}$.
- $o.at\_(i + 1) = \mathsf{null}$, for every attribute at of the entity c.
- $o.as\_(i + 1) \rightarrow \mathsf{isEmpty}()$, for every association-end as of the entity c.
- $c'.\mathsf{allInstances}().as'\_(i + 1) \rightarrow \mathsf{excludes}(o)$ for every entity c', and every association-end as' between c' and c.

Action update. For act the action of updating an attribute at of an instance o of an entity c with a value v, the difference between the states $(i + 1)$-th and i-th can be captured by the following expression in Execute$(\mathcal{D}, act, i)$:

- $o.at\_(i + 1) = v$.

---

[1] ActionGUI supports also *conditional* data actions, where the conditions are boolean OCL expressions. Notice that, when act is a conditional data action, we must also include in Execute$(\mathcal{D}, act, i)$, the expression that results from "projecting" its condition, using the function Project(), so as to refer to the i-th state in the sequence.

Action add. For *act* the action of adding an object o' to the objects that are linked with an object o through an association-end *as* (whose opposite association-end is as'), the difference between the states $(i+1)$-th and i-th can be captured by the following expressions in Execute($\mathcal{D}, act, i$):

- $o.as\_(i+1) = (o.as\_i) \rightarrow \text{including}(o')$.
- $o'.as'\_(i+1) = (o'.as'\_i) \rightarrow \text{including}(o)$.

Action remove. For *act* the action of removing an object o' to the objects that are linked with an object o through an association-end *as* (whose opposite association-end is as'), the difference between the states $(i+1)$-th and i-th can be captured by the following expressions in Execute($\mathcal{D}, act, i$):

- $o.as\_(i+1) = (o.as\_i) \rightarrow \text{excluding}(o')$.
- $o'.as'\_(i+1) = (o'.as'\_i) \rightarrow \text{excluding}(o)$.

To end this section, we list below the expressions in Execute($\mathcal{D}, act, i$) that capture the commonalities between the states $(i+1)$-th and i-th, for the case of the action updating an attribute *at* of an instance o of and entity c; the expressions for the other cases are entirely similar.

- $d.\text{allInstances}() \rightarrow \text{select}(x|x.st\_(i+1)) = d.\text{allInstances}() \rightarrow \text{select}(x|x.st\_i)$,   for every entity d.
- $d.\text{allInstances}() \rightarrow \text{select}(x|x.st\_i) \rightarrow \text{forAll}(x|x.at'\_(i+1) = x.at'\_i)$, for every entity d and every attribute at' of d, such that $at' \neq at$.
- $c.\text{allInstances}() \rightarrow \text{select}(x|x.st\_i) \rightarrow \text{excluding}(o) \rightarrow \text{forAll}(x|x.at\_(i+1) = x.at\_i)$.
- $d.\text{allInstances}() \rightarrow \text{select}(x|x.st\_i) \rightarrow \text{forAll}(x|x.as\_(i+1) = x.as\_i)$ for every entity d, and every association-end *as* of d.

4   Proving Invariants Preservation (Step 3)

Invariants are properties that are *required* to be satisfied in every system state. Recall that, in the case of data-management applications, the system states are the states of the applications' persistence layer, which can only be changed by executing the sequences of data actions associated to the applications' GUI events. Also recall that, within ActionGUI, (i) data invariants are specified along with the application's data model, and also that (ii) the sequences of actions triggered by the GUI events are specified in the application's GUI model. We can now formally define the invariant-preservation property as follows:

Definition 1 (Invariant preservation). *Let $\mathcal{D}$ be a data model, with invariants Φ. Let $\mathcal{A} = \langle act_1, \ldots, act_{n-1} \rangle$ be a sequence of data actions. We say that $\mathcal{A}$ preserves an invariant $\phi \in \Phi$ if and only if*

$$\forall \mathcal{F} \in [\![\text{Film}(\mathcal{D}, n), \bigcup_{i=1}^{n-1} \text{Execute}(\mathcal{D}, act_i, i)]\!]. \tag{1}$$

$$[\![\text{Project}(\mathcal{D}, \bigwedge_{\psi \in \Phi} (\psi), 1) \text{ implies Project}(\mathcal{D}, \phi, n)]\!]^{\mathcal{F}} = \text{true},$$

i.e., if and only if, for every $\mathcal{A}$-valid instance $\mathcal{F}$ of $\mathrm{Film}(\mathcal{D}, n)$ the following holds: if all the invariants in Φ evaluate to true *when "projected" over the first state of the sequence of states represented by $\mathcal{F}$, then the invariant ϕ evaluates to* true *as well when "projected" over the last state of the aforementioned sequence.*

Using SMT Solvers for Checking Invariant-Preservation

In [4,5] we proposed a mapping from OCL to first-order logic, which consists of two, inter-related components: (i) a map from ComponentUML models to first-order formulas, called ocl2fol$_{\mathrm{def}}$; and (ii) a map from boolean OCL expressions to first-order formulas, called ocl2fol. The following remark formalizes the main property of our mapping from OCL to first-order logic.

Remark 1. Let $\mathcal{D}$ be a data model, with data invariants Φ. Let ϕ be a boolean expression. Then,

$$\forall \mathcal{I} \in [\![\mathcal{D}, \Phi]\!] . ([\![\phi]\!]^{\mathcal{I}} = \text{true}) \Longleftrightarrow$$
$$\mathrm{ocl2fol}_{\mathrm{def}}(\mathcal{D}) \cup \{\mathrm{ocl2fol}(\gamma) \mid \gamma \in \Phi\} \cup \mathrm{ocl2fol}(\mathrm{not}(\phi)) \text{ is unsatisfiable.}$$

By the previous remark, we can reformulate Definition 1 as follows: Let $\mathcal{D}$ be a data model, with invariants Φ. Let $\mathcal{A} = \langle act_1, \ldots, act_{n-1} \rangle$ be a sequence of data actions. We say that $\mathcal{A}$ *preserves* an invariant $\phi \in \Phi$ if and only if the following set is unsatisfiable:

$$\mathrm{ocl2fol}_{\mathrm{def}}(\mathrm{Film}(\mathcal{D}, n)) \cup \{\mathrm{ocl2fol}(\gamma) \mid \gamma \in \bigcup_{i=1}^{n-1} \mathrm{Execute}(\mathcal{D}, act_i, i)\} \quad (2)$$
$$\cup\ \mathrm{ocl2fol}(\mathrm{not}(\mathrm{Project}(\mathcal{D}, \bigwedge_{\psi \in \Phi}(\psi), 1) \text{ implies } \mathrm{Project}(\mathcal{D}, \phi, n))).$$

In other words, using our mapping from OCL to first-order logic, we can transform an invariant-preservation problem (1) into a first-order satisfiability problem (2). And by doing so, we open up the possibility of using SMT solvers to automatically (and effectively) check the invariant-preservation property of non-trivial data-management applications, as we will report in the next section.

5   Case Study

In this section we report on a case study about using SMT solvers —in particular, Z3 [7]— for proving the invariant-preservation property. Satisfiability Modulo Theories (SMT) generalizes boolean satisfiability (SAT) by incorporating equality reasoning, arithmetic, fixed-size bit-vectors, arrays, quantifiers, and other first-order theories. Of course, when dealing with quantifiers, SMT solvers cannot be complete, and may return "unknown" after a while, meaning that neither they can prove the quantified formula to be unsatisfiable, nor they can find an interpretation that makes it satisfiable.

The data-management application for this case study is the eHealth Record Management System (EHRM) developed, using ActionGUI, within the European Network of Excellence on Engineering Secure Future Internet Software Services and Systems (NESSoS) [14]. The EHRM application consists of a web-based system for electronic health record management. The data model contains 18 entities, 40 attributes, and 48 association-ends. It also contains 86 data invariants. For the sake of illustration, we can group the EHRM's data invariants in the following categories:

G1. Properties about the population of certain entities. E.g., *There must be at least a medical center.*

MedicalCenter.allInstances()→notEmpty().

G2. Properties about the definedness of certain attributes. E.g., *The name of a professional cannot be left undefined.*

Professional.allInstances()→forAll(p|not(p.name.ocIsUndefined())).

G3. Properties about the uniqueness of certain data. E.g.: *There cannot be two different doctors with the same licence number.*

Doctor.allInstances()→forAll(d1,d2|d1<>d2 implies d1.licence<>d2.licence).

G4. Properties about the population of certain association-ends. E.g., *Every medical center should have at least one employee.*

MedicalCenter.allInstances()→forAll(m|m.employees→notEmpty()).

G5. Other properties: E.g., *A patient should be treated in a department where its assigned doctor works.*

Patient.allInstances()
→forAll(p|p.doctor.doctorDepartments→includes(p.department)).

In our case study, we have checked the invariant-preservation property for seven non-trivial sequences of data actions: namely, those that create a new admin staff, a new nurse, or a new doctor; those that reassign a doctor or a nurse to another department; and those that register a new patient, and move a patient to a different ward. The result of our case study is shown in Fig. 6. In particular, for each of the aforementioned sequences of actions, we indicate:

- The number of data actions (and conditions) in the sequence.
- The number of data invariants (potentially) affected by the actions in the sequence, indicating how many of them we have proved to be preserved by the sequence and how many to be violated.[2]

---

[2] Interestingly, when an invariant is violated, Z3 returns also an instance of the given filmstrip model responsibly for this violation. This *counterexample* can then be used to fix accordingly the given sequence of actions.

Sequences	Acts.	Conds.	Invariants			Time		
			affected	preserved	violated	min.	max.	avge.
Create an administrative	8	9	18	18	0	0.03s	0.20s	0.05s
Create a nurse	10	11	22	22	0	0.03s	0.22s	0.06s
Create a doctor	11	12	25	24	1	0.03s	27.00s	0.07s
Reassign a doctor	2	6	2	2	0	6.88s	11.10s	8.94s
Reassign a nurse	2	6	2	1	1	0.10s	17.01s	8.55s
Register patient	30	6	28	26	2	0.03s	0.20s	0.05s
Move a patient	2	3	3	3	0	0.03s	0.03s	0.03s
		Total	100	96	4			

Fig. 6. EHRM case study: summary

– The minimum, maximum, and average time taken for proving that the sequence preserves (or violates) each of the (potentially) affected invariants.

All the proofs have been ran on a machine with an Intel Core2 processor running at 2.83 GHz with 8GB of RAM, using Z3 versions 4.3.1 and 4.3.2. All the Z3 input files have been automatically generated with an ActionGUI plugin which implements our mapping from OCL to first-order logic. These files are available at `http://software.imdea.org/~dania/tools/ehrm.html`, where we also indicate which files are to be ran with which version.

Lessons learned. There are two main lessons that we can learn from this case study. The first lesson is that, when modelling non-trivial data-management applications, it is indeed not difficult to make errors, or at least omissions, even when using a high-level language like ActionGUI. In fact, the four *violated* invariants showed in Fig. 6 arise because the EHRM's modeler inadvertently omitted some conditions for the execution of the corresponding sequence of actions. As an example, for the case of creating a doctor, the invariant that is *violated* is "Every doctor has a unique licence number", and it is so because the modeler omitted a condition for checking that the licence number of the doctor to be created must be different from the licence numbers of the doctors already in the system. As another example, for the case of reassigning a nurse, the invariant that is *violated* is "There should be at least one nurse assigned to each department", and this is produced because the modeler omitted a condition for checking that the department where the nurse to be reassigned currently works must have at least two nurses working in it.

The second lesson that we have learned is that, using our methodology, and, in particular, using Z3 as the back-end prover, the invariant-preservation property can indeed be effectively checked for non-trivial data-management applications. As reported in Fig. 6, we are able to automatically prove that, for each of the sequences of actions under consideration, all the *affected* invariants are either *preserved* or *violated*. This means that Z3 does not return "unknown" for any of the 100 checks that we have to perform (corresponding to the total number of *affected* invariants), despite the fact that in all these checks there are (many) quantifiers involved. Moreover, regarding performance, Fig. 6 shows that, in most of the cases we are able to prove the invariant-preservation property in less than 100ms (worst case: 27s). This great performance is achieved even though, for each case, Z3 needs to check the satisfiability of a first-order theory containing on average 190 declarations (of function, predicate and constant symbols), 20 definitions (of predicates), and 550 assertions. Overall, these results improve very significantly those obtained in a preliminary, more simple case study reported in [6], where some checks failed to terminate after several days, and some others took minutes before returning an answer. However, we should take these new results with a grain of salt. Indeed, we are very much aware (even painfully so) that our current results depend on the (hard-won) interaction between (i) the way we formalize sequences of n states, OCL invariants, actions' conditions, and actions' executions, and (ii) the heuristics implemented in the verification back-end we use, namely Z3. This state-of-affairs is very well illustrated by the fact that, as indicated before, we have had to use two different versions of Z3 (4.3.1 and 4.3.2) to complete our case study for the following reason: there are some checks for which one of the versions returns "unknown", while the other version returns either "sat" or "unsat"; but there are some other checks for which precisely the opposite occurs.

6   Related Work

In the past decade, there has been a plethora of proposals for model-based reasoning about the different aspects of a software system. For the case of the static or structural aspects of a system, the challenge lies in mapping the system's data model, along with its data invariants, into a formalism for which reasoning tools may be readily available (see [10] and references). By choosing a particular formalism each proposal commits to a different trade-off between expressiveness and termination, automation, or completeness (see [16,3] and references). On the other hand, for the case of model-based reasoning about a system's dynamic aspects, which is our concern here, the main challenge lies in finding a suitable formalism in which to map the models specifying how the system can change over time. To this extent, it is worthwhile noticing the different attempts made so far to extend OCL with temporal features (see [12] and references). In our case, however, we follow a different line of work, one that is centered around the notion of *filmstrips* [8,18]. A filmstrip is, ultimately, a way of encoding a sequence of snapshots of a system. Interestingly, when this encoding uses the same language employed for modelling the static aspects of a system, then the tools available for reasoning about the latter can be used for reasoning about the former. This is precisely our approach, as well as the one underlying the proposals presented in [11] and [9]. However, the difference between our approach and those are equally important. It has its roots in our different way of mapping data models and data invariants (OCL) into first-order logic [4,5], which allows us to effectively use SMT solvers for reasoning about them, while [9] and [11] resort to SAT solvers. As a consequence, when successful, we are able to prove that all possible executions of a given sequence of data actions preserve a given data invariant. On the contrary, [9] can only validate that a given execution preserves a given invariant, while [11] can prove that all possible executions of a given sequence of data action preserve a given invariant, but only if these executions do not involve more than a given number of objects and links. Finally, [17] proposes also the use of filmstrip models and SMT solvers for model-based reasoning about the dynamic aspects of a system. This proposal, however, at least in its current form, lacks too many details (including non-trivial examples) for us to be able to provide a fair comparison with our approach.

7   Conclusions and Future Work

Data-management applications are focused around the so-called CRUD actions, namely, to create, read, update, and delete data from persistent storage. These operations are the building blocks for numerous applications, for example dynamic websites where users create accounts, store and update information, and receive customized views based on their stored data. In [2] we proposed a model-driven development environment, called ActionGUI, for developing data-management application. With ActionGUI, complete, ready-to-deploy, security-aware web applications can be automatically generated from the applications' data, security, and GUI models. In this paper, we present our work to enhance ActionGUI with a methodology for automatically proving that the application's data invariants, i.e., the properties that are required to hold in every state of the system, are indeed preserved after the execution of the sequences of data actions supported by the application's GUI. We have also reported on a non-trivial case study, in which we have successfully applied our methodology over an eHealth application whose data model contains 80 data invariants, and whose GUI model includes events possibly triggering more than 20 data actions in a sequence.

Finally, we are currently extending our methodology to deal with complex, non-atomic data action. The idea, of course, is to model the execution of these complex actions using OCL, as we have done for the case of CRUD actions. A more challenging goal, however, is to extend our methodology to deal with *iterations*. In ActionGUI, each iteration specifies that a sequence of data actions must be iterated over a collection of data elements. The idea here is to integrate in our methodology the notion of *iteration invariant*, taking advantage of the fact that the collection over which the sequence of data actions must be iterated is also specified using OCL. Finally, we are analyzing in depth the interaction between (i) the way we formalize data-invariants and data-action executions and (ii) the heuristics implemented in the verification back-end we use, namely Z3, to better understand its scope and limitations.

References

1. Basin, D., Doser, J., Lodderstedt, T.: Model driven security: From UML models to access control infrastructures. ACM Transactions on Software Engineering and Methodology 15(1), 39–91 (2006)

2. Basin, D.A., Clavel, M., Egea, M., García de Dios, M.A., Dania, C.: A model-driven methodology for developing secure data-management applications. IEEE Trans. Software Eng. 40(4), 324–337 (2014)
3. Cabot, J., Clarisó, R., Guerra, E., de Lara, J.: Verification and validation of declarative model-to-model transformations through invariants. Journal of Systems and Software 83(2), 283–302 (2010)
4. Clavel, M., Egea, M., García de Dios, M.A.: Checking unsatisfiability for OCL constraints. Electronic Communications of the EASST 24, 1–13 (2009)
5. Dania, C., Clavel, M.: OCL2FOL+: Coping with Undefinedness. In: Cabot, J., Gogolla, M., Ráth, I., Willink, E. (eds.) CEUR Workshop Proceedings OCL@MoDELS, vol. 1092, pp. 53–62. CEUR-WS.org (2013)
6. García de Dios, M.A., Dania, C., Basin, D., Clavel, M.: Model-driven development of a secure eHealth application. In: Heisel, M., Joosen, W., Lopez, J., Martinelli, F. (eds.) Engineering Secure Future Internet Services and Systems. LNCS, vol. 8431, pp. 97–118. Springer, Heidelberg (2014)
7. de Moura, L., Bjørner, N.: Z3: An efficient SMT solver. In: Ramakrishnan, C.R., Rehof, J. (eds.) TACAS 2008. LNCS, vol. 4963, pp. 337–340. Springer, Heidelberg (2008)
8. D'Souza, D., Wills, A.: Catalysis. Practical Rigor and Refinement: Extending OMT, Fusion, and Objectory. Technical report (1995), http://catalysis.org
9. Gogolla, M., Hamann, L., Hilken, F., Kuhlmann, M., France, R.B.: From application models to filmstrip models: An approach to automatic validation of model dynamics. In: Fill, H., Karagiannis, D., Reimer, U. (eds.) Modellierung. LNI, vol. 225, pp. 273–288. GI (2014)
10. González, C.A., Cabot, J.: Formal verification of static software models in MDE: A systematic review. Information & Software Technology 56(8), 821–838 (2014)
11. Jackson, D.: Software Abstractions: Logic, Language, and Analysis. The MIT Press (2006)
12. Kanso, B., Taha, S.: Temporal constraint support for OCL. In: Czarnecki, K., Hedin, G. (eds.) SLE 2012. LNCS, vol. 7745, pp. 83–103. Springer, Heidelberg (2013)
13. Kleppe, A.G., Warmer, J., Bast, W.: MDA Explained: The Model Driven Architecture: Practice and Promise. Addison-Wesley Longman Publishing Co., Inc., Boston (2003)
14. NESSoS. The European Network of Excellence on Engineering Secure Future internet Software Services and Systems (2010), http://www.nessos-project.eu
15. Object Management Group. Object constraint language specification version 2.4. Technical report, OMG (2014), http://www.omg.org/spec/OCL/2.4
16. Queralt, A., Artale, A., Calvanese, D., Teniente, E.: OCL-Lite: Finite reasoning on UML/OCL conceptual schemas. Data & Knowledge Engineering 73, 1–22 (2012)
17. Soeken, M., Wille, R., Kuhlmann, M., Gogolla, M., Drechsler, R.: Verifying UML/OCL models using Boolean satisfiability. In: DATE, pp. 1341–1344. IEEE (2010)
18. WieringaA, R.: survey of structured and object-oriented software specification methods and techniques. ACM Comput. Surv. 30(4), 459–527 (1998)

A   Technical Definitions

Definition 2 (Data models). *A data model is a tuple* $\langle C, AT, AS, ASO \rangle$ *such that:*

- C *is a set of class identifiers.*
- AT *is a set of triples* $\langle at, c, t \rangle$, *also represented as* $at_{(c,t)}$, *where at is an attribute identifier,* $c \in C$, $t \in C \cup \{$**Integer**, **Real**, **String**, **Boolean**$\}$, *and c and t are, respectively, the class and the type of the attribute at.*
- AS *is a set of tuples* $\langle as, c, c' \rangle$, *also denoted by* $as_{(c,c')}$, *where as is an association-end identifier,* $c, c' \in C$, *c and c' are, respectively, the source and the target classes of as.*
- ASO *is a symmetric relation,* $ASO \subseteq AS \times AS$, *where* $(as_{(c,c')}, as'_{(c',c)}) \in ASO$ *represents that as' is the association-end opposite to as, and vice versa, and* $c, c' \in C$.

Definition 3 (Object models). *Let* $\mathcal{D}$ *be a data model* $\langle C, AT, AS, ASO \rangle$. *Then, a* $\mathcal{D}$-*object model is a tuple* $\langle O, VA, LK \rangle$, *such that:*

- O *is a set of pairs* $\langle o, c \rangle$, *where o is an object identifier and* $c \in C$. *Each pair* $\langle o, c \rangle$, *also represented as* o_c, *denotes that the object o is of the class c.*
- VA *is a set of triples* $\langle o_c, at_{(c,t)}, va \rangle$, *where* $at_{(c,t)} \in AT$, $o_c \in O$, $t \in C \cup \{$**Integer**, **Real**, **String**, **Boolean**$\}$, *and va is a value of type t. Each triple* $\langle o_c, at_{(c,t)}, va \rangle$ *denotes that va is the value of the attribute at of the object o.*
- LK *is a set of triples* $\langle o_c, as_{(c,c')}, o'_{c'} \rangle$, *where* $as_{(c,c')} \in AS$, *and* $o_c, o'_{c'} \in O$. *Each tuple* $\langle o_c, as_{(c,c')}, o'_{c'} \rangle$ *denotes that the object o' is among the objects that are linked to the object o through the association-end as.*

Definition 4 (Filmstrip models). *Let* $\mathcal{D}$ *be a data model,* $\mathcal{D} = \langle C, AT, AS, ASO \rangle$. *Let n be a positive number. We denote by* $\mathrm{Film}(\mathcal{D}, n)$ *the model of the sequences of length n of* $\mathcal{D}$-*object models.* $\mathrm{Film}(\mathcal{D}, n)$ *is defined as follows:*

$$\mathrm{Film}(\mathcal{D}, n) = \langle C, (n \times \{\mathrm{st}\}) \cup (n \times AT), (n \times AS), (n \times ASO) \rangle$$

where

- $(n \times \{\mathrm{st}\}) = \{(\mathrm{st}\_i)_{(c, \mathrm{Boolean})} \mid c \in C \wedge 1 \le i \le n\}$.
- $(n \times AT) = \{(at\_i)_{(c,t)} \mid at_{(c,t)} \in AT \wedge 1 \le i \le n\}$.
- $(n \times AS) = \{(as\_i)_{(c,c')} \mid as_{(c,c')} \in AS \wedge 1 \le i \le n\}$.
- $(n \times ASO) = \{((as\_i)_{(c,c')}, (as'\_i)_{(c',c)}) \mid (as_{(c,c')}, as'_{(c',c)}) \in ASO \wedge 1 \le i \le n\}$.

Definition 5 (Project). *Let* $\mathcal{D} = \langle C, AT, AS, ASO \rangle$ *be a data model. Let n be positive number. Let* ϕ *be a* $\mathcal{D}$-*expression. For* $1 \le i \le n$, $\mathrm{Proj}(\mathcal{D}, \phi, i)$ *is the* $\mathrm{Film}(\mathcal{D}, n)$-*expression that "projects" the expression* ϕ *so as to refer to the i-th state in the sequences represented by the instances of* $\mathrm{Film}(\mathcal{D}, n)$. $\mathrm{Proj}(\mathcal{D}, \phi, i)$ *is obtained from* ϕ *by executing the following:*

- *For every class* $c \in C$, *replace every occurrence of* c.allInstances() *by* c.allInstances()$\rightarrow$select(o|o.st_(i)).
- *For every attribute* $at_{(c,t)} \in AT$, *replace every occurrence of* .at *by* .at_(i).
- *For every link* $as_{(c,c')} \in AS$, *replace every occurrence of* .as *by* .as_(i).

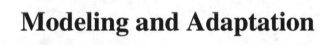

Modeling and Adaptation

Self-adaptive Software with Decentralised Control Loops

Radu Calinescu[1], Simos Gerasimou[1], and Alec Banks[2]

[1] Department of Computer Science, University of York, UK
[2] Defence Science and Technology Laboratory, Ministry of Defence, UK

Abstract. We present DECIDE, a rigorous approach to decentralising the control loops of distributed self-adaptive software used in mission-critical applications. DECIDE uses quantitative verification at runtime, first to agree individual component contributions to meeting system-level quality-of-service requirements, and then to ensure that components achieve their agreed contributions in the presence of changes and failures. All verification operations are carried out locally, using component-level models, and communication between components is infrequent. We illustrate the application of DECIDE and show its effectiveness using a case study from the unmanned underwater vehicle domain.

1 Introduction

A growing number of mission-critical software systems operate in uncertain scenarios characterised by internal failures and environment changes. These systems must *self-adapt* to comply with strict dependability, performance and other quality-of-service (QoS) requirements. Achieving QoS compliance is a great challenge of *self-adaptive software* [21]. To address it, recent research proposed the use of formal methods to drive self-adaptation within software systems. A promising approach in this area is *runtime quantitative verification* (RQV) [3, 6, 9], which uses quantitative model checking to reverify the QoS properties of software after environment or internal changes. This reverification identifies, and may in certain scenarios predict, QoS requirement violations, and supports the dynamic reconfiguration of the software for recovery from, or prevention of, such violations [3]. RQV has been successfully used to develop centralised-control self-adaptive software in domains including dynamic service selection [4], datacentre resource allocation [16] and dynamic power management [6].

Here we extend the applicability of RQV to distributed self-adaptive software. To this end, we introduce an RQV-driven approach for DEcentralised Control In Distributed sElf-adaptive software (DECIDE). DECIDE addresses two key objectives from the latest research roadmap for self-adaptive systems [21]:

1. *Decentralisation of control loops*, to eliminate the single point of failure created by centralised control loops, to improve the flexibility of self-adaptive systems, and to fulfil the original autonomic computing vision [18].
2. *Practical runtime verification and validation*, to guarantee compliance with the QoS requirements of mission-critical self-adaptive software.

© Springer-Verlag Berlin Heidelberg 2015
A. Egyed and I. Schaefer (Eds.): FASE 2015, LNCS 9033, pp. 235–251, 2015.
DOI: 10.1007/978-3-662-46675-9_16

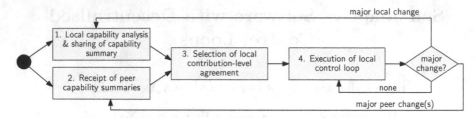

Fig. 1. Decentralised self-adaptation workflow for a DECIDE component

To the best of our knowledge, DECIDE is the first approach that uses formal verification to simultaneously decentralise the control loop of self-adaptive systems, and provide guarantees on their compliance with QoS requirements.

Overview: Each component of a DECIDE system executes a decentralised control workflow comprising the four stages shown in Fig. 1. First, local RQV is used in a *local capability analysis* stage, to establish a *capability summary*, i.e., a finite set of alternative contributions the component could make towards achieving the system-level QoS requirements. This stage is executed infrequently (e.g., when the component joins the system), and the capability summary is shared with the peer components. The local computation or the receipt of a peer capability summary triggers the *selection of a local contribution-level agreement* (CLA). This CLA is one of the alternative contributions from the capability summary of the local component, chosen such that the system complies with its QoS requirements as long as each component achieves its CLA. Most of the time, the *execution of a local control loop* is the only DECIDE stage carried out by a component. Its purpose is to ensure compliance with the selected component CLA through RQV-driven local adaptation. Infrequently, events such as significant workload increases or failures of component parts render a DECIDE local control loop unable to achieve its CLA. These events are termed *major changes*, and require the computation and selection of new local CLAs.

Contributions: The original contributions of the paper are (a) a theoretical foundation for decentralising the control loops of distributed self-adaptive software; (b) an RQV method for devising component capability summaries in distributed self-adaptive systems; (c) a method for the decentralised selection of component-level agreements; and (d) a case study that used DECIDE to develop a simulated distributed embedded system in the unmanned marine vehicle domain.

Structure of the paper: Sections 2–3 introduce the theoretical background underlying DECIDE and the distributed embedded system used for its illustration and evaluation. The stages of DECIDE are presented in Section 4, and its implementation and evaluation are described in Section 5. Section 6 presents related work, and Section 7 summarises our findings and discusses future work directions.

2 Preliminaries

DECIDE is applicable to systems that exhibit stochastic behaviour, and involves the runtime quantitative verification of formal models that describe the behaviour of their components. Here we present a class of such models called *continuous-time Markov chains* (CTMCs), and the temporal logic *continuous stochastic logic* (CSL), which is used to express the properties of CTMCs, as we will show for the running example we will introduce in Section 3. However, no change is required to use DECIDE with other types of probabilistic models, including discrete-time Markov chains [4, 5, 11] and probabilistic automata [16].

Definition 1. *A continuous-time Markov chain (CTMC) over a set of atomic propositions AP is a tuple*
$$M = (S, s_0, \mathbf{R}, L),\tag{1}$$
where:

- *S is a finite set of states, and $s_0 \in S$ is the initial state;*
- *$\mathbf{R} : S \times S \to [0, \infty)$ is a transition rate matrix such that for any state $s_i \in S$, the probability that the CTMC will transition from state s_i to another state within $t > 0$ time units is $1 - e^{-t \cdot \sum_{s_k \in S} \mathbf{R}(s_i, s_k)}$, and the probability that the new state is $s_j \in S$ is given by $\mathbf{R}(s_i, s_j) / \sum_{s_k \in S} \mathbf{R}(s_i, s_k)$.*
- *$L : S \to 2^{AP}$ is a labelling function.*

Quantitative or *probabilistic* model checkers operate on models expressed in a high-level, state-based language. Given a CTMC specified in this language, its representation (1) is derived automatically. We use the model checker PRISM [20], which supports the analysis of CTMCs extended with *costs/rewards*.

Definition 2. *A cost/reward structure over a CTMC with state set S is a pair of real-valued functions (ρ, ι), where*

- *$\rho : S \to \mathbb{R}_{\geq 0}$ is a state reward function that defines the rate $\rho(s)$ at which the reward is obtained while the Markov chain is in state s;*
- *$\iota : S \times S \to \mathbb{R}_{\geq 0}$ is a transition reward function that defines the reward obtained each time a transition occurs.*

Continuous stochastic logic (CSL) augmented with costs/rewards [19] is used to specify the quantitative properties to analyse for CTMC models.

Definition 3. *Let AP be a set of atomic propositions, $a \in AP$, $p \in [0, 1]$, I an interval in $\mathbb{R}$ and $\bowtie \in \{\geq, >, <, \leq\}$. Then a state formula Φ and a path formula Ψ in CSL are defined by the following grammar:*
$$\Phi ::= true \,|\, a \,|\, \Phi \wedge \Phi \,|\, \neg\Phi \,|\, P_{\bowtie p}[\Psi] \,|\, S_{\bowtie p}[\Psi]; \quad \Psi ::= X\Phi \,|\, \Phi \cup^{\leq I} \Phi \tag{2}$$
and the cost/reward augmented CSL state formulae are defined by the grammar:
$$\Phi ::= R_{\bowtie r}[I^{=T}] \,|\, R_{\bowtie r}[C^{\leq T}] \,|\, R_{\bowtie r}[F\Phi] \,|\, R[S] \tag{3}$$

CSL formulae are interpreted over states of a CTMC model. Path formulae only occur inside the probabilistic operator P and *steady-state* operator S, which define bounds on the probability of system evolution. For instance, a state s satisfies a formula $P_{\bowtie p}[\Phi]$ if the probability of the future evolution of the system meets the bound $\bowtie p$. For a path, the "next" formula $X\Phi$ holds if Φ is satisfied in the next state; the "bounded until" formula $\Phi_1 \cup^{\leq I} \Phi_2$ holds if before Φ_2 becomes true at time step $x \in I$, Φ_1 is satisfied continuously in the interval $[0, x) \cap I$. If $I = [0, \infty)$, the formula is termed "unbounded until". The notation $s \models \Phi$ and $M \models \Phi$ indicates that Φ is satisfied in state s and in the initial state of a CTMC model M, respectively. The semantics of the cost/reward operator R is as follows: $R_{\bowtie r}[I^{=T}]$ denotes the expected value of the reward at time instant T; $R_{\bowtie r}[C^{\leq T}]$ denotes the expected cumulative reward up to time T; $R_{\bowtie r}[F\Phi]$ gives the expected cumulative reward before reaching a state that satisfies Φ; and $R[S]$ is the average expected reward in the long-run.

3   Running Example

We will illustrate the application of DECIDE using a distributed multi-UUV (unmanned underwater vehicle) embedded system that extends our single-UUV system from [15]. UUVs are used for oceanic surveillance, survey and rescue operations, mine detection, and discovery of natural resources [24]. Enhancing UUV systems with self-adaptive capabilities is highly desirable to ensure their successful operation in the uncertain marine environment. This is particularly important given the limited ability to control UUV systems remotely, the criticality of their missions, and the need to minimise loss of expensive equipment.

We consider an n-UUV system deployed on a surveillance and data collection mission. The UUVs travel within proximity of each other, and the i-th UUV is equipped with $n_i > 0$ on-board sensors that can take periodic measurements of a characteristic of the ocean environment, e.g., dissolved oxygen, salinity or temperature. The l-th sensor of UUV i operates with varying rate $r_{il} \geq 0$, and the probability p_{il} that one of its measurements is sufficiently accurate for the purpose of the mission depends on the vehicle speed $sp_i \in [0, sp_i^{max}]$. This is typical for such devices, e.g., the measurement error of sonars can be approximated by a normal distribution with zero mean and standard deviation that increases with speed. For each measurement taken, an amount of energy e_{il} is consumed. Each UUV can switch on and off its sensors individually to save battery power; these operations consume energy given by e_{il}^{on} and e_{il}^{off}, respectively. The UUV system must meet the following system-level QoS requirements:

R1: The n UUVs should take at least 1000 measurements of sufficient accuracy per 60 seconds of mission time.

R2: At least two UUVs should have switched-on sensors at any time.

R3: Subject to R1–R2 being satisfied, the system should minimise energy use (so that the mission can continue for longer).

In addition, each UUV i must satisfy the local QoS requirements below:

R4: The energy e_i used by sensors in a minute should not exceed $e_i^{\max}$ Joules.

R5: No sensor with accuracy probability below $p_i^{\min}$ should be used.

R6: Subject to R4–R5 being satisfied, the UUV should minimise the local cost function $w_1 e_i + w_2 sp_i^{-1}$, where $w_1, w_2 > 0$ are UUV-specific weights.

In a dynamic environment, each UUV i should adapt to changes in the operating rate of its sensors and to sensor failures, by continually adjusting:

a) the UUV speed sp_i;

b) the sensor configurations $x_{i1}, x_{i2}, \ldots, x_{in_i}$, where $x_{ij} = 1$ if the j-th sensor is switched on and $x_{ij} = 0$ otherwise,

so that the system- and the UUV-level QoS requirements are met at all times.

4 Approach

DECIDE distributed self-adaptive systems comprise $n > 1$ components. We use Cfg_i and Env_i to denote the set of possible configurations and the set of possible environment states for the i-th component, respectively. Thus, Cfg_i corresponds to parameters that the local control loop of component i can modify, and Env_i to parameters that the component can only observe. In addition, component i has $m_i \geq 1$ QoS attributes $attr_{i1} \in V_1$, $attr_{i2} \in V_2$, $\ldots$, $attr_{im_i} \in V_{m_i}$, where the value domain V_j of the j-th attribute could be $\mathbb{R}$, $\mathbb{R}_+$, $\mathbb{B} = \{true, false\}$, etc. We further assume that the value of the j-th attribute depends on the current environment state $e \in Env_i$ and configuration $c \in Cfg_i$, and is given by:

$$attr_{ij}(e, c) = f_{ij}(e, c, M_i(e, c) \models \Phi_{ij}),\qquad(4)$$

where M_i is a Markov model parameterised by the state of the environment the component operates in and the configuration selected by its local control loop, Φ_{ij} is a probabilistic temporal logic formula, and $f(\cdot, \cdot, \cdot)$ is a function that can be evaluated in $O(1)$ time. The m_i attributes (Fig. 2) have the following roles:

1. Attributes $attr_{i1}, attr_{i2}, \ldots, attr_{im}$, $m < m_i$, are associated with the $m > 0$ QoS requirements of the DECIDE distributed system. Formally, the j-th system QoS requirement, $1 \leq j \leq m$, is specified as

$$expr_j(attr_{1j}, attr_{2j}, \ldots, attr_{nj}) \bowtie_j bound_j\qquad(5)$$

where a non-exhaustive list of options for the expression $expr_j$, relational operator $\bowtie_j$ and bound $bound_j$ is shown in Table 1.

2. Attribute $attr_{i,m+1}$ is a measure of the system-level cost associated with the current environment state and configuration of component i. Accordingly, $V_{m+1} = \mathbb{R}_+$ and the system-level cost $\sum_{i=1}^{n} attr_{i,m+1}$ needs to be minimised, subject to the m QoS requirements being satisfied.

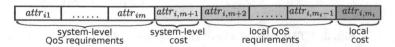

Fig. 2. QoS attributes of a DECIDE component and their roles

Table 1. Categories of DECIDE system-level QoS requirements from (5)

V_j	$expr_j(attr_{1j}, attr_{2j}, \ldots, attr_{nj})$	$\bowtie_j \in$	$bound_j \in$	Types of QoS requirements
$\mathbb{R}_+$	$\sum_{i=1}^n w_i \, attr_{ij}$, $w_i > 0$ weights	$\{<, \leq, \geq, >\}$	$\mathbb{R}_+$	throughput, energy usage, response time
$[0, 1]$	$\prod_{i=1}^n w_i \, attr_{ij}$, $w_i > 0$ weights	$\{<, \leq, \geq, >\}$	$[0, 1]$	reliability, availability
$\mathbb{B}$	$booleanExpr(attr_{1j}, \ldots, attr_{nj})$	$\{=, \neq\}$	$\mathbb{B}$	liveness, security

3. Attributes $attr_{i,m+2}, attr_{i,m+3}, \ldots, attr_{i,m_i-1} \in \mathbb{B}$ represent component-level QoS requirements that are satisfied iff

$$attr_{ij} = true \text{ for } j = m+2, m+3, \ldots, m_i - 1. \tag{6}$$

4. Attribute $attr_{i,m_i} \in \mathbb{R}_+$ is a measure of the component-level cost, which must be minimised subject to system and component QoS requirements being met.

Example 1. The set of configurations for UUV i of our distributed n-UUV system from Section 3 is $Cfg_i = Sp_i \times \{0, 1\}^{n_i}$, where $(sp_i, x_{i1}, x_{i2}, \ldots, x_{in_i}) \in Cfg_i$ give the UUV speed sp_i and sensor configurations $x_{i1}, x_{i2}, \ldots, x_{in_i}$ selected by the local control loop. The set of environment states for UUV i is $Env_i = \mathbb{R}_+^{n_i}$, where $(r_{i1}, r_{i2}, \ldots, r_{in_i}) \in Env_i$ gives the measurement rates for the n_i sensors.

The Markov model $M_i(e, c)$ used to compute the QoS attributes of UUV i in (4) is obtained through the parallel composition of CTMC models of the n_i sensors: $M_i = M_{i1} \parallel M_{i2} \parallel \ldots \parallel M_{in_i}$. Fig. 3 depicts the model of the l-th sensor, when this sensor is switched on ($x_{il} = 1$) or off ($x_{il} = 0$), hence the transition from the initial state s_0 to state s_1 or s_6, respectively. The transition $s_1 \to s_2$ corresponds to a measurement being taken with rate r_{il}. With probability p_{il}, the measurement is accurate and M_i transitions to state s_3; otherwise it transitions to state s_4. This operation continues while the sensor is active, as modelled by the transition $s_5 \to s_1$. The CTMC is augmented with two reward structures, whose non-zero elements are shown in Fig. 3 in rectangular boxes, and dashed rectangular boxes, respectively. The first structure ("*energy*") associates the energy used to switch the sensor on (e_{il}^{on}) and off (e_{il}^{off}) and to perform a measurement (e_{il}) with the transitions that model these events. The second structure ("*measure*") associates a reward of 1 to accurate measurements.

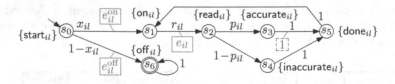

Fig. 3. CTMC model M_{il} of the l-th sensor from UUV i

Given the model M_i, the CSL formulae and the functions in Table 2 are used in (4) to establish the QoS attributes for requirements R1–R6. The $m = 2$ system-level requirements, R1 and R2, are given by the following instances of (5):

$$R1: \sum_{i=1}^{n} attr_{i1} \geq 1000 \quad \text{and} \quad R2: \bigvee_{1 \leq i_1 < i_2 \leq n} (attr_{i_1 2} \wedge attr_{i_2 2}) = true \quad (7)$$

4.1 DECIDE Stage 1: Local Capability Analysis

During this DECIDE stage, each component uses runtime quantitative verification to assemble a summary of its capabilities, as formally defined below.

Definition 4. *A finite set $CS_i \subset V_1 \times V_2 \times \cdots \times V_{m+1}$ is an α-confidence capability summary for the i-th component of a DECIDE system iff, for any $(a_{i1}, a_{i2}, \ldots, a_{i,m+1}) \in CS_i$, the local control loop of the component can ensure that:*
(i) $attr_{ij} \bowtie_j a_{ij}$, for $1 \leq j \leq m$; (ii) $attr_{i,m+1} \leq a_{i,m+1}$; and
(iii) $attr_{ij} = true$, for $m + 1 < j \leq m_i - 1$
with probability at least $\alpha \in (0, 1)$.

The DECIDE method for calculating the α-confidence capability summary of system component i, $1 \leq i \leq n$, involves the local execution of the steps below.

1. *Configuration analysis:* Select $N_i > 0$ disjoint configuration subsets Cfg_i^1, Cfg_i^2, $\ldots$, $Cfg_i^{N_i} \subset Cfg_i$ that correspond to different *modes of operation* for component i. What constitutes a mode of operation is component dependent. Examples include running different numbers of component instances, or operating with different degrees of accuracy. In our running example, UUV modes of operation correspond to different sensor sets being used.

2. *Environment analysis:* Identify subsets of environment states Env_i^1, Env_i^2, $\ldots$, $Env_i^{N_i} \subseteq Env_i$ associated with the N_i configuration subsets, such that the probability that the environment state is in Env_i^k is at least α, for any $1 \leq k \leq N_i$. These subsets can be identical. However, in the general case, each configuration subset Cfg_i^k may render different areas of the environment state irrelevant, and DECIDE exploits this as illustrated in Example 2.

3. *Attribute analysis 1:* Check that for any $1 \leq k \leq N_i$ and for any $1 \leq j \leq m$ with $\bowtie_j \in \{=, \neq\}$, the QoS attribute $attr_{ij}(c, e)$ has a single value, a_{ij}^k, for all $(c, e) \in (Cfg_i^k, Env_i^k)$. When this is not the case, further partition

Table 2. QoS attributes for UUV i, where val_{ij} is the value of $M_i(e, c) \models \Phi_{ij}$

j	V_j	Φ_{ij}	$attr_{ij} = f_{ij}(e, c, val_{ij})$
1	$\mathbb{R}_+$	$R_{=?}^{\text{"measure"}}\left[C^{\leq 60}\right]$	val_{i1}
2	$\mathbb{B}$	$P_{\geq 1}\left[F \; on_{i1}\|on_{i2}\|\ldots\|on_{in_i}\right]$	val_{i2}
3	$\mathbb{R}_+$	$R_{=?}^{\text{"energy"}}\left[C^{\leq 60}\right]$	val_{i3}
4	$\mathbb{B}$	$R_{\leq e_i^{\max}}^{\text{"energy"}}\left[C^{\leq 60}\right]$	val_{i4}
5	$\mathbb{B}$	$\bigwedge_{l=1}^{n_i}\left(read_{il} \Rightarrow P_{\geq p_i^{\min}}\left[X \; accurate_{il}\right]\right)$	val_{i5}
6	$\mathbb{B}$	$R_{=?}^{\text{"energy"}}\left[C^{\leq 60}\right]$	$w_1 val_{i6} + w_2 sp^{-1}$

the configuration set Cfg_i^k into disjoint subsets that satisfy this constraint. As shown in Table 1, one of the scenarios in which $\bowtie_j \in \{=, \neq\}$ is when $V_j = \mathbb{B}$. In this case, Cfg_i^k needs to be partitioned into two subsets. For other scenarios (e.g., when $V_j = \mathbb{R}_+$), DECIDE can be applied only if this operation partitions Cfg_i^k into a finite (and usually small) number of subsets. The rationale for this operation is that we want to associate each configuration set Cfg_i^k with a "bound" a_{ij}^k for each of $attr_{ij}$, $1 \leq j \leq m$, and the bounds a_{ij}^k are common values for QoS attributes $attr_{ij}$ for which $\bowtie_j \in \{=, \neq\}$.

4. *Attribute analysis 2:* For all $attr_{ij}$, $1 \leq j \leq m$, with $\bowtie_j \in \{<, \leq, \geq, >\}$, and for each configuration set Cfg_i^k, find simultaneous bounds $a_{ij}^k \in V_j$ such that

$$\forall e \in Env_i^k \bullet \exists c \in Cfg_i^k \bullet global(c, e) \land local(c, e), \qquad (8)$$

where $global(c, e) = \bigwedge_{\substack{1 \leq j \leq m \\ \bowtie_j \notin \{=, \neq\}}} \left(attr_{ij}(c, e) \bowtie_j a_{ij}^k \right)$ and $local(c, e) = \bigwedge_{j=m+2}^{m_i - 1}$
$attr_{ij}(c, e)$. When there is a single global QoS attribute $attr_{ij}$ with $\bowtie_j \in \{<, \leq, \geq, >\}$, its associated a_{ij}^k bound can be calculated as

$$a_{ij}^k = \begin{cases} \max_{e \in Env_i^k} \min_{c \in Cfg_i^k, local(c,e)} attr_{ij}(c, e), & \text{if } \bowtie_j \in \{<, \leq\} \\ \min_{e \in Env_i^k} \max_{c \in Cfg_i^k, local(c,e)} attr_{ij}(c, e), & \text{otherwise} \end{cases} \qquad (9)$$

Otherwise, a multi-objective optimisation technique [10, 13] needs to be used.

5. *Cost analysis:* Calculate the cost upper bound

$$a_{i,m+1}^k = \max_{e \in Env_i^k} \min_{c \in Cfg_i^k, global(c,e) \land local(c,e)} attr_{i,m+1}(c, e).$$

6. *Capability summary assembly:* Use the a_{ij}^k bounds from steps 3–5 to assemble

$$CS_i = \{cs_i^1, cs_i^2, \ldots, cs_i^{N_i}\}, \qquad (10)$$

where $cs_i^k = (a_{i1}^k, a_{i2}^k, \ldots, a_{i,m+1}^k)$, $1 \leq k \leq N_i$.

We are now ready for the following result, whose proof is available at http://www-users.cs.york.ac.uk/~simos/DECIDE.

Theorem 1. *The set CS_i in (10) is an α-confidence capability summary for component i of a DECIDE system.*

At the end of the local capability analysis stage of DECIDE, the local capability summary (10) is shared with the other components within the distributed system. For this purpose, we envisage DECIDE using recently emerged platforms for the engineering of distributed systems such as Kevoree [14] and DEECo [2].

Example 2. Suppose that the i-th UUV from our running example has $n_i = 2$ on-board sensors whose operating rates r_{i1} and r_{i2} are normally distributed with mean $2s^{-1}$ and standard deviation $0.2s^{-1}$, and with mean $4s^{-1}$ and standard deviation $0.3s^{-1}$, respectively. The UUV$_i$ environment state has the form (r_{i1}, r_{i2}), and the set of all environment states is $Env_i = [0, \infty]^2$. Also, assume that the UUV speed sp_i can be adjusted in the range $[1m/s, 5m/s]$. Hence, the UUV configuration set is $Cfg_i = [1, 5] \times \{0, 1\}^2$, where for any configuration $(sp_i, x_{i1}, x_{i2}) \in Cfg_i$, $x_{ij} = 1$ if sensor j is switched on and $x_{ij} = 0$ otherwise, for

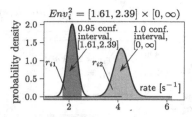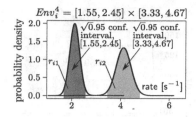

Fig. 4. Environment analysis for configuration sets Cfg_i^2 and Cfg_i^4 in Example 2

$j \in \{1, 2\}$. Finally, suppose that the bounds for local QoS requirements R4–R5 are $e_i^{\max} = 1000J$ and $p_i^{\min} = 0.9$, and that the energy used by the sensor operations are: $e_{i1} = 3J$, $e_{i1}^{\mathrm{on}} = 15J$, $e_{i1}^{\mathrm{off}} = 3J$, $e_{i2} = 2J$, $e_{i2}^{\mathrm{on}} = 10J$, $e_{i2}^{\mathrm{off}} = 2J$. An $(\alpha = 0.95)$-confidence capability summary for UUV i is built as follows:

1. *Configuration analysis*—A UUV mode of operation corresponds to using different subsets of sensors, so there are four configuration subsets: $Cfg_i^k = \{(sp_i, 0, 0)|sp_i \in [1, 5]\}$, $Cfg_i^2 = \{(sp_i, 1, 0)|sp_i \in [1, 5]\}$, $Cfg_i^3 = \{(sp_i, 0, 1)|sp_i \in [1, 5]\}$ and $Cfg_i^4 = \{(sp_i, 1, 1)|sp_i \in [1, 5]\}$.

2. *Environment analysis*—Assuming that the sensor rates r_{i1} and r_{i2} are independent, the environment state subsets Env_i^k, $1 \le k \le 4$, are obtained as Carthesian products of α_1 and α_2 confidence intervals for r_{i1} and r_{i2}, respectively, $\alpha_1\alpha_2 = 0.95$. When a single sensor $j \in \{1, 2\}$ is active for a configuration set Cfg_i^k, we use $\alpha_j = \alpha$ for it and $\alpha_{3-j} = 1$ for the inactive sensor when calculating Env_i^k. This allows the UUV to "promise" a stronger contribution towards the system requirements by disregarding the uncertainty in the state of switched-off sensors for configuration sets that have such sensors (Figure 4).

3. *Attribute analysis 1*—The relational operators for the $m = 2$ system requirements (7) are $\bowtie_1 = '\ge'$ and $\bowtie_2 = '='$, so DECIDE checks that the second attribute from Table 2 takes a single value within each configuration set Cfg_i^k. This check is successful because $attr_{i2} = false = a_{i2}^1$ for all configurations in Cfg_i^1 (as both sensors are switched off) and $attr_{i2} = true = a_{i2}^k$ for all configurations in Cfg_i^k, $2 \le k \le 4$. Hence, no partition of any Cfg_i^k set is required.

4. *Attribute analysis 2*—Requirement R1 in (7) is the only global requirement whose associated relational operator $\bowtie_1$ belongs to the set $\{<, \le, \ge, >\}$. Thus, DECIDE uses RQV to derive the bounds a_{i1}^k in (9) for $1 \le k \le 4$. Fig. 5a shows the analysis that establishes a_{i1}^2 using the model checker PRISM [20]. The worst-case environmental scenario in Env_i^2 is when $r_{i1} = 1.61s^{-1}$; the highest number of measurements in this scenario (i.e., a_{i1}^2) is achieved for $sp_i = 1m/s$.

5. *Cost analysis*—As shown in Fig. 5b, the cost $attr_{i3}$ is constant for each Env_i^k, and the maximum cost, a_{i3}^k, corresponds to the highest sensor rate(s) in Env_i^k.

6. *Capability summary assembly*—The bounds a_{ij}^k, $1 \le j \le 3$, $1 \le k \le 4$, obtained in steps 3–5 are organised into the four-element capability summary $CS_i = \{(0, false, 5), (94, true, 435), (193, true, 535), (279, true, 984)\}$.

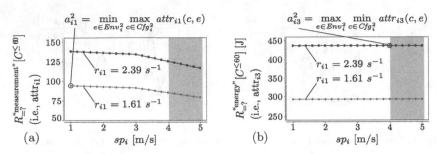

$$a_{i1}^2 = \min_{e \in Env_i^2} \max_{c \in Cfg_i^2} attr_{i1}(c,e) \qquad a_{i3}^2 = \max_{e \in Env_i^2} \min_{c \in Cfg_i^2} attr_{i3}(c,e)$$

(a)   (b)

Fig. 5. Verification of Φ_{i1} and Φ_{i3} from Table 2; shaded areas correspond to configurations that violate local requirement R5

4.2 DECIDE Stage 2: Receipt of Peer Capability Summaries

In this stage, the α-confidence capability summary (10) of a component is shared with all the other components within the system. DECIDE does not propose a new mechanism for sharing capability summaries. Instead, this DECIDE stage relies on the data sharing capabilities of recently emerged platforms for the engineering of distributed systems such as Kevoree [14] and DEECo [2].

4.3 DECIDE Stage 3: Selection of Component Contributions

In this stage, each of the n system components decides its contribution to the realisation of the system QoS requirements. To this end, each component uses the capability summaries $CS_1, CS_2, \ldots, CS_n$ to solve the optimisation problem:

$$\text{minimise} \quad \sum_{i=1}^n a_{i,m+1}$$
$$\text{subject to } expr_j(a_{1j}, a_{2j}, \ldots, a_{nj}) \bowtie_j bound_j, 1 \le j \le m \qquad (11)$$
$$\text{and} \quad (a_{i1}, a_{i2}, \ldots, a_{i,m+1}) \in CS_i, 1 \le i \le n$$

Assuming the problem has a solution, the CLA for the i-th component is given by

$$cla_i = (a_{i1}, a_{i2}, \ldots, a_{i,m+1}) \qquad (12)$$

from this solution, and we say that the i-th system component satisfies its CLA iff the QoS attributes of the component satisfy

$$\begin{aligned} attr_{ij} \bowtie_j a_{ij}, \text{ if } \bowtie_j \in \{<, \le, \ge, >\} \\ attr_{ij} = a_{ij}, \quad \text{otherwise (i.e., if } \bowtie_j \in \{=, \ne\}) \end{aligned}, \text{ for all } 1 \le j \le m. \qquad (13)$$

Remember from Section 4.1 that component configurations that satisfy (13) exist with probability at least α. We can now introduce the following theorem, whose proof is provided at http://www-users.cs.york.ac.uk/~simos/DECIDE.

Theorem 2. *Let $cla_1, cla_2, \ldots, cla_n$ be the CLAs (12) of a DECIDE system with QoS requirements (5). If component i satisfies cla_i for all $1 \le i \le n$, then the system QoS requirements are satisfied.*

DECIDE does not prescribe how the optimisation problem (11) should be solved, as this is application specific. Depending on the nature of the DECIDE system and its requirements, the best way to obtain the component CLAs (12) may be by using an efficient dynamic programming or greedy algorithm, a meta-heuristic or, when the solution space $CS_1 \times CS_2 \times \ldots \times CS_n$ is sufficiently small, by examining all options. The CLA calculation is performed independently by each system component (using the same deterministic method).

Example 3. Consider again our n-UUV system. The instance of the optimisation problem (11) solved by the DECIDE module running on each UUV is

$$
\begin{array}{ll}
\text{minimise} & \sum_{i=1}^{n} a_{i,3} \\
\text{subject to} & \sum_{i=1}^{n} a_{i1} \geq 1000 \text{ and } \bigvee_{1 \leq i_1 < i_2 \leq n} (a_{i_1 2} \wedge a_{i_2 2}) = true \\
\text{and} & (a_{i1}, a_{i2}, a_{i3}) \in CS_i, 1 \leq i \leq n
\end{array}
\tag{14}
$$

Our implementation (Section 5) casts this as a multiple-choice knapsack problem [17] and solves it using an efficient $O(n^2)$ dynamic programming algorithm. We provide this algorithm at http://www-users.cs.york.ac.uk/~simos/DECIDE.

4.4 DECIDE Stage 4: Execution of Local Control Loop

Most of the time, this is the only DECIDE stage being executed. The local control loop ensures that each component meets its CLA and local requirements by implementing the RQV-driven approach to developing (single control loop) self-adaptive software that we co-introduced in [6, 9], summarised in [3], and extended and used successfully in multiple application domains [4, 5, 15, 16].

The local control loop of component i uses RQV to establish the value of $M_i(e, c) \models \Phi_{ij}$ in (4), $1 \leq j \leq m_i$, either periodically and/or after events associated with environment or component changes. The aim is to verify if the QoS attributes of the component continue to satisfy the component CLA (12) and local requirements (6), and, if this is not the case, to identify a new configuration that does. The search for such new configurations starts with the configuration subset Cfg_i^k associated with the component CLA. When no configuration in Cfg_i^k is suitable, the search is extended to the entire configuration space Cfg_i. A component that is no longer able to meet its CLA and local requirements is affected by a "major change", and its capability summary is recalculated (Section 4.1). Describing single-control-loop RQV-driven adaptation is outside the scope of this paper, and we refer the reader to [3] for an overview of the approach.

Example 4. Suppose the CLA selected for the two-sensor UUV_i from Example 2 is $(193, true, 535)$. The local control loop will adjust the UUV configuration in response to changes in the sensor rates r_{i1}, r_{i2} such that the UUV achieves at least 193 accurate measurements, has at least an active sensor, and consumes at most 535J for each 60s of operation. Fig. 6 shows the RQV results when $r_{i2} = 3.68s^{-1}$, for the configuration subset $Cfg_i^3 = \{(sp_i, 0, 1)|sp_i \in [1, 5]\}$ associated with this CLA; as sensor 1 is switched off, the value of r_{i1} is irrelevant. Given these results, the control loop selects the configuration $(sp_i, x_1, x_2) = (3.6, 0, 1)$, which meets the CLA and local requirements, and minimises the local cost $attr_{i6}$.

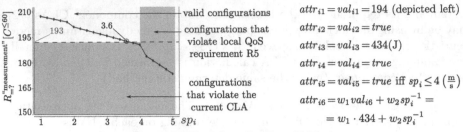

Fig. 6. RQV of $\Phi_{i1}-\Phi_{i6}$ from Table 2

4.5 Major Changes

Major changes trigger the execution of other DECIDE stages than the local control loop, as shown in Figure 1. There are two types of major changes.

A *local major change* occurs within a component when: (a) the local control loop cannot find a configuration that satisfies its CLA or local requirements; (b) failures within the component make certain modes of operation unavailable; and (c) the capability summary becomes overly conservative, due to a more favourable environment than anticipated or to recovery from a previous failure. In these scenarios, the component re-executes the local capability analysis stage.

A *peer major change* occurs when another component (a) joins the system; (b) undergoes a local major change; or (c) leaves the system. Component i learns about peer major changes of types (a) and (b) when it receives a new capability summary. For the last type of change, DECIDE requires that component failures are notified by the communication and synchronisation platform underpinning the interactions between components. This capability is supported by platforms such as Kevoree [14] and DEECo [2], and can be readily exploited by DECIDE.

5 Evaluation

Implementation — To evaluate DECIDE, we implemented a fully-fledged simulator for the multi-UUV self-adaptive system from our running example. We built our simulator on top of the open-source MOOS-IvP middleware (http://oceanai.mit.edu/moos-ivp), a widely used C++ platform for the implementation of autonomous applications on unmanned marine vehicles [1].

The simulator integrates the standard MOOS-IvP publish-subscribe and visualisation components with our MOOS component that implements the four DECIDE stages. Over 90% of our component is new code that implements the DECIDE local capability analysis, receipt of peer capability summaries, CLA selection and major change identification within local control loops. The rest is reused from our previous work on a single-UUV self-adaptive system with a centralised control loop [15]. The code for our multi-UUV simulator, the experimental results summarised in this section, and a video recording of a typical simulation are available at http://www-users.cs.york.ac.uk/~simos/DECIDE.

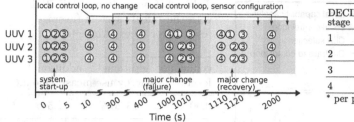

Fig. 7. Execution of DECIDE stages 1–4 during major changes and local sensor changes, and mean CPU and communication overheads for a three-UUV mission

Experimental setup — To evaluate DECIDE, we carried out a broad range of experiments using our multi-UUV system simulator. The system characteristics varied in these experiments include the number of UUVs n and UUV sensors n_i, $1 \leq i \leq n$, and the confidence level α used to assemble UUV capability summaries. To examine the impact of different types of failure, the experiments were seeded with failure patterns including of failures of sensors, sudden significant reductions in sensor measurement rates (i.e., sensors not meeting their specification) and failures of entire UUVs. All experiments were carried out on a 2.6GhZ Intel Core i5 Macbook Pro computer with 16GB memory, running Mac OSX 10.9.

Typical simulation scenario — Fig. 7 shows the execution of the DECIDE stages during key moments of a simulated 2000s mission carried out by a three-UUV system. Each UUV had three sensors, and the requirements enforced by DECIDE were requirements R1–R6 from Section 3. As shown in Fig. 7, the CPU overheads for the RQV-based local capability analysis and control loop (DECIDE stages 1, 4) and the knapsack problem solving in CLA selection (stage 3) are all negligible at under 40ms each, or below 0.4% when the local control loop is executed every 10s. The communication overhead, 71 bytes per peer UUV per major change, is very low too, even for a typical inter-UUV bandwidth of 0.5–5Kbps [23].

Adaptation effectiveness — In all experiments, the system recovered after sensor failures and performance drops, and UUV failures within 800ms from the moment when the last periodically run local control loop of an UUV started executing, for a typical inter-UUV bandwidth of 2.5Kbps. Thus, if the local control loop runs every 5s, the time to recovery was below 5.8s.

Adaptation efficiency — To assess the efficiency of the DECIDE self-adaptation decisions, we compared the number of measurements taken and the energy consumed by the three-UUV DECIDE system with the values of the same metrics for an "ideal" system (Table 3). In this "ideal" system (a) the sensor rates never varied from their nominal values; (b) the globally optimal set of sensors satisfying requirements R1–R6 were used at all times; and (c) all UUVs travelled with the minimum speed of 1m/s, to maximise the fraction of measurements that were accurate. This "ideal" system cannot be implemented in practice, but has the useful property that any practical system will use more measurements and

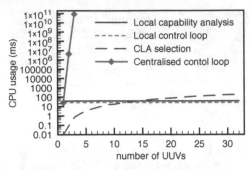

Fig. 8. Scalability analysis

Table 3. Comparison of DECIDE with the "ideal" system (average results over 10 experiments)

confidence level α	additional energy use	additional measurements
0.90	+18.26%	+12.54%
0.95	+18.30%	+12.58%
0.99	+20.62%	+9.97%

more energy than it does. Accordingly, the results in Table 3 show that DECIDE successfully decentralised the control loop of the UUV system with a modest loss in efficiency compared to any other solution that might be possible.

Role of confidence level α — Higher confidence levels make the component capability summaries (10) more conservative. This increases the system-level cost (e.g., the energy use for our system, see Table 3), but reduces the number of false positives from local control loop checks for major changes, as a fraction of α of the checks find the component operating in an expected environment state.

Scalability — As shown in Fig. 8, the two RQV-based DECIDE stages (i.e., the local capability analysis and the local control loop) use the same small amount of CPU time irrespective of the size of the n-UUV system. The $O(n^2)$ CPU time taken by the CLA selection stage stays below 200ms for systems of up to 32 UUVs. In contrast, using a centralised control loop that applies RQV to the entire system model $M_1 \parallel M_2 \parallel \ldots \parallel M_n$ takes over 4200s for $n = 2$ and is unfeasible for $n > 3$. The CPU time shown in Fig. 8 for the RQV of a complete model of a three-UUV system (i.e., 983.5 days) is an estimate we obtained based on the average verification time over a small subset of representative configurations from the configuration set that would need to be verified by this control loop.

Threats to validity — We identified several threats to external validity. First, as we evaluated DECIDE in a single case study, our approach may not be applicable to other systems because it may not be possible to cast their QoS attributes and requirements into the pattern given by (4)–(6) in Section 4. To limit this threat, we distilled this pattern from the growing body of research on RQV-driven self-adaptation in service-based, cloud-deployed and embedded software systems [3–6, 9, 11, 15, 16]. Second, for other systems it may not be possible to identify α-confidence subsets of environment states. This threat is mitigated by the fact that DECIDE can operate with approximations of such subsets, which impact only the frequency of major changes. Finally, major changes may occur too frequently, leading to unacceptable overheads and "jitter" in component reconfigurations. DECIDE can alleviate this by increasing the α confidence level (i.e., being more conservative), but our approach is not intended for systems with a high churn rate. Threats to internal validity originate from how experiments were performed. To reduce them, we developed our simulator using the well-established UUV software platform MOOS-IvP, we examined a wide range of scenarios, and we repeated all experiments many times.

6   Related Work

To the best of our knowledge, DECIDE is the first approach to using runtime quantitative verification (RQV) to decentralise the control loops of self-adaptive systems. Although RQV has attracted a lot of attention since its recent introduction in [3, 6, 9], the research so far (e.g., [4, 5, 11, 15, 16]) has focused on its use in centralised control loops. This is feasible only for systems whose stochastic models are small enough to be analysed fast and with acceptable overheads. Also, for distributed systems such as those in service-based applications [4, 5], centralised control introduces a single point of failure. DECIDE addresses both limitations. As all RQV steps analyse component models, our approach extends the applicability of RQV to larger component-based systems. Also, the use of RQV in DECIDE does not introduce a single point of failure, since the control loop of a component continues to operate when a peer component fails.

Decentralised-control self-adaptive systems have been developed using many other approaches, e.g. as multi-agent [7, 12, 25] and service-based systems [22]. Due to space constraints, we mention here only a few of these approaches, selected as representative for the field. Most of them take adaptation decisions using optimisation heuristics that cannot provide the strong guarantees required in mission-critical applications, e.g. bio-inspired [7], market-based [22] and gossip-style [25] heuristics. In contrast, DECIDE guarantees that the decentralised-control system meets its QoS requirements in the presence of changes, recovering from failures whenever feasible. More recent research explored the use of formal methods to guarantee that decentralised-control self-adaptive systems meet their functional requirements [8, 12, 26]. Our work complements this research, since DECIDE focuses on the QoS requirements of distributed self-adaptive systems.

7   Conclusion

We presented an approach to using runtime quantitative verification (RQV) to develop self-adaptive distributed systems with decentralised control loops. RQV-based decentralised control ensures that distributed systems developed using our approach continue to meet their QoS requirements after failures and environment changes. Compared to the current use of a centralised RQV control loop for the same purpose [3, 4, 6, 9, 11, 15, 16], our new approach achieves this: (a) with overheads that are several orders of magnitude lower; (b) scalably to much larger system sizes; (c) without introducing a single point of failure; and (d) with only a modest increase in system-level costs (18–21% in our case study).

In future work, we will assess the effectiveness of DECIDE in other domains, and examine its scalability for systems with larger component models (e.g.,

UUV systems with more sensors per UUV). In addition, we are extending DE-CIDE with support for using interface models as component QoS attributes, with assume-guarantee RQV used to verify system QoS properties as in [16].

Acknowledgments. This paper presents research sponsored by the UK MOD. The information contained in it should not be interpreted as representing the views of the UK MOD, nor should it be assumed that it reflects any current or future UK MOD policy.

References

1. Benjamin, M., et al.: Autonomy for unmanned marine vehicles with MOOS-IvP. In: Marine Robot Autonomy, pp. 47–90 (2013)
2. Bures, T., et al.: Deeco: An ensemble-based component system. In: CBSE 2013 (2013)
3. Calinescu, R., Ghezzi, C., Kwiatkowska, M., Mirandola, R.: Self-adaptive software needs quantitative verification at runtime. Comm. ACM 55(9), 69–77 (2012)
4. Calinescu, R., Grunske, L., Kwiatkowska, M., et al.: Dynamic QoS management and optimization in service-based systems. IEEE Trans. Softw. Eng. 37, 387–409 (2011)
5. Calinescu, R., Johnson, K., Rafiq, Y.: Developing self-verifying service-based systems. In: ASE 2013, pp. 734–737 (2013)
6. Calinescu, R., Kwiatkowska, M.Z.: Using quantitative analysis to implement autonomic IT systems. In: ICSE 2009, pp. 100–110 (2009)
7. Di Marzo Serugendo, G., Gleizes, M.-P., Karageorgos, A.: Self-Organization in Multi-Agent Systems. The Knowledge Eng. Rev. 20(2), 165–189 (2005)
8. D'Ippolito, N., et al.: Hope for the best, prepare for the worst: Multi-tier control for adaptive systems. In: ICSE 2014, pp. 688–699 (2014)
9. Epifani, I., Ghezzi, C., Mirandola, R., Tamburrelli, G.: Model evolution by runtime parameter adaptation. In: ICSE 2009, pp. 111–121 (2009)
10. Etessami, K., Kwiatkowska, M., Vardi, M.Y., Yannakakis, M.: Multi-objective model checking of markov decision processes. In: Grumberg, O., Huth, M. (eds.) TACAS 2007. LNCS, vol. 4424, pp. 50–65. Springer, Heidelberg (2007)
11. Filieri, A., Ghezzi, C., Tamburrelli, G.: Run-time efficient probabilistic model checking. In: ICSE 2011, pp. 341–350 (2011)
12. Fisher, M., Dennis, L., Webster, M.: Verifying autonomous systems. Comm. ACM 56(9), 84–93 (2013)
13. Forejt, V., Kwiatkowska, M., Norman, G., Parker, D., Qu, H.: Quantitative multi-objective verification for probabilistic systems. In: Abdulla, P.A., Leino, K.R.M. (eds.) TACAS 2011. LNCS, vol. 6605, pp. 112–127. Springer, Heidelberg (2011)
14. Fouquet, F., et al.: Kevoree modeling framework (KMF): Efficient modelling techniques for runtime use. CoRR, abs/1405.6817 (2014)
15. Gerasimou, S., Calinescu, R., Banks, A.: Efficient runtime quantitative verification using caching, lookahead, and nearly-optimal reconfiguration. In: SEAMS 2014 (2014)
16. Johnson, K., Calinescu, R., Kikuchi, S.: An incremental verification framework for component-based software systems. In: CBSE 2013, pp. 33–42 (2013)

17. Kellerer, H., Pferschy, U., Pisinger, D.: The multiple-choice knapsack problem. In: Knapsack Problems, pp. 317–347 (2004)
18. Kephart, J., Chess, D.: The vision of autonomic computing. Computer 36(1) (2003)
19. Kwiatkowska, M.: Quantitative verification: models, techniques and tools. In: ESEC-FSE Companion 2007, pp. 449–458 (2007)
20. Kwiatkowska, M., Norman, G., Parker, D.: Prism 4.0: verification of probabilistic real-time systems. In: CAV 2011, pp. 585–591 (2011)
21. Lemos, R., et al.: Software engineering for self-adaptive systems: A second research roadmap. In: Software Engineering for Self-Adaptive Systems II, pp. 1–32 (2013)
22. Nallur, V., Bahsoon, R.: A decentralized self-adaptation mechanism for service-based applications in the cloud. IEEE Trans. Softw. Eng. 39(5), 591–612 (2013)
23. Redfield, S.: Cooperation between underwater vehicles. In: Seto, M.L. (ed.) Marine Robot Autonomy, pp. 257–286 (2013)
24. Seto, M., Paull, L., Saeedi, S.: Introduction to autonomy for marine robots. In: Marine Robot Autonomy, pp. 1–46 (2013)
25. Sykes, D., Magee, J., Kramer, J.: Flashmob: Distributed adaptive self-assembly. In: SEAMS 2011, pp. 100–109 (2011)
26. Weyns, D., et al.: FORMS: Unifying Reference Model for Formal Specification of Distributed Self-Adaptive Systems. ACM Trans. Aut. Adapt. Syst. 7(1) (2012)

Model-Based Adaptation of Software Communicating via FIFO Buffers

Carlos Canal[1] and Gwen Salaün[2]

[1] University of Málaga, Spain
[2] University of Grenoble Alpes, Inria, LIG, CNRS, France

Abstract. Software Adaptation is a non-intrusive solution for composing black-box components or services (peers) whose individual functionality is as required for the new system, but that present interface mismatch, which leads to deadlock or other undesirable behaviour when combined. Adaptation techniques aim at automatically generating new components called adapters. All the interactions among peers pass through the adapter, which acts as an orchestrator and makes the involved peers work correctly together by compensating for mismatch. Most of the existing solutions in this field assume that peers interact synchronously using rendezvous communication. However, many application areas rely on asynchronous communication models where peers interact exchanging messages via buffers. Generating adapters in this context becomes a difficult problem because peers may exhibit cyclic behaviour, and their composition often results in infinite systems. In this paper, we present a method for automatically generating adapters in asynchronous environments where peers interact using FIFO buffers.

1 Introduction

The construction of new software in modern environments is mostly achieved by reusing and composing existing software elements. These elements (*peers* in this paper) can correspond to a large variety of software, such as Web servers, databases, Graphical User Interfaces, Software-as-a-Service in the cloud, Web services, etc. In order to make possible the composition of such heterogeneous software pieces, all peers are equipped with public interfaces, which exhibit their provided/required services as well as any other composition constraints that must be respected to ensure the correct execution of the composition-to-be. However, although a set of peers may appear as adequate for a new software system under construction, it is likely that their interfaces present mismatch, especially if they have been independently developed by third parties. Mismatch takes different forms such as disparate operation names or unspecified message receptions, and it prevents the direct assembly of the peers.

Software Adaptation [30,10] is a non-intrusive solution for composing black-box software peers that present interface mismatch, leading to deadlock or other undesirable behaviour when peers are combined. Adaptation techniques aim at automatically generating new components called *adapters*, and usually rely on

© Springer-Verlag Berlin Heidelberg 2015
A. Egyed and I. Schaefer (Eds.): FASE 2015, LNCS 9033, pp. 252–266, 2015.
DOI: 10.1007/978-3-662-46675-9_17

an *adaptation contract*, which is an abstract description of how mismatch can be worked out. All interactions pass through the adapter, which acts as an orchestrator and makes the involved peers work correctly together by compensating for mismatch. Many solutions have been proposed since the seminal work by Yellin and Strom [30], see, *e.g.*, [5,7,28,22,16,18].

These approaches vary in different aspects, such as expressiveness of interface descriptions (signatures, behaviour, Quality-of-Service, semantics), abstraction level (from abstract models to programming languages), algorithmic techniques (discrete controller synthesis, planning, enumerative approaches, etc.), or application areas (software components, Web services, agent-oriented systems etc.). Most existing approaches assume that the peers interact using synchronous communication, that is rendez-vous synchronizations. Nonetheless, asynchronous communication, *i.e.*, communication via buffers, is now omnipresent in areas such as cloud computing and Web development.

Asynchronous communication highly complicates the adapter generation process, because the corresponding systems are not necessarily bounded and may result into infinite systems. It is known that in this context, the verification problem and more particularly the boundedness property are undecidable for communicating finite state machines [6]. Therefore, if we want to generate an adapter in an asynchronous environment, how could we proceed? What bound should we choose for buffers during the generation process? Arbitrarily bounding buffers is an option, but we want to avoid imposing any kind of bounds on buffers, cyclic behaviour, or the number of participants, since it may unnecessarily restrict the behaviour of the whole system.

Recent results introduced the notion of *synchronizability* [3] and showed how to use it for checking certain properties on asynchronously communicating systems [24]. These results show that a set of peers is synchronizable if and only if the system generates the same sequences of messages under synchronous and unbounded asynchronous communication, considering only the ordering of the output messages and ignoring the ordering of input messages. Focusing only on output messages makes sense for verification purposes because: (i) output messages are the actions that transfer messages to the network and are therefore observable, (ii) input messages correspond to local consumptions by peers from their buffers and can therefore be considered to be local and private information. Synchronizability can be verified by checking the equivalence of the synchronous version of a given system with its 1-bounded asynchronous version (in which each peer is equipped with one input FIFO buffer bounded to size 1). Thus, this property can be verified using equivalence checking techniques on finite systems, although the set of peers interacting asynchronously can result in infinite systems.

In this paper, we rely on synchronizability for generating adapters for peers interacting asynchronously via (possibly unbounded) FIFO buffers. Given a set of peers modelled using Labelled Transition Systems and an adaptation contract, we first reuse existing adapter generation techniques for synchronous communication, *e.g.*, [12,22]. Then, we consider the system composed of the set of peers interacting through the generated adapter, and we check whether it satisfies the synchronizability property. If this is the case, this means that the system will behave exactly the same whatever bound we choose for buffers, therefore this adapter is a solution to our composition problem. If synchronizability is not preserved, a counterexample is returned, which is used for refining the adaptation contract. Our approach works iteratively by refining the contract until preserving synchronizability. It is worth observing that the main reason for non-synchronizability is due to output messages, which are uncontrollable in an asynchronous environment, hence have to be considered properly in the adaptation contract. Our approach is supported by tools for generating the adapter (Itaca [8]) and checking synchronizability (CADP [15]), and was applied to several case studies for evaluation purposes. A very early version of this work was sketched in [13] and is fully developed here.

The organization of this paper is as follows. Section 2 defines our models for peers and introduces the basics on (synchronous) software adaptation. Section 3 defines the synchronizability property for adapted systems. Section 4 presents our approach for generating adapters assuming asynchronous communication semantics. Finally, Section 5 reviews related work, and Section 6 concludes.

2   Models

In this section, we first present the interface model through which peers are accessed and used. Then, we define adaptation contracts and explain briefly how adapters are generated from peer interfaces and contracts.

2.1   Interfaces

We assume that peers are described using a behavioural interface in the form of a Labelled Transition System (LTS).

Definition 1 (LTS). *A* Labelled Transition System *is a tuple* (S, s^0, Σ, T) *where: S is a set of states, $s^0 \in S$ is the initial state, $\Sigma = \Sigma^! \cup \Sigma^? \cup \{\tau\}$ is a finite alphabet partitioned into a set $\Sigma^!$ ($\Sigma^?$, resp.) of send (receive, resp.) messages and the internal action τ, and $T \subseteq S \times \Sigma \times S$ is the transition function.*

The alphabet of the LTS is built on the set of operations used by the peer in its interaction with the world. This means that for each operation p provided by the peer, there is an event $p? \in \Sigma^?$ in the alphabet, and for each operation r required from its environment, there is an event $r! \in \Sigma^!$. Events with the same name and opposite directions ($a!$, $a?$) are complementary, and their match stands for inter-peer communication through message-passing. Additionally to peer communication events, we assume that the alphabet also contains a special τ event to denote internal (not communicating) behaviour.

Note that as usually done in the literature [19,2,26], our interfaces abstract from operation arguments, types of return values, and exceptions. Nevertheless, they can be easily extended to explicitly represent operation arguments and their associated data types, by using Symbolic Transition Systems (STSs) [22] instead of LTSs. However, this would render the definitions and results presented in this work much longer and cumbersome, without adding anything substantial to the technical aspects of our proposal.

2.2   Adaptation Contracts

Typical mismatch situations between peers appear when event names do not correspond, the order of events is not respected, or an event in one peer has no counterpart or matches several events in another one. All these cases of behavioural mismatch can be worked out by specifying adaptation rules. Adaptation rules express correspondences between operations of the peers, like bindings between ports or connectors in architectural descriptions. Adaptation rules are given as vectors, as defined below:

Definition 2 (Vector). *An* adaptation vector *(or* vector *for short) for a set of peers* $\{\mathcal{P}_1, \ldots, \mathcal{P}_n\}$ *with* $\mathcal{P}_i = (S_i, s_i^0, \Sigma_i, T_i)$, *is a tuple* $\langle e_1, \ldots, e_n \rangle$ *with* $e_i \in \Sigma_i \cup \{\epsilon\}$, ϵ *meaning that a peer does not participate in the vector.*

In order to unambiguously identify them, event names may be prefixed by the name of the peer, *e.g.*, $\mathcal{P}_i : p?$, or $\mathcal{P}_j : r!$, and in that case ϵ can be omitted. For instance, the vector $\langle p_1 : a!, p_3 : b?, p_4 : c? \rangle$ represents an adaptation rule indicating that the output event $a!$ from peer p_1 should match both input events $b?$ and $c?$ in p_3 and p_4, respectively, while peer $p2$ does not participate in this interaction.

In some complex adaptation scenarios, adaptation rules should be taken contextually (*i.e.*, vectors cannot be applied at any time, but only in certain situations). For this purpose, we use regular expressions (regex) on vectors, indicating a pattern for applying them that will constrain the adaptation process, enforcing additional properties on the adapter. In this work we use standard regex notation, where "|", and "$\star$" stand for alternation and Kleene star, respectively. For instance, $V_1 (V_2 \mid V_3) \star V_4$ states that the vector V_1 should be applied first, followed by several uses of V_2 and V_3, and always ending with V_4. In the absence of regex, we assume that adaptation rules are not contextually dependent and can be applied at any time during the adaptation process.

Definition 3 (Adaptation Contract). *An* adaptation contract V *for a set of peers* $\{\mathcal{P}_1, \ldots, \mathcal{P}_n\}$ *is a set of adaptation vectors for those peers, together with a (possibly empty) regex describing a pattern for applying the vectors.*

Writing the adaptation contract is the only step of our approach which is not handled automatically. This step is crucial because an inadequate contract would induce the generation of an adapter that will not make the composition of peers to behave correctly (for instance, some expected interactions may be discarded by the adapter, in order to avoid deadlock). However, the adaptation methodology that we propose is iterative (see Figure 3 in Section 4), which helps in writing the adaptation contract. For more details on the adaptation contracts and the kinds of adaptations that can be resolved with them, we refer to [12].

2.3   Adapter Generation

Given a set of interfaces and an adaptation contract, an adapter can be automatically derived using, *e.g.*, [12,22]. This approach relies on an encoding into process algebra together with on-the-fly exploration and reduction techniques. The adapter is given by an LTS which, put into a non-deadlock-free system yields it deadlock-free. All the exchanged events will pass through the adapter, which can be seen as a coordinator for the peers to be adapted. Code generation is also supported by our approach, thus BPEL adapters can be automatically synthesised from adapter LTSs. All these steps are automated by the Itaca toolset [8].

In order to generate an adapter, not only event correspondences stated in the adaptation rules must be taken into account, but also the LTSs describing the behaviour of the peers. Blindly applying adaptation rules without taking into account peers' behaviour may lead the system to a deadlock state if any of the events represented in a rule cannot be accepted by the corresponding peer in its current state. Hence, the adapter has not only the responsibility of following the adaptation rules and regex in the contract, but also to accommodate their use to the LTSs describing the behaviour of the peers, reordering and remembering events when required.

Notice that the adaptation algorithms in [12,22] generate *synchronous* adapters, that is, they assume a synchronous communication model for peers. In our present work we show how these results can be applied to asynchronous adaptation, where peers communicate asynchronously and are equipped with an input message buffer.

2.4   Case Study

This section describes the case study that will be used as running example throughout this work. Let us consider a multi-cloud scenario for creating virtual machines (VM) in IaaS clouds such as Google Compute Engine or Windows Azure. These clouds offer different APIs for VM creation and management, which allows us to show how adaptation can solve mismatch. The names of the events used here are inspired by the actual names of the corresponding operations in Google and Azure, although the scenario is conveniently simplified in order to abstract from many details that would make it unnecessarily long and complex.

The core element of the system is a Deployment Manager (DM). The LTS describing its behaviour is shown in Figure 1 (d). After receiving a request (`request?`), the DM creates a new VM instance (`instantiate!`), checks its status (`status?`) and returns it (`instance!`). Notice that the DM is not bound to any particular cloud (Google or Azure), nor it is described in the LTS how one of them is actually chosen. We will show later on how a specific cloud selection policy can be enforced by the adaptation contract.

The behaviour of Google Compute Engine, is shown in Figure 1 (b). In Google's IaaS cloud, the operation for creating a VM is named `addInstance`, and the status of a machine can be checked with `getInstance`. Additionally, we assume that the cloud sends statistical information about CPU and memory

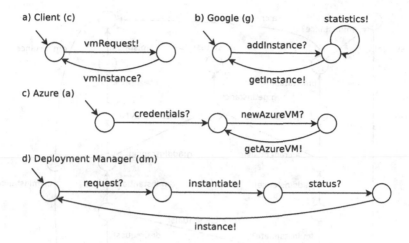

Fig. 1. LTSs describing the interfaces of the different peers

usage (`statistics!`). Figure 1 (c) shows the LTS corresponding to Windows Azure. We assume that some credentials must be received first (`credentials?`). Then, machine creation is performed with the operation `newAzureVM?`, while VM status is reported with `getAzureVM!`. The LTS describing the behaviour of a possible client, requesting several VMs, is shown in Figure 1 (a).

Finally, the vectors for composing the whole system, adapting the Client, the Deployment Manager, and Google's and Azure's clouds are as follows:

$$
\begin{aligned}
V_{request} &= \langle \texttt{c:vmRequest!}, \ \texttt{dm:request?} \rangle \\
V_{instantiateG} &= \langle \texttt{dm:instantiate!}, \ \texttt{g:addInstance?} \rangle \\
V_{statusG} &= \langle \texttt{dm:status?}, \ \texttt{g:getInstance!} \rangle \\
V_{credentialsA} &= \langle \texttt{a:credentials?} \rangle \\
V_{instantiateA} &= \langle \texttt{dm:instantiate!}, \ \texttt{a:newAzureVM?} \rangle \\
V_{statusA} &= \langle \texttt{dm:status?}, \ \texttt{a:getAzureVM!} \rangle \\
V_{instance} &= \langle \texttt{c:vmInstance?}, \ \texttt{dm:instance!} \rangle
\end{aligned}
$$

These vectors mostly show correspondence of events with different names. Note also that event `a:credentials?` has no correspondence in the DM, so it has no counterpart in the $V_{credentialsA}$ rule: this event will be issued by the adapter when required by the cloud. Additionally, a vector for event `g:statistics!` is omitted, since this event has no counterpart in the rest of the system. We can now automatically generate an adapter using Itaca's tools. The resulting adapter is shown in Figure 2.

3   Synchronizability of Adapted Systems

In this section, we present a few definitions characterizing the synchronizability property for adapted systems. The adapted synchronous composition of a set of

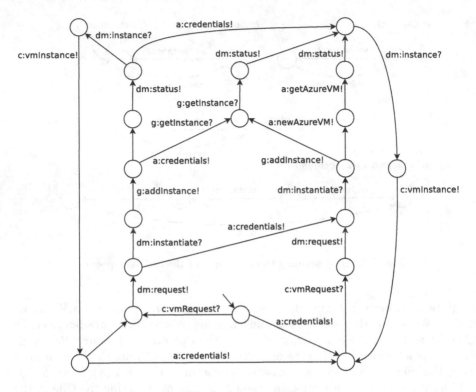

Fig. 2. Adapter LTS

peers corresponds to the system where a communication occurs when one peer can send (receive, *resp.*) an event and the adapter can receive (send, *resp.*) it.

Definition 4 (Adapted Synchronous Composition). *Given a set of peers* $\{\mathcal{P}_1, \ldots, \mathcal{P}_n\}$ *with* $\mathcal{P}_i = (S_i, s_i^0, \Sigma_i, T_i)$ *and an adapter* $\mathcal{A} = (S, s^0, \Sigma, T)$, *their synchronous composition is the labelled transition system* $LTS_{as} = (S_{as}, s_{as}^0, \Sigma_{as}, T_{as})$ *where:*

- $S_{as} = S_1 \times \ldots \times S_n \times S$
- $s_s^0 \in S_{as}$ *such that* $s_s^0 = (s_1^0, \ldots, s_n^0, s^0)$
- $\Sigma_{as} = \cup_i \Sigma_i \cup \Sigma$
- $T_{as} \subseteq S_{as} \times \Sigma_{as} \times S_{as}$, *and for* $s = (s_1, \ldots, s_n, s_a) \in S_{as}$ *and* $s' = (s'_1, \ldots, s'_n, s'_a) \in S_{as}$ *we have that*

(p2a) $s \xrightarrow{m} s' \in T_{as}$ *if* $\exists i \in \{1, \ldots, n\} : m \in \Sigma_i^! \cap \Sigma^?$ *where* $\exists s_i \xrightarrow{m!} s'_i \in T_i$, *and* $s_a \xrightarrow{m?} s'_a \in T$ *such that* $\forall k \in \{1, \ldots, n\}, k \neq i \Rightarrow s'_k = s_k$

(a2p) $s \xrightarrow{m} s' \in T_{as}$ *if* $\exists j \in \{1, \ldots, n\} : m \in \Sigma^! \cap \Sigma_j^?$ *where* $\exists s_a \xrightarrow{m!} s'_a \in T$, *and* $s_j \xrightarrow{m?} s'_j \in T_j$ *such that* $\forall k \in \{1, \ldots, n\}, k \neq j \Rightarrow s'_k = s_k$

(int) $s \xrightarrow{\tau} s' \in T_{as}$ *if* $\exists i \in \{1, \ldots, n\}, \exists s_i \xrightarrow{\tau} s'_i \in T_i$ *such that* $\forall k \in \{1, \ldots, n\}, k \neq i \Rightarrow s'_k = s_k$ *and* $s'_a = s_a$

However, in an asynchronous scenario, peers communicate with the adapter asynchronously via FIFO buffers. Hence, each peer $\mathcal{P}_i$ is equipped with an unbounded input message buffer Q_i, and the adapter $\mathcal{A}$ with an input buffer Q. A peer can either send a message $m \in \Sigma^!$ to the tail of the adapter buffer Q at any state where this send message is available, read a message $m \in \Sigma^?$ from its buffer Q_i if the message is available at the buffer head, or evolve independently through an internal τ transition. The adapter works in the same way. We recall that we focus on output events, since reading from the buffer is private non-observable information, which is encoded as an internal transition in the asynchronous system.

Definition 5 (Adapted Asynchronous Composition). *Given a set of peers* $\{\mathcal{P}_1, \ldots, \mathcal{P}_n\}$ *with* $\mathcal{P}_i = (S_i, s_i^0, \Sigma_i, T_i)$, Q_i *being its associated input buffer, and an adapter* $\mathcal{A} = (S, s^0, \Sigma, T)$ *with input buffer* Q, *their asynchronous composition is the labelled transition system* $LTS_{aa} = (S_{aa}, s_{aa}^0, \Sigma_{aa}, T_{aa})$ *where:*

- $S_{aa} \subseteq S_1 \times Q_1 \times \ldots \times S_n \times Q_n \times S \times Q$ *where* $\forall i \in \{1, \ldots, n\}$, $Q_i \subseteq (\Sigma_i^?)*$ *and* $Q \subseteq (\Sigma^?)*$
- $s_{aa}^0 \in S_{aa}$ *such that* $s_{aa}^0 = (s_1^0, \epsilon, \ldots, s_n^0, \epsilon, s^0, \epsilon)$ *(where* ϵ *denotes an empty buffer)*
- $\Sigma_{aa} = \cup_i \Sigma_i \cup \Sigma$
- $T_{aa} \subseteq S_{aa} \times \Sigma_{aa} \times S_{aa}$, *and for* $s = (s_1, Q_1, \ldots, s_n, Q_n, s_a, Q) \in S_{aa}$ *and* $s' = (s_1', Q_1', \ldots, s_n', Q_n', s_a', Q') \in S_{aa}$ *we have that*

(p2a!) $s \xrightarrow{m!} s' \in T_{aa}$ *if* $\exists i \in \{1, \ldots, n\} : m \in \Sigma_i^! \cap \Sigma^?$, *(i)* $s_i \xrightarrow{m!} s_i' \in T_i$, *(ii)* $Q' = Qm$, *(iii)* $s_a' = s_a$, *(iv)* $\forall k \in \{1, \ldots, n\} : Q_k' = Q_k$, *and* *(v)* $\forall k \in \{1, \ldots, n\} : k \neq i \Rightarrow s_k' = s_k$

(p2a?) $s \xrightarrow{\tau} s' \in T_{aa}$ *if* $m \in \Sigma^?$, *(i)* $s_a \xrightarrow{m?} s_a' \in T$, *(ii)* $mQ' = Q$, *(iii)* $\forall k \in \{1, \ldots, n\} : Q_k' = Q_k$, *and (iv)* $\forall k \in \{1, \ldots, n\} : s_k' = s_k$

(a2p!) $s \xrightarrow{m!} s' \in T_{aa}$ *if* $\exists j \in \{1, \ldots, n\} : m \in \Sigma^! \cap \Sigma_j^?$, *(i)* $s_a \xrightarrow{m!} s_a' \in T$, *(ii)* $Q_j' = Q_j m$, *(iii)* $Q' = Q$, *(iv)* $\forall k \in \{1, \ldots, n\} : k \neq j \Rightarrow Q_k' = Q_k$, *and (v)* $\forall k \in \{1, \ldots, n\} : s_k' = s_k$

(a2p?) $s \xrightarrow{\tau} s' \in T_{aa}$ *if* $\exists i \in \{1, \ldots, n\} : m \in \Sigma_i^?$, *(i)* $s_i \xrightarrow{m?} s_i' \in T_i$, *(ii)* $mQ_i' = Q_i$, *(iii)* $\forall k \in \{1, \ldots, n\} : k \neq i \Rightarrow Q_k' = Q_k$, *(iv)* $\forall k \in \{1, \ldots, n\} : k \neq i \Rightarrow s_k' = s_k$, *(v)* $Q' = Q$, *and (vi)* $s_a' = s_a$

(int) $s \xrightarrow{\tau} s' \in T_{aa}$ *if* $\exists i \in \{1, \ldots, n\}$, *(i)* $s_i \xrightarrow{\tau} s_i' \in T_i$, *(ii)* $\forall k \in \{1, \ldots, n\} : Q_k' = Q_k$, *(iii)* $\forall k \in \{1, \ldots, n\} : k \neq i \Rightarrow s_k' = s_k$ *(iv)* $Q' = Q$, *and* *(v)* $s_a' = s_a$

We use LTS_{aa}^k to define the *bounded adapted asynchronous composition*, where each message buffer is bounded to size k. The definition of LTS_{aa}^k can be obtained from Definition 5 by allowing send transitions only if the message buffer of the receiving peer has less than k messages in it. Otherwise, the sender is blocked, *i.e.*, we assume reliable communication without message losses.

The synchronizability property applies here by considering the adapter as a peer whose peculiarity is to interact with all the other participants.

Definition 6 (Branching Synchronizability). *A set of peers* $\{\mathcal{P}_1, \ldots, \mathcal{P}_n\}$ *and an adapter* $\mathcal{A}$ *are branching synchronizable if* $\forall k \geq 1$, $LTS_{as} \equiv_{br} LTS_{aa}^k$.

It was proved that checking the equivalence between the synchronous composition and the 1-bounded asynchronous composition, *i.e.*, $LTS_{as} \equiv_{br} LTS_{aa}^1$, is a sufficient and necessary condition for branching synchronizability [24].

Theorem 1 (Deadlock-freeness). *A synchronizable system consisting of a set of peers* $\{\mathcal{P}_1, \ldots, \mathcal{P}_n\}$ *and an adapter* $\mathcal{A}$ *is deadlock-free when all participants communicate asynchronously via k-bounded or unbounded FIFO buffers.*

Proof. An adapter generated using synchronous synthesis techniques is deadlock-free (DF) according to [12,22], that is, $LTS_{as} \models DF$. The system (peers interacting via an adapter) being synchronizable, we have $LTS_{as} \equiv_{br} LTS_{aa}$. Since branching equivalence [17] preserves deadlock-freeness, if LTS_{as} is deadlock-free then LTS_{aa} is deadlock-free, thus $LTS_{as} \models DF \Leftrightarrow LTS_{aa} \models DF$. □

4 Asynchronous Adaptation

In this section, we present our approach for adapter synthesis when peers interact via FIFO buffers, its application to our running example, and a short overview of tool support.

4.1 Methodology

Figure 3 shows how our approach works for generating adapter LTSs in asynchronous environments. First of all, we apply compatibility checking techniques, *e.g.*, [24], for understanding whether the set of selected peers can be reused and composed directly, that is, without using adaptation techniques for compensating mismatch. If an adapter is required, the user needs to provide an adaptation contract. Note that this is the only step of our approach that requires human intervention. Given a set of peer LTSs and an adaptation contract, an adapter LTS is automatically synthesised by means of synchronous adapter generation techniques, *e.g.*, [12,22]. Then, we check whether the adapted synchronous composition and the 1-bounded adapted asynchronous composition are equivalent. If this is the case, it means that the system is synchronizable and its observable behaviour will remain the same whatever bound is chosen for buffers. Thus, the adapter generated using generation techniques relying on synchronous communication can be used as is in an asynchronous context.

If the system is not synchronizable, the user should refine the adaptation contract using the diagnostic returned by equivalence checking. This counterexample indicates the additional behaviour present in the asynchronous composition and absent in the synchronous one, which invalidates synchronizability. The violation of this property has two main causes: either the adapter does not capture/handle all reachable output messages, or the adapter is too restrictive *wrt.* message orderings, *e.g.*, the adapter requires a sequence of two messages, which cannot be ensured in the asynchronous composition because both messages can be executed simultaneously. This latter case particularly arises when the adaptation contract enforces additional constraints by the use for instance of regex on vectors. This iterative process always terminates because these issues can be solved by modifying the adaptation contract, and the number of problems is finite since the input models are finite. It is worth emphasizing that the reasons for non-synchronizability can be used as guidelines when writing the adaptation contract. Keeping that in mind should help the user to converge more rapidly to a synchronizable system.

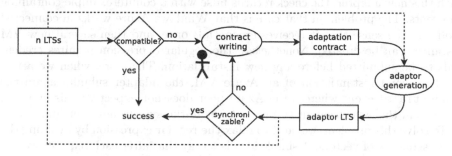

Fig. 3. Approach overview

4.2 Application to the Case Study

Let us go back to our multi-cloud running example. Given the participant LTSs and the set of vectors presented in Section 2, we can generate automatically the corresponding adapter. We first check synchronizability for this adapter composed with the peer LTSs. As a result, the verdict is false and we obtain the following counterexample: c:vmRequest!, dm:request!, dm:instantiate!, g:addInstance!, and g:statistics!, where the very last event appears in the asynchronous system but not in the synchronous one. Note that synchronizability checking focuses on output messages, hence the counterexample above contains only events sent by a peer to the adapter (c:vmRequest!, dm:instantiate!, g:statistics!) or by the adapter to a peer (dm:request!, g:addInstance!). This violation is due to the fact that the emission of statistics is not captured by a vector (yet), and this emission is inhibited in the synchronous system, while it is possible in the asynchronous system because reachable output messages cannot be inhibited under asynchronous communication.

In order to correct this problem, we extend the adaptation contract by adding the following vector: $V_{statisticsG} = \langle g:\texttt{statistics!} \rangle$. The corresponding adapter (not shown here) is generated and it consists of 25 states and 41 transitions. We check again synchronizability and the system composed of the four peers interacting through the adapter is synchronizable, which means that the adapter can be used under asynchronous communication and the system will behave exactly the same whatever bound is chosen for buffers.

However, in this system the Deployment Manager may always decide to instantiate the same kind of VM (Google or Azure). If we want to enforce the DM to instantiate a VM in one of the two clouds alternatively, we have to impose a specific sequence in the application of vectors during the adapter generation process. This can be specified by means of the following regex:

$$(\ V_{request} \ V_{instantiateG} \ V_{statisticsG} \ V_{statusG} \ V_{instance}$$
$$V_{request} \ V_{credentialsA} \ V_{instantiateA} \ V_{statusA} \ V_{instance} \ ) \ \star$$

The adapter generated using the aforementioned vectors and this regex contains 21 states and 24 transitions. However, when we check synchronizability with this new adapter, the check returns false with a counterexample containing 18 events. The problem in that case is that Windows Azure works in connected mode, in the sense that it receives credentials once, and then several new VM instances can be created. Nonetheless, the regular expression requires credentials to be submitted before any new instantiation. Therefore, when we arrive at the second instantiation of an Azure VM, the adapter submits again the `credentials!` event whereas the Azure peer does not expect it: this emission appears in the asynchronous system but not in the synchronous version.

To solve this problem, we need to relax the regular expression by avoiding the strict sequence of vectors. A simple idea is to say that after each request, we can execute in any order the vectors where one of the two VM providers (Google or Azure) is involved. This discards the problem encountered with the credentials, whose rule is executed the first time only. Here is the new regex:

$$(\ V_{request} \ (\ V_{instantiateG} \ | \ V_{statisticsG} \ | \ V_{statusG} \ | \ V_{instance} \ ) \ \star$$
$$V_{request} \ (\ V_{credentialsA} \ | \ V_{instantiateA} \ | \ V_{statusA} \ | \ V_{instance} \ ) \ \star \ ) \ \star$$

The corresponding adapter consists of 32 states and 38 transitions. When we check synchronizability with this new adapter, the system is synchronizable and accordingly this adapter can be used under asynchronous communication.

4.3   Tool Support

Tool support consists of two parts: a set of tools for generating adapters and some automated techniques for checking synchronizability. As for adapter synthesis, we reuse the Itaca toolbox [8]. Itaca takes as input a set of Symbolic Transition Systems (LTSs are STSs without message parameters) and an adaptation contract, and generates an adapter LTS, from which BPEL code can be generated, see [22] for details. As for synchronizability, we rely on process algebra encodings and equivalence checking. More precisely, we developed a Python script, which generates for all input LTSs (peers and adapter) some code in the LNT process algebra. Then, we use the CADP toolbox [15], which accepts LNT specifications as input. Particularly, we rely on CADP exploration tools for computing the required (synchronous/asynchronous) compositions and CADP equivalence checker for checking synchronizability.

Table 1 presents experimental results for some real-world examples. The table gives for each example the number of peers (P), the total number of states

(S) and transitions (T) involved in these examples, the size of the 1-bounded asynchronous system (minimised modulo branching reduction), and the overall time for checking synchronizability (including composition generations, minimisations, and equivalence checking). It is worth noting that out of these 14 examples, 7 of the adapters generated for synchronous communication can be directly reused as they are in asynchronous environments, while 7 require to use our approach in order to replay adapter synthesis techniques until obtaining an adapter which satisfies synchronizability. Computation times are quite short since all the examples found in the literature are quite small.

Table 1. Experimental results

Example	$|P|+1$	$|S|/|T|$	LTS_a^1 $(|S|/|T|)$	Synchro.	Time
FTP Transfer [5]	3	20/17	13/15	$\times$	52s
Client/Server [11]	3	14/13	8/7	$\checkmark$	54s
Mars Explorer [7]	3	34/34	19/22	$\times$	49s
Online Computer Sale [14]	3	26/26	11/12	$\checkmark$	53s
E-museum [12]	3	33/40	47/111	$\times$	53s
Client/Supplier [9]	3	31/33	17/19	$\checkmark$	49s
Restaurant Service [1]	3	15/16	10/12	$\checkmark$	55s
Travel Agency [28]	3	32/38	18/21	$\checkmark$	52s
Vending Machine [16]	3	15/14	8/8	$\checkmark$	49s
Travel Agency [4]	3	42/57	23/34	$\times$	45s
Client/Server [29]	4	19/24	18/32	$\times$	64s
SQL Server [27]	4	32/38	20/27	$\times$	62s
SSH Protocol [20]	4	26/28	16/18	$\checkmark$	56s
Booking System [21]	5	45/53	27/35	$\times$	85s

5   Related Work

In this section, we present the most relevant and recent results in the software adaptation area. First of all, notice that adaptation differs from automatic software composition approaches, particularly studied in the Web services area, where services involved into a new composition are assumed to perfectly match altogether with respect to certain compatibility property.

Van der Aalst *et al.* [1] propose a solution to behavioural adaptation based on open nets, a variant of Petri nets. Their generation algorithm produces an adapter which is obtained through several steps. First, a message transformation net, called engine, is generated from a set of message transformation rules. Then, a behavioural controller (a transition system) is synthesised for the product net of the services and the engine. Adapters are finally implemented in the BPEL orchestration language. In [23], the authors identify several kinds of mismatch between Web service interfaces. They provide a method for identification of the split/merge class of interface mismatch and a semi-automated, behaviour-aware approach for interface-level mismatch that results in identifying parameters of mapping functions that resolve that mismatch. They use and extend approaches in ontology matching for static matching of service interfaces to identify split/merge mismatch. In addition, they propose depth-based and iterative reference-based approaches that incorporate behavioural information during interface matching.

In [12,22], the authors proposed automated techniques for generating an adapter model from a set of service interfaces and a contract. The approach relies on an encoding into process algebra together with on-the-fly exploration and reduction techniques. Verification of contracts is also possible by using model checking techniques. Last, code is automatically generated from the adapter model to BPEL, which may finally be deployed. Inverardi and Tivoli [18] formalise a method for the automated synthesis of modular connectors. A modular connector is structured as a composition of independent mediators, each of them corresponding to the solution of a recurring behavioural mismatch. The paper proves that the connector decomposition is correct and shows how it promotes connector evolution on a case study. Bennaceur *et al.* [4] propose a technique for automated synthesis of mediators using a quotient operator, that is based on behavioural models of the components and an ontological model of the data domain. The method supports both off-line and run-time synthesis. The obtained mediator is the most general component that ensures deadlock-freedom and the absence of communication mismatch.

It is worth observing that, although all these papers present interesting approaches tackling software adaptation from different points of view, they assume that peers interact synchronously. There were a few attempts to generate adapters considering asynchronous communication. Padovani [25] presents a theory based on behavioural contracts to generate orchestrators between two services related by a subtyping (namely, sub-contract) relation. This is used to generate an adapter between a client of some service S and a service replacing S. An interesting feature of this approach is its expressiveness as far as behavioural descriptions are concerned, with support for asynchronous orchestrators and infinite behaviour. The author resorts to the theory of regular trees and imposes two requirements on the orchestrator, namely regularity and contractivity. However, this work does not support name mismatch nor data-related adaptation. Seguel *et al.* [28] present automatic techniques for constructing a minimal adapter for two business protocols possibly involving parallelism and loops. The approach works by assigning to loops a fixed number of iterations, whereas we do not impose any restriction, and peers may loop infinitely. Gierds and colleagues [16] present an approach for specifying behavioural adapters based on domain-specific transformation rules that reflect the elementary operations that adapters can perform. The authors also present a novel way to synthesise complex adapters that adhere to these rules by consistently separating data and control, and by using existing controller synthesis algorithms. Asynchronous adaptation is supported in this work, but buffers/places must be arbitrarily bounded for ensuring computability of the adapter.

6 Conclusion

Software adaptation is the only solution for building new systems by combining black-box services that are relevant from a functional point of view, but do not exactly match one with another and therefore require adjustments during the composition process. Most existing approaches focus on systems relying on synchronous communication. In this paper, we tackle the adapter generation question from a different angle by assuming that peers interact asynchronously via FIFO buffers. This highly complicates the synthesis process because we may have to face infinite systems when generating the adapter behaviour. Our approach provides a solution to this problem by using the synchronizability property and adapter generation techniques for synchronous communication. This enables us to propose an iterative approach for synthesising adapters, which work properly in asynchronous environments. Our approach is tool-supported and has been applied to a large variety of real-world examples found in the literature.

References

1. van der Aalst, W.M.P., Mooij, A.J., Stahl, C., Wolf, K.: Service Interaction: Patterns, Formalization, and Analysis. In: Bernardo, M., Padovani, L., Zavattaro, G. (eds.) SFM 2009. LNCS, vol. 5569, pp. 42–88. Springer, Heidelberg (2009)
2. de Alfaro, L., Henzinger, T.A.: Interface Automata. In: Proc. of ESEC/FSE 2001, pp. 109–120. ACM Press (2001)
3. Basu, S., Bultan, T., Ouederni, M.: Deciding Choreography Realizability. In: Proc. of POPL 2012, pp. 191–202. ACM (2012)
4. Bennaceur, A., Chilton, C., Isberner, M., Jonsson, B.: Automated Mediator Synthesis: Combining Behavioural and Ontological Reasoning. In: Hierons, R.M., Merayo, M.G., Bravetti, M. (eds.) SEFM 2013. LNCS, vol. 8137, pp. 274–288. Springer, Heidelberg (2013)
5. Bracciali, A., Brogi, A., Canal, C.: A Formal Approach to Component Adaptation. Journal of Systems and Software 74(1), 45–54 (2005)
6. Brand, D., Zafiropulo, P.: On Communicating Finite-State Machines. Journal of the ACM 30(2), 323–342 (1983)
7. Brogi, A., Popescu, R.: Automated Generation of BPEL Adapters. In: Dan, A., Lamersdorf, W. (eds.) ICSOC 2006. LNCS, vol. 4294, pp. 27–39. Springer, Heidelberg (2006)
8. Cámara, J., Martín, J.A., Salaün, G., Cubo, J., Ouederni, M., Canal, C., Pimentel, E.: ITACA: An Integrated Toolbox for the Automatic Composition and Adaptation of Web Services. In: Proc. of ICSE 2009, pp. 627–630. IEEE (2009)
9. Cámara, J., Martín, J.A., Salaün, G., Canal, C., Pimentel, E.: Semi-Automatic Specification of Behavioural Service Adaptation Contracts. Electr. Notes Theor. Comput. Sci. 264(1), 19–34 (2010)
10. Canal, C., Murillo, J.M., Poizat, P.: Software Adaptation. L'Objet 12(1), 9–31 (2006)
11. Canal, C., Poizat, P., Salaün, G.: Synchronizing Behavioural Mismatch in Software Composition. In: Gorrieri, R., Wehrheim, H. (eds.) FMOODS 2006. LNCS, vol. 4037, pp. 63–77. Springer, Heidelberg (2006)
12. Canal, C., Poizat, P., Salaün, G.: Model-Based Adaptation of Behavioural Mismatching Components. IEEE Trans. on Software Engineering 34(4), 546–563 (2008)

13. Canal, C., Salaün, G.: Adaptation of Asynchronously Communicating Software. In: Franch, X., Ghose, A.K., Lewis, G.A., Bhiri, S. (eds.) ICSOC 2014. LNCS, vol. 8831, pp. 437–444. Springer, Heidelberg (2014)

14. Cubo, J., Salaün, G., Canal, C., Pimentel, E., Poizat, P.: A Model-Based Approach to the Verification and Adaptation of WF/.NET Components. In: Proc. of FACS 2007. ENTCS, vol. 215, pp. 39–55. Elsevier (2007)

15. Garavel, H., Lang, F., Mateescu, R., Serwe, W.: CADP 2010: A Toolbox for the Construction and Analysis of Distributed Processes. In: Abdulla, P.A., Leino, K.R.M. (eds.) TACAS 2011. LNCS, vol. 6605, pp. 372–387. Springer, Heidelberg (2011)

16. Gierds, C., Mooij, A.J., Wolf, K.: Reducing Adapter Synthesis to Controller Synthesis. IEEE T. Services Computing 5(1), 72–85 (2012)

17. van Glabbeek, R.J., Weijland, W.P.: Branching Time and Abstraction in Bisimulation Semantics. Journal of the ACM 43(3), 555–600 (1996)

18. Inverardi, P., Tivoli, M.: Automatic Synthesis of Modular Connectors via Composition of Protocol Mediation Patterns. In: Proc. of ICSE 2013, pp. 3–12. IEEE / ACM (2013)

19. Magee, J., Kramer, J., Giannakopoulou, D.: Behaviour Analysis of Software Architectures, pp. 35–49. Kluwer Academic Publishers (1999)

20. Martín, J.A., Pimentel, E.: Contracts for Security Adaptation. J. Log. Algebr. Program. 80(3-5), 154–179 (2011)

21. Mateescu, R., Poizat, P., Salaün, G.: Adaptation of Service Protocols using Process Algebra and On-the-Fly Reduction Techniques. In: Bouguettaya, A., Krueger, I., Margaria, T. (eds.) ICSOC 2008. LNCS, vol. 5364, pp. 84–99. Springer, Heidelberg (2008)

22. Mateescu, R., Poizat, P., Salaün, G.: Adaptation of Service Protocols Using Process Algebra and On-the-Fly Reduction Techniques. IEEE Trans. on Software Engineering 38(4), 755–777 (2012)

23. Nezhad, H.R.M., Xu, G.Y., Benatallah, B.: Protocol-Aware Matching of Web Service Interfaces for Adapter Development. In: Proc. of WWW 2010, pp. 731–740. ACM (2010)

24. Ouederni, M., Salaün, G., Bultan, T.: Compatibility Checking for Asynchronously Communicating Software. In: Fiadeiro, J.L., Liu, Z., Xue, J. (eds.) FACS 2013. LNCS, vol. 8348, pp. 310–328. Springer, Heidelberg (2014)

25. Padovani, L.: Contract-Based Discovery and Adaptation of Web Services. In: Bernardo, M., Padovani, L., Zavattaro, G. (eds.) SFM 2009. LNCS, vol. 5569, pp. 213–260. Springer, Heidelberg (2009)

26. Plasil, F., Visnovsky, S.: Behavior Protocols for Software Components. IEEE Trans. on Software Engineering 28(11), 1056–1076 (2002)

27. Poizat, P., Salaün, G.: Adaptation of Open Component-based Systems. In: Bonsangue, M.M., Johnsen, E.B. (eds.) FMOODS 2007. LNCS, vol. 4468, pp. 141–156. Springer, Heidelberg (2007)

28. Seguel, R., Eshuis, R., Grefen, P.W.P.J.: Generating Minimal Protocol Adaptors for Loosely Coupled Services. In: Proc. of ICWS 2010, pp. 417–424. IEEE Computer Society (2010)

29. Tivoli, M., Inverardi, P.: Failure-Free Coordinators Synthesis for Component-Based Architectures. Sci. Comput. Program. 71(3), 181–212 (2008)

30. Yellin, D.M., Strom, R.E.: Protocol Specifications and Components Adaptors. ACM Trans. on Programming Languages and Systems 19(2), 292–333 (1997)

Lazy TSO Reachability

Ahmed Bouajjani[1], Georgel Calin[2], Egor Derevenetc[2,3], and Roland Meyer[2]

[1] LIAFA, University Paris 7
[2] University of Kaiserslautern
[3] Fraunhofer ITWM

Abstract. We address the problem of checking state reachability for programs running under Total Store Order (TSO). The problem has been shown to be decidable but the cost is prohibitive, namely non-primitive recursive. We propose here to give up completeness. Our contribution is a new algorithm for TSO reachability: it uses the standard SC semantics and introduces the TSO semantics lazily and only where needed. At the heart of our algorithm is an iterative refinement of the program of interest. If the program's goal state is SC-reachable, we are done. If the goal state is not SC-reachable, this may be due to the fact that SC under-approximates TSO. We employ a second algorithm that determines TSO computations which are infeasible under SC, and hence likely to lead to new states. We enrich the program to emulate, under SC, these TSO computations. Altogether, this yields an iterative under-approximation that we prove sound and complete for bug hunting, i.e., a semi-decision procedure halting for positive cases of reachability. We have implemented the procedure as an extension to the tool TRENCHER [1] and compared it to the MEMORAX [2] and CBMC [14] model checkers.

1 Introduction

Sequential consistency (SC) [19] is the semantics typically assumed for parallel programs. Under SC, instructions are executed atomically and in program order. When programs are executed on an Intel x86 processor, however, they are only guaranteed a weaker semantics known as Total Store Order (TSO). TSO weakens the synchronization guarantees given by SC, which in turn may lead to erroneous behavior. TSO reflects the architectural optimization of store buffers. To reduce the latency of memory accesses, store commands are added to a thread-local FIFO buffer and only later executed on memory.

To check for correct behavior, reachability techniques have proven useful. Given a program and a goal state, the task is to check whether the state is reachable. To give an example, assertion failures can be phrased as reachability problems. Reachability depends on the underlying semantics. Under SC, the problem is known to be PSPACE-complete [16]. Under TSO, it is considerably more difficult: although decidable, it is non-primitive recursive-hard [8].

Owing to the high complexity of TSO reachability, tools rarely provide decision procedures [2]. Instead, most approaches implement approximations. Typical approximations of TSO reachability bound the number of loop iterations [5,6], the number of context switches between threads [9], or the size of

© Springer-Verlag Berlin Heidelberg 2015
A. Egyed and I. Schaefer (Eds.): FASE 2015, LNCS 9033, pp. 267–282, 2015.
DOI: 10.1007/978-3-662-46675-9_18

store buffers [17, 18]. What all these approaches have in common is that they introduce store buffering in the *whole* program. We claim that such a comprehensive instrumentation is unnecessarily heavy.

The idea of our method is to introduce store buffering lazily and only where needed. Unlike [2], we do not target completeness. Instead, we argue that our lazy TSO reachability checker is useful for a fast detection of bugs that are due to the TSO semantics. At a high level, we solve the expensive TSO reachability problem with a series of cheap SC reachability checks — very much like SAT solvers are invoked as subroutines of costlier analyses. The SC checks run interleaved with queries to an oracle. The task of the oracle is to suggest sequences of instructions that should be considered under TSO, which means they are likely to lead to TSO-reachable states outside SC.

To be more precise, the algorithm iteratively repeats the following steps. First, it checks whether the goal state is SC-reachable. If this is the case, the state will be TSO-reachable as well and the algorithm returns. If the state is not SC-reachable, the algorithm asks the oracle for a sequence of instructions and encodes the TSO behavior of the sequence into the input program. As a result, precisely this TSO behavior becomes available under SC. The encoding is linear in the size of the input program and in the length of the sequence.

The algorithm is a semi-decision procedure: it always returns correct answers and is guaranteed to terminate if the goal state is TSO-reachable. This guarantee relies on one assumption on the oracle. If the oracle returns the empty sequence, then the SC- and the TSO-reachable states of the input program have to coincide. We also come up with a good oracle: robustness checkers naturally meet the above requirement. Intuitively, a program is robust against TSO if its partial order-behaviors (reflecting data and control dependencies) under TSO and under SC coincide. Robustness is much easier than TSO reachability, actually PSPACE-complete [10, 11], and hence well-suited for iterative invocations.

We have implemented lazy TSO reachability as an extension to our tool TRENCHER [1], reusing the robustness checking algorithms of TRENCHER to derive an oracle. The implementation is able to solve positive instances of TSO reachability as well as correctly determine safety for robust programs. The source code and experiments are available online [1].

The structure of the paper is as follows. We introduce parallel programs with their TSO and their SC semantics in Section 2. Section 3 presents our main contribution, the lazy approach to solving TSO reachability. Section 4 describes the robustness-based oracle. The experimental evaluation is given in Section 5.

Related Work

As already mentioned, TSO reachability was proven decidable but non-primitive recursive [8] in the case of a finite number of threads and a finite data domain. In the same setting, robustness was shown to be PSPACE-complete [11]. Checking and enforcing robustness against weak memory models has been addressed in [3, 7, 10–13, 24]. The first work to give an efficient sound and complete decision procedure for checking robustness is [10].

The works [2,21,22] propose state-based techniques to solve TSO reachability. An under-approximative method that uses bounded context switching is given in [9]. It encodes store buffers into a linear-size instrumentation, and the instrumented program is checked for SC reachability. The under-approximative techniques of [5,6] are able to guarantee safety only for programs with bounded loops. On the other side of the spectrum, over-approximative analyses abstract store buffers into sets combined with bounded queues [17,18].

2   Parallel Programs

We use automata to define the syntax and the semantics of parallel programs. A (non-deterministic) *automaton* over an alphabet Σ is a tuple $A = (\Sigma, S, \rightarrow, s_0)$, where S is a set of states, $\rightarrow \subseteq S \times (\Sigma \cup \{\varepsilon\}) \times S$ is a set of transitions, and $s_0 \in S$ is an initial state. The automaton is *finite* if the transition relation $\rightarrow$ is finite. We write $s \xrightarrow{a} s'$ if $(s, a, s') \in \rightarrow$, and extend the transition relation to sequences $w \in \Sigma^*$ as expected. The *language of A with final states* $F \subseteq S$ is $\mathcal{L}_F(A) := \{w \in \Sigma^* \mid s_0 \xrightarrow{w} s \in F\}$. We say that state $s \in S$ is *reachable* if $s_0 \xrightarrow{w} s$ for some sequence $w \in \Sigma^*$. Letter a *precedes* b *in* w, denoted by $a <_w b$, if $w = w_1 \cdot a \cdot w_2 \cdot b \cdot w_3$ for some $w_1, w_2, w_3 \in \Sigma^*$.

A parallel program P is a finite sequence of threads that are identified by indices t from TID. Each thread $t := (Com_t, Q_t, I_t, q_{0,t})$ is a finite automaton with transitions I_t that we call *instructions*. Instructions I_t are labelled by *commands* from the set Com_t which we define in the next paragraph. We assume, wlog., that states of different threads are disjoint. This implies that the sets of instructions of different threads are distinct. We use $I := \biguplus_{t \in \text{TID}} I_t$ for all instructions and $Com := \bigcup_{t \in \text{TID}} Com_t$ for all commands. For an instruction $inst := (s, cmd, s')$ in I, we define $cmd(inst) := cmd$, $src(inst) := s$, and $dst(inst) := s'$.

To define the set of commands, let DOM be a finite domain of values that we also use as addresses. We assume that value 0 is in DOM. For each thread t, let REG_t be a finite set of registers that take their values from DOM. We assume per-thread disjoint sets of registers. The set of expressions of thread t, denoted by EXP_t, is defined over registers from REG_t, constants from DOM,

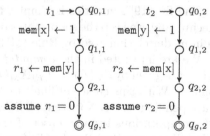

Fig. 1. Simplified Dekker's algorithm

and (unspecified) operators over DOM. If $r \in \text{REG}_t$ and $e, e' \in \text{EXP}_t$, the set of commands Com_t consists of loads from memory $r \leftarrow \text{mem}[e]$, stores to memory $\text{mem}[e] \leftarrow e'$, memory fences $\texttt{mfence}$, assignments $r \leftarrow e$, and conditionals $\texttt{assume}\ e$. We write $\text{REG} := \biguplus_{t \in \text{TID}} \text{REG}_t$ for all registers and $\text{EXP} := \bigcup_{t \in \text{TID}} \text{EXP}_t$ for all expressions.

The program in Figure 1 serves as our running example. It consists of two threads t_1 and t_2 implementing a mutual exclusion protocol. Initially, the addresses x and y contain 0. The first thread signals its intent to enter the critical section by setting variable x to 1. Next, the thread checks whether the second thread wants to enter the critical section, too. It reads variable y and, if it is 0, the first thread enters its critical section. The critical section actually is the state $q_{g,1}$. The second thread behaves symmetrically.

2.1 Semantics of Parallel Programs

The semantics of a parallel program P under memory model M = TSO and M = SC follows [23]. We define the semantics in terms of a *state-space automaton* $X_{\mathrm{M}}(P) := (E, S_{\mathrm{M}}, \Delta_{\mathrm{M}}, s_0)$. Each state $s = (\mathsf{pc}, \mathsf{val}, \mathsf{buf}) \in S_{\mathrm{M}}$ is a tuple where the program counter $\mathsf{pc} \colon \mathsf{TID} \to Q$ holds the current control state of each thread, the valuation $\mathsf{val} \colon \mathsf{REG} \cup \mathsf{DOM} \to \mathsf{DOM}$ holds the values stored in registers and at memory addresses, and the buffer configuration $\mathsf{buf} \colon \mathsf{TID} \to (\mathsf{DOM} \times \mathsf{DOM})^*$ holds a sequence of address-value pairs.

In the *initial state* $s_0 := (\mathsf{pc}_0, \mathsf{val}_0, \mathsf{buf}_0)$, the program counter holds the initial control states, $\mathsf{pc}_0(t) := q_{0,t}$ for all $t \in \mathsf{TID}$, all registers and addresses contain value 0, and all buffers are empty, $\mathsf{buf}_0(t) := \varepsilon$ for all $t \in \mathsf{TID}$.

The transition relation Δ_{TSO} for TSO satisfies the rules given in Figure 2. There are two more rules for register assignments and conditionals that are standard and omitted. TSO architectures implement (FIFO) store buffering, which means stores are buffered for later execution on the shared memory. Loads from an address a take their value from the most recent store to address a that is buffered. If there is no such buffered store, they access the main memory. This is modelled by the Rules (LB) and (LM). Rule (ST) enqueues store operations as address-value pairs to the buffer. Rule (MEM) non-deterministically dequeues store operations and executes them on memory. Rule (F) states that a thread can execute a fence only if its buffer is empty. As can be seen from Figure 2, events labelling TSO transitions take the form $E \subseteq \mathsf{TID} \times (I \cup \{\mathsf{flush}\}) \times (\mathsf{DOM} \cup \{\bot\})$.

The SC [19] semantics is simpler than TSO in that stores are not buffered. Technically, we keep the set of states but change the transitions so that Rule (ST) is immediately followed by Rule (MEM).

We are interested in the *computations* of program P under M $\in \{\mathrm{TSO}, \mathrm{SC}\}$. They are given by $\mathcal{C}_{\mathrm{M}}(P) := \mathcal{L}_F(X_{\mathrm{M}}(P))$, where F is the set of states with empty buffers. With this choice of final states, we avoid incomplete computations that have pending stores. Note that all SC states have empty buffers, which means the SC computations form a subset of the TSO computations: $\mathcal{C}_{\mathrm{SC}}(P) \subseteq \mathcal{C}_{\mathrm{TSO}}(P)$. We will use notation $Reach_{\mathrm{M}}(P)$ for the set of all states $s \in F$ that are reachable by some computation in $\mathcal{C}_{\mathrm{M}}(P)$.

To give an example, the program from Figure 1 admits the TSO computation τ_{wit} below where the store of the first thread is flushed at the end:

$$\tau_{\mathrm{wit}} = \mathsf{store}_1 \cdot \mathsf{load}_1 \cdot \mathsf{store}_2 \cdot \mathsf{flush}_2 \cdot \mathsf{load}_2 \cdot \mathsf{flush}_1.$$

Consider an event $\mathbf{e} = (t, inst, a)$. By $thread(\mathbf{e}) := t$ we refer to the thread that produced the event. Function $inst(\mathbf{e}) := inst$ returns the instruction. For flush events, $inst(\mathbf{e})$ gives the instruction of the matching store event. By $addr(\mathbf{e}) := a$

$$\frac{cmd = r \leftarrow \mathsf{mem}[e_a] \quad \mathsf{buf}(t){\downarrow}(\{a\} \times \mathsf{DOM}) = (a,v) \cdot \beta}{s \xrightarrow{(t,inst,a)} (\mathsf{pc}', \mathsf{val}[r := v], \mathsf{buf})} \text{ (LB)}$$

$$\frac{cmd = r \leftarrow \mathsf{mem}[e_a] \quad \mathsf{buf}(t){\downarrow}(\{a\} \times \mathsf{DOM}) = \varepsilon}{s \xrightarrow{(t,inst,a)} (\mathsf{pc}', \mathsf{val}[r := \mathsf{val}(a)], \mathsf{buf})} \text{ (LM)}$$

$$\frac{cmd = \mathsf{mem}[e_a] \leftarrow e_v}{s \xrightarrow{(t,inst,a)} (\mathsf{pc}', \mathsf{val}, \mathsf{buf}[t := (a,v) \cdot \mathsf{buf}(t)])} \text{ (ST)}$$

$$\frac{\mathsf{buf}(t) = \beta \cdot (a,v)}{s \xrightarrow{(t,\mathrm{flush},a)} (\mathsf{pc}, \mathsf{val}[a := v], \mathsf{buf}[t := \beta])} \text{ (MEM)} \qquad \frac{cmd = \mathsf{mfence} \quad \mathsf{buf}(t) = \varepsilon}{s \xrightarrow{(t,inst,\perp)} (\mathsf{pc}', \mathsf{val}, \mathsf{buf})} \text{ (F)}$$

Fig. 2. Transition rules for $X_{\mathrm{TSO}}(P)$ assuming $s = (\mathsf{pc}, \mathsf{val}, \mathsf{buf})$ with $\mathsf{pc}(t) = q$ and $inst = (q, cmd, q')$ in thread t. The program counter is always set to $\mathsf{pc}' = \mathsf{pc}[t := q']$. We assume $a = \widehat{e_a}$ to be the address returned by an address expression e_a and $v = \widehat{e_v}$ the value returned by a value expression e_v. We use $\mathsf{buf}(t){\downarrow}(\{a\} \times \mathsf{DOM})$ to project the buffer content $\mathsf{buf}(t)$ to store operations that access address a.

we denote the address that is accessed (if any). In the example, $thread(\mathsf{store}_1) = t_1$, $inst(\mathsf{store}_1) = q_{0,1} \xrightarrow{\mathsf{mem}[\mathsf{x}] \leftarrow 1} q_{1,1}$, and $addr(\mathsf{store}_1) = \mathsf{x}$.

3 Lazy TSO Reachability

We introduce the reachability problem and present our main contribution: an algorithm that checks TSO reachability lazily. The iterative algorithm queries an oracle to identify sequences of instructions that, under the TSO semantics, lead to states not reachable under SC. In Section 3.1, we show that the algorithm yields a sound and complete semi-decision procedure.

Given a memory model $\mathrm{M} \in \{\mathrm{SC}, \mathrm{TSO}\}$, the M reachability problem expects as input a program P and a set of *goal states* $G \subseteq S_{\mathrm{M}}$. We are mostly interested in the control state of each thread. Therefore, goal states $(\mathsf{pc}, \mathsf{val}, \mathsf{buf})$ typically specify a program counter pc but leave the memory valuation unconstrained. Formally, the *M reachability problem* asks if some state in G is reachable in the automaton $X_{\mathrm{M}}(P)$.

> **Given:** A parallel program P and goal states G.
> **Problem:** Decide $\mathcal{L}_{F \cap G}(X_{\mathrm{M}}(P)) \neq \emptyset$.

We use notation $Reach_{\mathrm{M}}(P) \cap G$ for the set of reachable final goal states in P.

Instead of solving reachability under TSO directly, the algorithm we propose solves SC reachability and, if no goal state is reachable, tries to lazily introduce store buffering on a certain control path of the program. The algorithm delegates choosing the control path to an *oracle function* $\mathcal{O}$. Given an input program R, the oracle returns a sequence of instructions I^* in that program. Formally, the oracle satisfies the following requirements:

- If $\mathcal{O}(R) = \varepsilon$ then $Reach_{SC}(R) = Reach_{TSO}(R)$.
- Otherwise, $\mathcal{O}(R) = inst_1inst_2 \ldots inst_n$ with $cmd(inst_1)$ a store, $cmd(inst_n)$ a load, $cmd(inst_i) \neq \mathtt{mfence}$, and $dst(inst_i) = src(inst_{i+1})$ for $i \in [1..n-1]$.

The lazy TSO reachability checker is outlined in Algorithm 1. As input, it takes a program P and an oracle $\mathcal{O}$. We assume some control states in each thread to be marked to define a set of goal states. The algorithm returns $true$ iff the program can reach a goal state under TSO. It works as follows. First, it creates a copy R of the program P. Next, it checks if a goal state is SC-reachable in R (Line 3). If that is the case, the algorithm returns $true$. Otherwise, it asks the oracle $\mathcal{O}$ where in the program to introduce store buffering. If $\mathcal{O}(R) \neq \varepsilon$, the algorithm extends R to emulate store buffering on the path $\mathcal{O}(R)$ under SC (Line 8). Then it goes back to the beginning of the loop. If $\mathcal{O}(R) = \varepsilon$, by the first property of oracles, R has the same reachable states under SC and under TSO. This means the algorithm can safely return $false$ (Line 10). Note that, since R emulates TSO behavior of P, the algorithm solves TSO reachability for P.

Algorithm 1. Lazy TSO Reachability Checker

Input: Marked program P and oracle $\mathcal{O}$
Output: $true$ if some goal state is TSO-reachable in P
$\quad\quad\quad$ $false$ if no goal state is TSO-reachable in P

1: $R := P$;
2: **while** $true$ **do**
3: $\quad$ **if** $Reach_{SC}(P) \cap G \neq \emptyset$ **then** $\quad$ {check if some goal state is SC-reachable}
4: $\quad\quad$ **return** $true$;
5: $\quad$ **else**
6: $\quad\quad$ $\sigma := \mathcal{O}(R)$; $\quad\quad\quad\quad\quad\quad\quad$ {ask the oracle where to use store buffering}
7: $\quad\quad$ **if** $\sigma \neq \varepsilon$ **then**
8: $\quad\quad\quad$ $R := R \oplus \sigma$;
9: $\quad\quad$ **else**
10: $\quad\quad\quad$ **return** $false$;

Let $\sigma := \mathcal{O}(R) = inst_1inst_2 \ldots inst_n$ and let $t := (Com_t, Q_t, I_t, q_{0,t})$ be the thread of the instructions in σ. The modified program $R \oplus \sigma$ replaces t by a new thread $t \oplus \sigma$. The new thread emulates under SC the TSO semantics of σ. Formally, the *extension of t by σ* is $t \oplus \sigma := (Com'_t, Q'_t, I'_t, q_{0,t})$. The thread is obtained from t by adding sequences of instructions starting from $\overline{q}_0 := src(inst_1)$. To remember the addresses and values of the buffered stores, we use auxiliary registers $ar_1, \ldots, ar_{\max}$ and $vr_1, \ldots, vr_{\max}$, where $\max \leq n-1$ is the total number of store instructions in σ. The sets $Com'_t \supseteq Com_t$ and $Q'_t \supseteq Q_t$ are extended as necessary.

We define the extension by describing the new transitions that are added to I'_t for each $inst_i$. In our construction, we use a variable $\mathtt{count}$ to keep track of the number of store instructions already processed. Initially, $Q'_t := Q_t$ and count := 0. Based on the type of instructions, we distinguish the following cases.

If $cmd(inst_i) = \mathtt{mem}[e] \leftarrow e'$, we increment count by 1 and add instructions that remember the address and the value being written in $ar_{\mathtt{count}}$ and $vr_{\mathtt{count}}$.

If $cmd(inst_i) = r \leftarrow \mathtt{mem}[e]$, we add instructions to I'_t that perform a load from memory only when a load from the simulated buffer is not possible. More precisely, if $j \in [1, \mathtt{count}]$ is found so that $ar_j = e$, register r is assigned the value of vr_j. Otherwise, r receives its value from the address indicated by e.

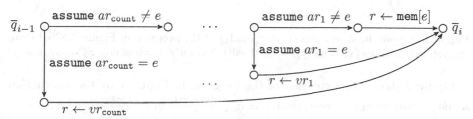

If $cmd(inst_i)$ is an assignment or a conditional, we add $(\overline{q}_{i-1},\, cmd(inst_i),\, \overline{q}_i)$ to I'_t. By the definition of an oracle, $cmd(inst_i)$ is never a fence.

The above cases handle all instructions in σ. So far, the extension added new instructions to I'_t that lead through the fresh states $\overline{q}_1, \ldots, \overline{q}_n$. Out of control state $\overline{q}_n$, we now recreate the sequence of stores remembered by the auxiliary registers. Then we return to the control flow of the original thread t.

$$\overline{q}_n \circ \xrightarrow{\mathtt{mem}[ar_1] \leftarrow vr_1} \circ \cdots \circ \xrightarrow{\mathtt{mem}[ar_{\max}] \leftarrow vr_{\max}} \circ\; dst(inst_n)$$

Next, we remove $inst_1$ from the program. This prevents the oracle from discovering in the future another instruction sequence that is essentially the same as σ. As we will show, this is key to guaranteeing termination of the algorithm for acyclic programs. However, the removal of $inst_1$ may reduce the set of TSO-reachable states. To overcome this problem, we insert additional instructions. Consider an instruction $inst \in I_t$ with $src(inst) = src(inst_i)$ for some $i \in [1..n]$ and assume that $inst \neq inst_i$. We add instructions that recreate the stores buffered in the auxiliary registers and return to $dst(inst)$.

$$\overline{q}_i \circ \xrightarrow{\mathtt{mem}[ar_1] \leftarrow vr_1} \circ \cdots \circ \xrightarrow{\mathtt{mem}[ar_{\mathtt{count}}] \leftarrow vr_{\mathtt{count}}} \circ \xrightarrow{cmd(inst)} \circ\; dst(inst)$$

Similarly, for all load instructions $inst_i$ as well as out of $\overline{q}_1$ we add instructions that flush and fence the pair (ar_1, vr_1), make visible the remaining buffered stores, and return to state q in the original control flow. Below, $q := src(inst_i)$ if $inst_i$ is a load and $q := dst(inst_1)$, otherwise. Intuitively, this captures behaviors that delay $inst_1$ past loads earlier than $inst_n$, and that do not delay $inst_1$ past the first load in σ.

$$\overline{q}_i \circ \xrightarrow{\mathtt{mem}[ar_1] \leftarrow vr_1} \circ \xrightarrow{\mathtt{mfence}} \circ \cdots \circ \xrightarrow{\mathtt{mem}[ar_{\mathtt{count}}] \leftarrow vr_{\mathtt{count}}} \circ\; q$$

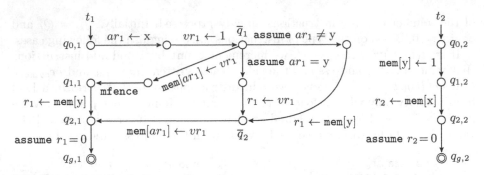

Fig. 3. Extension by $inst(\text{store}_1) \cdot inst(\text{load}_1)$ of the program in Figure 1. Goal state $(\text{pc}, \text{val}, \text{buf})$ with $\text{val}(x) = \text{val}(y) = 1$ and $\text{val}(r_1) = \text{val}(r_2) = 0$ is now SC-reachable.

Figure 3 shows the extension of the program in Figure 1 by the instruction sequence $inst(\text{store}_1) \cdot inst(\text{load}_1) := q_{0,1} \xrightarrow{\text{mem}[x] \leftarrow 1} q_{1,1} \xrightarrow{r_1 \leftarrow \text{mem}[y]} q_{1,2}$.

3.1   Soundness and Completeness

We show that Algorithm 1 is a decision procedure for acyclic programs. From here until (inclusively) Theorem 3 we assume that all programs are acyclic, i.e., their instructions and control states form directed acyclic graphs. Theorem 4 then explains how Algorithm 1 yields a semi-decision procedure for all programs.

We first prove the extension sound and complete (Lemma 1): extending R by sequence $\sigma := \mathcal{O}(R)$ does neither add nor remove TSO-reachable states. Afterwards, Lemma 2 shows that if Algorithm 1 extends R by σ (Line 8) then, in subsequent iterations of the algorithm, no new sequence returned by the oracle is the same as σ (projected back to P). Next, by the first condition of an oracle and using Lemma 2, we establish that Algorithm 1 is a decision procedure for acyclic programs (Theorem 3). Finally, we show that Algorithm 1 can be turned into a semi-decision procedure for all programs using a bounded model checking approach (Theorem 4).

Lemma 1. *Let $DOM \cup REG$ be the addresses and registers of program R and let $\sigma := \mathcal{O}(R)$. Then we have $(\text{pc}, \text{val}, \text{buf}) \in Reach_{TSO}(R)$ if and only if $(\text{pc}, \text{val}', \text{buf}) \in Reach_{TSO}(R \oplus \sigma)$ with $\text{val}(a) = \text{val}'(a)$ for all $a \in DOM \cup REG$.*

Let t be the thread that differs in R and $R \oplus \sigma$. To prove Lemma 1, one can show that for any prefix α' of $\alpha \in \mathcal{C}_{\text{TSO}}(R)$ there is a prefix β' of $\beta \in \mathcal{C}_{\text{TSO}}(R \oplus \sigma)$, and vice versa, that maintain the following invariants.

Inv-0 $s_0 \xrightarrow{\alpha'} (\text{pc}, \text{val}, \text{buf})$ and $s_0 \xrightarrow{\beta'} (\text{pc}', \text{val}', \text{buf}')$.

Inv-1 If pc and pc' differ, they only differ for thread t. If $\text{pc}(t) \neq \text{pc}'(t)$, then $\text{pc}(t) = dst(inst_i)$ and $\text{pc}'(t) = \overline{q}_i$ for some $i \in [1..n-1]$.

Inv-2 $\text{val}'(a) = \text{val}(a)$ for all $a \in DOM \cup REG$.

Inv-3 buf and buf' differ at most for t. If $\text{buf}(t) \neq \text{buf}'(t)$, then $\text{pc}'(t) = \overline{q}_i$ for some $i \in [1..n-1]$ and $\text{buf}(t) = (\widehat{ar_{\text{count}}}, \widehat{vr_{\text{count}}}) \cdots (\widehat{ar_1}, \widehat{vr_1}) \cdot \text{buf}'(t)$ where count stores are seen along σ from $src(inst_1)$ to $dst(inst_i)$.

We now show that the oracle never suggests the same sequence σ twice. Since in $R \oplus \sigma$ we introduce new instructions that correspond to instructions in R, we have to map back sequences of instructions $I_\oplus$ in $R \oplus \sigma$ to sequences of instructions I in R. Intuitively, the mapping gives the original instructions from which the sequence was produced. Formally, we define a family of projection functions $h_\sigma \colon I_\oplus^* \to I^*$ with $h_\sigma(\varepsilon) := \varepsilon$ and $h_\sigma(w \cdot inst) := h_\sigma(w) \cdot h_\sigma(inst)$. For an instruction $inst \in I_\oplus$, we define $h_\sigma(inst) := inst$ provided $inst \in I$. We set $h_\sigma(inst) := inst_i$ if $inst$ is a first instruction on the path between $\bar{q}_{i-1}$ and $\bar{q}_i$ for some $i \in [1..n]$. In all other cases, we delete the instruction, $h_\sigma(inst) := \varepsilon$. Then, if $R_0 := P$ is the original program, σ_j is the sequence that the oracle returns in iteration $j \in \mathbb{N}$ of the while loop, and w is a sequence of instructions in R_{j+1}, we define $h(w) := h_{\sigma_0}(\ldots h_{\sigma_j}(w))$. This latter function maps sequences of instructions in program R_{j+1} back to sequences of instructions in P.

We are ready to state our key lemma. Intuitively, if the oracle in Algorithm 1 returns $\sigma := \mathcal{O}(R)$ and $\sigma' := \mathcal{O}(R \oplus \sigma)$ then, necessarily, $h(\sigma') \neq h(\sigma)$.

Lemma 2. *Let $R_0 := P$ and $R_{i+1} := R_i \oplus \sigma_i$ for $\sigma_i := \mathcal{O}(R_i)$ as in Algorithm 1. If $\sigma_{j+1} \neq \varepsilon$ then $h(\sigma_{j+1}) \neq h(\sigma_i)$ for all $i \leq j$.*

We can now prove Algorithm 1 sound and complete for acyclic programs (Theorem 3). Lemma 2 and the assumption that the input program is acyclic ensure that if no goal state is found SC-reachable (Line 4), then Algorithm 1 eventually runs out of sequences σ to return (Line 7). If that is the case, $\mathcal{O}(R)$ returns ε in the last iteration of Algorithm 1. By the first oracle condition, we know that the SC- and TSO-reachable states of R are the same. Hence, no goal state is TSO-reachable in R and, by Lemma 1, no goal state is TSO-reachable in the input program P either. Otherwise, a goal state s is SC-reachable by some computation τ in R_j for some $j \in \mathbb{N}$ and, by Lemma 1, there is a TSO computation in P corresponding to τ that reaches s.

Theorem 3. *For acyclic programs, Algorithm 1 terminates. Moreover, it returns true on input P if and only if $Reach_{TSO}(P) \cap G \neq \emptyset$.*

To establish that Algorithm 1 is a semi-decision procedure for all programs, one can use an iterative bounded model checking approach. Bounded model checking unrolls the input program P up to a bound $k \in \mathbb{N}$ on the length of computations. Then Algorithm 1 is applied to the resulting programs P_k. If it finds a goal state TSO-reachable in P_k, this state corresponds to a TSO-reachable goal state in P. Otherwise, we increase k and try again. By Theorem 3, we know that Algorithm 1 is a decision procedure for each P_k. This implies that Algorithm 1 together with iterative bounded model checking yields a semi-decision procedure that terminates for all positive instances of TSO reachability. For negative instances of TSO reachability, however, the procedure is guaranteed to terminate only if the input program P is acyclic.

Theorem 4. *We have $G \cap Reach_{TSO}(P) \neq \emptyset$ if and only if, for large enough $k \in \mathbb{N}$, Algorithm 1 returns true on input P_k.*

4   A Robustness-Based Oracle

This section argues why robustness yields an oracle. Robustness [7,10,13,24] is a correctness criterion requiring that for each TSO computation of a program there is an SC computation that has the same data and control dependencies. Delays due to store buffering are still allowed, as long as they do not produce dependencies between instructions that SC computations forbid.

Dependencies between events are described in terms of the *happens-before* relation of a computation $\tau \in \mathcal{C}_{\mathrm{TSO}}(P)$. The happens-before relation is a union of the three relations that we define below: $\to_{hb} (\tau) := \to_{po} \cup \leftrightarrow \cup \to_{cf}$.

The *program order relation* $\to_{po}$ is the order in which threads issue their commands. Formally, it is the union of the program order relations for all threads: $\to_{po} := \bigcup_{t \in \mathrm{TID}} \to_{po}^{t}$. Let τ' be the subsequence of all non-flush events of thread t in τ. Then $\to_{po}^{t} := <_{\tau'}$.

The *equivalence relation* $\leftrightarrow$ links, in each thread, flush events and their matching store events: $(t, inst, a) \leftrightarrow (t, \mathtt{flush}, a)$.

The *conflict relation* $\to_{cf}$ orders accesses to the same address. Assume, on the one hand, that $\tau = \tau_1 \cdot \mathtt{store} \cdot \tau_2 \cdot \mathtt{load} \cdot \tau_3 \cdot \mathtt{flush} \cdot \tau_4$ such that $\mathtt{store} \leftrightarrow \mathtt{flush}$, events $\mathtt{store}$ and $\mathtt{load}$ access the same address a and come from thread t, and there is no other store event $\mathtt{store}' \in \tau_2$ such that $thread(\mathtt{store}') = t$ and $addr(\mathtt{store}') = a$. Then the load event $\mathtt{load}$ is an *early read* of the value buffered by the event $\mathtt{store}$ and $\mathtt{store} \to_{cf} \mathtt{load}$.

On the other hand, assume $\tau = \tau_1 \cdot \mathtt{e} \cdot \tau_2 \cdot \mathtt{e}' \cdot \tau_3$ such that $\mathtt{e}$ and $\mathtt{e}'$ are either load or flush events that access the same address a, neither $\mathtt{e}$ nor $\mathtt{e}'$ is an early read, and at least one of $\mathtt{e}$ or $\mathtt{e}'$ is a flush to a. If there is no other flush event $\mathtt{flush} \in \tau_2$ with $addr(\mathtt{flush}) = a$ then $\mathtt{e} \to_{cf} \mathtt{e}'$.

Figure 4 depicts the happens-before relation of computation τ_{wit}.

A program P is said to be *robust* against TSO if for each computation $\tau \in \mathcal{C}_{\mathrm{TSO}}(P)$ there exists a computation $\tau' \in \mathcal{C}_{\mathrm{SC}}(P)$ such that $\to_{hb} (\tau) = \to_{hb} (\tau')$. If a program P is robust, then it reaches the same set of final states under SC and under TSO:

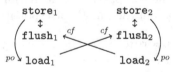

Fig. 4. The relation $\to_{hb} (\tau_{\mathrm{wit}})$

Lemma 5. *If P is robust against TSO, then $Reach_{SC}(P) = Reach_{TSO}(P)$.*

Our robustness-based oracle makes use of the following characterization of robustness from earlier work [10]: a program P is not robust against TSO iff $\mathcal{C}_{\mathrm{TSO}}(P)$ contains a computation, called *witness*, as in Figure 5.

Lemma 6 ([10]). *Program P is robust against TSO if and only if the set of TSO computations $\mathcal{C}_{TSO}(P)$ contains no witness.*

A witness τ delays stores of only one thread in P. The other threads adhere to the SC semantics. Conditions (W1) – (W4) in Figure 5 describe formally this restrictive behavior. Furthermore, condition (W5) implies that no computation $\tau' \in \mathcal{C}_{\mathrm{SC}}(P)$ can satisfy $\to_{hb} (\tau) = \to_{hb} (\tau')$.

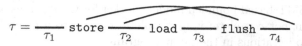

$$\tau = \underbrace{\qquad}_{\tau_1} \text{store} \underbrace{\qquad}_{\tau_2} \text{load} \underbrace{\qquad}_{\tau_3} \text{flush} \underbrace{\qquad}_{\tau_4}$$

Fig. 5. Witness τ with store $\leftrightarrow$ flush and thread $t := thread(\text{store}) = thread(\text{load})$. Witnesses satisfy the following constraints: (W1) Only thread t delays stores. (W2) Event flush is the first delayed store of t and load is the last event of t past which flush is delayed. So τ_2 contains neither flush events nor fences of t. (W3) Sequence τ_3 contains no events of thread t. (W4) Sequence τ_4 consists only of flush events e of thread t. All these events e satisfy $addr(\text{e}) \neq addr(\text{load})$. (W5) We require load $\rightarrow_{hb}^{+}$ e for all events e in $\tau_3 \cdot$ flush.

The computation τ_{wit} is a witness for the program in Figure 1. Indeed, in no SC computation of this program can both loads read the initial values of x and y. Relative to Figure 5, we have store $= \text{store}_1$, load $= \text{load}_1$, flush $= \text{flush}_1$, $\tau_3 = \text{store}_2 \cdot \text{flush}_2 \cdot \text{load}_2$, and $\tau_1 = \tau_2 = \tau_4 = \varepsilon$.

The *robustness-based oracle*, given input P, finds a witness τ as in Figure 5 and returns the sequence of instructions for the events in store $\cdot \tau_2 \cdot$ load that belong to thread t. If no witness exists, it returns ε. By Lemmas 5 and 6, this satisfies the oracle conditions from Section 3. Note that, given a robust program and the robustness-based oracle as inputs, Algorithm 1 returns within the first iteration of the while loop.

5 Experiments

We have implemented our lazy TSO reachability algorithm on top of the tool TRENCHER [1]. TRENCHER was initially developed for checking robustness and implements the algorithm for finding witness computations described in [10]. Our implementation reuses that algorithm as a robustness-based oracle. TRENCHER originally used SPIN [15] as back-end SC reachability checker. Currently, TRENCHER uses our own implementation of a simple SC model checker. This implementation exploits information about the instruction set for partial-order reduction and for live variable analysis. Moreover, it avoids having to compile the verifier executables (pan) as was the case for SPIN.

We have implemented Algorithm 1 with the following amendments. First, the extension does not delete the store instruction $inst_1$. This ensures the extended program has a superset of the TSO behaviors of the original program. Second, the extension only adds instructions along $\bar{q}_1, \ldots, \bar{q}_n$. The remaining instructions were added to ensure all behaviors of the original program exist in the extended program, once $inst_1$ is removed. The resulting algorithm is guaranteed to give correct results for cyclic programs. Of course, it cannot be guaranteed to terminate in general. Finally, our implementation explores extensions due to different instruction sequences in parallel, rather than sequentially.

We compare our prototype implementation against two other model checkers that support TSO semantics: MEMORAX [2] (revision 4f94ab6) and CBMC [14] (version 4.7). MEMORAX implements a sound and complete reachability checking procedure by reducing to coverability in a well-structured transition system.

CBMC is an SMT-based bounded model checker for C programs. Consequently, it is sound, but not complete: it is complete only up to a given bound on the number of loop iterations in the input program.

We describe three parameterized tests that we performed — more examples are available online [1]. The first one is Lamport's fast mutex [20] (see left-hand-side of Figure 6) where we varied the number of threads. The modified Dekker in Figure 7 is inspired by the examples of the fence-insertion tool MUSKETEER [4] and adds an "N-branching diamond" (see right-hand-side of Figure 7) to both program threads. Lastly, the program in Figure 8 has stores to address x on a length N loop in thread t_1: since t_1 expects to load the initial y value while t_2 expects to load 1 and then 0 from x, an execution that reaches the goal state goes through the length N loop twice.

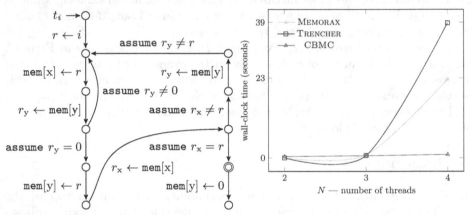

Fig. 6. The i-th Lamport mutex thread (left) and running times for N threads (right)

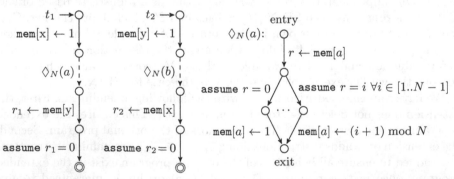

Fig. 7. Dekker's algorithm modified so that an "N-branching diamond" over distinct addresses $a, b \notin \{x, y\}$ is placed between the accesses to x and y. A final goal state is TSO-reachable if the first store is delayed past the last load in either t_1 or t_2.

5.1 Evaluation

We ran all tests on a QEMU @ 2.67GHz virtual machine (16 cores) with 8GB RAM running GNU/Linux. Our comparison does not include robust programs:

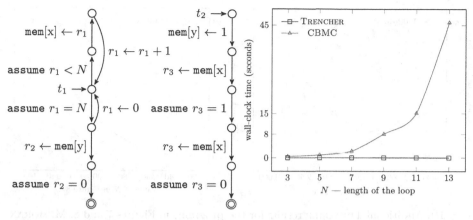

Fig. 8. A final goal state is TSO-reachable if t_1 goes through the (length N) loop two times: once to satisfy **assume** $r_3 = 1$ and the second time to satisfy **assume** $r_3 = 0$

TSO reachability for robust programs can be checked using SC reachability (if SC reachability returns false then one should account for verifying robustness). Moreover, CBMC implements an under-approximative method where the number of loop iterations is bounded. Our robust tests [1], however, contain unbounded loops.

The graph in Figure 6 shows that CBMC will be the fastest to verify Lamport's mutex when increasing the number of threads. This is the case since the smallest unwind bound suffices for CBMC to conclude reachability. For TRENCHER and MEMORAX, the considerable difference in verification time when increasing the number of threads is justified by the correlation between the program's data domain size and its thread count. Although not easily noticeable in Figure 6, MEMORAX's exponential scaling is better than TRENCHER's: TRENCHER is slightly faster than MEMORAX for $N \in \{2, 3\}$ but MEMORAX outperforms TRENCHER when $N = 4$. For both MEMORAX and TRENCHER our system runs out of memory when $N = 5$.

The graph in Figure 8 shows that our prototype is faster than CBMC for the second parameterized test. Indeed, with increasing N, an ever larger number of constraints need to be generated by CBMC. For TRENCHER, regardless of the value of N, it takes three SC reachability queries to conclude TSO reachability.

The graph in Figure 9 shows that, for the programs described by Figure 7, our prototype is faster than MEMORAX. It seems MEMORAX cannot cope well with the branching factor that the parameter N introduces.

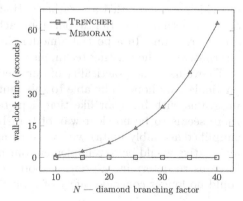

Fig. 9. Running times for Figure 7 tests

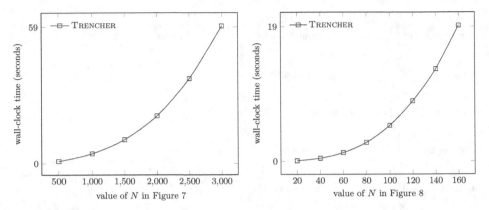

Fig. 10. Additional TRENCHER results for the programs in Figures 7 and 8. MEMORAX takes already 1 minute and 24 seconds for the program in Figure 7 and $N = 50$, while CBMC takes 8 minutes and 35 seconds for the program in Figure 8 and $N = 20$.

From Figures 8, 9, and 10 one can infer that TRENCHER scales better than MEMORAX and CBMC for the Figure 7 and Figure 8 examples, respectively.

5.2   Discussion

Because we find several witnesses in parallel, throughout the experiments our implementation required up to 2 iterations of the loop in Algorithm 1. In the case of robust programs, one iteration is always sufficient. This suggests that robustness violations are really the critical behaviors leading to TSO reachability.

The experiments indicate that, at least for some programs with a high branching factor, our implementation is faster than MEMORAX if a useful witness can be found within a small number of iterations of Algorithm 1. Similarly, our prototype is better than CBMC for programs which require a high unwinding bound to make visible TSO behavior reaching a goal state. Although the two programs by which we show this are rather artificial, we expect such characteristics to occur in actual code. Hence, our approach seems to be strong on an orthogonal set of programs. In a portfolio model checker, it could be used as a promising alternative to the existing techniques.

To evaluate the practicality of our method, more experiments are needed. In particular, we hope to be able to substantiate the above conjecture for concrete programs with behavior like that depicted in Figures 7 and 8. Unfortunately, there seems to be no clear way of translating (compiled) C programs into our simplified assembly syntax without substantial abstraction. To handle C code, an alternative would be to reimplement our method within CBMC. But this would force us to determine a-priori a good-enough unwinding bound. Moreover, we could no longer conclude safety of robust programs with unbounded loops.

Acknowledgements. The third author was granted by the Competence Center High Performance Computing and Visualization (CC-HPC) of the Fraunhofer Institute for Industrial Mathematics (ITWM). The work was partially supported by the PROCOPE project ROIS: *Robustness under Realistic Instruction Sets* and by the DFG project R2M2: *Robustness against Relaxed Memory Models*.

References

1. The Trencher tool, http://concurrency.informatik.uni-kl.de/trencher.html
2. Abdulla, P.A., Atig, M.F., Chen, Y.-F., Leonardsson, C., Rezine, A.: Counter-Example Guided Fence Insertion under TSO. In: Flanagan, C., König, B. (eds.) TACAS 2012. LNCS, vol. 7214, pp. 204–219. Springer, Heidelberg (2012)
3. Alglave, J.: A Shared Memory Poetics. PhD thesis, University Paris 7 (2010)
4. Alglave, J., Kroening, D., Nimal, V., Poetzl, D.: Don't Sit on the Fence. In: Biere, A., Bloem, R. (eds.) CAV 2014. LNCS, vol. 8559, pp. 508–524. Springer, Heidelberg (2014)
5. Alglave, J., Kroening, D., Nimal, V., Tautschnig, M.: Software Verification for Weak Memory via Program Transformation. In: Felleisen, M., Gardner, P. (eds.) ESOP 2013. LNCS, vol. 7792, pp. 512–532. Springer, Heidelberg (2013)
6. Alglave, J., Kroening, D., Tautschnig, M.: Partial Orders for Efficient BMC of Concurrent Software. CoRR, abs/1301.1629 (2013)
7. Alglave, J., Maranget, L.: Stability in Weak Memory Models. In: Gopalakrishnan, G., Qadeer, S. (eds.) CAV 2011. LNCS, vol. 6806, pp. 50–66. Springer, Heidelberg (2011)
8. Atig, M.F., Bouajjani, A., Burckhardt, S., Musuvathi, M.: On the Verification Problem for Weak Memory Models. In: POPL, pp. 7–18. ACM (2010)
9. Atig, M.F., Bouajjani, A., Parlato, G.: Getting Rid of Store-Buffers in TSO Analysis. In: Gopalakrishnan, G., Qadeer, S. (eds.) CAV 2011. LNCS, vol. 6806, pp. 99–115. Springer, Heidelberg (2011)
10. Bouajjani, A., Derevenetc, E., Meyer, R.: Checking and Enforcing Robustness against TSO. In: Felleisen, M., Gardner, P. (eds.) ESOP 2013. LNCS, vol. 7792, pp. 533–553. Springer, Heidelberg (2013)
11. Bouajjani, A., Meyer, R., Möhlmann, E.: Deciding Robustness against Total Store Ordering. In: Aceto, L., Henzinger, M., Sgall, J. (eds.) ICALP 2011, Part II. LNCS, vol. 6756, pp. 428–440. Springer, Heidelberg (2011)
12. Burckhardt, S., Musuvathi, M.: Effective Program Verification for Relaxed Memory Models. In: Gupta, A., Malik, S. (eds.) CAV 2008. LNCS, vol. 5123, pp. 107–120. Springer, Heidelberg (2008)
13. Burnim, J., Sen, K., Stergiou, C.: Sound and Complete Monitoring of Sequential Consistency for Relaxed Memory Models. In: Abdulla, P.A., Leino, K.R.M. (eds.) TACAS 2011. LNCS, vol. 6605, pp. 11–25. Springer, Heidelberg (2011)
14. Clarke, E., Kroning, D., Lerda, F.: A Tool for Checking ANSI-C Programs. In: Jensen, K., Podelski, A. (eds.) TACAS 2004. LNCS, vol. 2988, pp. 168–176. Springer, Heidelberg (2004)
15. Holzmann, G.J.: The Model Checker SPIN. IEEE Tr. Sof. Eng. 23, 279–295 (1997)
16. Kozen, D.: Lower Bounds for Natural Proof Systems. In: FOCS, pp. 254–266. IEEE Computer Society Press (1977)
17. Kuperstein, M., Vechev, M., Yahav, E.: Partial-Coherence Abstractions for Relaxed Memory Models. In: PLDI, pp. 187–198. ACM (2011)

18. Kuperstein, M., Vechev, M.T., Yahav, E.: Automatic Inference of Memory Fences. ACM SIGACT News 43(2), 108–123 (2012)
19. Lamport, L.: How to Make a Multiprocessor Computer that Correctly Executes Multiprocess Programs. IEEE Tr. on Com. 28(9), 690–691 (1979)
20. Lamport, L.: A Fast Mutual Exclusion Algorithm. ACM Tr. Com. Sys. 5(1) (1987)
21. Linden, A., Wolper, P.: An Automata-Based Symbolic Approach for Verifying Programs on Relaxed Memory Models. In: van de Pol, J., Weber, M. (eds.) Model Checking Software. LNCS, vol. 6349, pp. 212–226. Springer, Heidelberg (2010)
22. Linden, A., Wolper, P.: A Verification-based Approach to Memory Fence Insertion in Relaxed Memory Systems. In: Groce, A., Musuvathi, M. (eds.) SPIN Workshops 2011. LNCS, vol. 6823, pp. 144–160. Springer, Heidelberg (2011)
23. Owens, S., Sarkar, S., Sewell, P.: A Better x86 Memory Model: x86-TSO (extended version). Technical Report CL-TR-745, University of Cambridge (2009)
24. Shasha, D., Snir, M.: Efficient and Correct Execution of Parallel Programs that Share Memory. ACM Tr. on Prog. Lang. and Sys. 10(2), 282–312 (1988)

A Variability-Based Approach to Reusable and Efficient Model Transformations

Daniel Strüber[1], Julia Rubin[2], Marsha Chechik[3], and Gabriele Taentzer[1]

[1] Philipps-Universität Marburg, Germany
[2] Massachusetts Institute of Technology, USA
[3] University of Toronto, Canada
{strueber,taentzer}@mathematik.uni-marburg.de,
mjulia@csail.mit.edu, chechik@cs.toronto.edu

Abstract. Large model transformation systems often contain transformation rules that are substantially similar to each other, causing performance bottlenecks for systems in which rules are applied nondeterministically, as long as one of them is applicable. We tackle this problem by introducing *variability-based graph transformations*. We formally define variability-based rules and contribute a novel match-finding algorithm for applying them. We prove correctness of our approach by showing its equivalence to the classic one of applying the rules individually, and demonstrate the achieved performance speed-up on a realistic transformation scenario.

1 Introduction

Model-driven development emerged as a means to combat complexity of large-scale software development through the use of abstraction and refinement. Model-to-model and model-to-code transformations are key enablers of this development paradigm. While there have been many advances in understanding the formal properties of model transformations and devising their development environments, research on maintainability is still in preliminary stages [1]. Large model transformation systems often contain transformation rules that are substantially similar to each other. The most frequently applied mechanism for creating such rules is copying and modifying existing variants. This presents a maintainability obstacle (e.g., all related rules must be updated when a bug is found). The maintainability concern is often combined with a performance concern: In model-driven architecture [2], models go through a series of transformations such as optimizations and code generation, each introducing computational effort.

Inspired by product line engineering approaches [3, 4], a number of existing works, e.g., [5–7] tackle the reuse problem by introducing variability in model transformation rules. These works focus on representing a set of similar rules in a compact manner, providing the user with the ability to later *configure* the rules and produce specific variants. Rule variants are then matched and applied individually, using the classic approach. Since the number of desired configurations of each rule depends on the transformation input which may not be known upfront, the number of configured variants might be high. Thus, even though these works address the maintainability concern by providing a more compact representation of rule sets, they do not offer any performance-related benefits: all variants of a rule must still be considered by the transformation engine.

© Springer-Verlag Berlin Heidelberg 2015
A. Egyed and I. Schaefer (Eds.): FASE 2015, LNCS 9033, pp. 283–298, 2015.
DOI: 10.1007/978-3-662-46675-9_19

In this paper, we instead propose to augment the transformation engine itself by making it *variability-based*. We handle a scenario where *all* transformation rules need to be considered as long as one of them is applicable. Such an approach is useful in model refactoring suites or translators transforming models between a specific source and target languages. We introduce a novel algorithm for resolving variability *automatically* during the rule matching process, i.e., determination of application sites in the input model. Our central idea is to find matches for the common parts of all rule variants first and then to use them as starting points for the matching of the variable parts. We show that the transformation output produced by our algorithm is equivalent to the one produced when configuring and matching the rules individually, while our approach offers a substantial improvement in performance.

We present our approach to variability-based transformation using graph transformations [8], and, specifically, make the following contributions: (1) a formalization of variability-based rules, investigating their syntax and application semantics on the basis of graph transformation and proving their equivalence to the application of the corresponding classic rules; (2) a novel match-finding algorithm achieving a performance gain when compared to matching the rules individually; (3) an implementation of variability-based model transformation on top of Henshin, a rule-based model transformation language and tool; (4) an evaluation based on a real-life model transformation system that gives evidence of that performance gain.

The remainder of this paper is structured as follows: We introduce a motivating scenario in Sec. 2. In Sec. 3, we give the necessary background and, in Sec. 4, formally define the concept of variability-based graph transformation. We describe the algorithm for directly applying variability-based transformations in Sec. 5 and its implementation in Henshin in Sec. 6. Is effectiveness for model transformations when compared to manipulating a corresponding set of classic model transformation rules is evaluated in Sec. 7. In Sec. 8, we compare our approach with related work. We conclude in Sec. 9 with the summary and discussion of possible future directions.

2   Motivating Example

In this section, we give an example of variability-based transformation rules and their application. Our example is inspired by a set of real-life rules for optimizing and simplifying first-order logic expressions [9], aimed to improve performance of engines that process the expressions, e.g., theorem provers or SAT solvers.

Fig. 1 shows four transformation rules that simplify first-order logic formulas by removing redundant *not* symbols and thus reducing the "depth" of a formula. We present the rules in an integrated form, with the left- and right-hand sides of the transformation being represented in one graph. The elements of this graph have three kinds of labels: *delete*, *preserve*, and *create*. Elements labeled with *delete* and *preserve* are matched to an input model. The former are removed while the latter are kept in the output. Elements labeled with *create* just specify additions to the output.

For the example in Fig. 1, **Rule A** removes a $\neg\forall\neg$ segment of a formula and transforms it into an $\exists$ segment. This is done by removing nodes #2, #4 and their corresponding edges, replacing the quantifier of node #3 to be "exists" (node #7) rather than "forall" (node #8), and connecting the modified quantifier to the enclosing and the

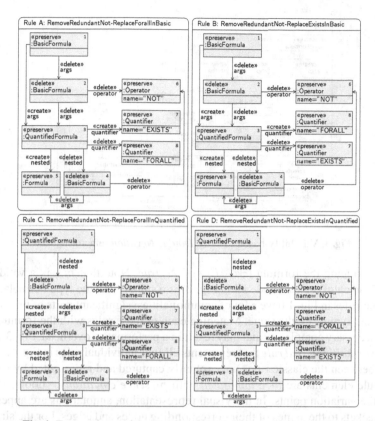

Fig. 1. Four variants of the *Remove Double Negation* refactoring rules

enclosed formulas – nodes #1 and #5, respectively. Similarly, Rule B removes a ¬∃¬ segment and transforms it into a ∀ segment. Rules C and D differ from A and B in the type and adjacent edges of the topmost enclosing formula (element #1): basic vs. quantified. A BasicFormula has an operator and a set of argument formulas, whereas a QuantifiedFormula has a quantifier and nests exactly one other formula. Note that there exists a third kind of formula, PredicateFormula, that encloses no other formulas.

Fig. 2 shows a first-order logic for-mula $\phi = (\neg\forall x \cdot \neg F(x)) \wedge true$ that can be simplified using one of these rules, namely, Rule A. The formula is also represented as a graph, with formula-specific elements depicted on the left-hand side of the figure. The right-hand side presents a library of "generic" reusable first-order logic operators. Elements #1-#5, #9, #11, #10 match with the corresponding elements #1-#8 of Rule A. We call this assignment a match m_A. Finding m_A triggers the application of

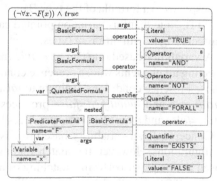

Fig. 2. Example first-order logic formula ϕ

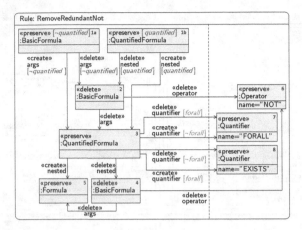

Fig. 3. Variability-based *Remove Double Negation* refactoring rule

Rule A, producing the formula $(\exists x \cdot F(x)) \wedge true$. Note that m_A is a valid match because PredicateFormula (node #5 in Fig. 2) is a sub-type of the type Formula.

The four rules in Fig. 1 have a lot of commonalities: significant parts of their internal structure and typing are the same. Matching each of these rules with the formula introduces unnecessary complexity and may result in a performance overhead. Fig. 3 shows a compact *variability-based rule* that represents all four individual rules in Fig. 1. The differences between the classic rules are explicitly captured and represented by *variation points*. Rule elements are then *annotated* with *presence conditions* – boolean formulas over the variation points. In the visual representation, annotations are appended in square brackets to the names of their corresponding nodes and edges. For the simplicity of presentation, we omit the presence condition *true*, e.g., for nodes #2-#8.

In our example, there are two variation points: (1) The *forall* variation point controls the direction of the quantifier inversion. When set to *true*, it corresponds to the $\neg\forall\neg$ to $\exists$ inversion, as in rules A and C; when set to *false*, it corresponds to the $\neg\exists\neg$ to $\forall$ inversion, as in B and D. (2) The *quantified* variation point controls the enclosing formula and its adjacent edges. When set to *true*, it corresponds to a formula of the type QuantifiedFormula with outgoing nested edges, as in C and D; when set to *false*, it corresponds to a formula of the type BasicFormula with outgoing args edges, as in rules A and B. Note that this variation pointed cannot be captured using node sub-typing, as it affects edges with different types.

A variability-based rule can be *configured* by setting variation point values and then selecting all elements whose presence conditions evaluate to *true* while removing those whose presence conditions evaluate to *false*. In our example, configuring the rule with *forall=true* and *quantified=false* produces Rule A in Fig. 1 while the configuration *forall=false* and *quantified=true* produces Rule D.

Conceptually, a variability-based rule is equivalent to a set of rules for all its valid configurations. However, the match-finding algorithm for a variability-based rule proposed in this paper performs matching of all its valid configurations at once, thus positively affecting both the maintainability and the performance of the transformation system. The algorithm *automatically* detects a configuration that induces a valid match using a two-step process. In the first step, it matches the *base rule* – the portion of the rule annotated with *true* and representing common parts of all individual rules. For the example in Figs. 3 and 2, this results in exactly one match, m_{base}, assigning elements #2, #6, #3, #8, #7, #4, #5 to #2, #9, #3, #11, #10, #4, #5 and connecting edges accordingly. In the second step, to match the variable parts the algorithm enumerates the valid configurations (in our example, Rules A to D) and tries to match them using m_{base}. This yields exactly one match for Rule A: m_A. The result of match-finding is m_A paired with the configuration *forall=true* and *quantified=false* that enabled this match.

3 Background: Algebraic Graph Transformation

We present our fundamental approach to variability-based transformation using graph transformation [8]. Graphs can be used to represent the underlying structure of visual models, and their conformance to a metamodel can be formally represented by typed attributed graphs mapped to type graphs. For simplicity, our treatment here uses basic graphs without types, attributes, and constraints, but our implementation and evaluation use the full power of typed attributed graphs, with inheritance, etc. since the concept of variability-basedness is orthogonal to these features. A *directed multi-graph*, simply called a *graph* in the following, comprises a set of nodes and a set of edges connecting these nodes. Structure-compatible mappings between graphs can be expressed in terms of *graph morphisms* which are compatible to source and target functions.

Definition 1 (Graph). *A graph $G = (G_N, G_E, src_G, trg_G)$ consists of a set G_N of nodes, a set G_E of edges, and source and target functions, $src_G, trg_G : G_E \to G_N$.*

Definition 2 (Total (Partial) graph morphism). *Given two graphs G and H, a pair of total (partial) functions (f_N, f_E) with $f_N : G_N \to H_N$ and $f_E : G_E \to H_E$ forms a total (partial) graph morphism $f : G \to H$, a.k.a. morphism, if it fulfills the following properties: (1) $f_N \circ src_G = src_H \circ f_E$ and (2) $f_N \circ trg_G = trg_H \circ f_E$. If both functions f_N and f_E are injective, f is called* injective. *If both functions f_N and f_E are inclusions, f is called* inclusion.

In the following, we recall the main definitions of the algebraic approach to graph transformation called the *gluing approach*. In this rule-based approach, graph elements occurring in the left and right-hand sides of a rule, i.e., in an *interface graph*, are used to glue new elements to already existing ones.

Definition 3 (Rule). *A (production) rule $p = L \xleftarrow{l} I \xrightarrow{r} R$ consists of graphs L, I and R, called* left-hand side, interface graph *and* right-hand side, *respectively, and two injective graph morphisms, l and r.*

A graph rule is applied along a match m of its left-hand side to a given graph G. The application of a graph rule consists of two steps: First, all graph elements in $m(L-l(I))$ are deleted. Nodes to be deleted may have adjacent edges which have not been matched, so the rule application may produce dangling edges. Therefore, all matches m have to satisfy the *gluing condition*: If a node $n \in m(L)$ is to be deleted by the rule application, it has to delete all adjacent edges as well. Afterwards, unique copies of $R - r(I)$ are added. This behavior can be characterized by a double-pushout [8]. Given a rule and a match, the resulting rule application is unique [8].

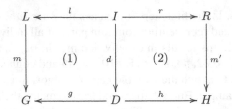

Fig. 4. Rule application by a double pushout (DPO)

Definition 4 (Rule application). *Let a rule* $p = L \xleftarrow{l} I \xrightarrow{r} R$ *and a graph G with a total graph morphism* $m : L \to G$ *be given. A* rule application *from G to a graph H, written* $G \Rightarrow_{p,m} H$, *is given by the diagram in Fig. 4 where (1) and (2) are pushouts. We refer to G, m and H as a* start graph, *a* match, *and a* result graph, *respectively.*

For example, the upper part of Fig. 2 shows a typed attributed graph which can be transformed by applying Rule A from Fig. 1. The rule match w.r.t. nodes has been described in Sec. 2. In addition, the match can be extended to edges. By rule application, nodes #2 and #4 are deleted, together with their adjacent edges. The edge between nodes #3 and #10 is also deleted. As no dangling edges are left behind, the gluing condition is satisfied. Edges between #3 and #9, #1 and #3, as well as between #3 and #4 are created yielding the graph structure for the formula $\phi' = (\exists x \cdot F(x)) \wedge true$.

4   Variability-Based Graph Transformation

In this section, we introduce variability-based graphs and transformation rules and show how to apply them. We provide proofs to all lemmas, propositions, and theorems in this section in an accompanying technical report [10].

4.1   Variability-Based Graphs and Rules

We denote variability using *presence conditions* – propositional expressions over a set of independent *variation points*. The set of these, called a *language of presence conditions*, is fixed for the set of rules and not changed by transformation steps.

Definition 5 (Language of presence conditions). *Given a set of variation points V, $\mathcal{L}_V$ is the set of all propositional expressions over V, called* presence conditions. *A total function cfg* $: V \to \{true, false\}$ *is a variability configuration. cfg satisfies a presence condition pc if pc evaluates to true when each variable v in pc is substituted by cfg(v). A presence condition is valid if there is a variability configuration satisfying it. A presence condition X is stronger than Y iff X $\implies$ Y.*

In the example in Sec. 2, $V = \{forall, quantified\}$. *true*, ¬*quantified*, and *forall* ∧ *quantified* are valid presence conditions; *forall* ∧ ¬*forall* is not valid.

Definition 6 (Variability-based graph). *Given a language of presence conditions $\mathcal{L}_V$, a variability-based graph $\hat{G}$ over $\mathcal{L}_V$ is a graph $G = (G_N, G_E, src_G, trg_G)$ and a pair of functions (pc_{G_N}, pc_{G_E}) with $pc_{G_N} : G_N \to \mathcal{L}_V$ and $pc_{G_E} : G_E \to \mathcal{L}_V$ such*

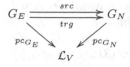

Fig. 5. Variability-based graph

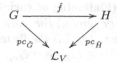

Fig. 6. Variability-based graph morphism

that (1) $\forall e \in G_E \cdot (pc_{G_E}(e) \implies pc_{G_N}(src_G(e))$ *and (2)* $\forall e \in G_E \cdot (pc_{G_E}(e) \implies pc_{G_N}(trg_G(e)))$ *(see Fig. 5). For brevity, we conflate* pc_{G_N} *and* pc_{G_E} *into a single function* $pc_G : (G_N \cup G_E) \to \mathcal{L}_V$ *assuming that* $G_N \cap G_E = \emptyset$.

This definition ensures that the presence condition of each edge is stronger than or equal to the presence conditions of both its source and target nodes. Note that pc_{G_N} and pc_{G_E} are total functions, i.e., all graph elements are annotated with presence conditions. Elements which are always present are annotated with *true*. Thus, any graph G without variability can be considered variability-based by defining $\forall x \in G \cdot pc_G(x) := true$.

For example, the left-hand side of the variability-based rule in Fig. 3, i.e., all preserved or deleted graph elements, forms a variability-based graph. All graph elements without annotation are mapped to the presence condition *true*, while nodes #1a and #1b and the adjacent edges as well as edges outgoing from node #3 are mapped to the depicted presence conditions.

In the following, we ensure that morphisms and rules over variability-based graphs preserve existing presence conditions.

Definition 7 (Variability-based graph morphism). *Given two variability-based graphs* $\hat{G}$ *and* $\hat{H}$ *over* $\mathcal{L}_V$ *as well as a graph morphism* $\hat{f} : G \to H$, $\hat{f}$ *is a variability-based graph morphism if* $pc_H \circ \hat{f} = pc_G$ *(see Fig. 6).*

Lemma 1 (Category of variability-based graphs). *Given a fixed* $\mathcal{L}_V$, *variability-based graphs and graph morphisms over* $\mathcal{L}_V$ *form a category.*

Definition 8 (Variability-based rule). *Given* $\mathcal{L}_V$, *a variability-based rule* $\hat{p} = \hat{L} \xleftarrow{\hat{l}} \hat{I} \xrightarrow{\hat{r}} \hat{R}$ *over* $\mathcal{L}_V$ *consists of a span of two variability-based graph morphisms* $\hat{l}$ *and* $\hat{r}$ *over* $\mathcal{L}_V$. *The underlying rule of* $\hat{p}$ *is* $p = (L \xleftarrow{l} I \xrightarrow{r} R)$.

For example, Fig. 3 shows a variability-based rule where all preserved graph elements do not change their presence conditions.

4.2 Application of Variability-Based Rules

We now show how to apply variability-based rules: (1) either by flattening them to a set of classic rules and applying a maximal among them in the classic way, or (2) directly, using a suitable variability configuration to identify the corresponding match. We then prove the equivalence of these two approaches.

Variability-Based Transformation through Flattening. We begin by showing how a variability-based rule can be *flattened*, i.e., represented by a set of classic rules.

Definition 9 (Flattening of variability-based graph). *Let a variability-based graph $\hat{G}$ over $\mathcal{L}_V$ be given. For each valid presence condition $c \in \mathcal{L}_V$, $G_c = (G_{c_N}, G_{c_E}, src_c, trg_c)$ is the* flattened graph *iff (1) $\forall n \in G_N \cdot n \in G_{c_N}$ if $c \implies pc_{G_N}(n)$; (2) $\forall e \in G_E \cdot e \in G_{c_E}$ if $c \implies pc_{G_E}(e)$; and (3) $src_c = src_G|_{G_{c_E}}$ and $trg_c = trg_G|_{G_{c_E}}$. Flat($\hat{G}$) is the set of all flattened graphs: $\{G_c \mid c \in \mathcal{L}_V \wedge c$ is valid$\}$.*

That is, a flattened graph G_c for presence condition c consists of those elements of $\mathcal{L}_V$ which are annotated by presence conditions implied by c. Note that different conditions can yield the same flattened graphs if the same set of used presence conditions is implied. The set of flattened graphs does not contain graphs for presence conditions equal to *false* since no variability configurations satisfy it.

For example, flattening the left-hand side $\hat{L}$ of the rule in Fig. 3 yields a set of graphs containing the left-hand sides $L_{forall \wedge quantified}$, $L_{\neg forall \wedge quantified}$, $L_{forall \wedge \neg quantified}$ and $L_{\neg forall \wedge quantifed}$ of all the rules in Fig. 1 as well as the intersection of all these – the base left-hand side L_{true}. In addition, *Flat($\hat{L}$)* contains four graphs where only one of the variation points is bound. For all other valid presence conditions $pc \in \mathcal{L}_V$, L_{pc} is equal to one from this list.

Lemma 2 (Smallest graph in flattening). *G_{true} is the smallest subgraph of G in Flat($\hat{G}$).*

The flattening of graphs can be lifted to graph morphisms and rules straightforwardly, yielding the rules ordered by the implication of their presence conditions to ensure that application of larger rules, modeling more specific cases, is attempted first.

Definition 10 (Flattening of variability-based graph morphism). *Let a variability-based graph morphism $\hat{f} : \hat{G} \to \hat{H}$ be given. Flattening of $\hat{f}$ is Flat($\hat{f}$) = $\{f_c : G_c \to H_c \mid c \in \mathcal{L}_V \wedge c$ is valid$\}$ with $G_c \in$ Flat($\hat{G}$), $H_c \in$ Flat($\hat{H}$) and $f_c = f|_{G_c}$.*

Definition 11 (Flattening of variability-based rule). *Given a variability-based rule $\hat{p} = \hat{L} \xleftarrow{l} \hat{I} \xrightarrow{r} \hat{R}$ over $\mathcal{L}_V$, we can apply the flattening of morphisms twice: Flat($\hat{p}$) = $(\{p_c : L_c \xleftarrow{l_c} I_c \xrightarrow{r_c} R_c \mid c \in \mathcal{L}_V \wedge c$ is valid$\}, \leq)$ with $l_c : I_c \to L_c \in$ Flat($\hat{l}$), $r_c : I_c \to R_c \in$ Flat($\hat{r}$). For the resulting rule set, a partial order between rules is defined through implication between their presence conditions: $p_{c_1} \leq p_{c_2}$ iff $(c_2 \implies c_1)$. Rule $p_{true} \in$ Flat($\hat{p}$) is also called* base rule.

For example, flattening the rule in Fig. 3 yields a set containing the four rules shown in Fig. 1 as well as their common maximal sub-rule (being the base rule) – the rule in Fig. 3 with only elements annotated by *true*.

The base rule is smaller than all the other rules in the set w.r.t. the partial order $\leq$. All rules of Fig. 1 are incomparable to each other. The additional four rules are larger than the base rule but smaller than the rules in Fig. 1.

Definition 12 (Ordered rule set). *An ordered rule set $\mathcal{R} = (\mathcal{R}_{rules}, \leq)$ consists of a set $\mathcal{R}_{rules}$ of rules and a partial order $\leq$ over this set.*

Definition 13 (Application of an ordered rule set). *Given an ordered rule set $\mathcal{R}$ and a graph G, the application of $\mathcal{R}$ to G is the set of rule applications: Trans($\mathcal{R}, G$) =*

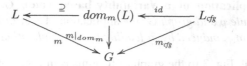

Fig. 7. A match induced by variability configuration

$\{G \Rightarrow_{p,m} H\}$ with $p \in \mathcal{R}_{rules}, p = (L \xleftarrow{l} I \xrightarrow{r} R)$ and a match $m : L \to G$ and $\forall p' \in \mathcal{R}_{rules}$ with $p' \geq p : \neg\exists$ a match $m' : L' \to G$ with $m'(L') \supset m(L)$.

For example, for the graph of formula ϕ in Fig. 2, there is exactly one match of base rule p_{true}. However, this rule is not maximal – Rule A = $p_{forall \wedge \neg quantified}$ in Fig. 1 can be matched as well. This match includes the match of the base rule, i.e., it is larger, and there is no larger one. For the graph structure of the formula $((\neg\forall x \cdot \neg F(x)) \wedge true) \wedge (\neg\forall x \cdot \neg F(x)) \wedge true)$, Rule A can be applied twice and there are no larger rules that match.

Direct Application of Variability-Based Rules. In the following, we consider the direct application of variability-based rules by finding a suitable variability-based match on-the-fly. The central task is to find a variability configuration such that the part of the left-hand side that can be matched is *locally maximal*, i.e., the match of a rule part cannot be extended by variable parts. If the resulting partial morphism of the left-hand side to graph G satisfies the gluing condition for the corresponding flat rule, the rule application can take place.

Definition 14 (Maximal partial morphism). *Given two graphs G and H, let $PM_{G,H}$ be the set of all partial graph morphisms from G to H. A partial morphism $m \in PM$ is maximal if $\forall m' \in PM \cdot \neg(dom_{m'}(G) \supset dom_m(G))$.*

Definition 15 (Variability-based match). *Given a variability-based rule $\hat{p}$ over $\mathcal{L}_V$ and a graph G, a variability-based match $\hat{m} = (m, cfg)$ over $\mathcal{L}_V$ consists of a maximal partial morphism $m \in PM_{L,G}$ and a variability configuration $cfg : V \to \{true, false\}$ such that $\forall x \in dom_m(L) \cdot cfg$ satisfies $pc_L(x)$. cfg induces a rule p_{cfg} s.t. cfg satisfies all presence conditions occurring in p_{cfg}. Moreover, reducing m to its domain, we get a morphism m_{cfg} which has to satisfy the gluing condition w.r.t. p_{cfg} (see Fig. 7).*

To apply the rule in Fig. 3 to the graph for formula ϕ in Fig. 2 by mapping to the same elements as Rule A in Fig.1, we choose the variability configurations $cfg(quantified) = false$ and $cfg(forall) = true$. Thus, p_{cfg} is Rule A. The resulting morphism $m_{cfg} = m_A$ satisfies the gluing condition, hence, it is a match for Rule A.

In the following, we show that the matched left-hand side of the variability-based rule is exactly the left-hand side of the chosen flat rule and there is no larger rule whose match would comprise the chosen one.

Proposition 1 (Variability-induced rule). *Given a variability-based rule $\hat{p}$ with a variability-based match $\hat{m} = (m, cfg)$ to graph G, $\hat{m}$ induces a rule p_{cfg} with the following properties: (1) $p_{cfg} \in Flat(\hat{p})$; (2) $L_{cfg} = dom_m(L)$, and (3) $\neg\exists p' \in Flat(\hat{p})$ s.t. $p_{cfg} \leq p'$ and cfg satisfies $pc_{L'}(x)$, $\forall x \in L'$.*

Definition 16 (Application of a variability-based rule). *Given a match $\hat{m}$ for variability-based rule $\hat{p}$ and graph G, the application of $\hat{p}$ at $\hat{m}$ is the classic rule application of p_{cfg} to m_{cfg} induced by $\hat{m}$ leading to rule application $G \Rightarrow_{p_{cfg}, m_{cfg}} H$.*

Applying the rule in Fig. 3 to the graph of formula ϕ in Fig. 2 at the variability-based match computed in the example after Def. 15 yields the graph structure of formula ϕ' described at the end of Sec. 3. Now, we show that the set of all applications of a variability-based rule $\hat{p}$ to a graph G is equal to the set of classic rule applications obtained from flattening $\hat{p}$ and applying these rules to G.

Theorem 1 (Equivalence of rule applications). *Given a variability-based rule $\hat{p}$ and a graph G, the following holds: $\{G \Rightarrow_{\hat{p}, \hat{m}} H | \hat{m} = (m, cfg) \text{ with } m \in PM_{L,G}\} = Trans(Flat(\hat{p}), G)$.*

5   Variability-Based Matching Algorithm

In this section, we describe an algorithm for implementing the concept of variability-based match (Def. 15). Our guiding intuition is to find matches for the base rule first, then expand these matches for the variable parts and finally filter the result to contain only maximal mappings.

Matching the base rule (see Def. 11) yields matches for the common parts that we store in a collection called *baseMatches*. Function FINDMATCHES in Fig. 8 extends *baseMatches* to find matches for the variable parts. It enumerates all consistent variability configurations, derives the corresponding rules and matches them classically. FINDMATCHES receives an input model, a variability-based rule, the *baseMatches* set, and two intermediate parameters: a data structure *bindings* that assigns each of the rule's presence conditions to one of the literals *true*, *false* or *unbound* (initially all entries are set to *unbound*) and a set to accumulate variability-based matches (initially empty). The function outputs the set of variability-based matches.

An execution of FINDMATCHES systematically binds all presence conditions, starting on Line 2 with an arbitrary one that we call pc_0. To enumerate all valid configurations, we first set pc_0 to *true* and then to *false* (Lines 3-4 and 5-6). In both calls to FINDMATCHESINNER, we first consider those presence conditions that were previously unbound and now are either contradicting or implied by the current bindings. On Lines 10 and 11, we compute them using a SAT solver, calling the results $bindings_{\downarrow}$ and $bindings_{\rightarrow}$ (for *false* elements and *true* elements, respectively). We update the bindings accordingly on Line 12. If all presence conditions are now bound, the problem becomes classic matching. We determine the classic rule to be matched by removing rule elements with a *false* presence condition on Line 14. The classic match-finder tries to bind the rule elements contained in the derived rule, but not in the base rule. The computed matches are translated into variability-based matches, being pairs of a classic match and the current variability configuration, on Lines 15-16. If some presence conditions have not been bound, we call FINDMATCHES again on Line 18. On Lines 7 and 19, we reset temporary bindings of variables to clean up before backtracking. To retain only the maximal matches, as demanded by Def. 15, we clean up after the outer FINDMATCHES call by removing all non-maximal entries from the result.

Input: *model*: Input model
Input: *rule*: Variability-annotated rule
Input: *baseMatches*: Classic matches of the base rule
Input: *bindings*: {Presence conditions used in *rule*} → {*true, false, unbound*}
Input: *matches*: Accumulated variability-based matches
Output: *matches*: Accumulated variability-based matches

```
 1: function FINDMATCHES(model, rule, baseMatches, bindings, matches)
 2:     pc₀ = bindings.select(unbound).get(0)
 3:     bindings.set(pc₀, true)
 4:     FINDMATCHESINNER(model, rule, baseMatches, bindings, matches)
 5:     bindings.set(pc₀, false)
 6:     FINDMATCHESINNER(model, rule, baseMatches, bindings, matches)
 7:     bindings.set(pc₀, unbound)
 8:     return matches
 9: function FINDMATCHESINNER(model, rule, baseMatches, bindings, matches)
10:     bindings↓ = bindings.select(unbound).select(p | bindings.contradicts(p))
11:     bindings→ = bindings.select(unbound).select(p | bindings.implies(p))
12:     bindings.setAll(bindings↓ → false, bindings→ → true)
13:     if bindings.select(unbound).isEmpty() then
14:         classicRule = rule.minus( {x ∈ rule | x.pc ∈ bindings.select(false)} )
15:         classicMatches = Matcher.matchClassically(model, classicRule, baseMatches)
16:         matches.addAll(createVariabilityBasedMatches(classicMatches))
17:     else
18:         FINDMATCHES(model, rule, baseMatches, bindings, matches)
19:     bindings.setAll(bindings↓ → unbound, bindings→ → unbound)
20:     return
```

Fig. 8. Pseudocode for recursive function FINDMATCHES

To exemplify our algorithm, we continue with the scenario at the end of Sec. 2. First, we create and match the base rule, comprising the elements annotated with *true*, by classic match-finding. The computed *baseMatches* set contains exactly match m_{base}. We arbitrarily select a presence condition ¬*qualified* and set it to *true* on Line 3, thus deriving *qualified* to be *false* on Lines 10-12. To bind the rest of the presence conditions, we call FINDMATCHES again on Line 18. We then select *forall* and set it to *true*, thus setting ¬*forall* to *false* and completing the binding of presence conditions. On Line 14, we remove all rule elements labelled ¬*forall* or ¬*qualified* to derive Rule A. Calling the classic match finder on this rule on Line 15 yields m_A. We pair this classic match with the current bindings to create a variability-based match. The remaining three configurations are determined analogously; however, they do not yield any additional matches.

Complexity of our algorithm is determined by the number of configurations which grows exponentially with the number of variation points. Of course, the configurations determine rules that in the classic approach would be matched individually. Thus, complexity of our algorithm is the same as that in classic matching. Yet, since we save matching effort by precomputing base matches and then extending them, we expect our algorithm to perform better than the classic one. We experimentally compare performance of our approach with classic in Sec. 7.

6 Implementation

Our implementation is based on the Henshin model transformation suite [11] which provides basic transformation functionalities for classic rules. Henshin consists of a transformation meta-model, a graphical editor for rule specification, and an interpreter engine for rule application. To *specify* variability-based rules, we extended the meta-model and editor of the Henshin language, allowing annotations of rule elements with presence conditions in the *properties* view. The user can highlight groups of rule elements sharing the same presence condition by assigning colors. To *apply* variability-based rules, we extended the Henshin interpreter engine, implementing the algorithm described in Sec. 5. We used FeatureExprLib [12], a tool which computes valid configurations of features using a SAT solver, for evaluating presence conditions. Finally, we cached the results of all evaluations in order to avoid repeating the same computations.

Our implementation also allows the user to restrict the set of valid configurations by defining relationships between variation points, such as *mutual exclusion* and *require*. These relationships can also be specified in terms of just presence conditions, e.g., setting a condition to $A \wedge \neg B$ if a variation point A excludes B.

7 Evaluation

In this section, we aim to answer two research questions: (RQ1) How compact are rule sets with variability-based rules compared to classic? (RQ2) What is the speedup of applying rules with variability instead of the corresponding classic ones?

Scenario. We investigated a transformation system comprised of 54 classic transformation rules. The rules constitute a translator from Object Constraint Language (OCL) expressions to nested graph constraints [9].

In this system, the main performance bottleneck, which we call *bottleneck rule subset* (BRS), is a subset of 36 rules that are applied nondeterministically, as long as one of them can be matched. The left-hand sides of the BRS rules have between 9 and 37 graph elements and share a considerable amount of commonalities. We applied the transformation system to 10 constraints described in [9] – an assortment of OCL constraints designed for a large coverage of applicable rules. The size of the input models, comprising individual constraints as well as the OCL standard library, containing operators and literals referenced by the constraints, ranges from 1832 to 1854 model elements.

Setup and Metrics. We manually refactored the 36 classic rules in BRS into 10 variability-based ones, relying on name similarities. We merged the original rules and annotated the result with presence conditions. To ensure correctness of the refactoring, we checked equality of the models yielded by both the original and the variability-based rule sets.

To investigate RQ1, we measured two metrics on both rule sets: *number of rules* and *number of elements per rule*, allowing us to quantify compactness. To investigate RQ2, we measured the *execution time* on both rule sets, allowing us to quantify performance. We determined the execution time on a Windows 7 workstation with a 3.40 GHz Intel i7-3770 processor and 8 GB of RAM.

Results of RQ1. In our example, variability-based rules help decrease the number of rules by 72% while increasing the number of elements per rule by 17%. Specifically, from 36 rules with the total of 1281 nodes and 1764 edges, we extracted 10 variability-based rules with 399 nodes and 589 edges and 2-3 variation points each. The ratio between common and variable parts increased with the size of the rule: the smallest rules had 10 common and 34 variable elements; the median – 69 common and 34 variable elements; the largest – 102 common and 60 variable elements.

Results of RQ2. Table 1 shows the result of applying the classic and the variability-based rule sets on each model, repeating the experiment 10 times.

We show the mean time *(mean)* and standard deviation *(sd)* for each rule set and model. For three of the input models, *ocl01* to *ocl03*, no performance difference was observable. For the remaining seven models, the execution time of transformations using rules with variability was on average 3.9 times faster than with the classic rules. To examine the cause of the performance difference more closely, we counted the number of successful and failed matching attempts (for a detailed account, please refer to [10]). In accordance with Theorem 1, the number of successful rule applications was always the same for both rule sets. In our approach, for *ocl04* to *ocl09* the number of failed match attempts is substantially lower, 1.72 times on average. We explain this observation by our reduced number of rules that increases the ratio of applicable to total ones. Overall, our experiments showed that in a scenario with a considerable amount of variability between rules, our approach allowed to create more compact rules and considerably improve the performance of their application.

Table 1. Running time

	time (sec) classic		time (sec) var.-based	
model	mean	sd	mean	sd
ocl01	**<.1**	<.1	**<.1**	<.1
ocl02	**<.1**	<.1	**<.1**	<.1
ocl03	**<.1**	<.1	**<.1**	<.1
ocl04	**56.7**	10.6	**14.2**	4.5
ocl05a	**65.1**	9.2	**13.0**	3.4
ocl05b	**96.7**	20.4	**19.7**	4.8
ocl06	**49.0**	13.4	**11.5**	3.9
ocl07	**389.4**	93.4	**78.4**	3.5
ocl08	**191.0**	11.7	**48.4**	12.7
ocl09	**11.6**	2.6	**5.0**	1.5
average	**85.9**	16.1	**19.0**	3.4

Threats to Validity and Limitations. The most important threat to validity is our choice of transformation rules and input models that may not be representative. We attempted to mitigate it by selecting a set of realistic transformation rules and input models already studied in the literature.

The performance gain achieved by our approach is affected by the amount of variability appearing within the rules. The maximum performance gain is observed for rule bases with large common parts which we match globally, paired with small variable parts which we match individually. Since the ratio of common and variable parts observed in our study may not be the same in all systems, the results might be different. Yet, matching common parts of similar rules only once is still expected to result in performance improvements. Furthermore, we are aware of the following caveats: (1) for very small examples, the overhead of variability processing might outweigh the reduced matching costs; and (2) if the left-hand side of the base rule does not represent a connected graph and the left-hand sides of the rule variants do, matching the base rule might become more expensive. We intend to investigate this issue in the future.

8   Related Work

The variability-based rules introduced in this paper are inspired by annotative representations of product lines [13–15] and augment representations proposed in earlier works.

While our focus is on the batch processing of *all* valid configurations of a variability-based rule, a number of related approaches, e.g., [5–7], target scenarios where a rule configuration is set externally to derive a desired classic rule. In such cases, [5, 6] report on a trade-off between better variability management and a performance overhead, the latter caused by the derivation of rules. In contrast, variability-based rules and matching improve both the compactness *and* the performance of a transformation system.

As for expressiveness, [5] and [7] are based on creating refinement rules for the variable parts and assigning them to one feature (or variation point). In turn, we support propositional presence conditions over variation points. In our evaluation example, we avoided several redundancies by assigning rule elements to a conjunction of two variation points. In this respect, [6] goes even further by allowing users to annotate a rule element with embedded C++ code, which, however, would produce an extremely large search space for variability-based matching.

Several model transformation languages implement *rule refinement* [1] – an important mechanism for reuse inside the same transformation system. In such languages, a base rule is refined by a set of sub-rules modifying it. Then, some approaches [16, 17] flatten the rules for application, i.e., compile them into simpler rules. The translational semantics in the approach proposed in RubyTL [18] is closest to ours – it applies the base rules first and then applies the refinement rules on the target model of the transformation. In contrast, our approach aims to efficiently find matches in the *source* model.

In [19], the authors propose an approach for transformation "lifting": given a classic model transformation, a transformation that operates on a family of related models is generated automatically. Instead, we do not focus on transforming a family of models but rather on creating and applying a family of related transformation rules in an efficient manner. [20] presents a reuse concept based on abstract transformation rules that can be instantiated for variants of similar meta-models. The abstract transformation rules are reverse engineered from existing transformation rules. In [21], the authors apply incremental graph pattern matching based on Rete networks to improve performance of transformation systems. However, they target the use case of successive application of the same set of rules on a modified input model and do not deal with variability inside the transformation system. These approaches are orthogonal to ours, and we intend to combine them with ours in the future.

9   Conclusion

In this paper, we proposed a novel approach to improve reuse and performance in model transformation systems. Aiming to handle a class of problems where rules with many commonalities are to be applied nondeterministically as long as one of them is applicable, we introduced variability not only to the rules but also to transformations using them. We proved correctness of our approach and contributed an efficient matching algorithm evaluated using a realistic model transformation system.

In this work, the refactoring of classic to variability-based rules was performed manually. As a future work, we intend to automate this step, possibly by applying techniques proposed by the product line engineering community for determining commonalities and variabilities in models. Moreover, while this work focused on rule application, other computationally expensive operations performed on rules, such as state-space exploration or critical pair analysis, might also benefit from explicit variability management. We intend to investigate this in the future. Providing an efficient solution for the matching of base rules represented as disconnected graphs is also subject for possible future work, as is to compare our approach against existing algorithms aiming at specific tasks in compilers and theorem provers. Finally, we aim to apply variability-based rules to distributed modeling scenarios with multiple variants of editing steps, e.g., synchronous and asynchronous ones [22].

Acknowledgements. We thank Thorsten Arendt and Frank Hermann for providing input for our evaluation.

References

1. Kusel, A., Schönböck, J., Wimmer, M., Kappel, G., Retschitzegger, W., Schwinger, W.: Reuse in Model-to-Model Transformation Languages: Are We There Yet? In: SoSyM, pp. 1–36 (2013)
2. Soley, R.: Model Driven Architecture. Object Management Group (2000)
3. Clements, P.C., Northrop, L.: Software Product Lines: Practices and Patterns. Addison-Wesley (2001)
4. Pohl, K., Boeckle, G., van der Linden, F.: Software Product Line Engineering: Foundations, Principles, and Techniques. Springer (2005)
5. Sijtema, M.: Introducing Bariability Rules in ATL for Managing Variability in MDE-based Product Lines. In: Proc. of MtATL 2010, pp. 39–49 (2010)
6. Kavimandan, A., Gokhale, A., Karsai, G., Gray, J.: Managing the Quality of Software Product Line Architectures through Reusable Model Transformations. In: Proc. of QoSA/ISARCS 2011, pp. 13–22. ACM (2011)
7. Trujillo, S., Zubizarreta, A., De Sosa, J., Mendialdua, X.: On the Refinement of Model-to-Text Transformations. In: Proc. of JISBD 2009, pp. 123–133 (2009)
8. Ehrig, H., Ehrig, K., Prange, U., Taentzer, G.: Fundamental Theory for Typed Attributed Graphs and Graph Transformation based on Adhesive HLR Categories. Fundamenta Informatica 74, 31–61 (2006)
9. Arendt, T., Habel, A., Radke, H., Taentzer, G.: From Core OCL Invariants to Nested Graph Constraints. In: Giese, H., König, B. (eds.) ICGT 2014. LNCS, vol. 8571, pp. 97–112. Springer, Heidelberg (2014)
10. Strüber, D., Rubin, J., Chechik, M., Taentzer, G.: A Variability-Based Approach to Reusable and Efficient Model Transformation - Technical Report,
https://www.uni-marburg.de/fb12/swt/research/publications

11. Arendt, T., Biermann, E., Jurack, S., Krause, C., Taentzer, G.: Henshin: Advanced Concepts and Tools for In-Place EMF Model Transformations. In: Petriu, D.C., Rouquette, N., Haugen, Ø. (eds.) MODELS 2010, Part I. LNCS, vol. 6394, pp. 121–135. Springer, Heidelberg (2010)
12. Kenner, A., Kästner, C., Haase, S., Leich, T.: TypeChef: Toward Type Checking #ifdef Variability in C. In: Proc. of FOSD 2010, pp. 25–32 (2010)
13. Czarnecki, K., Antkiewicz, M.: Mapping Features to Models: A Template Approach Based on Superimposed Variants. In: Glück, R., Lowry, M. (eds.) GPCE 2005. LNCS, vol. 3676, pp. 422–437. Springer, Heidelberg (2005)
14. Kästner, C., Apel, S.: Integrating Compositional and Annotative Approaches for Product Line Engineering. In: Proc. of the Wksp. on Modularization, Composition and Generative Techniques for PLE (McGPLE) at GPCE 2008, pp. 35–40 (2008)
15. Rubin, J., Chechik, M.: Combining related products into product lines. In: de Lara, J., Zisman, A. (eds.) Fundamental Approaches to Software Engineering. LNCS, vol. 7212, pp. 285–300. Springer, Heidelberg (2012)
16. Anjorin, A., Saller, K., Lochau, M., Schürr, A.: Modularizing Triple Graph Grammars Using Rule Refinement. In: Gnesi, S., Rensink, A. (eds.) FASE 2014 (ETAPS). LNCS, vol. 8411, pp. 340–354. Springer, Heidelberg (2014)
17. Jouault, F., Allilaire, F., Bézivin, J., Kurtev, I., Valduriez, P.: Atl: A qvt-like transformation language. In: Companion to the 21st ACM SIGPLAN Symposium on Object-Oriented Programming Systems, Languages, and Applications, pp. 719–720. ACM (2006)
18. Cuadrado, J.S., Molina, J.G.: A Model-Based Approach to Families of Embedded Domain-Specific Languages. IEEE TSE 35, 825–840 (2009)
19. Salay, R., Famelis, M., Rubin, J., Sandro, A.D., Chechik, M.: Lifting Model Transformations to Product Lines. In: Proc. of ICSE 2014, pp. 117–128 (2014)
20. Sánchez Cuadrado, J., Guerra, E., de Lara, J.: Reverse engineering of model transformations for reusability. In: Di Ruscio, D., Varró, D. (eds.) ICMT 2014. LNCS, vol. 8568, pp. 186–201. Springer, Heidelberg (2014)
21. Bergmann, G., Ráth, I., Szabó, T., Torrini, P., Varró, D.: Incremental pattern matching for the efficient computation of transitive closure. In: Ehrig, H., Engels, G., Kreowski, H.-J., Rozenberg, G. (eds.) ICGT 2012. LNCS, vol. 7562, pp. 386–400. Springer, Heidelberg (2012)
22. Strüber, D., Taentzer, G., Jurack, S., Schäfer, T.: Towards a distributed modeling process based on composite models. In: Cortellessa, V., Varró, D. (eds.) FASE 2013 (ETAPS 2013). LNCS, vol. 7793, pp. 6–20. Springer, Heidelberg (2013)

Applications

Exploring Scenario Exploration

Nuno Macedo, Alcino Cunha, and Tiago Guimarães

HASLab — High Assurance Software Laboratory
INESC TEC & Universidade do Minho, Braga, Portugal

Abstract. Model finders are very popular for exploring scenarios, helping users validate specifications by navigating through conforming model
instances. To be practical, the semantics of such scenario exploration operations should be formally defined and, ideally, controlled by the users,
so that they are able to quickly reach interesting scenarios.

This paper explores the landscape of scenario exploration operations,
by formalizing them with a relational model finder. Several scenario exploration operations provided by existing tools are formalized, and new
ones are proposed, namely to allow the user to easily explore very similar (or different) scenarios, by attaching preferences to model elements.
As a proof-of-concept, such operations were implemented in the popular
Alloy Analyzer, further increasing its usefulness for (user-guided) scenario
exploration.

1 Introduction

With the ever-growing adoption of model-driven engineering (MDE) practices
in software development, it becomes increasingly important to easily verify and
validate the evolving specifications. The first step of this "debugging" process
is typically *scenario exploration* [15], the generation of conforming model instances that provide quick feedback about the specifications and help to flag
problems at early stages of development. *Model finders*, tools whose goal is precisely to find models that conform to given constraints, play an essential role in
such tasks. Among these, Alloy [7] and its underlying model finder Kodkod [17],
with a lightweight approach to formal methods, an object-oriented flavor and
the ability to provide quick feedback through the generation of snapshots, have
proven to be well-suited to handle MDE tasks. This is patent in the number
of techniques that have been proposed to verify and validate with such tools
essential MDE artifacts, like model specifications [1,8,10,3] and model transformations [5,2]. Unfortunately, model finders like Alloy have limited usefulness in
scenario exploration, since they do not enable the user to control the criteria
through which returned instances are selected from among those rendered consistent. In fact, it is not even possible to formalize the order under which the
instances are enumerated, as this is typically imposed by the underlying opaque
solving procedure.

Consider, as an example, the OwnGrandpa Alloy module from [7], distributed
with the Alloy Analyzer and depicted in Fig. 1, designed to explore the popular song *"I'm My Own Grandpa"*. This module consists of Person elements

A. Egyed and I. Schaefer (Eds.): FASE 2015, LNCS 9033, pp. 301–315, 2015.
DOI: 10.1007/978-3-662-46675-9_20

```
1   abstract sig Person {
2     father  : lone Man,
3     mother  : lone Woman }
4   sig Man extends Person {
5     wife    : lone Woman }
6   sig Woman extends Person {
7     husband : lone Man }
8   fact {
9     no p:Person | p in p.^(mother+father)      // Biology
10    wife = ~husband                            // Terminology
11    no (wife+husband) & ^(mother+father)       // SocialConvention
12    Person in                                  // NoSolitary
13       Person.(mother+father+~mother+~father+wife+husband) }
14  run {} for exactly 2 Man, exactly 2 Woman
```

Fig. 1. The OwnGrandpa Alloy module

(called *atoms*, in Alloy) that are either Man or Woman, introduced by *signature* declarations (ll. 1–7). Each person may have another person with appropriate gender as father or mother, as well as a wife or husband. These relations are declared by *fields* within the signatures. An additional *fact* (ll. 8–13) imposes some restrictions on these relations: the mother and father fields must not be cyclic (**Biology**), wife and husband are each others inverse (**Terminology**), no one is married to an ancestor (**SocialConvention**) and there are no solitary persons (**NoSolitary**, not present in the original version but introduced to provide richer exploration scenarios). To validate this module and identify potential problems, the user is able to generate model instances that conform to it. The *run* command (l. 14) instructs the Analyzer to find instances with exactly 2 men and 2 women. Once an initial model is calculated, the user is able to iterate through others until there are no more valid instances left. Figure 2 presents a possible sequence of returned instances (this procedure is non-deterministic but the selected ones are representative of the result of multiple executions).

It is easy to grasp that these instances show little resemblance with one another. In fact, there is no clear order in which they are produced, which hinders the usefulness of the finder in the exploration of scenarios, since it is not predictable when problematic instances have not been generated. For instance, the user could be interested in exploring variations of the family tree m_1 (Fig. 2b), in which case instances similar to the one from Fig. 3a should be calculated. Ideally, the users should be able to go even further and customize the notion of "similar instance" for each particular context. This would allow them, for instance, to ask for models close to m_1 but prioritizing changes on marital relations, resulting instead in instances resembling the one at Fig. 3b, which quickly reveals a potential problem: this version of the OwnGrandpa module allows siblings to marry each other. Finding an instance that flags this problem using regular model findering would require an arbitrary, and possibly large, number of steps.

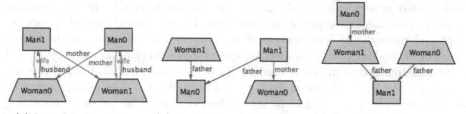

(a) Initial instance m_0.   (b) Succeeding instance m_1.   (c) Succeeding instance m_2.

Fig. 2. Regular model finding results

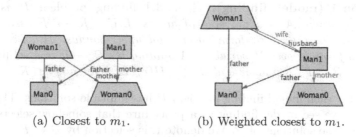

(a) Closest to m_1.   (b) Weighted closest to m_1.

Fig. 3. Target-oriented model finding results

This paper explores this landscape of scenario exploration operations and formalizes them over relational model finding problems. While previous research on controlled scenario exploration exists—particularly on the generation of minimal instances [9,15,6] and on allowing the user to ask for similar instances through the introduction of additional facts [15]—a systematic study of such operations is still lacking. During this exploration it also becomes clear that many interesting operations are not supported by any existing system. We advocate that a Kodkod extension with support for *weighted target-oriented model finding* provides a formalism that is sufficiently flexible to support many interesting scenario exploration operations, including those proposed in previous studies and user-parametrizable ones that allow the generation of the instances from Fig. 3. As a proof-of-concept, we instantiate and implement some of these operations in the Alloy Analyzer, further improving its capabilities as a scenario exploration tool.

Section 2 introduces the notion of weighted target-oriented model finding, essential to define interesting operations. Section 3 formalizes scenario exploration operations on top of it, which are then deployed in an extension to the Alloy Analyzer in Section 4. Section 5 compares our formalization with existing work, while Section 6 draws conclusions and points directions to future work.

2 Relational Model Finding

The model finding formalism followed in this paper is inspired by the relational model finder Kodkod [17]. While alternative formalizations could be followed, this one has proven to be simple and flexible enough to enable the formalization of interesting scenario exploration operations. In this context, model finders are deployed through the specification of *problems* $\mathcal{P}$, which establish the search space of the finder. A problem specifies a set of bounded relation variables $\mathcal{R}$, and solving it amounts to finding a binding $B : \mathcal{R} \rightarrow \mathcal{T}$ that assigns to each relation $r \in \mathcal{R}$ a tuple set $t \in \mathcal{T}$ drawn from a fixed universe $\mathcal{A}$. While relations may be of arbitrary arity (greater than 0), its binding $B(r)$ must be uniform, containing only tuples of the same arity. This arity is imposed by its bounds, which must themselves be uniform. Bindings are isomorphic to models by translating classes as unary relations (i.e., sets) and attributes and associations as binary relations.

Definition 1 (model finding). *A* model finding problem P *is a tuple* $\langle \mathcal{A}, L, U, \phi \rangle$ *where* $\mathcal{A}$ *is a universe of atoms,* $L, U : \mathcal{R} \rightarrow \mathcal{T}$ *assign to each relation variable* $r \in \mathcal{R}$ *uniform lower- and upper-bounds, with* $L(r) \subseteq U(r)$, *and* ϕ *is a formula over* $\mathcal{R}$ *variables. A binding* $B : \mathcal{R} \rightarrow \mathcal{T}$ *is a solution of* P, *denoted by* $B \models P$, *if* ϕ *holds and* $B(r) \subseteq U(r) \backslash L(r)$ *for any* $r \in \mathcal{R}$.

Typically, each model finding problem P has multiple solutions. Throughout this paper, we see model finding as a procedure that somehow selects a single model from the solutions of P. We denote this selection by $B \leftarrow P$.

In previous work [4] we extended model finding problems to a *target-oriented* version, that allowed a finer control over the range of solutions of a problem. Let $\Delta : (\mathcal{R} \rightarrow \mathcal{T}) \times (\mathcal{R} \rightarrow \mathcal{T}) \rightarrow \mathbb{N}_0$ be a distance function over two bindings defined as the symmetric difference between them, defined as

$$\Delta(B, B') = \sum_{r \in \mathcal{R}_B \cap \mathcal{R}_{B'}} |B(r) \ominus B'(r)|$$

where $\mathcal{R}_B$ denotes the set of relation variables bound by B. This is equivalent to measuring the graph-edit distance between two models. Equipped with this metric we can define model finding problems whose goal is to, besides producing consistent model instances, approximate, according to Δ, a given target.

Definition 2 (target-oriented model finding). *A* target-oriented model finding problem P_T *is a tuple* $\langle \mathcal{A}, L, U, T, \phi \rangle$ *where* $\langle \mathcal{A}, L, U, \phi \rangle$ *is a model finding problem* P *and* $T : \mathcal{R} \rightarrow \mathcal{T}$ *assigns targets to a set of relation variables, with* $L(r) \subseteq T(r) \subseteq U(r)$ *for any* $r \in \mathcal{R}_T$. *A binding* $B : \mathcal{R} \rightarrow \mathcal{T}$ *is a solution of* P_T, *denoted by* $B \models P_T$, *if* $B \models P$ *and, for any other solution* $B' \models P_T$:

$$\Delta(B, T) \leqslant \Delta(B', T)$$

If no targets are defined, this degenerates into a regular model finding problem.

Target-oriented problems do not have necessarily a single solution, but the set of acceptable solutions is in general much smaller than the equivalent target-free problem. Nonetheless, plain graph-edit distance is too rigid to allow the user to finely control the generation of solutions. Thus, in this paper we propose a new class of *weighted* model finding problems, where the user is able to assign different weights to each relation variable, and thus control modifications over their valuation. Given a weight function $w : \mathcal{R} \to \mathbb{N}_0$, let $\Delta_w : (\mathcal{R} \to \mathcal{T}) \times (\mathcal{R} \to \mathcal{T}) \to \mathbb{N}_0$ be defined as

$$\Delta_w(B, B') = \sum_{r \in \mathcal{R}_B \cap \mathcal{R}_{B'}} |w(r)(B(r) \ominus B'(r))|$$

Given such distance function, the model finder will try to minimize the overall weighted distance between the two bindings, and as a consequence prioritize modifications on relations with smaller weight.

Definition 3 (weighted target-oriented model finding). *A weighted target-oriented model finding problem P_w is a tuple $\langle \mathcal{A}, L, U, T, w, \phi \rangle$ where $\langle \mathcal{A}, L, U, \phi \rangle$ is a model finding problem P, $T : \mathcal{R} \to \mathcal{T}$ assigns targets to a set of relation variables, with $L(r) \subseteq T(r) \subseteq U(r)$ for any $r \in \mathcal{R}_T$ and $w : \mathcal{R} \to \mathbb{N}_0$ is a weight function with $\mathcal{R}_T \subseteq \mathcal{R}_w$. A binding $B : \mathcal{R} \to \mathcal{T}$ is a solution of P_w, denoted by $B \models P_w$, if $B \models P$ and, for any other solution $B' \models P$:*

$$\Delta_w(B, T) \leqslant \Delta_w(B', T)$$

Weighted problems may still have multiple solutions. If w is a constant function, such problems degenerate into regular target-oriented ones. We will denote such weight function by $\underline{1}$. If a relation has weight 0, changes on it do not count towards the update distance, meaning that these may change freely between the target and the solutions. If all relations have weight 0, all solutions will be at the same minimal distance 0 from the target, thus degenerating into a regular model finding problem.

3   Scenario Exploration Operations

Relational model finding problems provide the base over which we formalize scenario exploration operations. Two operations are typically supported: init : $\mathcal{S} \to \mathcal{P}$ creates an initial model finding problem from a specification $\mathsf{S} \in \mathcal{S}$ (for instance, an Alloy module), and next:$\mathcal{P} \times (\mathcal{R} \to \mathcal{T}) \to \mathcal{P}$, that given the previously produced instance, updates the problem to produce a succeeding solution. Each model finding problem P that results from these operations may have multiple solutions; a single one is typically drawn from them and presented to the user. This section presents various instantiations of these two operations.

For any specification S, the embedding $[\![\mathsf{S}]\!]$ derives an appropriate weighted target-oriented model finding problem $\langle \mathcal{A}_\mathsf{S}, L_\mathsf{S}, U_\mathsf{S}, \{\,\}, \underline{1}, \phi_\mathsf{S} \rangle$ (which is equivalent to a regular model finding problem $\langle \mathcal{A}_\mathsf{S}, L_\mathsf{S}, U_\mathsf{S}, \phi_\mathsf{S} \rangle$). The embedding of the module $\mathsf{OwnGrandpa}$ from Fig. 1, which will be used as a running example, results in the model finding problem presented in Fig. 4 for the scope provided in the run command, 2 men and 2 women (atom names are abbreviated for readability).

Although model finding problems act upon relation variables, sometimes it is useful to refer to the individual atoms of the universe, which requires the reification of the atoms into relations. For instance, for universe $\{\mathsf{M0}, \mathsf{M1}, \mathsf{W0}, \mathsf{W1}\}$, this would give rise to 4 new singleton unary relations with exact bounds:

```
{M0,M1,W0,W1}

Man      : ({M0,M1},{M0,M1})
Woman    : ({W0,W1},{W0,W1})
father   : ({},{(M0,M0),(M0,M1),(M1,M0),(M1,M1),
                (W0,M0),(W0,M1),(W1,M0),(W1,M1)})
mother   : ({},{(M0,W0),(M0,W1),(M1,W0),(M1,W1),
                (W0,W0),(W0,W1),(W1,W0),(W1,W1)})
wife     : ({},{(M0,W0),(M1,W0),(M0,W1),(M1,W1)})
husband  : ({},{(W0,M0),(W1,M0),(W0,M1),(W1,M1)})

all p:Man | lone p.wife && all p:Woman | lone p.husband
all p:Man+Woman | lone p.father && lone p.mother
all p:Man+Woman | !(p in p.^(mother+father))
wife = ~husband
no ((wife+husband) & ^(mother+father))
Man+Woman in (Man+Woman).(father+mother+~father+~mother+wife+husband)
```

Fig. 4. Kodkod embedding of the OwnGrandpa problem

```
M0 : ({M0},{M0})     W0 : ({W0},{W0})
M1 : ({M1},{M1})     W1 : ({W1},{W1})
```

Since these are bound exactly, they do not affect the performance of the solver. Throughout this section, every model finding problem is assumed to have the atoms from its universe $\mathcal{A}$ reified into relations in $\mathcal{R}$, which allow concrete B instances to be referred in its formula ϕ. Given an operator $\approx$ that compares tuple sets, formula $[B]_\approx$ compares the valuation of relation variables $\mathcal{R}$ with their binding in B. For instance, for model m_1 (Fig. 2b), this takes the shape:

```
M0 + M1            ≈ Man     && W0 + W1      ≈ Woman    &&
M1->M0 + W1->M0 ≈ father  && M1->W0      ≈ mother    &&
none->none         ≈ wife    && none->none ≈ husband
```

Relation **none** represents the empty set in Kodkod, and **none->none** the empty binary relation. Instantiating the operation with equality as $[B]_=$ results in a formula that holds iff the relations are assigned the exact same valuation as B.

3.1   Generation Operations

Regular generation. The most basic instantiation of the generation operation, offered by Kodkod and most model finders, simply defines a problem that returns every consistent instance, amounting to a regular model finding problem:

$$\text{init}(\text{S}) = \langle \mathcal{A}_\text{S}, L_\text{S}, U_\text{S}, \{\,\}, \underline{1}, \phi_\text{S} \rangle$$

That is, the regular embedding $[\![\text{S}]\!]$. Figure. 2a already presented a possible solution drawn from init(OwnGrandpa), but since the generation followed no criteria, any other model $B \models [\![\text{S}]\!]$ could have been returned instead.

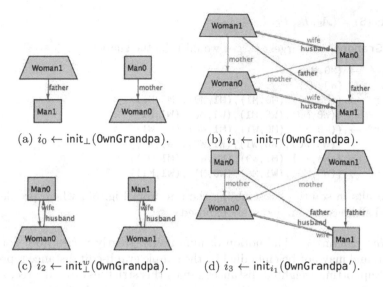

(a) $i_0 \leftarrow \text{init}_{\perp}(\text{OwnGrandpa})$.   (b) $i_1 \leftarrow \text{init}_{\top}(\text{OwnGrandpa})$.

(c) $i_2 \leftarrow \text{init}_{\perp}^{w}(\text{OwnGrandpa})$.   (d) $i_3 \leftarrow \text{init}_{i_1}(\text{OwnGrandpa}')$.

Fig. 5. Instantiations of the generation operation init

Minimal generation. Equipped with target-oriented problems, we are able to define more refined scenario exploration operations. For instance, we can define a version of init that always returns minimal solutions according to the Δ distance function, which is useful since, often, the problems of the specification are patent in even small examples. This may be achieved by trying to approximate the minimal model accepted by the problem's bounds:

$$\text{init}_{\perp}(S) = \langle \mathcal{A}_S, L_S, U_S, L_S, \underline{1}, \phi_S \rangle$$

Note that the target cannot simply be an empty model, as that could fall below the lower bounds of $[\![S]\!]$. Thus, the problem should instead try to approximate L_S. For instance, in OwnGrandpa, the smallest potential instance amounts to:

```
Man                           ↦ {M0,M1}
Woman                         ↦ {W0,W1}
father,mother,wife,husband    ↦ {}
```

Figure 5a shows a solution that results from applying $\text{init}_{\perp}$ to OwnGrandpa, which must relate some of its elements due to the NoSolitary constraint (without this constraint, there would be a single minimal solution, with the four persons unconnected). Since constraint Terminology forces wife and husband tuples to be paired, minimal generation will always prioritize parenthood relations.

Maximal generation. A dual instantiation of minimal generation, is that of the generation of maximal solutions according to Δ, which forces the binding to assign as many tuples as possible to the relations. This is useful because it allows the exploration of boundary scenarios. Likewise to minimal generation, the largest potential instance of $[\![S]\!]$ is represented by the problem's upper-bound:

$$\text{init}_\top(S) = \langle \mathcal{A}_S, L_S, U_S, U_S, \underline{1}, \phi_S \rangle$$

In `OwnGrandpa`, the largest target would take the shape:

```
Man      ↦ {M0,M1}
Woman    ↦ {W0,W1}
father   ↦ {(M0,M0),(M0,M1),(M1,M0),(M1,M1),
            (W0,M0),(W0,M1),(W1,M0),(W1,M1)}
mother   ↦ {(M0,W0),(M0,W1),(M1,W0),(M1,W1),
            (W0,W0),(W0,W1),(W1,W0),(W1,W1)}
wife     ↦ {(M0,W0),(M1,W0),(M0,W1),(M1,W1)}
husband  ↦ {(W0,M0),(W1,M0),(W0,M1),(W1,M1)}
```

This results in solutions resembling the one from Fig. 5b, where problems like married siblings are immediately exposed.

Weighted generation. The notion of minimality greatly varies from context to context, and may not be embodied by the simple graph-edit distance represented by Δ. Supporting weighted distances tames this strictness to a degree, allowing the user to customize the notion of minimal or maximal solution. This allows a controlled generation of boundary solutions, that can more easily trigger the detection of problems. Given a weight function w and support for weighted target-oriented model finding, this can be simply defined as:

$$\text{init}_\perp^w(S) = \langle \mathcal{A}_S, L_S, U_S, L_S, w, \phi_S \rangle$$
$$\text{init}_\top^w(S) = \langle \mathcal{A}_S, L_S, U_S, U_S, w, \phi_S \rangle$$

For instance, the order proposed in Section 1 for `OwnGrandpa`, that prioritizes the ancestry tree, could be embodied by the following weight function:

```
Man,Woman,father,mother ↦ 3
wife,husband            ↦ 1
```

Applying $\text{init}_\perp^w$ to `OwnGrandpa` using this weight function would only yield the solutions with persons connected by marriage rather than parenthood, as depicted in Fig. 5c, because a pair of tuples `wife`/`husband` weighs less than a single parenthood tuple; if instead parenthood relations were assigned weight 2, minimal solutions would combine both parenthood and marriage connections.

Generation from instance. Imagine that the developer found the problematic instance i_1 (Fig. 5b) and as a consequence modified the module to a `OwnGrandpa'` version by adding a constraint that supposedly forbids siblings from marrying each other. When returning to exploration, the developer could want to search for instances that resemble i_1, to make sure that no similar problems persist. Of course in this simple scenario an assertion could be defined to check that there are no marriages between siblings, but as the complexity of the properties increases, it may be simpler to explore the solutions around the problematic instance before defining assertions. This is not possible in regular model finding, but is straight-forward in target-oriented model finding, for a binding $B : \mathcal{R} \to \mathcal{T}$ representing a pre-existing model:

$$\text{init}_B(\mathsf{S}) = \langle \mathcal{A}_\mathsf{S}, L_\mathsf{S}, U_\mathsf{S}, B, \underline{1}, \phi_\mathsf{S} \rangle$$

If B is still a valid solution, it is guaranteed to be returned; otherwise the one closest to it will, allowing the user to assess whether the fix to the specification was successful. If OwnGrandpa' is well defined, then the instance from Fig. 5d will be returned, which is the solution closest to i_1 without married siblings. This scenario hints at the application of such operation in the context of model repair, restoring the consistency of inconsistent instances through minimal updates.

3.2   Iteration Operations

Regular iteration. The most basic iteration operation, as provided by Kodkod and most existing model finders, generates arbitrary fresh solutions, i.e., solutions that have not been previously returned. This can be defined as:

$$\text{next}(\langle \mathcal{A}, L, U, \_, \_, \phi \rangle, B_0) = \langle \mathcal{A}, L, U, \{\,\}, \underline{1}, \phi \wedge \neg\, [B_0]_= \rangle$$

Recall that $[B_0]_=$ is a formula that tests whether the relation variables have the valuation of B_0; negating it removes such instance from the search space. This basic instantiation of next returns arbitrary solutions, for instance the sequence already presented in Fig. 2.

Least-change iteration. Target-oriented model finding can greatly benefit iteration operations. The most evident instantiation is to always search for instances that are close to each other. This can be easily instantiated by setting the previous instance as the target of the problem for the succeeding solution:

$$\text{next}_\perp(\langle \mathcal{A}, L, U, \_, \_, \phi \rangle, B_0) = \langle \mathcal{A}, L, U, B_0, \underline{1}, \phi \wedge \neg\, [B_0]_= \rangle$$

Essentially, the target is now updated at each iteration to the current binding. Like the standard next operation, $\text{next}_\perp$ negates the current solution in ϕ, guaranteeing that the iteration will not loop between two close instances. Figures 6a and 6b exemplify this for OwnGrandpa, assuming m_1 was returned by the preceding generation problem.

Most-change iteration. In scenario exploration it is sometimes useful to iterate through solutions that greatly differ from each other, in order to explore the whole search space. Using target-oriented problems, this can be specified as:

$$\text{next}_\top(\langle \mathcal{A}, L, U, \_, \_, \phi \rangle, B_0) = \langle \mathcal{A}, L, U, \overline{B_0}, \underline{1}, \phi \wedge \neg\, [B_0]_= \rangle$$

Binding $\overline{B_0}$ represents the complement of B_0 in relation to the upper-bound of the problem, i.e., for any $r \in \mathcal{R}$, $\overline{B_0}(r) = U(r) \backslash B_0(r)$, which is the potential solution further away from B_0. A possible run for OwnGrandpa is depicted in Figs. 6c and 6d, assuming m_1 as the previous solution.

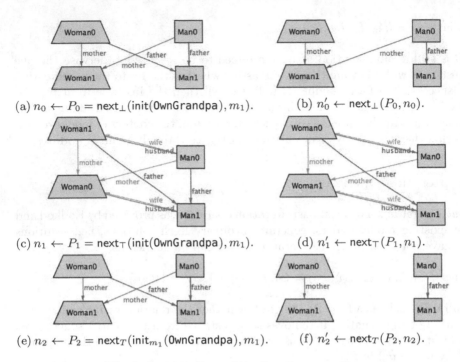

(a) $n_0 \leftarrow P_0 = \text{next}_\perp(\text{init}(\text{OwnGrandpa}), m_1)$.   (b) $n_0' \leftarrow \text{next}_\perp(P_0, n_0)$.

(c) $n_1 \leftarrow P_1 = \text{next}_\top(\text{init}(\text{OwnGrandpa}), m_1)$.   (d) $n_1' \leftarrow \text{next}_\top(P_1, n_1)$.

(e) $n_2 \leftarrow P_2 = \text{next}_\top(\text{init}_{m_1}(\text{OwnGrandpa}), m_1)$.   (f) $n_2' \leftarrow \text{next}_\top(P_2, n_2)$.

Fig. 6. Instantiations of the iteration operation next

Circular iteration. The user may find one of the returned instances interesting and wish to explore all solutions that are similar to it. Such kind of iteration that "circulates" an instance is specified by simply fixing the target of the problem:

$$\text{next}_T(\langle \mathcal{A}, L, U, T, \_, \phi \rangle, B_0) = \langle \mathcal{A}, L, U, T, \underline{1}, \phi \wedge \neg [B_0]_= \rangle$$

Pairing this operation with $\text{init}_\perp$ will iteratively produce minimal solutions by circulating the minimal model, while pairing it with init_B will enumerate all solutions that resemble model B. While not formalized, this would be the behavior embodied by the iteration operation in [4]. Figures 6e and 6f present a possible trace created by this operation for OwnGrandpa and m_1. As one circulates around the fixed target, solutions may begin to show little resemblance with each other.

Weighted iteration. The scenario exploration operations presented hitherto allow the generation of solutions in an ordered manner, but do not allow the user to control that order. Equipped with weighted target-oriented model finding problems, the user is able to fine-tune the generation of solutions. Each of the above presented operations may be adapted to a weighted scenario, like:

$$\text{next}_\perp^w(\langle \mathcal{A}, L, U, \_, \_, \phi \rangle, B_0) = \langle \mathcal{A}, L, U, B_0, w, \phi \wedge \neg [B_0]_= \rangle$$
$$\text{next}_\top^w(\langle \mathcal{A}, L, U, \_, \_, \phi \rangle, B_0) = \langle \mathcal{A}, L, U, \overline{B_0}, w, \phi \wedge \neg [B_0]_= \rangle$$

For instance, once $\text{init}_\perp^w$ kickstarts a problem with weights generating a minimal solution, iteration using $\text{next}_\perp^w$ can be used to search for the next minimal ones.

Note that such formalization allows the weight function to be modified at each iteration. Considering the same weight function from Section 3.1 for OwnGrandpa, searching for close instances prioritizes changes in the marital status, while preserving the biological characteristics of the model; searching for far instances would have the opposite effect, modifying the latter as much as possible.

Cone iteration. Other works on scenario exploration consider a notion of minimality that differs from ours [15]. In these, the order on solutions is defined by inclusion, i.e., a binding B is considered smaller than B' if for every $r \in \mathcal{R}$, $B(r) \subseteq B'(r)$. Minimal solutions are thus those where further removing any tuple results in an inconsistent solution. Thus, each minimal solution B has a "cone" of augmented solutions, containing instances obtained by introducing elements in B. To generate minimal solutions, the technique from [15] finds arbitrary solutions and then iteratively removes tuples until finding a minimal solutions from its cone. In our setting, this is simulated by a target-oriented problem:

$$\mathsf{next}_{\subseteq}(\langle \mathcal{A}, L, U, \_, \_, \phi \rangle, B_0) = (\langle \mathcal{A}, L, U, L, \underline{1}, \phi \wedge \neg [B_0]_{\subseteq} \rangle$$

Clause $\neg [B_0]_{\subseteq}$ introduced in each iteration guarantees that no more solutions from the cone of B_0 will be produced (this differs from $\neg [B_0]_=$, where B_0 will not be produced but other solutions from its cone may). The smallest target L guarantees that the minimal solution from the new cone is selected. The solutions generated by $\mathsf{init}_{\perp}$ are guaranteed to be the minimum of a cone, thus it can be used to kickstart the iteration with $\mathsf{next}_{\subseteq}$. In OwnGrandpa, this results in solutions other than the ones considered minimal by Δ: besides those similar to i_0 (Fig. 5a), connected by parenthood tuples, those connected by marriage would also be considered minimal, since removing any of those tuples would render the solutions inconsistent (in fact, it will return the same solutions as $\mathsf{init}_{\perp}^w$ with weight 1 and 2 for marriage and parenthood links, respectively).

Extended iteration. Once a problem is being explored, it may be useful to control the generation of the next solution by introducing additional constraints without restarting the model finding procedure. For a formula ψ, this is formalized as:

$$\mathsf{next}_{\psi}(\langle \mathcal{A}, L, U, \_, \_, \phi \rangle, B_0) = \langle \mathcal{A}, L, U, B_0, \underline{1}, \phi \wedge \psi \rangle$$

This generates the solutions closest to B_0 where ψ also holds, including itself: the negation of B_0 is left out of the formula because the user may be assessing whether B_0 remains a solution with ψ. Since the atoms are assumed to be reified in the problem, this operation can also be used to perform the augmentation operation proposed in [15] through the insertion of tuples into relations. However, since their notion of minimality differs from ours, the resulting solutions could vary in certain scenarios. This operation is related to the generation from instance: next_{ψ} may be used when the user wishes to explore solutions without persisting ψ in the original specification; init_B must be used if the specification is effectively updated, requiring the restart of the iteration process.

4   Deployment in the Alloy Analyzer

Some of the proposed scenario exploration operations were implemented in an extension to the Alloy Analyzer. The Analyzer is built over Kodkod, which only supports regular model finding. Thus, first, Kodkod was extended to support weighted target-oriented model finding, and second, Analyzer was modified to be able to communicate with that extended version of Kodkod.

4.1   Weighted Kodkod

Regular Kodkod problems $\langle \mathcal{A}, L, U, \phi \rangle$ are solved through an embedding into boolean logic and the deployment of SAT solvers. This embedding is performed by interpreting each n-ary relation $r \in \mathcal{R}$ as a matrix with n dimensions of size $|\mathcal{A}|$. For each tuple $\langle A_{i_1}, ..., A_{i_n} \rangle$ in the lower-bound $L(r)$, the value in $r[i_1, ..., i_n]$ is set to 1; for those outside the upper-bound $U(r)$, the value in $r[i_1, ..., i_n]$ is set to 0. For each tuple $\langle A_{i_1}, ..., A_{i_n} \rangle$ in-between the bounds $(U(r)\backslash L(r))$, a new boolean variable $r_{i_1,...,i_n}$ is created, that establishes the presence of that tuple in r. Formula ϕ is then embedded by translating operations over relations to the corresponding matrix operations. If the SAT solver is able to find a valid valuation for the variables, it represents a valid model instance of the problem.

In [4] we extended this procedure to deal with targets using *maximum satisfiability* (Max-SAT) problems, whose goal is to find an assignment that maximizes the number of satisfied clauses. Since clauses emerging from constraint ϕ should be prioritized over those introduced by the targets, we relied on *partial maximum satisfiability* (PMax-SAT) problems, where two kinds of clauses, *soft* and *hard*, can be defined: the solver must satisfy all hard clauses and maximize the number of soft clauses satisfied. Hard clauses consist of those emerging from the standard Kodkod embedding of ϕ into boolean logic; soft clauses consist of a clause $r_{i_1,...,i_n}$ for every tuple $\langle A_{i_1}, ..., A_{i_n} \rangle$ in the target $T(r)$ and a clause $\neg r_{i_1,...,i_n}$ for every tuple $\langle A_{i_1}, ..., A_{i_n} \rangle$ outside the target but within the bounds $U(r)\backslash T(r)$. Maximizing the number of soft clauses satisfied amounts to finding solutions that differ as little as possible from the target.

Max-SAT solvers typically support *weighted* clauses, in which case the solver maximizes the weighted sum of satisfied clauses (in fact, hard clauses in PMax-SAT are enforced by assigning them weights greater than the weighted sum of all soft clauses). Thus, given a weight function $w : \mathcal{R} \to \mathbb{N}_0$, it is easy to deploy weighted target-oriented model finding problems. For each n-ary relation $r \in \mathcal{R}$ with $w(r) \neq 0$, for every tuple $\langle A_{i_1}, ..., A_{i_n} \rangle$, either a soft clause $r_{i_1,...,i_n}$ or $\neg r_{i_1,...,i_n}$ with weight $w(r)$ is introduced, depending on the tuple belonging to $T(r)$ or $U(r)\backslash T(r)$ respectively. The targets of relations whose weight is 0 are simply ignored, as their valuation does not affect the target-oriented procedure. We implemented such procedure on top of SAT4J (http://www.sat4j.org), a pure Java SAT solver that natively handles weighted PMax-SAT problems.

4.2 Scenario Exploration in Alloy

The Alloy Analyzer is built on top of Kodkod, so implementing interesting scenario exploration operations in it requires only an adaptation to the introduced weighted target-oriented Kodkod. The current prototype has support for minimal and maximal instance generation ($init_\perp$ and $init_\top$) as well as weighted minimal and maximal iterations ($next_\perp^w$ and $next_\top^w$). These are triggered by buttons introduced alongside those for issuing regular init and next commands in the Analyzer.

One of the main advantages of the Alloy Analyzer over plain Kodkod is its ability to automatically present the solutions as graphs through an embedded visualizer. Moreover, the user is able to easily customize the presentation of the solutions through the definition of *themes*. In order to provide a seamless experience to the user, we extend the theme editor to also support the assignment of weights to each signature and field (which are both translated into relations in Kodkod), which is retrieved every time the iteration commands are called. By default, all weights are set to 1, representing a regular target-oriented model finding problem. The user is able to increase them, or set them to 0, in which case the atoms corresponding to that relation are discarded from the target.

The other scenario exploration operations could have also been implemented in Alloy in a straight-forward way. Since the theme is persisted through iterations, $init_\perp^w$ and $init_\top^w$ could have been implemented instead of plain $init_\perp$ and $init_\top$; the Analyzer allows the persistence of generated solutions as XML files, which could be used to implement $init_B$. Extended iteration $next_\psi$ could be deployed by allowing the specification to be updated in a controlled way during the iteration of solutions. The implementation of these operations is left as future work.

It is worth noting that, instead of reifying the atoms into the Kodkod problem, the Analyzer short-circuits the introduction of constraint $\neg\ [B_0]_=$ at each next step directly into the SAT problem where tuples can be directly referred to, avoiding the creation of additional relations. Our implementation follows the same approach on the introduction of targets into the PMax-SAT solver.

5 Related Work

A large number of techniques have been proposed for the generation of model instances from first-order logic constraints. The most relevant to this work are those following the "MACE-style" [14], where finite models are found through an embedding of problems into propositional logic and the deployment of off-the-shelf SAT solvers, of which Kodkod is a paradigmatic example. However, while techniques for the efficient generation of models abound, few allow the user to control how they are selected. Among the operations explored in Section 3, the best-studied one is the generation of minimal models. Such techniques [9,15,6] usually rely on an iterative procedure that removes elements from found solutions, until a minimal model is reached (according to the inclusion order presented in Section 3), that can be simulated by our "cone iteration".

More closely to our work is Aluminum [15], a tool built over Alloy whose focus is precisely to allow the user to guide the solver through scenario exploration.

Two exploration operations are proposed: the generation of minimal instances and their augmentation through introduction of tuples into relations. While the proposed next$_\psi$ operation also allows the introduction of elements (since atoms are reified), our notion of distance varies from theirs, and thus the set of generated solutions may differ. Nonetheless, its behavior could be simulated by an embedding similar that of "cone iteration" next$_\subsetneq$, that minimizes solutions within independent cones. Thus, the proposed operations subsume those of Aluminum.

Relational model finders have been applied in model repair, where the ability to enforce least-change iteration is essential. The authors from [16] assess the suitability of Kodkod to repair inconsistencies. Given an inconsistent solution, a consistent one is found by relaxing the bounds of the original to allow the addition or removal of tuples suspected of causing the inconsistencies. However there is no control over how close the new model is to the original one and the authors do not reason on how to manage the creation of new atoms. Our next$_\perp$ operation, based on previous work on target-oriented model finding [4] guarantees that the closest solution is returned. Previously, we had attempted to produce models with least-change directly over Alloy using an iterative procedure, which was applied in the context of model repair [13] and inter-model consistency management [11,12]. While less scalable, working at the Alloy level rather than at Kodkod's directly allowed for more expressive model distance functions.

6   Conclusion

In this paper we explored scenario exploration operations, formalizing them on top of weighted target-oriented model finding problems. To assess the usefulness of the defined operations in real MDE scenarios, an in-depth empirical study would be needed. At any rate, we believe that our formalism has shown to be sufficiently expressive and flexible to allow the specification of interesting operations, including those proposed in previous work.

We have extended Kodkod to support such class of problems by relying on PMax-SAT solver with weights, and implemented some of the proposed scenario exploration operations in the Alloy Analyzer as to prove their feasibility. In the future we intend to expand this set, converting the Analyzer into a fully fledged scenario exploration tool, as well as to assess the performance of this embedding. Nonetheless, [4] shows that such approach is viable for medium-sized models, which would be adequate for this kind of application. Managing the user expectations is also a concern. While the proposed operations allow the user to customize the order of generation by assigning weights to relations, the connection between the weights and the resulting order may not be completely clear. We are studying mechanisms to automatically derive those weights through user input of what exactly is considered a "close" solution.

Acknowledgments. This work is co-financed by the North Portugal Regional Operational Programme (ON.2 – O Novo Norte), under the National Strategic Reference Framework (NSRF), through the European Regional Development

Fund (ERDF), within project NORTE-07-0124-FEDER-000062. The authors thank Antónia Lopes for suggesting interesting operations regarding maximal change.

References

1. Anastasakis, K., Bordbar, B., Georg, G., Ray, I.: On challenges of model transformation from UML to Alloy. In: SoSyM, vol. 9, pp. 69–86 (2010)
2. Büttner, F., Egea, M., Cabot, J., Gogolla, M.: Verification of ATL transformations using transformation models and model finders. In: Aoki, T., Taguchi, K. (eds.) ICFEM 2012. LNCS, vol. 7635, pp. 198–213. Springer, Heidelberg (2012)
3. Cunha, A., Garis, A., Riesco, D.: Translating between Alloy specifications and UML class diagrams annotated with OCL. In: SoSyM (2013)
4. Cunha, A., Macedo, N., Guimarães, T.: Target oriented relational model finding. In: Gnesi, S., Rensink, A. (eds.) FASE 2014 (ETAPS). LNCS, vol. 8411, pp. 17–31. Springer, Heidelberg (2014)
5. Garcia, M.: Formalization of QVT-Relations: OCL-based static semantics and Alloy-based validation. In: MDSD 2008, pp. 21–30. Shaker Verlag (2008)
6. Iser, M., Sinz, C., Taghdiri, M.: Minimizing models for tseitin-encoded SAT instances. In: Järvisalo, M., Van Gelder, A. (eds.) SAT 2013. LNCS, vol. 7962, pp. 224–232. Springer, Heidelberg (2013)
7. Jackson, D.: Software Abstractions: Logic, Language, and Analysis. MIT Press, revised edition (2012)
8. Kleiner, M., Del Fabro, M.D., Albert, P.: Model search: Formalizing and automating constraint solving in MDE platforms. In: Kühne, T., Selic, B., Gervais, M.-P., Terrier, F. (eds.) ECMFA 2010. LNCS, vol. 6138, pp. 173–188. Springer, Heidelberg (2010)
9. Koshimura, M., Nabeshima, H., Fujita, H., Hasegawa, R.: Minimal model generation with respect to an atom set. In: FTP 2009, pp. 49–59 (2009)
10. Kuhlmann, M., Gogolla, M.: From UML and OCL to relational logic and back. In: France, R.B., Kazmeier, J., Breu, R., Atkinson, C. (eds.) MODELS 2012. LNCS, vol. 7590, pp. 415–431. Springer, Heidelberg (2012)
11. Macedo, N., Cunha, A.: Implementing QVT-R bidirectional model transformations using alloy. In: Cortellessa, V., Varró, D. (eds.) FASE 2013 (ETAPS 2013). LNCS, vol. 7793, pp. 297–311. Springer, Heidelberg (2013)
12. Macedo, N., Cunha, A.: Least-change bidirectional model transformation with QVT-R and ATL. In: SoSyM (2014) (to appear)
13. Macedo, N., Guimarães, T., Cunha, A.: Model repair and transformation with Echo. In: ASE 2013, pp. 694–697. IEEE (2013)
14. McCune, W.: A Davis-Putnam program and its application to finite first-order model search: quasigroup existence problem. Technical Report ANL/MCS-TM-194, Argonne National Laboratory, Argonne, IL (May 1994)
15. Nelson, T., Saghafi, S., Dougherty, D.J., Fisler, K., Krishnamurthi, S.: Aluminum: principled scenario exploration through minimality. In: ICSE 2013, pp. 232–241. IEEE/ACM (2013)
16. Van Der Straeten, R., Pinna Puissant, J., Mens, T.: Assessing the kodkod model finder for resolving model inconsistencies. In: France, R.B., Kuester, J.M., Bordbar, B., Paige, R.F. (eds.) ECMFA 2011. LNCS, vol. 6698, pp. 69–84. Springer, Heidelberg (2011)
17. Torlak, E., Jackson, D.: Kodkod: A relational model finder. In: Grumberg, O., Huth, M. (eds.) TACAS 2007. LNCS, vol. 4424, pp. 632–647. Springer, Heidelberg (2007)

Data-Oriented Characterization of Application-Level Energy Optimization

Kenan Liu[1], Gustavo Pinto[2], and Yu David Liu[1]

[1] State University of New York, Binghamton, NY, US
kliu20@binghamton.edu, davidL@cs.binghamton.edu
[2] Federal University of Pernambuco, Recife, PE, Brazil
ghlp@cin.ufpe.br

Abstract. Empowering application programmers to make energy-aware decisions is a critical dimension of energy optimization for computer systems. In this paper, we study the energy impact of alternative data management choices by programmers, such as data access patterns, data precision choices, and data organization. Second, we attempt to build a bridge between application-level energy management and hardware-level energy management, by elucidating how various application-level data management features respond to Dynamic Voltage and Frequency Scaling (DVFS). Finally, we apply our findings to real-world applications, demonstrating their potential for guiding application-level energy optimization. The empirical study is particularly relevant in the Big Data era, where data-intensive applications are large energy consumers, and their energy efficiency is strongly correlated to how data are maintained and handled in programs.

Keywords: Energy consumption, Application-level data management.

1 Introduction

Modern computing platforms are experiencing an unprecedented diversification. Beneath the popularity of the Internet of Things, Android phones, Apple iWatch and Unmanned Aerial Vehicles, a critical looming concern is energy consumption. Traditionally addressed by hardware-level (*e.g.*, [11,5]) and system-level approaches (*e.g.*, [7,18]), energy optimization is gaining momentum at the level of application development [1,3,4,13,15,23]. These *application-level energy management* strategies complement lower-level strategies with an expanded *optimization space*, yielding distinctive advantages: first, applications are viewed as a white box, whose structural features may be considered for energy optimization; second, the knowledge of programmers and their design choices can influence energy efficiency. Recent studies [16] show application-level energy management is in high demand among application developers.

The grand challenge ahead is the lack of systematic guidelines for application-level energy management. Unlike lower-level energy management strategies that often happen "under the hood," application-level energy management requires

© Springer-Verlag Berlin Heidelberg 2015
A. Egyed and I. Schaefer (Eds.): FASE 2015, LNCS 9033, pp. 316–331, 2015.
DOI: 10.1007/978-3-662-46675-9_21

the participation of application software developers. For example, programmers need to understand the energy behaviors at different levels of software granularities in order to make judicious design decisions, and thus improve the energy efficiency. As indicated in recent studies, the devil often lies with the details [2,17], and the guidelines are often anecdotal or incorrect [16]. Should we pessimistically accept that the optimization space of application-level energy management as unchartable waters, or is there wisdom we can generalize and share with application developers in their energy-aware software development?

This paper is aimed at exploring this important yet largely uncharted optimization space. Even though the energy impact of arbitrary developer decisions — e.g., using encryptions when the battery level is high and no security otherwise — is impossible to generalize and quantify, we believe a sub-category of such design decisions — those related to *data* — have interesting and generalizable correlations with energy consumption. With Big Data applications on the rise, we believe the data-oriented perspective on studying application-level energy management may in addition have the forward-looking appeal on future energy-aware software development. In particular, we attempt to answer the following research questions:

RQ1. How does the choice of application-level data management features impact energy consumption?

RQ2. How does application-level energy management interact with hardware-level energy management?

For **RQ1**, we consciously look into features "middle-of-the-road" in granularity: they are coarser-grained than instructions [22] or bytecode [10,14] to help retain the high-level intentions of application developers, yet at the same time finer-grained than software architectures or frameworks to facilitate reliable quantification. Specifically, we study the impact of energy consumption over different choices of:

- *data access pattern*: For a large amount of data, does the pattern of access (sequential vs. random, read vs. write) impact energy consumption?
- *data organization and representation*: Do different representations of the same data (unboxed vs. boxed data, a primitive array vs. an `ArrayList`, an array of objects vs. multiple arrays of primitive data) have impact on energy consumption?
- *data precision*: Do precision levels (*e.g.*, `short`, `int`, and `long`) of data have impact on energy consumption?
- *data I/O strategies*: For I/O-intensive applications, do different choices of data processing — such as buffering — have impact on energy consumption?

To answer **RQ2**, we are aimed at connecting application-level energy management and its lower-level counterparts. It is our belief that energy consumption is the combined effect of interactions through application software, system software, and hardware; the best energy management strategy should be the harmonious coordination of all layers of the compute stack. Concretely, we rein-vestigate the aforementioned data-oriented application features in the context of Dynamic Voltage and Frequency Scaling (DVFS) [11], arguably the most classic hardware-based energy management strategy. This exploration expands the en-ergy optimization space where "software meets hardware," over a frontier where software engineering research joins forces with hardware architecture research.

Overall, this paper makes the following contributions:

- It performs the first empirical study that systematically characterizes the optimization space of application-level energy management, from the fresh perspective of *data*. The multi-dimensional study ranges from data access pattern, data organization and representation, data precision, and data I/O intensity.
- It conducts experiments to bridge application-level and hardware-level en-ergy management, and constructs a unified optimization space connecting hardware and application software.
- It reports the release of jRAPL, an open-source library to precisely and non-invasively gather energy/performance information of Java programs running on Intel CPUs.

2   Methodology

In this section, we introduce our research methodology and the details of our experimental environment.

2.1   The Open-Source jRAPL Library

We have developed a set of APIs for profiling Java programs running on CPUs with Running Average Power Limit (RAPL) [5] support. Originally designed by Intel for enabling chip-level power management, RAPL is widely supported in today's Intel architectures, including Xeon server-level CPUs and the popular i5 and i7. RAPL-enabled architectures monitor the energy consumption infor-mation and store it in Machine-Specific Registers (MSRs). Such MSRs can be accessed by OS, such as the msr kernel module in Linux. RAPL is an appealing design, particularly because it allows energy/power consumption to be reported at a fine-grained manner, *e.g.*, monitoring CPU core, CPU uncore (L3 cache, on-chip GPUs, and interconnects), and DRAM separately.

Our library can be viewed as a software wrapper to access the MSRs. The RAPL interface itself has broader support for energy management, whereas our library only uses its capability for information gathering, a mode in RAPL named "energy metering." Since the msr module under Linux runs in privileged kernel mode, jRAPL works in a similar manner as system calls.

The user interface for jRAPL is simple. For any block of code in the application whose energy/performance information is to the interest of the user, she simply needs to enclose the code block with a pair of statCheck invocations. For exam-ple, the following code snippet attempts to measure the energy consumption of the doWork method, whose value is the difference between beginning and end:

```
double beginning = EnergyCheck.statCheck();
doWork();
double end = EnergyCheck.statCheck();
```

Additional APIs also allow time and other lower-level hardware performance counter information (for diagnostics) to be collected. The API can flexibly collect either CPU time, User Mode time, Kernel Mode time, and Wall Clock time. If not explicitly specified, all time reported in the paper is Wall Clock time. When a CPU consists of multiple cores, jRAPL can report data either individually or combined. Throughout the paper, all energy/power data for multi-core CPUs are reported as combined.

Compared with traditional approaches based on physical energy meters, the jRAPL-based approach comes with several unique advantages:

- *Refined Energy Analysis*: thanks to RAPL, our library can not only report the overall energy consumption of the program, but also the breakdown (1) among hardware components and (2) among program components (such as methods and code blocks). As we shall see, refined hardware-based analysis allows us to understand the relative activeness of different hardware components, ultimately playing an important role in analyzing the energy behaviors of programs. In meter-based approaches, hardware design constraints often make it impossible to measure a particular hardware component (such as CPU cores only, or even DRAMs because they often share the power supply cable with the motherboard).
- *Synchronization-Free Measurement*: in meter-based measurements, a somewhat thorny issue is to synchronize the beginning/end of measurement with the beginning/end of the program execution of interest. This problem is magnified for fine-grained code-block based measurement, where the problem *de facto* becomes the synchronization of measurement and the program counter. With jRAPL, the demarcation of measurement coincides with that of execution; no synchronization is needed.

One drawback of the jRAPL-based approach is the energy data collection itself may incur overhead. Fortunately, the time overhead for MSR access is in the microseconds, orders of magnitude lower than the execution time of our experiments.

2.2   Experimental Environment

We run each experiment in the following machine: a 2×8-core (32-cores when hyper-threading is enabled) Intel(R) Xeon(R) E5-2670, 2.60GHz, with 64GB of DDR3 1600 memory. It has three cache levels (L1, L2 and L3) with 64KB per core (128KB total), 256KB per core (512KB total) and 3MB (smart cache), respectively. It is running Debian 6 (kernel 3.0.0-1-amd64) and Oracle HotSpot 64-Bit Server VM (build 20.1-b02, mixed mode), JDK version 1.6.0_26. The processor has the capability of running at several frequency levels, varying from 1.2, 1.4, 1.6, 1.8, 2.0, 2.2, 2.4 and 2.6 GHz.

For the JVM, the parallel garbage collector is used, and just-in-time (JIT) compilation is enabled to be realistic with real-world Java applications. The initial heap size and maximum heap size are set to be 1GB and 16GB respectively. We run each benchmark 6 times within the same JVM; this is implemented by a top-level 6-iteration loop over each benchmark. The reported data is the average of the last 4 runs. We chose to report the last 4 runs because JIT execution tends to stabilize in the later runs [17]. If the standard deviation of such 4 runs is greater than 5%, we executed the benchmark again until results stabilize. All experiments were performed with no other load on the OS. Unless explicitly specified in the paper, the default **ondemand** governor of Linux is used for OS power management. Turbo Boost feature is disabled.

3   Application-Level Energy Management

This section explores the optimization space of application-level energy management through five data-oriented characterizations.

3.1   Data Access Patterns

We first examine how energy consumption differs under sequential and random access. By access, we consider both read and write operations. The read micro-benchmark traverses a large **int** array (of size N=50,000,000) and retrieves the value at each position, while the write counterpart micro-benchmark assigns integer 1 to each position. To construct a fair comparison between sequential and random access, we resort to an "index array" preloaded with index numbers: numbers from 1 to N in that order for sequential access, and a random permutation of numbers between 1 and N for random access. Thanks to the index array, the program logic is identical for sequential and random access. The reported results do not consider index array preloading.

The figure on the right shows[1] the benchmarking results, with bars for energy data and lines for power data. We do not explicitly show the execution time, which by physics, can be derived as the division of energy and power. There are 10 bars for each figure, the first five of which 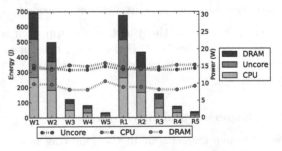 (with prefix W) indicate write access, and the remaining five (with prefix R) indicate read access. In each group, suffix 1 represents 100% randomness in access, 2 for 25% randomness, 3 for 1% randomness, and 4 for 0.1% randomness, and 5 for 0% randomness, *i.e.*, sequential access. The level of randomness is controlled by

---

[1] Throughout the paper, all bar charts follow the same legends as those in this figure.

index range: *e.g.*, we imitate 1% random access by allowing random permutation within each N × 1% interval of the array.

The data reveals the significant impact of access randomness on energy consumption. The more random data access is, the more energy is consumed. This is consistent with hardware behaviors due to cache locality. Further observe that read vs. write accesses make little difference on energy consumption. The conventional folklore is that writes are often more expensive than reads, but this effect, if any, appears to be small on energy consumption. In fact, in one combination R3 vs. W3, the opposite is true.

3.2 Data Representation Strategies

Let us now investigate the impact of different data representation strategies on energy consumption. First, we look into the difference between representing a sequence of integers as a primitive array and as an `ArrayList`. We construct a similar experiment as one described in Section 3.1, by traversing an `ArrayList` of `Integer`'s of a large size (N = 50,000,000). We mimic "read" through the `List.get(int i)` method, and "write" through the `List.set(int i, Object o)` method.

The results of the `ArrayList` implementation are shown the figure on the right, where SEQ/RAN/R/W labels denote sequential, 100% random, read, and write access, respectively. Compared with Section 3.1, energy consumption is much higher: the RAN-R configuration with primitive array representation consumes around 670J, whereas its counterpart result here is around 1550J. This does not come as a surprise. `ArrayList` uses boxed data (of `Integer` type) whereas our primitive array implementation uses unboxed data (of `int` type). Furthermore, the getter/setter required by `ArrayList` are method invocations, more expensive than primitive array read/write.

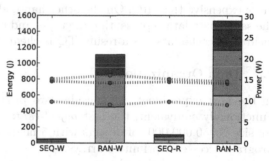

This experiment motivated us to answer a more general question related to object-oriented languages: when we say an object is accessed, which representation of the object is being accessed: a reference to it, a value it holds, or the type it has? Do they have the same effect on energy consumption? We construct the next experiments, in three groups:

- *Reference Query (RQ):* accesses the reference of an `Integer` object;
- *Type Query (TQ):* accesses the type held by an `Integer` object;
- *Value Query (VQ):* accesses the value that an `Integer` object holds;

The result on the right is
divided into three groups as
above. In each group, postfix
1 denotes 100% random access,
2 denotes 25% random access,
and 3 denotes sequential access.
For the TQ experiment, our
benchmark applies `instanceof`
operator to the object. To avoid
source-level compiler optimiza-

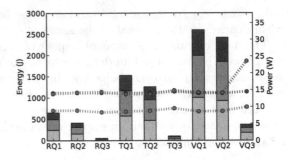

tion performed by modern Java compilers such as transforming expression `x`
`instanceof Integer` to a no-op if `x` is only assigned to hold an `Integer` object, our micro-benchmark assigns objects of different types to reference `x`, and
the `instanceof` operator cannot be optimized away through standard points-
to analysis.

RQ and TQ are both more efficient than VQ. According to the runtime semantics of object-oriented programs, RQ only entails a stack access, whereas VQ
includes access to the heap, a much more expensive operation.

Less obvious is the case of TQ. On one hand, the type of an object is stored
as object metadata, whose access also requires heap access. As a result, TQ is
more expensive than RQ. On the other hand, all objects of the same type share
the same metadata representing the type, and repeated queries of the same type
yield high cache hits. As a result, TQ is cheaper than VQ.

3.3 Data Organization

In the next experiment, we consider two programs in Figure 1 and Figure 2.
Functionally equivalent, the first *object-centric* program accesses a large array
(of size N=50,000,000) of objects with 5 fields, and the second *attribute-centric*
program accesses 5 primitive arrays.

As shown here, the object-
centric data grouping consumes
about 2.62x energy. The results here may reveal a trade-
off   between   programming
productivity and energy efficiency. Object-oriented encapsulation is known to have many
benefits, such as modularity, information hiding, and maintain-

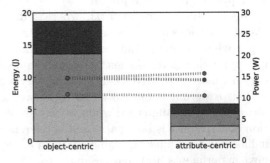

ability. That being said, it does pay a toll on energy consumption, likely due to
garbage collection. Another plausible cause is that there is no guarantee that
objects in the array are allocated in contiguous space on the heap. As a result,
even though Fig. 1 may be cache-friendly for retrieving the 5 fields for the same
object, it may incur more cache misses when the entire array is traversed.

```
class Grouped {
  int a, b, c, d, e = ...;
}
class Main {
  Grouped[] group = ...;
  void calc() {
    for (int i = 0; i < N; i++) {
      group[i].e = group[i].a * group[i].b * group[i].c * group[i].d;
}}}
```

Fig. 1. Object-Centric Data Grouping

```
class Main {
  int[] a = ..; int[] b = ..; int[] c = ..; int[] d = ..; int[] e = ..;
  void calc() {
    for (int i = 0; i < N; i++) {
      e[i] = a[i] * b[i] * c[i] * d[i];
}}}
```

Fig. 2. Attribute-Centric Data Grouping

3.4   Data Precision Choices

We next analyze the impact of data precision choices on energy consumption. Our micro-benchmark performs the multiplication of two 1000 × 1000 matrices. For our experiments, we vary the matrix element type, declared with the short, int, float, double, and long types respectively for each variation of the benchmark. In our environment, short/int/float/double/long data types are 16/32/32/64/64 bits respectively. To set a fair comparison, we pre-fill matrices with double values through random number generation. All other variations of the benchmark pre-fill their matrix data through data conversion from the double matrix. In other words, all experiments operate on matrices of comparable values, only with different precisions. Our reported results exclude the pre-filling/converting stage above.

Our experiments show that energy consumption grows with the number of bits (a) among the non-floating point data types, as reflected by the relative standings between short, int, and long. (b) among floating point data types, as seen in the relative standings between float and double. Both are 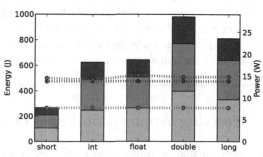 consistent with architecture-level comparisons, where instructions operating on more bytes/words are more expensive.

It is however unreliable to use the number of bits to cross-compare between non-floating point types and floating point types. Programs with floating point types involve the use of FPUs. Based on our experience, one must be cautious to draw generalizations from cross-comparisons between FPU-intensive programs and those otherwise. For instance, the two 32-bit types used in our benchmarking — `int` and `float` — appear to incur similar amounts of energy consumption. As we shall see in the Section 5 however, the two may also lead to drastically different consumptions. It is a reminder for energy-conscious programmers who wish to save energy by modifying their `float`-precision program to one with `int` precision — the strategy may or may not be effective.

3.5 Data I/O Configurations

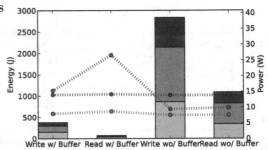

Finally, we analyze the energy behaviors of I/O operations. We construct two microbenchmarks that read and write 50MB data from/to a file, using `FileInputStream` and `FileOutputStream` objects respectively. For the read benchmark, we create two variations, one with buffering through the use of the `BufferedInputStream` object, and the other without. Similarly, the write benchmark has two variations. The one with buffering uses the `BufferedOutputStream` object.

As the figure reveals, buffering has significant impact on improving energy efficiency. Indeed, buffer removal in essence disables bulking of I/O operations, so its effect on energy consumption is dramatic. Furthermore, observe that data output is significantly more energy-consuming than data input. Third, the power consumption of unbuffered file access (about 10W) is lower than that of buffered access. Unbuffered file access leads to a much higher level of I/O intensity. As a result, CPU is more likely to remain idle, and more likely to be scaled down by Linux's default power management strategy, the **ondemand** governor.

> **RQ1 Summary:** *Random access, object-centric data organization, unbuffered I/O consume significantly more energy. The energy consumption for memory read and write are on par, but file write is significantly more expensive than file read. Data types with more bits tend to consume more energy, but there is no simple generalization to cross-compare FPU-intensive types and those that are not.*

4   Unifying Application-Level Optimization with DVFS

This section places application-level energy management in a broader context, investigating its combined impact with hardware-based energy management.

Background. DVFS [11] is a common CPU feature where the operational frequency and the supply voltage of the CPU can be dynamically adjusted. DVFS is a classic and effective power management strategy. The dynamic power consumption of a CPU, denoted as P, can be computed as $P = C * V^2 * F$, where V is the voltage, F is the frequency, and C is a (near constant) factor. The energy consumption E is an accumulation of power consumption over time t, i.e., through formula $E = P * t$.

Result Summary. We have conducted the same experiments reported in the previous section, except that the executions are conducted at different CPU frequencies. Due to page limit, we defer the complete data set in the online repository (see Section 8 for information). Figure 3 and Figure 4 report selected results. All figures are represented as heat map matrices.

A common trend among these experiments is that downscaling CPU often leads to less "favorable" results: in the majority of experiments, not only there will be a performance loss, but also increased energy consumption. The root cause is that DVFS only directly influences the CPU power consumption. The power consumptions for the Uncore and the DRAM sub-systems remain roughly constant. Thus, since time increases as frequency decreases, energy consumption for these sub-systems increases as well when a lower CPU frequency is selected. This is a sober reminder of the applicability of DVFS as an energy management strategy: whereas downscaling can be effective in some scenarios, blind DVFS is likely to fall short in goals. This somewhat pessimistic conclusion does have a positive "coda" — thanks to the difference between micro-benchmarks and real-world applications — a discussion we will continue in Section 5.

Furthermore, observe that we have adopted a very narrow view to equate "being favorable" as being able to save energy. As an example beyond this view, running CPUs at the lowest frequency may reduce heat dissipation, and improve the reliability of program execution.

Overall, our results can serve as a "lookup" chart to guide energy-aware programmers to desirable combinations of application-level energy management and hardware-level energy management. For example, if a programmer wishes to randomly access an array and query the value held by the array element object (*VQ+Randomness*) with a fixed energy budget, she can look up the results from Figure 3, and run the program either at 2GHz or at 2.6Ghz. The former may reduce heat dissipation, whereas the latter may produce results faster.

Specific Findings. In Figure 3, observe that for *VQ+Randomness*, 100% random access or 25% random access at frequencies of 2.4GHz, 2.2GHz, 2GHz, and 1.8GHz can all yield energy savings. There is a performance loss in these configurations, but the loss is also smaller than their more sequential counterparts. These configurations may be useful for energy management since they represent a possible trade-off between energy saving and performance loss. The more random access patterns react to DVFS more gracefully because random access leads to more cache misses and instruction pipeline stalls. As a result, the CPU more frequently "waits for" data fetch. When the CPU frequencies are lowered, the relative impact on performance is smaller.

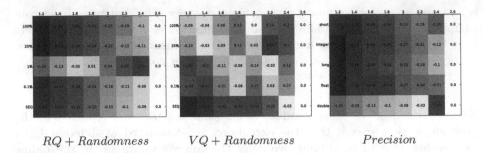

RQ + Randomness   VQ + Randomness   Precision

Fig. 3. Selected Energy Results of DVFS Combined with Data Access, Data Representation, and Data Precision. (Labels on top are CPU frequencies, and labels to the left are random/sequential access patterns. All data are normalized energy consumption against the 2.6Ghz data of the same row. Red indicates savings, whereas Blue indicates loss. The darker the Red shade, the more "favorable" the configuration is, *i.e.*, greater energy savings. The darker the Blue shade, the more "unfavorable" the configuration is *i.e.*, greater energy loss.)

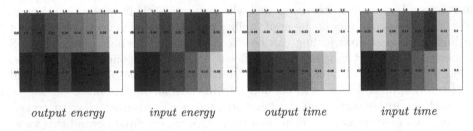

output energy   input energy   output time   input time

Fig. 4. DVFS and Data I/O (O: Output, I: Input, B: Buffered, U: Unbuffered)

The most encouraging results come from Figure 4. Here, especially in the buffered I/Os, lowering CPU frequency can often yield energy savings. This is dramatic for cases such as buffered input (I/B), where the energy consumption for 2.2GHz is less than half of that of 2.6GHz, whereas the execution time at 2.2GHz turns out being shorter than that of 2.6GHz. This is a "sweet spot" in energy management: the program is not only more energy-efficient, but also runs faster. The cause behind this behavior is that CPUs running such I/O-intensive benchmarks are mostly idle, so lowering the CPU frequency has little impact on performance, but can significantly save energy. The improved performance may come as a mild surprise to some; we believe this demonstrates the execution time is not bound by CPU, but the storage system. The operations of the latter are often less deterministic, causing delays at unpredictable times.

RQ2 Summary: *Blindly downscaling CPU frequency often leads to increased energy consumption and performance loss. Downscaling can play a prominent role in the energy optimization of I/O-intensive benchmarks.*

5   Case Study

In this section we apply our findings to two real-world benchmarks, SUNFLOW and XALAN, from the well-known DaCapo suite benchmark[2].

SUNFLOW renders a set of images using ray tracing, a CPU-intensive benchmark. The original program represents rendering data in type `double`. We performed our experiments by varying the data types appearing in the rendering method from `double` to `short`, `int`, `float`, and `long`. The rest of the source code remained unchanged.

The results here confirm some patterns from micro-benchmarking: for instance, `short` still consumes less energy than `int`, and `float` is still cheaper than `double`. The figure here highlights the non-comparability between floating point types and non-floating point types. The rendering process of SUNFLOW involves

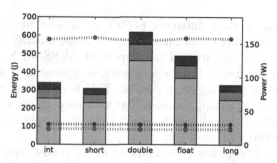

complex floating point operations (such as division), leading to heavy overhead on FPU operations (such as rounding [8]). In other words, these heavy operations significantly outpace their `short/int/long` counterparts in execution time, and subsequently energy consumption.

Another observation is that the difference in energy consumption of `short`, `int` and `long` is not as drastic as the one in micro-benchmarking. The same also holds for the difference between `float` and `double`. Real-world programs such as SUNFLOW are more likely to lead to instruction pipeline stalls (due to branching, synchronization, *etc*) than micro-benchmarks, and we speculate these additional stalls may help mask some of the difference.

Even though SUNFLOW is a complex application — it has more than 22,000 lines of Java code — we observed that a simple modification on the data types of a single method can have a considerable influence on the overall energy consumption of the application. In this example, the energy-aware programmer needs to balance the trade-off between energy efficiency and accuracy.

XALAN transforms XML documents into HTML. This benchmark performs reads and writes from input/output channels, and it has 170,572 lines of Java code. In its default version, the benchmark does not use a buffer. We add buffers to two program points in the XSLTBench class. With this modification, we observed an energy saving of 4.29%. Execution time kept roughly the same. The first figure in Figure 5 shows the results. On one hand, the savings here are not as "dramatic" as what micro-benchmarking showed. On the other hand, real-world applications often consume more energy, so a small percentage of savings can

---

[2] http://www.dacapobench.org

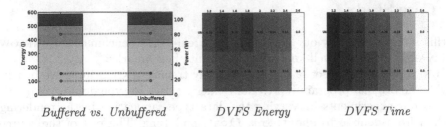

Buffered vs. Unbuffered   DVFS Energy   DVFS Time

Fig. 5. XALAN Results

still make a difference (4.29% for XALAN implies more than 20J). The insights from micro-benchmarking guide us to identify and perform this optimization.

We also studied the impact of DVFS on XALAN, with results shown in the same figure. In all configurations, executing XALAN can lead to energy savings than running it at 2.6Ghz. This is consistent with our findings in the micro-benchmarking, because XALAN does perform significant I/O operations on files. DVFS may be useful for XALAN when one is willing to trade performance for energy savings.

The power consumptions of SUNFLOW and XALAN also deserve attention. Different applications operate on very different power levels: the CPU power for SUNFLOW nearly doubles that for XALAN. Our power analysis is consistent with the established fact that SUNFLOW is a CPU-intensive benchmark.

Finally, the gap between CPU power consumption and Uncore/DRAM power consumption is much larger than those in micro-benchmarks. This is good news for CPU-centric energy management strategies such as DVFS: they may sometimes be ineffective for micro-benchmarks because Uncore/DRAM power consumption has a large proportion to offset the savings from CPUs, the proportional offset is smaller when we apply these strategies to real-world benchmarks. To validate this, we conducted the data precision experiment of SUNFLOW over different CPU frequencies and produced a counterpart of the *Precision* heat map of Fig. 3. As it turns out, unlike all cells are blue in the *Precision* heat map of Fig. 3, most cells are red for SUNFLOW. In other words, 2.6GHz is not the most energy-saving frequency for data precision choices. Readers can find the detailed data of this result in our online repository.

6   Threats to Validity

Internal factors: First, accessing MSRs also consumes energy (see discussions in Section 2.1). This overhead cannot be ignored if MSR accesses are too frequent, *e.g.*, at microsecond intervals. We mitigate this problem by using the RAPL interface only at the beginning and at the end of the benchmark execution. Second, the readings from the RAPL interface are hardware (CPU core or socket)-based. It cannot isolate the energy consumption of OS execution, VM execution, and application execution. As our experiments are mostly set up to be *comparative* — such as demonstrating the difference in energy consumption between sequential vs. random access — and our OS/VM settings remain unchanged throughout experiments, the root cause of relative difference in energy consumption for different experiments is likely to be the (direct and indirect) effect of the application, not OS or VM. Third, analyzing code with a short execution time may disproportionally amplify the noise from hardware and OS. We mitigate this problem by increasing the execution length of our benchmarks (such as via designing the benchmark to operate on a large amount of data) and averaging the results of multiple executions.

External factors: First, our results are limited by our selection of benchmarks. Second, there are other possible data manipulations beyond the scope of this paper. With our tool, we expect similar analysis can be conducted in the future when other aspects of data-related application features become relevant. Third, our results are reported with the assumption that JIT is enabled. This stems from our observation that later runs of JIT-enabled executions do stabilize in terms of energy consumption and performance. We experienced differences in standard deviation of over 30% when comparing the warmup run (first 2 executions) and later runs, but less than 5% when comparing the last 4 runs.

7 Related Work

Application-level energy management. In recent years, a number of studies have explored energy management strategies at the application level as an attempt to empower the application programmer to take energy-aware decisions. Some focus on the design of new programming models, with examples such as Green [1], Energy Types [4], and Eco [23]. In these systems, recurring patterns of energy management tasks are incarnated as first-class citizens. Approximated programming [3] trades and reasons about occasional "soft errors", *i.e.*, errors that may reduce the accuracy of the results, for a reduction in energy consumption. The relationship between this line of work and our work is complementary: existing work provides language support to facilitate energy optimization, whereas our work experimentally and empirically establishes the room of the energy optimization space.

Energy measurement. Energy measurement is a broad area of research. Prior work has attempted to model energy consumption at the individual instruction level [22], system call level [6], and bytecode level [20]. Recent progress also includes fine-grained measurement for Android programs [10,14], with detailed energy measurement of different hardware components such as camera, Wi-Fi and GPS. RAPL-based energy measurement has appeared in recent literature (*e.g.*, [12,21]); its precision and reliability has been extensively studied [9].

Empirical studies. Existing research that dealt with the trade-off of comparing individual components of an application and energy consumption has covered a wide spectrum of applications. These studies vary from concurrent programming [17], VM services [2,12], cloud offloading [13], and refactoring [19]. To the best of our knowledge, our study is the first in exploring how different choices of fine-grained data manipulation impact on the energy consumption of different hardware sub-systems, and how application-level energy management and lower-level energy management interact.

8   Conclusion

In this paper, we take a data-centric view to empirically study the optimization space of application-level energy management. Our investigation is distinctive for several reasons: (1) it focuses on application-level features, instead of hardware performance counters, CPU instructions, or VM bytecode; (2) it is carried out from the data-oriented perspective, charting an optimization space often known to be too "application-specific" to quantify and generalize; (3) it offers the first clues on the impact of unifying application-level energy management and hardware-level energy management; (4) it provides an in-depth analysis from a whole-system perspective, considering energy consumption not only resulting from CPU cores, but also from caches and DRAM.

The focus of this paper lies upon "charting" the optimization space. In the future, we are interested in applying the findings in this paper — together with the library we developed — to application-level energy optimization. Two directions that appear to fit nicely with our study are (1) energy co-optimization through program refactoring and deployment-site configuration; (2) energy optimization through search-based software engineering, such as applying the data-oriented characterizations described in the paper as the dimensions of search space, and jRAPL as a tool, for software energy optimization.

A full set of the experimental results, the source code of jRAPL, the benchmarks, and all raw data, can be found online at http://kliu20.github.io/jRAPL/.

Acknowledgments. We thank the anonymous reviewers for their high-quality and thorough comments and suggestions. We also thank Jianfei Hu, Amol Patil, and Harry Xu for useful discussions. This work is partially supported by US NSF CCF-1054515 and CAPES-Brazil.

References

1. Baek, W., Chilimbi, T.: Green: A framework for supporting energy-conscious programming using controlled approximation. In: PLDI (2010)
2. Cao, T., Blackburn, S., Gao, T., McKinley, K.: The yin and yang of power and performance for asymmetric hardware and managed software. In: ISCA (2012)
3. Carbin, M., Kim, D., Misailovic, S., Rinard, M.: Proving acceptability properties of relaxed nondeterministic approximate programs. In: PLDI (2012)
4. Cohen, M., Zhu, H., Emgin, S., Liu, Y.: Energy types. In: OOPSLA (2012)

5. David, H., Gorbatov, E., Hanebutte, U., Khanna, R., Le, C.: Rapl: Memory power estimation and capping. In: ISLPED (2010)
6. Dong, M., Zhong, L.: Self-constructive high-rate system energy modeling for battery-powered mobile systems. In: MobiSys (2011)
7. Farkas, K., Flinn, J., Back, G., Grunwald, D., Anderson, J.: Quantifying the energy consumption of a pocket computer and a java virtual machine. In: SIGMETRICS (2000)
8. Goldberg, D.: What every computer scientist should know about floating-point arithmetic. ACM Comput. Surv. 23(1), 5–48 (1991)
9. Hähnel, M., Döbel, B., Völp, M., Härtig, H.: Measuring energy consumption for short code paths using rapl. SIGMETRICS Perform. Eval. Rev. 40(3), 13–17 (2012)
10. Hao, S., Li, D., Halfond, W., Govindan, R.: Estimating mobile application energy consumption using program analysis. In: ICSE (2013)
11. Horowitz, M., Indermaur, T., Gonzalez, R.: Low-power digital design. In: IEEE Symposium Low Power Electronics (1994)
12. Kambadur, M., Kim, M.A.: An experimental survey of energy management across the stack. In: OOPSLA, pp. 329–344 (2014)
13. Kwon, Y., Tilevich, E.: Reducing the energy consumption of mobile applications behind the scenes. In: ICSM (2013)
14. Li, D., Hao, S., Halfond, W., Govindan, R.: Calculating source line level energy information for android applications. In: ISSTA (2013)
15. Liu, Y.D.: Energy-efficient synchronization through program patterns. In: Proceedings of GREENS 2012 (2012)
16. Pinto, G., Castor, F., Liu, Y.: Mining questions about software energy consumption. In: MSR (2014)
17. Pinto, G., Castor, F., Liu, Y.: Understanding energy behaviors of thread management constructs. In: OOPSLA (2014)
18. Ribic, H., Liu, Y.: Energy-efficient work-stealing language runtimes. In: ASPLOS (2014)
19. Sahin, C., Pollock, L., Clause, J.: How do code refactorings affect energy usage? In: ESEM (2014)
20. Seo, S.C., Malek, Medvidovic, N.: Estimating the energy consumption in pervasive java-based systems. In: PerCom (2008)
21. Subramaniam, B., Feng, W.-c.: Towards energy-proportional computing for enterprise-class server workloads. In: ICPE (2013)
22. Tiwari, V., Malik, S., Wolfe, A., Lee, M.: Instruction level power analysis and optimization of software. Journal of VLSI Signal Processing 13, 1–18 (1996)
23. Zhu, H.S., Lin, C., Liu, Y.D.: A programming model for sustainable software. In: ICSE 2015 (May 2015)

Resource Specification
for Prototyping Human-Intensive Systems

Seung Yeob Shin[1], Yuriy Brun[1], Leon J. Osterweil[1],
Hari Balasubramanian[2], and Philip L. Henneman[3]

[1] School of Computer Science, University of Massachusetts, Amherst, MA, USA
{shin,brun,ljo}@cs.umass.edu
[2] Department of Industrial Engineering, University of Massachusetts, Amherst, MA, USA
hbalasubraman@ecs.umass.edu
[3] Department of Emergency Medicine, Tufts-Baystate Medical Center, Springfield, MA, USA
henneman@baystatehealth.org

Abstract. Today's software systems rely heavily on complex resources, such as humans. Human-intensive systems are particularly important in our society, especially in the healthcare, financial, and software development domains. One challenge in developing such systems is that the system design must account for the constraints, capabilities, and allocation policies of their complex resources, particularly the humans. The resources, their capabilities, and their allocation policies and constraints need to be carefully specified, and modeled. Toward the goal of supporting the design of systems that make effective use of such resources, we introduce a resource specification language and a process-aware, discrete-event simulation engine that simulates system executions while adhering to these resource specifications. The simulation supports (1) modeling the resources that are used by the system, and the ways in which they are used, (2) experimenting with different resource capability mixes and allocation policies, and (3) identifying such undesirable situations as bottlenecks, and inefficiencies that result from these mixes and policies. The joint use of detailed resource specifications and simulation supports rapid evaluation of human-intensive system designs. We evaluate our specification language and simulation framework in the healthcare domain, on a software system for managing a hospital emergency department.

1 Introduction

Many software systems constantly interact with humans and other complex resources. Insufficient attention to these interactions at system design time can reduce the quality and effectiveness of the system. In this paper, we tackle the development of software systems that interact with complex resources. We argue that understanding both the *process* the resources follow, and the resources themselves in terms of their *availability*, *skills*, and *constraints*, early in the development process can improve system quality, ease validation by directly involving domain experts and customers in the design process, and allow for documentation of assumptions and requirements, communication among the developers, and traceability and improved debugging.

We provide a language for formally specifying and modeling complex resources and their interactions with one another and the software components, and an automated

© Springer-Verlag Berlin Heidelberg 2015
A. Egyed and I. Schaefer (Eds.): FASE 2015, LNCS 9033, pp. 332–346, 2015.
DOI: 10.1007/978-3-662-46675-9_22

discrete-event simulator to support dynamically analyzing the effects of different re-source mixes and resource-allocation policies.

We motivate and evaluate our work through a representative example scenario based on a hospital's emergency department (ED) modeled after the Baystate Medical Center ED, in Springfield, MA, USA. An ED administrator is tasked with making the ED more efficient. The ED sees an average of 288 patients per day, employs 26 doctors, 41 nurses, 5 triage nurses, and 16 clerks, and houses 48 beds, 2 x-ray rooms, and 4 CT-scan ma-chines. The administrator notices that the patients' average length of stay (LoS) is 297 minutes, exceeding the national average, and that patients spend, on average, 20 minutes in the waiting room before being seen. Further, the doctors and nurses are underutilized during the night and overutilized during the day. The administrator decides that the ED needs a modern software system to manage patient care, billing, supplies, and staff. Part of this system is a patient-management software component that will track each patient and allocate doctors, nurses, and other resources. This component has to make deci-sions about resource allocations, manage resources, such as beds and equipment, and also interact with the human resources, such as doctors, nurses, and technicians. The administrator's goals are to (1) automate the patient handling process, (2) evaluate re-source allocation policies, (3) understand the constraints that impact resource utilization to develop shift schedules that balance utilization, and (4) understand the hospital's ef-ficiency bottlenecks. To design and implement the patient-management component, the developers will need to interact with domain experts to model the process patients un-dergo, and the involved resources. This model will serve as documentation, enable sim-ulation to evaluate resource-allocation policies, detect resource utilization inefficiencies, and support the administrator's decisions about how to best spend money on resources.

This paper makes the following three contributions:

1. A precise resource specification language for capabilities, interactions, allocation policies, and scheduling constraints of complex resources.
2. A process-aware discrete-event simulator JSim that respects the resource specifica-tions and constraints.
3. A case study applying our approach to discover implications of resource allocation and scheduling policies, and thus helping guide the design of a hospital ED patient-management software system.

2   Resource Modeling

This section describes our language for specifying resources, their capabilities, and the constraints and policies governing their allocation.

2.1   Resource Characteristics

We identified six aspects of resources that must be specified to enable accurately as-signing resources to tasks:

1. the resource's *capabilities*, (e.g. the tasks it may perform),
2. *attributes* (e.g., certifications and experience),

3. a *guard* qualification of those capabilities and attributes based on the dynamic state of the system (e.g., a doctor's availability is affected by the number of patients she is already caring for),
4. an *assignment policy* for enforcing resource constraints (e.g., the doctor who performed a surgery is the one who discharges the patient),
5. a *contention policy* for activity selection when multiple activities require the same resource instance (e.g., when one doctor is caring for multiple patients, the critical patients must come first), and
6. a *selection policy* for resource selection when multiple resource instances satisfy the needs of an activity (e.g., assigning a doctor to a new patient).

We designed our resource-specification language around the ability to easily and precisely specify each of the above aspects. In our language, a resource is a collection of *capabilities* and *attributes*. Each of a resource's capabilities is qualified with a *guard*, a predicate that can specify constraints and policies for allocating resources. For example, the specification of a resource with two capabilities, triage and treat, may have guards indicating that the resource's triage skills are high for all patients except gunshot-wound patients, and are particularly low late in the evening.

Each capability's *contention policy* specifies how the system decides what to do when that resource is requested by multiple activities. The contention policy is evaluated dynamically, based on an activity's priority, resource needs, and attributes. For example, a doctor may be allocated to patients on a first-come first-served basis, based on the severity of the illness, randomly, or some combination of these.

Finally, each capability's *selection policy* similarly specifies which of a set of suitable resources (e.g., a set of qualified and available doctors) is chosen. Again, this policy is evaluated dynamically.

2.2 Resource Model

Figure 1 shows the static relations among the entities that define a resource. This metamodel is an extension of an earlier, less expressive resource metamodel [14]. As already noted, a resource is composed of *capabilities*, tasks the resource can perform, and *attributes*, which describe the characteristics of the resource. Thus, for example, a cost attribute should be included in the specification of the doctor resource if the cost effectiveness of the doctor is to be analyzed. A particularly

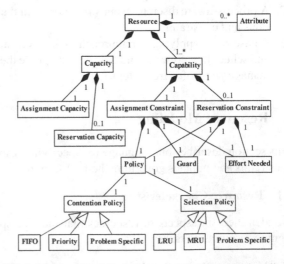

Fig. 1. The metamodel of a resource specification describes the static relations of the entities that define a resource

Attribute Declaration

```
<declare-attribute name="location" type="string" />
<declare-attribute name="working" type="boolean" />
```

Resource Model

```
<resource type="TrRN">
<attribute name="location" value="" />
<attribute name="working" value="" />
<capacity assignment_available="1" />
<capability name="Triage">
<assignment guard="working==true" effort_needed="1"
        contention_policy="FIFO" selection_policy="LeastUtilizedFirst : ProblemSpecific" />
</capability>
</resource>
```

Resource Instances

```
<instantiate type="TrRN" number="2" />
<instance type="TrRN" id="1" set_attribute="location" value="shared" />
<instance type="TrRN" id="1" set_attribute="working" value="true" />
<instance type="TrRN" id="2" set_attribute="location" value="shared" />
<instance type="TrRN" id="2" set_attribute="working" value="true" />
```

Fig. 2. The resource model for the process of handling patients specifies a triage nurse resource (TrRN). The attributes of the resource model (top) are used by the triage nurse model (middle). Two instances (bottom) of the resource show two sample triage nurses.

key attribute is capacity, comprised of assignment capacity and reservation capacity, This attribute bounds the number of activities a resource may participate in simultaneously, and is used to ensure that the simulator does not allocate to any resource more activities than that resource can handle. Both assignment and reservation capacities are needed because, for example, a doctor may care for multiple patients (up to the reservation capacity bound), but can only work on one at a time (assuming the assignment capacity is set to 1).

Figure 2 shows an example of a resource specification. It defines the attributes of the resource model (top), the resource model itself (middle), and two instances of triage nurse resources (TrRN).

Allocating resources to a given activity requires knowing more than the capability and capacity of the resources. It also requires knowing (1) the availability of each resource, (2) the (estimated) effort the given activity requires from a resource, and (3) constraints on reserving and assigning to each resource. Each capability consists of a reservation and an assignment constraint. Each constraint is specified in the form of a guard, a Boolean expression defined over the dynamic variable values of the process. For example, an assignment guard might be used to specify that only a triage nurse who is working can be assigned as a resource to an activity (<assignment guard = "working==true"> in Figure 2). The guards can also specify what shift a nurse works,

Step	Resource request specification
Triage	triage_nurse: Triage, `blocking`
Register	clerk: Register, `blocking`
PlaceInBed	bed: PlaceInBed, `blocking`
Treat	reserved_doctor: MDTreat, 1, `replaceable`, `blocking`
Treat	reserved_nurse: RNTreat, 1, `replaceable`, `blocking`
RNAssess, RNDischarge	nurse: RNTreat, `blocking`, reserved_nurse
MDAssess, Procedure, MDDischarge	doctor: MDTreat, `blocking`, reserved_doctor

Fig. 3. Resource request specifications. Each step in Figure 4 has a resource request specification associated with it.

when the nurse takes breaks and eats meals, and when personal considerations allow the nurse to work late, or leave early.

Human resources exert effort in performing activities, whereas other resources (e.g., beds and equipment) do not. For resources that exert effort, the amount of effort can be estimated using optional `skill level` and `experience` attributes. (Our triage nurse example does not employ these optional attributes.)

Finally, constraints on resource contention (multiple activities requesting the same resource instance) and activity contention (multiple resource instances capable of providing the capability requested by a given activity) are specified by the *contention policy* and *selection policy*, respectively. First-come first-serve (`FIFO`) is an example of a built-in policy, but custom policies can be defined as arbitrary functions over the dynamic variables of the process. Least utilized resource first (`LeastUtilizedFirst`, see Figure 2) is an example of a custom policy. Other built-in policies not shown in Figure 2 include least (`LRU`) or most (`MRU`) recently used policies, and a policy based on the priority of the request (`Priority`).

2.3   Resource Request Model

The resource model includes specifications of resource requests. We separate resource requests from process activities (described in Section 3) into two types, a reservation request and an assignment request. Each activity generates a separate request for each resource it needs. Figure 3 shows several examples of resource requests:

Reservation Request: reserved-resource: capability, count, [`replaceable`,] `blocking` | `nonblocking`
Assignment Request: resource: capability, `blocking` | `nonblocking` [, reserved-resource]

Both reservation and assignment requests ask for an available resource that performs a particular capability. Which resource is returned depends on the dynamic state of the process. For example, a doctor may be assigned to drawing a patient's blood, but only when all nurses are fully assigned, and only when the blood draw task is considered to require a small amount of effort and a low skill level. Our request model supports the use of blocking requests (see the `blocking` and `nonblocking` keywords in the request definitions) to ensure that only fully qualified resources are allocated to the activity. The `replaceable` keyword means that a resource may be replaced by another, under certain situations.

3   Process Modeling

Our approach represents processes by an executable language that describes a sequences of steps. Each step specifies the need for one or more resources. We use of the Little-JIL process definition language [19], which has been used in previous work to support the definition of complex processes in the medical, election, software development, and other domains [3, 13, 15, 20, 21]. Little-JIL is not a contribution of this paper. We did, however, enhance Little-JIL by augmenting each step specification with an allocation (either reservation or assignment) request.

We now outline the Little-JIL features most relevant to our work on resource specification. We refer the reader to prior work for a complete language definition [19]. A Little-JIL activity specification is defined using hierarchically decomposed steps. A step represents an activity or a task that is part of the modeled process. Each step has a name and a set of badges to represent control flow among its substeps, its interface (a specification of its input and output artifacts and the resources it requires), and the exceptions it handles. A step with no substeps is called a leaf step and represents an activity to be performed without any explicitly defined process guidance.

Every non-leaf step has a sequencing badge (an icon embedded in the left portion of the step bar), which defines the order of substep execution, such as sequential (right arrow), in parallel (equal sign), one chosen from a set (circle with a horizontal line), or in sequence in which substeps are to be tried as alternatives (right arrow with an × on its tail). The latter two kinds of steps enable specification of certain kinds of uncertainties that might arise during process execution.

Each Little-JIL step interface specifies the types of resources the step requires. Allocating a resource instance to the step happens dynamically, during process execution by the resource manager. We use the ROMEO resource manager [12]. Every step requires at least one resource, specially designated as the step's agent. Little-JIL agents may be either humans or automated devices.

Figure 4 shows an example high-level process definition in Little-JIL that specifies the process of handling patients in an ED. When a patient arrives, she is received, which consists of being triaged, registered, and then placed in a bed. Being placed in a bed involves being treated: assessed by a nurse and then a doctor, undergoing procedures,

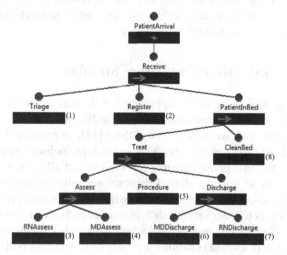

Fig. 4.   A patient treatment process, specified with the Little-JIL process model language [19]. This high-level model abstracts away lower-level steps, denoted in (parentheses). The full, detailed model can be found at http://people.cs.umass.edu/~shin/ed/.

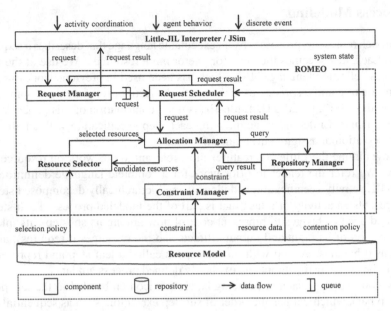

Fig. 5. A view of the resource-aware JSim discrete-event process simulator that focuses on ROMEO, the resource management component

and being discharged, first by a doctor and then by a nurse. Finally, the bed is cleaned and made available for assignment to support the treatment of another patient.

While this process activity flow is relatively simple, its execution depends on details of the resource model that may contain intricate dependencies among the doctors, nurses, beds, and other resources.

4   JSim Resource-Aware Simulator

The final piece of our approach is a discrete-event simulator that simulates processes whose activities are modeled in Little-JIL, and whose resources are modeled in ROMEO. To this end, we have extended JSim [14], an existing discrete-event simulator of Little-JIL/ROMEO processes. Our extensions include support for (1) resource instances, (2) the two-phase resource reservation and allocation, and (3) contention policy constrains to select preferred requests, selection policy constrains to select preferred resources. These extensions enable the simulator to support such scenarios as (1) allowing doctors to have varying shift constraints, (2) enforcing the same doctor always handles a given patient, unless the doctor's shift ends, at which point the patient is handed off to a new doctor, (3) enabling a variety of scheduling policies, such as handing the sickest patient first, or using the least utilized resource first. Additionally we have redesigned the simulator's architecture to improve the separation of concerns and localization of key aspects of the system.

Figure 5 shows the extended JSim architecture, focusing on the resource handling aspects of the simulator. The architecture separates the activity issues from resource concerns, which makes it easy to keep track of resource allocations, utilizations, waiting times, and other properties that other simulators have difficulty reporting (see Section 6). In addition, extended JSIM treats resource constraints as a separate concern, which eases changing them, facilitating experimentation with different resource allocation strategies.

The Little-JIL Interpreter is an abstract representation of a number of JSim components not related to resource management. The activity coordination artifact represents the Little-JIL activity definition. The agent behavior artifact specifies details (such as speed and cost) of the way in which resource instances provide their capabilities. The discrete event clock is an event arrival stream that triggers the execution of process activities. During simulation, activities first acquire and then release resources by sending requests to ROMEO, which evaluates the dynamic guards and constraints on each resource and determines which resources satisfy the request, and responds with either a satisfactory resource, or a message that the needed resource is unavailable.

The Request Manager receives and responds to reservation, assignment, and release requests, which are queued by contention policies in the resource model. The Allocation Manager allocates resources in collaboration with the Resource Selector, Constraint Manager, and Repository Manager components. When the Allocation Manager receives an allocation request for a capability, the Repository Manager identifies candidate resources, the Constraint Manager evaluates the resources' guard constraints to remove unsuitable resources, and the Resource Selector evaluates the selection policies to select a candidate. For a release request, the Allocation Manager interacts with the Repository Manager to adjust released resources' allocated capacity values.

This architecture yields flexibility for exploring resource constraint specifications effectively. For example, the Request Manager can be instrumented to record the history of requests, and identify resource bottlenecks by finding which resources spend the most time waiting for activities, and which activities spend the most time waiting for resources. The Allocation Manager likewise can be instrumented to record the resource allocation history and compute resource utilization levels over various time granularities (e.g., hourly), even taking into account resource unavailability due to such events as lunch times and breaks.

5   Case Study: Emergency Department

We evaluated our approach by using our resource-aware discrete-event simulator to expedite the simulation and evaluation of a range of ED operations management strategies. Our aim was to show that our approach can suggest the characteristics and design of a system that has superior operational behavior, and that respects even very intricate resource characteristics and constraints. We used specifications of various ED operational practices, resource characteristics and mixes, and allocation approaches to run JSim simulations aimed at understanding the effects of these specifications on such key operational characteristics as patient waiting time, resource allocation levels, and overall costs. Our domain expert, who both helped us develop the specifications and validate the models and simulation results, has decades of experience as an emergency physician and an ED manager at the Baystate Medical Center Emergency Department, in Springfield, MA, USA. He further has significant experience with research in discrete-event simulation of EDs [2].

5.1 Emergency Department Characteristics

ED resources range from beds, blood, and x-ray devices, to a spectrum of human resources, from receptionists and porters, to nurses of varying kinds, to doctors with various specialties and skill levels. Resources are always scarce in order to keep down the costs of operating the ED. Therefore, wise allocation of these resources is necessary to assure timely and competent care. A full description of the ED activities, resources, constraints, and policies is beyond the scope of this paper. Instead, we describe only a few details to illustrate the complexity of the models. Some ED characteristics that posed interesting challenges for us include:

Six acuity levels: ED patients are classified into six acuity levels based on the severity of their ailments. The care process varies based on the acuity. A level-six (sickest) patient is immediately allocated a doctor (MD), a nurse (RN), and a bed. These patients also get highest priority in x-ray room and CT room allocation. In contrast, a level-one patient undergoes fewer procedures, each of which with a lower resource allocation priority.

Arrivals: Our process definition allows patients to arrive in two ways: Critical patients, by definition, always arrive by ambulance, while other patients arrive on their own. Critical patients are the sickest (acuity level six), while the others are categorized into the remaining five acuity levels. Patient arrival rates over the 24-hour period are specified by a Poisson distribution, based on actual arrival rates at the Baystate Medical Center.

Staffing: Human resources work on a shift system; the number of available humans varies over 24 hours. Typically, an MD or an RN will work one of three different 8-hour shifts, although our simulations suggest greater flexibility in the start times and durations of shifts could lead to shortening the patients' LoS.

Same MD-RN constraints: A patient assigned to a bed is cared for by the same MD and RN throughout the stay, with changes only when the MD's or RN's shifts end, or they are on a break.

Workload: Estimates of the effort required to perform activities are specified by triangular distributions, based on the Baystate Medical Center data. These estimates, along with the specifications of the skill levels of the resources, dictate the amount of time required by each of the activities.

Fast & Main tracks: The ED operates two tracks. The fast track cares for low acuity patients (levels 1–3), and the main track, high acuity (4–6). Each track has its own beds and MD and RN resources. At night, the fast track closes and its patients are transferred to the main track. During this transfer, fast track resources are deallocated and appropriate main track resources are allocated for the patients.

5.2 Emergency Department Activity Model

While we omit the full models from this paper, for exposition, we present a small subset of the ED process and resource specifications. Figure 6 illustrates the patient-testing process for an acuity-level-four patient. The `AL4Test` step at the root is a parallel step, meaning the lab test process, `AL4LabProc`, can be done in parallel with `AL4Test`. The 70% annotation on `AL4LabProc`'s pre-requisite means that 70% of acuity-level-four patients require the lab test. For the other tests, a nurse checks a patient's ECG (`RNECG`), and then a doctor checks the ECG result (`MDCkECG`), since `AL4ECGProc` is a sequential step. After the ECG test, a nurse gives a medication to the patient (`RNMedHi`), and the patient is transferred to the CT or x-ray room.

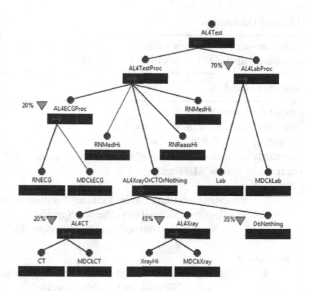

Fig. 6. The Little-JIL definition of the patient testing process, which is part of the care an acuity-level-four patient undergoes in an ED

This behavior is represented by the `AL4XrayOrCTOrNothing` choice step, which means only one of its child steps will be executed, with step pre-requisites indicating the probability of each alternative. While space constraints prevent us from describing the full patient care process and resource models, they can be found at `http://people.cs.umass.edu/~shin/ed/`.

Step	Resource request specification
RNECG, RNMedHi, RNReassHi	nurse: RNTreat, blocking, reserved_nurse
MDCkECG, MDCkCT, MDCkXray, MDCkLab	doctor: MDTreat, blocking, reserved_doctor
CT	ct_room: CTScan, blocking
XrayHi	x-ray_room: X-rayScan, blocking

Fig. 7. The resource request specifications associated with each step in Figure 6

Figure 7 shows the resource requests made by the leaf steps of the process. All requests are blocking, meaning step execution cannot begin until the resource is assigned. For each patient, the MD and RN requests can only be satisfied by the previously reserved resources.

5.3 Emergency Department Resource Model

Figure 8 describes the resource model for MD, and shows three example instances of MDs. The full model (omitted here), also defines the RN, TrRN, clerk, bed, x-ray room, and

Attribute Declaration

```
<declare-attribute name="location" type="string" />
<declare-attribute name="shift" type="string" />
```

Resource Model

```
<resource type="MD">
<attribute name="location" value="" />
<attribute name="shift" value="" />
<capacity assignment_available="1" reservation_available="1"/>
<capability name="MDTreat">
<reservation
    guard="location==artifact(patient.location) && time>=start(shift) && time<end(shift)"
    contention_policy="SickestFirst : ProblemSpecific"
    selection_policy="LeastUtilizedFirst : ProblemSpecific"
    effort_needed="0" />
<assignment
    guard="location==artifact(patient.location) && time>=start(shift) && time<end(shift)"
    contention_policy="SickestFirst : ProblemSpecific"
    selection_policy="LeastUtilizedFirst : ProblemSpecific"
    effort_needed="1" />
</capability>
</resource>
```

Resource Instances

```
<instantiate type="MD" number="3" />
<instance type="MD" id="1" set_attribute="location" value="main-track" />
<instance type="MD" id="1" set_attribute="shift" value="7AM--3PM" />
<instance type="MD" id="2" set_attribute="location" value="main-track" />
<instance type="MD" id="2" set_attribute="shift" value="3PM--11PM" />
<instance type="MD" id="3" set_attribute="location" value="main-track" />
<instance type="MD" id="3" set_attribute="shift" value="11PM--7AM" />
```

Fig. 8. The MD resource model, specifying attributes, capabilities, and allocation policies

CT room resources. Human resource attributes include their work shift and location (fast track or main track), and bed attributes include a location.

Every capability of every MD and RN resource has a guard that specifies when the resource is available to provide the capability. One use of this guard is specifying that fast track doctors are only available for fast track patients and only during their shifts.

In our ED model, MD and RN resources are always reserved before being assigned (whereas our language also allows for assignment without reservation). When a shift change occurs, a reserved resource becomes unavailable, prompting ROMEO to reserve a replacement. This approach enforces both same MD-RN constraints, and ED shift change policies. A similar approach allows for fast track and main track bed resource allocation policies.

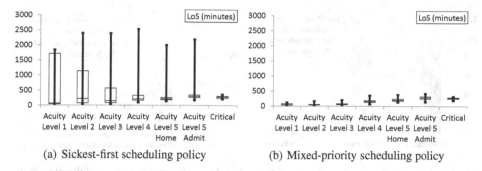

(a) Sickest-first scheduling policy   (b) Mixed-priority scheduling policy

Fig. 9. Using the mixed-priority scheduling policy greatly reduces the LoS for patients across all acuity levels

5.4 Simulation Results

Effective ED management has multiple competing goals, including decreasing patients' LoS, increasing net revenue, and increasing service quality. An ED can decrease patients' LoS by hiring more staff and building more facilities; but this increases cost and reduces net revenue. Thus, EDs seek resource allocation approaches that decrease patients' LoS without increasing cost or sacrificing quality. While LoS and revenue are straightforward to measure, there are multiple ways to measure quality of care. Because handoffs can cause miscommunication we use the number of patient handoffs due to shift changes to measure care quality.

We next present the results of three ED simulation studies that demonstrate how our approaches and tools can expedite exploring the effects of changing resource mixes and allocation strategies on LoS, resource utilization levels, and number of handoffs.

> Situation 1: The ED wishes to explore how different resource allocation policies affect the patients' LoS.

Our domain expert wanted to explore the consequences of changing the sickest-first policy to treat acuity levels 1–4 as equal. Figure 9 shows how the two policies affect the LoS. Figure 9(a) shows that with the sickest-first policy, the average LoS for all patients is 388 minutes. Low acuity patients experience high LoS variation because they are resource-starved when there are many sicker patients. Figure 9(b) shows that with the mixed-priority policy, overall LoS is decreased to 275 minutes, and the starvation problem for low acuity patients is ameliorated. Our approach expedited this study by requiring only a simple modification to the resource specification (`contention_policy = "MixedPriority : ProblemSpecific"`) and a simple definition of the policy.

> Situation 2: ED beds fill quickly and waiting time increases when patient arrival rates increase. The ED seeks guidance about what investments are likely to be most cost-effective in reducing waiting time.

EDs routinely deal with the problem of insufficient numbers of beds by creating *hallway beds*, beds placed in the ED hallways. This is a low-cost, temporary solution, but

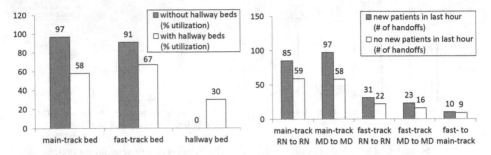

Fig. 10. Allowing the creation of hallway beds greatly reduces the bed resource utilization

Fig. 11. The number of handoffs decreases when doctors and nurses stop accepting new patients 1 hour before their shifts end

hallway beds cause problems of privacy, noise, and poor traffic flow. We modeled the allocation of hallway beds specifying that they are only allocatable to stable patients, and only when the ED is sufficiently crowded. Figure 10 shows how bed utilization decreases dramatically when hallway beds are added. Hallway beds decrease the waiting times for both tracks, with overall patient LoS dropping from 388 to 159 minutes. Our approach expedited this study by requiring only a modest change to a guard in the specification of the hallway bed resource.

> Situation 3: The ED recognizes that handoffs are error-prone and seeks a strategy for reducing handoffs.

Our domain expert suggested that if an MD does not accept *new* patients in the last hour of the shift, that time might be used for more careful handoffs, leading to better quality of care, but increasing patient LoS. Figure 11 compares the number of handoffs in each track when MDs do and do not accept new patients in the last hour of their shifts. The main track handoffs reduce significantly, while the fast track improvement is relatively small. However, this changed working policy causes an increase in overall LoS from 159 to 170 minutes. Our approach expedited this study, again by requiring only a modest change to a guard (reservation_guard = time >= start(shift) && time < end(shift)-1) for the MD and RN resources.

5.5 Discussion

Complex domains like hospital EDs benefit substantially from systems that enforce careful resource management and respect resource complexity and constraints. The design of such systems can be suggested by analysis of simulations that reflect accurately and precisely the effects of resource policies on overall system characteristics.

Our work has shown that flexibility in resource specification and management, facilitated by its implementation as a separate architectural component, can expedite the rapid development and evaluation of simulations that can serve as prototypes of such systems. Our approach and tools helped us to model behavior such as shift changes and handoffs easily. We showed that easy modifications to resource specifications sufficed to support creating simulations that compared resource scheduling strategies, and allocation criteria, and that introduced new resources types and uses. The architecture of our simulation approach facilitated these comparisons by concentrating needed changes in the resource and constraint management components.

6 Related Work

Simulating less-detailed resource models is common, exploring domains such as software development [1, 7, 11], healthcare [2, 4, 10] and other domains that employ intricate processes. Some discrete-event simulation approaches offer enhanced flexibility in defining process event flow [5, 18]. Others have built distributed discrete-event simulators [6, 17] to exploit the power of a distributed environment, but have not focused on the resources.

System dynamics approaches [7,8] incorporate resource issues more prominently, integrating representations of both discrete and continuous dynamics into discrete-event simulations. However, even these approaches fail to represent humans behavior in sufficient detail. Incorporating human behavior in software development, Hanne et al. [16] discuss how human factors influence software development productivity, but focuses on the relation between productivity and learning, time pressure, and other psychological factors. However, their work considers these human factors only as stochastic variables. Lee et al. [9] propose a simulation framework with resource management modules for resource intensive service and business modeling, but their resource models are simplistic, and do not address how system context can dynamically change a resource's capabilities and allocation constraints.

7 Contributions and Future Work

We have developed a resource specification language that allows for precise specification of the capabilities of complex resources, their interactions with one another and with processes that use them, their allocation policies, and their scheduling constraints. We evaluated our language by specifying, in considerable detail, a hospital emergency department's patient handling software component that tracks patients and assigns resources. This evaluation showed that our language is expressive enough to describe complex resources, such as humans, restrictions on their use, and constraints on their allocation policies. Our work suggests that discrete event simulations based on careful resource specification can expedite the design of complex human-intensive systems.

Encouraged by these results, we next will explore (1) developing measures of the reliability of these simulations, (2) identifying static analysis approaches to validating the correctness of these simulations, and (3) measuring flexibility and implementation speed gains deriving from separating resource management from activity management.

Acknowledgments. Alexander Wise helped in developing and supporting various Little-JIL tools. This material is based upon work supported by the National Science Foundation under grants IIS-1239334, CNS-1258588, and IIS-0705772.

References

1. Alan, M.J.S., Christie, M.: Organizational and social simulation of a software requirements development process. Software Process: Improvement and Practice 5, 103–110 (2000)
2. Beck, E.: A discrete event simulation approach to resource management, process changes and task prioritization in emergency departments. Master's thesis, Department of Mechanical and Industrial Engineering, University of Massachusetts, Amherst, MA, USA (2009)
3. Clarke, L., Gaitenby, A., Gyllstrom, D., Katsh, E., Marzilli, M., Osterweil, L.J., Sondheimer, N.K., Wing, L., Wise, A., Rainey, D.: A process-driven tool to support online dispute resolution. In: dg.o, pp. 356–357 (May 2006)
4. Duguay, C., Chetouane, F.: Modeling and improving emergency department systems using discrete event simulation. Simulation 83(3), 311–320 (2007)
5. Hubl, A.: Flexible model for analyzing production systems with discrete event simulation. In: WSC, pp. 1554–1565 (December 2011)
6. Jacobs, P.H.M., Lang, N.A., Verbraeck, A.: Web-based simulation 1: D-SOL; a distributed Java based discrete event simulation architecture. In: WSC, pp. 793–800 (December 2002)
7. KeungSik Choi, T.K.: Doo-Hwan Bae. An approach to a hybrid software process simulation using the devs formalism. Software Process: Improvement and Practice 11, 373–383 (2006)
8. Kofman, E.: Discrete event simulation of hybrid systems. SIAM Journal on Scientific Computing 25, 1771–1797 (2004)
9. Lee, Y.M., An, L., Bagchi, S., Connors, D., Kapoor, S., Katircioglu, K., Wang, W., Xu, J.: Discrete event simulation modeling of resource planning and service order execution for service businesses. In: WSC, pp. 2227–2233 (December 2007)
10. McCarthy, M.L., Ding, R., Pines, J.M., Zeger, S.L.: Comparison of methods for measuring crowding and its effects on length of stay in the emergency department. Academic Emergency Medicine 18(12), 1269–1277 (2011)
11. Podnar, I., Mikac, B.: Software maintenance process analysis using discrete-event simulation. In: CSMR (March 2001)
12. Raunak, M., Osterweil, L.: Resource management for complex and dynamic environments. IEEE Transactions on Software Engineering 39(3), 384–402 (2012)
13. Raunak, M.S., Chen, B., Elssamadisy, A., Clarke, L.A., Osterweil, L.J.: Definition and analysis of election processes. In: SPW/ProSim 2006, vol. 3966, pp. 178–185 (May 2006)
14. Raunak, M.S., Osterweil, L.J., Wise, A., Clarke, L.A., Henneman, P.L.: Simulating patient flow through an emergency department using process-driven discrete event simulation. In: SEHC (May 2009)
15. Shin, S.Y., Balasubramanian, H., Brun, Y., Henneman, P.L., Osterweil, L.J.: Resource scheduling through resource-aware simulation of emergency departments. In: SEHC, pp. 64–70 (May 2013)
16. Hanne, H.N.T.: Simulating human resources in software development processes. Technical Report 64, Fraunhofer-Institut fur Techno- und Wirtschaftsmathematik (2004)
17. Vanmechelen, K., De Munck, S., Broeckhove, J.: Conservative distributed discrete event simulation on Amazon EC2. In: CCGrid, pp. 853–860 (May 2012)
18. Wagner, G.: Extending discrete event simulation by adding an activity concept for business process modeling and simulation. In: WSC, pp. 2951–2962 (December 2009)
19. Wise, A.: Little-JIL 1.5 language report. Technical Report 2006–051, Department of Computer Science, University of Massachusetts, Amherst (2006)
20. Zhao, X., Brun, Y., Osterweil, L.J.: Supporting process undo and redo in software engineering decision making. In: ICSSP, pp. 56–60 (May 2013)
21. Zhao, X., Osterweil, L.J.: An approach to modeling and supporting the rework process in refactoring. In: ICSSP, pp. 110–119 (June 2012)

The Prophecy of Undo

Martín Abadi*

University of California, Santa Cruz, USA

Abstract. Prophecy variables are auxiliary program variables whose values are defined in terms of current program state and future behavior. This paper explains their relevance to reasoning about systems with "undo" operations, and develops an approach that facilitates their use.

1 Introduction

Auxiliary variables are often helpful in reasoning about systems and in proving their correctness. The most common auxiliary variables are history variables, whose values are defined in terms of current system state and past behavior. On the other hand, the definitions of prophecy variables, which can be seen as dual to history variables, refer to the future behavior of a system rather than to its past behavior [1]. Prophecy variables are considerably less mundane and well-understood than history variables. Although they may seem counter-intuitive, prophecy variables are sometimes necessary for the completeness of reasoning methods. They have not been employed frequently in reasoning about actual systems, but their uses (for example, linearizability proofs [6,5]) have been compelling and significant. This paper aims to contribute to their study and to their practical application.

Specifically, this paper highlights a class of important applications for prophecy variables, namely reasoning about systems with "undo" operations. These operations play a variety of roles, such as rolling back the effects of aborted transactions, restoring from snapshots in case of a failure, and recovering from attacks (e.g., [3,4,8]). In all these cases, the correctness of "undo" is both delicate and critical. In particular, although an "undo" may be selective (for example, in security, applying only to the effects of an attack), the "undo" should not give rise to inconsistencies in a system's observable behavior. When one system component rolls back a non-deterministic computation, other components should generally roll back any of their own actions influenced by the relevant non-deterministic choices; those choices may later be revisited, leading to different results. Prophecy variables can help in reasoning about the state of the system, basically because they can predict which computations will be rolled back.

Work on these applications leads us to the development of proof strategies that facilitate the use of prophecy variables. In the presence of liveness properties, the soundness of prophecy variables generally requires a certain finiteness condition

---

* Most of this work was done while M. Abadi was at Microsoft Research. He is now at Google.

© Springer-Verlag Berlin Heidelberg 2015
A. Egyed and I. Schaefer (Eds.): FASE 2015, LNCS 9033, pp. 347–361, 2015.
DOI: 10.1007/978-3-662-46675-9_23

(roughly, that for each state there are only finitely many possible prophecies). For instance, when a variable represents an internal decision on how long a system will run, the condition helps ensure that this decision cannot be "undone" infinitely often and that the system cannot run forever. Even when this finiteness condition can be satisfied, it complicates the definition of prophecy variables. We devise an approach that allows us to ignore the condition during the bulk of the reasoning, and then ensure finiteness via a separate quotient construction. (To date, the experience with this approach is all related to "undo"; but the approach is more general, at least in theory.)

The paper focuses on two small, instructive examples. In both cases, we prove that a lower-level system with "undo" is a correct refinement of a higher-level system without "undo". The same ideas and techniques apply to reasoning about larger systems, and indeed the origin of this paper is ongoing research on a practical dataflow computing platform named Naiad [12]. The small examples of this paper have the advantage of not including the peculiarities of Naiad and other intricate features not directly relevant to our present purposes.

The literature contains a few other, somewhat related examples. In particular, Lampson has observed the relevance of prophecy variables to refinements proofs for protocols for reliable message delivery despite crashes [10]. His writings, however, do not include a precise definition of the required prophecy variables. Lampson's ideas are, to our knowledge, the most closely related to the present paper. Other work deals with the use of prophecy variables in proofs of program properties, rather than in refinement proofs, sometimes with the support of automated tools (e.g., [2]), which we do not consider in this paper. Thus, Sezgin, Tasiran, and Qadeer have developed a method for static verification of concurrent programs that includes prophecy variables [13]; they employed prophecy variables for expressing the consequences of interference between threads.

The literature also contains variations on the notion of prophecy variable and related concepts, such as backwards simulation relations [11]. In particular, Jonsson relaxed the finiteness requirement so that it needs to apply only infinitely often [7]. (He also provided an explanation of the connections between extant proof techniques, to which we refer the reader for additional background.) Those variations may well be helpful in reasoning about some systems with "undo" operations, complementing the present work.

The next section is a review of our framework for specifications and refinement proofs. Section 3 presents the first example. Section 4 introduces an approach to finiteness. Section 5 presents the second example, which leverages the results of Section 4. Section 6 concludes. Because of space constraints, we give the proofs for examples but omit those for the metatheory.

2   Specifications and Refinement Proofs (Review)

This section reviews our framework for specifications and the basic machinery of refinement mappings and prophecy variables (mostly from [1]). It contains no technical novelties.

2.1   State Spaces, Behaviors, and Properties

We assume a fixed set Σ_E of externally visible states. A *state space* Σ is a subset of $\Sigma_E \times \Sigma_I$ for some set Σ_I of internal states, or the set Σ_E itself. We let Π_E be the obvious projection mapping from $\Sigma_E \times \Sigma_I$ onto Σ_E.

The sequence $\langle\!\langle s_0, s_1, s_2, \ldots \rangle\!\rangle$ is said to be *stutter-free* if, for each i, either $s_i \neq s_{i+1}$ or the sequence is infinite and $s_i = s_j$ for all $j \geq i$. We define $\natural\sigma$ as the stutter-free sequence obtained from σ by replacing every maximal finite subsequence $s_i, s_{i+1}, \ldots, s_j$ of identical elements with the single element s_i. When S is a set of sequences, we let $\Gamma(S) = \{\tau : \exists\sigma \in S.\natural\sigma = \natural\tau\}$, and we say that S is *closed under stuttering* if $S = \Gamma(S)$.

For any set Σ, we write Σ^ω for the set of all infinite sequences of elements in Σ. We write $\sigma|_m$ for the prefix of σ of length m. We say that an infinite sequence $\langle\!\langle \sigma_0, \sigma_1, \sigma_2, \ldots \rangle\!\rangle$ of sequences in Σ^ω *converges* to the sequence σ in Σ^ω if for all $m \geq 0$ there exists $n \geq 0$ such that $\sigma_i|_m = \sigma|_m$ for all $i \geq n$. In this case, we define $\lim \sigma_i = \sigma$. We say that σ is a *limit point* of a set S if there exist elements σ_i in S such that $\lim \sigma_i = \sigma$. (While every element of S is trivially a limit point of S, in general S may have additional limit points.)

If Σ is a state space, then a Σ-*behavior* is an element of Σ^ω. A Σ_E-behavior is called an *externally visible behavior*. A Σ-*property* is a set of Σ-behaviors that is closed under stuttering. If the property contains all its limit points, then it is called a *safety property*. A Σ_E-property is called an *externally visible property*. If P is a Σ-property, then $\Pi_E(P)$ is a set of externally visible behaviors but not necessarily an externally visible property because it need not be closed under stuttering. The externally visible property *induced* by a Σ-property P is the set $\Gamma(\Pi_E(P))$. When Σ is clear from context or is irrelevant, we may use the terms *behavior* and *property* instead of Σ-behavior and Σ-property. We sometimes apply the adjective "complete", as in "complete behavior", to distinguish behaviors and properties from externally visible behaviors and properties.

2.2   State Machines

A *state machine* is a triple (Σ, F, N) where

- Σ is a state space,
- F, the set of *initial* states, is a subset of Σ,
- N, the *next-state relation*, is a subset of $\Sigma \times \Sigma$.

The *(complete) property generated by* a state machine (Σ, F, N) consists of all infinite sequences $\langle\!\langle s_0, s_1, \ldots \rangle\!\rangle$ such that $s_0 \in F$ and, for all $i \geq 0$, either $\langle s_i, s_{i+1} \rangle \in N$ or $s_i = s_{i+1}$. (We use angle brackets for elements of N, as in $\langle s_i, s_{i+1} \rangle$.) This set is closed under stuttering, so it is a Σ-property. It is also a safety property. The *externally visible property generated by* a state machine is the externally visible property induced by its complete property. In general, this externally visible property need not be a safety property.

For simplicity, we do not consider fairness conditions or other explicit liveness properties that can be imposed on state machines. Even without them, the externally visible properties generated by state machines can imply non-trivial liveness properties (see [1, Section 3] and the example of Section 5), so the finiteness condition on prophecy variables cannot be ignored.

We loosely follow the TLA approach for specifying state machines [9]. Thus, we write specifications as logical formulas, of the form:

$$\exists y_1, \ldots, y_n. \, F \wedge \Box [N]_v$$

where:

- the state is represented by a set of state functions, which we write as variables $x_1, \ldots, x_m, y_1, \ldots, y_n$;
- we distinguish external variables and internal variables, and the internal variables (in this case, $y_1, \ldots, y_n$) are existentially quantified;
- F is a formula that may refer to the variables;
- $\Box$ is the temporal-logic operator "always";
- N is a formula that may refer to the variables and also to primed versions of the variables (which denote the values of those variables in the next state);
- v is a list of variables $v_1, \ldots, v_k$, and $[N]_v$ abbreviates $N \vee ((v_1' = v_1) \wedge \ldots \wedge (v_k' = v_k))$.

The role of the subscript v is to guarantee closure under stuttering.

Such formulas do not describe state spaces, which we define separately.

2.3   Implementations and Refinement Mappings

A state machine **S** *implements* a state machine **S'** if and only if the externally visible property induced by **S** is a subset of the externally visible property induced by **S'**. In other words, **S** implements **S'** when every externally visible behavior allowed by **S** is also allowed by **S'**.

A *refinement mapping* from a state machine $\mathbf{S} = (\Sigma, F, N)$ to a state machine $\mathbf{S}' = (\Sigma', F', N')$ is a mapping $f : \Sigma \to \Sigma'$ such that:

R1. For all $s \in \Sigma$, $\Pi_E(f(s)) = \Pi_E(s)$.
R2. $f(F) \subseteq F'$.
R3. If $\langle s, t \rangle \in N$ then $\langle f(s), f(t) \rangle \in N'$ or $f(s) = f(t)$.

The following is a straightforward specialization of the soundness theorem for refinement mappings [1]:

Proposition 1. *If there exists a refinement mapping from* **S** *to* **S'**, *then* **S** *implements* **S'**.

Thus, refinement mappings, which work at the level of states, offer a convenient method for proving containment between sets of sequences of states.

2.4   Very Simple Prophecy Variables

Sometimes one needs to prove invariants and add auxiliary variables before constructing refinement mappings. As indicated in the Introduction, the most common auxiliary variables are history variables; their values are defined in terms of current system state and past behavior. For instance, for a program with an integer variable x, a history variable h may record the largest value of x seen so far; formally, h would be defined by the initial condition $h = x$ and the transition relation $h' = \mathtt{max}(h, x')$, which says that at every step the new value of h is the maximum of the previous value of h and the new value of x. Conversely, a prophecy variable might be defined by $h = \mathtt{max}(h', x)$, going from the future to the past, without an initial condition. The exact requirements on prophecy variables are, unfortunately, somewhat more intricate.

Formally, our starting point will be the notion of *simple* prophecy variables [1]. (The difference with "full-scale" prophecy variables has to do with stuttering.) Moreover, since we focus on refinement but not equivalences, and since our state machines do not include fairness conditions or other explicit liveness properties, we can omit requirements named P3 and P5 in [1]. We say that a state machine $\mathbf{S^P} = (\Sigma^P, F^P, N^P)$ *is obtained from* $\mathbf{S} = (\Sigma, F, N)$ *by adding a very simple prophecy variable* when the following requirements are satisfied:

P1. $\Sigma^P \subseteq \Sigma \times \Sigma_P$ for some set Σ_P.
P2'. $F^P = \{(s, p) \in \Sigma^P \mid s \in F\}$.
P4'. If $\langle s, s' \rangle \in N$ and $(s', p') \in \Sigma^P$
      then there exists $(s, p) \in \Sigma^P$ such that $\langle (s, p), (s', p') \rangle \in N^P$.
P6.   For all $s \in \Sigma$, the set $\{(s, p) \in \Sigma^P\}$ is finite and nonempty.

The following is a special case of the soundness theorem for prophecy variables [1]:

Proposition 2. *If $\mathbf{S^P}$ is obtained from $\mathbf{S}$ by adding a very simple prophecy variable, then $\mathbf{S}$ implements $\mathbf{S^P}$.*

3   First Example

Our first example is rather minimal. Its purpose is to illustrate why and how prophecy variables are useful for proving that a lower-level system with "undo" refines a higher-level system without "undo". Non-deterministic choice is prominent in this example and in the second one, because non-determinism typically complicates "undo", as suggested in the Introduction. More technically, the example also demonstrates how the definition of a state space with a prophecy variable can play a role similar to that of an invariant.

3.1   High-Level Specification (No "undo")

In our high-level system, an integer is chosen internally and then revealed, once. The internal choice is made by assigning a value to the internal variable y.

The publication of that choice consists in copying that value to the external variable x. Both variables have the value **ready** before those assignments.

The state space Σ_{High} is thus $(\mathbb{Z} \cup \{\text{\bf ready}\}) \times (\mathbb{Z} \cup \{\text{\bf ready}\})$.

Initial condition:

$$InitProp \stackrel{\Delta}{=} (x = y = \text{\bf ready})$$

Steps:

1. Choosing an integer:

$$Choose \stackrel{\Delta}{=} ((x = x' = y = \text{\bf ready}) \wedge (y' \in \mathbb{Z}))$$

2. Publishing the choice:

$$Publish \stackrel{\Delta}{=} ((x = \text{\bf ready}) \wedge (y \in \mathbb{Z}) \wedge (x' = y) \wedge (y' = y))$$

The high-level specification:

$$SpecH \stackrel{\Delta}{=} \exists y.(InitProp \wedge \Box[Choose \vee Publish]_{x,y})$$

3.2   Low-Level Specification (with "undo")

In the low-level specification, additional transitions can undo choices. The specification is silent on why rollbacks happen—whether because of failures or as deliberate steps. Accordingly, for simplicity, we do not model failure detection, nor do we distinguish a "redo" from an original choice.

The state space Σ_{Low} equals Σ_{High}; moreover, the initial condition and the actions for choosing and for publishing a choice are exactly as above in the high-level specification. We have one additional action for undoing a choice:

$$Undo \stackrel{\Delta}{=} ((x = x' = \text{\bf ready}) \wedge (y \in \mathbb{Z}) \wedge (y' = \text{\bf ready}))$$

The low-level specification:

$$SpecL \stackrel{\Delta}{=} \exists y.(InitProp \wedge \Box[Choose \vee Undo \vee Publish]_{x,y})$$

3.3   Prophecy Variable

There is no direct refinement mapping from the low-level specification to the high-level specification, basically because there is no way to know whether to map a low-level state $(\text{\bf ready}, n)$ to $(\text{\bf ready}, n)$ or to $(\text{\bf ready}, \text{\bf ready})$ without predicting whether the choice of n will persist. To be conservative, we could always map $(\text{\bf ready}, n)$ to $(\text{\bf ready}, \text{\bf ready})$, but then a low-level transition that publishes n would need to be expanded into two high-level transitions, something that plain refinement mappings do not support. In more realistic variants of this example, the number and complexity of the additional high-level transitions may be larger; in the example of Section 5, the conservative approach is not viable at all.

On the other hand, we can find a suitable refinement mapping after introducing a prophecy variable, as we show next. This prophecy variable is an internal variable that we add by defining an enriched state space:

Construction 1. *The state space Σ_{Low}^P consists of tuples (x, y, D) where*

1. $(x, y) \in \Sigma_{\text{Low}}$,
2. $D \in \{\text{done}, \text{notdone}\}$,
3. $x \in \mathbb{Z}$ *implies* $D = \text{done}$.

Intuitively, **done** indicates that a choice is final; **notdone** that it is not.

Initial condition:

$$InitPropP \triangleq InitProp$$

Steps:

1. Choosing an integer:

$$ChooseP \triangleq (Choose \wedge (D = D'))$$

2. Undoing the choice:

$$UndoP \triangleq (Undo \wedge (D = \text{notdone}))$$

3. Publishing the final choice:

$$PublishP \triangleq (Publish \wedge (D = D'))$$

The enriched low-level specification:

$$SpecP \triangleq \exists y, D.(InitPropP \wedge \Box [ChooseP \vee UndoP \vee PublishP]_{x,y,D})$$

Note the absence of an initial condition on D, and that the value of D affects the enabledness of the action *UndoP*. These features clearly indicate that D is not an ordinary history variable. In other respects, D is quite tame: trivial equations such as $D = D'$ and $D = \text{notdone}$ are easy to handle in reasoning with these definitions.

Proposition 3. *SpecP is obtained from SpecL by adding a very simple prophecy variable.*

Proof: The conditions on the state space (P1), on initial states (P2′), and on existence and finiteness (P6) are immediate.

The condition on backward steps (P4′) is the only non-trivial one, but it is still easy. Since *Choose* $\vee$ *Undo* $\vee$ *Publish* implies $x \notin \mathbb{Z}$, the choice of D is unconstrained by condition (3) in Construction 1. So, for backward steps, taking whatever value of D the corresponding action suggests is appropriate ($D = D'$ or $D = \text{notdone}$, depending on whether the transition corresponds to *Choose* or *Publish* or to *Undo*). □

3.4   Refinement Mapping

Next we construct a refinement mapping from the low-level specification with a prophecy variable to the high-level specification:

Proposition 4. *Let* $f : \Sigma_{\text{Low}}^{P} \to \Sigma_{\text{High}}$ *be such that:*

$$f(x, y, \text{done}) = (x, y)$$
$$f(x, y, \text{notdone}) = (\text{ready}, \text{ready})$$

Then f *is a refinement mapping from SpecP to SpecH.*

Proof: – The constraint that $x \in \mathbb{Z}$ implies $D = \text{done}$ (condition (3) in Construction 1) entails that $f(x, y, \text{notdone}) = (\text{ready}, \text{ready})$ preserves the value of the external variable x.

- Initial states are mapped to initial states, trivially.
- *ChooseP* transitions are mapped to stutters if $D = \text{notdone}$ and to *Choose* transitions otherwise: in a *ChooseP* transition, $(x, y, D) = (\text{ready}, \text{ready}, D)$ and $(x', y', D') = (\text{ready}, y', D')$ with $y' \in \mathbb{Z}$; hence $f(x, y, D) = (\text{ready}, \text{ready})$ and $f(x', y', D') = (\text{ready}, \text{ready})$ if $D = \text{notdone}$ and $= (\text{ready}, y')$ otherwise.
- *UndoP* transitions are mapped to stutters: in a *UndoP* transition, $(x, y, D) = (\text{ready}, y, \text{notdone})$ and $(x', y', D') = (\text{ready}, \text{ready}, D')$; hence $f(x, y, D) = (\text{ready}, \text{ready})$ and $f(x', y', D') = (\text{ready}, \text{ready})$.
- *PublishP* transitions are mapped to *Publish* transitions: in a *PublishP* transition $(x, y, D) = (\text{ready}, y, D)$ where $y \in \mathbb{Z}$ and $(x', y', D') = (y, y, D)$; hence $x' \in \mathbb{Z}$, so $D' = D = \text{done}$ by condition (3) in Construction 1, so $f(x, y, D) = (\text{ready}, y)$ where $y \in \mathbb{Z}$ and $f(x', y', D') = (y, y)$.

$\square$

3.5   Main Result

We conclude:

Proposition 5. *SpecL implements SpecH.*

Proof: By Propositions 3 and 2, *SpecL* implements *SpecP*. By Propositions 4 and 1, *SpecP* implements *SpecH*. The claim follows by transitivity. $\square$

4   An Approach to Finiteness

In this section we present results that can facilitate proofs with prophecy variables. Although they do not constitute a panacea, they conveniently enable us to shift the finiteness requirement on prophecy variables through a quotient construction. We demonstrate their use in the example of Section 5, below. (They would also have been helpful in the example of Section 3 if we had foolishly allowed not only **done** and **notdone** but all strings as possible values of D.)

4.1   Quotients

When $\mathcal{Q}$ is an equivalence relation on Σ, the *quotient* of the state machine $\mathbf{S} = (\Sigma, F, N)$ by $\mathcal{Q}$ is the state machine $\mathbf{S}_{/\mathcal{Q}} = (\Sigma_{/\mathcal{Q}}, F_{/\mathcal{Q}}, N_{/\mathcal{Q}})$ such that:

Q1. $\Sigma_{/\mathcal{Q}} = \Sigma/\mathcal{Q}$ (the set of equivalence classes of states from Σ).
Q2. For $s \in \Sigma_{/\mathcal{Q}}$, $s \in F_{/\mathcal{Q}}$ if and only if there exists $s' \in s$ such that $s' \in F$.
Q3. For $s, t \in \Sigma_{/\mathcal{Q}}$, $\langle s, t \rangle \in N_{/\mathcal{Q}}$ if and only if
       there exist $s' \in s$ and $t' \in t$ such that $\langle s', t' \rangle \in N$.

We represent each equivalence class in $\Sigma/\mathcal{Q}$ by an arbitrary member (say, the smallest in a fixed ordering of Σ), so that $\Sigma/\mathcal{Q} \subseteq \Sigma \subseteq \Sigma_E \times \Sigma_I$ for some set Σ_I.

4.2   Refinement Mappings via Quotients

We say that a function f with domain Σ *respects* the equivalence relation $\mathcal{Q}$ on Σ when, for all $s, t \in \Sigma$, if $s\mathcal{Q}t$ then $f(s) = f(t)$.

Proposition 6. *Let* $\mathbf{S} = (\Sigma, F, N)$ *and* $\mathbf{S}' = (\Sigma', F', N')$, *and let* $\mathbf{S}_{/\mathcal{Q}}$ *be the quotient of* $\mathbf{S}$ *by an equivalence relation* $\mathcal{Q}$ *on* Σ. *Assume that:*

- *f is a refinement mapping from* $\mathbf{S}$ *to* $\mathbf{S}'$,
- *f respects* $\mathcal{Q}$.

Let $f_{/\mathcal{Q}} : \Sigma/\mathcal{Q} \to \Sigma'$ *be such that, for all* $s \in \Sigma/\mathcal{Q}$, $f_{/\mathcal{Q}}(s) = f(s)$. *Then* $f_{/\mathcal{Q}}$ *is a refinement mapping from* $\mathbf{S}_{/\mathcal{Q}}$ *to* $\mathbf{S}'$.

4.3   Very Simple Prophecy Variables via Quotients

We define a state machine $\mathbf{S}^P = (\Sigma^P, F^P, N^P)$ to be *obtained from* $\mathbf{S} = (\Sigma, F, N)$ *almost by adding a very simple prophecy* when the usual conditions P1, P2', and P4' hold, and instead of P6 we have only part of it:

P6'. For all $s \in \Sigma$, the set $\{(s, p) \in \Sigma^P\}$ is nonempty.

The following proposition enables us to recover a simple prophecy variable:

Proposition 7. *Let* $\mathbf{S} = (\Sigma, F, N)$ *and* $\mathbf{S}^P = (\Sigma^P, F^P, N^P)$, *and let* $\mathbf{S}^P_{/\mathcal{Q}} = (\Sigma^P_{/\mathcal{Q}}, F^P_{/\mathcal{Q}}, N^P_{/\mathcal{Q}})$ *be the quotient of* $\mathbf{S}^P$ *by the equivalence relation* $\mathcal{Q}$ *on* Σ^P. *Assume that:*

1. *$\mathbf{S}^P$ is obtained from* $\mathbf{S}$ *almost by adding a very simple prophecy variable,*
2. *for all* $(s_1, p_1), (s_2, p_2) \in \Sigma^P$, *if* $(s_1, p_1)\mathcal{Q}(s_2, p_2)$ *then* $s_1 = s_2$ *(in other words, projecting to the first component respects* $\mathcal{Q}$),
3. *for all* $s \in \Sigma$, *the set* $\{(s, p) \in \Sigma^P\}/\mathcal{Q}$ *is finite.*

Then $\mathbf{S}^P_{/\mathcal{Q}}$ *is obtained from* $\mathbf{S}$ *by adding a very simple prophecy variable.*

4.4   Invariants and Quotienting

Invariants are often needed before other arguments in proofs. In particular, the required conditions for refinements mappings (R1 and especially R3) sometimes hold only for reachable system states, and the role of invariants is to focus attention on those states. The propositions in this section enable us to combine invariants with quotienting.

We say that Inv is an *inductive invariant* of the state machine $\mathbf{S} = (\Sigma, F, N)$ if $Inv \subseteq \Sigma$, $F \subseteq Inv$, and, for all $s, t \in \Sigma$, if $\langle s, t \rangle \in N$ and $s \in Inv$ then $t \in Inv$. Given a subset Inv of Σ and an equivalence relation Q on Σ, we write $Inv_{/Q}$ for the subset of $\Sigma_{/Q}$ such that $s \in Inv_{/Q}$ if and only if there exists $s' \in s$ such that $s' \in Inv$. (This notation generalizes the definition of $F_{/Q}$.) We say that Inv *respects* Q when, for all $s, t \in \Sigma$, if sQt and $s \in Inv$ then $t \in Inv$.

Proposition 8. *Assume that:*

- *Inv is an inductive invariant of $\mathbf{S} = (\Sigma, F, N)$,*
- *Inv respects the equivalence relation Q on Σ.*

Then $Inv_{/Q}$ is an inductive invariant of $\mathbf{S}_{/Q} = (\Sigma_{/Q}, F_{/Q}, N_{/Q})$.

Given a specification $\mathbf{S} = (\Sigma, F, N)$ and a subset Inv of Σ, we write $\mathbf{S} + Inv$ for $(\Sigma, F, N \cap (Inv \times \Sigma))$.

Proposition 9. *Assume that Inv is an inductive invariant of $\mathbf{S} = (\Sigma, F, N)$. Then $\mathbf{S}$ and $\mathbf{S} + Inv$ generate the same complete property.*

Proposition 10. *Assume that Inv respects Q. Then the complete property that $\mathbf{S}_{/Q} + Inv_{/Q}$ generates is included in that of $(\mathbf{S} + Inv)_{/Q}$.*

5   Second Example

Our second example is slightly longer and much trickier than the first. It illustrates how the finiteness requirement on prophecy variables can be conveniently ignored in the core of a refinement argument.

5.1   High-Level Specification (No "undo")

In the high-level system, integers are chosen internally in ascending order, and then revealed, gradually. The choice is made by adding elements to an internal variable y that holds a finite set. The publication of a choice consists in moving the largest element of y to the external variable x, which also holds a finite set.

The state space Σ_{High} is thus $\mathcal{P}_f(\mathbb{Z}) \times \mathcal{P}_f(\mathbb{Z})$ where $\mathcal{P}_f(\mathbb{Z})$ is the set of finite sets of integers.

Initial condition:

$$InitProp \triangleq (x = y = \emptyset)$$

Steps:

1. Choosing one more integer:

$$Choose \triangleq \exists n \in \mathbb{Z}.((n > \max(x \cup y)) \wedge (y' = y \cup \{n\}) \wedge (x' = x))$$

2. Publishing the largest pending choice:

$$Publish \triangleq \exists n \in \mathbb{Z}.((n = \max(y)) \wedge (y' = y - \{n\}) \wedge (x' = x \cup \{n\}))$$

The high-level specification:

$$SpecH \triangleq \exists y.(InitProp \wedge \Box[Choose \vee Publish]_{x,y})$$

Note that *SpecH* allows all behaviors where x takes a sequence of values $\emptyset$, $\{0\}$, $\{0, -1\}$, ..., $\{0, -1, ..., -k\}$, but not their limit, so it is not a safety property.

5.2   Low-Level Specification (with "undo")

In the low-level specification, additional transitions can undo choices. Again, the state space Σ_{Low} equals Σ_{High}; moreover, the initial condition and the actions for choosing and for publishing a choice are exactly as above in the high-level specification. We have one additional action for undoing choices:

$$Undo \triangleq \exists S \subseteq \mathbb{Z}.((y' = y \cap S) \wedge (x' = x))$$

This action models a selective rollback, in which we keep choices only if they are in a given set S of "survivors".

The low-level specification:

$$SpecL \triangleq \exists y.(InitProp \wedge \Box[Choose \vee Undo \vee Publish]_{x,y})$$

5.3   Prophecy Variable

Again, we cannot directly find a refinement mapping from the low-level specification to the high-level specification. The constraints on the order in which integers are chosen and published contribute to this difficulty.

- For instance, suppose that we were to map the low-level state $(\{4\}, \{2, 3\})$ to the high-level state $(\{4\}, \{2, 3\})$, naively. This trivial mapping cannot possibly be satisfactory. According to the low-level specification, $(\{2, 4\}, \emptyset)$ is reachable from $(\{4\}, \{2, 3\})$ (via an "undo" of 3 and the publication of 2), while according to the high-level specification no state of the form $(\{2, 4\}, \cdot)$ is reachable from $(\{4\}, \{2, 3\})$.
- On the other hand, unlike in the first example (see Section 3.3), we cannot pretend that choices are not made "until the last minute". For instance, we cannot map the low-level state $(\{4\}, \{2, 3\})$ to the high-level state $(\{4\}, \emptyset)$. According to the low-level specification, $(\{2, 3, 4\}, \emptyset)$ is reachable from $(\{4\}, \{2, 3\})$ (by publishing 3 and then 2), while according to the high-level specification no state of the form $(\{2, 3, 4\}, \cdot)$ is reachable from $(\{4\}, \emptyset)$.

So we introduce a prophecy variable. We add the prophecy variable as an internal variable in an enriched state space:

Construction 2. *The state space* Σ_{Low}^P *consists of tuples* (x, y, D) *where*

1. $(x, y) \in \Sigma_{\mathrm{Low}}$,
2. $D \subseteq \mathbb{Z}$,
3. $x \subseteq D$.

Intuitively, choices of the integers in D will never be undone in the future. Accordingly, condition (3) says that choices that have been revealed cannot be undone.

Initial condition:

$$InitPropP \triangleq InitProp$$

Steps:

1. Choosing one more integer:

$$ChooseP \triangleq (Choose \wedge (D = D'))$$

2. Undoing some choices:

$$UndoP \triangleq \exists S \subseteq \mathbb{Z}.((y' = y \cap S) \wedge (x' = x) \wedge (D = (D' \cap S) \cup x))$$

3. Publishing a choice:

$$PublishP \triangleq (Publish \wedge (D = D'))$$

The enriched low-level specification:

$$SpecP \triangleq \exists y, D.(InitPropP \wedge \Box[ChooseP \vee UndoP \vee PublishP]_{x,y,D})$$

Note the equation $D = (D' \cap S) \cup x$ in $UndoP$, which defines D from D'. Such definitions are typical for prophecy variables. In this case, the equation might be read as saying that the choices of integers that will never be undone henceforth are the choices of integers already in x or the choices that "survive" this $UndoP$ step and will never be undone afterwards.

Several variants are possible. In particular, we could change the state space so that D is included in $x \cup y$, thus ensuring that for each (x, y) there are only finitely many possible values for D. Accordingly, we would have to make other adjustments, not all of them attractive. For instance, in $ChooseP$, we would have to replace $D = D'$ with a more complicated equation, such as $D = D' \cap (x \cup y)$. Such expressions would then appear pervasively throughout proofs. In a larger example (like the one of interest to us in the context of Naiad), such a change can create more work than it avoids. So we proceed without a finiteness guarantee; quotienting will nevertheless allow us to complete the verification.

Proposition 11. *SpecP is obtained from SpecL almost by adding a very simple prophecy variable.*

Proof: The conditions on the state space (P1), on initial states (P2′), and on existence (P6′) are again immediate.

The condition on backward steps (P4′) is the only non-trivial one: it requires care in order to ensure that $x \subseteq D$. In the cases of transitions *Choose* and *Publish*, we take $D = D'$ as suggested by the definitions of *ChooseP* and *PublishP*, and the desired result follows since $x \subseteq x'$ in both cases. In the case of a transition *Undo*, we take $D = (D' \cap S) \cup x$ for a set S as suggested by the definition of *UndoP*, and immediately obtain that $x \subseteq D$. ▯

5.4   Refinement Mapping

We let *Inv* be the predicate $x \cap y = \emptyset$, which says that x and y are disjoint. It is a straightforward inductive invariant of *SpecH*, *SpecL*, and *SpecP*. Relying on *Inv*, we construct a refinement mapping:

Proposition 12. *Let $f : \Sigma_{\text{Low}}^P \to \Sigma_{\text{High}}$ be such that:*

$$f(x, y, D) = (x, y \cap D)$$

Then f is a refinement mapping from SpecP + Inv to SpecH.

Proof: – The mapping trivially preserves the external variable x.
  – It maps initial states to initial states.
  – It maps *ChooseP* transitions to *Choose* transitions or to stutters, depending on whether the integer chosen is in D.
  – It maps *PublishP* transitions to *Publish* transitions: if a *PublishP* transition adds n to x, then $n \in y$ and $n \in x'$, so $n \in D'$ by condition (3) in Construction 2, so $n \in D$ since $D = D'$, so $n \in y \cap D$.
  – It maps *UndoP* transitions to stutters: for some $S \subseteq \mathbb{Z}$, we have $y' \cap D' = (y \cap S) \cap D' = y \cap (D' \cap S) = y \cap ((D' \cap S) \cup x) = y \cap D$ since $D = ((D' \cap S) \cup x)$. The equation $y \cap (D' \cap S) = y \cap ((D' \cap S) \cup x)$ exploits the invariant *Inv*.

▯

5.5   Main Result (via Quotienting)

At this point, we have the main ingredients of a proof that *SpecL* implements *SpecH*: an auxiliary variable that (almost) satisfies all expected conditions, an invariant, and a refinement mapping. It remains to put them together. The recipe for this purpose has several steps but is easy and fairly generic. The steps are much as in the first example (Proposition 5), but with an extra layer of quotienting. Crucially, the statement of the final result (Proposition 13) does not mention inductive invariants or quotients.

Proposition 13. *SpecL implements SpecH.*

Proof: We quotient Σ^P_{Low} by a relation $\mathcal{Q}$:

$$(x_1, y_1, D_1)\mathcal{Q}(x_2, y_2, D_2)$$
$$\text{if and only if}$$
$$(x_1, y_1) = (x_2, y_2) \text{ and } y_1 \cap D_1 = y_2 \cap D_2$$

We prove that *SpecL* implements $SpecP_{/\mathcal{Q}}$ and that $SpecP_{/\mathcal{Q}}$ implements *SpecH*. The claim follows by transitivity.

1. For each x and y, the set of equivalence classes $\{(x, y, D) \in \Sigma^P_{\text{Low}}\}/\mathcal{Q}$ is finite, because y is finite. Therefore, by Propositions 11 and 7, $SpecP_{/\mathcal{Q}}$ is obtained from *SpecL* by adding a very simple prophecy variable. By Proposition 2, *SpecL* implements $SpecP_{/\mathcal{Q}}$.

2. Both *Inv* and f respect the equivalence relation $\mathcal{Q}$: the definition of *Inv* does not even mention D, and that of f uses it only in a context of the form $y \cap D$. Since *Inv* is an inductive invariant of *SpecP*, $Inv_{/\mathcal{Q}}$ is an inductive invariant of $SpecP_{/\mathcal{Q}}$ by Proposition 8. Therefore, $SpecP_{/\mathcal{Q}}$ implements $SpecP_{/\mathcal{Q}} + Inv_{/\mathcal{Q}}$ by Proposition 9. In turn, $SpecP_{/\mathcal{Q}} + Inv_{/\mathcal{Q}}$ implements $(SpecP + Inv)_{/\mathcal{Q}}$ by Proposition 10. Finally, $(SpecP + Inv)_{/\mathcal{Q}}$ implements *SpecH* by Proposition 12 (which constructs a refinement mapping), Proposition 6 (which quotients the mapping), and Proposition 1 (which asserts the soundness of refinement mappings). We deduce that $SpecP_{/\mathcal{Q}}$ implements *SpecH* by transitivity.

$\square$

6   Conclusion

Prophecy variables are generally useful for manipulating the timing of non-deterministic choices. Specifically, they help in constructing refinement mappings when a low-level specification makes its non-deterministic choices later than a corresponding high-level specification. Therefore, prophecy variables are broadly relevant to reasoning about systems with "undo" operations: those operations can roll back computations that include non-deterministic choices, which are effectively not made until they are committed, perhaps by a later output action.

The examples of this paper focus on the delicate interaction between "undo" operations and non-determinism. Of course, actual systems have many other aspects, including non-trivial deterministic computations and sophisticated methods for rollback based on logging and checkpointing (e.g., [3]). Nevertheless, reasoning about those systems can benefit from prophecy variables and from the techniques described in this paper. Our ongoing work on Naiad, for instance, features non-deterministic scheduling choices; "undo" is typically a rollback caused by a failure. Prophecy variables are crucial in the proof that a low-level specification with failures refines a high-level specification where such failures are assumed impossible. As in this paper, prophecy variables predict which choices will persist and which will be revisited.

Acknowledgments. I am grateful to Michael Isard, Leslie Lamport, and Butler Lampson for discussions on the subject of this paper.

References

1. Abadi, M., Lamport, L.: The existence of refinement mappings. Theoretical Computer Science 82(2), 253–284 (1991)
2. Cook, B., Koskinen, E.: Making prophecies with decision predicates. In: Proceedings of the 38th Annual ACM SIGPLAN-SIGACT Symposium on Principles of Programming Languages, pp. 399–410 (2011)
3. Elnozahy, E.N., Alvisi, L., Wang, Y., Johnson, D.B.: A survey of rollback-recovery protocols in message-passing systems. ACM Computing Surveys 34(3), 375–408 (2002)
4. Harris, T., Larus, J.R., Rajwar, R.: Transactional Memory, 2nd edn. Synthesis Lectures on Computer Architecture. Morgan & Claypool Publishers (2010)
5. Henzinger, T.A., Sezgin, A., Vafeiadis, V.: Aspect-oriented linearizability proofs. In: D'Argenio, P.R., Melgratti, H. (eds.) CONCUR 2013 – Concurrency Theory. LNCS, vol. 8052, pp. 242–256. Springer, Heidelberg (2013)
6. Herlihy, M., Wing, J.M.: Linearizability: A correctness condition for concurrent objects. ACM Transactions on Programming Languages and Systems 12(3), 463–492 (1990)
7. Jonsson, B.: Simulations between specifications of distributed systems. In: Groote, J.F., Baeten, J.C.M. (eds.) CONCUR 1991. LNCS, vol. 527, pp. 346–360. Springer, Heidelberg (1991)
8. Kim, T., Wang, X., Zeldovich, N., Kaashoek, M.F.: Intrusion recovery using selective re-execution. In: 9th USENIX Symposium on Operating Systems Design and Implementation, pp. 89–104 (2010)
9. Lamport, L.: Specifying Systems, The TLA+ Language and Tools for Hardware and Software Engineers. Addison-Wesley (2002)
10. Lampson, B.W.: Reliable messages and connection establishment. In: Mullender, S. (ed.) Distributed Systems, pp. 251–281. Addison-Wesley (1993)
11. Lynch, N.A., Vaandrager, F.W.: Forward and backward simulations: I. Untimed systems. Information and Computation 121(2), 214–233 (1995)
12. Murray, D.G., McSherry, F., Isaacs, R., Isard, M., Barham, P., Abadi, M.: Naiad: a timely dataflow system. In: ACM SIGOPS 24th Symposium on Operating Systems Principles. pp. 439–455 (2013)
13. Sezgin, A., Tasiran, S., Qadeer, S.: Tressa: Claiming the future. In: Leavens, G.T., O'Hearn, P., Rajamani, S.K. (eds.) VSTTE 2010. LNCS, vol. 6217, pp. 25–39. Springer, Heidelberg (2010)

Author Index

Printed in the United States
By Bookmasters